# THE ENGLISH  ...TS

# OF THE

# TWENTIETH CENTURY

A History of the English Baptists
Volume 4
General Editor: Roger Hayden

# THE ENGLISH BAPTISTS

# OF THE

# TWENTIETH CENTURY

## Ian M. Randall

The Baptist Historical Society
2005

This is the fourth volume in the series on the English Baptists originally planned under the editorship of the late Dr E.A. Payne, subsequently under Dr B.R. White, and now edited by Dr Roger Hayden.

*Already published*

THE ENGLISH BAPTISTS OF THE SEVENTEENTH CENTURY
by B.R. White (1983, 1996)

THE ENGLISH BAPTISTS OF THE EIGHTEENTH CENTURY
by Raymond Brown (1986)

THE ENGLISH BAPTISTS OF THE NINETEENTH CENTURY
by J.H.Y. Briggs (1994)

The right of Ian M. Randall to be identified as the Author of this Work has been asserted by him in accordance with the Copyright, Designs and Patents Act 1988

© 2005                                    The Baptist Historical Society
Baptist House, 129 Broadway, Didcot OX11 8RT

ISBN 0 903166 35 6 (paperback)
ISBN 0 903166 36 4 (casebound)

To
Barrie White
with appreciation

# THE ENGLISH BAPTISTS
# OF THE TWENTIETH CENTURY

## CONTENTS

# FOREWORD

D r Ian Randall's present book completes the series that was begun by the Baptist Historical Society in 1983, telling the story of Baptists in England from the seventeenth to the twentieth century. The four century volumes have each been well served by their respective authors, Dr B.R. White, Dr Raymond Brown, Professor J.H.Y. Briggs, and now Dr Ian Randall.

Dr Keith Clements had begun the process of looking at the twentieth century by editing a helpful Summer School volume on *Baptists in the Twentieth Century* (1983). The former Secretary and President of the Society, the Revd Dr W. Morris West, began work on the twentieth-century volume, but was unable to finish it before his death in 1999. His various papers and personal autobiography about the twentieth century were published by the Society as *Baptists Together* in 2000. These last two volumes have helped Dr Randall in his demanding task. Dr Randall has unusually allowed the whole Baptist family to be involved in telling the story, by his in-depth consultation of the *Baptist Times* over the whole century. Dr Randall's use of this unique source to amplify the broad outline of our Baptist story is revealed through his detailed study of the life and work of the Baptist Union, its Council and Committees. This provides a fascinating chronological account of the Baptist family as it has faced the large themes of ministry, mission, social concern and ecumenical involvement.

The Society is deeply indebted to the four writers of the denominational history, now including Dr Randall for this final volume. Together they provide a comprehensive account of our Baptist past. It is for Baptists of the twenty-first century to discover what the future is for our life together, and this Society hopes that this Baptist story, 'warts and all', will enable contemporary Baptists to avoid 'the fate of those who forget their past', which is 'having to relive it.'

The Society also wishes to acknowledge the vital part played by Faith Bowers in the detailed work of preparing the manuscripts for publication, and also to their printers, Tyndale Press of Lowestoft, for their efficient production of each volume.


ROGER HAYDEN
Series Editor and President, Baptist Historical Society
Advent 2004

# PREFACE
# AND ACKNOWLEDGEMENTS

W hen I was asked by the committee of the Baptist Historical
Society to write this volume, I was delighted to accept. It is a
privilege to contribute to the fine series of volumes produced
by the Society on English Baptists over four centuries. Writing the book
has been both enjoyable and daunting. The enjoyment has come from
entering into the experiences of Baptists as they have witnessed to their
faith throughout the century. At times, however, it has been a difficult
task. With a mass of material available, it is not easy to decide what to
include and what to omit. Also, in writing about events in the past few
decades through which I have lived, there has been the challenge of
seeking to do justice to a variety of viewpoints. Despite my best efforts,
I am sure that I have not been completely successful.

Many people have helped me significantly in my work on this book.
In particular, I want to thank three colleagues within the Baptist
Historical Society who have played a key role: Roger Hayden, the
President of the Society, John Briggs, the editor of the *Baptist Quarterly*,
and Faith Bowers, the sub-editor of the *Quarterly*. Each of these has read
and commented in detail on my early drafts, and Faith has also done
wonderful work in editing my revised version. I am deeply appreciative
of their support and guidance.

In addition, a number of people have kindly read and made many
helpful comments on the whole of my manuscript. My particular thanks
go to the following: Basil Amey, the former Assistant General Secretary
of the British Council of Churches; David Bebbington, Professor of
History at Stirling University; Brian Bowers, a deacon at Bloomsbury
Central Baptist Church; David Coffey, General Secretary of the Baptist
Union of Great Britain; John Colwell, my colleague at Spurgeon's
College, who teaches doctrine and ethics; Keith Jones, the Rector of the

International Baptist Theological Seminary, Prague; Janice Randall, my wife, who is an English language teacher; and Douglas Sparkes, former Deputy General Secretary of the Baptist Union. I am also grateful to others who have read chapters relating to certain periods: Rod Badams, Roy Freestone, Bernard Green, David Harper, Keith Hobbs, Sharon James, Simon Jones, Douglas McBain, David Milner, David Russell, Michael Taylor and Nigel Wright. The feedback I have received has been of great value and I have been able to make important changes as a result. As is always the case, any errors which remain are my own responsibility.

As I was beginning to think about how I would undertake the research, I was given valuable assistance by the late Morris West, formerly Principal of Bristol Baptist College and President of the Baptist Historical Society. It has also been most helpful to interview David Russell and Bernard Green, who have served as General Secretaries of the Baptist Union, David Coffey, the current General Secretary, and Michael Taylor, former Principal of Northern Baptist College. Each of these has provided me with crucial insights and I am indebted to them.

I have made many visits to the Angus Library at Regent's Park College, Oxford, during the course of writing this book. I have made extensive use of material kept there - the *Baptist Times*, the minutes of the Baptist Union Council and its committees, the personal papers of Ernest A. Payne, former General Secretary of the Baptist Union, as well as many other items relevant to this volume. Sue Mills, the Librarian, and Jennifer Thorp, the BMS archivist, have been unfailingly helpful in responding to my frequent requests for material. Here at Spurgeon's my colleague, Judy Powles, the Librarian, has, as always, been most obliging.

In the early period when I was working on this volume I was the Academic Dean and Director of Baptist and Anabaptist Studies at the International Baptist Theological Seminary (IBTS), Prague, and I wish to express my thanks to the Rector, Keith Jones, and the members of the IBTS Board of Trustees, who kindly gave me three months of sabbatical leave so that I could give my full time to writing. Without that sabbatical this book would have taken considerably longer to write. I am also grateful to the Whitley Lectureship for a grant towards research expenses.

The illustrations were gathered by Faith and Brian Bowers. Many come from the *Baptist Times*, whose staff were very helpful. Some come from the Angus Library. A number are drawn from the picture collections of the Baptist Historical Society and of Bloomsbury Central Baptist Church. Others were kindly supplied by individuals, as indicated in the list of illustrations on pp.xvi-xxiv. To all I am grateful.

I wish, finally, to thank two other people. My wife, Janice, has been a constant source of strength and an example to me of how to live as a committed Baptist Christian, and I am deeply grateful to her for her love and support. The second person is Dr B.R. White, one of the outstanding Baptist historians of the twentieth century, who was the Principal of Regent's Park College in the 1980s when I studied there in preparation for Baptist ministry. He both encouraged me to pursue research in Baptist history and was a model of historical scholarship at its best. This book is dedicated to Barrie White.

Ian M. Randall
Spurgeon's College
London
Advent 2004

# LIST OF ABBREVIATIONS

| | | | |
|---|---|---|---|
| ACCR | Advisory Committee for Church Relations (BUGB) | COPEC | Conference on Politics, Economics and Citizenship, 1924 |
| ACEA | African and Caribbean Evangelical Alliance | COs | Conscientious Objectors |
| ACUTE | (Evangelical) Alliance Commission for Unity and Truth among Evangelicals | CSSM | Children's Special Service Mission |
| AEBC | Association of Evangelical Baptist Churches | CTBI | Churches Together in Britain and Ireland |
| AIM | Action in Mission (BUGB) | CTE | Churches Together in England |
| BA | Bachelor of Arts | CTP | Christian Training Programme |
| BBC | British Broadcasting Corporation | *CW* | *Christian World* |
| BBU | Baptist Bible Union | DSO | Distinguished Service Order |
| BCC | British Council of Churches | DTh | Doctor of Theology |
| BD | Bachelor of Divinity | EBF | European Baptist Federation |
| BEC | British Evangelical Council | | |
| BEM | *Baptism, Eucharist and Ministry* | ECUM | Evangelical Coalition for Urban Mission |
| BMM | Baptist Men's Movement | ed./eds | editor/s |
| BMS | Baptist Missionary Society | edn | edition |
| *BQ* | *Baptist Quarterly* | FBCC | Fellowship of Baptist churches for Covenanting |
| BRF | Baptist Revival Fellowship | | |
| BSF | Baptist Students' Federation | FCFC | Free Church Federal Council (Before 1940 this referred to the Federal Council of the Evangelical Free Churches) |
| *BT* | *Baptist Times* | | |
| BUGB/BU | Baptist Union of Great Britain, sometimes shortened to BU (until 1988 BUGBI for Baptist Union of Great Britain and Ireland) | | |
| | | Free Church Council - short form for the National Council of the Evangelical Free Churches | |
| *BW* | *British Weekly* | | |
| BWA | Baptist World Alliance | FIEC | Fellowship of Independent Evangelical Churches |
| BWL | Baptist Women's League | | |
| CBE/OBE | Commander/Officer of the Order of the British Empire | GP&F | General Purposes and Finance Committee (BUGB) |
| CCBI | Council of Churches for Britain and Ireland | HTB | Holy Trinity Church, Brompton |
| CCLEPE | Consultative Committee for Local Ecumenical Projects | ICCC | (American) International Council of Christian Churches |
| CE | Christian Endeavour | | |
| CEC | Conference of European Churches | ICP | Inter-Church Process |

| | | | |
|---|---|---|---|
| ITV | Independent Television | RSC | Residential Selection |
| IVF | Inter-Varsity Fellowship | | Conference (BUGB) |
| JP | Justice of the Peace | SALT | Spurgeon's Adaptable |
| KC | King's Counsel | | Leadership Training |
| LBA | London Baptist Association | | Programme |
| LBC | London Bible College | SCM | Student Christian |
| LCC | London County Council | | Movement |
| LEPs | Local Ecumenical | SDP | Social Democratic Party |
| | Projects/Local Ecumenical | SPCK | Society for Promoting |
| | Partnerships | | Christian Knowledge |
| MA | Master of Arts | TV | television |
| MARCEA | Merseyside and Region | UCCF | Universities and Colleges |
| | Churches Ecumenical | | Christian Fellowship |
| | Assembly | | (formerly IVF) |
| MC | Military Cross | URC | United Reformed Church |
| MP | Member of Parliament | WCC | World Council of Churches |
| MRA | Moral Re-Armament | WIEA | West Indian Evangelical |
| MTh | Master of Theology | | Alliance |
| n.d. | no date given | WORGLEP | Working Group on LEPs |
| n.p. | no publisher given | | (BUGB) |
| NIE | Nationwide Initiative for | YBA | Yorkshire Baptist |
| | Evangelism | | Association |
| NFCC | National Free Church | YFC | Youth for Christ |
| | Council | YMCA | Young Men's Christian |
| p./pp. | page/pages | | Association |
| p.p. | private publication | YWL | Young Worshippers' |
| PHAB | physically handicapped and | | League |
| | able bodied | | |
| RAF | Royal Air Force | | |

# BIBLIOGRAPHIC REFERENCES

Full bibliographic details will be found in the Bibliography at the back, with shorter references in the footnotes.

# THE ILLUSTRATIONS

Note: Many of the photographs reproduced here are old and those from the *Baptist Times* had already been screened for printing, so the quality is variable. Nevertheless, they offer a contemporary record of Baptist life through the century.

The illustrations on pages 7, 22, 37, 44, 45, 68, 82, 85, 88, 105, 106, 107, 108, 124, 127, 137, 139, 143, 150, 157, 158, 172, 192, 195, 213, 223, 247, 253, 274, 276, 277, 278, 279, 307, 310, 314, 315, 318, 329, 340, 356, 358, 364, 383, 390, 391, 397, 402, 405, 408, 419, 424, 426, 447, 448, 460, 463, 474, 498, 500, 507, 511 and 513 come from pages of the *Baptist Times*, or from the journal's collection of loose photographs. The staff, especially Mark Woods, Alan O'Sullivan and Phil Creighton were very helpful over this.

Those on pages 49, 70, 87, and 264 are from the collections in the Angus Library, Regent's Park College, Oxford. The librarian, Sue Mills, and her archivist colleague, Jennifer Thorp, kindly supplied these.

Those on pages 120, 134, 169, 262, 296, 372, 401, 412, 413, 428, 472 and 478 come from *Baptist Handbooks* and *Baptist Directories.* These used to carry photographs of new church buildings, and continue to provide a portrait of each year's president of the Baptist Union.

Those on pages 23, 26, 65, 75, 176, 177, 178, 184, 193, 208, 261, 334, 351, 423, 464, and 528 are drawn from the picture collection of the Baptist Historical Society.

Those on pages 42, 59, 145, 191, 210, 216, 241, 246, 322, and 514 come from the photographic collection of Bloomsbury Central Baptist Church.

Individuals who kindly supplied other photographs are acknowledged in the detailed list that follows.

Chapter 1
page
7        Memorial stone-laying of the new Baptist Church House, Wednesday, 24 April 1901. Miss Ruth Elsie Marnham presents a bouquet to Alexander Maclaren DD LittD, BU President 1875-

6 and 1901-2. From the *Baptist Times* 1901, where it was reproduced as a full page; the journal rarely carried illustrations at that date, advertisements apart. The photograph was taken by E.H. Mills, 19 Stanley Gardens, Belsize Park.

Chapter 2

# Chapter 1
# INTRODUCTION
# 'MISSIONARY PURPOSES'

In his analysis of evangelism and spirituality within Protestant Nonconformity in England in the twentieth century, David Bebbington contrasts the position of the Free Churches at the beginning and at the end of the century. At the beginning, a common body of popular evangelicalism united most of the Nonconformist churches and chapels, and these congregations willingly co-operated in the wider Free Church Council movement. At the end, Bebbington notes, there was 'astonishing diversity', with many new groups and fellowships having emerged alongside 'the rumps of Methodism, the United Reformed Church and the Baptist Union'.[1] Perhaps 'rump', which suggests a small remnant, does not do full justice to the continuing significance of the historic Free Churches, but there is no doubt about the extent to which Nonconformity was transformed during the twentieth century. The Free Churches lost their sense of self-identity, part of which had been their belief that they could act as 'conscience' to the nation.[2] As one institutional mark of this transformation, at the end of the century it was decided that the Free Church Council would become

---

1    D.W. Bebbington, 'Evangelism and Spirituality in Twentieth-Century Protestant Nonconformity', in A.P.F. Sell and A.R. Cross, eds., *Protestant Nonconformity in the Twentieth Century* (Carlisle: Paternoster Press, 2003), p.215.
2    For background see D.W. Bebbington, *The Nonconformist Conscience: Chapel and Politics, 1870-1914* (London: George Allen and Unwin, 1982); E.K.H. Jordan, *Free Church Unity: History of the Free Church Council Movement, 1896-1941* (London: Lutterworth Press, 1956); J.W. Grant, *Free Churchmanship in England, 1870-1940* (London: Independent Press [n.d. but 1940]).

a Free Churches' group in association with the larger ecumenical body, Churches Together in England. This change took place on 1 April 2001.[3] The decline experienced by the Free Churches, Baptists included, was representative of a wider trend within society. Whereas about 33% of British people were members of one of the Christian Churches in 1900, a hundred years later, in an increasingly multi-faith environment, the figure was 12%, with regular attendance at church services dipping from 9.9% in 1989 to 7.5% in 1998.[4] Robin Gill, in *The 'Empty' Church Revisited* (2003), compared the 1903 and 1993 church-going figures for Bromley, Kent, which in 1903 was a place of fairly high church-going. Gill's estimate, from the data available, is that 31% of the Bromley population was in church in 1903, but only 10.5% by 1993. Baptist church-going in Bromley was remarkably resilient, the earlier figure for Baptist attendance being 2.7%, only falling by 1993 to 2.1%. Nationally, significant growth during the later part of the century in independent and Pentecostal churches meant that in the English Church Census in 1998 Free Church attendances were two-fifths of all church-goers. In a century marked by overall decline in church involvement, the achievement of Baptists, together with some other Free Churches, compared favourably with that of the Anglican and Roman Catholic Churches.[5]

Because of the degree of change that was experienced during the century, this study of Baptist life is structured on a decade by decade basis. This is different from the thematic approach adopted in the fine volume, *English Baptists in the Nineteenth Century*, by Professor John Briggs, editor of the *Baptist Quarterly*. Earlier volumes in the Baptist Historical Society's series on English Baptists looked at specific time

---

3     *Free Church Chronicle*, November 2000, p.1; B. Amey, 'The Free Church Federal Council', *The Journal of the United Reformed Church History Society*, Vol.7, No.3 (2003), p.196.

4     P. Brierley, *Religious Trends: 2000/2001, No.2* (London: Christian Research Association, 1999), p.8.17; P. Brierley, *The Tide is Running Out* (London: Christian Research Association, 2000), p.27.

5     R. Gill, *The 'Empty' Church Revisited* (Aldershot: Ashgate, 2003), pp.163-7.

periods and at the major groups within Baptist life.[6] The allocation in the present volume of one chapter to each decade is, inevitably, somewhat artificial: Baptist life does not shift gear every ten years. This in turn mirrors the limitation, on a larger scale, of looking only at one particular century. Thus it can be argued that the optimism of the later Victorian era continued into the Edwardian age, and that in the early twentieth century Baptists in England were still shaped by a typically Victorian belief in inexorable progress. The difficulty of sticking rigidly to the century is particularly acute just at its end. In 1999-2000 English Baptists were moving towards a new form of organizational life, which came into being formally in 2002. Not only does this organizational development, then, belong to the story of Baptists in the twenty-first century, but it is also too early to assess the effect of the various changes in Baptist life that were agreed in the 1990s.

There are other limitations to this study. In looking only at Baptists in England in the twentieth century, the Baptists in Scotland, in Ireland and in Wales are by definition excluded. However, a series of essays on Baptists in Scotland was published in 1988, and Brian Talbot has written more recently on Scottish Baptist origins.[7] Joshua Thompson produced a history of the Baptist Union of Ireland in 1995.[8] T.M. Bassett wrote on the Baptists in Wales,[9] and Densil Morgan's *Span of the Cross* (1999)

---

6    B.R. White, *The English Baptists of the Seventeenth Century* (Didcot: Baptist Historical Society, 1996, 2nd edn.); R. Brown, *The English Baptists of the Eighteenth Century* (London: Baptist Historical Society, 1986); J.H.Y. Briggs, *The English Baptists of the Nineteenth Century* (Didcot: Baptist Historical Society, 1994).

7    D.W. Bebbington, ed., *The Baptists in Scotland: A History* (Glasgow: The Baptist Union of Scotland, 1988); B.R. Talbot, *The Search for a Common Identity: The Origins of the Baptist Union of Scotland 1800-1870* (Carlisle: Paternoster Press, 2003).

8    J. Thompson, *Century of Grace: The Baptist Union of Ireland: A Short History, 1895-1995* (Belfast: Baptist Union of Ireland, 1996).

9    T.M. Bassett, *The Baptists of Wales and the Baptist Missionary Society* (Swansea: Ilston Press, 1991).

is a definitive work on the churches in Wales in the twentieth century.[10] In addition, there are groups of English Baptists and individual Baptist churches that do not appear here. Strict and Particular Baptists, some known as Gospel Standard Strict Baptists and others now as Grace Baptists, have their own historian, Kenneth Dix, Secretary of the Strict Baptist Historical Society. He has written a comprehensive account of Strict Baptists in the nineteenth century,[11] and is currently working on the twentieth century. At the beginning of the century there were about 600 Strict Baptist churches in England.[12] In the 1960s a new movement of Reformed Baptists emerged, and this development is described in a study by Tim Grass.[13] Other Baptist churches in England are completely independent or belong to the Fellowship of Independent Evangelical Churches (FIEC), founded in 1922 by a former Baptist minister, E.J. Poole-Connor. The FIEC grew from ten churches in 1923 to 425 in 1991.[14] The churches traced in the chapters that follow are only those English Baptist churches that belong to the Baptist Union of Great Britain.

A history of the English Baptists who belong to the Union is not, however, a history of the Union as an institution. In 1959 a valuable history of the Baptist Union, by Ernest A. Payne, was published, and this has as its focus the central workings of that part of the Baptist denomination affiliated to the Union.[15] Yet Baptist churches were, from the beginning, autonomous, and until the early twentieth century they were never tightly organized. Thus it is appropriate to look at the

---

10    D. Morgan, *Span of the Cross: Christian Religion and Society in Wales 1914-2000* (Cardiff: University of Wales Press, 1999).

11    K. Dix, *Strict and Particular: English Strict and Particular Baptists in the Nineteenth Century* (Didcot: Baptist Historical Society, 2001).

12    I am grateful to Kenneth Dix for this information.

13    T. Grass, 'Strict Baptists and Reformed Baptists in England, 1955-76', in *Baptist Myths* (forthcoming, Paternoster, 2005).

14    D.G. Fountain, *E.J. Poole-Connor, 1872-1962: Contender for the Faith* (Worthing: Henry E. Walter, 1966), p.124; T.H. Bendor-Samuel, *Keeping the Faith* (Croydon: FIEC, 1992), p.70.

15    E.A. Payne, *The Baptist Union: A Short History* (London: Carey Kingsgate Press, 1959).

machinery of the Union as one part of the story of Baptist life, while also bringing out many other elements connected with grass-roots Baptist existence. The way in which Baptists drew more closely together in the twentieth century has been well told by Peter Shepherd in his life of J.H. Shakespeare (1857-1928), who was General Secretary of the Union during the first quarter of the twentieth century,[16] and many details are also to be found in *The Home Mission Story* and *An Accredited Ministry*, by Douglas Sparkes, former Deputy General Secretary of the Union.[17] Further information about the Union in the first two-thirds of the century can be found in the perceptive assessment by Morris West, former Principal of Bristol Baptist College, of three General Secretaries: Shakespeare, M.E. Aubrey (1885-1957) and E.A. Payne (1902-80).[18]

Baptists within the Baptist Union of Great Britain (and Ireland, until 1988) have been in membership of the Baptist World Alliance (BWA), formed in 1905, since its inception.[19] They have also been fully involved in the European Baptist Federation (EBF), formed at the end of the 1940s. The contribution of British Baptists to the world Baptist community has been significant and there have been particularly strong Baptist links across Europe, as outlined by Bernard Green, a former General Secretary of the Union, in his two books, *Tomorrow's Man*, which is the story of a European Baptist statesman, J.H. Rushbrooke, and *Crossing the Boundaries*.[20] The world vision of Baptists has, too, been embodied for British Baptists – not only English Baptists - in the Baptist Missionary Society (BMS), now known as BMS World Mission.

---

16    P. Shepherd, *The Making of a Modern Denomination: John Howard Shakespeare and the English Baptists, 1898-1924* (Carlisle: Paternoster Press, 2001).

17    D.C. Sparkes, *The Home Mission Story* (Didcot: Baptist Historical Society, 1995); D.C. Sparkes, *An Accredited Ministry* (Didcot: Baptist Historical Society, 1996).

18    W.M.S. West, *Baptists Together* (Didcot: Baptist Historical Society, 2000). Morris West was also President of the Baptist Historical Society.

19    For the celebration of the centenary of the BWA in 2005 a history volume is being produced.

20    B. Green, *Tomorrow's Man: A Biography of James Henry Rushbrooke* (Didcot: Baptist Historical Society, 1997); B. Green, *Crossing the Boundaries: A History of the European Baptist Federation* (Didcot: Baptist Historical Society, 1999).

The two- hundred–year history of the BMS was told in a magisterial work by Brian Stanley in 1992,[21] and since then the work of BMS World Mission has expanded. The continuing story of Baptist involvement in overseas mission, although of great importance in the life of the denomination, necessitates an account in its own right, rather than appearing as an adjunct to this record of Baptists in England.

One wider area of Baptist involvement which is dealt with in this book, appearing in most of the chapters, is the relationship between Baptists and transdenominational and ecumenical endeavours.[22] A major milestone in the Churches' search for unity was the World Missionary Conference in Edinburgh in 1910. Long before then, Baptists had a desire to see Christians coming together, especially for the purposes of mission. Thus Baptists have been prominent in the Evangelical Alliance, which was formed in 1846, and in the Free Church movement, dating from the 1890s, although the ecumenical and the evangelical vision have seemed to some Baptists in the twentieth century to be in opposition to one another.[23] Indeed, some Baptists have accused the ecumenically-inclined of abandoning evangelicalism. In 1943 the *Baptist Times* insisted that the denomination was 'evangelical through and through',[24] but for various reasons, not all to do with ecumenism, there were Baptists who wished to dispute this claim. These disputes will be examined. While a section of the Baptist denomination eschewed ecumenism, other Baptists considered that wider co-operation was consistent with the values of the broader pan-denominational evangelical movement, a movement outlined by Professor David Bebbington, himself a Baptist, in his seminal volume, *Evangelicalism in Modern*

---

21    B. Stanley, *The History of the Baptist Missionary Society, 1792-1992* (Edinburgh: T & T Clark, 1992).
22    For an overview of the search for unity in England in the twentieth century, see D.M. Thompson, 'The Unity of the Church in Twentieth-Century England: Pleasing Dream or Common Calling?', in R.W. Swanson, ed., *Unity and Diversity in the Church* (Oxford: Blackwell, 1996), pp.507-31.
23    See I.M. Randall and D. Hilborn, *One Body in Christ: The History and Significance of the Evangelical Alliance* (Carlisle: Paternoster Press, 2001).
24    *Baptist Times* [hereafter *BT*], 6 May 1943, p.1.

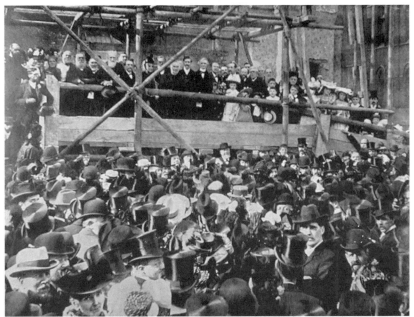

*The memorial stone laying for Baptist Church House on 24 April 1901.
A little girl, Miss Ruth Elsie Marnham, presents a bouquet to
Dr Alexander Maclaren, President of the Baptist Union.*

*Britain.*[25] For such Baptists, their evangelicalism afforded them freedom to be both distinctively Baptist and also committed to playing a constructive part in the wider Church.

In tracing the way in which Baptist communities have changed and developed through the century, the main source used here has been the *Baptist Times.* In 1899 two newspapers, the *Baptist Times* and the *Freeman,* came together to become the *Baptist Times and Freeman,* which was established as the official organ of the denomination. J.H. Shakespeare, and his brother, Alfred, were editors. Until 1910 there was another paper, the *Baptist,* edited by T.H. Stockwell, which was often

25    D.W. Bebbington, *Evangelicalism in Modern Britain: A History from the 1730s to the 1980s* (London: Routledge, 1995).

quite critical of the official Baptist Union line and which provided, therefore, a valuable alternative perspective on Baptist affairs. In 1910, however, the *Baptist* was taken over by the *Baptist Times*. In 1924 Shakespeare resigned as *Baptist Times* editor, and J.C. Carlile, a journalist as well as a Baptist minister, took over, continuing as editor for the next twenty years. Carlile was succeeded by F. Townley Lord, minister of Bloomsbury Central Baptist Church, London. The first full-time editor, Walter Bottoms, edited the *Baptist Times* from 1956 to 1973, during a period when there were some severe criticisms of the Union, especially from the Baptist Revival Fellowship (BRF). The views of the BRF were promulgated in their own *Bulletin*. Geoffrey Locks, who followed Walter Bottoms and who was the first lay person to edit the *Baptist Times*, built on the editorial line taken by Bottoms; by then there was much less emphasis on promoting an official Union position. Locks was editor until 1990, and was succeeded by John Capon, another Baptist layman, who had been editor of the *Church of England Newspaper* and founder editor of *Third Way* magazine.²⁶

A number of other important Baptist archives provide material on English Baptists in the twentieth century. These include the minutes of the Baptist Union Council and its committees; a small collection of papers from M.E. Aubrey, a Welshman whose General Secretaryship of the Union lasted from 1925 until 1951; the massive personal archive of E.A. Payne, who was the Union's enormously influential General Secretary from 1951 until 1967; the extensive papers of David S. Russell, a Scotsman who served as General Secretary from 1967 to 1982; and the correspondence and papers of Bernard Green, who held this office from 1982 to 1991. The *Baptist Handbook* provides a year by year account of Baptist Assemblies, records of denominational statistics, details of ministers, and obituaries. Other weekly religious newspapers produced during the century, particularly in the earlier part of the century, provided useful coverage of the Baptist denomination, notably the *British Weekly*, the *Christian World*, the *Christian*, and the *Christian Herald*. The thinking of Baptist ministers is found in *The Fraternal*, later

---

26    For a summary of the history see the *BT*, 11 December 2003, pp.8-9.

the *Baptist Ministers' Journal.* Michael Goodman, who has written on Baptist life in the 1930s, has brought together valuable information from ministers of that period.[27]

A few books offer an overall picture of aspects of Baptist or wider ecclesiastical life throughout the whole century. *Baptism and the Baptists: Theology and Practice in Twentieth-Century Britain* (2000), by Anthony R. Cross, is a meticulously researched study of changing Baptist thinking throughout the century, covering especially the areas of baptism and of ecumenical relationships. *Baptists in the Twentieth Century* (1982), a series of Baptist Historical Society papers, sheds light on areas such as worship, ecumenism and politics.[28] The *Baptist Quarterly*, the journal of the Baptist Historical Society, is a rich source of interpretative articles. A number of histories have appeared throughout the century looking at the development of regional Baptist Associations in England. The histories of the East Midland Association and of the Baptists in Yorkshire, Lancashire and Cheshire, both of which were published in the 1980s, are particularly valuable.[29] Much has been written about the wider Church in the twentieth century. Adrian Hastings' volume, *A History of English Christianity, 1920-2000,*[30] is in a class of its own. Although stronger on the Anglican and Catholic Churches than on the Free Churches, it illuminates the context in which Baptists operated.

Drawing from all these and from other sources, this book seeks to examine what Baptists in England – or at least some Baptists in England

---

27 See M. Goodman, 'Numerical Decline amongst English Baptists, 1930-1939', *Baptist Quarterly* [hereafter *BQ*], Vol.36, No.5, 1996; 'A Faded Heritage: English Baptist political thinking in the 1930s', *BQ*, Vol.37, No.2, 1997.

28 K.W. Clements, ed., *Baptists in the Twentieth Century* (London: Baptist Historical Society, 1982).

29 F.M.W. Harrison, *It All Began Here: The Story of the East Midland Baptist Association* (London: East Midland Baptist Association, 1986); I. Sellers, ed., *Our Heritage: The Baptists of Yorkshire, Lancashire and Cheshire, 1647-1987* (Leeds: Yorkshire Baptist Association and Lancashire & Cheshire Baptist Association, 1987).

30 A. Hastings, *A History of English Christianity, 1920-2000* (London: SCM, 4th edn., 2001).

- have experienced throughout the one hundred years beginning in 1900. It is impossible to do justice to all that took place. Much local Baptist church life is recorded in the minutes of church members' meetings. With their congregational form of church government, Baptists discuss and make decisions about major issues regarding this communal life in such meetings. Many histories have been written about local churches, but these have not been widely used here. The ways in which Baptist lay people sought to apply their faith in their working lives also require further detailed study. Several Baptists have received knighthoods, and a considerable number have received other honours such as the Commander of the Order of the British Empire (CBE) or the Officer of the Order of the British Empire (OBE), all recognizing their contribution to society. Only a few of these are mentioned. There are sources which offer pointers to the activities of Baptist lay people, such as the publications of the Baptist Men's Movement, *Baptist Layman*, later *Layman*, and *World Outlook*. The Baptist Women's League and its successor bodies have given attention to women's changing roles in society. But much of the data that would enable studies of Baptist laity to take place has not yet been collected. An oral history project, under the auspices of the Baptist Historical Society, has begun to address this question.

Some other topics have not been included because they would require more specialist treatment than is possible here. There is no detailed analysis, for example, of sermons preached through the century. *Baptist Worship To-day*, a comprehensive report produced in 1999 by Christopher (Chris) Ellis, minister of Cemetery Road, Sheffield, shows that in the 1990s Baptist sermons were usually closely based on scripture and most were described as 'teaching' or 'expositional'. The report includes other valuable data relating to the conduct of worship, for example the dominance of the New International Version of the Bible in

Baptist churches.[31] Although Baptists have prized preaching, such details are not available for earlier periods. The constitutions of local churches have not been examined, although these provide valuable insights into administrative issues, such as how lay leaders – deacons, and sometimes elders – are elected or otherwise appointed by church members.[32] Church architecture, although not described, has been a crucial issue at local level, since during the century huge sums of money have been spent by Baptists on new church buildings or modifications of existing premises. Generally, there has been a movement away from traditional Baptist chapels to multi-purpose church centres. Pews and pulpits have often been removed, organs have become less popular and worship bands have become more common, and community facilities for offering ministry to old and young have become a normal part of church premises.[33] A number of these moves are indicators of the mission priorities of Baptists.

In part because of the seemingly inexorable decline in Christian practice that has taken place in Britain in the twentieth century, the place of mission has been increasingly emphasized by Baptists and by Christians of other denominations. This book will seek to highlight that emphasis. However, a number of other themes have been central to Baptist life throughout the century. These include the place and function of the preaching and pastoral ministry, authentic spiritual experience, the

---

31   C.J. Ellis, *Baptist Worship To-day* (Didcot: Baptist Union, 1999), pp.5, 10. This report was based on two worship surveys undertaken by the Doctrine and Worship Committee of the Baptist Union. The surveys collected data on leadership and participation in worship, use of scripture, preaching, prayer, hymns and songs, the Lord's Supper, and baptism and membership. Dr Ellis's work has now been incorporated into his book, *Gathering* (Canterbury Press, 2004).

32   Many details about administration in Baptist churches are included in F. Bacon, *Church Administration* (Bristol: Bristol and District Association of Baptist Churches, 1981 [with subsequent reprintings and revision]). This book offers guidance as well as description.

33   The leading commentator in this field is Clyde Binfield. For a superb example, see C. Binfield, 'Strangers and Dissenters: The Architectural Legacy of Twentieth-Century English Nonconformity – Context, Case Study and Connexion', in Sell and Cross, eds., *Protestant Nonconformity in the Twentieth Century*, chapter 6.

social context, the role of the Baptist Union and its relationship to the churches, inter-church and inter-denominational relationships, and Baptist identity. All of these are considered in each of the chapters that follow. At the end of 1999, David Coffey, who became Baptist Union General Secretary in 1991, spoke of the reforms that were then taking place in the Union and affirmed a typically Baptist belief: 'God is leading us on this journey of reform', he affirmed, 'for his missionary purposes'.[34] In a century of church decline, the challenge of shaping communities that are relevant to and effective in mission has been seen by Baptists in England as of paramount importance.

---

34    *BT*, 23 September 1999, p.11.

# Chapter 2
# 'THE FUTURE RESTS WITH
# THE FREE CHURCHES'
# (1900-1909)

Writing in 1906 from Thame Baptist Church, Oxfordshire,
William Chambers quoted a piece of conventional Baptist
'wisdom'. It was said regarding Baptists that '75 per cent of
the ministers want to change their pastorate and 50 per cent of
the churches wish they would'.[1] The awareness that a range of
denominational problems existed and that changes were necessary was to
set the agenda for Baptist leaders, especially for J.H. Shakespeare, who
was the visionary Secretary of the Baptist Union from 1898 to 1924.
Shakespeare was deeply committed to achieving effective ministry and
mission within and through the Baptist Union. To achieve change, both in
the denomination and more widely in society, Baptists engaged in internal
re-organization, in evangelism and in socio-political action. The most
notable examples of Baptist engagement with the wider society in this
period were an intense campaign against legislation in the field of
education and Baptist support for the Liberal Party in the General
Election of 1906. In that year the *Christian World*, which was widely read
among members of the Free Churches – Methodists, Congregationalists
and Baptists being the largest such denominations - said that if figures
regarding numbers of church members in Britain had any value at all, then
'the future rests with the Free Churches'.[2] This was a decade of
considerable Free Church confidence.

---

1   *Baptist*, 27 September 1906, p.203.
2   *Christian World* [hereafter *CW*], 8 February 1906, p.11.

MINISTERS AND MEMBERS

What were the Free Church figures? By 1900 there were 239,114 members in 1,744 Baptist churches in England, as listed in the *Baptist Handbook* produced by the Baptist Union. This included churches not in the Union. The figure for Baptist membership compared with 257,435 Congregationalists and 410,384 members to be found in Wesleyan Methodism. The Easter Day communicants in the Church of England in 1900 were 1,902,000.[3] It is likely that on an average Sunday – Easter Day was not average - there were more people in Free Church chapels than in Anglican churches, since many people attended the chapels regularly who were not members.[4] Throughout the nineteenth century Free Church figures had been rising nationally, although in 1904 one observant Baptist, W.Y. Fullerton, later Home Secretary of the Baptist Missionary Society, pointed out that the number of worshippers in proportion to the population was decreasing. Few people were aware of this until after 1906. Fullerton's estimate in 1904 was that one in five of the people of London were regular worshippers.[5] There had in fact been a decline in overall church-going in London over the course of the later nineteenth century, but Baptists had increased their membership and also their percentage of London's population.[6]

Particular attention was able to be paid by Baptists to their strength in London because of a detailed survey undertaken in 1902-3 by Richard Mudie-Smith, a deacon at Westbourne Park Baptist Church, for the *Daily News*. As the results were published, the *Baptist Times and Freeman* (hereafter the *Baptist Times*), the official organ of the Baptist

3    R. Currie, A. Gilbert and L. Horsley, *Churches and Churchgoers: Patterns of Church Growth in the British Isles since 1700* (Oxford: Clarendon Press, 1977), pp.128, 142, 149; *Baptist Handbook* (London: Baptist Union, 1901). Baptists had 2,812 chapel buildings.
4    Bebbington, *The Nonconformist Conscience*, p.2.
5    *BT*, 29 April 1904, supplement, p.x.
6    J. Munson, *The Nonconformists: In Search of a Lost Culture* (London: SPCK, 1991), pp.11-12; cf. H. McLeod, *Class and Religion in the Late Victorian City* (London: Croom Helm, 1974).

denomination, seized on them with delight. Mudie-Smith reported that of the worshippers in London, 538,477 were Church of England, 545,317 were in the Free Churches and 96,218 were Roman Catholic. Baptists, with 163,052 worshippers, were the largest of the Free Church denominations, followed by Congregationalists with 158,913, Wesleyan Methodists with 122,607, the Salvation Army with 38,896 and the Presbyterians with 38,021. Attendance at the best-attended Baptist churches showed that certain preachers could still draw crowds. The largest attendance at one Baptist service was 2,210, at the huge Metropolitan Tabernacle, founded at the Elephant and Castle by the Victorian 'prince of preachers', C.H. Spurgeon. This church was not, however, a member of the Baptist Union. The largest Baptist Union causes - with more than 1,000 people at one service - were the East London Tabernacle, founded and built up by Archibald Brown, a friend of Spurgeon's, followed by Tabernacles or Chapels at Woolwich, Westbourne Park, Shoreditch, Upper Holloway, Ferme Park, West Norwood, West Croydon and Peckham.[7] Baptists appeared to be setting the pace in London.

Outside London, too, there were large Baptist churches. Broadmead Baptist Church, in Bristol, ranked with the largest London congregations. The best-attended church in the Midlands was Melbourne Hall, Leicester, where the pastor was W.Y. Fullerton, who had been trained as a pastor-evangelist under C.H. Spurgeon and had also been influenced by the founding minister of Melbourne Hall, F.B. Meyer. In 1906 the Melbourne Hall membership was 1,200. Queen's Road Baptist Church, Coventry, was another leading Midlands church. W.E. Blomfield, minister there at the beginning of the century, became President of Rawdon College, Leeds, in 1904. In his last three church meetings at Queen's Road, Blomfield received sixty people into church membership.[8]

---

7   *BT*, 12 February 1904, p.127.
8   E.E. Kendall, *Doing and Daring* (Rushden: Stanley L. Hunt, 1955), pp.70-5; C. Binfield, *Pastors and People: The Biography of a Baptist Church, Queen's Road, Coventry* (Coventry: Queen's Road Baptist Church, 1984), pp.111-12.

In the North West, Manchester had Union Chapel, Oxford Road, where the famous preacher, Alexander Maclaren, was pastor from 1858 to 1903, and Moss Side Baptist Church, both with over 800 members in the early twentieth century. In Liverpool, Myrtle Street Chapel, together with its branch causes, had almost 900 members. Another Baptist church of comparable size in Lancashire was in Accrington. The Swindon Tabernacle and Oxford's New

*Horfield Baptist Church, Bristol*

Road Baptist Church, which had several branch causes, both had around 750 members. The minister at New Road, James Dann, urged commitment to evangelism, arguing that 'every one of us is called to be a missionary'.[9]

A continuing challenge for Baptists was to establish churches in areas

*Horfield interior*

where the population was growing. This period saw the development of the phenomenon of sub-urbanization. The middle-class movement to the outer fringe of cities was to have a profound effect on the life of inner-city Baptist churches and meant that new churches had to be built to serve the spreading suburbs. At Horfield, Bristol, a 'large and handsome new chapel', as the *Baptist Times* put it, was built to seat over 1,000 people. The foundation stone was laid in 1900, at a time of remarkable growth. This church was designed to serve a new area of the city and its membership would

---

9     R. Chadwick, ed., *A Protestant Catholic Church of Christ* (Oxford: New Road Baptist Church, 2003), p.181.

overtake that of the historic Broadmead church.[10] West Bridgford was an example of advance in the Nottingham area. A church was formed in 1903

*Westgate Chapel, Bradford*

and a site was purchased on which a chapel was built in 1907.[11] In the same period the Baptists in Leeds and Bradford built new buildings in expanding residential communities. In Bradford, Baptists were able to point to their new Westgate Chapel, in the then leafy suburbs of Manningham, built in mock gothic style and able to accommodate 750 people. Westgate was not as large as Bradford's premier Baptist cause, Sion Jubilee, but new churches were symbols of what was perceived to be continuing Free Church advance. The architecture of this period spoke of

Baptist confidence. Box-shaped chapels with straight pews and galleries gave way to churches with spires, large organs and stained glass windows.[12]

Yet Baptist life remained varied. An analysis in the *Baptist Times* in 1902 showed that over one-third of Baptist churches in England had a membership of under 100, and many could not

*Westgate Chapel, Bradford*

10   *BT*, 8 February 1900, p.105; *Horfield Baptist Church: Diamond Jubilee Celebrations* (Bristol: p.p., 1952).
11   Harrison, *It All Began Here*, p.90.
12   Sellers, ed., *Our Heritage*, p.73.

afford to pay a pastor.[13] Smaller chapels, often in villages, were an important part of Baptist witness, but chapels struggled in many rural areas as people moved to the towns and cities. By contrast with other areas of the country, in the London Baptist Association (LBA) only eighteen out of 165 churches in the Association in 1902 had a membership of under 100.[14] It seemed in the early part of the century that churches which were strategically situated could grow rapidly. The Baptist chapel in Ferme Park, Hornsey, for example, which began with a membership of seventy-one in 1889, had 1,041 members by 1906. The minister there from 1890 to 1925 was the highly respected Charles Brown, who had trained at Bristol Baptist College. Henry Cook, Brown's successor and biographer, said that Ferme Park, was 'filled with devout people of the best stamp'. Cook saw the neighbourhood as 'coming to the peak of its development', with the Ferme

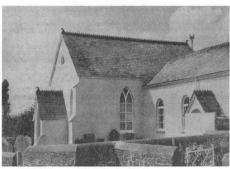

*A rural chapel: Newton St Petrock Baptist Church, Devon, built in 1904 but in an older style; the 1830 chapel to right.*

Park church reaping that benefit. Although most Baptist churches abandoned the system of pew rents around 1900, in favour of voluntary offerings, Ferme Park had a waiting list for rented pews.[15] Ferme Park was also an example of a church that encouraged a wide range of activities. Like other progressive chapels, it offered sporting facilities. In 1901 the Ferme Park Baptist Tennis Club had to reply to allegations that

---

13   *BT*, 9 May 1902, supplement p.ii.
14   *BT*, 11 July 1902, p.525.
15   H. Cook, *Charles Brown* (London: Kingsgate Press, 1939), pp.40-9; cf. B. and F. Bowers, 'Baptists and their Money', unpublished paper to the Third International Conference on Baptist Studies, Prague, July 2003, p.9. Copy deposited in the Angus Library, Regent's Park College, Oxford.

single men and women meeting at the Club were indulging in 'improper behaviour'. Tennis clubs were regarded as 'marriage markets'.[16]

There were at times considerable tensions between the outlook of rural pastors and that of more sophisticated urban Baptist pastors. One village minister, H.C. Field, from the Baptist Old Stevington Meeting in Bedfordshire, writing in May 1903 in the *Baptist*, saw the difference in terms of education. Field claimed that university-educated Baptist ministers 'will not take poor pastorates but are always on

*Interior, Newton St Petrock*

the look-out for the wealthiest churches with the biggest salaries'.[17] Not surprisingly, there was an indignant reply from a 'Baptist undergraduate', who claimed that Baptist ministers he knew without university training had 'manifested not a little of the unlovely spirit of competition and self-seeking which Mr Field attributes to University men'. His view was that university-educated ministers as a whole had no less devotion than others.[18] Field's perspective was, nonetheless, probably quite widespread. However, it was not the case that large Baptist churches invariably had more highly educated ministers. Indeed R.E. Willis, from Ipswich, a correspondent who contributed regularly to the *Baptist*, sought to prove that ministers with university degrees were relatively ineffective and that a high proportion of them were pastors in small churches.[19]

---

16  H. McLeod, '"Thews and Sinews": Nonconformity and Sport', in D.W. Bebbington and T. Larsen, eds., *Modern Christianity and Cultural Aspirations* (Sheffield: Sheffield Academic Press, 2003), p.42.
17  *Baptist*, 15 May 1903, p.310.
18  *Baptist*, 22 May 1903, p.326.
19  *Baptist*, 22 May 1906, p.329.

Although it is important to look at the role played by ministers in the progress or otherwise of local Baptist churches and of the denomination, the part played by prominent lay people was crucial. Sir George White, from Norwich, was returned as Liberal MP for North Norfolk in 1900 and soon became a leader of the Free Church opposition in Parliament to the Conservative government's Education Bill.[20] Sir George Macalpine, a member of Accrington Baptist Church, was a local colliery and brick company owner who found time to serve in the church as a deacon and a Sunday School teacher. He was an effective lay preacher, served the Baptist Missionary Society (BMS), was President of the Union in 1910, and was also an accomplished Greek and Hebrew scholar.[21] In London, Regent's Park Chapel, a uniquely upper-middle-class Baptist church, was ably led by E.G. Gange, the minister, and his preaching no doubt contributed to the attendance of 1,400 on a Sunday. But the overall ministry at Regent's Park Chapel owed a great deal to leading church families. For example, the Chapel's fine hall was constructed as a result of money given by Lord Justice and Lady Lush, who were wealthy members. Dr Percy Lush, a doctor, and Samuel Lithgow, a solicitor, were involved in helping working people through the church's Stanhope Institute.[22]

Three laymen were elected to the Baptist Union presidency (a one-year office) in the Edwardian period. In 1903 Sir George White was President, and two years later the office was held by Judge William Willis, KC, a member of Dereham Baptist Church, Norfolk, and a lay preacher, who had been MP for Colchester in the 1880s.[23] The third lay President was Sir George Macalpine. Such lay leaders often offered insights into the state of the denomination. An active layman from a noted

20   B.M. Doyle, ' "Through the Windows of a Baptist Meeting House": Religion, Politics and the Nonconformist Conscience in the Life of Sir George White MP', *BQ*, Vol.36, No.6 (1996), pp.294-307.
21   Sellers, ed., *Our Heritage*, p.54.
22   *BT*, 19 January 1900, p.45.
23   D.W. Bebbington, 'Baptist MPs in the Nineteenth Century', *BQ*, Vol.29, No.1 (1981), pp.14-15.

Baptist family, John William Jewson, the Secretary of St Mary's Baptist Church, Norwich, chaired the Norfolk Association in 1906 and took as his theme 'Our deficiencies as a denomination'. Jewson spoke rather gloomily about lack of unity between Baptist churches, lack of unity within fellowships, lack of charity towards other denominations, and lack of charity towards the working classes.[24] Lay people were often in touch with the huge social needs and significant changes evident in Britain in the twentieth century and the challenges faced in terms of mission. A continuing problem, for instance, was that large new areas of housing, such as Walthamstow, in London, were neglected by the churches, and church attendance by Baptists who moved to such areas often lapsed.[25] Although some churches were harnessing lay leadership, the loss of lay people would become a major preoccupation.

## A STRONGER UNION

The person in the early twentieth century who did most to draw Baptist churches together and give them a common vision was a formidable church leader, John Howard Shakespeare. Born in Malton, Yorkshire, in 1857, the son of a Baptist minister, Shakespeare spent his boyhood in the Midlands.[26] He studied at Regent's Park College, obtaining an MA from London University, and in 1883, when almost twenty-six, became minister of St Mary's, Norwich. Shakespeare had a compelling personality and in 1892 he made his mark at a Baptist Assembly when he set out, with characteristic passion and attention to detail, a plan for starting new churches ('church extension') to reach the expanding urban population. When the health of Samuel Harris Booth, the Secretary of the Union, began to fail in the 1890s, Shakespeare was approached about becoming the next Secretary. Although reluctant to leave pastoral ministry, he

---

24    C.B. Jewson, *The Baptists in Norfolk* (London: Carey Kingsgate Press, 1957), pp.137-8.
25    *BT,* 13 April 1906, p.259.
26    See Sir Geoffrey Shakespeare, *Let Candles be Brought In* (London: MacDonald, 1949), chapter XVII.

accepted the invitation and took up the post in 1898. He had, as Shepherd puts it, dramatic and far-reaching ambitions for the Union;[27] his concept of what it was to be an effective denomination with an efficient ministry was to shape much of organized Baptist life in the twentieth century.

*Southampton Row in 1908*
*Baptist Church House is on the left beyond the tunnel entrance*

---

27    Shepherd, *The Making of a Modern Denomination*, p.20.

The first major project which Shakespeare undertook was the promotion of what was called a Twentieth Century Fund for the denomination, a suggestion that had come in 1898 from Samuel Vincent of Plymouth when he was President of the Union.[28] The goal was to raise £125,000 for evangelizing and for church extension; £30,000 for the Union's Annuity Fund; £6,000 for student scholarships; £34,000 for a new Baptist Church House in London, and £25,000 for educational and other projects approved by the Baptist Union Council.[29] This was a massive target. Money had been coming in only very slowly for an existing Extension fund, launched in 1892. In 1898 only £10,000 had been collected.[30] The churches, however, responded to the fresh challenge that Shakespeare put before them. The *Baptist Times*, reflecting Shakespeare's views, spoke in 1900 about many churches 'in a state of semi-paralysis', and argued for denominational efforts to help such churches.[31] Shakespeare was aware, however, that the Union was far from united. One major

*J.H. Shakespeare*

division was between closed-communion churches, which accepted only those baptized as believers to communion, and open-communion churches, which welcomed all Christians. Closed-communion churches could earmark gifts to the Twentieth Century Fund for churches with that practice.[32] Through this and other policies, Shakespeare was seeking to be an inclusive leader, drawing the Union together.

Shakespeare was prone to depression, and his health gave way for a time in 1901, partly due to extreme pressure of work. Despite this, the

---

28    J.H. Shakespeare, *The Story of the Baptist Union Twentieth Century Fund* (London: Baptist Union Publications Department, 1904), p.9.

29    Sparkes, *The Home Mission Story*, p.17.

30    West, *Baptists Together*, pp.36-8.

31    *BT*, 14 September 1900, p.746.

32    *Baptist*, 5 January 1900, p.10.

fund-raising campaign was successful. Herbert Marnham, a young London stockbroker and treasurer of the Union, and Sir John Barran, MP, from Leeds, the founder of a successful clothing business and the first treasurer of Leeds University, were joint Fund treasurers. Shakespeare travelled widely, sometimes with John Clifford of Westbourne Park Baptist Church, London, the best-known Baptist leader of the time. In March 1902 there was a 'Simultaneous Collection' for the Fund and it was reckoned that for the first time the same hymns were used in 1,200 Baptist churches. A million and a half leaflets and hymnsheets were distributed.[33] The *British Weekly*, edited by W. Robertson Nicoll, which had the largest readership of any religious newspaper in England, discerned deep Baptist loyalty, with Shakespeare and Alexander Maclaren from Manchester (then the 'Grand old Man' of Baptist life) seen as key Baptist figures.[34] Perhaps the response of the denomination was not so much due to old loyalties as to new enthusiasm. This reached a pitch of excitement on 1 May 1902, at the spring Assembly, when Shakespeare announced to the 1,500 people present that gifts and promises amounting to £250,000 had been received. In fact a promise of £5,000 from the Chivers family (the jam manufacturers) had come that day. Wealthier Baptists had contributed generously.[35] This Fund was an astonishing achievement and signalled Baptist denominational renewal.[36]

Impetus towards more united action among Baptists was to be found in the regional Baptist Associations of churches as well as the Union. Ministers and lay  people in Associations were taking  their own initiatives. In 1901 the LBA, the largest Association, appointed John Bradford, minister of a strong church, Fairlop Road, Leytonstone, as its first full-time Secretary. During his period as Secretary, the London

---

33   *British Weekly* [hereafter *BW*], 27 March 1902, p.612.
34   *BW*, 8 May 1902, p.83.
35   Payne, *The Baptist Union*, p.159.
36   P. Shepherd, 'Denominational Renewal', *BQ*, Vol.37, No.7 (1998), pp.336-50.

Baptist Property Board was formed.[37] In 1904 the East Midland Baptist Association appointed its first full-time Secretary, C.G. Croome, who had been pastor of the Palm Street Church, Nottingham. Associations were keen to see Baptist churches established in towns where none existed. By 1906 seventy-five new churches had been helped from the Twentieth Century Fund. Not all succeeded: Matlock, in Derbyshire, for example, began with services in the town hall in 1902, and two years later the prospects for starting a church looked good. The sum of £750 was offered from the Twentieth Century Fund, but to build a chapel cost £2,600, and the services were discontinued in 1907.[38] Others met with more success. At Brighton, a growing town, it was felt that a strong central Baptist church was needed and two of the existing four Baptist churches, Sussex Street and Queen Street, agreed to merge to form Gloucester Place, which opened in 1904.[39]

Although there were advances in the operations of the local Associations across the country, the trend that was more evident under Shakespeare was towards denominational centralization. This was especially visible in the re-location in 1903 of the Union headquarters to Baptist Church House in Southampton Row, in the Holborn area of London. Previously the Union had rented three rather dingy rooms in premises in Furnival Street, near Holborn Circus, used primarily for the BMS. Before Shakespeare's period, the BMS took the lead in many denominational matters. Union income was relatively small. Some Baptists took exception to Shakespeare's ambitious plans to spend £34,000 (in the event it was £50,000) on Church House. 'Fair Play Layman', writing to the *Baptist*, deplored this 'big house' which most ordinary Baptists would be too shy to enter, but which would be 'a nice centre for capitalists to debate the merits of ministers  for vacant

37    W.C. Johnson, *Encounter in London: The Story of the London Baptist Association, 1865-1965* (London: Carey Kingsgate Press, 1965), p.58.
38    Harrison, *It All Began Here*, pp.90-2.
39    F. Buffard, *Kent and Sussex Baptist Associations* (Faversham: Kent and Sussex Baptist Associations, 1963), p.120.

pulpits'.[40] Many other Baptists, however, took considerable pride in the centre, with its panelled oak Council Chamber and other fine features. A bronze statue of C.H. Spurgeon was sculpted and placed in the reception area in Baptist Church House.[41] The stress on the place of London in Baptist life was evident within the LBA, with Bloomsbury Chapel becoming Bloomsbury Central Baptist Church, a church for which both the LBA and the Union took partial responsibility.[42] Baptist Church House became the hub of denominational life, a fruit of what J.C. Carlile, Baptist minister and journalist (editor of the *Baptist Times* from 1925), called Shakespeare's genius for organization and push to centralization.[43]

As part of the new organization, Union committee structures were elaborated. In this Baptists were following the same path as other denominations, notably the Congregationalists. The *Baptist*, representing a more independent strain in Baptist life, featured trenchant criticisms of these trends, such as the remarks of a 'Minister' who asked in 1906: 'Have we degenerated into a Roman hierarchy with Mr Shakespeare as the Pope?'[44] Yet Shakespeare, although somewhat autocratic, gathered around him able men and women as colleagues.[45] One of these was F.B. Meyer, who had been the visionary evangelistic minister of Melbourne Hall, Leicester, and then of Regent's Park Chapel, London. As President of the Union in

*F.B. Meyer*

1906, Meyer argued that Baptist churches – he added, in a phrase that implied centralization, 'may I not say the Baptist Church?' - with other Free Churches could give leadership to the nation in a way which the

---

40    *Baptist*, 26 January 1900, p.58.
41    For further details, see D.C. Sparkes, *The Offices of the Baptist Union of Great Britain* (Didcot: Baptist Historical Society, 1996), pp.8-17.
42    Johnson, *Encounter in London*, p.58.
43    J.C. Carlile, *My Life's Little Day* (London: Blackie, 1935), pp.152, 158.
44    *Baptist*, 18 January 1906, p.36.
45    Payne, *Baptist Union*, pp.164-5.

Established Church could not do.[46] When Meyer was elected President he had strong backing from central Union figures, although at that time he was minister of Christ Church, Westminster Bridge Road, Lambeth, which was a Congregational church.[47] There was a perceived need for leaders who would not only serve on committees but would travel and bind the churches together. Meyer was an inveterate traveller, and he and Shakespeare drove extensively around England in 1906-7. Shakespeare commented: 'We have accomplished the redemption of the motor car.'[48] Such initiatives were intended to create a stronger Union.

## A NEW FUND AND A NEW FEDERATION

In May 1902 W.E. Blomfield, then minister of Queen's Road, Coventry, delivered an address at the spring Baptist Assembly which was later seen as crucial for a further Union fund, designed partly to support the stipends of pastors. In his address, Blomfield paid tribute to the thinking of the Baptist businessman, William Chivers, from Histon, Cambridgeshire, who had died that year. Chivers had been influenced by the way in which the Free Church of Scotland had set up in the 1840s a successful 'Sustentation Fund'. Blomfield suggested a Baptist Sustentation Fund, incorporating the existing Home Mission and Augmentation Funds, to ensure a minimum stipend for all approved or 'recognised' Baptist Union ministers and also to make provision for evangelistic endeavour. Ministerial recognition committees had begun to operate in the Baptist Union from 1898.[49] In this period there were about 2,000 ministers listed in the *Baptist Handbook*, of whom approximately eighty per cent had received official Union recognition.[50] There were particular worries about ministry for small churches which could not pay a stipend. Shakespeare, in a *Baptist Times* editorial in 1902 written to influence the Baptist Union

46   *BT*, 27 April 1906, p.308.
47   *BT*, 29 April 1904, supplement, p.11; *BT*, 14 July 1905, supplement, p.v.
48   *BT*, 27 July 1906, p.551.
49   *BT*, 9 May 1902, supplement, pp.ii-5; Sparkes, *An Accredited Ministry*, pp.9-12.
50   Shepherd, *The Making of a Modern Denomination*, pp.56-8.

Council (a body of about 160 people) as well as the Assembly, described small churches as 'often depressed almost to despair'. In Shakespeare's mind there was an urgent need for action.[51]

Backing for the Sustentation Fund was forthcoming. The developments are covered in detail by Douglas Sparkes in *The Home Mission Story*.[52] Early in 1903 the Union established a Sustentation Fund Committee, which became the Ministerial Settlement and Sustentation Committee, with the settlement issue arising from Union concern to help pastors move from one church to another.[53] There was much debate about questions of stipends and settlement in 1903-5. Some saw Baptist independency being undermined by the moves towards help from central funds. A 'young layman', G.H. Tomlin, was highly critical of Shakespeare in the *Baptist*, saying that the true preacher would work regardless of stipend. The *Baptist Times* had refused to print Tomlin's letter.[54] Radical ideas were discussed in the Union committee, chaired by J. G. Greenhough, minister until 1905 at Victoria Road Church, Leicester. In 1906 there were references to the possibility of Baptist churches in a geographical area forming a 'common church' with 'one eldership'. On settlement, there was discussion of the possibility of ministers settling in a new church every four years, on a given date. Methodism was the model. In the light of poor ministerial remuneration, fully centralized payment of ministers' stipends was mooted. Thomas Greenwood, who was intimately associated with C.H. Spurgeon's Pastors' College and also became Secretary of the LBA, tabled these proposals.[55]

---

51   *BT*, 17 January 1902, pp.46-7.
52   D.C. Sparkes, *The Home Mission Story* (Didcot: Baptist Historical Society, 1995).
53   Ibid., p.22.
54   *Baptist*, 20 February 1903, p.118.
55   Minutes of the Baptist Union Ministerial Settlement and Sustentation Committee, 29 January 1906; 20 February 1906. The Minutes of the BU Council and its associated committees are bound together in a series of volumes now at Regent's Park College Oxford, Angus Library. Greenwood was later Chairman of Spurgeon's College Council.

At the 1906 spring Assembly a motion asked the Council to ascertain to what degree Baptist ministers and churches would be willing to accept 'the Periodic Exchange of Pastorates through the agency of a special Committee of the Baptist Union'.[56] It was agreed to test this far-reaching idea, although a considerable number of pastors demurred, believing that an increasingly central control of ministers was being mooted. One minister, 'Called, not Chosen', said in the *Baptist* that if such control became a reality he would be one of the first to join an alternative 'Union of ostracized men'.[57] About 1,300 questionnaires were sent out to test opinion. Shakespeare received only 115 replies, eighty-three in favour and thirty-two against. The Union Council, chaired by F.B. Meyer as Union President, decided early in 1907 that despite this low level of interest a joint meeting of the Ministerial Settlement and Ministerial Recognition Committees should be asked to draft a plan.[58] Precedents could be used: the Lancashire and Cheshire Association had set up its own advisory committee to assist in settlements. At a meeting of the Sustentation and Ministerial Recognition Committees in February 1907, a plan was produced which proposed that churches and ministers would be eligible to join a voluntary union, 'The Circle'. Churches in the Circle would appoint pastors from within the Circle and pastors would move every four years, unless the church voted that they stay. Information about pastors would be circulated to help with settlements.[59]

This scheme, as Sparkes comments, threatened to divide the denomination.[60] Only the eighty-three churches interested in the new ideas (which represented Shakespeare's thinking) were sent the details of the 'Circle'. A conference was proposed. By the end of 1907 there were only thirty replies. Twelve churches said they would send representatives to a

---

56    *BT*, 27 April 1906, p.306.
57    *Baptist*, 25 January 1906, p.52.
58    Minutes of the Baptist Union Council, 17 December 1906; 15 January 1907.
59    Minutes of a Joint Meeting of the Baptist Union Ministerial Settlement and Sustentation Committee and the Ministerial Recognition Committee, 19 February 1907. Bound in with BU Council minutes, Angus Library., Regent's Park College, Oxford.
60    Sparkes, *The Home Mission Story*, pp.26-7.

conference on the subject. Eight others expressed general approval of the plan but wanted amendments.[61] When the Ministerial Settlement and Sustentation Committee met on 13 January 1908 it seemed that there was negligible support from the churches or the Associations for radical change.[62] Shakespeare dropped the idea of a 'Circle' and began instead to talk of a 'Federation' - language which was common in wider Free Church circles at the time. The only part of a 'Federation' paper presented at a meeting of Union Officers on 19 May 1908 to draw an enthusiastic response, however, was the proposal for a fund to ensure minimum stipends.[63] Even this had centralizing overtones, since churches being 'sustained' would send to the Union what they raised for ministerial support, and where this sum was less than the minimum stipend it would be supplemented. The scheme included fixed terms for pastorates - three, five or seven years. The proposals were trailed in the *Baptist Times* on 22 January 1909.[64]

There was, not surprisingly, considerable debate at the next Council, with the formidable Richard Glover, of Tyndale Baptist Church, Bristol, opposing Shakespeare's ideas. James Logan Moffat, minister of the large Baptist congregation in Accrington, was similarly unimpressed. Both Glover and Logan had grown up in the Presbyterian tradition and their opposition to Shakespeare's plans may have sprung in part from a fear that the Baptist Union might become more Presbyterian.[65] Differing views appeared in the *Baptist Times*. Although some feared the new centralized system, others highlighted the suffering village ministers were experiencing because of extreme independency. In the Union as a whole 36.8% of the ministers were earning under £120 per annum, although in

---

61    Minutes of the Baptist Union Ministerial Settlement and Sustentation Committee, 17 December 1907 (bound with BU Council minutes, Angus Library).
62    Minutes of the Baptist Union Ministerial Settlement and Sustentation Committee, 13 January 1908.
63    Minutes of a Meeting of Baptist Union officers and others, 19 May 1908.
64    *BT*, 22 January 1909, p.56.
65    I am indebted to Douglas Sparkes, former Deputy General Secretary of the Baptist Union, for this suggestion.

London only 9% earned under £120.[66] With the debate still on-going, revised proposals were presented by Shakespeare to the 1909 spring Assembly of the Union.[67] There was still no resolution, but Shakespeare was undaunted, continuing to insist that churches and ministers would be helped by the scheme.[68] At the Council on 4 October 1909 it was reported that ten Associations had approved the scheme and another eleven had referred it to their churches. Of the 132 churches that had responded, 106 were in favour, eighteen were against and eight were neutral.[69] After seven years of debate, the 1,608 accredited ministers who were in Baptist pastorates in 1909 were still uncertain about how Shakespeare's thinking might or might not affect their ministries and their salaries.

THE 'WEAK PLACE' - HOME MISSION

The tendency in much of this discussion was to focus on the inner workings of the churches rather than on mission, although for Shakespeare effective mission was the goal. 'The weak place in our Denomination', said the *Baptist Times* in 1900, 'is in our Home Missions'.[70] The fact that £125,000 was allocated to home mission from the Twentieth Century Fund was important. F.C. Spurr, who began his ministry in Cardiff, was the missioner of the Union from 1890 to 1904, before moving to Maze Pond, Old Kent Road, London, as pastor. As part of his mission enterprise, Spurr involved himself (with many other Baptists) in the huge Free Church 'Simultaneous Mission' in 1901. This pan-denominational outreach began in London and moved to other parts of the country. In Birmingham, which was a major centre, the chief missioners were Gipsy Smith, an evangelist associated with Methodism, and John Clifford, who had a strongly evangelistic vision. Visitation took place all over the city. Birmingham Town Hall was filled every night and

---

66    *BT*, 11 July 1902, p.525.
67    *BT*, 30 April 1909, supplement, pp.iv-viii.
68    *BT*, 9 July 1909, p.500.
69    Minutes of the Baptist Union Council, 4 October 1909.
70    *BT* 5 January 1900, p.9.

there were overflow meetings. This kind of impact was paralleled in other cities. There was considerable analysis of the Simultaneous Mission, with some commentators taking the view that it had not made a great impression on the masses of people who were outside the churches. [71]

Some Baptist churches were, nonetheless, growing significantly in this period. The findings of the census by Mudie-Smith in 1902 were followed closely, and the *British Weekly* noted that the Baptist Tabernacle in Poplar, with 1,235 worshippers, had the highest attendance of any Protestant church in the district. This attendance compared with forty-four people four and a half years earlier when the innovative minister, Alfred Tildsley, who had a particular interest in the use of films, began his ministry.[72] Under its much-loved pastor, John Wilson, the Woolwich Baptist Tabernacle, with a membership of 1,497 at the time of the Mudie-Smith survey, had 2,444 in attendance, including children. The core of the church, according to the survey, comprised solid middle-class artisans, who were at least partially successful in drawing in working-class people. Wilson was minister in Woolwich from 1878, when the membership of the church was ninety, to 1939. His contribution to the neighbourhood was such that he was elected only the second Freeman of the Borough of Woolwich.[73] Mudie-Smith's data showed that the Free Churches were at their least prosperous in the West End of London. Chelsea, for example, had only one Baptist church, Lower Sloane Street, although this cause offered some encouragement to Baptists since it had grown from 506 members in 1886 to 936 in 1903.[74] There were also examples of growth outside London. The Norfolk Association reported in 1902 that there had been 192 baptisms in the previous year, the highest number yet recorded.

---

71   E.K.H. Jordan, *Free Church Unity*, p.69; *BT*, 12 April 1900, p.239; see D.J. Tidball, 'Evangelical Nonconformist Home Missions, 1796-1901', University of Keele PhD (1981).

72   *BW*, 26 February 1903, p.519; D.R. Rapp, 'A Baptist Pioneer: The exhibition of film to London's East End working classes, 1900-1919', *BQ*, Vol.40, No.1 (January 2003), pp.6-21.

73   H. Moncrieff, *Roots of Labour* (Yeovil: Linden Hall, 1990), pp.54-60.

74   *BW*, 4 June 1903, p.107.

But it also noted a drift to the cities, with young people being lost to the country churches.[75] Growth was uneven.

Part of the national growth in the years 1902-4 may have been due to the evangelistic missions conducted by two Americans, R.A. Torrey and Charles Alexander, who followed the model of Dwight L. Moody and his singer-colleague, Ira Sankey. Large Torrey-Alexander meetings were held in cities such as Birmingham. T.E. Titmuss, pastor of Spring Hill Baptist Church and an influential leader within the strong Birmingham Baptist constituency, was largely responsible for organizing the Torrey-Alexander mission in 1904 in Birmingham's Bingley Hall.[76] In 1904 the *British Weekly* asked ministers to report on the results of the extensive campaigns across Britain. David Davies, at Holland Road Baptist Church, Hove, said that after the meetings in the Dome, Brighton, he had received a number of names to follow up, but these were mainly Sunday School children. He was, however, baptizing three people converted at the mission. Davies commented that 'the converts with comparatively few exceptions have been drawn from the churchgoers and not from the masses, who seldom, if ever, attend religious services'. Davies spoke of the problems of reaching people 'in a pleasure-seeking town like Brighton'. David Llewellyn, pastor at Florence Road Baptist Church, Brighton, said that there were reportedly 3,000 converts in Brighton, but he estimated only 300 additions to the churches. Richard Evans, at Girlington Baptist Church, Bradford, told a similar story. Churches were receiving new members, but few, according to most pastors who reported, attributed their spiritual experiences to the mission.[77]

Considerable Baptist advance took place in 1905, and it was regarded as significant that this was the year in which the Welsh Revival was at its height. The impact of this Revival spread to England through ministers who visited Wales. In 1905 the Berkshire Association reported over 200

---

75   Jewson, *The Baptists in Norfolk*, p.132.
76   A.S. Langley, *Birmingham Baptists: Past and Present* (London: The Kingsgate Press, 1939), p.168.
77   *BW*, 3 November 1904, p.84; 10 November 1904, p.108.

baptisms in the previous twelve months, following a period of stagnation. The fresh vitality was attributed to the influence of the Revival.[78] The number of people baptized by the East Midland Association churches in 1905 was 1,686, by far the highest figure ever. From then on, however, this number dropped steadily.[79] At the Metropolitan Tabernacle in London a mission conducted by students from the Pastors' College, inspired by the Revival, lasted for several weeks and hundreds were added to the congregation. A report by Archibald McCaig, the College Principal, in 1906, emphasized, however, that this was not a passing revivalist phenomenon.[80] McCaig was justified in arguing that there had been on-going Baptist growth. The Pastors' College received reports in 1903 from 418 former students who were currently pastors, indicating that in their churches there had been 3,954 converts baptized in the previous year.[81] Such figures were used in unashamedly partisan, pro-Spurgeonic reports in the *Baptist*, which noted that of the nine churches in the Union with over 900 members, seven were led by ministers trained at the Pastors' College.[82]

This pattern of growth was not to continue, despite much evangelistic activity. Many churches, larger and smaller, went into decline. For several Baptist Associations, the years after 1906 were years in which this began to be evident. This was not the case in all Associations. The Western Association, for example, saw continued growth up to 1918.[83] For London, however, the year 1907, when Charles Brown from Ferme Park was president of the LBA, represented a peak, with a total of 57,331 members in 199 churches. Ominously, 1907 also saw 3,173 erasures from

78   E.A. Payne, *The Baptists of Berkshire* (London: Carey Kingsgate Press, 1951), p.124.
79   Harrison, *It All Began Here*, p.87.
80   A. McCaig, 'The Pastors' College Jubilee', *The Sword and the Trowel*, June 1906, pp.278-9.
81   *BT*, 20 November 1903, p.805.
82   *Baptist*, 24 April 1903, p.265.
83   F.H. Cockett, *Partnership in Service: A Brief History of the Western Baptist Association, 1823-1973* (Bridport, n.p., n.d.), p.17.

LBA membership, a very high figure. In 1908 the Kent and Sussex Association was commenting on 'the decline of membership, the indifference to public worship, the neglect of the prayer meeting, the paucity of conversions'. There had in fact been a level of gloom in Kent and Sussex for some time. Discussions in 1903 had dealt with the question 'Why are conversions so rare?' Methods of making worship more attractive to the unchurched were debated.[84] 1906 saw membership peak in the Yorkshire Association, and Lancashire and Cheshire followed the same trend. There had already been a decline in membership of the Free Churches relative to the population, but when decline became absolute Baptists began to take notice.[85]

Questions about decline would dominate much Baptist thinking in the first half of the twentieth century. The natural response made by Shakespeare and others was to reaffirm the place of mission. In 1907, A. Weaver Evans, who had been a minister in the Free Church of England and the Countess of Huntingdon's Connexion, became Union missioner. Applications from churches wanting Weaver Evans to help them were sent to Shakespeare, thus emphasizing that this appointment was central to the Union's vision.[86] In the same year, George Macalpine from Accrington, as Moderator of the Lancashire and Cheshire Association, spoke on 'The Arrested Progress of the Church'. It was a phrase taken up by others in the Union's leadership. Macalpine bluntly blamed this 'arrested progress' on a lack of attention to conversion, unnecessary concern about biblical scholarship, and a lost sense of sin and of a Saviour. He was not enthusiastic about the newly-popular Pleasant Sunday Afternoon or Brotherhood meetings for men that were held – as a means of outreach - in many Free Churches. 'Christianity', the fairly conservative Macalpine declared, 'is not a religion of pleasure, but of sorrow.'[87] Two years later the Union set up the Arrested Progress Committee, to plan initiatives, and

---

84    Buffard, *Kent and Sussex Baptist Associations*, p.122.
85    See Bebbington, *The Nonconformist Conscience*, p.2.
86    *BT*, 6 September 1907, p.664.
87    Sellers, ed., *Our Heritage*, p.77.

from this came Association Spiritual Welfare Committees. Baptists were seeking denominational progress through mission.

EDUCATIONAL PRINCIPLES

Most Baptists in this period were also committed to some level of engagement with society. In 1902-3 the focus of this engagement became education. Equality of opportunity in the field of education had been an important objective of Nonconformists in the nineteenth century and there was thus considerable Free Church resentment when the Conservative government led by Arthur Balfour began to plan a reorganization which would fund church schools (Anglican and Roman Catholic) from local rates. A Bill was introduced into Parliament in March 1902. There was strong opposition not only from the Free Churches but also from the trades unions to a scheme which gave money from the rates to church schools yet did not give any control of the schools to the public. Parliamentary debates carried on through sixty-five sittings. On 4 December 1902 the Bill was passed by 246 votes to 123 and it came into force in March 1903. Free Church leaders, in opposing the Bill, pointed out that 16,000 teaching posts in Church schools were not open to Free Church members, and at the Baptist Union Assembly in autumn 1902 there was support for the principle of refusing to pay the new rate. This stance was seen by those present as being like a 'Solemn League and Covenant', reminiscent of periods when those who dissented from the state suffered for their faith.[88]

---

88    *BT,* 17 October 1902, p.763.

Baptist ministers were highly active in the campaign of resistance to the Education Act. The strong anti-Catholicism of many Protestants was a factor. There were denunciations of 'Rome on the rates'. Baptist feelings may also have been stimulated by a sense of social exclusion.[89] One of the main Baptist opponents of the Act, however, was George White, who as a shoe manufacturer and Liberal MP was certainly not socially deprived. In 1902, when MPs were debating the Education Bill, White had been Chairman for seventeen years of the Norwich School Board. White also launched the Technical Institute, which became the Norwich City College. When it came to educational reform, White was not negatively oppositional. Indeed he and his Conservative opposite number tried to resolve the difficulties caused by the government's proposals, but their ideas were not acceptable at Westminster.[90] Did Baptist ministers who opposed the legislation feel socially excluded? It seems more likely that they were inspired by their convictions. On 4 December 1902, Thomas Spurgeon, who as minister of the Metropolitan Tabernacle had a certain standing in

*The Revd Charles Brown addresses a protest meeting in October 1903, backed by the Revds J.R. Wood, F.B. Meyer and Dr Rowlands, following the trial of passive resisters before the Hornsey magistrates.*

Edwardian London, stated in the *British Weekly* that he would not pay the new rate. 'The law', he said defiantly, 'must seize our goods.' The question of the law was sensitive. 'Some', Spurgeon asserted, 'will persist

---

89    K.D. Brown, *A Social History of the Nonconformist Ministry in England and Wales, 1800-1930* (Oxford: Clarendon Press, 1988), p.213.

90    Jewson, *The Baptists in Norfolk*, pp.133-4.

in calling us law-breakers. So be it. We are in good company.' He cited Peter and John ('we must obey God rather than men') and other precedents.[91]

Shakespeare, who was concerned to mould a Baptist witness that would have credibility in society, would have preferred to avoid the campaign. He admitted in December 1902 his internal struggle. 'I thoroughly dislike fads and faddists', he remarked, 'and I am out of sympathy with extreme people generally.' The Act, however, as he saw it, was an unjust measure.[92] Shakespeare was, therefore, willing to have the spring 1903 Assembly used as an occasion when publicity could be given to the campaign of 'passive resistance', as it became known. In reality, Shakespeare did not have much option. George White, as Union President, gave a speech at the Assembly which was a call to battle and which attracted sustained applause. White pronounced: 'Consequences are nothing; principles are everything.' He saw the consequences of resisting – seizures of personal property and even imprisonment - as important ways of highlighting the battle, but as being meaningless without principles. The Assembly rose at the end of his speech. Shakespeare, who was seated next to John Clifford, stood and said that Clifford had remarked delightedly to him that the Union had found its voice. White's address was reckoned one of the ablest delivered by a President of the Union.[93]

A month later, in May 1903, many Baptists joined a huge demonstration against the new Act. This was staged in Hyde Park and attracted more than 140,000 people. Clifford and Meyer, together with Silvester Horne, a Congregational minister and later an MP, were the main speakers on this unparalleled occasion.[94] Then, in July 1903, 15,000 people packed the Royal Albert Hall, when Thomas Spurgeon opened the meeting with prayer and Clifford roused the willing audience. As Clifford employed his fiery rhetoric, handkerchiefs and programmes were waved,

91    *BW*, 4 December 1902, p.192.
92    *BW*, 18 December 1902, p.283.
93    *BW*, 30 April 1903, p.60.
94    *BW*, 28 May 1903, p.164.

and often what he had to say was drowned by cheering.[95] The *British Weekly* covered news each week of what it called the 'persecutions' of those who refused to pay the new, unjust rate. By this time not only Conservative, but also some Liberal politicians were becoming annoyed. Lord Rosebery, a Liberal, was upset by the 'absolute misstatements' he thought Clifford was making.[96] For their part, the Free Churches, determined that they would make their mark, formed a National Committee for Passive Resistance. The Committee reported in July 1903 that J.H. French, the President of the LBA, had refused to pay the rate. French was taken before the magistrate, who was personally sympathetic but had to impose a fine.[97]

Some individual cases of passive resistance received special publicity. Walter Parker, a member of Sutton Baptist Church, Surrey, who was aged about sixty, was sent to prison for non-payment. It was a severe ordeal for this law-abiding citizen to spend a week in Wandsworth Prison. His health was adversely affected. To Parker's great surprise, 200 to 300 people, including his minister, George Turner, were at the prison door to welcome him on his release and to accompany him home. Parker's was a celebrated case and he was warmly acclaimed at a large passive resistance meeting in the City Temple, London.[98] One Baptist pastor, W.J. Potter, from Stourbridge, was imprisoned (for one day) in March 1904 and his congregation managed to recruit a sympathetic Anglican vicar, W.J. Spriggs-Smith, who spoke at a protest meeting.[99] The magistrate, perhaps making a point, sentenced Potter to a month in prison when he next appeared as a resister.[100] In Kegworth, in the East Midlands, the Baptist minister, G.C. Leader, after refusing to pay the rate, had his organ sold. It fetched two guineas at auction. The Shepshed Brass Band was present

95  *BT*, 17 July 1903, p.497.
96  G.K.A. Bell, *Randall Davidson: Archbishop of Canterbury* (London: Oxford University Press, 1952), p.376.
97  *BT*, 3 July 1903, p.463.
98  *BW*, 8 October 1903, p.620; 10 December 1903, p.258.
99  *BW*, 31 March 1904, p.671.
100 *BW*, 20 October 1904, p.31.

at the auction and when it struck up the 'Dead March' the auctioneer, 'pale and nervous', disappeared. A protest meeting attracted 1,500 people, and the organ, which had been bought by a sympathizer, was returned to Leader. At another East Midlands auction of a Baptist minister's possessions one lady hit the auctioneer on the head with her umbrella.[101] Such tactics naturally attracted attention.

The passive resistance campaign, although defiant and well organized, did not change government policy. By February 1905 there had been 40,000 summonses for refusal to pay,[102] but it seems that many of the small fines were paid by friends. Also, although there were some high profile resisters such as Judge Willis, most of those fined or even imprisoned did not attract widespread comment. On occasions Baptists probably alienated public opinion. Controversy broke out in *The Times* in April 1904 over allegations by F.B. Meyer that a child in a village school had been caned simply because of the stance made by the child's Free Church parents on education.[103] Furthermore, Free Church people were not united. Wesleyan Methodists, the largest Free Church group in England, were often ambivalent. For example, at Worthing in Sussex (admittedly not a town noted for its militancy), of fifty passive resisters summoned in February 1904, twenty-eight were Baptists but only four were Wesleyan Methodists.[104] Even among Baptists, not all were enthusiastic. S.W. Bowser, Principal of the Midland College, refused to commit himself to the campaign.[105] It was hoped when a Liberal government was elected in 1906 that the education minister, Augustine Birrell, whose father had been a Baptist pastor, would deliver what the Free Churches wanted. Birrell's ideas, however, were opposed in the House of Lords.[106] For the time being Baptist hopes were unfulfilled.

---

101   Harrison, *It All Began Here*, p.97.
102   *BT*, 10 February 1905, p.106.
103   *The Times*, 18 April 1904, p.12; 28 April 1904, p.10.
104   *BW*, 3 March 1904, p.559.
105   Harrison, *It All Began Here*, p.97.
106   *BW*, 16 August 1906, p.455; *BT*, 16 November 1906, p.825; 7 December 1906, p.891.

## 'ACTIVE AGAINST ALL WRONG'

Other issues were taken up by Baptists in their on-going desire to change society. Like other Free Churches, Baptists were active in campaigns to control and restrict the drink trade, to limit gambling, to oppose Sunday games, to seek better housing for the poor and to bring to an end sweated labour. Exerting social pressure was seen as part of the outworking of wider mission, since the churches were called upon to oppose sin. George White said in his presidential address to the Union Assembly in 1904 that Baptists should be active against 'all wrong', and added that they should especially oppose 'those social conditions which hinder the work of evangelization amongst the masses'.[107] The issue of alcoholic drink was one which aroused strong feelings. Over 2,000 Baptist churches in Britain (about two-thirds of the total) had temperance Band of Hope groups for children. In response to the Conservative government's Licensing Bill of 1904, Free Church leaders organized mass rallies against the Bill in Hyde Park and in the Royal Albert Hall. Meyer, a prominent Free Church spokesman, was typical in vehemently denouncing the 'pro-Beer government'.[108] Kenneth Brown suggests that many Presidents of the Baptist Union urged that social work should not be allowed to be a distraction from evangelism.[109] There were also those, nonetheless, who affirmed the proper place of social action.

On some issues, however, Baptists were seriously divided. The most obvious division was over the Boer War, which began in 1899. A good number of leading Baptist ministers opposed British involvement, most notably John Clifford, Alexander Maclaren, F.B. Meyer and J.C. Carlile. On 14 December 1901 the *Daily News*, which was owned by the Quaker, George Cadbury, and was opposed to the War, printed the names of 5,270 Nonconformist ministers who had signed a 'Peace Manifesto'. But W.E. Blomfield, at Queen's Road Baptist Church, Coventry, pointed out that there were 14,609 Nonconformist ministers in the United Kingdom, most

---

107   *Baptist Handbook* (1904) p.108.
108   *CW*, 26 May 1904, p.3.
109   Brown, *A Social History of the Nonconformist Ministry*, p.212.

of whom had not signed. Half of the total number of Baptist pastors, it was revealed, had not been signatories. In other Free Church denominations the signatories were a minority of ministers. Among Wesleyan ministers a massive eighty per cent had not signed.[110] Because of the differing opinions held by Baptists, the official statements made at Union Assemblies tended to be rather general. War as a whole was condemned and the creation of the new International Court at The Hague in Holland was welcomed. In 1901, in a 'Patriotic Declaration' which expressed loyalty to the new King, Edward VII, the Union hoped that the 'horrors of war' would pass and that there would be 'an honourable and lasting peace'.[111]

*Deaconesses taking part in a temperance procession.*
*The shield banner proclaims 'Less Beer, More Boots'*

110  Munson, *The Nonconformists*, pp.235-6.
111  *Baptist Handbook* (1901), p.132; (1902), p.110.

Loyalty to the King was only to be expected, but loyalty to political leaders was qualified. Baptists felt free to oppose those who did not seem to them to be upholding the standards of morality which would offer the right example to the country. This was the essence of what has been called the

*The Baptist deaconesses, 1907*

'Nonconformist conscience'. The possible inclusion of Sir Charles Dilke in a future Liberal government was carefully considered by the Committee of the National Council of the Evangelical Free Churches (often referred to as the Free Church Council) in 1904. The reason for the caution was that in the 1880s Dilke's wife had brought a case for divorce to court. Her grounds were her husband's adultery, grounds which were accepted by the court. Free Church leaders, including Clifford and Meyer, opposed Dilke's inclusion in governmental ranks since Dilke had neither confessed his sin nor been exonerated.[112] Surprisingly, the spotlight was never to be turned by Free Church leaders on the relationship that David Lloyd George, later Prime Minister, had with Frances Stevenson. Baptists noted that Lloyd George was baptized at the age of thirteen (in the Criccieth Church of Christ) and counted him as a Baptist.[113] Clifford had a cordial relationship with Lloyd George, meeting him at, for example, the National Liberal Club. Clifford and Shakespeare were among those trying to use political contacts to urge Free Church views.

---

112  Bebbington, *The Nonconformist Conscience*, p.45.
113  *BT,* 2 October 1903, p. 675; M. Goodman, 'A Faded Heritage: English Baptist political thinking in the 1930s', *BQ,* Vol.37, No.2 (1997), pp.60-1.

Was this commitment to a socio-political agenda and to the reform of society reflected at the level of local Baptist churches? The indications suggest that for many churches this was the case, at least to some degree. The *British Weekly* reported in 1902 on mayors in England who were Baptists – at Accrington, Camberwell, Halifax, High Wycombe, Luton, Plymouth, Stepney, Tunbridge Wells, and Wolverhampton.[114] The total number of Baptist mayors was thought to be at least thirteen, which was believed to be a record, and is indicative of an interest in local politics among a significant number of Baptist lay people. Two years later six members of the Woolwich Tabernacle – two deacons and four others – were elected to the local Borough Council.[115] It was in part because of the belief that Free Church members should be properly

*The Deaconesses' Mission, half a mile from their Institute in Guilford Street, 1901. They ran a clinic here and held evangelistic meetings every evening.*

represented in all sections of society that Baptists felt strongly about the Education Act. In 1904 both W.E. Blomfield, in Coventry, and J.W. Ewing, minister of the 900-member Rye Lane Chapel, Peckham, in London, highlighted the injustice of the exclusion of those who were not Anglicans from posts as head teachers of schools.[116]

An important gauge of Baptist social involvement is the activity of Baptist churches in deprived areas. Here the work of Baptist deaconesses was crucial. In 1890 a Baptist Deaconesses' Home and Mission had been

114  *BW*, 20 November 1902, p.133.
115  *BW*, 7 April 1904, p.691.
116  *BW*, 10 March 1904, p.583; *BW*, 23 June 1904, p.267.

*A Sister with a young patient, 1901*

founded under the direction of F.B. Meyer and the London Baptist Association, and medical, social and evangelistic work was undertaken.[117] In one year, 1910, the deaconesses' medical work treated 27,000 patients. Charles Booth's survey in 1902, *Life and Labour of the People of London*, underlined London's pressing social needs. The best known deaconess was Hettie Bannister, who began work in 1905 at the Barking Road Tabernacle, West Ham, East London, where she was involved with the poor and with many young men and women employed in factories. The Tabernacle, which launched the West Ham Central Mission, offered alternatives to public houses through clubs and further education. Sister Hettie was passionately concerned about poverty: it was estimated in 1905 that out of 140,000 people in Barking, 35,000 were in a state of semi-starvation, with many families living in one-room dwellings.[118] A year later, William Cuff, pastor of Shoreditch Baptist Tabernacle, a church with over 900 members, spoke about East End churches in which many members were poor, had large families and tried to escape to the suburbs.[119] In 1907 the Deaconess Order advertised for more trainees, under the superintendency of Sister Constance. At that time

---

117  D.M. Rose, *Baptist Deaconesses* (London: Carey Kingsgate Press, 1954), p.10; N. Morris, *Sisters of the People: The Order of Baptist Deaconesses, 1890-1975, CCSRG Research Paper 2* (Bristol: University of Bristol, 2002), p.10. Their first home was at 59 Doughty Street, and then at 98 Guilford Street.

118  *BT*, 17 March 1905, p.198; P. Rowntree Clifford, *Venture in Faith: The Story of the West Ham Central Mission* (London: Carey Kingsgate Press, 1950), chapter 4. A century later this Mission continues to serve the disadvantaged in society.

119  *BT*, 4 May 1906, supplement, pp.i-ii; *CW*, 3 May 1906, p.21.

there were about twenty deaconesses working with Baptist churches, with the main premises being in Gough Street, Leather Lane, London.[120]

Spurred on by their opposition to the Education Act, Nonconformists fought hard for the return of the Liberals in the 1906 election.[121] Free Church voters rallied to the Liberal cause.[122] It seemed in 1906, when the Liberals came in with a huge majority, that a great Free Church battle had been won: it was reckoned that there were nearly 200 Free Church MPs in the new Parliament. A victory banquet was held at the Hotel Cecil in London at which Lloyd George and John Clifford were among the speakers. 'I hail this victory', said Clifford, 'with the deepest joy and thankfulness.'[123] Seventeen Baptists were elected, more than ever before.[124] But Baptists began to discover that the new government was unable to bring about the hoped-for radical changes. A major obstacle to reformist legislation was the House of Lords, and John Clifford spoke about the out-dated nature of the Lords. As he saw it, the days of the House of Lords were numbered. 'The hereditary principle', he stated in 1906, 'is bound to go', and he referred derisively in 1908 to the 'Philistines of the Upper House'. By contrast, he had words of praise for the new socialist society which he saw emerging, suggesting that Labour MPs 'received their training where I got mine, in a village pulpit'.[125] At least some Baptists were seeking radical change.

WIDER CONTACTS

The identity of Baptists as part of the Free Churches was strong in 1900, especially in the area of socio-political action, and this was to lead to

---

120   *BT*, 4 January 1907, supplement, p.v.
121   Bebbington, *Nonconformist Conscience*, pp.142-7; D.A. Hamer, *Liberal Politics in the Age of Gladstone and Rosebery* (Oxford: Clarendon Press, 1972), p.311.
122   *BW*, 18 July 1901, p.319; D.W. Bebbington, 'Nonconformity and Electoral Sociology, 1867-1918', *Historical Journal*, Vol.27, No.3 (1984).
123   *BW*, 8 March 1906, p.619.
124   D.W. Bebbington, 'Baptist Members of Parliament in the Twentieth Century', *BQ*, Vol.31, No.6 (1986), pp.254-5.
125   *BW*, 27 September 1906, p.583; *BT*, 28 February 1908, p.149.

many discussions about greater Free Church unity. In 1901 joint assemblies of the Baptist and Congregational Unions were held at the City Temple, London. Joseph Parker spoke about the possibility of a united Congregational Church which would bring the two denominations together. This was also the period when Free Churches were working closely together across the country in mission. In 1907, Meyer resigned from Christ Church, Westminster Bridge Road, and received what he called a 'second ordination' to wider mission, including acting as a 'travelling Bishop' of the Free Churches.[126] Later, from 1910 to 1920, he was Secretary of the Free Church Council. The combination of Free Church evangelism and social comment in the early twentieth century attracted the attention of political figures. Arthur Balfour (Prime Minister, 1902 to 1905) admitted that John Clifford's pamphlet *The Fight Against the Education Bill* had circulated in hundreds of thousands and had stimulated innumerable sermons and addresses.[127] In 1902 Clifford became President of the Liberation Society and David Lloyd George, then a cabinet minister, became Vice-President. The Liberation Society was committed to religious equality and the disestablishment of the Church of England. The 1906 election result gave strength to the Society.[128] Baptists gained confidence from their wider Free Church identity.

They also gained strength from their evangelical links with those who might or might not be Free Church members. An organization that was crucial in training many Baptist young people in the early twentieth century was the interdenominational and increasingly international Young People's Society for Christian Endeavour (CE). It began in 1881 at a Congregational Church in Maine, USA. Although Christian Endeavour, as it was always called, was formed in some evangelical churches in England in the 1890s, many more local societies were started in the first few decades of the twentieth century. The purpose of these CE groups was to foster spiritual growth and activity. The motto of the movement was

---

126   *Free Church Year Book* (London: National Free Church Council, 1907), p.81; *Free Church Year Book* (London: NFCC, 1908), p.33.
127   Jordan, *Free Church Unity*, p.83.
128   *BW*, 7 March 1907, p.583.

'For Christ and the Church'. Baptists and Congregationalists had by far the largest number of Christian Endeavour societies and many young people found in CE their first opportunities to give leadership or speak publicly. Other youth movements, especially the Boys' Brigade, the Boys' Life Brigade, the Girls' Guildry and the Girls' Life Brigade, were also important in an increasing number of Baptist churches.[129] At Bloomsbury Central Baptist Church, Christian Endeavour and Boys' Brigade were introduced in 1901, followed by the Girls' Guildry. Thomas (Tom) Phillips, the minister, was concerned that Christian Endeavour appealed only 'to the pious twenty-five per cent'.[130]

Unity with other evangelicals in renewal and mission, especially through the Evangelical Alliance, was a further wider link for many Baptists. The early twentieth century saw the Evangelical Alliance stressing 'comprehensiveness within the truth'.[131] The traditional Calvinist-Arminian divide had disappeared to a large extent as evangelicals saw themselves committed to a common cause. In 1904 the Kent and Sussex Association stressed its commitment to evangelical faith and to conversion followed by baptism. From its formation in 1835 its rules stated that 'this Association consists of Particular Baptist churches in Kent and Sussex', but this was altered in 1904 to say that 'this Kent and Sussex Association of Baptist churches consists only of evangelical churches practising believers' baptism'.[132] There were a number of Baptist ministers who travelled widely and whose influence in wider evangelical circles was considerable. Baptists played a continuing role in organizations such as the Bible Society, and joined in organizing and speaking at interdenominational conventions. F.B. Meyer was a leading

---

129  For Christian Endeavour in this period see E.J.T. Bagnall, *The British Manual of Christian Endeavour* (London: Christian Endeavour Union, 1936). For the Boys' Brigade see J. Springhall, *Sure and Steadfast: A History of the Boys' Brigade, 1883 to 1983* (London: Collins, 1983).

130  F. Bowers, *A Bold Experiment: The Story of Bloomsbury Chapel and Bloomsbury Central Baptist Church, 1848-1999* (London: Bloomsbury Central Baptist Church, 1999), pp.215, 220, 248.

131  Randall and Hilborn, *One Body in Christ*, pp.183-4.

132  Buffard, *Kent and Sussex Baptist Associations*, pp.123-4.

*The Baptist World Congress in 1905:*
*Miss Nannie Helen Burroughs from Kentucky addresses a gathering in Hyde Park.*

speaker at the largest of these, the Keswick Convention, which was held each year in the Lake District and which emphasized the message of holiness.[133]

Finally, Baptists expressed their wider sense of identity through the formation in 1905 of the Baptist World Alliance (BWA). Shakespeare and Meyer were deeply involved in the Baptist international scene, but the idea for an international Baptist congress seems to have come initially from A.T. Robertson, of the Southern Baptist Theological Seminary, Louisville, Kentucky, USA, and from J.N. Prestridge, also of Louisville, with an article appearing in the American *Baptist Argus* (edited by

---

133  For Keswick see Charles Price and I.M. Randall, *Transforming Keswick* (Carlisle: Paternoster/OM, 2000).

Prestridge) in 1903.[134] In January 1904 copies of the article were sent by Prestridge to many Baptist leaders world-wide. Shakespeare was, not surprisingly, fascinated, and spoke to the Union's General Purposes Committee in June of that year about the concept of a congress. It was quickly decided to plan for a 'Pan-Baptist Conference in London' to be held in the summer of 1905. The Union Council and the BMS worked together, under Shakespeare's leadership, in the massive preparatory work. It was agreed that some contentious theological issues, such as the relationship of baptism to church membership, should be excluded from platform pronouncements at the congress, and that the emphasis should be on promoting Baptist links, stimulating Christian service, expressing Baptist principles and considering the oppression of Baptists in many parts of the world.[135] Theological reflection on questions of Baptist ecclesiology was to be subservient to the promotion of a sense of wider Baptist community.

This first World Congress opened on 10 July 1905 in Exeter Hall in London. Shakespeare, as the congress secretary, welcomed the delegates with the ambitious (and inaccurate if judged strictly numerically) claim that Baptists were probably 'the greatest Protestant evangelical community on earth'. The tone of the congress was described by Shakespeare as 'distinctly evangelical' and 'optimistic', the conviction being expressed that Baptist beliefs were going to triumph in the world.[136] Notable Baptists from both sides of the Atlantic delivered addresses, and David Lloyd George (acclaimed at the congress as 'a good Baptist'), gave a stirring speech on the then-current controversy over education.[137] Indoor and outdoor events exuded Baptist confidence and the congress closed at the end of a week of meetings with a 'demonstration' in the Royal Albert

---

134  *First Baptist World Congress, London, 1905* (London: Baptist Union, 1905), p.v; F.T. Lord, *Baptist World Fellowship* (London: Carey Kingsgate Press, 1955), pp.2-4.

135  Minutes of joint Baptist Union/BMS Committee, 3 October 1904. Bound in BU volumes in Angus Library.

136  *First Baptist World Congress, London, 1905*, p.vi.

137  Munson, *The Nonconformists*, chapter 9.

Hall, which attracted 10,000 people. At this meeting Alexander Maclaren and Meyer were particular heroes. Maclaren had led the congress in the words of the Apostles' Creed to emphasize Baptist solidarity with the universal Church. Meyer, who called the congress a 'veritable Pentecost', was greeted with tremendous excitement, the galleries breaking into a 'white foam of handkerchiefs'.[138]

Shakespeare was giving thought before and during the congress to the possibility of 'federating' the international Baptist community to enable the achievement of common purposes, and before the congress closed it was resolved to appoint J.N. Prestridge and Shakespeare himself as convenors of a committee to arrange future congresses and to form a Baptist World Alliance. Prestridge and Shakespeare became joint secretaries of the Alliance, and John Clifford, as a seasoned Baptist campaigner on political as well as ecclesiastical matters, became the BWA President. English Baptists were to the fore. The co-ordination of ongoing activities was inevitably problematic, given the global nature of an organization like the Alliance. One of the most significant initial benefits, however, was the development of a greater pan-European Baptist consciousness, in line with Shakespeare's exalted dream that 'the evangelical and spiritual life of the Continent of Europe will gravitate to Baptist teaching and fellowship'.[139] This grand vision was not to be fulfilled to the extent that Shakespeare hoped, but there was to be a strong sense of the wider Baptist community across Europe and subsequently within other continents.

## EVANGELICAL THEOLOGY

Although theological reflection was subservient to activism within the BWA, English Baptists were concerned to enunciate their identity. J.W. Ewing, one of the London Baptists involved in Evangelical Alliance affairs, set out in 1900 some of the beliefs which he considered held Baptists together - a church of regenerate persons, the will of Christ made

---

138  *BW,* 20 July 1905, p.363.
139  Rushbrooke, *First Baptist World Congress, London, 1905,* p.viii.

known in Scripture, freedom of individuals to interpret scripture, and baptism by immersion.[140] Yet within London, Baptists were not united. Out of 239 Baptist churches in 1900, only 155 were in the LBA. Another sixty were Strict and Particular Baptist churches. The Metropolitan Tabernacle, the largest Baptist cause, was not in the LBA (it had left over C.H. Spurgeon's concerns in the 1880s about broader theology in the Union), and some churches associated with the Tabernacle formed the Home Counties Association, which was not in the Union for the same reason.[141] When a question about the Downgrade Controversy – a term that was used to describe C.H. Spurgeon's conflict with the Union - was raised in January 1900, E.G. Gange, of Regent's Park Chapel, who had trained at the Pastors' College, stated that the matter was practically forgotten. He denied the claim that Spurgeon had been censured by the Union at the time of the controversy.[142] Archibald Brown, to whom C.H. Spurgeon had been a mentor and who would become a ministerial colleague of Thomas Spurgeon at the Metropolitan Tabernacle, retorted that Gange was ignorant of the deep convictions that C.H. Spurgeon had held.[143] Theological tensions remained.

These tensions were underlined a few months later by William Cuff, who had trained under C. H. Spurgeon and had a long and effective ministry at the Shoreditch Tabernacle. He spoke about the commitment of the Tabernacle to the gospel, a commitment which, he pointed out, led 250-300 voluntary workers to take responsibility for mission services on Sunday evenings. Cuff was typical of a large number of Baptists in saying that he had no faith in the 'Social Gospel'.[144] This did not mean that Cuff opposed social ministry, but he believed that the priority was the gospel of salvation by faith in Christ. Differing theological perspectives regarding the gospel and society could be found across the churches in the

---

140  *BT*, 23 November 1900, p.947.
141  *BT*, 7 December 1900, p.981. Dix lists sixty-five Strict and Particular Baptist Churches in London in 1900: Dix, *Strict and Particular*, pp.286-7.
142  *BT*, 19 January 1900, p.45.
143  *BT*, 26 January 1900, p.64.
144  *BT*, 16 March 1900, p.205.

Baptist denomination. In Liverpool two extremes were evident. Charles Aked, who built up Pembroke Chapel before leaving for America in 1906, was a Fabian socialist and a leading Baptist advocate of a social gospel. On the other hand, forthright opposition to the social gospel was the stance taken by another Liverpool Baptist minister, the outspoken John Thomas at Myrtle Street.[145]

The Union was seeking in this period an evangelical position around which the different elements in the denomination could unite. Alexander Maclaren, with the authority of old age and of his presidency of the Union, argued at the autumn Assembly in 1901 for 'evangelical mysticism'.[146] It was well known that John Clifford favoured unity that was grounded in spiritual experience, not in credal statements seeking to enunciate evangelical beliefs. John Wilson of Woolwich, a popular choice in 1903 as Union President, was described as 'evangelical to the core of his being'. In this respect, commented the *Baptist Times* in May 1903, he was fully representative of the whole denomination.[147] But how was this evangelicalism to be expressed? Council discussions took up this matter. At the autumn Assembly held in Derby in October 1903 it was proposed that the brief Declaration of Principle of 1873 be enlarged, to affirm:

The sole and absolute authority of our Lord Jesus Christ in all matters pertaining to faith and practice.

The recognition of the liberty of every Church to interpret and administer the laws of Christ as contained in the Holy Scriptures, and

That Christian Baptism is the immersion in water of those who have professed repentance toward God and faith in our Lord Jesus Christ, into the Name of the Father, the Son and the Holy Ghost.

The proposed changes to the Declaration, plus other constitutional changes, were outlined and advocated by Shakespeare in a 'statesmanlike

145  Sellers, ed., *Our Heritage*, p.54.
146  *BT*, 11 October 1901, supplement p.i.
147  *BT*, 1 May 1903, p.313.

speech', but Shakespeare said that given the objections to the changes –
some objected to the lack of reference to evangelism - the
recommendations would be withdrawn for further consideration by the
Council, Associations and churches.[148]

Revised proposals were put to the autumn Assembly in 1904, held at
Broadmead Baptist Church, Bristol. The proposed Declaration of
Principle now stated that the Basis of the Union was:

> That our Lord Jesus Christ is the sole and absolute authority in all
> matters pertaining to faith and practice, as revealed in the Holy
> Scriptures, and that each Church has liberty to interpret and
> administer His laws.
>
> That Christian Baptism is the immersion in water, into the Name of
> the Father, the Son and Holy Ghost, of those who have professed
> repentance toward God and faith in our Lord Jesus Christ, Who 'died
> for our sins according to the Scriptures; was buried, and rose again the
> third day'.
>
> That it is the duty of every disciple to bear personal witness to the
> Gospel of Jesus Christ, and to take part in the evangelization of the
> world.

This proposal, with its inclusion of the clause on evangelism, was
unanimously adopted. The objects of the Union were affirmed, which
included cultivating 'love and respect for one another and for all who love
the Lord Jesus Christ'; spreading the gospel through ministers and
evangelists, the establishing of churches, Sunday Schools and scripture
distribution; united action at home and abroad; declaration of opinion on
public questions; and religious equality. In 1906 it was agreed that the

---

148  D.C. Sparkes, *The Constitutions of the Baptist Union of Great Britain* (Didcot:
Baptist Historical Society, 1996), p.21.

phrase, 'our God and Saviour' be added after 'our Lord Jesus Christ' in the first clause of the Declaration.[149]

In a separate but related development, the members of the General Purposes Committee of the Union spoke in March 1905 about a proposal by Thomas Greenwood to remove any reference to the Downgrade Controversy from the past minutes of the Baptist Union. A committee was set up which discussed the issue.[150] Greenwood was the son of a deacon of C.H. Spurgeon's, had trained at the Pastors' College, had pastorates in London - at Catford Hill and Ramsden Road, Balham - and became the LBA Secretary in 1906. His concern was to eliminate what was regarded by some as the 'censure' motion against Spurgeon in the minutes. In May 1905, D.J. Hiley (known at that time for his ministry at Broadmead, Bristol, and later a President of the Union), seconded by Richard Glover, moved that certain parts of the minutes of 1888 and 1889 be deleted. This proposal was brought, they said, with a desire to promote unity. To remove these parts was to remove what for some - it was accepted – was a source of pain. The General Purposes Committee voted in favour of removal, by twenty votes to ten, but the Council was divided and the proposal was dropped.[151] Divergent theological and historical perspectives contributed to these difficulties.

The vulnerability of the denomination to theological division was again highlighted in 1907 when R.J. Campbell, Congregational minister of the City Temple, London, produced a widely-publicised book entitled *The New Theology*. Campbell, in arguing that humanity and divinity were parts of one great consciousness, drastically revised traditional

---

149  Payne, *Baptist Union*, pp.160-3, 212; Sparkes, *Constitutions* (1996), pp.21-7, 37-8; R.L. Kidd, ed., *Something to Declare: A Study of the Declaration of Principle* (Oxford: Whitley Publications, 1996), pp.20-3.
150  Minutes of the Baptist Union General Purposes Committee, 21 March 1905; 27 April 1905.
151  Minutes of the Baptist Union General Purposes Committee, 1 May 1905; Minutes of the Council, 1 May 1905.

Christology.[152] Although Campbell was a Congregationalist, it was inevitable that Baptists would be drawn into the debate. One Baptist to support Campbell was Clifford. In February 1907 Clifford preached for Campbell at the City Temple and spoke about 'the gross and culpable misrepresentations to which he [Campbell] has been subjected during the past three weeks by a small section of the daily press'. Clifford said he disagreed with some of Campbell's statements, but spoke of his 'high and holy aims'. There was applause.[153] Clifford's support was in marked contrast to most Baptist responses. Thomas Spurgeon did not know how Campbell could remain in Christian ministry, and Charles Brown, who was booked to preach at the City Temple, offered to withdraw from the engagement, as his views were diametrically opposed to Campbell's.[154] In the event Brown did preach, in an electric atmosphere. He pronounced: 'Christ is here this morning, ready to do for you what he has already done for so many of us through faith in His sacrificial death.' Many people who had come to hear Brown applauded, and there were shouts of 'Glory!', 'Praise God!' and 'Amen'. Brown's positive evangelical stance was one Baptists were eager to affirm.[155]

## WORSHIP AND SPIRITUAL EXPERIENCE

For Baptist ministers who wished their evangelical message to be relevant to early twentieth-century society, the question of what kind of worship should characterize Baptist services was a pressing one. The sermon remained central to Baptist worship. As a contribution to progress in other aspects of worship, a new *Baptist Church Hymnal* was produced in 1900 in conjunction with the Psalms and Hymns Trust. This book, which

---

152  R.J. Campbell, *The New Theology* (London: Chapman & Hall, 1907); K.W. Clements, *Lovers of Discord: Twentieth Century Theological Controversies in England* (London: SPCK, 1988), p.39.

153  *BW*, 7 February 1907, p.491.

154  *BW*, 24 January 1907, p.439; 14 February 1907, p.515.

155  *BW*, 14 February 1907, p.515; Cook, *Charles Brown*, pp.55-6.

introduced new hymns and chants, attracted both criticism and praise.[156] Some recognized that change was inevitable. The *Baptist Times* suggested in 1901 that the kind of music which might be heard and enjoyed in Baptist chapels a hundred years in the future would split the churches in 1901 if it was even considered.[157] It was a statement that anticipated later, often acrimonious splits which would take place over music, and was made in the context of a debate beginning to emerge. Devotional hymns from the Keswick Convention were becoming increasingly popular in Free Church circles.[158] Perhaps, it was suggested in 1901, timidity was frightening Baptist congregations into 'dull mediocrity' in worship.[159] A.T. Brainsby, known for his unconventional ministry in Barnoldswick, Lancashire, wanted to avoid this trap. He was reported in 1903 as having used as soloists in his services 'first class artists' who were all Christians.[160] Choirs were common, and at the well-known Woolwich Tabernacle, as Charles Booth noted in his report *Life and Labour of the People of London*, a full orchestra was playing at the services.[161]

One change taking place without any kind of co-ordination was the increasing use at Baptist communion services of single glass cups instead of a common cup. The use of single cups began in Congregationalism in the 1890s, and it was suggested in the *Baptist Times* in 1901 that people were avoiding Baptist communion services because they were not happy with the common cup.[162] From a temperance standpoint, churches should use non-alcoholic wine at communion and by 1904 unfermented wine was used in most Baptist churches. But the single cup was thought by some to

---

156  For an overview see A.E. Peaston, *The Prayer Book Tradition in the Free Churches* (London: James Clarke & Co., 1964). In 1905 J.H. Shakespeare and G.P. Gould produced a *Manual for Free Church Ministers* with orders of service for weddings, funerals, baptisms and dedications of infants.

157  *BT*, 8 March 1901, p.157.

158  For example, *Hymns of Consecration and Faith* (London: Marshall Bros, [n.d. but 1903]).

159  *BT* 8 March 1901, p.157.

160  *BT*, 30 October 1903, p.747.

161  Munson, *The Nonconformists*, p.48.

162  *BT*, 16 August 1901, p.552.

be unhygienic when non-alcoholic wine was used. Linked with the temperance issue, therefore, was the late Victorian concern for hygiene.[163] Many letters about individual cups, for and against, were published in the *Baptist Times*. One theme taken up by those arguing for the common cup was that this expressed unity in a way that was not true of individual cups. In September 1901, the Baptists in London Road, Lowestoft, suggested that they had found a way to overcome this problem. All the members now drank from individual cups simultaneously.[164] Over the next year many Baptist churches adopted the practice of passing round individual cups on a tray and the idea of the members 'drinking together' became more popular.[165]

Sensitivity to opinions about worship is illustrated by the response of William Cuff at Shoreditch Tabernacle, in 1903, to the survey by Charles Booth. For Booth, the Tabernacle was 'perfect in its way, but its way is not that of being a house of God. No feeling of sacredness attaches to it'. William Cuff was amazed at this 'wild' statement. Booth had talked to William Cuff, but in Cuff's view the Tabernacle had been sadly misunderstood. Cuff's own focus was on the people who worshipped there. 'Under my ministry here, of over thirty years', he stated, 'all that is holy, sacred and blessed has become a real experience to them.' Cuff described the enthusiastic Tabernacle meetings, characterized by the preaching of the word of God, prayer and praise.[166] Booth, for his part, was looking for what might be termed a 'sacred space', a concept foreign to Cuff. Given Cuff's concern that worship should meet the needs of his people, he was achieving his objective. The same concern was evident in F.B. Meyer's ministry. In 1903 he announced that he was shifting the time of the evening service at Christ Church from 6.30pm to 7.00pm, and that the Liturgy he had used would be discontinued to make the services more

---

163   Sellers, ed., *Our Heritage*, p.81.
164   *BT*, 6 September 1901, p.606 (report by J. Edgar Ennals).
165   *BT*, 13 June 1902, p.441.
166   *BW*, 16 April 1903, p.4.

accessible. Young men and women from the church would go out into the neighbourhood before the service to invite people in.[167]

*A Baptist church choir, 1909*

A somewhat different approach to relevance in worship was seen at Westbourne Park, where John Clifford was minister. There was a marked intellectual tone at the Westbourne Park services. A visitor in 1907 recorded that the Bible reading was from the recent Weymouth translation of the Bible, a telegram was read about the progress of the Hague Peace Conference, and the sermon, which had no text, was entitled 'Sabatier and the present condition of Roman Catholicism'. Yet the climax of the sermon was an evangelistic appeal. Indeed Clifford had to abandon the last hymn because he was carried away by his theme.[168] Clifford was not afraid to include all kinds of topics and approaches in the experience of public worship. Other Baptist ministers were keen to show that what happened in chapel worship was relevant to political life. J. Glynn

---

167  *BW*, 7 May 1903, p.85.
168  *CW*, 22 August 1907, p.5.

Edwards, the minister of St Mary's Baptist Church, Norwich, spoke on a Sunday morning in 1909 about the atrocities being perpetrated in the Congo. He moved a resolution calling on the British government to intervene, and his congregation carried the resolution unanimously by standing in their pews. Copies of the resolution were sent to the Prime Minister and the Foreign Secretary.[169]

Arguably a deeper issue than the outward form of worship was the spiritual vitality of Baptist life. At the Union Assembly in spring 1900, William Cuff spoke about the importance of being 'saturated with the Holy Ghost'. In his view everything else in spiritual experience was useless.[170] Baptist pastors took for granted that members read the Bible and prayed, but accepted that there could still be a lack of vibrant spiritual life. The Secretary of the East Midland Association bemoaned the fact that many members were 'apathetic and asleep'.[171] In 1903 a booklet by Charles Williams of Accrington described the Baptist practice of church discipline, intended to ensure high standards of spirituality: he said it was marked by 'indulgence and laxity', and observed that the unspiritual character of the monthly church members' meeting in Baptist churches was well known.[172] There were attempts to address such problems. The presidential address at the Assembly in 1906, delivered by Meyer, was judged by the perceptive Newton Marshall, who had grown up under Clifford at Westbourne Park, to have 'intense spirituality'. Marshall, who was taking up ministry at Heath Street, Hampstead, commented: 'God was showing to the Baptist denomination the way in which they should go.'[173] At this stage some evangelicals were moving towards Pentecostal spirituality. Commenting in 1908 on the gift of tongues, Tom Phillips argued that Edward Irving and others in the nineteenth century had

---

169  Jewson, *The Baptists in Norfolk*, p.142.
170  *BT*, 27 April 1900, supplement, p.v.
171  Harrison, *It All Began Here*, pp.87-8.
172  C. Williams, *The Principles and Practices of the Baptists* (London: Baptist Tract Society, 1903), pp.99, 102; J.W. Grant, *Free Churchmanship in England, 1870-1940* (London: Independent Press, 1940), p.148.
173  *BW*, 26 April 1906, p.48.

claimed these 'endowments' and that there was no *a priori* objection to this gift.[174] Denominational leaders were looking for a deeper spirituality.

It was in part because of this search that Baptists showed great interest in the Welsh Revival. Evan Roberts, the young Revival leader, was seen by some as rather an enigma, but several Baptist leaders who visited Wales came back with positive reports. Tom Phillips, himself Welsh, was one. 'There is no doubt', he reported, 'that the Revival is a very real thing.' Speaking of the emotion of the meetings, he said: 'I would welcome such ecstasy, just for a change, at some of our Nonconformist assemblies.' The need in England, he suggested, was not the Welsh Revival but the Spirit that brought it.[175] J.W. Ewing from Rye Lane Chapel, Peckham, London, said in 1905, after his visit to Wales: 'I seemed to be searched through and through by the white light of the Spirit of Holiness'.[176] Charles Brown, who also went to Wales, did not want Evan Roberts to be brought to England. 'This would savour', he suggested, 'too much of the showman.'[177] Always the organizer, Shakespeare proposed a meeting for ministers to discuss the Revival. This was held at Meyer's church, Christ Church, and leading London Free Church ministers contributed, including the Methodist, Dinsdale Young, and the Congregationalist, Campbell Morgan. Among Baptists, Tom Phillips reported on the effects of the Revival on his own church, with petitions at prayer meetings indicating a new spiritual mood.[178] Revived churches seemed to augur well for the future.

CONCLUSION

Many Baptists, ministers and members, looked forward to the twentieth century with optimism. J.H. Shakespeare, the dominant figure in this period, typified this outlook, and worked hard to bring the denomination

---

174  *BT*, 26 June 1908, p.449.
175  *BW*, 22 December 1904, p.315.
176  *BT*, 6 January 1905, p.5.
177  *BT*, 10 February 1905, p.98.
178  *BW*, 2 March 1905, p.544.

closer together so that it could be more effective in mission. Alexander
Maclaren, speaking in 1900, said that it was necessary for Free Churches
to address the 'Heathenism of England'.[179] Free Church identity was
reinforced in 1902-6 as Baptists committed themselves to socio-political
action. Here the power of John Clifford was crucial. Describing a speech
by Clifford at the City Temple in 1905, F.B. Meyer said that 'a moral
hurricane swept through the building'.[180] There were fears among some
Baptists, however, that the social agenda was being given too much
prominence. One Baptist, George Freeman, stated in 1909: 'The ministry
that departs from the great mission of saving sinners and making souls is
a discredit in the world and a degradation to itself.'[181] Certainly, despite
the optimism, there was concern about spiritual malaise. Many Baptist
churches that had grown in the nineteenth century now had to deal with
lapsed members. There were also theological tensions and the Union had
at times to work hard to achieve unity. Often what held the churches
together was a common commitment to evangelism and spiritual revival.
Local Associations were happy when they could report encouraging
examples such as that of a small church like Battle, Sussex, which in
1908 had 150 men meeting each week on Sunday afternoons.[182] Aspects
of Baptist life did appear promising, but as the century progressed this
promise was to prove hard to fulfil.

---

179  *BT*, 23 February 1900, supplement, p.ix.
180  *BT*, 3 November 1905, p.768.
181  *Anti-Socialist*, Sept. 1909, p.90, cited by Brown, *A Social History of the Nonconformist Ministry*, p.212.
182  Buffard, *Kent and Sussex Baptist Associations*, p.118.

# Chapter 3
# 'CATHOLIC AND
# COMPREHENSIVE'
# (1910-19)

A t the 1910 National Free Church Council meetings, which were held in Hull, the *British Weekly* report spoke about the 'catholic and comprehensive note' struck in the speeches by J.H. Shakespeare. It is true that Shakespeare was 'catholic' in his thinking, a feature that would become more and more evident as the decade progressed. He was also remarkably radical. Denominationalism, asserted Shakespeare in 1910, was 'a tree which was rapidly becoming hollow'. He saw it as 'propped by the iron bands of trust deeds', and he prophesied that 'one day, in the general storm, it will come down with a crash.' More constructively, Shakespeare called for a United Free Church working together in England and proposed a Commission of Inquiry to look into this possibility. The real issue, for Shakespeare, was not that of denominationalism, but of reaching a society in which church commitment was in decline. His belief was that mission was hindered by denominational divisions, and he argued that his ultimate concern was for 'the Cross, and the Word, and the personal God Himself'.[1] Up until 1919, at which point his views were strongly challenged, Shakespeare's comprehensive vision had an enormous influence on Baptist denominational life. Yet for many Baptists in this decade the ecumenical agenda set out by Shakespeare was not his most important contribution. Many ministers and lay people welcomed Shakespeare's ideas because they believed that he would help to ensure effective ministry within Baptist churches.

---

1    *BW*, 17 March 1910, p.680; 10 November 1910, p.170.

RECOGNITION OF MINISTRY

As indicated previously, there was considerable concern in the denomination to raise the quality of the ministry. The early years of the twentieth century saw what was perceived to be a surfeit of Baptist ministers, with a proportion viewed by the Union leadership as inadequately trained. J.G. Greenhough, who in 1905 completed a long ministry at Victoria Road Baptist Church, Leicester, was the strong-minded chairman of the Union's Ministerial Recognition Committee from 1896 to1911. Given that there was an apparent oversupply of ministers, with at least 100 ministers out of pastoral charge,[2] Greenhough addressed the question of how to limit the number of ministers. Shakespeare's inclination was to insist that only those who had matriculated at a recognized university be accepted into Baptist ministry, but in 1901 only eight per cent of Baptist ministers had been connected with a university.[3] Indeed some of those elected as deacons in Baptist churches held the belief that 'Ministers empty churches by degrees'.[4] The leading article in the *Baptist* on 14 September 1905, reflecting the uncertainties and even bitterness among rank-and-file ministers about plans for compulsory Baptist Union examinations, said that it seemed as if 'it is the weakest who go to the wall'. The people intent on limiting entry to accredited Baptist ministry in England, the article continued, included 'not a few spiritual non-efficients', who were seeking to 'erect a fence of scholasticism around the ministry'.[5]

In 1910 new Union procedures formalized a 'probationary' period in ministry and examinations for both 'collegiate' and 'non-collegiate' ministers (those who had trained through a Baptist college and those who had not) before transfer to the list of recognized Union ministers. The acceptance of these procedures, however, was fraught with difficulty. In 1906 there was a storm of protest when the *Baptist Handbook*

---

2    See Sparkes, *An Accredited Ministry*, p.15.
3    J.E.B. Munson, 'The education of Baptist ministers, 1870-1900', *BQ*, Vol.26 (1976), p.321.
4    Sellers, ed., *Our Heritage*, p.128.
5    *The Baptist*, 14 September 1905, p.176.

differentiated between ministers recognized by the Union and about 400 (twenty per cent of the total) who were not. The symbol printed against these 400 was referred to as a 'dagger', and they were soon being described in the *Baptist*, which printed letters from non-collegiate ministers that the *Baptist Times* had refused to print, as having been 'made outcasts' or, more dramatically, 'daggered'.[6] There was talk of forming another Union. Writing in the *Baptist,* F.B. Meyer, the incoming Union President, a natural conciliator, said: 'I quite appreciate the position of the brethren who count themselves aggrieved; but surely it is premature to speak of a new association and sustentation funds. There must be some solution short of this. Let us pray that it may be revealed to us.'[7] Calls were made for a public protest at the Assembly at Huddersfield. T.W. Medhurst, however, who had been C.H. Spurgeon's first student in 1856, showed little sympathy with the complainers in the pages of the *Baptist*, which came as a surprise since the *Baptist* usually relied on support from 'Spurgeon's men'.[8]

*T.W. Medhurst*

In the light of the strong feelings generated, the Council decided that the 'dagger' would not appear again.[9] The new recognition procedures were then put to the spring Assembly held in Bloomsbury Central Baptist Church in 1907. To smooth the path to acceptance, those ministers who had entered the pastorate prior to 1900, and had Association backing, were exempted from sitting examinations and there were special arrangements for those who had entered the ministry between 1900 and 1907.[10] It was widely felt that the deciding speech at Bloomsbury was by

---

6    *The Baptist*, 8 February 1906, p.93; 14 June 1906, p.380; 5 July 1906, p.2.
7    *The Baptist*, 15 February 1906, p.106.
8    *The Baptist*, 12 July 1906, p.24; 2 August 1906, pp.73-4; 23 August 1906, p.118; 13 September 1906, p.169.
9    *The Baptist*, 4 October 1906, p.217.
10   Sparkes, *An Accredited Ministry*, p.20.

W.J. Fox, of West Hendon, a non-collegiate minister who said that he had passed a Union examination through sitting up a little later at night and getting up earlier in the morning to study. At the end of the debate, only about fifteen of those present voted against the new scheme.[11] Later George Sage, another non-collegiate minister, who had begun his ministry in 1896 at St Neots, Cambridgeshire, spoke about how he had fared with the Union examinations. He had failed the first time, in part because he had two village churches to look after and five services to take every week, but he was glad that he had persevered and passed.[12] The *Baptist* continued to object to a Baptist Union examination as 'an entire departure from Scripture teaching, Apostolic practice and Baptist belief', but the tide was moving against it.[13]

Because of the interim arrangements regarding accreditation, which allowed many previously non-accredited ministers to be recognized, it was only in 1910 that the new rules began to 'bite'. At the 1910 autumn Assembly, which was held in Glasgow, there was what Newton Marshall, the scholarly pastor-theologian of Heath Street, Hampstead, called 'a root-and-branch denunciation of the whole present system of the recognition of ministers'. This attack came from Hugh Brown, a well-known Baptist minister in Dublin who was not accredited. Brown complained about the imposition of the 'man-made tests', as he termed them, on ministers. There were sharp exchanges at the Assembly between Brown and Greenhough. Hugh Brown failed to persuade the Assembly, although his intervention did have an impact. Marshall, who had no personal stake in the outcome of the debate, was unimpressed by Brown's position. What would Brown, Marshall wondered, put in the place of a proper accreditation system? Any alternative seemed to Marshall 'exceedingly vague', and a recipe for chaos.[14] The *Baptist Times* made the Union's position clear in a leader of 4 November 1910.

---

11 *The Baptist*, 2 May 1907, p.286.
12 *The Baptist*, 30 May 1907, p.344.
13 *The Baptist*, 13 June 1907, p.381.
14 *BW*, 6 October 1910, p.4.

> It is not reasonable that the Baptist Union should be expected to put upon its Accredited List any man who is called to the pastorate of a Church, even though he may be deficient in education, in scriptural knowledge, without any theological training, and through his tactlessness a real source of weakness and danger to the Churches.[15]

The rules of the scheme as amended were generally viewed as equitable. They were seen as necessary to provide an effective ministry, without which Baptist churches would not flourish.

Opposition, however, continued. In November 1910 Roland J. French, from Leytonstone, complained in the *Baptist Times* on behalf, he claimed, of 140 probationers who had trained in the Baptist colleges. Previously most complaints about the changes up to that point had been from non-collegiate ministers. French claimed that the Union's Ministerial Recognition method was coercive, compelling probationer ministers who had spent at least four years studying in one of the Baptist colleges to sit a further examination. His letter also revealed something of the tension between those who had been trained in Baptist colleges and those who had not. The non-collegiate route was, French alleged, a 'cheap and easy way' into the Baptist ministry. He advised his fellow-probationers not to sit the further examination and to make the whole 'slip-shod' scheme, designed by 'a few men at headquarters', unworkable.[16] Concern about French's outburst was such that Sir George Macalpine replied as President of the Union, saying that there had been much consultation about the Scheme and urging co-operation by probationers, who he recognized could render it inoperable. But not all probationer ministers agreed with French. Indeed one said that French's letter was 'hysterical' and that in the light of it an examination for probationers was a desirable thing, if not a necessity.[17]

At the 1911 autumn Assembly, after consultation with probationers and with Hugh Brown, a concession was made by the Union. It was now

---

15   *BT*, 4 November 1910, p.720.
16   *BW*, 17 November 1910, p.202.
17   *BW*, 24 November 1910, p.234; 24 November 1910, p.252 ('Probationer').

*W.T. Whitley*

proposed that probationary ministers who were college-trained could come on the fully Accredited List after four years of pastoral service, while for non-collegiate probationers an alternative to the Union examination was six years of pastoral service before coming on the fully Accredited List. The support of the Association for probationers was made obligatory.[18] By this time the constituency that had been represented by the *Baptist* did not have the same opportunity to express its opinion about the changes, since the *Baptist* had closed.[19] John Thomas of Myrtle Street, Liverpool, who had been a critic of Shakespeare's, said of the demise of the *Baptist*: 'At length the time has come when whatever dividing line may have existed between the 'independent' and 'official' organs has broken down.'[20] Probably opinion among ministers had swung in favour of Shakespeare, given his evident desire to help the churches. In 1911 the Ministerial Recognition rules, revised yet again, were adopted unanimously. Greenhough, however, was tired of making concessions, and resigned as chairman of the Ministerial Recognition Committee. His place was to be taken by P.T. Thomson, who had succeeded him at Victoria Road, Leicester. Greenhough was, as Douglas Sparkes puts it, 'brusque and frequently sarcastic', but he was also committed to high-quality Baptist ministry and wished 'to recognise and approve standards of excellence'.[21]

The initial achievement of the standards set was to a large extent in the hands of the Colleges. The historian, W.T. Whitley, who had previously been Principal of the Baptist College of Victoria, Australia,[22]

---

18    Sparkes, *An Accredited Ministry*, pp.24-6; Shepherd, *The Making of a Modern Denomination*, p.72.

19    *The Baptist,* 29 September 1910, p.613.

20    *The Baptist*, 29 September 1910 p.613.

21    Sparkes, *An Accredited Ministry*, pp.15, 26-7.

22    K. Manley, ' "The right man in the right place": W.T. Whitley in Australia (1891-1901)', *BQ*, Vol.37, No.4 (1997), pp.174-92.

investigated the situation regarding training in 1908. He found that 555 Baptist ministers had been trained at the Pastors' College, 144 at Regent's Park, London, 128 at Bristol, 124 at Rawdon, Leeds, 109 at Manchester, and 78 at the Midland College, Nottingham. Others had trained at the Welsh and Scottish colleges. Whitley believed there were too many colleges, but attempts to amalgamate the Manchester, Rawdon and Midland colleges had failed. Whitley acknowledged the benefit colleges were receiving from nearby universities.[23] From 1900 Regent's Park College was one of the Divinity Schools of the University of London and tutors became 'recognized teachers'.[24] Later the Pastors' College made arrangements with London University so that students could study for a London BD. In 1909 Bristol University College became Bristol University, and Bristol Baptist College, under the able presidency of W.J. Henderson and with the respected Bristol businessman and benefactor, Edward Robinson, as treasurer, became an Associated College of the University. The College decided to move to Tyndall's Park, close to the University, and the College building was opened there in 1919.[25] At Manchester College, where J.T. Marshall was the long-serving President, a Manchester University BD could be taken.[26] Some Baptist colleges shared classes with Congregational colleges and gained benefit from Congregational theologians.[27] Desire for higher academic standing was typical of the period.

---

23   *BT*, 21 February 1908, pp.130-1. For the failed attempts to unite the colleges see P. Shepherd, *The making of a northern Baptist College* (Manchester: Northern Baptist College, 2004), chapter 7.

24   E.A. Payne, 'The Development of Nonconformist Theological Education in the Nineteenth Century, with Special Reference to Regent's Park College', in E.A. Payne, ed., *Studies in History and Religion* (London: Lutterworth Press, 1942), p.245.

25   *Bristol Baptist College: 250 years, 1679-1929* (Bristol: The Baptist College, 1929), pp.37, 53; N.S. Moon, *Education for Ministry: Bristol Baptist College, 1679-1979* (Bristol: Bristol Baptist College, 1979), pp.67-70.

26   C. Rignal, *Manchester Baptist College, 1866-1916* (Bradford & London: William Byles & Sons Ltd, 1916), p.174.

27   For Congregational developments, see Grant, *Free Churchmanship in England*, pp.206-67.

*Staff and students of Regent's Park College, 1919-20,*
*including the first woman student, Violet Hedger (see p.72)*

What was it like to be a student in one of the colleges? R.E. Cooper spoke of the 'serenity' of the atmosphere at Regent's Park.[28] John Owen Hagger, who completed his training at Regent's Park College in 1911, described one element of his college experience in this way: 'There was an atmosphere of liberation and liberty. Liberation from inadequate theology, from the dull monotony of the outside world...I honestly think that had someone kept a log of the rags that went on day after day, it would be incredible reading, and to none more than the good deacons of the churches which had supported our applications.' This was not the full picture. There was also, as this student put it, 'the tension of study and preparation'. In addition, George P. Gould, the College President, was a demanding mentor. Hagger highlighted the experience students had of sermon class: 'There is no denying that to preach before the Doctor was an ordeal. His standards were exacting. He insisted upon strictly

---

28    R.E. Cooper, *From Stepney to St Giles': The Story of Regent's Park College, 1810-1960* (London: Carey Kingsgate Press, 1960), p.76.

historical exegesis, sometimes I should say, to the point of pedantry'.[29] It seems clear that college training was invigorating, but there were many who felt called to the ministry whose personal circumstances – often relating to finance - meant that they were unable to enter a Baptist college. Of those who settled as ministers in Baptist churches in the years 1910 to1915, 237 had been trained at one of the Baptist colleges, while 106 had prepared in other ways.[30]

Women were also, at this point, outside the collegiate system. In 1910 a Miss Clark from Glasgow wrote to Shakespeare to say that she was a first-year Arts student at Glasgow University intending to take MA and BD degrees. She asked about future settlement as a Baptist minister. The Ministerial Recognition Committee replied that it was unable to consider 'those who were not actually engaged in pastoral work' and, perhaps as a result of this lack of encouragement, nothing more was heard from Miss Clark.[31] In 1918 Miss Edith Gates became minister of Little Tew and Cleveley Baptist Church, Oxfordshire, at a time when normal procedures in the churches had been affected by the war, and four years later she became the first woman on the list of probationer ministers.[32] When Regent's Park College and the two London Congregational colleges were re-opened after the war women were admitted for training: 'the war-time service of womanhood', it was noted, 'had made previous restrictions impossible'. The first Congregational woman minister had already been recognized. In 1924

---

29   J.O. Hagger, *RPC Magazine*, No. 38, p.2, cited by Cooper, *From Stepney to St Giles'* p.76. On facing page the photograph shows left to right from back: R.T. Tyrrell, C.W. Gray, E.L. James; N.G. Barrow, H.W. Hunt, J.A. Whitcombe, F.J. Gay, G.B. Girvan, J.N. Schofield, R.V.C. Thompson, G.C.Matthews, W.G. Legassick, R.L. Child, A.R.D. Simpson; G.W. Williams, S.N. Fisher, E.F. Pepper, P.E. Dennis, H.V. Larcombe, Miss V. Hedger, F.G. Hastings, H.J. White, F.L. Stubinton, A.W. Austin; A.J. Klaiber, H.J. Flowers, Prof. S.W. Green, Dr G.P. Gould, Prof. Farrer, A. Small, W.G. Addison, R.D. Black.

30   Sparkes, *An Accredited Ministry*, pp. 28-9.

31   Minutes of the Baptist Union Ministerial Recognition Committee, 18 July 1910; Sparkes, *An Accredited Ministry*, p. 27.

32   R.M.B. Gouldbourne, *Reinventing the Wheel: Women and Ministry in English Baptist Life* (Oxford: Whitley Publications, 1997), p. 27. Nancy Astor became the first woman MP in Britain in 1919.

the first woman, Violet Hedger, appeared on the list of Regent's Park College students seeking settlement.[33] Women were eligible for admission to Bristol Baptist College from 1919, although it was not until the 1930s that the first woman ministerial student, Gwenyth Hubble, studied there. Ordained Baptist ministry was an almost exclusively male preserve in the first half of the twentieth century.

## THE SUSTENTATION SCHEME

Closely linked with ministerial recognition was the question of sustaining the ministry. Those ministers receiving aid from the Sustentation Fund had to be accredited. There was a concern that the procedures should safeguard the Fund. After the years of debate, on 8 April 1910 the full details of the Union's proposed Ministerial Settlement and Sustentation scheme were given in the *Baptist Times*.[34] Shakespeare had reluctantly accepted that there had to be changes to his earlier proposals. There was now no mention, for instance, of an obligatory fixed term in a pastorate. The annual stipends guaranteed for ministers were £100-£120 for an unmarried man, and £120-£150 for a married man. This would raise the stipends of a considerable number, since there was evidence that half the English Baptist ministers received less than £150. Probably over a quarter received less than £100. By comparison, the minimum for an accredited Wesleyan minister was £140.[35] A survey in 1911 showed that out of 1,974 Baptist churches in England, 534 had a membership of fifty or less, 410 had from fifty to 100 members and 270 had from 100 to 149 members. Most churches with under 150 members found it almost impossible to pay a stipend of £150, yet 823 of them had pastors. The problem at local level was perceived to be that most Baptists were 'wage-earners and people in business with many anxieties and not much of the world's wealth'.[36]

---

33    Sparkes, *An Accredited Ministry*, p. 32.
34    *BT*, 8 April 1910, p.222.
35    Sparkes, *The Home Mission Story*, pp.32-3. See Brown, *A Social History of the Nonconformist Ministry*, pp.156-61.
36    *BT*, 7 July 1911, p.424.

The 1910 spring Assembly marked a significant step forward in the adoption of the Ministerial Settlement and Sustentation scheme. J.R. Wood, who had been Union President in 1902, and who was pastor at Upper Holloway, with S.G. Morris as his assistant, moved a resolution recommending the new scheme for accrediting and supporting ministers. He suggested to the Assembly that the scheme would 'tend to mitigate many of the evils of our present system, while at the same time maintaining the unity which so happily prevails in our midst'.[37] Wood was right. There was a sense of unity at the Assembly, with only nine delegates voting against the motion. Among the churches themselves, however, there was less enthusiasm, an indication that the Assembly was not wholly representative. Shakespeare wrote to churches and Associations to tell them about the Assembly decision and to seek a response from them by 23 September. Only 504 churches responded, with 378 being in favour of the scheme, ninety-three opposed and thirty-three neutral.[38] It was clear that further persuasive work needed to be done, and at the 1911 spring Assembly a younger minister, F.G. Benskin, from Broadmead, Bristol, outlined the burden of poverty that many Baptist ministers and their families had to endure. The new scheme, it was argued, would alleviate that poverty. It was agreed at the July 1911 Council meeting that Benskin's address be circulated to all the churches.[39]

A year later, at the 1912 spring Assembly, with the groundwork finally completed, there was general agreement that the new arrangements were widely acceptable. Churches still had the option whether or not to be part of the scheme, but only those joining the new 'Federation' would receive the benefits. Shakespeare was confident enough to move a resolution (seconded by John Clifford) that the Assembly should adopt the scheme. His impassioned speech drew on Baptist history. Four years earlier the Baptist Historical Society had been formed, with W.T. Whitley, as Secretary, to encourage systematic

---

37   *BT*, 6 May 1910, p.296.
38   Sparkes, *The Home Mission Story*, p.35.
39   Minutes of the Baptist Union Council, 18 July 1911, p.4.

historical study.⁴⁰ Shakespeare referred to Andrew Fuller, the great eighteenth-century Baptist theologian and the first Secretary of the BMS. Fuller's salary from his church at Soham, said Shakespeare, 'became inadequate to provide for the expenses of a rising family....he was greatly depressed and nearly brought down by sorrow and sickness to the grave'. Shakespeare's argument in favour of ministerial sustentation was persuasive. 'It is false economy', he pronounced, 'to starve an Andrew Fuller'. He explained that there would be a Federation of those churches wishing to join the new scheme. His address was rapturously received and the resolution put to the Assembly was passed unanimously. Sir John Horsfall, JP, who owned the Hayfield Mills near Keighley, Yorkshire, seconded by Charles Brown of Ferme Park, moved that the appeal for the Sustentation Fund should be launched, and the Assembly again voted unanimously.⁴¹

The challenge now was to raise the £250,000 which was needed for the Fund. As usual, Shakespeare had undertaken preliminary work and had secured promises of £51,685, over £4,000 of this from ministers themselves. He also announced at the Assembly that five leading laymen would be the Treasurers of the Fund. These were Sir John Horsfall, Sir George Macalpine, Herbert Marnham (by now a successful stockbroker), John Chivers (brother of the late William Chivers from Histon), and Percy Illingworth, MP, the Chief Whip of the Liberal Party. In addition, Shakespeare had been intent on recruiting F.B. Meyer, who was respected by all parts of the Baptist constituency, to give his weight to the appeal. With his sound psychological understanding of his colleagues, Shakespeare played on Meyer's instinct for hard work and sympathy for poorer ministers. As early as July 1908 Meyer had responded positively to Shakespeare about the 'great work' that was to be done 'for Christ and our denomination'.⁴² The success of the appeal owed a great deal to the fund-raising and organisational endeavours of

---

40    I. Sellers, 'W.T. Whitley: A Commemorative Essay', *BQ*, Vol.37, No.4 (1997), pp.159-73.

41    *BT*, 26 April 1912, supplement, pp.iii-v.

42    F.B. Meyer to J.H. Shakespeare, 28 July 1908, quoted in W.Y. Fullerton, *F.B. Meyer: A Biography* (London: Marshall, Morgan & Scott [1929]), p.89.

a small group: Meyer, J.H. Rushbrooke, minister of Hampstead Garden Suburb Free Church (where Herbert Marnham was a deacon and Sunday school superintendent), F.A. Jones of Cranbrook Road, Ilford, F.G. Benskin, and Mrs C.S. Rose, the gifted organizing secretary of the Baptist Women's League (BWL), formed in 1908 through Shakespeare's initiative. Soon after the 1912 Assembly, Shakespeare suffered a breakdown in health and was off work for almost eight months.[43]

*Hampstead Garden Suburb Free Church, built in 1911 by architect Edwin Lutyens it is the only Baptist Grade 1 Listed Building*

During the appeal, Meyer conceived the idea of using as a visual publicity motif the building of Nehemiah's wall, with 250 stones, each stone being equivalent to £1,000. Almost every week for over a year Meyer had a page in the *Baptist Times* in which he reported on the

43   Sparkes, *The Home Mission Story*, pp.48-9.

accumulation of the Fund and the ideas that were being generated for this purpose. Meyer commended, for example, the making of 'Sustentation Marmalade', which he described as a 'brilliant suggestion'. It could, he added improbably, be bought by bachelors keen to impress their ladies.[44] Still more bizarre was the case he reported of the lady with a 'Sustentation dog', which caught rabbits to be sold for the benefit of the Fund.[45] By the spring Assembly of 1913, £138,511 had been given or promised to the Fund. A special Sustentation Day was convened by London Baptists on 28 October 1913. The occasion was marked in a number of ways. Marnham and Illingworth hosted a lunch at the Hotel Metropole at which Sir Alfred Pearce Gould, Treasurer of the BMS (and Vice-Chancellor of London University), was the speaker; in the afternoon there was an enthusiastic women's meeting which filled the City Temple; and in the evening David Lloyd George, then Chancellor of the Exchequer, spoke at a meeting in Westminster Chapel. The very substantial sum of £26,698 was raised during the course of the day.[46]

Even some of those who had been quite suspicious of Shakespeare's centralizing ministerial scheme became involved in supporting the practical endeavours. An example was Archibald McCaig, Principal of the Pastors' College. Shakespeare's comprehensive vision had included drawing the Baptist colleges more closely together, but the Pastors' College would not take part in a proposed united College Board, stating flatly that it would not agree to any interference with its 'absolute and sole authority in the matter of the choice and training of the students of the Pastors' College'.[47] Nonetheless, McCaig was supportive of Meyer's fundraising activities.[48] At a Sustentation Fund meeting in the Metropolitan Tabernacle in 1914, A.C. Dixon, the Tabernacle's minister, another deeply conservative Baptist, admitted that he had been converted

---

44   *BT*, 31 January 1913, p.93.
45   *BT*, 23 May 1913, p.397.
46   *BT*, 31 October 1913, pp.825-30.
47   Spurgeon's College, London: College Minute Book, 4 March 1909; see M. Nicholls, *Lights to the World: A History of Spurgeon's College, 1856-1992* (Harpenden: Nuprint, 1994), p.124, and Shepherd, *The Making of a Modern Denomination*, p.66. The Board met in 1912 and survived for 3½ years.
48   *BT*, 11 April 1913, p.289.

to the Fund. Dixon presided at the Fund meeting, and Meyer, Shakespeare and Charles Brown spoke.[49] Some individual Baptist congregations gave very large amounts. Regent's Park Chapel, for example, where Meyer was pastor, gave £4,888. In September 1913 Meyer divulged, however, that as many as three out of every four Baptist churches had not participated financially, and on Sunday, 8 March 1914, when it was hoped to raise £20,000 through a Simultaneous Collection, extremely bad weather kept many people at home and only £11,000 was collected.[50]

At the 1914 spring Assembly, during a Thanksgiving Meeting at the Royal Albert Hall, Shakespeare was able, with enormous satisfaction, to announce that the target of £250,000 had been reached. He was given a standing ovation. The BWL had set its own target of raising £50,000 and had exceeded this figure. Charles Brown, who paid enthusiastic tribute to the leadership of Shakespeare, stated that the Baptist denomination had 'entered upon a new relationship to the ministry, of responsibility, of honour, of respect'.[51] The euphoria was understandable; the financial reality was somewhat different. Although the new sense of responsibility had been emphasized, it was reported in October 1914 that only £157,000 had actually been received. The full amount did not come in until 1917. Also, the Simultaneous Collection which was taken in the churches in March of each year never reached the targets set. Many churches still gave little or no financial support to the Union. In 1917, however, when 462 grants to ministers were made, the figure of £120 per annum as a minimum salary was increased to £130 (£150 for those living in London)[52] and allowances for children were added. Sustaining the ministry from central funds became an integral part of Union life.

49   *BW*, 5 March 1914, p.673.
50   *BT*, 12 September 1913, p,693; Sparkes, *The Home Mission Story*, pp.49-50.
51   *BT*, 1 May 1914, supplement, pp.1-6.
52   This 'London weighting' appears to have ceased by 1923.

FORCED INTO WAR

J.H. Shakespeare had further ideas which he wished to implement in his comprehensive reform of the denomination, but the outbreak of war had far-reaching implications for such plans. The psychological effect on Baptists of the declaration of war against Germany was profound. Many Baptists had been deeply committed to the cause of international peace. John Clifford and J.H. Rushbrooke were publicly associated with efforts to link the Churches of the world, involving themselves, for example, in a World Alliance for Promoting International Friendship through the Churches. Initiatives by Allen Baker, a Liberal MP and a Quaker, led to the formation in 1910 of 'The Associated Councils in the British and German Empires for Fostering Friendly Relations between the Two Peoples'. Baker also helped launch the journal, *The Peacemaker*.[53] Clifford, Meyer, Shakespeare, Charles Brown, Sir George Macalpine and Sir George White were Vice-Presidents of the British Council's committee, and Newton Marshall, who had gained his doctorate in Halle, Germany, was active in fostering German-English contacts. Rushbrooke, who was to undertake considerable work in Europe and would become General Secretary of the Baptist World Alliance, was editor of *The Peacemaker*, which by 1914 had achieved a circulation of 67,000.[54]

In January 1914, John Clifford told his Westbourne Park congregation: 'A new era is coming nearer and nearer every year…Militarism belongs to the dark ages; it is not fit for our time. It must go. It is going.'[55] A mere seven months later, however, the situation was very different. Following the outbreak of war, and in particular the violation of Belgian neutrality, there was considerable re-thinking. The congregation at Haven Green, Ealing, was one of the churches that took in Belgian refugees. Preaching at a Sunday evening service in August

---

53    K. Robbins, *The Abolition of War: The 'Peace Movement' in Britain, 1914-1919* (Cardiff: University of Wales Press, 1976), p.18. See also, K. Robbins, 'Protestant Nonconformists and the Peace Question', in Sell and Cross, eds., *Protestant Nonconformity*, pp.216-39.

54    *BT*, 6 January 1914, p.24; K.W. Clements, 'Baptists and the Outbreak of the First World War', *BQ*, Vol.26, No.2 (1975), p.80.

55    *CW*, 8 January 1914, p.7.

1914 at Westbourne Park on 'The Churches and the War', Clifford suggested: 'Our business is not to condemn the nations now engaged in strife.' The truth, he considered, was very difficult to find. But as he warmed to his theme he became surprisingly partisan. 'The progress of humanity', he informed his hearers, 'in my judgement hinges upon this war...We are forced into it.' This was not, for Clifford, a war in which Britain and Germany could both point to factors that favoured their position. Rather, he claimed, 'the best and noblest elements of the human race are with us.' As he saw it, this was a battle for humanity. Clifford received an unambiguous congregational affirmation, with calls of 'Hear, hear!'[56] A month later Meyer, preaching at Ferme Park for Charles Brown, announced somewhat mysteriously that he believed 'the heavenly legions themselves are moving forward'.[57]

War drastically affected historic German-British Baptist relationships. J.H. Rushbrooke, who had studied in Berlin, and whose wife, Dora, was German, was deeply torn by the conflict. With Shakespeare and Newton Marshall, he had shared in the organization of the first European Baptist Congress in Berlin in 1908, which had attracted 1,800 delegates. Newton Marshall was the 'father' of the congress. Rushbrooke was also prominent in the second European Congress, held in Stockholm in 1913, and in the following year he travelled to Constance in Germany with John Clifford to attend a Protestant Peace Conference. This had to be abandoned because of the war, and Rushbrooke tried to reach the Baltic coast to join his wife and daughter. He was under close surveillance, and, believing that he was going to be interned indefinitely, he tendered his resignation to his church in Hampstead Garden Suburb. He also gave his congregation specific advice: 'Love your land, as true Englishmen: but do not forget to be Christians. Have room in your hearts for those who are called your "enemies", multitudes of whom serve the same Lord.'[58] The church did not accept his resignation and the Rushbrookes were able to return to England at the end of October 1914. For Rushbrooke the war was an

---

56    *BW*, 20 August 1914, p.525.
57    *BW*, 17 September 1914, p.589.
58    Green, *Tomorrow's Man*, pp.61-3.

'awful fact' which had seemed impossible and in the face of which, he admitted, his personal faith had 'almost reeled'.[59]

The Baptist Union Council, in a manifesto in late September 1914, concentrated not on internal struggles of faith but on the struggle against the enemy. 'We believe', said the Council, 'the call of God has come to Britain to spare neither blood nor treasure in the struggle to shatter a great anti-Christian attempt to destroy the fabric of Christian civilisation'. At the same time as casting the German offensive as 'anti-Christian', the manifesto called for prayers of penitence, prayers for enemies and prayers for Baptists in Germany and Austria. It also expressed delight that 'many of the young men of our Churches have dedicated themselves ... to the service of their country'.[60] By the end of November Baptist churches were publicizing the number of those who had enlisted from their congregations: Ferme Park, 120; Westbourne Park, 100; Horfield, Bristol, 50; Bloomsbury, 40-50. As Keith Clements comments: 'Pride stirred in the hearts of previously peace-loving Baptists as they watched their young men go.'[61] Most Baptists turned out not to be pacifists but 'pacificists': war was inhumane but sometimes necessary.[62] The 1915 Yorkshire Baptist Association Assembly passed a resolution declaring hatred of war, but noting that most delegates recognized that national honour, duty and obligation to international law left no alternative. One layman in the North West expressed in the same year his bewilderment: 'Twelve months ago I considered myself a member of the Peace Society and to an extent I am still.'[63]

Shakespeare, Clifford, Meyer and Richard Glover from Bristol were among the Baptists who, on 23 September 1914, signed a firmly-worded reply by British Church leaders to an appeal from some German theologians who had claimed that their country had been the victim of conspiracy. 'We have taken our stand', said the British Church leaders

---

59    *BW*, 10 September 1914, p.573.
60    *BT*, 25 September 1914, p.719.
61    Clements, 'Baptists and the Outbreak of the First World War', p.76.
62    M. Ceadel, *Pacifism in Britain, 1914-1945: The Defining of a Faith* (Oxford: Clarendon Press, 1980), p.3.
63    Sellers, ed., *Our Heritage*, pp.84-5. (W. Sargent of Moss Side).

firmly, 'for international good faith, for the safeguarding of smaller nationalities, and for the upholding of the essential conditions of brotherhood among the nations of the world.'[64] Amongst Baptists, with their history of being a small minority, there was a particular concern for the welfare of small nations. In October 1914 the Archbishop of Canterbury, Randall Davidson, called a conference at Lambeth to study the implications of the war. Clifford and Shakespeare participated. On 10 November 1914 they, together with Meyer, Tom Phillips of Bloomsbury and Free Church leaders of other denominations, were on the platform with Lloyd George at a meeting in the City Temple to rally support for the war.[65] The meeting was chaired by Sir William Robertson Nicoll, editor of the *British Weekly*, and he and Shakespeare became two of the leading advocates of the war effort.[66] By 1917, John Clifford could be referred to with approval as a 'veteran recruiting sergeant'.[67]

By 1917, however, the feelings in local churches were rather different, with the full horror of war becoming evident. The large number of Baptist recruits meant considerable Baptist losses. Baptist churches in the north, for example, reported: 'Lost several boys in action … 63 serving King and country … suffering from absence of young men at war … four Deacons on active service, one wounded, the youngest has fallen in battle, one decorated for attending wounded under heavy shell fire … three members have made the supreme sacrifice … 70 of the lads engaged in war … 110 names on roll of honour … mourn loss of three members in battle … mourn loss of a promising young scholar who has fallen.'[68] At Ferme Park, Hornsey, seventy people, described as 'the finest flower of the life of the Church', were killed in battle.[69] There was talk of soldiers as saints. Campbell Morgan, minister at the Congregational Westminster Chapel, London, said that 'the sign of the

---

64    See Bell, *Randall Davidson*, pp.740-4.
65    Jordan, *Free Church Unity*, pp.140-1.
66    Shepherd, *The Making of a Modern Denomination*, pp.75-6.
67    *BW*, 4 January 1917, p.280.
68    Sellers, ed., *Our Heritage*, p. 86.
69    Cook, *Charles Brown*, pp.59-61.

Cross is on every man that marches to his death'.[70] But Tom Phillips at Bloomsbury insisted on the need for a turning to God from sin - the only way in which a soldier could be a saint.[71] Traditional evangelical thinking about the fate of those who were not clearly believers and who were killed in battle was being challenged, but for most Baptists the challenge was to reach out with the message of Christ to all those who were fighting.

Care for Baptists in the forces was a major concern. Determined representations by Shakespeare and R.J. Wells, the Secretary of the

*E.L. Watson, Baptist chaplain in France, 1914*

Congregational Union, led to Baptist and Congregational pastors being accepted as chaplains, under a United Navy and Army Board. Lord Kitchener, Secretary of State for War, was opposed to the plan, but Lloyd George and Percy Illingworth lent support.[72] By 1916 sixty-one Baptist ministers had been appointed as chaplains. For Shakespeare the United Board was an example of how a united Free Church could work in England. Baptist chaplains developed new ecumenical ministries. F.C. Spurr described a Roman Catholic soldier requesting a blessing from a Baptist chaplain.[73] Chaplaincy work also contributed to changing views of Baptist ministry, since chaplains were serving the Crown. But Baptist ministers who became chaplains saw themselves as exercising substantially the same evangelistic and pastoral ministries as they had done in their churches. Some described baptismal services held at the Front. Baptisms were reported in France, one in a 'bath-house' and another in a stream. A.J. White, a Garrison chaplain,

---

70    A. Wilkinson, *Dissent or Conform? War, Peace and the English Churches, 1900-1945* (London: SCM, 1986), pp 25-7.

71    *BT*, 2 December 1915, p.782.

72    In 1914 the *Baptist Times* ran articles about Baptist chaplains, such as E.L. Watson and C.S. Rose. See Shepherd, *The Making of a Modern Denomination*, pp.96-103.

73    F.C. Spurr, *Some Chaplains in Khaki: An account of the work of Chaplains of the United Navy and Army Board* (London: H.R. Allinsen, 1916), p.1.

conducted a baptism in the sea in Alexandria, Egypt.[74] Several Baptist ministers took shorter-term assignments with the YMCA in France.

One serious problem for Baptists was the Military Service Acts, which introduced conscripted service in 1916. Tribunals (which often included members who had been recruiting agents) were given the task of assessing the cases of 14,000 applicants seeking exemption from military service. Most Conscientious Objectors (COs) were willing to accept non-combatant duties during the war, but about 1,500 requested total exemption. A number of these were subjected to brutal punishment. Clifford denounced the Acts because they violated liberty of conscience, and he joined with pacifists on the executive of the National Council Against Conscription, which became the National Council for Civil Liberties. Shakespeare, judging by the stance of the *Baptist Times*, seems to have seen conscription as a necessary evil, although he protested to the government about its harsh policies. Meyer visited thirty-four COs sentenced to death in France for refusing to obey military orders, and he reported to Herbert Asquith, the Prime Minister, about the brutality he discovered.[75] The philosopher, Bertrand Russell, supplied material for Meyer's book on conscientious objection, *The Majesty of Conscience.*[76] Preaching at a Sunday service in 1916 at Haven Green, Ealing, Arnold Streuli, the minister, condemned tribunal attitudes, instancing a tribunal member who, when a CO quoted Jesus' words, replied dismissively, 'Jesus is not here'.[77] Streuli's views contributed to a split in his church after the war. J.G. Greenhough, by contrast with Streuli, believed those who fought were better Christians than the COs.[78] War divided the Baptist community.

74   *BT*, 26 May 1916, p.327; 29 December 1916, p. 808; 28 March 1919, p.182.
75   Clements, 'Baptists and the Outbreak of the First World War', p.76; *The Times*, 9 June 1916, p.9; 22 June 1916, p 7; Sir Wyndham Childs, *Episodes and Reflections* (London: Cassell & Co., 1930), pp.152-3.
76   J. Vellacott, *Bertrand Russell and the Pacifists in the First World War* (Brighton: Harvester, 1980), p.213; cf. P.R. Dekar, 'Twentieth-Century British Baptist Conscientious Objectors', *BQ*, Vol.35, No.1 (1993), pp.35-44.
77   *BW*, 30 March 1916, p.529.
78   *BT*, 7 September 1917, p.549.

## SOCIAL INVOLVEMENT

There was a widely shared desire of Baptists through this period – before, during and after the war – for a better society to be created. David Bebbington suggests that by 1910 the period of the influence of the Nonconformist conscience, which had been declining in importance, had come to an end.[79] This was the year when Thomas Law, who had been fully involved in the political fray as Secretary of the Free Church Council, committed suicide while in a state of depression, and Meyer was invited by the Council to accept the Honorary Secretaryship of the Council.[80] Although Meyer's emphasis was on the spiritual work of the Council, in the context of the bitter controversy in 1909-10 about the veto powers of the House of Lords over the Commons, Meyer could describe the Upper House as 'warped by class prejudice'.[81] There was resentment that the House of Lords had blocked educational reform, and although the passive resistance campaign against rates being paid towards church schools was losing momentum, there were those who continued that battle. By 1910, P.T. Thomson, of Victoria Road, Leicester, and later the Baptist Union's Commissioner for Education, had been in prison on eight occasions. In 1913 Passive Resistance meetings, held under the auspices of the Free Church Council, were still being attended by major figures such as Clifford and Robertson Nicoll, with their deliberations being reported to Lloyd George.[82]

Some Baptists hoped that through Baptist representatives in Parliament the concerns of the Baptist and wider Free Church constituency would be addressed. After the second 1910 General Election, when the Liberals were again returned to power (although with a reduced majority), there were fourteen Baptist Members of Parliament. This was despite the fact that some Baptist MPs had retired.[83] There had

79    Bebbington, *The Nonconformist Conscience*, p.160.
80    Ibid., p.81.
81    *CW*, 9 December 1909, p.3.
82    S. Koss, *Nonconformity in Modern British Politics* (London: B.T. Batsford, 1975), p.123.
83    D.W. Bebbington, 'Baptist Members of Parliament in the Twentieth Century', *BQ*, Vol.31 (1986), p.255.

been seventeen Baptist MPs after the 1906 election, but it was claimed that no Baptist MPs who had offered themselves for re-election in 1910 had been defeated.[84] There was continuing interest in and support for Lloyd George among Baptists, with Shakespeare especially keen to capitalize on Lloyd George's Baptist sympathies. However, by 1913 there was increasing disillusionment about the will of the Liberal government to tackle such contentious issues as educational reform and temperance legislation. On the temperance question, the Baptist Total Abstinence Association was vigorous, and there were temperance Bands of Hope in most large Baptist churches; but there was no evidence at that point that the government would align itself with any temperance campaign.

*'Waiting their turn to take food from the Invalid Kitchen to their Sick Relatives' West Ham Central Mission, 1912*

Clifford described the Liberal government's record in 1913 as a 'betrayal', and Shakespeare blamed the Free Church Council for being ineffective in achieving the goals of its constituency.[85]

With the onset of war, some social priorities inevitably changed. Against the background of the suffragette movement and the role of women in the war effort, there was a strong emphasis on the place of women in Baptist life. Branches of the Baptist Women's League were established in many churches and large central meetings were held for women. The BWL opened a hostel, Newington Court, for business girls

84   Koss, *Nonconformity in Modern British Politics*, p.111.
85   Ibid., pp.122-3.

in central London, in 1912.[86] Mrs Illingworth, the wife of Percy Illingworth, MP, was the speaker in 1913 at a large BWL rally. During the war, the League turned its attention to the needs of the troops, and through the channels of chaplains it supplied extra help to them, such as clothing. It also gave practical assistance to homeless French Protestant refugees and to British Prisoners of War.

Nurses were mobilized to care for wounded soldiers. There was co-operation between the BWL and the Deaconess Order in medical work. Hettie Rowntree Clifford (formerly Deaconess Hettie Bannister),[87] at Barking Road Tabernacle (the West Ham Central Mission), and Mrs C.S. Rose, the energetic leader of the BWL, who were probably the two best known women in the denomination, led the way in social ministry during the war. Others worked with them. Meyer, who had stimulated the beginnings of the deaconess movement and remained a supporter, was concerned about the sexual *mores* of soldiers. He helped to make the YMCA in Waterloo Road, London, available for soldiers experiencing what he termed 'serious moral dangers'.[88]

*Hettie Rowntree Clifford*

A number of the Baptist colleges were utilized for the purpose of meeting social needs during the war. Thus Regent's Park College was used from 1916 for the re-training of war-blinded sailors and soldiers. By this time the number of students there had fallen to ten. They went into residence at the Congregational Hackney College, with the responsibility for their training being taken up by the eminent Congregational theologian, P.T. Forsyth. Many students in the colleges volunteered for work connected with the war. One-third of the Bristol College's students

---

86  *BT*, 4 October 1912, supplement, p.iv.
87  Deaconesses left the Order when they married. Hettie Bannister married Robert Rowntree Clifford.
88  *The Times*, 12 November 1915, p.9.

were engaged in such work in 1915. Midland Baptist College, already small, had only two students in 1917 and the war was to result in its permanent closure.[89] Many who had been about to begin training for ministry took up other activities instead, often social service associated with the war. Others entered the ministry, but not via the colleges. This meant that in the period 1917 to 1922, of the new ministers settled in churches, only 104 had Baptist college training, whereas 117 were non-collegiate.[90] The strength of these new ministers was their practical experience in war-time, but not all were equipped for the challenges they would face in the 1920s and 1930s. Deaconess training at this stage was under the leadership of Isabel James, who was a friend of Shakespeare's and a leading figure in the BWL. Bloomsbury Central Church was the spiritual home of the deaconesses.[91]

*Isabel James*

What about political influence? At national level Baptists suffered a considerable loss during the war through the early death, in his mid-forties, of Percy Illingworth, the Chief Whip of the Liberal Party. Illingworth was MP for Shipley, Yorkshire, and it was after he was elected to Parliament that he was baptized in Girlington Baptist Church. In London he attended Bloomsbury. His memorial service was attended by nearly all the members of the Cabinet.[92] An institute was built in 1916 on land belonging to the War Office in Aldershot as a memorial to Illingworth. The war saw other Baptists take up new political posts. From 1917 the Chairman of the Parliamentary Labour Party and the Leader of the Party in the Commons was a Baptist, William Adamson,

---

89  W.J. Avery, 'The Late Midland College', *BQ*, Vol.1 (1922-3), pp.218-22, 263-9, 327-36.
90  Sparkes, *An Accredited Ministry*, p.29.
91  *BT*, 7 November 1919, p.650; F. Bowers, *A Bold Experiment*, pp.267-72. From 1912 the Deaconess Home was at 37 Mecklenburgh Square.
92  *BT*, 8 January 1915, p.20; 15 January 1915, p.39; and see D.C. Sparkes, 'Percy Illingworth and the last Liberal Government', *BQ*, Vol. 34, No 7 (2002), pp.328-46.

MP.[93] The biggest boost to Baptist hopes of national influence, however, came in December 1916 when Lloyd George succeeded Asquith as Prime Minister. Shakespeare became a frequent visitor to 10 Downing Street and one of the Prime Minister's advisors.[94] It may well be that Shakespeare welcomed this role because of his ideas about Baptists as part of the wider Church in England. Problems, however, emerged. Rifts between Asquith and Lloyd George, and the acceptance by Lloyd George of Conservative backing, caused Free Church unease. In October 1917, at the suggestion of Shakespeare, Lloyd George invited several leading Free Church ministers to breakfast at 10 Downing Street. Lloyd George was keen to have the support of ministers, but, as G.I.T. Machin argues, resultant socio-political Free Church gains were almost non-existent.[95]

After the war there was some movement on the part of individual Baptists in the direction of the Labour Party. In November 1918,

Clifford, then aged eighty-two, said that he could not trust the political coalition with the Conservatives into which Lloyd George had entered. In the following month Clifford took the chair at a Free Church demonstration in support of the Labour Party. For Clifford this was not a huge shift of political position. He had already been associated with the Fabian Society. Indeed it was 'New Liberalism', with its social vision, which laid the foundation of the welfare state. Clifford now saw future reforms as lying with the Labour Party.[96] He was not alone. Nearly one-third of Baptist parliamentary candidates in the 1918 General Election were Labour. However, Church issues hardly surfaced; the concerns were about peace

*John Clifford*

93    Bebbington, 'Baptist Members of Parliament in the Twentieth Century', p.263.
94    Payne, *The Baptist Union*, p.181.
95    G.I.T. Machin, *Politics and the Churches in Great Britain, 1869 to 1921* (Oxford: Clarendon Press, 1987), p.313.
96    Koss, *Nonconformity in Modern British Politics*, p.147; Bebbington, *The Nonconformist Conscience*, p.60.

and reconstruction.[97] As an illustration of Free Church divisions over Lloyd George, Ferme Park's Charles Brown was pleased that at North Islington the candidate in the 1918 election was not 'chosen by the Lloyd George caucus'. If that had been the case, said Brown, 'I should vote Labour, as I approve of its programme and I admire immensely men like Arthur Henderson... I wish from the bottom of my heart that there could be a coalition of the forces of Liberalism and Labour.' Even James Nicholas, minister of East Castle Street Welsh Baptist Church, London, reckoned as Lloyd George's church, campaigned for Labour.[98]

## SUPERVISION OF BAPTIST LIFE

The period of the war was one in which Baptists saw changes in the way the denomination was led. In 1912, in connection with the new scheme of ministerial settlement, Shakespeare stated that it was intended to set up 'a thoroughly organized and representative committee' to oversee the settlement process and associated matters.[99] It was not clear at that point how this was to be achieved. The thinking in the denomination was, however, moving in the direction of greater centralization. Congregationalism was not being defended as robustly or as uniformly as before. J.C. Carlile, for example, said in 1911 that it was 'hardly possible to prove any one exclusive form of Church Government from the New Testament history'. He argued that churches could not afford to continue in isolation; there was a need for ministers to co-operate.[100] In the same year global co-operation was emphasized at the second Baptist World Congress, held in Philadelphia, USA, in June 1911, under the presidency of Clifford. This event reinforced the idea of a wider fellowship of Baptists. Prior to the Congress, Shakespeare visited the United States and was involved in a range of preparatory work. It was

---

97    Machin, *Politics and the Churches*, p.315.
98    *BT*, 22 June 1917, p.384.
99    *BT*, 26 April 1912, supplement, p.iii.
100   *BT*, 13 January 1911, pp.24-5.

also in this period that Shakespeare, together with Newton Marshall and J.H. Rushbrooke, developed the European Baptist network.[101]

The insights Shakespeare gained from involvement with Hungarian Baptists in this period were important because, as Peter Shepherd argues, they provided him at a pragmatic level with a possible model for a more centrally-orientated form of national Baptist organization. Shakespeare had worked with Hungarian Baptists in 1907 to produce a framework for their Union in which the whole of Hungary was divided into convenient geographical areas. Baptists living and worshipping in each area were to form one church, 'though these may be attached to different local meetings or preaching stations', and it was decided that the payment of all ministerial stipends would be the responsibility of the geographical areas. Shakespeare's later observations on this development are significant. His hope was that the new constitution would mean that the Baptists of Hungary would 'avoid the faults and the weaknesses which Independency exhibits among ourselves' and he also voiced his wish that the work of the Hungarian Commission might serve 'as an object lesson to ourselves'. Baptist independency in Britain, he suggested, would be all the stronger if tempered with that 'dash of Presbyterianism' which had been infused into the constitution of the new United Hungarian Church.[102] This experience was to influence Shakespeare in his thinking about geographical supervision of Baptist life in England.

It was at a meeting of the Secretaries and Treasurers of the Associations, held in November 1914, that reference was first made to the 'division of the country into districts under the charge of general superintendents'. There appears to have been little discussion of this very far-reaching change.[103] The next mention was at a Sustentation Fund sub-committee on 18 January 1915 when, after considerable discussion (the minutes say nothing more than that), the six members present 'agreed to recommend that the country be divided into the following

---

101   For this story see Green, *Crossing the Boundaries.*
102   Shepherd, *The Making of a Modern Denomination*, p.40.
103   Sparkes, *The Home Mission Story*, p.58, citing minutes of a meeting of 18 November 1914.

districts, with a general superintendent over each'.[104] Ernest Payne spoke later about Shakespeare's elaborate and carefully worked-out scheme for ministerial settlement and removal, and the appointment of the superintendents.[105] Other writers have relied on Payne in seeing superintendents as an integral part of the whole sustentation scheme. The idea may have been in Shakespeare's mind for some time, especially as a result of exploring models of operation with the Hungarians, but Geoffrey Reynolds, in *First Among Equals*, suggests that the superintendency arrangements might have been an afterthought.[106] Whether or not Shakespeare saw superintendents as integral to the sustentation scheme, they were certainly part of a bigger, comprehensive ecclesiological picture which was in his mind.

The Sustentation Fund sub-committee, at its meeting on 16 February 1915, put more flesh on the bones. The superintendents would be responsible for the Sustentation Fund in their area, would be the Baptist Union's representatives dealing with settlements, would be involved in issues connected with grouping of churches and would be a point of contact for churches. The stipends of the superintendents would be paid by the Union.[107] The activities of the Union were, therefore, being increased once more. As well as operating from Baptist Church House, the Union would, in effect, operate in a direct way across the country. As this new development was made public – at the 1915 spring Assembly in the first instance – some questions were raised by Associations. In 1915 Shakespeare attended the Yorkshire Baptist Association Assembly and in the light of his visit J. Holmes, the incoming Association President, did not deliver a presidential address but gave Shakespeare the opportunity to talk about his plans for the Union. The main concern at this point seems to have been about the idea of superintendents. In order to counter worries that Associations would be side-lined, Shakespeare

---

104 Minutes of the Baptist Union Sustentation Fund Sub-Committee, 18 January 1915. Bound with BU Council Minutes, Angus Library.
105 Payne, *Baptist Union*, p.175.
106 G.G. Reynolds, *First among Equals* (Didcot: Baptist Union, Southern Area, 1993), p.65.
107 Minutes of the Baptist Union Sustentation Fund Sub-Committee, 16 February 1915.

stressed that in six of his proposed nine (later ten) areas across the country there were already full-time Association Secretaries in operation.[108]

There was, however, more to it than that, as was made clear by George Gould, the incoming President of the Union, who seconded the resolution concerning superintendents at the 1915 spring Assembly. As Principal of Regent's Park College, Gould was keenly aware of the place and importance of ministry in the denomination. His speech at the Assembly in support of the Sustentation appeal referred to a 'new order of ministry' in the Baptist denomination.[109] Was superintendency a new order? A.J. Klaiber, in a contribution to *The Baptist Union General Superintendents* (1949) on 'Superintendency in Baptist History', claimed that a communication from A.C. Underwood, the Baptist historian (and Principal from 1928 of Rawdon College, Leeds), showed that Shakespeare's thinking about superintendents was indebted to Lutheran Church models of superintendency.[110] Indeed, Shakespeare made this connection in his 1915 spring Assembly address, referring to John Clifford's experience of staying with a Lutheran superintendent in Germany. There was laughter (perhaps nervous laughter on the part of some) when Shakespeare told the Assembly that he was not trying to impose a system of episcopacy on Baptists. To assuage Baptist fears, Shakespeare referred to the seventeenth-century General Baptist Messengers as officers appointed to 'supervise the Churches'.[111] This comparison was taken up by others.[112] Shepherd argues that the primary function of the Messengers was evangelistic and also suggests that Shakespeare's interest throughout all of this discussion was basically pragmatic.[113]

Shakespeare was a pragmatist, but his 'catholic and comprehensive' ecclesiological vision made him question congregationalism. He would

---

108  Sellers, ed., *Our Heritage*, p.80.
109  *BT*, 30 April 1915, supplement, p.iii.
110  A.J. Klaiber, *et al.*, *The Baptist Union General Superintendents* (London: Baptist Union, 1949), p.8.
111  *BT*, 30 April 1915, supplement, p.iii.
112  Payne, *Baptist Union*, p.182.
113  Shepherd, *The Making of a Modern Denomination*, pp.79-81.

have been delighted by a comment in 1916 from William Hogan, President of the Western Association, that Baptists had, in appointing superintendents, 'produced an ideal Bench of Bishops'.[114] The 'bench' was Hector V. Thomas (North West), Secretary of the Lancashire and Cheshire Association; J. Gyles Williams (North East), Secretary, Yorkshire Association; C.G. Croome (East Midland), Secretary, East Midland Association; R.M. Julian (West Midland), Secretary, West Midland Association; Frank Durbin (Western), Secretary, Devon and Cornwall Association; N. Hardingham Patrick (Eastern), minister of Brockley Road, London; C.T. Byford (Central), BWA Commissioner in Europe; Thomas Woodhouse (Southern), minister of Brownhill Road, Catford, London; J.W. Ewing (Metropolitan), minister of Rye Lane Chapel, Peckham; and J. Meredith Jones (South Wales), minister of Alma Street, Newport. Five had trained at the Pastors' College, two at Pontypool, one at Midland College, one at Bristol, and one was non-collegiate. Their first conference was in November 1915. The *Baptist Times* in March 1916 (reflecting Shakespeare's views) hoped their work - 'settling disputes, arranging the removal and settlement of ministers, visiting, encouraging and advising rural Churches, exercising a sympathetic supervision and linking the whole Denomination' - would be the 'most fruitful effort we have ever made'.[115]

Linking together the denomination was seen as important. At the Union's spring Assembly in 1916 a resolution was approved which hoped that 'a General Superintendent shall not be unduly absorbed in business and financial cares, but that he may be enabled, through the blessing of God, to exercise a spiritual ministry in the Churches of the area and promote their closer union and more effective co-operation'.[116] By 1918 a pattern had been established by which the superintendents met

---

114  Devon and Cornwall Baptist Association Minute Book, 1916, cited by Shepherd, *The Making of a Modern Denomination*, p.80. For a more extended discussion see I.M. Randall, 'A Good Bench of Bishops?', in S. Murray Williams, ed., *Translocal Ministry* (Didcot: Baptist Union, 2004), pp.33-43.

115  *BT*, 3 March 1916, p.132. The General Superintendents were often referred to as Area Superintendents or simply Superintendents, and these terms will be used in this book.

116  *Baptist Handbook* (1916), pp.276-7.

monthly to deal with the needs of the 1,357 Baptist churches that had chosen to join the Federation.[117] Other ways by which the Union was strengthened included the annual Assembly (it was decided in 1915 to have only one per year) and the efforts of the Secretary. Shakespeare fostered relationships at a personal level, not only at Baptist Church House but also on the golf course. In 1918 the highly competitive Shakespeare was awarded the joint first prize in the ministerial section of the Arundel House golf competition.[118] Part of the responsibility for Union relationships also lay with the Presidents. Tom Phillips of Bloomsbury, a Welshman, was President in 1916, and an Irishman, W.Y. Fullerton, Home Secretary of the BMS, followed. Wider links across the UK as well as Union-BMS co-operation were affirmed. J.E. Roberts, who followed Maclaren as pastor at Union Chapel, Oxford Road, Manchester, used his presidency in 1918 to urge the establishment of Spiritual Welfare Committees.[119] Superintendents were, nonetheless, key to denominational cohesion.

## 'TRULY HOLY, TRULY CATHOLIC'

In 1910 Shakespeare made an eloquent plea to a National Free Church Council audience for a United Free Church of England. He also gave an illuminating interview to the *British Weekly*. In the light of the World Missionary Conference in 1910 in Edinburgh, it might have seemed that Christian unity was simply a topic of current interest, but Shakespeare explained that he had been pondering the subject of wider union for at least three years. 'I recognise', he said, 'that any attempts which have been made in England towards the union of different denominations have resulted in failure.' The way forward, he suggested, was through an alliance or federation of denominations, rather than through one 'sect' (the word he used) being absorbed into another. He continued: 'The plain fact is that Denominationalism today is maintained largely by vested

---

117  Minutes of the Baptist Union Council, 22-25 April 1918, p.9.
118  Minutes of the Arundel House Golf Trophy Committee of the Baptist Union, 11 October 1918. Bound with BU Council Minutes, Angus Library.
119  Sellers, ed., *Our Heritage*, p. 87.

interests – by colleges, funds, and officials. Our members move freely from one church to another.' The most serious problem, for Shakespeare, was that the churches were not coping with evangelizing England. Shakespeare envisaged a board appointed by the evangelical (i.e. Free Church) denominations which would look at redistributing Free Church forces. His far-sighted vision was that in every village there would be the Anglican Church, 'with its helpful traditions', and a Free Church (with 'simpler worship'), attached to one Free Church denomination, e.g. 'United Free Church of England, Baptist Section'.[120]

The call by Shakespeare was echoed by others. Charles Brown said in April 1911 that in his recent work as President of the Free Church Council he had 'almost forgotten that he was a Baptist in the glowing consciousness that he was a Christian'. Indeed he had even regretted the name 'Baptist', he claimed, since the denomination stood for much more than baptism. Also, he added controversially, Baptists actually laid less stress on baptism than most other Christians. However, Brown insisted that the Baptist testimony to baptism was needed. He shared Shakespeare's vision: 'I long to see one competent, well organised Free Church of England'. But any such move would have to allow freedom to Baptists to preach about and administer believer's baptism.[121] Later that year, Meyer preached at the Free Church in Amersham-on-the-Hill, Buckinghamshire, on a similar theme. He stated that he would like to see in all country districts in England, instead of a number of small buildings, one good building, such as in Amersham, for Christians of all denominations. As an indication of his own commitment to a weekly observance of Holy Communion, he suggested that the celebration of the Lord's Supper according to different Christian traditions could be done weekly at midweek services.[122]

---

120  *BW*, 10 November 1910, p.170; cf. D.M. Thompson, 'The Unity of the Church in Twentieth-Century England: Pleasing Dream or Common Calling?', in R.W. Swanson, ed., *Unity and Diversity in the Church* (Oxford: Blackwell, 1996), pp.515-16.

121  *BW*, 9 March 1911, p.662; 27 April 1911, p.84.

122  *BW*, 31 August 1911, p.529.

It took three years, and further prompts from Shakespeare, for the Free Church Council to set up an investigation into the question of a United Free Church. At the 1913 Free Church Council meetings, which were attended by 1,200 people, Meyer supported Shakespeare and proposed a Free Church Commission of Enquiry to look into the 'union' ideas. It was decided that Free Church leaders would meet together at Mansfield College, Oxford, over Easter.[123] There was also interest in inter-communion with the Anglican Church. At an inter-church conference convened in June 1913 in Kenya (in a village called Kikuyu), a conference that marked a concern for unity found in some regions of Africa following Edinburgh 1910,[124] a united service of Holy Communion was held. During this service, conference members (including non-Anglicans) received communion from a bishop. Evangelicals were distressed by the subsequent adverse reaction from high Anglicans to the openness displayed at Kikuyu.[125] With the outbreak of war in 1914 the impetus towards unity slowed down, but a decisive stimulus came through Shakespeare's presidential message to the Free Church Council at Bradford in 1916. This address, entitled 'The Free Churches at the Cross-Roads', has been reckoned to be 'one of the most brilliant and penetrating papers ever delivered by a Free Churchman'.[126]

'We have reached a stage in the religious life of this country', Shakespeare said in his Bradford address, 'when, if we are simply denominations and not a united Church, we are doomed. The principle of division has spent its force. The era of Union must begin.' He believed that the emphasis on denominationalism did not express the mind of Christ and was 'a decaying idea'. 'We may', he suggested, 'be called by God to turn our back on our own past ... The feeling is advancing with the inevitableness of the dawn and springtime, that the differences between the Evangelical Free Churches are not sufficient ground for

---

123  *BW*, 20 March 1913, p.716.
124  W.R. Hogg, *Ecumenical Foundations*, (New York: Harper & Brothers, 1952), p.159. Edinburgh 1910 was the World Missionary Conference.
125  *Evangelical Christendom*, January-February 1914, pp.17-19; cf. Randall and Hilborn, *One Body in Christ*, pp.150-7.
126  Jordan, *Free Church Unity*, p.128.

separation.' Shakespeare appealed again for a federation of Free Churches.[127] There was considerable acclamation, and the address, of which tens of thousands of copies were printed, was widely distributed. Shakespeare travelled all over the country to put his case and further conferences of Free Church leaders were held, at Mansfield College, Oxford, in 1916, and in Cambridge a year later, to discuss the issues. A brief statement of faith for the new Federation was produced.[128] This was accepted by the Free Church Council in March 1917, and in April 1918 the proposals for federation came to the Baptist Union Assembly.

The Baptist denomination was the first Free Church denomination officially to consider federation. It was known that there would be opposition, and those who favoured the scheme knew that it was important to show that it would not interfere with any denomination's autonomy. Before the Assembly, Shakespeare drew together a high-powered committee which he felt would be helpful in the crafting and bringing of the resolution about the issue. The members were F.G. Benskin from Broadmead, Bristol, W.E. Blomfield, Principal of Rawdon College, Charles Brown, Clifford, Fullerton, George Gould, J.G. Greenhough, Meyer, Phillips, and J.E. Roberts. All of these were leading ministerial figures. There were also two laymen, Herbert Marnham, by now an important Baptist Union figure, and H.G. Wood.[129] In a passionate speech urging federation, Shakespeare told the Assembly that it was 'unthinkable that Baptists should wreck the movement'. He called for unity 'for the salvation of our fellow-countrymen'. This was a call to warm Baptist hearts.[130] Not all hearts, however, were warmed. A dissenting group had previously circulated a pamphlet, 'Shall Baptists Forfeit their Honour?', and when Roberts, as Union President, moved a

---

127 *BW*, 9 March 1916, p.464; *Free Church Year Book* (London: NFCC, 1916), pp.9-24.
128 Hayden, 'Still at the Crossroads?: Revd J.H. Shakespeare and Ecumenism', in Clements, ed., *Baptists in the Twentieth Century*, p.45.
129 A.R. Cross, *Baptism and the Baptists: Theology and Practice in Twentieth-Century Britain* (Carlisle, Paternoster Press, 2000), p.45.
130 *BT*, 3 May 1918, p.277.

resolution in favour of federation, with Charles Brown seconding it, there was further dissent.[131]

James Mountain, the patriarchal minister of St John's Free Church, Tunbridge Wells, led the opposition.[132] Mountain claimed that the proposed Federation's Declaration of Faith was inadequate in respect of Scripture and the Doctrine of Christ, and he asked for the proposal to go back to local churches. Each mover and seconder – for and against the motion - received twenty-five minutes between them to put their case. Mountain was, typically, so determined to convince the audience that he left only three minutes for his seconder, C.T. Cook, the minister from 1918 at Tollington Park, London, and later the editor of the *Christian*. Charles Brown vigorously opposed Mountain. In his speech Brown used the title of the dissenting group's pamphlet and argued that 'we should forfeit our honour and our claim to be a vital part of the Holy Catholic Church if we refuse to federate'. After two hours of discussion the motion by Mountain was overwhelmingly defeated. Other Free Churches were to follow the Baptist lead, and the Federal Council of the Evangelical Free Churches came into being in 1919, with Shakespeare as Moderator. Rushbrooke, commenting on the 1918 Baptist Assembly, was pleased that Mountain and his group were so clearly defeated.[133] Opposition from Mountain, however, would not go away.

In November 1918, Shakespeare published his most important book, *The Churches at the Cross-Roads*. The change from his 1916 address, 'The Free Churches at the Cross-Roads', is significant. Shakespeare was now advocating unity with the Church of England. His own 'grand passion' had become 'a Church truly holy, truly Catholic; a Church which can, if needs be, override its past'.[134] Shakespeare had been part of discussions on unity within the Faith and Order movement which grew out of Edinburgh 1910, and had become convinced that reunion

---

131   Shepherd, *The Making of a Modern Denomination*, p.106.
132   For Mountain see D.W. Bebbington, 'Baptists and Fundamentalism in Inter-War Britain', in K. Robbins, ed., *Protestant Evangelicalism: Britain, Ireland, Germany and America, c1750-c1950* (Oxford: Blackwell, 1990), pp.297-326.
133   *BW*, 25 April 1918, p.59; 2 May 1918, p.68.
134   J.H. Shakespeare, *The Churches at the Cross-Roads* (London: Williams & Norgate, 1918), p.58.

must take place 'upon the basis of episcopacy'. This was set out explicitly in *The Churches at the Cross-Roads*,[135] which Adrian Hastings sees as one of the most important books of twentieth-century English Christianity.[136] But Shakespeare, the 'wayfarer who has come into a larger country' (as he described himself),[137] was not able to take Baptists into his uncharted territory. Robertson Nicoll, in the *British Weekly*, published a stinging attack on possible episcopal re-ordination of Free Church ministers in a united Church. During the war, he said, people had not noticed 'private conclaves of ecclesiastics', but now – and his remarks were personal - Shakespeare would 'find no followers along the steep gradient down which he is pointing them'.[138] This was largely true. At the 1919 Union Assembly, in an electric atmosphere, T.R. Glover, a classical scholar, a Fellow of St John's College and Public Orator in the University of Cambridge (and son of Richard Glover of Bristol), ranged himself against Shakespeare over a united Church in England.[139] The Assembly backed Glover, dealing Shakespeare's ecumenical aspirations a severe blow.

## THEOLOGICAL TRENDS

Ecumenical issues were linked with broader theological issues, but it would be simplistic to associate those who were pro-ecumenical with more liberal theology, or those who were anti-ecumenical with more conservative thought. T.R. Glover would later be attacked by Fundamentalists, yet in his opposition to Shakespeare's ideas Glover found himself on the same side as James Mountain, who anticipated with delight, in early 1919, that Shakespeare's ecumenical ideas would be 'slain and decently buried'.[140] But contact with those outside their own circles broadened Baptist thinking. At the beginning of the decade the

---

135 Shakespeare, *The Churches at the Cross-Roads*, p.178; Hayden, 'Still at the Crossroads?: in Clements, ed., *Baptists in the Twentieth Century* (1982), p.45-7.
136 Hastings, *A History of English Christianity*, p.98.
137 Shakespeare, *The Churches at the Cross-Roads*, p.208.
138 *BW*, 5 December 1918, p.146.
139 *BW*, 1 May 1919, p.109.
140 *BW*, 16 January 1919, p.262.

conservative Archibald McCaig, Principal of the Pastors' College, gave a report on the Edinburgh 1910 Conference in which he appreciated the contribution of the high churchman, Bishop Charles Gore.[141] The Free Church Fellowship, which began when about a dozen friends gathered at Mansfield College at Easter 1911, attracted many future Free Church leaders, and by 1913 had 250 members.[142] There was desire to appropriate 'the experience of all the saints concerning the practice of the Presence of God' and hope for 'a Free Church so steeped in the spirit and traditions of the entire Church Catholic as to be ready in due time for the reunion of Christendom'[143] M.E. Aubrey, minister of St Andrew's Street Baptist Church, Cambridge, who from 1925 would be Secretary of the Baptist Union, was among the Baptists who joined the Fellowship. In 1916, at its annual conference, meditations from Julian of Norwich and Thomas à Kempis were utilized. [144]

A common trend, which can be discerned among some Baptist and other Free Church leaders, was the appropriation of currents of theological thought not only for the sake of deeper understanding but also because they opened up fresh possibilities in the area of spirituality. Paying tribute in 1914 to Newton Marshall, whose early death in that year deprived the denomination of a fine thinker, Shakespeare highlighted the last words that Marshall - who had been chairman of the Union's Spiritual Welfare Committee – had said to him. Marshall had spoken of the need for a 'Retreat movement' for ministers, concentrating on prayer and penitence. 'Alas!', observed Shakespeare, 'We have no room in our bustling life for Retreats.' It was perhaps a comment on Shakespeare's own life. Shakespeare did encourage, however, what he termed the 'mystical way' to be taken.[145] Two years later F.C. Spurr, then at Regent's Park Chapel, was among those advocating an advance in Spiritual Welfare in the denomination. He wanted Sunday evening

141  *BW*, 7 July 1910, p.340.
142  G. Edmonds, *The Free Church Fellowship, 1911-1965: An Ecumenical Pioneer* (Gerrards Cross: Free Church Council, 1965).
143  *The Grounds of our Fellowship*, (n.p.: Free Church Council, [n.d. but 1911]), p.7.
144  *Free Church Fellowship Notes*, No.16, September 1916, p.3.
145  *BT*, 20 March 1914, p.243.

conferences for the purpose of study, rather than always having standard services. Another proposal from Spurr, echoing the thinking of Marshall, was to have congregational retreats for spiritual renewal. Spurr linked this to deeper fellowship in church meetings, service to the community and the need for every Christian to be involved in witness.[146]

One increasingly significant Baptist who was seeking in his writings to connect theology and spirituality was H. Wheeler Robinson, then a tutor at Rawdon College. Robinson was especially interested at this time in two areas: the theology of baptism and the theology of the Holy Spirit. He argued in 1914 that thinking about water baptism among Baptists placed too much emphasis on the personal act of faith and not enough on 'the spiritual energies which that act of faith mediates'. Robinson argued for a close association between the gift of the Spirit and baptism.[147] This provoked former President of the Union, Sir George Macalpine, to take issue with Robinson. For Macalpine it was conversion, not baptism, which was *the* overwhelming experience.[148] Despite his deep commitment to serious biblical exposition and also to the life of the Spirit, Robinson was regarded with a degree of suspicion by more conservative Baptists. In 1919 Robinson wrote in the *Baptist Times* on the Bible and eschatology, and condemned the 'acrobatic contortions of the literalists, treating as their trapeze the books of Daniel and Revelation'.[149] L.C. Parkinson, minister of Burlington Baptist Church, Ipswich, who had studied at Christ's College, Cambridge, and Regent's Park College, complained about Robinson's remarks, and asserted that there was 'a large body' of Baptist ministers holding premillennial views of the Second Advent.[150] Divisions over theology and spirituality were to continue to surface.

The question of the interpretation of the 'end times', however, was not one that was taken up by many prominent Baptist figures. It was,

---

146  *BT*, 3 November 1916, p.671.
147  *BT*, 24 July 1914, p.601; cf. A.R. Cross, 'The Holy Spirit: Key to the Baptismal Sacramentalism of H. Wheeler Robinson', *Baptist History and Heritage*, Vol.36, Nos.1&2 (2001), pp.174-89.
148  *BT*, 31 July 1914, p.616.
149  *BT*, 17 April 1919, p.223.
150  *BT*, 25 April 1919, p.245.

therefore, rather a surprise when F.B. Meyer became a prime mover in a new initiative to draw attention to the Second Advent. On 8 November 1917 a manifesto was widely published in the British Christian press which affirmed that Jesus might return 'at any moment', that Israel would be territorially restored and converted by Christ's appearing, and that under the reign of Christ there would be a 'great effusion of the Holy Spirit'.[151] The origins of the manifesto can be traced to a visit to Meyer made a few weeks earlier by two Baptist ministers, J.S. Harrison and Alfred Bird, who had trained at the Pastors' College in the 1860s-1870s. They urged Meyer to call the church to a perception of prophecy being fulfilled. In due course Meyer became Secretary of the Advent Testimony and Preparation Movement.[152] The first public meetings of the movement were held at the Queen's Hall in London on 13 December 1917, when 3,000 enthusiasts came together. Meyer drew household evangelical names, like Prebendary H.W. Webb-Peploe, John Stuart Holden (both Anglican leaders), Dinsdale Young (Methodist) and Campbell Morgan (Congregational), into his plan.[153] Baptist denominational leaders generally remained outside this circle, although a number of Baptist pastors were or became advocates of premillennialism.

One issue to which the denominational leadership was again forced, very reluctantly, to give attention, was the view that should be taken of the Downgrade controversies of the 1880s within the Union. At the 1915 Union Assembly, this matter was raised, with J. Moffat Logan, of Accrington, moving the following motion:

> That without seeking to re-interpret the past, but simply in the interests of spiritual unity and denominational effectiveness, this Assembly thinks that the time has come to delete from its records the Minute of 23rd April 1888, which has reference to the late C.H. Spurgeon.[154]

---

151  For the full manifesto, see, for example, *Christian World*, 8 November 1917, p.7.

152  *Monthly Bulletin of the Advent Preparation Prayer Union*, June 1919, p.1.

153  Fullerton, *F.B. Meyer: A Biography*, pp.157-9; D.W. Bebbington, *Evangelicalism*, pp.192-3; *CW*, 22 November 1917, p.10; 29 November 1917, p.7.

154  Payne, *Baptist Union*, p.188.

The thinking was that to delete the minute would answer those supporters of C.H. Spurgeon who alleged that the Union had, in 1888, effectively censured Spurgeon for the criticisms he had made of theological trends in the denomination. John Clifford, who had been personally involved in the 1880s, moved an amendment to Logan's motion, and Clifford was seconded by D.J. Hiley, the respected minister of the 800-member Chatsworth Road Baptist Church, West Norwood, London, who had trained at the Pastors' College and had been minister of Broadmead, Bristol. The 'amendment' was in fact a counter-motion. It suggested that 'this Assembly of the Baptist Union of Great Britain and Ireland declines to re-open the question of the Minute of 23rd April 1888, referred to by the mover of the resolution'. After differing views were expressed in discussion, the counter-motion was carried by a large majority, indicating that a determinedly 'Spurgeonic' element was not dominant at the Assembly. An additional sentence was added by J.C. Carlile: 'But the Assembly earnestly hopes that the Council will seek some means by which English Baptists now separated may be united in one organization.' This was a reference to the Metropolitan Tabernacle, where A.C. Dixon was pastor, and to other churches similarly outside the Union.[155]

There was a concern on the part of many ministers in the Union to emphasize straightforward evangelical beliefs, rather than issues which might cause division. William Cuff at Shoreditch, who often quoted from Spurgeon in his sermons, admitted that he found some of the writings of the great American Calvinist theologian, Jonathan Edwards, 'very confusing'.[156] J.W. Ewing, who had studied at the Pastors' College and who was President of the Union in 1912, was committed to the inclusive evangelicalism of the Evangelical Alliance.[157] W.Y. Fullerton, another Pastors' College product, talked in 1918 of an 'up-grade movement' in the denomination, stating that, as Union President, he knew that 'our men [ministers] are true to the evangelical faith in the broad sense, while not

155 Ibid.
156 See Randall and Hilborn, *One Body in Christ*, chapter 8.
157 *BW*, 7 November 1912, p.170.

out of touch with the thought of the day.'[158] This was virtually indistinguishable from the view of the incoming President in 1918, J.E. Roberts, who had trained at Regent's Park College. Roberts talked in his presidential address about the role of the 'Evangelical Church', claiming: 'Applications of the Gospel widen with the developing life of the world.' Roberts was critical because 'the Church has dwelt too long in academic aloofness, afraid to face the facts of life, the facts of science, the facts about the Bible'. Evangelicalism, he argued, must be 'broad and deep'.[159] It was this more open theological outlook which most Union leaders wished to foster.

REACHING THE PEOPLE

The Union leadership also wished to stress the priority of evangelism. In 1911 H.C. Wagnell was appointed as the evangelist of the Union, in succession to A. Weaver Evans. The question was raised: what sort of evangelist would he be? The *Baptist Times* was pleased that evangelists of the 'sweating, shouting, auctioneer' type were no longer popular, but it still wanted 'holy zeal'. An evangelist had to speak directly to people. Wagnell had ministered in the North of England, his ministry having included church planting in Blackpool, and on one occasion he had baptized twenty-three people in the public baths. On other occasions he had conducted baptisms in the sea.[160] Soon Wagnell was leading local missions in connection with Baptist churches around the country. For example, in 1912 he was at the Penge Tabernacle in south London for ten days of mission. Some thirty or forty 'decisions' were registered.[161] Some were worried about such instant decisions. In 1911 the Baptist Church at Lenton, Nottingham, reported that the names of all those who had been added as a result of a mission in 1908 had subsequently been removed, and the church's view was that 'it would have been better for the church

158  *BT*, 19 April 1918, p.5.
159  *BW*, 25 April 1918, p.53.
160  *BT*, 6 January 1911, supplement, p.vi.
161  *BW*, 19 December 1912, p.393.

and those individuals if the mission services had never been held'.[162] Wagnell, however, largely gained the confidence of the churches.

Much outreach carried out by local Baptist churches went on without outside evangelistic help. The *Baptist Times* reported in 1911 on Sister Lizzie Hodgson, a deaconess at West End Baptist Chapel, Hammersmith. The report described her as educated and cultured, a good preacher with a literary gift, and someone who was capable and well organized. She was attracting 500 each week to her women's meeting. More remarkably, she was also preaching on Sunday nights in the Lyric Theatre, Hammersmith, which seated 1,400 people, and was filling it, with two-thirds of the audience present being men. The Hammersmith church's membership in that period was between 400 and 500, so clearly many from outside the church were attending. During the first ten weeks of these evangelistic services there had been 200 enquirers. At the beginning

*Sister Lizzie Hodgson*

of the venture, Sister Lizzie felt she lacked confidence, but she grew through experience. She also preached in the 'open air' and helped to get young people out of the workhouse.[163] Hammersmith was not the only example of preaching taking place in cinemas. In the same year Douglas Brown, who had an 800-strong congregation (which included many young people) at Ramsden Road, Balham, was holding evangelistic services on Sunday evening in the Empire Theatre.[164] The significant feature at Hammersmith, however, was the role of a local woman leader.

---

162  Harrison, *It All Began Here*, p.92.
163  *BT*, 16 June 1911, supplement, p.i. She became a member of Hammersmith Borough Council, and served for twelve years.
164  *BT*, 24 March 1911, supplement, p.2.

Women were active in many forms of mission. Deaconesses supported the work of the Union's Caravan Mission, formed in 1907 and led by the Revd and Mrs C.S. Rose. The contribution of women was to increase during the war. The BWL began to organize visits in 1914 to 'places of business' in order to bring young women into touch with the churches.[165] Many more girls were now breadwinners. The openings for well-educated young women were regarded as numerous. According to the *British Weekly*, good salaries could be earned by

Caravan Mission: Revd and Mrs C.S. Rose, Revd F.B. Meyer and Revd G.A. Ambrose

shorthand typists if they spoke two languages. In a household where the father might be unemployed, two girls could provide the needed family income.[166] On the other hand, F.C. Spurr spoke about women's conditions of work as generally poor.[167] It was recognized that the churches had to adapt to changed social conditions in which women were seeking equality. A much-quoted example of dynamic female leadership in Baptist life was Hettie Rowntree Clifford, who in 1914 was often preaching to 900 people at the West Ham Central Mission. Although working alongside her well-known husband Robert, who was the West Ham minister, she was the 'life and soul' of the Mission.[168] Among the Mission's many initiatives were a hostel and a Settlement Home with a community of eighteen people. In 1919 a Union committee on women's work suggested a new Union agency, the Baptist Sisterhood, to oversee the Deaconess work and also a Sisterhood Training College. Soon the

165  *BW*, 7 May 1914, p.156.
166  *BW*, 9 April 1914, p.37.
167  *BT*, 7 May 1915, supplement, p.vi.
168  *BT*, 12 June 1914, p.493.

*Caravan Mission, 1912: F.B. Meyer speaking, Mrs Rose at the harmonium*

Sisterhood Committee was in operation.[169] The role of women was receiving greater prominence.

There was also considerable concern about ministry to children and young people. Sunday schools remained strong. At Christ Church, Westminister Bridge Road, F.B. Meyer was responsible for the oversight of the Southwark Sunday School Society, which attracted 4,000 children.[170] But there were increasing concerns that Sunday schools were not sufficiently connected with the worship life of the churches. Baptist and other churches began to set up Young Worshippers' Leagues

---

169  Minutes of a Baptist Union Joint Committee Re Baptist Women's Work and the Deaconesses' Home and Mission, 1 April 1919;  Minutes of Sisterhood Committees, 12 June 1919; 23 June 1919. Bound with BU Council Minutes, Angus Library.

170  For Meyer at Christ Church, see I.M. Randall, *Spirituality and Social Change: The Contribution of F.B. Meyer* (Carlisle: Paternoster Press, 2003), chapters 1, 2 and 6.

*Barefoot Children of Plaistow, 1910, another aspect of the work of West Ham
Central Mission: 'This is how some of the children come to Sunday School. It is most
touching to hear the Superintendent warn children with boots to be careful not to
tread upon the poor little bare feet.'*

(YWL), an idea proposed by W. Robertson Nicoll.[171] The Baptist church
at Wavertree, Dovedale Road, Liverpool, under the leadership of J.
Fleming Shearer, began monthly services for 'Worshipping Children'.
These were inspiring events, with over 200 children present.[172] In the
same year, 1913, Mitcham Lane Baptist Church, Streatham, had 400 in
the Sunday school and seventy-eight in the YWL.[173] New ideas spread
rapidly. In Leicester a 'League of Worshipping Families' began in one
Baptist church in 1914, while in north London there was a 'Children's
Church'.[174] Some thought that expecting children to go to morning
Sunday school at 10.00 a.m., church at 11.00 am, and perhaps also to
afternoon Sunday school, was unrealistic. But in 1917 Robertson Nicoll
bemoaned the fact that in hundreds of Free Churches there were no

---

171   See William Robertson Nicoll and J.W. Butcher, *The Children for the Church: The
      Young Worshippers' League* (London: Hodder & Stoughton, 1913).
172   *BW*, 30 January 1913, p.532.
173   *BW*, 3 April 1913, p.10.
174   *BW*, 30 April 1914, p.108.

children at the main services.[175] In that year Baptist churches in England had 372,805 Sunday scholars on their books, with 41,429 teachers.[176] By 1917, Charles Street Chapel, Leicester, had run a Young Worshippers' League for six years. The YWL awarded four silver medals to those who had achieved six years of attendance.[177] In 1918 the Young People's Committee of the Union encouraged a 'Young People's Fellowship of the Baptist Union'.[178] Considerable attention was being paid to the problem of integrating children and young people into the services.

The desire to reach and retain young people was reinforced by an awareness that most experiences of personal commitment to Christ took place at this stage of life. A survey in 1913, which looked at the question of the age of conversion, indicated that, out of 3,500 adult professing Christians, 75% of the males and 85% of the females assigned their age of decision to the years between ten and eighteen, mostly fourteen to eighteen. George Gould, of Regent's Park College, utilized this survey in a speech in 1913 as Union Vice-President, urging work among children as a priority. Gould reminded his hearers that there were more children in the Protestant Sunday Schools in Britain than in public elementary day schools. He called, however, for fresh thinking, and questioned whether afternoon Sunday schools were suited to senior classes. Gould recalled that afternoon services had been terminated because 'preachers and hearers had proved [the afternoon] to be the least suited to mental and spiritual activity', and so afternoons were devoted to Sunday schools - presumably thought to be less demanding. Afternoon schools, Gould suggested, suited younger children, but many senior classes did not want to meet with juniors. His suggestion was that seniors could meet on Sunday evenings, at a time when young people were often wandering the streets. The over-riding aim, Gould emphasized, should be to bring young people to mature faith.[179]

---

175  *BW*, 12 March 1914, p.682; 21 May 1914, p.210.
176  *Baptist Handbook* (1917), p.195.
177  *BW*, 10 July 1918, p.287.
178  Minutes of the Young People's Committee of the Baptist Union, 28 January 1918, bound with BU Council minutes, Angus Library.
179  *BW*, 1 May 1913, p.121.

This vision, if it were to be properly fulfilled, meant that efforts had to be made to integrate Baptist communities more fully, so that young and old were included. Carey Bonner, a Baptist minister who was General Secretary of the interdenominational National Sunday School Union, encouraged churches to arrange Young People's Socials and provide other recreational activities. He and others, however, were concerned about young people and adults at church events engaging in 'the folly of kissing games'.[180] At Haven Green, Ealing, a church of nearly 500 members, Arnold Streuli, who had been much involved with young people when at Moss Side, in Manchester, started a YWL in 1916. He introduced a periodic shorter morning service which concluded with a fifteen-minute rally designed for children and young people up to the age of fourteen. They were present during the whole service and for the final part they came forward and filled the first seven pews in the church. A reporter who was present in 1916 noted, however, that, although a proportion of the adults remained for the last part of the service, hundreds left.[181] It was difficult to achieve all-age integration. Ferme Park was an example of a church that tried to cater in worship for the range of people within the congregation. There were many trained musicians in the membership and there was a fine choir, which led worship that included hymns, anthems and a chant. Children's hymns were included in the services as a matter of policy.[182]

Some churches were drawing in new members, young and old, in this period. London Road Baptist Church, Portsmouth, for example, had 530 members in 1918, which was more than double the number in 1915, when John Edmonds became the pastor.[183] But the overall picture was of decline. In one year, 1913, one church in the East Midland Association deleted fifty-six names, another deleted fifty, and another thirty.[184] It

---

180   Carey Bonner referred in 1904 to protests by F.B. Meyer about 'the absurd lengths to which such games were carried on in the north of England': Carey Bonner to L.W. Phillips, 25 November 1904; letter in the possession of Peter Conlan of Bromley.

181   *BW*, 30 March 1916, p.529.

182   *BW*, 22 August 1912, p.495.

183   *BW*, 21 March 1918, p.455.

184   Harrison, *It All Began Here*, p.87.

seems that people had joined who were not deeply committed. There was also a debate in the pre-war period about whether middle-class Baptist churches were out of touch with the Labour Movement.[185] In other cases, churches lacked leaders who could adapt to changed situations. J.C. Jones, in Spalding, only began to contemplate retirement at the age of ninety. At that point, in 1913, he had been pastor of the same church for sixty-six years.[186] In 1912 the Lancashire and Cheshire Association reported its first drop in membership. The two largest churches in the North West, Union Chapel and Moss Side, both of which had over 800 members and both of which placed great emphasis on work with young people, reached their peak membership in 1913-14. Although decline was evident before the war, the war itself severely damaged the life of many churches. About 170 people associated with Union Chapel were serving in the Army in 1917 and nineteen had been killed.[187] Many churches, like Ferme Park, Hornsey, never recovered from the losses. As well as those who lost their lives, others lost their faith.[188]

CONCLUSION

This period was one in which there was great concern to ensure good quality ministry within Baptist churches. From J.H. Shakespeare's point of view, this could be achieved only by greater centralization and thorough, structured accreditation procedures, ideas that were at odds with traditional Baptist thinking. The period saw not only internal denominational changes but also massive social upheaval, not least due to the war. Baptists responded by becoming involved in wider issues. Superintendents were introduced, and they would form the backbone of Union activity. After the war, King George V and Queen Mary attended a Free Church Thanksgiving service, a historic moment for the Free Churches. Shakespeare, always alive to the bigger picture, was pushing for greater ecumenical involvement: Adrian Hastings describes him as

185  *BT*, 21 February 1913, p.144.
186  *BW*, 6 March 1913, p.665.
187  *BW*, 4 January 1917, p.280.
188  Cook, *Charles Brown*, pp.59-61.

'the most deeply and consistently ecumenical of all the Church leaders of the time'.[189] Yet moves towards unity raised profound questions about Baptist identity, with the vision of Shakespeare for a united Church in England failing to gain support from most Baptists. Many Baptists were more concerned about spirituality and mission. J.C. Carlile said in 1916: 'The problem behind all the problems for the Church is spirituality.' He asked how many churches took responsibility for the 'cure of souls'.[190] Too many churches seemed to be losing touch with younger people and efforts to reverse this trend met with only limited success. The 'catholic and comprehensive' vision of the Church was to attract some Baptists throughout the twentieth century, but others saw it as a diversion from Baptist priorities.

*A group of children for whom the West Ham Central Mission was seeking to care*

189   Hastings, *A History of English Christianity*, p.98.
190   *BT*, 15 September 1916, p.560.

# Chapter 4
# 'MUCH PROGRAMME
# AND LITTLE POWER'
# (1920-29)

The 1920s proved to be difficult for Baptist churches. The high hopes that J.H. Shakespeare had entertained for wider Church unity were not to be fulfilled. D.J. Hiley, minister of Chatsworth Road Baptist Church, London, as President of the Union in 1920, argued that people were not remotely interested in 'Episcopacy', but were intensely interested in 'character, pure goodness, spirituality'.[1] This was a clear rebuttal of Shakespeare's views about unity. Hiley's relationship with Shakespeare was good-natured; Shakespeare advised Hiley in 1920 to 'accept me as your bishop, and do what I tell you', adding that he would be 'in a great succession, for all the really great presidents have done that'.[2] Joining with the Established Church, however, did not appeal to Baptists. Attempts at unity were hampered because the Church of England resisted Free Church calls for inter-communion and because of the trend in the Church of England towards high church practices, as seen in the contentious campaign for revision of the Prayer Book.[3] In addition, Baptists had internal problems, such as a decrease in numbers of students for the ministry.[4] Douglas Brown, the best known Baptist evangelist of the period, wrote in 1926: 'Our spiritual birth rate is alarmingly small; our standard of church membership unsatisfactory.' He continued: 'There is a painful lack of driving force in our church life. We

---

1    *BW*, 6 May 1920, p.109.
2    *BW*, 13 May 1920, p.130.
3    I. Machin, 'Reservation under Pressure: Ritual in the Prayer Book Crisis, 1927-1928', in R.N. Swanson, ed., *Continuity and Change in Christian Worship* (Woodbridge, Suffolk: Boydell Press, 1999), pp.447-63.
4    *BT*, 22 April 1926, p.303.

seem to be living in days of much programme and little power, many schemes and little sanctity, multitudinous activity and small progress'.[5] If his analysis was right, the denomination needed renewal. This was a theme of the 1920s.

## ECUMENISM: THE UNITY OF THE BODY OF CHRIST

In the summer of 1920 an *Appeal to All Christian People* was issued by the Anglican Lambeth Conference – held once every ten or twelve years - which called on all churches to 'unite in a new and great endeavour to recover and to manifest to the world the unity of the Body of Christ'.[6] On behalf of the 250 bishops at the conference, the *Appeal* asked for conversations about unity to take place between representatives of the Church of England and the Free Churches. Among Congregationalists, A.E. Garvie, Principal of New College, London, was enthusiastic. Baptist responses were varied. Charles Brown of Ferme Park, writing in August 1920, welcomed the gracious spirit of the *Appeal*, but did not see the feasibility or advantages of organic union.[7] A month later a 'Provisional Statement' from the Federal Council of the Evangelical Free Churches (usually referred to as the Free Church Federal Council) and the National Council of the Evangelical Free Churches echoed Brown's approach. It welcomed 'religious intercourse' and called for inter-communion, but saw fundamental problems with the Anglican position.[8] T.R. Glover of Cambridge University was vocal in his opposition to any union that might involve episcopal re-ordination. Glover wrote a defence of the Free Churches in a series of articles in the *British Weekly* and this was published as *The Free Churches and Reunion* (1921). The book had a preface by John Clifford, who boldly suggested that Glover had articulated 'the convictions and experiences of Baptists everywhere'.[9]

5    *BT*, 8 April 1926, p.262.
6    G.K.A. Bell, *Documents on Christian Unity, 1920-4* (London: Oxford University Press, 1924), p.5.
7    *BT*, 27 August 1920, pp.566-7.
8    Bell, *Documents on Christian Unity*, p.119.
9    T.R. Glover, *The Free Churches and Re-Union*, Preface, (Cambridge: W Heffer & Sons, 1921) n.p.

As Anthony Cross has shown, determined Baptists such as Glover did not rule out working with Anglicans.[10] Some Baptists saw opportunities to spread their beliefs in this way. Thus J. Ivory Cripps, who in 1925 became Superintendent of the West Midland Area, argued in January 1921 that if Baptists were part of a United Church of England their witness to believer's baptism would have 'unanswerable appeal'.[11] Shakespeare seems to have been more concerned to introduce Anglican thinking to Baptists. Before the April 1921 Baptist Union Assembly, Shakespeare persuaded the Archbishop of York, Cosmo Lang, to address the approximately 2,000 people at the Assembly on the *Appeal*. Lang was well received and Shakespeare, thrilled with the event - which was a breakthrough - wrote to Lang: 'Your address was so persuasive that I said afterwards that if someone had risen and moved that we accept episcopal ordination, it could have been carried. I think perhaps this is an exaggeration, but something very near it would have been reached.' Given the setbacks Shakespeare had experienced, his optimism was remarkable. Lang commented that 'the reception was very cordial to me personally, but I do not think these good people have any real care about a visible church at all. I am afraid they are still content if only they can preach at St Paul's and communicate at our altars.'[12] Lang's coolness, rather than Shakespeare's talk of the powerful 'finger of God' at work, reflected the ecclesiastical reality.[13]

Although Shakespeare was unusual in his high expectations about unity, the Free Churches continued, through their representatives, to work on the issues raised by the *Appeal*, and a report was published in May 1921. It asked if the Church of England was prepared to recognize non-episcopal churches as corporate parts of the Church of Christ. It seemed that Anglicans were moving in this direction, but crucial matters required clarification. Twenty-five Free Church leaders were nominated

---

10    Cross, *Baptism and the Baptists*, pp.54-5: Glover, *Free Churches and Re-Union*, pp.54-5.
11    *BT*, 14 January 1921, p. 23.
12    J.G. Lockhart, *Cosmo Gordon Lang* (London: Hodder and Stoughton, 1949), p.274.
13    See R. Hayden, 'Still at the Crossroads?' in Clements, ed., *Baptists in the Twentieth Century*, p.49.

to continue the discussions, particularly aiming for 'explications of expressions in the Appeal which are felt to have an ambiguous character'. The Baptist representatives were Charles Brown from Ferme Park, W.Y. Fullerton as Home Secretary of the BMS, Sir Alfred Pearce Gould, a distinguished surgeon (specializing in cancer research) and also treasurer of the BMS, and Shakespeare.[14] E.A. Payne notes that during the conversations which followed the *Appeal*, and which continued for five years, important memoranda were prepared, making plain the differences between the episcopal and non-episcopal churches. Shakespeare, Charles Brown, Fullerton, J.C. Carlile and Herbert Marnham – treasurer of the Union and first among equals of Baptist laity - were the Baptists mainly engaged in the talks.[15]

What Payne does not mention is the tension generated along the way. T.R. Glover raised questions in 1922 in the *British Weekly* and at the Union Council concerning an 'interim report' that had been published which seemed to him to give ground to Anglican doctrine and practice, and he pointedly asked if Shakespeare, Brown and Marnham considered that infant baptism was true baptism. 'I venture to hope', he commented in his typically provocative style, 'that there are still Baptists who hold to a more Scriptural and intelligent view of Baptism.' Glover was outraged at the non-recognition of Baptist ministry by Anglicans, suggesting: 'The issue is not Christian brotherhood or charity or tolerance. It is the question of sheer truthfulness.'[16] W.E. Blomfield, Principal of Rawdon College, entered the ranks, asserting that Glover's letter was 'like a healthy wind after a week of fog'. Blomfield objected to Free Church leaders lending their support to what were at best 'ambiguities' regarding baptism, the nature of the eucharist and episcopacy. He also observed that British Baptists were part of a 'great international communion of nearly nine millions in church membership',

---

14    Bell, *Documents on Christian Unity,* pp.131, 142.
15    Payne, *The Baptist Union,* p.187.
16    T.R. Glover to the editor: *BW,* 8 June 1922, p. 203; Minutes of the Baptist Union Council, 11 July 1922.

and argued that there should have been scholarly examination of the issues by a committee representing world Baptist life.[17]

Henry Townsend, the outspoken President of Manchester College, went further. He stated that in Baptist theology membership was for those who had 'personal faith in Jesus Christ our Lord and Saviour', which was not the viewpoint of the interim Reunion report. Townsend was firmly evangelical, though open to advances in biblical criticism, and was also a deeply committed Baptist, contending that it was not possible to reconcile Baptist congregationalism with episcopacy. Pulling no punches, he referred to Baptist 'control' from Baptist Church House and said the denomination was being asked to agree that in the interests of unity Baptist ministers would be episcopally ordained. 'As principal of a Baptist College', he declared, 'I feel that I am asked to do a horrible thing. I am asked to consent to episcopal ordination for the students under my charge, when I am teaching them that episcopacy as we know it is fundamentally opposed to the truth of the New Testament.' Townsend suggested that Baptist churches in the North believed their principles were 'being given away behind their backs' and that it was the Union's policy to silence any criticism. For Shakespeare to sign the interim report, he added, was humiliating for Baptists. Becoming even more personal, Townsend said he believed Shakespeare could split the denomination.[18] This was an indication of tension between Baptist churches in the North and South.

Shakespeare himself did not reply to Townsend, but Charles Brown was willing to defend what had been done in the unity discussions. Brown was adamant that Shakespeare had not signed anything on behalf of Baptists. Further, Brown emphasized that the issues would be debated and that Townsend would be able to contribute. In specific defence of Shakespeare, Brown said that the Union General Secretary had told the archbishops and bishops that Baptists would not accept re-ordination.[19] At this stage, therefore, in 1922, those Baptists involved in ecumenical discussions were still hopeful that they might achieve something, while

---

17  *BW*, 15 June 1922, p.222.
18  Ibid.
19  *BW*, 22 June 1922, p.242.

aware that progress was difficult. The fact that in the following months hopes for progress were dampened was due not only to Baptist opposition to the Anglican stance but also due to high-church attitudes. The powerful Anglo-Catholic group in the Church of England had little desire for discussions with Free Church leaders to succeed. In addition, problems arose due to parallel conversations in which, from 1921, some high-church Anglicans met with some progressive Roman Catholics.[20]When these Catholic-Anglican conversations, held at Malines, France, seemed to accept the Roman Catholic view of the eucharist, a deeply depressed Shakespeare urged Baptist withdrawal from Free Church-Anglican discussions.[21]

An even more serious blow to discussions about unity, in the eyes of many Baptists, was a leaked Anglican statement in July 1923 (from an Anglican-Free Church conference) affirming the necessity of episcopal ordination for valid ministry. This statement was received with regret by the Free Church Federal Council on 18 September 1923.[22] W.E. Blomfield, then Baptist Union President, was blunt. In a letter to *The Times* on 27 September 1923, he stated that the Baptist denomination was 'uncommitted by any of the proceedings which have followed the Lambeth Conference'.[23] Two years later, when discussions with the Anglicans came to an end, Blomfield reiterated that in his view nothing could come of the Lambeth proposals, and he encouraged Baptists to carry on their own work, while cherishing 'an ardent affection for all who love our common Lord'.[24] The Union Council, in February 1926, was unenthusiastic about the discussions. A fuller Baptist response to the *Appeal* came in a *Reply* adopted unanimously by the Baptist Assembly meeting at Leeds in May 1926. The *Reply* was appreciative of the Anglican initiative. It then stressed Baptist belief in 'the Catholic Church as the holy Society of believers in our Lord Jesus Christ'; in the

---

20    Hastings, *A History of English Christianity*, pp.208-12.
21    Carlile, *My Life's Little Day*, pp.180-1.
22    Bell, *Documents on Christian Unity*, pp. 160, 165; Cross, *Baptism and the Baptists*, p.61.
23    *The Times*, 27 September 1923, p.8.
24    *BT*, 22 October 1925, p.748.

Scriptures, which 'possess for us supreme and unique authority'; and (significantly) in baptism and the Lord's Supper as 'means of grace to all who receive them in faith'. Baptists, however, rejected the belief that the commission to ministry could be only through an episcopate.[25]

Although the Lambeth *Appeal* ultimately ran out of steam, it did open up the thinking of some Baptists to the ecumenical dimension. Inter-church discussions held at Murren, Switzerland, in 1924 included Charles Brown, T.R. Glover and Tom Phillips as participants.[26] There were endeavours arising from the Edinburgh 1910 Conference in which Baptists were involved. At a meeting of the Baptist Union Council in January 1914, three Baptist leaders who had come over from the USA - Newman Smyth of New Haven, Peter Ainslie of Baltimore, and W.H. Roberts of Philadelphia – spoke about plans for a World Conference on Faith and Order being canvassed by Charles Brent, an American Episcopalian. The Council agreed to appoint a Baptist Commission of fourteen people 'to represent the Baptist Union of Great Britain and Ireland with a view to co-operating with the other Commissions with regard to the arrangements'. Because of the First World War this did not materialize, but in 1920 J. E. Roberts, from Union Chapel, Oxford Road, Manchester, represented British Baptists at a preliminary Faith and Order committee meeting in Switzerland.[27] The World Conference on Faith and Order was held in Lausanne in 1927 and two Baptists, W.T. Whitley, the leading British Baptist historian, and Roberts, attended at their own expense. Payne suggests that many British Baptists were deeply disappointed at the Union's decision not to send official delegates, but there was also considerable Baptist suspicion of ecumenical developments.[28]

---

25  Minutes of the Baptist Union Council, 9 and 10 February 1926; *Reply of the Churches in Membership with the Baptist Union to the "Appeal to all Christian People" issued by the Lambeth Conference of 1920*, in Bell, *Documents on Christian Unity*, pp.85-91.

26  *CW*, 11 September 1924, p.4.

27  W.M.S. West, 'Baptists in Faith and Order', in Clements, ed., *Baptists in the Twentieth Century*, pp.55-6.

28  Payne, *Baptist Union*, p.197; Shepherd, *The Making of a Modern Denomination*, p.182.

## BAPTIST FUNDAMENTALISM

What had caused this attitude? One movement that would have liked to claim an influence was what came to be termed Fundamentalism. The interest in Fundamentalism in the 1920s – an interest not confined to Baptists - was such that the *British Weekly* devoted many articles to it. Fundamentalists opposed such things as biblical criticism, the teaching of evolution and advances towards church unity, and James Mountain's attempt to frustrate Free Church federation at the 1918 Baptist Union Assembly was an example of the Fundamentalist agenda at work. There

was a fear in Fundamentalist circles that unity meant theological compromise. In 1920 Mountain took his battle against those with broader theological sympathies to the annual interdenominational Keswick Convention. Mountain had been associated with Keswick from its beginning in 1875, and had been influenced by F.B. Meyer, Keswick's leading international speaker. After serving as a minister of the Countess of Huntingdon's Connexion, Mountain became convinced of believer's baptism and was baptized by Meyer in 1893, thereafter persuading some members of his Countess of Huntingdon Chapel in Tunbridge Wells to join him in founding a Free

*A church of this period, Mitcham Lane, Streatham (1927)*

Church with Baptist convictions.[29] Commenting on the place of James Mountain in British Fundamentalism, Bebbington suggests: 'Tunbridge Wells was the place where organized Baptist Fundamentalism was born.'[30]

---

29    J. Mountain, *My Baptism and what led to it*, 2<sup>nd</sup> edn. (London: n.p., n.d.).
30    Bebbington, 'Baptists and Fundamentalism in Inter-War Britain', p.303.

Although Mountain subscribed to Keswick's motto, 'All One in Christ Jesus', he was not inclined to define 'all' in an expansive way, and he became very agitated in 1920 about three first-time Keswick speakers who held to broader evangelical views. One was R.T. Howard, Principal of the Anglican St Aidan's College, Birkenhead, who was to be associated with the growing liberal evangelical movement in Anglicanism in the 1920s. The other two were Baptists: Charles Brown of Ferme Park, and F.C. Spurr, then pastor of Regent's Park Chapel, London. Brown's initial response to Keswick was positive. He reported: 'I am bound to say I never saw a happier crowd'.[31] Before going to Keswick, Spurr had believed that the attitude to the Bible that was held at Keswick was narrowly obscurantist. This was rather dismissive of such leading Baptist speakers at Keswick as Meyer, W.Y. Fullerton and Graham Scroggie, minister of Charlotte Chapel, Edinburgh. But Spurr was delighted to say in August 1920 that among the Keswick speakers that year, some had 'the broadest sympathies with everything that is truly progressive in religion'.[32] Spurr's breadth was anathema to Mountain. Charles Brown was also in Mountain's sights. In 1920 Brown took issue with the views of Archibald McCaig, from the Pastors' College, who objected to Sunday school material written by R.H. Coats of Hamstead Road, Handsworth, Birmingham, on the grounds that it contained 'higher criticism' of the Bible.[33] Brown defended Coats, arguing that there was no need for the Bible to be infallible at every point.[34] This put Brown in the Fundamentalist firing line.

James Mountain had some success in discrediting the Anglican, R.T. Howard, since Howard's main Convention address carried overtones of pantheism. It was more difficult to undermine Brown or Spurr. The address given by Brown, in the opinion of many, had been the finest at the Convention.[35] Spurr had been a Baptist Union evangelist and then a

31 *BW*, 19 August 1920, p.397.
32 *CW*, 5 August 1920, p.4; I.M. Randall, ' "Capturing Keswick": Baptists and the Changing Spirituality of the Keswick Convention in the 1920s', *BQ*, Vol.36, No.7 (1996), pp.331-48.
33 *BT*, 9 January 1920, p.27.
34 *BT*, 16 April 1921, pp.256-7; cf. Charles Brown in *BT*, 9 November 1923, p.782.
35 *Christian*, 29 July 1920, p.15.

pastor in Melbourne, Australia, before succeeding Meyer at Regent's Park Chapel in 1914. Also, Spurr's address at Keswick elicited appreciative comment from unimpeachably orthodox evangelicals like W.Y. Fullerton, who said that Spurr had spoken 'winged words which have been used of God'.[36] Nonetheless, Mountain targeted Spurr, warning that if he addressed Keswick in 1921 (as he was booked to do) there would be public protests. The *Baptist Times* was anticipating in June 1921 that Spurr would speak, but Spurr withdrew and appealed to F.B. Meyer and Stuart Holden, the Anglican Keswick leader, for a tribunal to investigate his vilification.[37] Mountain stipulated that he must vet the tribunal's membership. Meyer and Holden, while sympathizing with Spurr's complaint that those trumpeting orthodoxy lacked 'orthodoxy of courtesy and goodwill', felt that a tribunal was pointless.[38] From Brown's standpoint, Keswick's Council culpably failed to support Spurr.[39] The whole episode alienated Brown, and was enormously embarrassing to Stuart Holden, a close friend of Brown's. Spurr declared himself sickened by 'this miserable Keswick controversy'.[40] The well-spring of the controversy was British Fundamentalism.

How did this British phenomenon relate to the American Fundamentalist movement? British Fundamentalism was never as pervasive as the American variety. Baptists in Britain recognized the contribution of biblical scholars: H. Wheeler Robinson was well known, as was T.H. Robinson, a Baptist minister who from 1927 was Professor of Semitic Languages in University College, Cardiff.[41] In the USA, a Baptist, W.B. Riley, led the World's Christian Fundamentals

36   *Life of Faith*, 28 July 1920, p.725.
37   James Mountain wrote against Spurr in J. Mountain, *Rev. F.C. Spurr and Keswick* (Tunbridge Wells: n.p., 1921); *BT*, 24 June 1921, p.390; *Christian*, 7 July 1921, p.11; *BW*, 7 July 1921, p.254.
38   *Life of Faith*, 6 July 1921, p.746; *BW*, 14 July 1921, p.276; 21 July 1921, p.290; 28 July 1921, p.306; 11 August 1921, p.330.
39   *BW*, 14 July 1921, p.276.
40   *BT*, 29 July 1921, p.472.
41   M.P. Matheney, Jnr, 'Teaching Prophet: The Life and Continuing Influence of Theodore Henry Robinson', *BQ*, Vol.29, No.5 (1981), pp.199-216.

Association, which sought to combat 'modernist' scholarship.[42] Mountain, mirroring American developments, set up a Fundamentalist group, the Baptist Bible Union (BBU), and the first BBU annual meeting, in May 1919, was chaired by J.W. Thirtle, editor of the *Christian* from 1920 and treasurer of the Baptist Historical Society. Two Baptist ministers, C.T. Cook of Tollington Park, London, and F.E. Marsh from Weston-super-Mare, were also involved. These three supporters could not, however stomach the BBU's belligerence.[43] The aggression that was typical of American Fundamentalism had limited attraction in England. The journal of the BBU, the *Bible Call*, nothing daunted, launched an attack in 1922 upon the 'Modernist movement' as an agent of anarchy and Bolshevism.[44] A year later, the BBU held a convention at Raleigh Park Baptist Church, Brixton Hill, where the pastor was a probationer minister trained at the Pastors' College. The convention was designed to 'uphold the Fundamentals of the Faith and to deepen Spiritual Life'.[45] The *Bible Call* added to its title *and Fundamentalist Advocate* in 1924, explaining that it was in 'hearty sympathy' with American Fundamentalists.[46]

There were attempts to nurture British-American Fundamentalist links through networks such as the inter-denominational Bible League, founded in 1892. Of the twenty-two vice-presidents of the League in 1923, nine were Baptists, including the American, A.C. Dixon, who from 1911 to 1919 had been pastor of the Metropolitan Tabernacle, London, and the Canadian, T.T. Shields. Transatlantic connections were evident. One British vice-president of the League was Dixon's successor at the Tabernacle, H. Tydeman Chilvers, formerly a Strict and Particular Baptist. The Tabernacle was not in the Union, although the Home

42  M. Marty, *Modern American Religion: The Noise of Conflict, 1919-1941* (Chicago: University of Chicago, 1991), p.170.
43  Bebbington, 'Baptists and Fundamentalism in Inter-War Britain', in Robbins, *Protestant Evangelicalism*, pp.300-1. For J.W. Thirtle, who had been a Christadelphian, see H.W. Robinson, 'In Memoriam', *BQ*, Vol.7 (1934-35), p.287. C.T. Cook was later editor of the *Christian*.
44  *Bible Call*, June 1922, p.41.
45  *Life of Faith*, 14 March 1923, p.301. The pastor was T.D. Robinson.
46  *Bible Call*, 24 July 1924, p.102.

Counties Association, which had been organized by churches that were sympathetic to Spurgeon's stance during the Downgrade controversy, joined the Union in 1927. Chilvers wrote in the early 1920s about the necessity of holding firmly to the sound doctrine of former years.[47] A.C. Dixon had been involved in London Baptist Association affairs, and referred to J.C. Carlile as his 'dear friend' and Fullerton as his 'dear brother', but in 1922 he used the *Western Recorder* (a Baptist journal in the USA) to describe Carlile as a 'destructive critic' of the Bible and to allege that Fullerton had lost his passion for the gospel.[48] A.C. Dixon's views were regarded as extreme, but were mild compared with those of his brother Thomas, who wrote racist novels.[49]

An example of an English Baptist minister being subjected to a transatlantic Fundamentalist pincer movement was the case of Laurance Marshall, former minister of Queen's Road Baptist Church, Coventry. In

1925 Marshall left Coventry and moved to Toronto, Canada, to take up the post of Professor of Practical Theology at McMaster University, a Baptist foundation. W.M. Robertson, pastor of the Toxteth Tabernacle, Liverpool, which had left the Union in 1920 because of 'the departure from the faith' of some Baptist ministers, pursued a campaign against Marshall. Robertson wrote to T.T. Shields in Toronto accusing Marshall of discrediting the Old Testament by questioning the historicity of, for example, the book of Jonah. Shields, who was already waging war against what he alleged was

*L.H. Marshall*

McMaster's modernism, seized on the information from Robertson, and Marshall found that he had to defend himself with a robust speech to his Canadian fellow-Baptists. Queen's Road, Coventry, affirmed that

---

47    *Life of Faith*, 12 December 1923, p.1535; Bebbington, 'Baptists and Fundamentalism in Inter-War Britain', in Robbins, *Protestant Evangelicalism*, p.303.

48    *BT*, 9 June 1922, p.368; 27 July 1922, p.52.

49    P. Harvey, *Redeeming the South* (Chapel Hill: University of North Carolina Press, 1997), pp.2, 220.

Marshall was a preacher of 'the full gospel of Jesus Christ', and for his part Marshall reported back to Queen's Road that 'the more I am attacked the more I thrive and the more friends I make'. In 1930 Marshall returned to England, becoming minister of Victoria Road, Leicester. He moved to Rawdon College in 1936, where he was tutor and then (from 1948) Principal.[50]

The Fundamentalist reverberations could be heard among some Baptists beyond Britain and America. An attack was launched on the Baptist Missionary Society in 1922 when R. Wright Hay, of the Bible League, who had served with the BMS, criticized George Howells, a BMS missionary in India, for his apparent rejection of belief in an 'infallible Bible'. Watkin Roberts, a former BMS missionary to Assam was so concerned that he wrote *The Ravages of Higher Criticism in the Indian Mission Field,* and there were calls from other conservatives, especially within Welsh churches, for the BMS to investigate the theological views of its missionaries. The pastor of Upper Tooting Baptist Church, Henry Oakley, resigned from the BMS General Committee because of his worries about the Society, and three missionaries also resigned.[51] When the BMS refused to impose doctrinal tests on candidates, an alternative Missionary Trust Fund was created to collect money and support one of those who had resigned, D.T. Morgan. At the 1923 Assembly, the much-respected W.Y. Fullerton spoke of the Society's loyalty to the evangelical faith and this speech was received warmly. Spurr remarked that Fullerton felt keenly the 'almost criminal attacks by a few fanatics'.[52] Fullerton's role was crucial in avoiding the kind of split that took place in the Church Missionary Society. Bebbington comments that this Fundamentalist campaign 'produced

---

50   Binfield, *Pastors and People*, pp.188-90. The resignation of Toxteth Tabernacle from the Union is recorded in the Baptist Union's General Purposes Committee Minutes, 16 March 1920.

51   *Bible Call*, January 1923, p.10; B.P. Jones, *The King's Champions* (Cwmbran, Gwent: Christian Literature Press, 1986), pp.192-3.

52   *BW*, 26 April 1923, p.62; *BT*, 27 April 1923, pp.296, 302; cf. Stanley, *The History of the Baptist Missionary Society*, pp.377-81.

scant results except ill feeling'.[53] The Fundamentalist movement among Baptists, despite its varied attempts to gain wider influence, remained small.

## BAPTIST DISTINCTIVES

More important than Fundamentalism as a reason for Baptist reservations about ecumenism was the strong commitment in the 1920s to Baptist distinctives. Why was this stress so significant? In part it represented the passing of the dominance of Shakespeare and the emergence of other voices. In 1921 Shakespeare indicated that he intended to retire in 1922 shortly after his sixty-fifth birthday. Although he did not retire until 1924, he was not the force he had been previously. In his later period, Shakespeare's ecumenical focus made him somewhat isolated among Baptists; in private he professed himself 'at heart an Episcopalian'. An illuminated address was presented to Shakespeare in 1919 - signed by the Prime Minister, several MPs, four archbishops, thirty-three bishops, and Free Church leaders - which spoke of his 'able and zealous advocacy of the cause of Christian unity'.[54] Hostility to Shakespeare's agenda, however, was forcefully expressed in the early 1920s by T.R. Glover, by then more widely known through a column he wrote in the *Daily News*. Glover was elected in 1923 as Union Vice-President and told his friend Carlile, who was deputizing as Union General Secretary: 'I was elected as a protest against Shakespeare... you know quite well that he has left his original Baptist ideas.' Glover was deeply antipathetic towards what Shakespeare had achieved. 'How I hate that Church House', he told Carlile, 'and all the toadying sneaking cadging atmosphere!'[55] Glover saw his presidency as an opportunity to achieve change.

Another figure who was keen to highlight Baptist distinctives was Melbourn Evans Aubrey, a Welshman who in 1913, at the age of twenty-

53   Bebbington, 'Baptists and Fundamentalism in Inter-War Britain', in Robbins, *Protestant Evangelicalism*, p.319.
54   Shepherd, *The Making of a Modern Denomination*, pp.111, 117-18.
55   T.R. Glover to J.C. Carlile, 30 November 1923, cited by Shepherd, *The Making of a Modern Denomination*, p.159.

seven, became pastor of St Andrew's Street Baptist Church, Cambridge. Aubrey, born in 1885, the son of a minister, had studied at the South Wales Baptist College and Mansfield College, Oxford, and by the early 1920s he was known as an outstanding preacher and pastor. Aubrey wrote in 1922 about aspects of Baptist ministerial formation, alleging that some students entered ministry 'with little enough knowledge, not merely of our denominational story and the historical development of our principles, but of the whole of the Evangelical and Free Church progress since Reformation times'.[56] He felt Baptist principles were not being given priority. In 1923, when Gilbert Laws, who had trained at the

Pastors' College and was at St Mary's Baptist Church in Norwich, defended a higher view of ministry and warned against the thinking of the Plymouth Brethren (who rejected the pastoral office), Aubrey criticized Law. Aubrey wanted to distance Baptists from anything resembling episcopal views of ministry. For him episcopacy was 'a lost cause'.[57] Just over a year later, Aubrey's name was submitted as candidate for Union General Secretary. Neither Carlile (as interim Union Secretary) nor J.H. Rushbrooke wished to be considered, and both backed Aubrey. With the support of Glover, who was a deacon at St Andrew's Street as well as Union President, Aubrey's name was

M.E. Aubrey

proposed to the Council and warmly received.[58] Shakespeare's influence was fading.

The next step was for Aubrey's name to go to the 1925 Assembly. Glover anticipated that the appointment of Aubrey would give the

56   M.E. Aubrey, 'The Future of our Ministry', *BQ*, Vol.1 (1922-1923), p.178.
57   *BT*, 21 December 1923, p.882; 28 December 1923, p.897; Shepherd, *The Making of a Modern Denomination*, pp.159-60.
58   Minutes of the Baptist Union Council, 20 January 1925; *BT*, 23 January 1925, p.54; West, *Baptists Together*, pp.48-63.

128     THE ENGLISH BAPTISTS OF THE 20$^{TH}$ CENTURY

denomination a healthier direction, and his eagerness, combined with some political manoeuvring, led him to write to the *Baptist Times* to say that Aubrey had indicated his willingness to accept the secretaryship. To an extent Glover pre-empted the Assembly by saying that 'with all Baptists I am happy in the prospect of such a man at the helm'.[59] Aubrey himself had struggled with the decision. 'Some of the convictions I hold most strongly', he said, 'are not those of many of my brethren.' In fact it would turn out that Aubrey was closer to many Baptists than was Shakespeare. Aubrey was dismayed (as were his deacons) at the prospect of his leaving a thriving congregation which greatly appreciated his ministry, but there was a stronger call: to serve the wider Baptist cause. 'If I were to decline', Aubrey concluded, 'I think I should never feel happy about my decision.' In his letter to the Council he commented that if the Assembly decided on someone else, he would not complain.[60] In fact the Assembly received Aubrey's nomination with acclamation. The *Baptist Times* commented that there were 'dangers which might easily become grave perils, but we have faith in God and in the new pilot'.[61] Choosing his words carefully, Aubrey said: 'The superstructure of the Baptist Union is the splendid monument of Dr Shakespeare's work. The foundations are the faith and loyalty of our Baptist people in the churches, and they need constant care.'[62]

Under Aubrey's leadership, attention was directed away from the superstructure and towards the substructure. He asked that Baptists should 'think of me seldom as an official and always as a friend'.[63] As someone who believed in the role of the churches as an influence in the world, he was anxious to visit local churches and Associations. Fullerton, for the BMS, looked forward to working with Aubrey, and said they would 'do their best to be the two focal points of a decent ellipse'.[64] Carlile was optimistic about the future, expressing in early 1925 his faith

59   *BT*, 13 February 1925, p.99.
60   *BT*, 13 February 1925, p.104; Minutes of the Baptist Union Council, 17 March 1925.
61   *BT*, 1 May 1925, p.294.
62   *BT*, 8 May 1925, p.323.
63   *BW*, 30 April 1925, p.93.
64   *BT*, 1 May 1925, p.310.

in the wider Baptist fellowship.[65] Yet there were profound challenges facing the denomination in the mid-1920s. F.C. Spurr asked in September 1925 why people were leaving Baptist churches. He suggested a number of reasons: quarrels that took place in church members' meetings, weaker denominational allegiance because of the stress on ecclesiastical unity, queries about rigid Baptist approaches to conversion, and an absence of order and beauty in Baptist worship. Spurr looked for a new Baptist *apologia*.[66] Aubrey sought to offer this, especially addressing younger people, who were allegedly lacking in denominational loyalty. By 1928 Aubrey could assert that he was meeting younger Baptists who were good denominationalists. Significantly, he drew a contrast with an 'older generation' that had wanted to eliminate denominational frontiers.[67] Was Shakespeare in view?

The new generation gained support in their emphasis on Baptist principles from the stance of Baptists in America. In July 1920 a small, international conference met at Baptist Church House and at that conference J.H. Rushbrooke was appointed as Baptist Commissioner for Europe. Rushbrooke was already well regarded in English Baptist life and would soon become widely known among US Baptists. In 1928 he became the General Secretary of the Baptist World Alliance. At the BWA Congress in Stockholm in 1923, Rushbrooke paid wholehearted tribute to the moral leadership of America in the world Baptist community. The incoming President of the BWA in that year was E.Y. Mullins, President of the Southern Baptist Seminary in Louisville, Kentucky, since 1899. J.H. Rushbrooke's pro-American speech was greeted with tremendous enthusiasm. There were English pastors, however, such as J.G. Greenhough, who bitterly criticized Rushbrooke's pro-American internationalism. Despite this, the stress on Baptist distinctives, now being pushed by American and English Baptist leaders, drew widespread support. Gilbert Laws, chairman of the British Baptist Continental Committee, called for Baptist denominational self-

---

65   *BT*, 2 January 1925, p.3.
66   *BT*, 10 September 1925, p.639.
67   *BT*, 16 February 1928, p.103.

consciousness: conversion, churches based on the New Testament, and believer's baptism were all seen as Baptist distinctives.[68]

A robust declaration of Baptist principles agreed at Stockholm in 1923 opposed unity with 'any centralized organization wielding power over the individual conscience' and condemned infant baptism as 'utterly irreconcilable with the ideal of a spiritual Christianity'.[69] Fullerton described this forthright Congress declaration as likely to go far 'to clear our position amongst other churches, and to establish it amongst ourselves'.[70] The declaration was also another sign of the way Shakespeare's vision was being replaced by a different approach. Shakespeare was delighted to be asked to preach during the Stockholm meetings at a special service in Uppsala Cathedral, arranged by the Lutheran ecumenical statesman, Archbishop Söderblom. However, as Shakespeare arrived at the pulpit to preach, the huge pulpit Bible accidentally fell down. This caused him great consternation. Later that evening Shakespeare told J.C. Carlile that the Bible's fall was a sign: 'My work is done.' Nervous exhaustion was suddenly in evidence as he cried uncontrollably.[71] Rushbrooke considered Shakespeare to be thoroughly out of step with the general mood among Baptists at Stockholm and Rushbrooke confided to his wife, Dora, that the only question regarding Shakespeare was 'whether he means to fall into line, or begin new intrigues'.[72] Shakespeare never regained his confidence, and this made it easier for Aubrey to set out new priorities for the denomination.

---

68   *BT*, 20 July 1923, pp.518-20; 27 July 1923, p.542; Green, *Tomorrow's Man*, pp.98-100.
69   *BT*, 24 August 1923, pp.602-3; W.T. Whitley, ed., *Third Baptist World Congress* (London: Kingsgate Press, 1923).
70   W.Y. Fullerton, 'The Stockholm Congress and Exhibition', *BQ*, Vol.1 (1923), pp.291-3.
71   Carlile, *My Life's Little Day*, p.167.
72   Green, *Tomorrow's Man*, p.104.

'THE CARDINAL DOCTRINES OF EVANGELICAL CHRISTIANITY'

A Baptist 'position' could be set out in a short declaration, but harder theological work was required to elaborate Baptist beliefs. Probably the most creative theologian among British Baptists in the 1920s was H. Wheeler Robinson. He became Principal of Regent's Park College in 1920 and would be the driving force in the strategic move of the college from London to Oxford, a move which was to be completed by the Second World War.[73] In the 1890s Robinson had studied for an Arts degree at Edinburgh University and he followed this by theological study at Mansfield College, Oxford, during which time he also made two visits to the continent of Europe to broaden his theological awareness. This period was decisive for his development. Robinson then held pastorates at Pitlochry, Perthshire, and at St Michael's Baptist Church, Coventry, before joining W.E. Blomfield at Rawdon College in 1905. When he was appointed Principal at Regent's Park, the College was looking for someone 'at the height of his powers, who is willing to live for his post and who may be expected in the providence of God to give twenty years or so to the service of the College. He must be able in all directions to impress himself upon his men, a scholar, a University man, a Baptist, a saint, and with marked administrative ability'. Robinson ably met these requirements.[74]

Although Robinson's work on the theology of baptism sprang from strong Baptist commitment, he was by no means narrow. He encouraged co-operation between Regent's Park and two London Congregational Colleges, New College and Hackney College. But Robinson was determined to put his own stamp on Regent's Park. He began a weekly Communion Service, which became the heart of college life. His talks on these occasions showed 'catholicity and depth', characteristics also to be

---

73   Cooper, *From Stepney to St Giles'*, pp.86-90.
74   Cooper, *From Stepney to St Giles*, p. 81. For H. Wheeler Robinson as a scholar see also R. Mason, 'H. Wheeler Robinson Revisited', *BQ*, Vol.37, No.5 (1998), pp.213-26.

observed in his writings.[75] In 1911 Robinson had written *Baptist Principles*, and he later contributed regularly to the *Baptist Times*. For Robinson the common Baptist understanding of baptism was inadequate. Writing in 1921, Robinson argued that in baptism God gives the gift of the Holy Spirit.[76] He followed this with an important article in the *Baptist Quarterly* expressing concern about the playing down of baptism in Baptist churches. Robinson noted that most British Baptist churches now had open communion, a change reflecting 'the essential unity of the Church'. But Robinson was unhappy about the trend towards open membership. Normal Baptist procedure was for those applying for membership to give testimony about personal faith, and closed membership churches also required applicants to have been baptized as believers. With open membership, Robinson observed, there were 'members of Baptist Churches who have never been baptized in any external sense'. He argued for the 'evangelical sacramentalism of the New Testament': conversion and baptism together being 'the channel of the Spirit'.[77]

Both T.H. Robinson and Wheeler Robinson were leading Old Testament scholars, and throughout the century Old Testament studies in Britain owed a great deal to Baptist scholars. Through books such as *Prophecy and the Prophets in Ancient Israel* (1923), T.H. Robinson made an outstanding contribution to an understanding of the prophets. In particular he explored the place of ecstasy in prophetic experience.[78] Wheeler Robinson's most influential work in the area of Old Testament studies was his concept of corporate personality. His argument, which was that for the Hebrew people the individual had meaning only in relation to the group, opened up new understandings of the world of the Old Testament. A paper by Wheeler Robinson on 'corporate personality'

75    E.A. Payne, *Henry Wheeler Robinson* (London: Nisbet & Co, 1946), p.71.
76    *BW*, 27 January 1921, p.369.
77    H.W. Robinson, 'The Place of Baptism in Baptist Churches To-day', *BQ*, Volume 1 (1922-1923), pp.212-18.
78    T.H. Robinson, *Prophecy and the Prophets in Ancient Israel* (London: Duckworth, 1923), pp.40-6; cf. J.T. Williams, 'The Contribution of Protestant Nonconformists to Biblical Scholarship in the Twentieth Century', in Sell and Cross, eds., *Protestant Nonconformity* , pp.1-32.

has been called 'a classic of British Old Testament scholarship'.[79] Wheeler Robinson's interest in corporate personality led him to explore how it was possible for human beings to be open to various outside influences, including the influence of the Spirit of God. A Baptist Old Testament scholar of a later generation, Rex Mason, writing in 1998, saw Wheeler Robinson's ideas about the way in which the human personality could be accessible to spiritual revelation as his most important contribution to theology.[80]

The early 1920s saw Wheeler Robinson having to defend his scholarly work in the area of biblical studies. Regent's Park College received an annual grant from the Particular Baptist Fund, but in 1921 theological queries were raised by some of the Fund's trustees about a commentary on Deuteronomy that Robinson had written fourteen years previously. When application was made for the annual grant in 1921 the Fund managers said that no grants were to be made to colleges 'unless the Fundees are satisfied that the teaching is not in conflict with Particular Baptist Doctrine'. The College committee, with an eye to the College's tradition (as Stepney College), believed 'the teaching of the college to be in full and loyal accord with the evangelical faith as held by the Baptist Churches generally and by the founders of the Particular Baptist Fund and of Stepney College'. For three or four years there was some doubt about whether the grant would be awarded, but Robinson convinced those criticizing him that he was loyal to 'the cardinal doctrines of evangelical Christianity'. By 1926 the Fund managers had become distributors of Robinson's book, *Baptist Principles*.[81] Two years later Robinson's *The Christian Experience of the Holy Spirit*, a profound

---

79    C.S. Rodd, in 'Introduction', H.W. Robinson, *Corporate Personality* (Edinburgh: T&T Clark, 1981, 2nd ed.), p.7.

80    See H.W. Robinson, 'Hebrew Psychology', in A.S. Peake, ed., *The People and the Book: Essays on the Old Testament* (Oxford: Clarendon, 1925), pp.353-72; Mason, 'H. Wheeler Robinson Revisited', p.220.

81    Cooper, *From Stepney to St Giles'*, p.83; Payne, *Henry Wheeler Robinson*, p.74. For the Fund's history, see T. Valentine, *Concern for the Ministry* (Teddington: Particular Baptist Fund, 1967).

exploration of pneumatology, was published.[82] Wheeler Robinson became the leading example of a Baptist scholar connecting biblical theology with experience and practice.

T.R. Glover's approach was rather different from that of Robinson, and was perhaps best set out in his book *The Jesus of History* (1917), which had an introduction by Randall Davidson, Archbishop of Canterbury. It sold 50,000 copies in three years and the profits that accrued to the Student Christian Movement (SCM) helped to establish SCM as a publishing house. Glover was a highly popular SCM speaker at a time when the SCM was very strong within British higher education. In *The Jesus of History*, and also in *Jesus in the Experience of Men* (1920), Glover attempted to bring out the human personality of Jesus.

Conservatives, however, were deeply suspicious about Glover's theology and in particular his failure to say anything about Jesus' miracles.[83] In 1923-24 a few Baptist churches of a conservative disposition, including Octavius Street in Deptford, Newton Avenue in Acton, and Abbey Street in Bermondsey, left the Union on doctrinal grounds. James Mountain himself left the Union and tried, with little success, to promote an alternative 'New Baptist Union, free from Modernism'.[84] One speaker at the annual Pastors' College

*A new church and school of this decade, Monton, Manchester, 1928*

---

82    H.W. Robinson, *The Christian Experience of the Holy Spirit* (London: Nisbet & Co, 1928).

83    H.G. Wood, *Terrot Reaveley Glover: A Biography* (Cambridge: Cambridge University Press, 1953), p.109; Clements, *Lovers of Discord*, pp.114-19; B. Stanley, ' "The Old Religion and the New": India and the making of T.R. Glover's *The Jesus of History*', in D.W. Bebbington, ed., *The Gospel in the World* (Carlisle: Paternoster Press, 2002), pp.295-312.

84    Minutes of the Baptist Union Council, 15 January 1924; 8 July 1924. Three further withdrawals - Drummond Road in Bermondsey, Romney Street in Westminster,

conference in 1923 saw the denomination as 'dying', claiming only Spurgeon's men could save it.[85] Gilbert Laws, who was a moderate Pastors' College figure, disliked the extreme views being purveyed, but defended those 'on the conservative wing of our denomination' and asked Glover in 1924 not to ridicule these 'devout and holy people', a reference to acerbic articles by Glover in the *Daily News*.[86]

Given this background, there were understandable worries on the part of the Union leadership that there might be protests from conservatives when Glover took the presidency of the Union at the 1924 Assembly. Glover, however, delivered a presidential address on 'Preaching Christ' which disarmed many critics. He assured his hearers: 'As I grow older I want more and more to preach Christ without theory, to tell people the tremendous facts associated with Him – the fact of victory over sin, the changed life, and the most amazing fact of all, Himself'.[87] It may be questioned whether there can be such a thing as a Christ 'without theory', but Glover made clear his belief in the deity of Christ. The Assembly hymns he chose were, deliberately, mainly by Isaac Watts. He also asked three speakers, Arthur Dakin, Percy Evans and Albert Law, to give addresses on the theme 'God in Christ'. The speakers represented three college traditions - Bristol, Spurgeon's and Regent's Park- and all the addresses affirmed orthodox Christology: F.C. Spurr spoke of them as being of a very high order. Indeed Spurr was insistent that no-one who heard Glover as President could doubt his evangelicalism. Percy Evans, recently appointed as a tutor at Spurgeon's College (as the Pastors' College was known from 1923), and an Assembly speaker for the first time, said: 'I hope my appearance here may be accepted as a symbol of unity.'[88]

In the face of attempts in the early 1920s to move the denomination either in the direction of Fundamentalism or towards a more overtly

---

and Onslow in South Kensington – are noted by Bebbington, 'Baptists and Fundamentalism in Inter-War Britain', in Robbins, *Protestant Evangelicalism*, p.318.
85 *BT*, 11 May 1923, p.336.
86 *BT*, 18 January 1924, p.44.
87 Wood, *Terrot Reaveley Glover*, p.156.
88 *BW*, 8 May 1924, p.121; Clements, *Lovers of Discord*, pp.107-42.

liberal evangelicalism, the theological course that was charted by
emerging leaders like Aubrey can be described as central evangelicalism
which had Christ as its focus. Thus at the 1922 Union Assembly,
Wheeler Robinson's address, which had the title 'The Centrality of
Christ in Christian Life and Thought', was cordially received. In
affirming Robinson, the Assembly would have been aware that his
theology had been questioned.[89] At the 1924 Assembly, Spurr
commented that uneasiness had been generated by 'the action of a few
insignificant men who have set up as Popes.' Charges of liberalism in the
Union had been made in pamphlets posted to church secretaries. Spurr
believed the Assembly answered the false charges and showed that
Baptists were soundly evangelical.[90] Theological debates would
continue, but in 1926, as Union President, Rushbrooke struck a note
which appealed to a wide cross-section of the Baptist constituency. He
argued that to be a Baptist was not inconsistent with catholicity and he
also affirmed that Baptists held, as the 'source and governing principle
of their distinctive faith and practice', the Protestant motto, *sola fide*, by
faith alone. Baptists had taken seriously the 'great, simple, splendid
Gospel whose rediscovery and reassertion is the glory of the
Reformation'.[91]

## LEADERSHIP AND MINISTRY

Baptist pastors might be preaching the gospel, but were they being paid
enough to live by the gospel? The concerns that had been highlighted in
the first two decades of the century about the support of Baptist pastors
were still to the fore in the 1920s. The needs of retired ministers were
also pressing. The widow of James A. Spurgeon had presented Arundel
House, Brighton, to the Union, and this functioned until the 1970s as a
welcome rest home for a significant number of ministers and their wives,
but it was feared that many more ministers were suffering from

89   *BW*, 11 May 1922, p.124.
90   *BW*, 15 May 1924, p.150.
91   J.H. Rushbrooke, *et al.*, *The Faith of the Baptists* (London: The Kingsgate Press, 1926), pp.61, 70; cf. *BT*, 20 May 1926, p.347.

**WHY NOT ENJOY**

The warmth and sunshine of the South Coast?

Within easy reach of London and with through connections from other parts of the country.

**ARUNDEL HOUSE BRIGHTON**

OFFERS EITHER A RESTFUL OR STRENUOUS HOLIDAY WITH HAPPY FELLOWSHIP

ARUNDEL HOUSE was established in memory of Dr. J. A. Spurgeon as a place of rest for ministers and other Christian workers.

*An advertisement for Arundel House in 1964*

exhaustion and poverty. H.P. Gould of Norwich asked at the 1920 Assembly that the case for increasing stipends should not be based on 'the hardships of the ministers' lot; the day had gone for charitable doles'. He wished to see an appeal founded on reason, not sympathy.[92] One reason was clear: the Industrial Court had stated that living costs in 1920 were 150% above 1914 levels, so that a stipend of £160 in 1920, judged by pre-war standards, had a buying power of only £64.[93]

An appeal was duly launched for a United Fund of £250,000, half for Union purposes and half for the BMS, which was facing a financial crisis.[94] The Union's share would be divided: £100,000 for sustentation purposes; £20,000 for deaconesses, in particular for a new Women's Training College, Havelock Hall, Hampstead; and £5,000 for relief work and the establishment of Baptist seminaries in Europe. As with previous appeals, several leading individuals gave energy to fund-raising. Sir Alfred Pearce Gould, as treasurer of the BMS, committed himself fully to this cause until his death in 1922. He and Herbert Marnham, the Union treasurer, were the United Fund's treasurers; Shakespeare, Fullerton and

---

92   *BT*, 14 May 1920, p.325.
93   *BT*, 23 July 1920, p.485.
94   Stanley, *The History of the Baptist Missionary Society*, pp.381-6.

C.E. Wilson were the secretaries; and John Chown was chief
commissioner. The appeal was forcefully publicized in the *Baptist Times*
and through meetings across the country. Baptists were shocked to be
told that a rat-catcher working for the East Sussex County Council was
earning much more than the average pastor. There was a speedy response
to the appeal, perhaps showing that the denomination had become a
stronger entity. After little more than a year, £270,000 was in hand or
promised, although all the money did not come in until 1923. The
minimum ministerial stipend was raised to £160 per annum, with
children's allowances of £10. Of 1,683 Union churches, 1,489 had joined
the Union's 'Federation' (established in 1912), which meant they were
eligible for aid, and about 600 ministers were grant aided.[95]

Following this appeal, another major and very significant project
was the raising of £300,000 for a Superannuation Fund. The first
Annuity Fund had been opened in 1875 but was underfunded and
underused. There were 2,069 recognized ministers in the Union in 1926,
but only 692 were members of the Annuity Fund. Often older ministers
had to remain in office because they had no other means of livelihood.
The main proposals for a Superannuation Fund had been agreed before
Aubrey took office, but these were formally presented at the 1926
Assembly. At the 1927 Assembly in London, a prominent Baptist
layman, Thomas Penny, moved the resolution that a new Scheme should
be set up and an appeal launched. This was carried with great
enthusiasm. The letter of appeal after the Assembly was signed by sixty-
three leading Baptist lay men and women. By 1929, £312,750 had been
given or promised.[96] Aubrey put great effort into promoting the
Superannuation Scheme, although he expressed disappointment that
people were writing to him about the scheme as if it was 'the big thing
in front of us'. It was, Aubrey agreed, 'very big', but, typically, he
insisted that evangelism was of greater importance.[97] The concern for

---

95   Sparkes, *The Home Mission Story*, pp.76-80.
96   D.C. Sparkes, *Pensions – Provision for Retired and Disabled Ministers* (Didcot:
     Baptist Historical Society, 1996), chapters 4 and 5. The full amount of £300,000
     did not come in until 1935.
97   *BT*, 6 January 1927, p.3.

ministerial pensions should be seen in the context of an approach to Baptist ministry that had been shaped by Shakespeare's thinking about the ministerial office. Also, new social conditions demanded a more professional view of ministry. The Union believed it had the responsibility for the selection, training, accreditation and support of ministers.[98]

The vision for a well-trained and competent ministry motivated the work of the Baptist colleges. W.E. Blomfield, as Union President, referred in 1923 to criticisms of the colleges on theological grounds - probably a reference to what had been said about Wheeler Robinson -

*Spurgeon's College, South Norwood*

and insisted that the colleges gave Christ supreme place. Yet they also, rightly in his view, incorporated critical studies.[99] The *Baptist Quarterly* carried articles relevant to these issues. Aubrey argued for spiritual priorities in training: 'We need trained men, efficient men, more and more of them, but above all, in the future as in the past, men whose names are written in heaven, men well-known at the throne of God.' He applauded examples of 'true piety': those 'reading on their knees'.[100] Regarding theological college principals, the historian W.T. Whitley believed that 'the personal influence of the head was all important over the members of the "family"'.[101] Certainly principals such as Robinson, Henry Townsend at Manchester, and Arthur Dakin, appointed Principal at Bristol in 1924, were having significant influence.

---

98   Shepherd argues that what developed was a clerical concept of ministry that was new among Baptists: Shepherd, *The Making of a Modern Denomination*, p.179.
99   See *BW*, 26 April 1923, p.62; *BT*, 27 April 1923, p.301.
100  Aubrey, 'The Future of our Ministry', pp.178-9.
101  W.T. Whitley, 'Our Theological Colleges', *BQ*, Vol.1 (1922-3), p.26.

In 1923 the Pastors' College moved to South Norwood, taking the new name of Spurgeon's College, and two years later the college appointed Percy Evans, a capable scholar, as Principal. There had been rumours that Spurgeon's, which subscribed to the Evangelical Alliance basis of faith, might become a general evangelical training centre,[102] but Evans drew it closer to the life of the Union.

Yet there were problems in Baptist ministry in the 1920s. There was concern about low numbers entering ministry - the five English Baptist colleges were turning out a total of only twenty students a year, compared to fifty before the war.[103] Blomfield spoke in 1923 about gifted novices whom churches were scrambling to secure, and large churches that were vacant through lack of competent leaders. In line with Union thinking, Blomfield wanted to encourage promising younger people into ministry. On ministerial standards he commented: 'We see cultured men and women drift away from our Churches... It may be that our type of worship and ministry does not appeal to refined and thoughtful folk.'[104] A year later Blomfield reflected on the brevity of many pastorates. He estimated that many ministries lasted only about three years, which meant that a pastor did not gain the trust and affection of his flock. Blomfield believed this was a cause of people drifting away.[105] P.T. Thomson, Union Commissioner for Education and chairman of the Ministerial Recognition Committee, introduced proposals in 1922 to make a Baptist Union examination for non-collegiate probationers compulsory, while removing examinations for college-trained probationers. One critic of this change, W.T. Andress of Calstock, Cornwall, said the Holy Spirit and a church might call someone, but 'the Baptist Union will forbid him'. In 1923, however, the substance of Thomson's thinking was accepted by the Assembly.[106] There was also

102  *BT*, 6 October 1922, p.638.
103  Brown, *A Social History of the Nonconformist Ministry*, p.225.
104  See *BW*, 26 April 1923, p.62; *BT*, 27 April 1923, pp.296, 302; cf. Minutes of a Special Committee on the Ministry, 2-4 January 1923; bound with BU Council minutes, Angus Library.
105  W.E. Blomfield, 'A Few Reflections on my Presidential Experiences', *BQ*, Vol.2 (1924-1925), p.52.
106  Sparkes, *An Accredited Ministry*, pp.28-9; *BT*, 31 March 1922, p.200.

discussion of how to raise the status of lay preachers, who served 900 churches. In 1923 a three-year training course for lay preachers was introduced and a year later the Union published, for the first time, a list of recognized lay preachers.[107] Concern for quality in ministry was still high on the agenda.

The difficulty some churches were facing in finding the right kind of minister is highlighted by a case in January 1926. An advertisement appeared in the *British Weekly* (probably the *Baptist Times* would not have carried it) which read: 'Strong, healthy, North Midland Baptist Church, net membership 300, S.S. and institutional interests, salary up to £500, requires Pastor, age 34 to 45, married with family preferred.' Henry Cook, a Scot who had recently been appointed as minister at Ferme Park, London, in succession to Charles Brown, said he hoped no Baptist ministers would apply. He argued that because of the superintendency system, ministers were no longer 'touting' for posts: the advertisement was to be deplored. No doubt part of the disquiet was that the salary advertised was far in excess of the minimum stipend. It is not certain, however, that the settlement scheme was working as well as might have been hoped. Edgar Washbourne from Warwickshire wrote to the *British Weekly* in response to Cook's letter to say that most churches considered the superintendents'

*Violet Hedger*

recommendations were 'often both unsuitable and unsuccessful'. He defended advertisements, and hoped that churches and ministers would learn from 'the proved efficient methods of the business world in the matter of advertising'. [108]

Violet Hedger, writing in 1925, believed that the churches were lagging behind the world at large in making use of the gifts of women. She said women were successful as doctors, barristers and politicians,

---

107   J.E.T. Hough, *Servants of the Word* (London: Carey Kingsgate Press, 1963), p.12.
108   *BW*, 7 January 1926, p.372; 14 January 1926, p.378; 21 January 1926, p.398.

whereas in church life men filled the executive offices. Hedger trained for the ministry at Regent's Park College with the encouragement of her minister, Charles Brown, although Wheeler Robinson was not supportive. She said that there was a growing need for women ministers and spoke about women's understanding in delicate matters. The ideal, she suggested, might be churches with both a male and female pastor.[109] Hedger obtained a BD and settled in 1926 at Littleover, Derby, as a probationer minister. She was not the first female Baptist minister, although she became the best known. Edith Gates, at Little Tew and Cleveley, Oxfordshire, qualified as a probationer through the Union examination in 1922.[110] Gates was to become President of her Association. Maria Living-Taylor trained at the Universities of London and Dijon, and in 1924, after four years of ministry, was accepted on to the Union's ministerial list. Sion Jubilee, the most significant church in the Bradford District, called her husband John and herself as joint pastors, but Maria rarely conducted Sunday worship.[111] In the light of the fact that women were entering ministry, the Council commissioned a report on the subject. Advocates of women in ministry referred to there being neither male nor female 'in Christ'.[112] The Council stated in 1926 that although churches were reluctant to invite women as pastors, according to Baptist belief and practice gender was no bar to service.[113] This became Union policy.

109  *BT*, 16 January 1925, pp.35-6.
110  Minutes of the Baptist Union Ministerial Recognition Committee, 7 November 192; bound with BU Council minutes, Angus Library.
111  Sellers, ed., *Our Heritage*, p.87.
112  Minutes of the Baptist Women's Training College and Sisterhood Committee, 14 July 1920; Minutes of the Baptist Union Ministerial Recognition Committee, 17 October 1924; bound with BU Council minutes, Angus Library; *BT*, 1 May 1925, p.309.
113  Minutes of the Baptist Union Council, 9 and 10 February, 1925; *BT*, 11 February 1926, p.100; J. Briggs, 'She-Preachers, Widows and other Women: The feminine dimension in Baptist life since 1600', *BQ*, Vol.31, No.7 (1986), pp.337-52; Sparkes, *An Accredited Ministry*, pp.31-5; 49-50.

## SPIRITUAL LIFE AND HEALTH

Within the life of the churches, the role of women was crucial. Havelock Hall, as a Women's Training College for deaconesses, was opened in 1920 and attempts were made to ensure for deaconesses a minimum stipend of £100 per annum.[114] Kathleen Dunn, the college's first Principal, resigned after a few months. There had been some tensions over the content of the education, with Wheeler Robinson stating that the curriculum was 'fundamentally wrong' and that he had never taught classes which 'dragged so heavily'.[115] Dunn was succeeded by Miss J.J. Arthur, a

*Havelock Hall*

graduate of Glasgow University and a secondary school teacher. The Baptist Women's League, which gave support to deaconesses, continued to grow, with Mrs C.S. Rose as its inspiring leader. In 1921, 1,000 women attended the BWL meeting at the Assembly. The position of women was becoming more prominent. At the 1925 Assembly, Hettie Rowntree Clifford spoke about the role of deaconesses: there were over forty, and a few were taking charge of churches. The Lancashire and Cheshire Association appointed an itinerant Sister to help smaller churches. Birmingham's *Daily Mail* reported in 1924 on Sister Ida Evans, in Birmingham, who was making 3,000 visits each year in the slums. At Bloomsbury the deaconesses took on much of the daily work of the church.[116] Increasingly, women were also church secretaries. This

---

114  Minutes of the Baptist Women's Training College and Sisterhood Committee, 27 January 1920, 9 November 1920.

115  H. Wheeler Robinson to P.T. Thomson, 11 December 1920, Baptist Union Minute Book, 1920; Minutes of the Baptist Women's Training College and Sisterhood Committee, 28 April 1921.

116  *BT*, 8 May 1925, p.323; D.M. Rose, *Baptist Deaconesses* (London: Carey Kingsgate Press, 1954), p.16; Bowers, *A Bold Experiment*, pp.266-71; G. Lee, 'Women in Baptist Ministry in the 20th Century' (unpublished paper, 2001).

*The Sunday School, Littleover Baptist Church, Derby, 1926*
*The minister, Violet Hedger, in a dark suit, is almost central*

meant involvement in finance, membership issues and denominational affairs.[117]

Another area to which churches gave continuing attention was ministry to children. By now a service of dedication of infants, something which had been encouraged by J.H. Shakespeare and by J.H. Rushbrooke, was becoming more common.[118] The 1920s had seen excitement about the Young Worshippers' League, but in some instances only a 'straggling half-dozen' children were found in churches. There was debate about whether children should come into church or have a

---

117  S.J. Price, 'The Office of Church Secretary', *BQ*, Vol.2 (1924-1925), pp.253-62.
118  For developments, see W.M.S. West, 'The Child and the Church: A Baptist Perspective', in W.H. Brackney, P.S. Fiddes and J.H.Y. Briggs, eds., *Pilgrim Pathways: Essays in Honour of B.R. White* (Macon, Ga.: Mercer University Press, 1999), pp.82-7. In 1911 J.H. Rushbrooke had produced a 'Form for the Dedication of Infants'.

parallel children's church.[119] In 1926 there was a considerable decrease in Baptist Sunday scholars, after a period of growth, and Aubrey asked: 'Why have our Sunday Schools lost the fruit of their work?' This, he believed, was a challenge for young people's groups and for the many Christian Endeavour societies in Baptist churches.[120] A series of articles in the *Baptist Times* allowed issues to be raised. The denomination was now losing 5,000 scholars per year. Carey

*Girls' Guildry, Bloomsbury, mid-1920s*

Bonner, General Secretary of the National Sunday School Union and President of the Baptist Union in 1931, said that it was necessary to re-evaluate training, week-day activities and use of premises.[121] The secretary of the Welfare of Youth Committee in the East Midland Association wrote in 1929 about a lack of definite teaching in Sunday schools.[122] In fact, as Jeffrey Cox has shown, because of the decline in the number of children under fifteen in England and Wales between 1901 and 1931, the decline in Baptist Sunday school membership as a percentage of that age group was only one per cent.[123] Many Baptist churches also had uniformed organizations like the Boys' Brigade and Girls' Guildry.

A generally lively spirit was to be found among the groups of older teenagers and young adults associated with Baptist churches in the 1920s, although these groups were not to be found in all churches. Aubrey, who had attracted many young people in his ministry in Cambridge, was on the lookout for signs of hope. In 1926 he wrote, in

119  *BW*, 7 August 1924, p. 408; 14 August 1924, p.426.
120  *BT*, 15 April 1926, p.279.
121  *BT*, 16 February 1928, p.104.
122  Harrison, *It All Began Here*, p.117.
123  J. Cox, *The English Churches in a Secular Society: Lambeth, 1870-1930* (Oxford: Oxford University Press, 1982), pp.226-7.

what was a weekly letter by him in the *Baptist Times*: 'I find a spirit of confidence and loyalty everywhere.'[124] It was noted in 1927 that most new members of Baptist churches were in their teens or early twenties.[125] Baptists were proud of the fact that they sent the largest delegation of any single denomination to the Christian Endeavour Annual Convention.[126] In 1928 Aubrey reported with some excitement that a number of able young business and professional men in London had banded themselves together to learn in fellowship how to serve Christ and the churches. Although this Baptist Young Men's Movement remained relatively small, it did provide fellowship for those who found that in their churches they lacked friends who understood the pressures they faced in the business and professional world. [127]

One movement which appealed to people in their twenties was the Oxford Group, an informal interdenominational network, with a base in Oxford, which flourished from the late 1920s.[128] It was started by an American Lutheran minister, Frank Buchman. In 1912 F.B. Meyer spoke at Pennsylvania State College and during his visit he advised Buchman, who was working there, that he should give an hour a day to listening to God and should make personal relationships the focus of his evangelism. Meyer found Buchman so busy that he was using two telephones, and Meyer insisted that the voice of God was more important than human voices.[129] Buchman's view was that in his own witness to individuals he was a failure before meeting Meyer. From then on, according to Buchman, people became his priority and in addition he 'decided to

---

124  *BT*, 8 July 1926, p.491.

125  *BT*, 28 April 1927, p.297.

126  *BT*, 16 June 1927, p.430.

127  *BT*, 16 February 1928, p.103. For the Baptist Young Men's Movement, which was linked to the Baptist Laymen's Missionary Movement, see K.W. Bennett, *God at Work with Men* (Pontesford, Shrewsbury: BMM, 1997).

128  D.W. Bebbington, 'The Oxford Group Movement between the Wars', in W.J. Sheils and D. Wood, eds., *Voluntary Religion* (Oxford: Blackwell, 1986), pp.495-507.

129  K.D. Belden, *Reflections on Moral Re-armament* (London: Grosvenor Books, 1983), p.38.

devote an hour, from 5 a.m. to 6 a.m ... in a daily time of quiet'.[130] Buchman was influenced by another Baptist, Oswald Chambers, and in the 1920s Buchman was committed to reading through Chambers' books, with Chambers' *My Utmost for His Highest* having pride of place.[131] T.R. Glover first met Buchman in 1914, and contact continued during the 1920s. Comparing himself with Buchman, Glover wished in 1928 that he had more gift for 'arresting people for Christ'.[132] The Keswick Convention's message, which included a call to 'full surrender', influenced Buchman. A *Baptist Times* correspondent in 1928 noted how Glover and Meyer, a Keswick speaker, had contributed to the Oxford Group.[133]

The influence on Baptists of the Oxford Group, with its relational spirituality, would grow in the 1930s, but in the 1920s a more important development in the area of spirituality was the interest taken in 'higher' churchmanship. Anglo-Catholic forms of worship, which were spreading significantly in the Church of England, were usually criticized by Baptists. Spurr spoke in 1922 of an Anglo-Catholic self-styled High Mass in Birmingham Cathedral which included a song about the 'blood drops in the chalice'. Spurr asked: 'Is it with this neo-paganism that we Evangelicals are invited to make common cause?'[134] Yet Ernest Payne, as a theological student in the 1920s, was not satisfied with the Baptist worship he experienced. Payne observed that there were many Baptist churches where ministers who ventured to read prayers as well as engaging in extempore prayer were regarded with undisguised suspicion. But Payne suggested that cultural progress meant that there was a more critical attitude to public worship on the part of many worshippers. Extempore prayer, he thought, was the ideal in a small group, but for larger congregational worship he preferred an ordered form, and he

---

130  T. Spoerri, *Dynamic out of Silence* (London: Grosvenor Books, 1976), p.30.
131  A. Jarlert, *The Oxford Group, Group Revivalism and the Churches in Northern Europe, 1930-1945* (Lund, Sweden: Lund University Press, 1995), p.60.
132  T.R. Glover to F. Buchman, 3 August 1928: Library of Congress, Washington DC, MRA Archive, Box 35.
133  *BT*, 21 June 1928, p.460 (Name not given).
134  *BW*, 29 June 1922, p.268. For background see W.S.F. Pickering, *Anglo-Catholicism* (London: SPCK, 1989).

ventured the opinion – which would shape his later work on liturgy - that a litany made worship a properly corporate act.[135]

There were others who believed that the health of the churches depended on fostering a deeper spirituality through spiritual retreats. Spurr himself, despite his antipathy towards Anglo-Catholicism, regretted in 1925 that a year or two previously there had been a Free Church retreat movement in progress but that it had died down. He wanted more emphasis on the inner life.[136] Tait Patterson, the minister at Dewsbury, had a strong sense of spirituality and liturgy not often seen in the Baptist community of this period. He produced a manual of prayers for worship, *Call to Worship*, and, with financial help from a manufacturer in Dewsbury, who was a committed Baptist, Patterson organized a retreat at Kiplin Hall, Yorkshire, which started a pattern of annual retreats.[137] Another minister who found retreats of value was Wheeler Robinson. His book, *The Christian Experience of the Holy Spirit* (1928), owed a great deal to his own experiences in prayer. He had become increasingly interested in John Henry Newman, attended prayer retreats at the high-church Mirfield Community led by W.H. Frere, and led Baptist ministerial retreats in which time was given to quiet worship introduced by simple litanies.[138] The Baptist Ministers' and Missionaries' Prayer Union, which amalgamated with the Baptist Ministers' Fraternal Union, also had a tradition of retreats.[139]

The issue of the spiritual health of the denomination was put starkly by Gilbert Laws at the 1926 Assembly. Rushbrooke, as President, had asked a number of Assembly speakers to take up the theme, 'The Faith of the Baptists', and these addresses were later published in a book. Laws, one of the contributors, said that he wished to be perfectly frank: 'Many of us are tired in mind, a little perplexed in our efforts to find the right emphasis for today in our preaching, conscious of our lack of touch with the ever flowing intellectual life of our time, and, above all ... very

135  E.A. Payne 'Public Prayer', *BQ*, Vol.2 (1924-1925), pp.128-32.
136  *BW*, 19 November 1925, p.178.
137  Sellers, ed., *Our Heritage*, p.91.
138  Payne, *Henry Wheeler Robinson*, pp.59-60.
139  Randall, *Spirituality and Social Change*, pp.62-5.

conscious of our lack of power to cast out demons.' In speaking about casting out demons, Laws was probably not talking about exorcism, but rather about the general power of Christian ministry over evil in the world. He offered some suggestions, among them a retreat 'to place ourselves in the hands of some master of the interior life'.[140] Laws was well aware of the attempts to promote spiritual welfare in the churches and the struggles that seemed to accompany such efforts. There were worries in this period about the decline in family worship. But Laws was not addressing his remarks primarily to Baptist lay people, as if they were the ones who had to initiate change. He quoted one Baptist layman who said, regarding the Sunday services at his church: 'My soul gets a cold bath in the city every day; I do not want two more on Sunday.' For Laws, change had to be evident in the ministry, which needed 're-vitalizing by a fresh contact with the sources of power'.[141]

## EVANGELISM AND REVIVAL

Fresh contact seemed to be possible. On 20 July 1921, Hugh Ferguson, minister of London Road Baptist Church, Lowestoft, and John Hayes, Vicar of Christ Church, Lowestoft, reported at the Keswick Convention that an unexpected revival had come to East Anglia. In the view of Hayes, Ferguson had been 'one of the coldest icicles I had dropped across in the whole of my life', but he had had a new spiritual experience and, despite the fact that he was an unemotional Scot, he wept with joy. Powerful prayer meetings started in the London Road church.[142] In the autumn of 1920 Ferguson had visited Douglas Brown, minister of the 800-member Ramsden Road Baptist Church, Balham, to ask if he would conduct a mission in Lowestoft. Brown accepted the invitation, and from 7 March 1921, when the mission began, until 2 April, when the first phase ended, Brown addressed several meetings per day. The number of

---

140  Rushbrooke, *et al.*, *The Faith of the Baptists*, p.16.
141  Ibid., p.17.
142  *Keswick Week*, 1921, pp.242, 246.

conversions was reckoned to have been over a thousand.[143] Brown's impact was felt by the Baptist denomination when he spoke at the 1921 Assembly. His address was 'pure volcanic energy'. Brown stretched out his hands at the end of his message and said: 'All hail the power of Jesus' name'. J.C. Carlile stood up to pray, but the audience had to express itself in song. A voice began to sing and the audience followed. 'It is safe to say', the *Baptist Times* reporter commented on 6 May 1921, 'that never before has such a scene been witnessed at any session of the Baptist Union Assembly.'[144]

During the remainder of 1921, Brown was in constant demand as a preacher. Many of the churches in which he preached were Baptist,

*Douglas Brown*

although his meetings were almost always interdenominational. In June he held meetings at Burlington Baptist Church, Ipswich, where L.C. Parkinson was minister. The format was prayer in the mornings, Bible studies in the afternoons (many on the Second Advent) and evening gospel services, which attracted 1,100 people. At the close of all the evening services Brown asked people wishing to commit their lives to Christ to go to the 'enquiry room'. Meetings in Great Yarmouth followed, initially at Park Baptist Church and then at St George's Church. A report in the *Baptist Times* spoke of two Anglican clergy and three Baptist ministers 'on their knees dealing with anxious enquirers'.[145] Later this revival would be remembered for its impact

on fishermen, but Brown reached beyond the fishing communities. By the end of October 1921 he had conducted special meetings in Lymington ('Our services last Sunday were full of the fire of God, and

---

143   S.C. Griffin, *Forgotten Revival* (Bromley: Day One Publications, 1992), pp.20-40.
144   *BT*, 6 May 1921, p.279.
145   *BT*, 17 June 1921, p.375.

the power of God was present to heal.'), Ramsgate, Worthing, Bournemouth, the Isle of Wight, London (Chatsworth Road), Bath (Manvers Street), Redhill and Worthing. A typical report stated that ministers, deacons and church members, many in tears, knelt round the communion table making solemn vows of dedication.[146]

As Brown addressed more and more congregations, it became clear that he was moving from a ministry that was primarily evangelistic to one in which he stressed the renewal of the churches. Some, such as J.C. Carlile, were fearful that this would be simply an emotional revival.[147] There is no doubt that Brown did emphasize experience. He spoke in September 1921 of a 'baptism of the Holy Ghost', which he had experienced eight months earlier, as the key to what happened in Lowestoft.[148]Yet his terminology was designed to play down excessive emotion. Rooms for enquirers were called 'Quiet Rooms'. Brown deliberately did not encourage ecstatic 'hallelujahs' or repeated singing of choruses, to the disappointment of some traditional revival-seekers. Brown also reached out to his critics. Speaking at Bloomsbury Central Baptist Church in February 1922, he asked Carlile to lead in prayer. Responding to some who asked him why he did not preach on hell, Brown replied that his message was the love of God in Jesus.[149] In March 1922, Tom Phillips at Bloomsbury expressed delight that 'revival or Pentecost' had come to London. By then Brown had conducted 1,000 revival services, thousands were responding to his appeals, and Associations were being encouraged by the Union to appoint Evangelistic Committees.[150]

At the 1922 Assembly Brown spoke again, although not with the same effect as the previous year. It was noted at the beginning of 1922 that he was looking weary and somewhat discouraged. Having visited many churches, Brown's controversial view was that without an

146  *BT*, 28 October 1921, p.657.
147  *BT*, 3 June 1921, p.345; 3 July 1921, p.344; 16 September 1921, p.556.
148  Griffin, *Forgotten Revival*, p.55.
149  *BT*, 17 February 1922, p.100.
150  *BT*, 17 March 1922, p.173; Minutes of a Baptist Union Evangelisation Committee and Commission of Enquiry on the Ministry, 21 March 1922; bound with BU Council minutes, Angus Library.

evangelical revival the churches in England would be closed in ten years.[151] In his address to the Assembly he took up denominational issues, making it clear to the Assembly that he had no sympathy with 'heresy hunters' in the denomination. Also, Brown was no longer stressing the Second Advent to the extent that he had done a year before.[152] This kind of re-positioning by Brown was significant, since some of his supporters, such as the active layman, Benjamin I. Greenwood, were identified with very conservative elements within the denomination. The hope of denominational leaders in 1922 was that Brown's stress on revival would help the denomination, but Tom Phillips – who had voiced admiration of Brown - queried in October 1922 whether Brown was in touch with modern thinking. He noted that Brown had recently spoken on 'Death' and had referred to the death of his own father (the well-known Archibald Brown), but that people had not been moved by the address as they might have been in the past.[153] Nonetheless, the Union continued to see Brown as a crucial evangelistic figure; his statement in November 1922 that he saw signs of 'a general evangelical awakening' was welcomed.[154]

It was clear early in 1923 that Brown was struggling with physical exhaustion. He began to cancel some engagements. While at the Baptist World Alliance Congress in Stockholm, however, he found the wider fellowship a healing experience.[155] Later in 1923, he conducted large meetings in Carr's Lane Congregational Church, Birmingham, and J.E. Roberts in Manchester suggested in September 1923 that Brown might become involved in official denominational evangelism.[156] There appeared to be evidence of Baptist advance in the early 1920s, following a period of stagnation. As examples of decline, in 1920 the Berkshire Association saw its lowest ever recorded number of baptisms, and the Western Association had five years of decline from 1918. But from 1920

---

151  *BT*, 6 January 1922, p.11.
152  *BT*, 17 March 1922, p.173; *BW*, 11 May 1922, p.124; cf. *Christian*, 28 April 1921, p.11.
153  *BT*, 13 October 1922, p.658.
154  *BW*, 30 November 1922, p.208.
155  *BT*, 17 August 1923, p.586.
156  *BT*, 28 September 1923, p.680.

to 1923 there was an increase in overall Baptist membership in England.[157] The wish of Roberts regarding Brown was to be fulfilled. At the Council meeting on 20 November 1923, Carlile proposed that Brown should become the Union's Commissioner of Evangelism, and on 9 September 1924, during a service at Bloomsbury, Brown was set apart as part-time (and unpaid) Commissioner of Evangelism. In early 1925 Carlile spoke warmly of the great evangelistic movement connected with 'our beloved Commissioner', but only a few months later Brown resigned from the work due to complete nervous collapse.[158]

Throughout the period 1921 to 1925, Brown had continued to be the pastor of Ramsden Road Church, although he had often been away from there. By November 1926 he was back in full-time local ministry, pronouncing that he was 'as fit as a fiddle'. He spoke in December about wider Baptist issues, declaring that the Modernists and the theologically orthodox in the denomination were like a team playing against itself.[159] Aubrey was eager to use Brown once more to stimulate evangelism - as far as Brown's health allowed – and several people now saw the possibility of his influence being felt as President of the Union. In 1928 he was duly elected Vice-President and to the delight of the Assembly he spoke during his presidential address in 1929 about his own spiritual experiences, describing in detail how, following weeks of mental struggle, he had an experience in early 1921 in the middle of the night: 'I awoke with a sense of a Royal Presence; I dressed and went into the study. Sitting at my desk I was conscious of a Divine Companion. He was in front of me, questioning, awaiting a verdict.' Brown had bowed in a profound moment of self-surrender and on the very next day Hugh Ferguson from Lowestoft appeared in his congregation. The result was what Brown called 'three months of miracles and four years of

---

157 Payne, *The Baptists of Berkshire*, p.130; F.H. Cockett, *Partnership in Service: A Brief History of the Western Baptist Association (1823-1973)* (Bridport: n.p.: [n.d. but 1973]), p.17; *BT*, 9 January 1925, p.17.
158 Minutes of the Baptist Union Council, 20 November 1923; 8 July 1924; *BT*, 12 September 1924, p.600; 2 January 1925, p.3; 24 April 1925, p.281; 14 May 1925, p.345.
159 *BT*, 18 November 1926, p.832; 30 December 1926, p.960.

harvesting'.[160] The story was exciting, but it seemed from the way he told it that in Brown's mind the harvesting was over.

Douglas Brown's work was, however, by no means the only evangelistic contribution being made to Baptist life in this period. In 1920 the *Baptist Handbook* listed six Baptist evangelists.[161] From West Ham, one of the poorest boroughs in England, Robert Rowntree Clifford issued a powerful challenge - a 'Call for Personal Evangelism'. Clifford, the son of a shipwright, came from Sunderland. He studied at Regent's Park College and after a rural ministry was called to the East End, to a church in decline and set in an area marked by unemployment and poverty. He and his wife, Hettie, shared a vision for mission.[162]In the light of these and other ventures, Aubrey sounded an optimistic note in 1926: 'I believe we are beginning to wake up to the new day...Our churches are calling for more than able sermons and beautiful services. They want to prove the power of the Gospel of Christ.'[163] As if in confirmation of this assessment, Baptists in Woking told Aubrey in 1927 that their young men held open-air meetings each Sunday. Aubrey was enthusiastic: 'Think of the experience they are gaining...and the strengthening of faith and character that will grow out of this.' Aubrey urged people to get out 'and speak a word for Jesus Christ'.[164] Interdenominational revival meetings were held in London in 1928, at a time when Pentecostal evangelists were making an impact in England. Baptist participants in these revival

*Robert Rowntree Clifford*

160   *BT*, 9 May 1929, p.353.
161   *Baptist Handbook* (1920), p.220. Four of these were in active ministry: William Hardiman in Winstone, Cirencester; S. Silvester in Datchworth, Stevenage; Charles Whatley at Elsted Station, Midhurst; and D. Wilkinson in Birmingham.
162   Johnson, *Encounter in London*, p.67. See also P. Rowntree Clifford, *Venture in Faith: The Story of the West Ham Central Mission* (London: Carey Kingsgate Press, 1950).
163   *BT*, 18 November 1926, p.827.
164   *BT*, 2 June 1927, p.395.

meetings included J.W. Ewing, the Area Superintendent, Tydeman Chilvers, F.B. Meyer, and John Martin from Erith, Kent.[165] With or without gifted evangelists like Douglas Brown, evangelism was a Baptist priority.

## SOCIO-POLITICAL QUESTIONS

Although revival could be conceived in rather narrow terms, there were Baptists who were seeking in the 1920s to understand how the gospel related to the needs of a society that was experiencing massive tensions. The life of the churches could not be dissociated from the life of society. Distress experienced in mining areas sparked off coal disputes, and 1926 saw the General Strike. Along with other denominations, Baptists called for a resumption of negotiations.[166] A group of Baptist ministers who attempted to put together an appropriate statement about the strike, however, abandoned the task.[167] Gyles Williams, North Eastern Superintendent, retired in 1929 feeling deeply the demoralization of the churches, not least those in mining communities. He recognized that decline was often due to economic causes, as well as the failure of ministers and members to revive congregations. In the North there were attempts to establish new congregations on municipal housing estates, for example in Leeds and Sheffield, but often people on these estates who joined the churches set their sights on buying their own houses, which meant they moved away. Building on a discipleship campaign in Yorkshire at the end of the 1920s, J.B. Middlebrook at New North Road, Huddersfield, set out a programme that encouraged Baptists to take commitment more seriously. But as Baptist membership continued to fall, fewer Baptists were confident that their churches could effect political change.[168]

---

165  *BW*, 27 September 1928, p.534. For the Pentecostal contribution, see K. Warrington, ed., *Pentecostal Perspectives* (Carlisle: Paternoster Press, 1998), chapters 1 and 2.
166  Machin, *Churches and Social Issues*, pp.35-40.
167  D.W. Bebbington, 'Baptists and Politics since 1914', in Clements, ed., *Baptists in the Twentieth Century*, p.85.
168  Sellers, ed., *Our Heritage*, pp.88, 91.

There was debate in the 1920s about the extent to which politics had any place in Baptist churches. This represented a striking contrast to earlier Free Church confidence. As a sign of the changed climate, Blomfield insisted that political statements belonged outside the pulpit, since ministers lacked the knowledge to make pronouncements and often their hearers had more expertise. Baptist congregations were, he argued, more sharply divided politically than forty years earlier. The role of ministers in this situation, he suggested, was to be 'character-builders'.[169] On the other hand, H. Ingli James, known later for his ministry at Queen's Road, Coventry, was committed to 'the Gospel and the claims of Labour'.[170] Some politically active Baptists shared in 1924 in COPEC (the Conference on Politics, Economics and Citizenship), which drew together 1,400 people in Birmingham under the overall chairmanship of William Temple, then Bishop of Manchester. Hugh Martin, a Baptist minister who was active in SCM, was chairman of the COPEC executive. J. Ivory Cripps, minister of the Church of the Redeemer, Birmingham, and then West Midland Superintendent, who had been Emmeline Pankhurst's chaplain during her hunger strike in prison in 1912 on behalf of suffragettes, played a full part in COPEC.[171] Mrs Vera Barson, the outspoken wife of the minister at Claremont, Bolton, suggested that COPEC speakers should tour Baptist churches.[172]

Many Baptists, however, rightly felt that the trends in society meant they were having decreasing influence. Jeffrey Cox has argued that by the early 1920s Lambeth Borough Council assumed that it, not the churches or other agencies that had been so important, had responsibility for social services.[173] Commenting on the East Midland Association in the 1920s, F.M.W. Harrison indicates that the social events churches had provided were becoming irrelevant. The Labour Party was attracting idealistic people who had previously looked to the churches.[174] Statements about

---

169  W.E. Blomfield, 'A Few Reflections on My Presidential Experiences', BQ, Vol. 2 (1924-1925), p.53; cf. Bebbington, 'Baptists and Politics since 1914', pp.77-83.
170  For H. Ingli James see Binfield, *Pastors and People*, chapters 11-13.
171  *BT*, 13 March 1925, p.175.
172  Sellers, ed., *Our Heritage*, p.88.
173  Cox, *The English Churches in a Secular Society*, p.273.
174  Harrison, *It All Began Here*, p.117.

declining Sunday school attendance often bemoaned children being at cinemas on Sundays. Gloom was evident, although it could be mixed with hope, as in a report which stated that whereas the pattern was for

churches to become cinemas, in Hayes, Middlesex, a cinema had become a Baptist church.[175] Baptists and other evangelicals supported restrictions on what facilities were open on Sundays, although F.C. Spurr argued against legal prohibitions on what could be done on Sunday.[176] Spurr was well aware of trends in church-going: when a survey in 1926 showed that in poor working-class areas churchgoing had halved since 1902-3, he noted that one church where he used to preach to 1,200 people now had a congregation of fifty.[177] Some argued that society could be changed only through ministry that was socially-orientated, but Arthur Dakin, discussing ministry and social leadership, argued that the minister was primarily a preacher of the Word.[178] The socio-political agenda was much less clear than it had been before.

*Arthur Dakin*

Yet plenty of Baptists were involved in public life. In the legal field, Sir Charles Montague Lush and Sir Clement Meacher Bailhache were well-known judges.[179] For most of the 1920s there were at least ten Baptist MPs. Lloyd George still courted Free Church leaders and was able, as Adrian Hastings puts it, to 'bewitch them again and again with the rhetoric of Welsh Nonconformity'.[180] Speaking to a breakfast meeting in 1922 at 10 Downing Street, at which Charles Brown, Shakespeare, Carlile and Tom Phillips were present, Lloyd George talked about

---

175  *BT*, 22 June 1923, p.453; 22 April 1926, p.303.
176  *BT*, 26 March 1920, p.203.
177  *BW*, 8 March 1926, p.547.
178  *BT*, 23 July 1925, p.52.
179  A.C. Underwood, *A History of the English Baptists* (London: Carey Kingsgate Press, 1947), p.259.
180  Hastings, *A History of English Christianity*, p.120. Hastings (p.24) calls Lloyd George 'extremely untrustworthy, devious, a twister of words'.

religious revival preceding social reform.[181] A year later, Lloyd George spoke at a luncheon at the Cecil Hotel, in connection with support for Spurgeon's College. During the campaign to raise funds for the Baptist Superannuation Fund, Lloyd George addressed a meeting at the City Temple on behalf of the Fund. G. Hay Morgan, KC, a Baptist, an able lawyer, and a former MP, was another speaker. In 1929 a Superannuation Fund dinner was held in a London hotel at which not only Lloyd George spoke but also the Prime Minister, Stanley Baldwin. The host and hostess, H.O. Serpell, a JP and Sheriff of Surrey, and Miss F. Oliver, from Woking Baptist Church, covered the costs. Serpell was a considerable Baptist benefactor. Arthur Newton, a leading layman within the LBA and Union President in 1930, was Chief Commissioner of the Fund and helped with arrangements. This was judged the greatest such event Baptists had ever staged. In his speech Baldwin showed – to Baptist delight - that he was knowledgeable about Baptists, mentioning well-known preachers such as Robert Hall.[182]

A continued feature of Baptist life in the 1920s was the number of prominent lay people who gave their time to Union affairs. Some were rewarded by Union presidency. The contribution of Thomas Penny, JP, a distinguished Taunton citizen, was recognized when he became Union President in 1925. Another significant Baptist layman was C.T. Le Quesne, KC, a barrister of growing influence, whose wife was Eileen Pearce Gould, daughter of Sir Alfred Pearce Gould. Le Quesne was a keen Liberal.[183] A.R. Doggart, JP, managing director of a multiple drapery concern in County Durham and – like many other Baptists

*C.T. Le Quesne*

181   *BT*, 10 March 1922, p.149.
182   *BT*, 31 January 1929, pp.76-80.
183   *BT*, 13 March 1925, p.173.

- a vigorous temperance advocate, served the churches in the Northern Association and was Union President in 1928. Lay people on the Union Council in the 1920s included Richard Jewson, JP, a leading member of St Mary's, Norwich, who had been Lord Mayor of the city. The Council itself had 115 ministerial and 45 lay members, though average attendance was half that figure. The Union had over thirty committees and to a large extent was run by a group that had the time to devote to the many meetings that were convened. Morris West speaks about a 'them' and 'us' feeling in the denomination, and critics spoke of impersonal decision-making procedures.[184] That was not how most hard-working committee members saw it, but Baptists whose social circumstances allowed them to attend regular meetings in London were probably not always aware of the thinking at the grass-roots.

On the wider international front, Baptists were taking an increasing interest in difficulties faced by Baptists in other parts of the world. Relief efforts under the auspices of the Baptist World Alliance extended into Russia, and Rushbrooke paid visits to the Soviet Union and other Eastern European countries. There was great concern about the repression of Baptists and other Christians in Communist Russia: in 1923 John Clifford and F.C. Spurr signed a protest prepared by the Archbishop of Canterbury about attacks on the Orthodox Church.[185] Rushbrooke also invested a great deal of time in the 1920s in seeking freedom of worship for Baptists in Romania. In the 1930s, when almost all the approximately 1,600 Baptists churches in Romania were closed through government decree, Rushbrooke organized an international campaign.[186] Baptist internationalism also enabled Baptists in England to see a bigger picture. English Baptists were delighted to have links with Dr Prochazka, a well-known theological teacher in Prague, who had studied at Regent's Park College, and with Josef Novotny from Prague who was at Midland

184  *BT*, 23 July 1925, p.531; Shepherd, *The Making of a Modern Denomination*, pp.177-8; West, *Baptists Together*, p.47.
185  Bell, *Randall Davidson*, pp.1079-80.
186  Green, *Rushbrooke*, pp.150-3.

College.[187] Another example of internationalism was the Northamptonshire Association's affirmation that 'the idea of a League of Nations is in essential accord with the ideals of the Kingdom of God'. The Association encouraged churches to form branches of the League (which many did), 'so that by faith, study and propaganda they may make effective witness to the ideals of world peace'.[188]

CONCLUSION

The 1920s saw the end of the voyage by J.H. Shakespeare towards an ecumenical haven. Probably the principal rocks on which it foundered were episcopal re-ordination of Baptist ministers and the question of believer's baptism. Baptists wished to stress their own distinctives and also to support their own ministries. Within the denomination, further progress was made in raising money for important Union and BMS Funds. Yet there was a widespread feeling that all was not well. Attention was being given in the 1920s to questions of spiritual vitality and revival. It was reported in 1921 that, generally speaking, prayer meetings were weak in Baptist churches. Indeed there were hundreds of churches where the numbers at the mid-week prayer meeting were 'dismal'. The report suggested that the best prayer meetings were to be found in the 'ultra-evangelical or evangelistic Churches, where a vigorous soul-winning work is always in progress'. By contrast, it continued, 'a largely attended prayer meeting in connection with a broad-evangelical Church is a singularly rare occurrence'.[189] M.E. Aubrey, as successor to Shakespeare, attempted to address issues of renewal. When Shakespeare died in 1928, after a long illness marked by physical incapacity and depression, his legacy was a much more centralized Baptist organization. But was there, as Douglas Brown alleged, a fine programme but little power? Shepherd

187  BT, 13 July 1923, p.497.
188  T.S.H. Elwyn, The Northamptonshire Baptist Association (London: Carey Kingsgate Press, 1964), pp.85-6.
189  BT, 26 August 1921, p.519.

argues that although Shakespeare's achievements were substantial, he did not base them securely on the ecclesiology that lay at the heart of Baptist identity and thus he 'left Baptists without a clear sense of where responsibility for mission and ministry really lay'.[190] The recovery of this sense of spiritual responsibility on the part of the churches was to be a continuing challenge - one to which Aubrey was to give attention in the 1930s.

---

190  Shepherd, *The Making of a Modern Denomination*, p.187.

# Chapter 5
# 'A STIRRING OF DEEPER LIFE'
# (1930-39)

In January 1931, as he looked at the year ahead, M.E. Aubrey wrote that it seemed to him that there was 'a stirring of deeper life in a great many of our churches'. He said that as Union General Secretary he was often described as a 'statesman', but he wished to be known as an evangelist.[1] It was this concern for the spiritual effectiveness of the denomination that would characterize Aubrey's approach to his task in the 1930s. It is difficult, however, to avoid the conclusion that the stirrings failed to revive the denomination as a whole. Despite evangelistic campaigns, the churches were not able to reverse the decline in membership. Internally there were theological imbroglios over issues such as the doctrine of the atonement and externally there were wider social changes militating against Baptist growth. Yet obstacles served in some cases to stimulate desire for renewal. In 1936 Henry Townsend, President of Manchester College, speaking as incoming President of the Union, said that he was yearning that 'the Church we love may be baptised of the Holy Spirit', and he believed that a 'Forward Movement' which had been launched in the denomination was genuinely 'of God'.[2] As part of his presidential comment on the state of the churches, Townsend made the provocative statement that evangelical experience had been largely absent from modern evangelical Christianity.[3] Such observations by a prominent Baptist thinker highlighted weaknesses within and challenges for the denomination, but the call to address these was itself evidence of the spiritual stirring in the 1930s that Aubrey discerned.

---

1    *BT*, 1 January 1931, p.3.
2    *BT*, 16 April 1936, p.294.
3    *CW*, 30 April 1936, p.7.

## THE DISCIPLESHIP CAMPAIGN

After five years in office, Aubrey launched his first major denominational campaign. He laid the groundwork carefully and in 1931 the Union Council endorsed what was envisaged as a three-year period of co-ordinated activity under the title of 'The Discipleship Campaign'. The circumstances seemed to be right. Although Baptist church membership was in overall decline, the report in 1931 on the number of baptisms showed that there had been an increase of 917 on the previous year, taking the figure to 11,297.[4] It appeared that there were significant numbers of people coming to personal faith. The challenge for some Baptist churches was to retain people. In some parts of the country Baptist witness had not kept up with shifts in population. The *Baptist Times* noted in July 1931, as it covered plans for evangelism, that over 200,000 people lived in London's Shoreditch and Bethnal Green and yet there was only one Baptist church, the Shoreditch Tabernacle, which was finding it hard to continue its work. Ernest O. Clifford and his wife had moved there from the West Ham Central Mission in 1929, and the Shoreditch church was attracting increasing numbers of people, but the building needed a huge injection of cash to put it right.[5] This was an enormously challenging situation which had parallels in many places.

Because the needs across the country were varied, Aubrey emphasized that the momentum for the Discipleship Campaign should come from local Associations. Whereas Shakespeare had drawn from the example of the seventeenth-century Baptist Messengers to argue for superintendents, Aubrey utilized the same history to press for regionalized evangelistic strategies. He suggested that each Association should appoint 'Campaign Messengers' to liaise with the Union. Some Associations acted quickly, appointing a committee to initiate evangelistic activities. In Yorkshire, for example, there was considerable enthusiasm, and J.B. Middlebrook, pastor of New North Road Baptist Church, Huddersfield (later Home Secretary of the BMS), was the

---

4    *BT*, 8 January 1931, p.23.
5    *BT*, 23 July 1931, pp.517-20.

Yorkshire Messenger.[6] Others Associations were hesitant. One unnamed Association asked a Council member in December 1931 about the job of Messenger. The member replied that he was 'dreadfully foggy' but would discuss it. Aubrey, hearing about this, wrote scathingly: 'Just think of it: here is "a member of the Council" ready even to discuss doing something!' Aubrey said people should not wait for the Union. 'Our grandfathers', he commented acidly, 'didn't wait to be told by the Baptist Union what to do.' He even spoke of the danger of leaning on headquarters. The contrast with Shakespeare's philosophy was considerable. The chairman of the Campaign Committee, Alfred Ellis, JP, from Amersham, who was an able solicitor (Ellis & Fairbairn, the Union's solicitors) and an active lay preacher, insisted that there was no rigid Campaign method.[7]

In February 1932, a few weeks after this incident, it was announced that the Messengers would be meeting at Baptist Church House. Aubrey had still not recovered from the remark about 'fogginess', but he was optimistic about the Campaign. He wrote in the *Baptist Times*: 'There is a good deal of fogginess about. That is the worst of fires – they so often begin with a lot of smoke, especially if the wood has got a bit damp! But let us cheer up – we shall by God's grace, get things blazing merrily before long.'[8] As the Campaign became better known, Aubrey received a great deal of feedback from the Associations. He considered that much of the advice offered was 'diametrically conflicting', with some people, for instance, advocating personal evangelism, and others organized distribution of literature. Many of these issues Aubrey handed back to the Associations and encouraged them to bring together men and women with leadership ability and evangelistic fervour. Aubrey's view was that each Association should appoint two Messengers, a man and a woman, to encourage people to pray, discuss, and plan new initiatives.[9] Middlebrook spoke at the first meeting of Messengers, on 10 March

6    Personal memoir by J.B. Middlebrook: Regent's Park College Oxford, Angus Library, Baptist Missionary Society Archive, file H 94-95/4.
7    *BT*, 31 December 1931, p. 340; 7 January 1932, pp. 3, 6.
8    *BT*, 11 February 1932, p. 87.
9    *BT*, 28 July 1932, p.55.

1932, about what was being done in Yorkshire. Three main aspects were to emerge and were to characterize the Campaign.

In the first place, there was considerable stress on the role of lay people. In January 1933 Alfred Ellis, as Campaign chairman (and in 1932-33 Union President), spoke of the way in which lay people could be 'soul winners'. He also referred to the crucial role of lay preachers in the Baptist denomination, pointing out that they had the spiritual oversight of at least 40,000 people week by week.[10] At a meeting of the Discipleship Campaign committee a month later George Evans, minister of Oxford Road Baptist Church, Manchester, argued for a central place in the Campaign for young men and women working in business. He also urged that Baptist churches, as part of their discipleship, should foster more intimate fellowship. 'The call', said Evans, using language that was drawn from movements of renewal such as Keswick, 'should not only be to surrender to Christ, but to surrender to the Holy Spirit.' At this meeting the use of personal testimony by lay people was considered, although two of those present, Gilbert Laws and Douglas Brown, both very experienced in evangelism, indicated that there were dangers in any standardized approach.[11] There was, however, unanimity about the need for full lay participation in the Campaign.

A second emphasis was on the importance of team-work, illustrated most dramatically by developments in Essex.[12] The Essex Baptist Association had been planning to implement the work of the Discipleship Campaign but there was a degree of apathy until Hugh Redwood, of the *News Chronicle*, spoke at a meeting at Dagenham Baptist Church chaired by Hugh McCullough, the church's minister. Stanley A. Baker, minister at Tabernacle Baptist Church, Grays, was also present. The idea emerged that a number of ministers could work together as an evangelistic team in the Essex churches. After months of prayer and thought, four young

---

10   *BT*, 5 January 1933, p.9.
11   Minutes of the Baptist Union Discipleship Campaign Committee, 13 February 1933.
12   See REKABAS, *An Adventure for God* (London: Kingsgate Press, 1934); Doris Witard, *Bibles in Barrels: A History of Essex Baptists* (Southend-on-Sea: Essex Baptist Association, 1962), chapter 22.

ministers, McCullough, Baker, Fred G. Missen from Burnham-on-Crouch, and George Banks from Rayleigh, met in August 1933 to consider such a commitment. Within days of agreeing to move forward, the minister at Laindon, Essex, Tom Shepherd, joined them. The ministers in pastoral charge asked their churches for permission to spend a week each month, from Monday to Saturday, in wider evangelism. During these weeks there were mornings of prayer, Bible study and self-examination. Afternoons were for house visitation or meetings in the local churches that invited the team. Evening meetings were evangelistic and also encouraged believers to a deeper commitment to Christ. The 'follow up' was the local church's responsibility. Invitations came from many churches.

The 'Essex Five', as they were called, constituted a diverse team. The leader was McCullough, who was born in Ireland, was brought up in Barnardo's Homes in the East End of London, and had ministered at Rayleigh, Dagenham, and later Clacton-on-Sea. Stanley Baker was another product of the East End. He was listening to Douglas Brown in Bloomsbury Central Baptist Church after the First World War when Brown pointed to him in the gallery: 'You, young man! What God wants from you is a little bit of movement!' This brought Baker into Baptist ministry. He became the secretary of 'the Five'. Baker's later ministries were varied and included pastorates in Norwich (where he was involved in 'Christian Commando' campaigns), Birmingham, Cambridge (Zion) and Wisbech. He also became Secretary for the Movement for World Evangelisation and travelled widely as Christian Endeavour President in 1949-50. Fred Missen had been in business at Woking, and after his involvement with the Essex Five had a successful ministry at the Central Baptist Church, Walthamstow, before moving to Teddington, Middlesex. George Banks, the only unaccredited minister among the Five, was a Bible teacher and pianist. The group's members, therefore, brought a variety of abilities and experience to their evangelism.

With encouragement from Aubrey, Messengers shared their experiences at regular meetings in London. In January 1934, Hugh McCulloch reported on what was being experienced in Essex Baptist churches through his team. He considered that what had happened in some cases was 'nothing less than revival', with as many as thirty or forty people coming to the enquiry rooms at the end of meetings. Ministers had also been encouraged. 'In three instances', McCulloch related, 'ministers had become so depressed that they had decided to give up their Churches', but he was delighted to say that they were now going on with their work. Nor was the impact due only to preaching by the team of ministers. Often church members spoke at evangelistic meetings, usually on the theme of 'What Jesus Christ means to me', such testimonies being restricted to two or three minutes. Methods used in Essex showed that both ministerial and lay teams could function effectively. Within the Dagenham church, McCulloch had brought together six to eight young men as a team. Similarly, R. Rowntree Clifford, from the West Ham Central Mission, spoke to the Messengers about his own work, which saw over sixty young people meeting regularly for special prayer, individuals 'in their teens' giving short addresses, and people regularly coming forward to give themselves to Christ.[13]

The final element in the Campaign was the contribution of the Union leadership. Aubrey knew that the 'forward movement' he had promoted did not resemble a Fund, which could be measured. In 1933 he wrote: 'We have a stiff job before us. It is not like raising money. It is raising the temperature. A crust, like ice, seems to have formed in some places over the life of our Churches…That must be broken.'[14] Aubrey's strategy was to keep the Campaign at the forefront of the minds of Council members and of those at Assemblies. He urged the setting up of study circles, the development of teams, and the importance of having congregations that welcomed outsiders. Douglas Brown, who was strongly supportive of the Campaign, suggested in 1934 that the responsibilities of church membership needed to be better understood by

---

13    Minutes of the Baptist Union Discipleship Campaign – Meeting of Messengers, 25 January 1934.

14    *BT*, 2 February 1933, p.75.

Baptists.[15] Partly in response to this concern, Arnold Clark, a businessman (a glass merchant) who became treasurer of the Union that year, wrote three booklets, *Why should a fellow be baptised?*, *Should a fellow pray?*, and *Should a fellow follow Christ?* Perhaps as a counter to the stress on 'fellows', there was space at the 1934 Assembly for women to speak. Aubrey, fired by the Essex Five, arranged for six ten-minute contributions at the Assembly on aspects of practical evangelism. McCullough and Sister Margaret Evans, a deaconess at Dagenham, were among the speakers. Planting new churches was discussed, and this was supported by Arthur Dakin of Bristol.[16] Evangelism was to the fore.

*Arnold Clark*

## THE FUNDAMENTALS AGAIN

The campaign also, however, coincided with theological tensions within the denomination. The Fundamentalist lobby had been quiet during the first few years of Aubrey's secretaryship; attacks launched against the Union in the first half of the 1920s had spent their force. In 1925, the year of the Fundamentalist-generated 'Monkey Trial' in Dayton, Tennessee, USA (about teaching evolution in schools), the *Baptist Times* commented that the view that evolution was God's method of creation was held by many younger Baptist ministers.[17] It seemed in 1930 that a calmer decade for English Baptists might lie ahead. Storm clouds, however, were gathering. The superintendents noted in June 1929 that W.E. Dalling, a non-collegiate probationer at Stanningley, Yorkshire, had failed to follow the advice of A.C. Underwood (recently appointed to the principalship at Rawdon College) concerning his probationary reading. Dalling was due to complete the final Baptist Union

---

15  *BT*, 15 March 1934, p.180.
16  *BT*, 26 April 1934, pp.296, 303; 17 May 1934, p.369.
17  *BT*, 13 August 1925, pp.575, 577.

Examination.[18] The problem was that he refused to read some of Underwood's recommended books. Underwood demanded academic rigour; his own education had been at London and Oxford Universities. Although Dalling had also had a university education – at Fitzwilliam Hall, Cambridge – he now, apparently, restricted himself to books matching his convictions. He pronounced in March 1930 with reference to the Union: 'I feel it to be the distinct leading of the Holy Spirit to cut myself off from such a Christ-dishonouring Union.' His resignation was accepted.[19]

The case became something of a *cause célèbre*. The Ministerial Recognition Committee, meeting on 17 November 1930, received a letter of protest about Dalling's treatment from a group of six ministers and lay leaders including Owen Owen, pastor of South Street Baptist Church, Exeter (the largest Baptist cause in Exeter), and Benjamin I. Greenwood of Sevenoaks, a Baptist deacon and company director. The letter spoke about books being recommended to probationers that were 'subversive' of evangelical Christianity. The Council replied that in their desire to assist those preparing for ministry they had always endeavoured 'to help them to be faithful, efficient and evangelical pastors and preachers' and argued that the books prescribed were by evangelical scholars, although they differed from each other on certain issues. The Council appealed to the signatories to support freedom of thought, 'subject only to complete loyalty to Christ as Lord and Saviour, which is the proud tradition and trust of the Baptist denomination'.[20] The reply did not satisfy Dalling or his supporters, and in February 1931 Dalling launched a bitter attack in the *Baptist Times* on 'the Modernist propaganda which proceeds and grows in Baptist Colleges'. He saw the same modernism in the Union Council and the Ministerial Recognition Committee.[21]

18   Minutes of a Baptist Union Ministerial Recognition Special Committee, 18 June 1929; Minutes of the Baptist Union Council, 19 November 1929.
19   Minutes of the Baptist Union Council, 11 and 12 March 1930; *Bible League Quarterly*, July-September 1930, p.127.
20   Minutes of the Baptist Union Ministerial Recognition Committee, 17 November 1930.
21   *BT*, 5 February 1931, p. 92.

Owen Owen, the prime mover in the protest about Dalling, who had been deeply affected by the Welsh Revival three decades before, suggested that Dalling was being penalized for views 'which are those that our denomination has held throughout the past centuries'. A Union committee was set up to consider this, and, clearly keen to find an accommodation, it said that Dalling could re-apply for accreditation. The committee noted in March 1931 that he had done two years of his reading (and had, therefore, only one to do), and said that a new supervisor could be appointed. But by this time the dispute was beyond resolution. Polygon Baptist Church, Southampton, where Dalling was now minister, had sent out circular letters attacking the Union. Polygon's actions were deprecated by the local district of Baptist churches.[22] At a meeting of the Council in November 1931, J.M. Soper, a layman who had defended Dalling but also unsuccessfully urged Dalling to accept the overtures of the Council, suggested the Council should take responsibility for books recommended to probationers. Percy Evans, Principal of Spurgeon's College, did not agree. Evans noted that Wheeler Robinson's scholarly book, *The Religious Ideas of the Old Testament*, had been criticized, but it was a book he recommended to students at Spurgeon's. Council members took the view that the choice of probationary reading was not a task for them.[23]

Another issue was ticking away like a time bomb ready to explode. T.R. Glover was asked to prepare notes on basic aspects of the Christian faith for Discipleship Campaign study groups. In 1931 Glover produced *Fundamentals*, a booklet covering Sin, Punishment, Repentance, Conversion, Salvation, Atonement, Justification and Sanctification. On the atonement, Glover said that the term had no standard meaning in the

---

22   *BT*, 5 February 1931, p.92; 19 March 1931, p.196; Minutes of a Baptist Union
     Council Sub-Committee, 24 March 1931.
23   Minutes of the Baptist Union Council, 24 and 25 November 1931.

Bible and in the popular sense was hardly found
in the New Testament.[24] By February 1932,
5,000 copies of *Fundamentals* had been printed.
What Glover wrote was, however, seen by some
as an attack on traditional doctrine. The pastor
of the Metropolitan Tabernacle, Tydeman
Chilvers, stated in *The Sword and the Trowel* in
February 1932 that he was thankful the
Tabernacle was not in the Union. He wanted
Baptists to reject Glover's publication.[25]
Chilvers continued a month later: 'The old and

*T.R. Glover*

precious idea of a personal, vicarious, substitutional sacrifice for sin, and
Christ bearing sin's penalty is scouted.' *Fundamentals*, he asserted, had
not enough gospel to save one soul, far less inspire a campaign among
'our great and beloved Baptist denomination'.[26] Another publication, the
*Fundamentalist*, sought to put pressure on Percy Evans to separate
himself from the 'soul-destroying errors rampant within the Baptist
Union'. One anonymous Baptist minister writing in the *Fundamentalist*
asserted that the Union was composed of 'pseudo-Baptists' and was
almost a synonym for infidelity.[27]

Such incidents were irritants, but by the time of the Council meeting
on 7 March 1932 the issue looked as if it could become serious. A
proposal was made to the Council by Thomas Greenwood, Chairman of
the Spurgeon's College Council, that Glover's booklet be withdrawn.
Greenwood, who had previously written a forceful yet eirenic letter to the
Discipleship Campaign committee about the issue, said that he honoured
Glover for his work but that the booklet was 'an attack on one of the
truths which was most precious to a large section of the Union'. Aubrey
was torn. His private letters before the Council show his appreciation of

---

24    T.R. Glover, *Fundamentals* (London: Baptist Union, 1931), p.23. For the
       controversy, see Clements, *Lovers of Discord*, pp.120-4.

25    *The Sword and the Trowel*, February 1932, pp.31-2.

26    *The Sword and the Trowel*, March 1932, p.68.

27    *Fundamentalist*, November 1931, p.260; January 1932, p.19; March 1932, p.53;
       April 1932, p.81; May 1932, p.100.

Glover, who had 'plenty of friends on the Committee and the Council', and also of Greenwood, whom he saw as worth more than 'lots of your modernists'.[28] Although Glover had previously refused to withdraw the booklet, at the Council he offered to do so. However, a majority of the Council did not want this to happen. A proposal was made by F.J. Walkey, Central Area Superintendent, that a second pamphlet be produced, presenting other views. An adjournment was called and Alfred Ellis consulted with Greenwood and Percy Evans. Ellis then stated that if Greenwood withdrew his motion he would propose that another pamphlet be issued. This was done with Glover's support. Glover added personal testimony to Christ as Saviour and Lord, telling the Council he believed the mystery of the cross was unfathomable but that all could say: 'He loved me and gave Himself for me.'[29]

A crisis seemed to have been averted. The Council supported the suggestion that Percy Evans should write the further pamphlet, and Evans was open to this.[30] He later wrote *The Saving Work of Christ*. But Glover had an unpleasant surprise in store. On 11 March 1932 *The Times* carried an article by him saying that the 1925 Dayton court case had no parallel in Britain because openness to modern thought had been secured through the Union's stand against Spurgeon during the Downgrade Controversy. Glover contrasted the higher level of education of younger Free Church ministers with Spurgeon's 'rather amateur' training of ministers.[31] Aubrey was appalled. He immediately wrote to *The Times* dissociating the Union from the article. Percy Evans telephoned Aubrey to say that Glover's article had 'plunged him in the depths'. An unusually forceful Aubrey told Glover about 'the half warmed ineffective bunch that too many of our Colleges have been turning out in this past generation'. The academics that Glover lauded had, according to Aubrey, little of the spiritual passion that 'sustained Spurgeon's men through long, long

28  W.M.S. West, 'The Reverend Secretary Aubrey: Part 1', *BQ*, Vol.34, No.5 (1992), pp.201-2. Thomas Greenwood was the brother of Benjamin Greenwood.
29  Minutes of the Baptist Union Council, 7-9 March 1932; *BT*, 10 March 1932, p.158; 17 March 1932, p.175.
30  Minutes of Baptist Union Council, 7-9 March 1932.
31  *The Times*, 11 March 1932, p.8; *BT*, 17 March 1932, p.180.

ministries – Wilson fifty-four years, Cuff a lifetime in Shoreditch, Carlile thirty odd years at Folkestone, Douglas Brown twenty-five years at Balham.'[32] Subsequently Upper Tooting, a 400-member church where Henry Oakley was minister, left the Union in protest at its doctrinal weakness,[33] but Aubrey's stance seemed to satisfy the constituency.

In this period Congregationalism was experiencing severe theological tensions, and these affected Baptists. In 1931 J.S. Whale, of Mansfield College, opposed the theology of Frank Lenwood, previously Foreign Secretary of the London Missionary Society. Lenwood stated in his *Jesus - Lord or Leader?* (1930) that Christ was divine 'only in the sense in which it is possible to use the word of any other good and great man'.[34] The year 1931 saw Nathaniel Micklem begin a powerful column in the *British Weekly* which gained him a reputation as an 'arch-anti-liberal'.[35] His position as Principal of Mansfield College was to ensure great influence and he had a powerful ally in B.L. Manning, the Cambridge historian.[36] Some liberal Congregationalists, including Lenwood, produced in 1933 a 'Re-statement of Christian thought', which for Micklem bore no clear relationship to Christian faith.[37] In 1934-35 there was much concern at the Baptist Union Council that E.J. Roberts, a minister influenced by Lenwood, could not subscribe to the wording in the Union's Declaration of Principle regarding the deity of Christ. Scottish Baptists had voted in 1933 to remove Roberts (at that time a minister in Scotland) from their accredited list. Roberts returned to

---

32   M.E. Aubrey to T.R. Glover, 13 March 1932, cited by West, 'The Reverend Secretrary Aubrey: Part 1', p.203.

33   Henry Oakley, who had been trained at Regent's Park College, said that his deacons wanted to leave the Union: Minutes of the Baptist Union Council, 22 and 23 November 1932.

34   J.S. Whale, 'Jesus - Lord or Leader?', *Congregational Quarterly*, Vol.8, No.1 (1930), pp. 54-7; F. Lenwood, *Jesus - Lord or Leader?* (London: Constable & Co., 1930), p.4; B. Stanley, 'Manliness and Mission: Frank Lenwood and the London Missionary Society', *The Journal of the United Reformed Church History Society*, Vol.5, No.8 (1996).

35   N. Micklem, *The Religion of a Sceptic* (London: Acton Society Trust, 1976), p.53.

36   I.M. Randall, *Evangelical Experiences: A Study of the Spirituality of English Evangelicalism, 1918-1939* (Carlisle: Paternoster Press, 1999), chapter 7.

37   *CW*, 16 February 1933, p.9.

ministry in England, at Tottlebank Baptist Church in the Lake District, and asked the Council, which was considering whether his name should be deleted from the accredited list of ministers, to accept his personal affirmation that Jesus was the Son of God. A number of exchanges took place and in March 1935 the Council agreed that Roberts could remain on the accredited list.[38] The Union was concerned to uphold Christological fundamentals.

UNITY AND IDENTITY

If under Aubrey's leadership evangelism was a priority, there was rather less emphasis on ecumenical endeavour. Following the Lambeth Conference of 1930, Cosmo Lang, the Archbishop of Canterbury, issued an invitation to the Federal Council of the Evangelical Free Churches to resume conversations about unity. Seymour Price, a leading London Baptist layman (later director of the Temperance Permanent Building Society), was adamant that organic unity was not practical.[39] Despite such doubts, eighteen representatives were put forward by the Free Churches, the Baptists being Aubrey, Gilbert Laws and Hugh Martin. Both Aubrey and Laws, minister of St Mary's Church, Norwich, and Union President in 1934, were cautious, whereas Hugh Martin was an enthusiast for ecumenism. Martin had worked for the Student Christian Movement since 1917 and was responsible for its publication work. He was from 1929 the editor of the SCM Press and Secretary from 1933 of Friends of Reunion.[40] In 1932 a Free Church Unity Group, which included Charles Brown and other leading Baptists, published a leaflet entitled *A Plea for Unity*; responses to this showed once again the different opinions within

---

38    *CW*, 2 November 1933, p.13; Minutes of the Baptist Union Council, 20 and 21 November 1934; 5 and 6 March 1935; K. Roxburgh, 'Eric Roberts and orthodoxy among Scottish Baptists', *BQ*, Vol.34, No.2 (2001), p.90; Sparkes, *The Constitutions of the Baptist Union of Great Britain*, pp.37-8.
39    S.J. Price, 'Laymen and Reunion', *BQ*, Vol.5 (1931), p.299.
40    A.R. Cross, 'Dr Hugh Martin: Publisher and Writer, Part 1', *BQ*, Vol.37, No.1 (1997), pp.33-49; A.R. Cross, 'Revd Dr Hugh Martin: Ecumenist, Part 2', *BQ*, Vol.37, No.2 (1997), pp.71-86. For the SCM see T. Tatlow, *The Story of the Student Christian Movement* (London: SCM Press, 1933).

Baptist life.[41] In November 1932 there were discussions regarding unity between Congregationalists, Baptists and Presbyterians and a 'Special Committee' of the Baptist Union was set up. Aubrey commented guardedly: 'I believe every good Baptist will welcome unity if it can be shown to be possible without sacrifice of any principle which we regard as essential to the presentation of the Gospel of Christ in its fulness.'[42]

The next two years saw continuing debates about unity. Gilbert Laws delivered a paper to the Baptist World Congress in Berlin in 1934 on 'Baptists and Christian Unity: What is Possible?' Baptist beliefs about believer's baptism and infant baptism meant he could not see possibilities for union with paedobaptists. Instead he encouraged Baptists to draw closer to one another.[43] The *Baptist Times* fostered on-going discussion

*The BWA Congress Hall in Berlin, 1934*

of this address. Robert Wilson Black, from Twynholm Baptist Church, Fulham, supported Laws. The Twynholm church had been in membership with the Churches of Christ, a denomination which practised believer's baptism, and Twynholm had joined the Baptist Union as recently as 1931. Black, who had become very wealthy through his estate agency business, was Twynholm's leading personality.[44] Any sacrifice of Baptist principles, Black argued, was a disaster. By contrast, Hugh Martin suggested that denominational divisions hindered the gospel.[45] More practically, Edith Laws, as

---

41   A.R. Cross, *Baptism and the Baptists* (2000), pp.71-2.
42   *BT*, 10 November 1932, p.775.
43   J.H. Rushbrooke, ed., *Fifth Baptist World Congress, Berlin, 1934* (London: BWA, 1934), pp.172-4.
44   For Black, see H. Townsend, *Robert Wilson Black* (London: Carey Kingsgate Press, 1954).
45   *BT*, 23 August 1934, p.601; 30 August 1934, p.612; 6 September 1934, p 628.

President of the Free
Church Council in Norwich,
commented in 1934 that
among young people
denominational convictions
could be combined with
appreciation of different
traditions.[46] Also in 1934,
Martin edited *Towards
Reunion*, published by
SCM, in which contributors
spoke about their

*British Group in Berlin, 1934*

denominations. The Baptist position was outlined by F. Townley Lord,
from 1930 the minister of Bloomsbury. He noted that although infant
baptism was unacceptable to Baptists, infant dedication services were part
of Baptist practice.[47]

In a number of different ways Baptists in the 1930s wrestled with
theological issues of unity and Baptist identity. The influential Union
Special Committee, under the chairmanship of C.T. Le Quesne, spent five
years working on issues connected with possible union with
Congregationalists and Presbyterians. The denomination's theologians
were enlisted to assist in this task. For example, Wheeler Robinson and
Percy Evans studied questions of baptism in relation to Congregational
and Presbyterian practice and produced a detailed joint memorandum.[48]
There were also extensive discussions in the Special Committee of the
practices of open membership, closed membership and closed
communion. Further contributions were made by the historian, W.T.
Whitley, and by A.C. Underwood, Principal of Rawdon College, who
were both involved in theological work associated with the Faith and
Order movement. This movement would sponsor a crucial Conference in
1937 and would pave the way for the establishment of the World Council

---

46  *BT*, 27 September 1934, p.680.
47  F.T. Lord, 'The Baptists', in Hugh Martin, ed., *Towards Reunion: What the Churches Stand For* (London: SCM Press, 1934), pp.25-8.
48  Minutes of a Baptist Union Enquiry, 11 July 1933.

of Churches (WCC).[49] Underwood argued that Baptists were 'the only Christian body which has preserved the full sacramental value of Christian baptism'.[50] The Congregationalist Nathaniel Micklem, however, challenged Baptist theology by demanding whether Baptists believed baptism was a sacrament.[51] Henry Townsend replied angrily to Micklem, accusing him of mischief-making, and he insisted on the view that there was a 'further access of Divine grace' in baptism.[52]

This bad-tempered exchange was in contrast to the normally harmonious relationships between Congregationalists and Baptists, who saw themselves as sharing much in common. A factor contributing to theological tensions may well have been the publication in 1937 of the Report of the Union's Special Committee that had been working, over the

course of five years, on the question of union with the Congregationalists and Presbyterians. The considered view of the committee was that believer's baptism, 'whether it be called an ordinance or a sacrament', was 'of the most serious import'. It was agreed that Baptists could not recognize infant baptism as valid baptism and that any attempt to force the Union to do so would be divisive. At the Council in November 1937 there was a recommendation that Associations consider this report. Wilson Black, however, who had been upset by a recent *Plan for Unity* which Martin and some other Baptists had signed, asked

*R. Wilson Black*

for an amendment to say that Baptists were in favour of co-operation with Congregationalists and Presbyterians but that union would entail

---

49    W.T. Whitley, 'Lambeth and Murren', *BQ*, Vol.5 (1930), p.149; Payne, *The Baptist Union*, pp.197-8.

50    A.C. Underwood, 'Views of Modern Churches (g) Baptist (2)', in R. Dunkerley, ed., *The Ministry and the Sacraments* (London: SCM Press, 1937), pp.225-6; R.L. Child, 'The Ministry and the Sacraments': A Free Church Point of View', *BQ*, Vol.9, No.3 (1938), pp.132-8.

51    *BW*, 30 December 1937, p.255.

52    *BW*, 13 January 1938, p.291; *BT*, 20 January 1938, p.51.

disloyalty to Christ. The lack of support for the ecumenical perspective of Martin was seen by the fact that Wilson Black's amendment was carried by a majority at the Council, although it was then withdrawn in favour of a milder statement that organic church unity was impracticable 'at the present'. This was carried unanimously.[53]

In the meantime, the wider Anglican-Free Church conversations had carried on throughout most of the 1930s and in 1938 an *Outline of a Reunion Scheme* was produced.[54] Even before this was released, J.C. Carlile said there were – entirely predictable – questions and problems in it for Baptists, notably baptism, episcopacy and church and state. Wilson Black, not surprisingly, was outspoken in his opposition: 'The Report', he stated, 'is a radical and deplorable contradiction of Baptist principles, and I cannot understand how it could have received the approval of any Baptists. I can conceive of nothing more calculated to injure the Forward Movement and the establishment of new Baptist churches.'[55] The names of Aubrey, Charles Brown and Gilbert Laws were listed as assenting to the *Outline* but they distanced themselves from it. Only Hugh Martin spoke in favour. During discussions at the Union Council in March 1938, and in the *Baptist Times*, Gilbert Laws pressed for a statement that organic unity with the Church of England was impossible, since Baptists objected to episcopacy, infant baptism, the authority of tradition, and a state church. Laws was strongly supported by Black. Henry Townsend was also hostile to the *Outline*. A resolution setting out Laws' position was carried at the Council with only four votes against, and an official *Reply* from the Council in November 1938 confirmed that for Baptists the *Outline* did not form a basis for organic union.[56] It seemed that in

---

53  Report by the Special Committee Appointed by the Baptist Union Council on the Question of Union between Baptists, Congregationalists and Presbyterians, 1937; Minutes of the Baptist Union Council, 16 and 17 November 1937; Cross, *Baptism and the Baptists*, pp.79-84.

54  See G.K.A. Bell, *Documents on Christian Unity, 1920-4* (London: Oxford University Press, 1924), pp.71-101.

55  *BT*, 27 January 1938, pp.62, 71-2.

56  Minutes of the Baptist Union Council, 8 and 9 March 1938; *BT*, 3 February 1938, p.83; 17 February 1938, p.124; Cross, *Baptist and the Baptists*, pp.133-4; Townsend, *Robert Wilson Black*, pp.103-8; Payne, *The Fellowship of Believers*,

eighteen years of discussion with the Church of England about unity relatively little had been achieved.

During this period, Baptists in England were also thinking about greater internal unity – between the Union and the BMS. In 1936 it seemed likely that the Government would seek to purchase the BMS Mission House in Furnival Street and the leadership of the BMS raised at the Council the possibility of a joint building for the BMS and the Union. There were protracted discussions during 1936 and 1937.[57] Wilson Black pressed for a leasehold site in Russell Square to be obtained. Among those opposed to this idea were Arnold Clark, Union treasurer, Gordon Fairbairn, the new legal adviser, H.L. Taylor, BMS treasurer and Union President for 1937-38 (and a director of eight companies, mostly in the paper industry), and Aubrey himself. When the Council voted on 8 March 1938 in favour of the proposed scheme (64 votes to 28), however, Aubrey indicated he would support it.[58] But when it came to the Assembly on 25 April, the opposition triumphed. Government proposals to buy Furnival Street had been abandoned, and there was unease about the Union taking a leasehold property. J.B. Middlebrook described the Assembly session as dreadful, with catcalls greeting speakers. The proposal was overwhelmingly defeated. Wilson Black felt he had lacked support from Aubrey, and he tendered his resignation from the Council.[59] Through the mediation of Arthur Dakin, Black stayed on the Council, but Middlebrook considered that Aubrey was so badly shaken that his leadership never recovered its poise.[60]

pp.148-9; Jordan, *Free Church Unity*, pp.175-9.

57  See Minutes of the Baptist Union Council, 17 and 18 November 1936; 16 and 17 November 1937; W.M.S. West, 'The Reverend Secretary Aubrey: Part II', *BQ*, Vol.34, No.6 (1992), pp.263-81; Sparkes, *The Offices of the Baptist Union*, chapter 3.

58  Minutes of the Baptist Union Council, 8 and 9 March 1938; West, 'The Reverend Secretary Aubrey: Part II', pp.268-70.

59  Minutes of the Baptist Union Council, 28 April 1938.

60  Personal Memoir by J.B. Middlebrook.

## FULL SURRENDER

Although efforts to achieve unity institutionally seemed to be marked by failure, whether this was unity between Baptists and others or even between Baptist organizations, there were movements in the 1930s which eschewed institutional unity and which instead achieved success in drawing Christians together in informal ways. The best known of these was Keswick, where a Baptist, W. Graham Scroggie, was the leading speaker. In 1938 Scroggie commenced ministry at the Metropolitan Tabernacle, a church not associated with Keswick's holiness message, and he paved the way with a series of messages on the deepening of the spiritual life.[61] Another popular Baptist speaker at Keswick in the 1930s was John MacBeath, a lecturer at the Scottish Baptist College and later minister of Haven Green, Ealing. When MacBeath's Keswick addresses were published, Aubrey commended their coverage of the heights and depths of Christian experience and service.[62] But in a number of Baptist churches in the early 1930s more attention was given to Frank Buchman's Oxford Group, which drew ideas from Keswick, than to Keswick itself.[63] In 1933 F.C. Spurr, perhaps still smarting from vilification he had received in the 1920s from Keswick's Fundamentalist supporters, was glad to report that an Oxford Group event he had attended was unlike Keswick. He appreciated the testimonies from engineers, bank managers, financiers and teachers, and hoped people affected by the Group would not become Fundamentalist.[64] There was never any possibility that this would happen. The Group consciously embraced and reflected a new cultural mood.[65]

People associated with the Group met in small local groups, and much of the impact was on the laity. F.C. Bryan of the Downs Chapel,

---

61  *Life of Faith*, 29 September 1937, p.1020; *The Sword and the Trowel*, November 1937, p.333.
62  *BT*, 20 October 1932, p.719.
63  See I.M. Randall, '"Arresting People for Christ": Baptists and the Oxford Group in the 1930s', *BQ*, Vol.38, No.1 (1999).
64  *CW*, 13 July 1933, p.5; 20 July 1933, p.13.
65  For more on this see Bebbington, *Evangelicalism in Modern Britain*, pp.233-42.

Clapton, described in 1931 examples of what Buchman called 'life-changing'. Bryan wrote in the *Baptist Times*: 'A front-rank surgeon addicted to drink, a young teacher of philosophy lost in a maze of speculation, a churchgoing businessman whose religion was formal and frigid, a minister whose ministry lacked converting power – all delivered by Christ and made powerful, life-changing witnesses to Him!' A 'Baptist Reader', describing Group meetings, commented: 'It seems to me that the movement introduces a Free Church atmosphere to the Established Church, but perhaps it would do more good in the Free Churches if we could recapture the "meeting-house" atmosphere for ourselves.'[66] A member of St Andrew's Street Baptist Church, Cambridge, Ada Brooks, after two years of Group meetings, gained deeper knowledge of the Bible and hoped to help the Discipleship Campaign.[67] H.C. Kemp, a Leeds University graduate who trained at Rawdon College and became minister of Pellon Baptist Church, Halifax, spoke about a young man in his church who had been a Sunday school teacher but had drifted away when - like many in the north of England - he became unemployed. Through the Group he found renewed faith and broke off his engagement to a non-Christian girl. It was a classic tale of restoration. Kemp suggested that those who feared such experiences could hinder the Discipleship Campaign.[68]

Those preparing for ministry also felt the challenge of the Group. Bill Jaeger, a Baptist who became prominent in Oxford Group outreach to the East End of London in the 1930s, exemplified the way in which the Group encouraged deeper spiritual commitment. Born in Stockport, Jaeger was baptized at the age of thirteen by George Combe at Green Street Baptist Church, became a helper in the Green Street Sunday school and began to preach at the age of sixteen.[69] In 1931 he entered Regent's Park College to train for Baptist ministry. During his first week in college

66    *BT*, 17 December 1931, p.904; 24 December 1931, p.920.
67    *BT*, 9 February 1933, p.92.
68    *BT*, 6 July 1933, p.461.
69    *Greek Street Baptist Church, Stockport, Manual* (Stockport: p.p., 1930), p.28; C. Jaeger, *Never to Lose my Vision: The Story of Bill Jaeger* (London: Grosvenor Books, 1995), p.21.

Jaeger met members of the Group and was challenged by their set of standards - absolute honesty, purity, unselfishness and love - and by their determination to surrender fully to Christ and 'remake the world'. Jaeger 'felt filled with a new energy and freedom'and saw this experience as equipping him to help build a better society. For him this was not a new direction, but 'a development of the work he had felt called to do since his baptism'. Soon Jaeger's mother was affected.[70] Although Wheeler Robinson, as College Principal, was at one stage concerned that Jaeger was spending too much time with the Group, Jaeger took seriously the responsibility of a two-year student pastorate in Leavesden Road, under the care of Beechen Grove, Watford. Congregations at Leavesden Road doubled during his period of leadership.[71]

Congregations were affected spiritually as well as numerically. George Evans, minister at Oxford Road, Manchester, which at that time had about 400 members, described in 1932 how he had been lonely and in despair, worried by the spiritual inertia in the church, until the Group effected a profound change. He had been deeply concerned, over two decades, about how to see a release of God's power through his ministry. He claimed that since his new surrender he had known God revealing himself in the church in fresh ways.[72] A young Baptist minister described in the *Baptist Times* in 1933 how he had been spiritually challenged at Keswick in the previous year. Group members to whom he spoke had subsequently pin-pointed wrongdoing in his life. His conservative background made him cautious about the Group, but he took a step of surrender, followed Group advice and confessed his faults to a Baptist leader, and was now preaching the cross with new dynamism (according to his deacons), seeing frequent conversions and baptisms.[73] H.C. Kemp similarly felt new power in his preaching and pastoral work through contact with the Group. He was aware of deeper spiritual communion among church members and was sure that 'the revival for which all loyal Baptists are earnestly praying will come about if our churches will get in

---

70   Jaeger, *Never to Lose*, pp.25-9.
71   Interview with Bill Jaeger, 9 May 1997; Jaeger, *Never to Lose*, p.32.
72   *CW*, 11 August 1932, p.7.
73   *BT*, 16 February 1933, p.108.

touch with the Group and then form a Group within their own fellowship'.[74]

At a Group 'house-party' (as residential Group gatherings were called) in Oxford in 1933, which attracted 5,000 people and filled six Oxford colleges, J.C. Carlile was impressed by the joy, informality and lack of rigidity that he encountered. This kind of atmosphere, which was in tune with some of the cultural changes to be seen in the period, was an important factor in the Group's appeal. Carlile met Frank Buchman and felt that he was pioneering a return to the experience of the early church. Compared to the overall numbers at this massive house-party, the Baptist contingent was relatively small. Spurr noted that 1,000 ministers were present, including some of the most scholarly Free Church leaders. Carlile led a camp of ten lay

*J.C. Carlile*

people and about forty Baptist ministers and students. Communal 'sharing' was a Group practice, and some ministers at the house-party testified openly to having 'grown stale in their pulpit work because they had lost the wonder of Christ's love to them individually'. For Carlile the experience of Group fellowship was genuinely baptistic, although he had some reservations about the practice of sharing - especially where sins and failures were spoken about in public - and also about the way in which Group members claimed to receive direct divine guidance. When Carlile put his worries to Buchman, he received the reply: 'A live faith takes risks.' However, Carlile was not entirely satisfied. He valued an intelligent faith and thus wanted more emphasis within the Group on properly understanding the Bible.[75]

74   *BT*, 6 July 1933, p.461.
75   *BT*, 13 July 1933, p.477; *BW*, 13 July 1933, p.295; 20 July 1933, p.493; *CW*, 20 July 1933, p.13.

The reservations felt by Carlile were indicative of tensions that surrounded the Group's activities. In some cases involvement with the Group seemed to result in people leaving Baptist life. G.H. Boobyer, who trained at Bristol College and had a DTh from Heidelburg University, commenced ministry in 1931 at King's Road Baptist Church, Reading, but after only two years he resigned and devoted himself fully to Group activities.[76] It is likely that Boobyer felt guided to do that, but this kind of Group guidance was coming under increasing scrutiny. J.B. Middlebrook declined to join the Group despite being told by Group members whom he knew that all the 'guidance' pointed to the rightness of his joining. A wealthy Group member offered him total financial backing if he worked for the Group. Middlebrook was worried by what he heard from Regent's Park College about students who were Groupers 'playing fast and loose with preaching engagements in the churches at the behest of the Spirit', and about several 'first class men' being lost to the Baptist denomination.[77] One forthright young Baptist, Cyril Petch from Isleham, near Ely, said in 1933 that he felt there were many younger Baptists who, like himself, were 'on fire' for Christ, but had no contact with 'Groups'. He quoted the chorus, 'Now none but Christ can satisfy'.[78] There was a concern that a focus on the Group meant that specifically Baptist activities received less attention.

Aubrey commented in his typically judicious style in October 1933 that he was grateful for what the Oxford Group had done for some Baptist churches and ministers, but he also recognized that it was dangerous to over-emphasize certain points. No doubt he had ideas about sharing and guidance in mind. It also seemed that the Group's consciously contemporary approach, which included avoidance of traditional religious terminology, had polarized opinion in some churches. Aubrey said that some Baptists wanted to go back to doctrines emphasized fifty years before, whereas others, usually younger people, believed there was no hope as long as the 'same old story' was told every week.[79] Two years

76   Payne, *The Baptists of Berkshire*, p.130. Boobyer later became a Quaker.
77   Personal Memoir by J.B. Middlebrook.
78   *BT*, 27 July 1933, p.504.
79   *BT*, 19 October 1933, p.703.

later, Spurr recalled how F.B. Meyer had opened his heart to a group of ministers. This kind of sharing was of great benefit. Spurr wanted more open spiritual expression among ministers and lay people, since there could be no such thing as an authentic spiritual life that was merely personal. He stressed that communal approaches to spiritual experience did not originate with Buchman, but he acknowledged that the Group had encouraged it.[80] By the later 1930s, however, enthusiasm for the Group was waning within Baptist circles. In the face of the challenges of Fascism and Communism, Buchman was to give priority to general 'moral re-armament'. Some of the Group's achievements had by that stage proved questionable. Spurr wrote in 1937: 'Three men known to me are now worse than they were before they joined the Group. Their enthusiasm has not only evaporated; they are colder than ever.'[81] Nonetheless, the contemporary spirituality of the Group had contributed to a deepening of spiritual life in sections of the denomination.

MINISTERIAL EFFICIENCY

The renewing influence of the Oxford Group suggested that there was sometimes a lack of spiritual vitality among ministers. Much attention was paid in the 1930s to 'ministerial efficiency'. A Union report, *Matters Affecting the Efficiency of the Ministry*, was discussed by the Council in 1930. A Commission on the issue, chaired by F.J. Humphrey, formerly at St Mary's Baptist Church, Norwich, and Union President in 1938-39, had reported in 1928. Commission members included B. Grey Griffith, Home Secretary of the BMS, S.W. Hughes, Secretary of the Free Church Council, J.B. Middlebrook, and John Wilson of Woolwich. The report referred to the shortfall in the number of probationers coming out of the colleges but concentrated on issues of quality rather than quantity. It suggested that there should be a clear procedure for testing a call to ministry, which would involve recommendation by the local church and the Association, and would include pre-collegiate training. The report

---

80    *BT*, 14 February 1935, pp.134-7.
81    *BT*, 3 June 1937, p.428.

spoke about the importance of intellectual ability, physical fitness, character and spirituality in ministry, and called for more practical training. It was suggested that 'the spirit of consecration and Christian zeal is in danger of evaporating in an atmosphere dominated by intellectual and technical studies'. The report also argued for more training in areas such as leading young people, church administration, understanding modern society, preaching – the 'prophetic ministry' - and the care of souls.[82]

The Commission's work was introduced by Middlebrook and A.C. Underwood to the Baptist ministers present at a Pastoral Session of the Union Assembly. The ministers did not take kindly to references in the report to problems in ministry: neglect of study, lack of dedication, tactlessness, pugnacity, laziness, and restlessness. Indeed the report was shouted down.[83] Nor were the college principals willing to accept it. At a United Collegiate Board Sub-Committee in 1932 convened to look at the issues, it was pointed out that there were considerable difficulties in trying to introduce into college courses more of the practical elements suggested by the Commission. Often it could take two years of college training to bring students to a basic school-leaving level of education. Addressing the suggestion that colleges were failing to make spirituality central, Arthur Dakin and Wheeler Robinson, who worked closely together in a scheme by which some Bristol students moved on to Regent's Park to do post-graduate work, insisted 'many things were done to foster the spiritual welfare of the students'. During the 1930s, the number of Regent's Park students in Oxford increased and a central feature of college life in Oxford was a weekly communion service.[84] R.W. Thomson, later Assistant General Secretary of the Union, recalled that as a Regent's Park student in this period – he took up his first ministry, in Notting Hill, in 1931 - he found the communion services very

---

82   Report, *Matters Affecting the Efficiency of the Ministry* (London: Baptist Union, April 1928).
83   Personal Memoir by J.B. Middlebrook.
84   Cooper, *From Stepney to St Giles'*, p.87;  Moon, *Education for Ministry* , pp.77-8.

moving.[85] The charge that intellectual considerations took precedence over spirituality was refuted. The Principals were adamant that worship was crucial to college life.[86] Deliberations on the topic continued throughout the 1930s.[87]

There was, however, more to ministerial effectiveness than college training. There was a need for on-going development in ministry, and the Yorkshire Association retreats for ministers at Kiplin Hall were offered as one model of how spiritual growth could be fostered. Some church members complained that ministers were failing to connect with people's needs. A letter in the *Baptist Times* in 1934, 'A Woman's View of the Church', made the surprising statement that ministers were able to enjoy sport and foreign travel, and mixed in a higher social circle. In the North East, where Baptists generally were poor, such ministers were seen as remote from their flocks. J.R. Ashby, moderator of the annual assembly of the Northern Baptist Association, defended the ministers.[88] George Barnes, from Bacup, alleged (somewhat unconvincingly) that churches had been told that as a result of the Sustentation Fund ministers would be free from anxiety about stipends and there would be revival. This had not happened. Another correspondent, Percy Austin, pointed out that George Barnes was a well-off layman – a solicitor – and that for him to blame ministers for wishing to have a reasonable stipend was hardly fair.[89] It seemed, however, that there was some resentment about a lack of ministerial involvement with congregations. 'A deacon in the Industrial North' wrote: 'If our ministers became pastors also, and carried out a systematic visitation of their people, they would at times not show such a lack of understanding of the struggle that so many of the people have to face.'[90]

---

85   R.W. Thomson, 'A Round Unvarnish'd Tale' (unpublished manuscript, 1979), p.8: Regent's Park College Oxford, Angus Library, Acc.60.
86   Minutes of the United Collegiate Board Sub-Committee 4 April 1932.
87   Minutes of the Baptist Union Ministerial Recognition Sub-Committee meeting with College Principals, 7 April 1938.
88   *BT*, 18 January 1934, p.48; 8 February 1934, p.92.
89   *BT*, 8 February 1934, p.92; 1 March 1934, p.142.
90   *BT*, 15 March 1934, p.178.

In some cases ministers themselves placed more emphasis on preaching than on pastoral work. Michael Walker described Baptist churches in this period where 'preaching was central to the life and strength of the congregation'. The pastors of these churches – J.B. Middlebrook in Huddersfield, H. Ingli James at Queen's Road, Coventry, and Henry Cook, with a 1,000-strong congregation at Ferme Park – were 'scholar pastors, evangelical to their core, widely read, liberal in their politics, and radical in their sympathies'.[91] It was not surprising that others sought to emulate such preachers. At the same time, there was a recognition that the social context was changing. A leading article in the *Baptist Times* in 1930 on preaching stated: 'The old style of pulpit exposition makes little appeal to the new generation.'[92] Aubrey was not complacent about Baptist worship. He had produced a *Minister's Manual* (1927) to raise standards and he argued in 1930 for greater use of read prayers in services. He considered that when people who were not regular churchgoers decided to go to church they went 'primarily to worship and to pray, and our order gives them too little help'. Aubrey accepted that he might not convince most of his readers.[93] At the same time, he argued against any diminution of the role of preaching. In his view arrangements at church anniversary services, which as Union Secretary he often took, conspired against preaching. Hymns were innumerable, the choir-master chose the longest anthems, and announcements rivalled sermons in length. Aubrey recalled an occasion when the congregation looked exhausted before the sermon began: 'What chance', he asked, 'had the preacher?'[94]

There were other problems, such as a continued struggle in the 1930s to meet the demands made on the Sustentation Fund. Increasing numbers of Baptist churches were without ministerial leadership.[95] Some of these,

---

91    M. Walker, 'Baptist Worship in the Twentieth Century', in Clements, ed., *Baptists in the Twentieth Century*, p.22.
92    *BT*, 3 April 1930, p.225.
93    *BT*, 20 November 1930, p.815. The *Manual* contained orders of service for various occasions, including an order for the dedication of infants.
94    *BT*, 27 November 1930, p.834.
95    Sparkes, *The Home Mission Story*, chapter 7.

it was suggested, might need to be closed. In other cases trained lay leaders were sought. Norfolk had an average of 120 lay preachers serving Baptist congregations between the wars.[96] There was regular discussion in the 1930s about the Lay Preachers' Federation and how it could recruit and train young men and women. Alfred Ellis, who had been chairman of the Lay Preachers' Committee and who championed lay ministries, died in 1936.[97] While lay preachers such as Ellis were seeking to develop younger leaders, ordained ministry faced an opposite challenge. Aubrey noted that often churches would not consider someone as minister for a vacant pastorate who was over fifty. Aubrey opposed this approach. His article was entitled 'Too Old at Fifty?' Virtually every church consulting him about a minister, said Aubrey, told him that they wanted a young man. He was often asked: 'Do you know a good student?'[98] Finally, the ministry of women was still not encouraged in many churches. One estimate was that eighty per cent of Baptist churches did not even know about deaconesses. Hettie Rowntree Clifford made it plain in 1935 that in her view a 'onesided' (male only) ministry was neither effective nor acceptable. She said that the days when men discussed what women could do had 'long gone'.[99]

## SOCIAL CHANGES AND SOCIAL MINISTRY

The comment by Hettie Rowntree Clifford highlighted the changing social background. Societal developments meant that the role of women in Baptist churches received more attention and was also re-shaped. In the later 1920s there was agreement in the Union leadership that Havelock Hall was not viable as a training centre.[100] A new Training College for deaconesses was opened in Camden Town in 1930 under the leadership of Sister Gertrude Kendall. From 1935 the Deaconess movement operated

---

96    Jewson, *The Baptists in Norfolk* (1957), p.151.
97    Minutes of Meeting of General Superintendents, 14 February 1929; Minutes of Lay Preachers' Federation Committee, 5 November 1930.
98    *BT*, 14 May 1931, p.343.
99    *BT*, 31 October 1935, p.796.
100   Minutes of a Baptist Union Conference re Havelock Hall, 20 May 1925.

*A deaconess of this period, Sister Doris (Margaret Curry)*

under the title 'The Order of Baptist Deaconesses and Women's Training College'. The college moved to Carlton Drive, Putney in 1936.[101] Greater emphasis was placed on deaconesses using modern methods to reach people and less emphasis was placed on ministry to the poor. Vernon Baptist Church, King's Cross, became the main centre for practical training. By 1932, eleven Sisters were in charge of Baptist churches and others were assistant pastors, with the BWL financing many of the posts.[102] Sister Margaret Evans, for example, was appointed to take charge of Wood Lane, Dagenham. Deaconesses often worked in such growing areas of population. An estimated eight million people were living in new housing areas: some new housing was privately owned, but there were also massive municipal estates, in part a product of 'slum clearance'. Dagenham and Becontree, for instance, had 750,000 people. Baptist work in this area was seen by A.J. Burgoyne, moderator of the Becontree church, as 'a drop in a bucket'.[103]

The support given to women's ministry by the BWL, which in 1930 had branches in 1,000 Baptist churches, was substantial. Carey Hall, the United Missionary College for Women (Selly Oak, Birmingham), where a Baptist minister, Gwenyth Hubble, was Principal from 1945, began to be used for deaconess' training.[104] The BWL supported the Business Girls' Hostel in London, where Jennie Hughes, a deaconess, was warden. Mrs C.S. Rose concluded her leadership of the BWL and a search took place in 1933 for a new organizing secretary. Names were submitted to Aubrey. It is fascinating, given Aubrey's strictures about ageism, that it was expected that the new post-holder would be between thirty and

101 Rose, *Baptist Deaconesses*, pp.18-20. See chapter 6 below for further developments in the 1940s.
102 Morris, *Sisters of the People*, pp.14, 18.
103 *BT*, 15 January 1931, p.44.
104 Townsend, *Robert Wilson Black*, pp.169, 204.

*Doris M. Rose*

thirty-five.[105] Doris Rose (not related to C.S. Rose), the successful Headquarters Secretary of the Girls' Life Brigade, was appointed to the post. She was from a strong Baptist family, her parents having founded Acocks Green Baptist Church, Birmingham, and it was hoped that her skills would encourage women's activities. During discussions about the use of the gifts of women, Gilbert Laws applauded Eva Booth's appointment as Salvation Army General, seeing the Army as 'the most wonderful instrument that Christ has in the world today'.[106] More Baptist diaconates now included women. One 'Woman Deacon' told the *Baptist Times* in 1938 that about twelve years previously her minister (probably at Abingdon Baptist Church) proposed that women could join the diaconate. The older people 'gasped in astonishment', especially when two women in their thirties were elected.[107]

Although social changes were acknowledged, there was little analysis among Baptists of the prevailing social conditions. References to the 'Industrial North' were indicative of an awareness of an increasing North-South divide, created largely by economic circumstances. Many churches in the North were seeking to alleviate the economic plight of people in their communities, and the Union Council urged the government to do more for the two million unemployed, but Baptists more often spoke about problems associated with personal responsibility, such as drunkenness and gambling.[108] The temperance Band of Hope still operated in many larger Baptist churches, and T.G. Dunning was the Union's Director of Education, Temperance, Social Service and Youth. In 1932 Wilson Black became President of the prohibitionist United Kingdom Alliance.[109] There was deeply-felt concern about Sunday

---

105  *BT*, 21 September 1933, p.631.
106  *BT*, 25 October 1934, p.762.
107  *BT*, 27 January 1938, p.64.
108  Bebbington, 'Baptists and Politics since 1914', in Clements, ed., *Baptists in the Twentieth Century*, p.86.
109  Townsend, *Robert Wilson Black*, pp.169, 204.

observance. Most Baptists opposed the Sunday opening of cinemas and Townley Lord spoke about village churches competing with whirrs and hoots from cars driven by Sunday pleasure seekers.[110] On the subject of smoking, Aubrey's policy was freedom: predictably, the example of C.H. Spurgeon's cigar smoking was adduced. It was increasingly noted, however, that tobacco was addictive.[111] At times the Union's Moral and Social Questions Committee dealt with more complex issues. In 1935, for example, it discussed a Bill to legalize the voluntary sterilization of people with mental deficiency or hereditary physical defects. Wider church opinion was divided.

*Dr T.G. Dunning (left) with the Revd McKay and Mr Lavender on visit to Germany 1934*

Surgeon Rear-Admiral Eric Pearce Gould, at Middlesex Hospital, who gave medical advice to the Union, saw the Bill as acceptable.[112]

Some discussions took Baptists into the area of politics. In the past this had been familiar territory, but, as Bebbington argues, a major shift had taken place by the 1930s. No longer were Baptists automatically Liberals. Communal politics gave way to class politics.[113] Whereas Baptists had historically opposed Conservative administrations, in 1932 Alfred Ellis, in his Union presidential address, seemed to affirm the Conservative-dominated National Government led by Ramsay MacDonald.[114] Baptist allegiances were becoming varied. There was support for Baptist Labour MPs such as William Adamson, Secretary of State for Scotland from 1929 to 1931, who was active in Dunfermline

---

110 *BT*, 10 January 1929, p.18.
111 *BT*, 18 August 1932, p.567; 1 September 1932, p.600.
112 Minutes of the Baptist Union Moral and Social Questions Committee, 13 February 1935.
113 Bebbington, 'Baptists and Politics since 1914', p.79.
114 M. Goodman, 'A Faded Heritage: English Baptist political thinking in the 1930s', *BQ*, Vol.37, No.2 (1997), p.60.

West Baptist Church, and for Henry Thomas, Secretary for the Colonies, who was involved in the work of Swindon Tabernacle.[115] Baptists were delighted in 1934 when MacDonald, the Prime Minister, spoke knowledgeably about Spurgeon at a centenary celebration in the Royal Albert Hall of the preacher's birth.[116] There was declining interest in battles with Anglicans, although Baptists complained in the 1930s of continuing injustices: 12,000 schools existed in which a Free Church teacher could not be head.[117] Aubrey reported that a Baptist teacher at training college was told she would have better career prospects as an Anglican.[118] But Aubrey now saw the bitter early twentieth-century education feud as an episode lacking 'the blessing of God'.[119] Aubrey contributed to the distancing of the Union from politics. For him, politicking was a threat to spirituality.[120]

Nonetheless, Aubrey did look to the Liberals to press for educational reforms. Strains emerged in 1931 between Aubrey and Lloyd George, then in his late sixties, when Aubrey made plain his unhappiness with Liberal efforts in this area. Lloyd George, in response, spoke of Aubrey's 'unjust and rather ill-considered attack upon the Liberal Party' and insisted that he still held the same opinion as when he and Clifford had campaigned in 1902: it was Aubrey who was compromising. Aubrey was deeply hurt.[121] Against this background, Aubrey was not predisposed to back Lloyd George's 1935 'Call to Action' on behalf of peace and unemployment, nor his Council of Action for Peace and Reconstruction. Several Baptists, such as S.W. Hughes and Wilson Black, supported Lloyd George, but Aubrey refused, seeing the 'Call' as 'an electioneering manifesto', an opportunist move by Lloyd George to attack the National

---

115　Bebbington, 'Baptist Members of Parliament in the Twentieth Century', suggests there is doubt about Thomas' Baptist membership, pp.263, 285.

116　*BT*, 3 May 1934, pp.317-18.

117　*BT*, 20 February 1930, p.123.

118　*BT*, 22 January 1931, p.59.

119　M.E. Aubrey to S.W. Hughes, 11 June 1935, cited by Goodman, 'A Faded Heritage: English Baptist political thinking in the 1930s', p.63.

120　Bebbington, 'Baptists and Politics since 1914', p.83.

121　*BT*, 5 March 1931, p.169; 12 March 1931, p.179; 19 March 1931, p.200; 26 March 1931, p.215.

Government and attract support to himself. The *Call to Action* was issued on 12 June 1935, with the backing of senior Free Church figures, and the following day Aubrey resigned from the Free Church Council.[122] Affirmation for Aubrey came from several quarters, including from Thomas Greenwood and from Theo Bamber, minister of Rye Lane Chapel, Peckham. Aubrey said to William Olney, a layman connected with the Metropolitan Tabernacle, that he had 'made perfectly clear to the Prime Minister and others when they have consulted me, that as leader of the Baptist Union, I could never play any party game'.[123] The 'Call' attracted much Press attention, but soon fizzled out.

By the 1930s, as Michael Goodman has argued, the Liberal Party had lost credibility with many Baptists.[124] MPs in or on the fringe of the National Government included Baptists such as Sir Geoffrey Shakespeare (the son of J.H. Shakespeare), who was Parliamentary Secretary to the

*Ernest Brown*

Minister of Health, and Ernest Brown, a member of Upton Vale Baptist Church, Torquay, and then of Bloomsbury Central Baptist Church, who from 1935 was Minister of Labour. Only between five and seven Baptists were MPs in the 1930s. Brown, the best-loved politician among Baptists, had been told in 1923 by John Clifford that he should never be down-hearted about the Christian Evangel, and this message continued to inspire him. His wife Eva became the first chair of the Women's Committee of the Baptist World Alliance in 1939.[125] Aubrey had an open relationship with Brown, who was a Liberal but

---

122   West, 'The Reverend Secretary Aubrey: Part I', pp.204-12; see Koss, *Nonconformity in Modern British Politics*, pp.187-215.
123   Goodman, 'A Faded Heritage', p.60; West, 'The Reverend Secretary Aubrey: Part I', p.212.
124   Goodman, 'A Faded Heritage', pp.67-8
125   Bebbington, 'Baptist Members of Parliament in the Twentieth Century', pp.252, 260, 264-5.

was not a rigidly party political figure. Party political allegiance was not a priority for most Baptists in the 1930s. R. Rowntree Clifford captured the mood of many Baptists in a speech he made in 1933, as Union President, in which he described the break-up of family life, the growing secularism of Sunday, and neglect of the Bible. Many, he argued, 'hold the ideals of the Church, but they spend themselves in all kinds of social enterprises and recognize no Church loyalty'.[126] Baptists were increasingly detached from socio-political activity.

## PEACE AND WAR

Europe in the 1930s was itself uncertain how to deal with wider political changes, especially issues of war and peace. There was general Baptist support for the work of the League of Nations, although in 1931 Theo Bamber, of Rye Lane, Peckham, expressed doubts about a body 'seeking to establish a world of peace in a world of sin'. By contrast, a large Sunday morning congregation at Ferme Park in 1931, led by Henry Cook (later Metropolitan Superintendent), passed this resolution: 'We desire to reiterate our faith in the League of Nations as the only hope of peace in the world.' This wording was later criticized, but it indicates clearly the views of some Baptists. Perhaps typical of Baptist thinking was the 1931 Northamptonshire Association statement which both supported the League and argued that 'the Christian teaching of neighbourliness and goodwill is the only remedy for military rivalry'.[127] In the same year W.H. Haden, minister in West Bridgford, Nottingham, spoke to Baptist ministers at the Assembly about the formation of a ministers' peace group. In 1934 a Baptist Ministers' Pacifist Fellowship was formed, with 580 ministers becoming members. Another leading Baptist pacifist was Herbert Dunnico, Labour MP for Consett from 1922 to 1931, who was Secretary of the Peace Society. Pacifist influence among Baptists in this period led to the Assembly of 1936 agreeing a motion that 'modern war

---

126  *BT*, 4 May 1933, p.307.
127  *BT*, 18 June 1931, p.428; 2 July 1931, p.462; 9 July 1931, p.476; Elwyn, *The Northamptonshire Baptist Association*, p.86.

means the organized killing of men, women and children on a wide scale, and is manifestly contrary to the will of God'.[128]

This stance was somewhat at odds with the conclusions that emerged from a group set up by the Baptist Union Council in 1933 to consider 'The Attitude of the Baptist Denomination to War'. The group was chaired by Ernest Brown, who was later succeeded by J.H. Rushbrooke, and its report urged the surrender of a measure of national sovereignty to secure the formation of an appropriate World Organization to keep the peace. It admitted some hesitation about the contention, which was endorsed by a majority of the committee, '... that a peaceful world cannot be ensured apart from force organized in such form and on such a scale as to be equal to the task of restraining disloyal and aggressive states'.[129] In this period the *Baptist Times* aired differing views on the subject. There was much interest in the efforts to achieve disarmament, and Ernest Bacon, from Little Kimble in Buckinghamshire, was one of those calling for total disarmament, arguing that nothing less than '100 per cent disarmament' was compatible with the mind of Christ.[130] Even among those who did not take this position, there was great concern about the build-up of arms. The Bristol and District Association was typical in passing resolutions in 1935 and 1937 declaring its 'continued support for international peace' and expressing a strong desire 'for an equitable adjustment of economic and territorial advantage as between different nations of the world'.[131]

By this time there was much anxiety among Baptists and others in Britain about developments in Germany. The British Evangelical Alliance Council, on 27 April 1932, deplored the persecution of Jews in Germany, who, it stated, were suffering 'at the hands of those who profess and represent the Christian faith'. This resolution was received

---

128  P.R. Dekar, 'Twentieth-Century British Baptist Conscientious Objectors', *BQ*, Vol.35, No.1 (1993), pp.37-8.
129  Payne, *Baptist Union*, p.207, citing 'The Attitude of the Baptist Denomination to War', pamphlet, 1937.
130  *BT*, 30 March 1933, p.204.
131  L.G. Champion, *Bristol and District Association of Baptist Churches*, 1823-1973 (Bristol: p.p., 1973), p.31.

unfavourably by some evangelicals in Germany, among them some Baptists, who protested to the British Alliance, but in June 1933 the Alliance formulated an even stronger resolution on the subject. This stated that 'the discrimination now being exercised against the Jews is contrary to the basic principles of tolerance and equality which are accepted in the modern world in relation to the treatment of religious and racial minorities'.[132] Similar sentiments were expressed in 1933 by British Baptists, and there was coverage in the *Baptist Times* of the resistance of some church leaders in Germany to the Nazis, although, as K.W. Clements has shown, there was considerable ignorance among British Baptists about the Protestant scene in Germany.[133] The theology of Karl Barth was appreciated by Henry Townsend, but such awareness did not necessarily extend to Barth's anti-Nazi political endeavours.[134] Clarity was not helped by the hostile attitudes of the German Baptists to statements that were critical of Nazi policies.[135]

The problem about how to respond to German Baptist thinking came to a head over the issue of whether to have the Baptist World Alliance Congress in Germany in 1934. There was considerable debate, but finally J.H. Rushbrooke's view, that the Congress should go ahead, prevailed. Rushbrooke, who was the leading Baptist champion of religious freedom in countries such as Russia and Romania, argued that a demonstration of the freedom of the Baptist family to express its views was important. Aubrey used the Congress, which attracted 8,000 Baptists (only 300 from Britain), to speak about freedom of conscience, but Carl Schneider of the Hamburg Baptist Seminary also used it to praise the Third Reich.[136] By 1936 the British Evangelical Alliance was seeking to help Jews leaving Germany and was taking a special interest in the German Confessing

132  *Evangelical Christendo*m, July-August 1933, p.150.
133  *BT*, 30 March 1933, p.205; K.W. Clements, 'A Question of Freedom? British Baptists and the German Church Struggle', in Clements, ed., *Baptists in the Twentieth Century*, p.99.
134  *BT*, 14 January 1932, p.28.
135  *BT*, 18 May 1933, p.345; 31 August 1933, p.589.
136  Rushbrooke, ed., *Fifth Baptist World Congress, Berlin, 1934*, pp.182, 192-3; B. Green, *Tomorrow's Man* (1997), pp.118-21; chapter 8.

Church, in particular Martin Niemoller and Karl Barth. When Barth was in London in 1937 the Alliance sponsored a meeting at the Russell Hotel to pay tribute to him.[137] Barth's pleas for solidarity did not fall on completely deaf ears in this period.[138] But Baptists were uncertain how to view some of the issues in Germany, with Ernest Payne, from 1932 the BMS's Young People's Secretary, encouraging English Baptists to understand that German Baptists were appreciative of the freedoms they were experiencing.[139]

Some Baptists, such as Ingli James in Coventry, continued in the later 1930s to give considerable priority to peace. They drew strength from well-known Christian pacifists such as Muriel Lester, who had Baptist roots, and Donald Soper, a leading Methodist minister in London. In Coventry, Thelma Raven, aged seventeen, was invited by a school friend to Queen's Road Baptist Church to hear Ingli James. She had not been to church for years, but was attracted by the way in which James addressed current situations. Her diary for 20 March 1938 recorded: 'Ingli gave a grand address on "Could Christ save Europe?" He was preaching pacifism and internationalism.' As Clyde Binfield puts it: 'The pervasive, dogged motif which made Queen's Road precious to Thelma Raven and her friends was its testimony for peace.'[140] By this time, however, peace was becoming less likely. In the same year Hans Luckey, of the Hamburg Baptist Seminary, while defending political developments in Germany, admitted that German Baptist young people were able to spend little time in the churches since serving the state was filling up their time.[141] The persecution by the Nazis of German Confessing Church members was taken up by Aubrey in a speech to the

---

137  *Evangelical Christendom*, January-February 1936, p.24; March-April 1937, p.44.
138  This is the suggestion by Clements in 'A Question of Freedom?' in Clements, ed., *Baptists in the Twentieth Century*, p.109.
139  *BT*, 29 July 1937, pp.567-8; 12 August 1937, p.600.
140  Binfield, *Pastors and People*, pp.247-55; P.R. Dekar, 'Twentieth-Century British Baptist Conscientious Objectors', *BQ*, Vol.35, No.1 (1993), pp.39-40.
141  *BT*, 11 August 1938, p.625; 1 September 1938, p.673.

BWA Congress in Atlanta, USA, in August 1939. Aubrey issued a forthright denunciation of Nazism.[142] Hopes for peace were receding.

A month later war broke out. By contrast with the belligerent outlook which characterized much of mainstream British Christianity during the First World War, the predominant mood at the beginning of the Second World War was one of restraint. As Adrian Hastings puts it: 'For the Church, as for the nation as a whole, war was seen by September 1939 as inevitable and just, but it was entered into soberly and rather sadly.'[143] The Baptist Union set up an Emergency Committee and a War Services Committee. The United Navy, Army and Air Force Board, formed to a large extent as a result of Shakespeare's efforts during the First World War, had continued to function during the inter-war years, and now once more came into its own. By the end of 1939 there were reports of considerable involvement in chaplaincy work by Baptist ministers. As early as October 1939, thirty-six Baptist pastors, along with thirty-five Congregationalists, had applied for Commissioned Chaplaincies.[144] By December forty-nine Baptists were chaplains in the regular Army, ten in the RAF and two in the Navy.[145] For the second time in the twentieth century, war was to have a profound impact on Baptist life.

SIGNS OF RENEWAL?

Throughout the 1930s, Baptist decline was a continued cause of heart-searching in the denomination. Michael Goodman has suggested several reasons for the decline: the failure of Sunday schools to attract as many children as before, the social aspirations of Baptists which cut them off from the working classes, a defeatist attitude, and lack of social and political engagement.[146] It is true that a considerable reduction in Sunday

---

142   J.H. Rushbrooke, ed., *Sixth Baptist World Congress, 1939* (Atlanta, Georgia: BWA, 1939), pp.198-206.

143   Hastings, *A History of English Christianity*, p.373.

144   Minutes of the United Navy, Army and Air Force Board, 13 October 1939.

145   Minutes of the War Services Committee, 4 December 1939.

146   See Goodman, 'Numerical Decline amongst English Baptists, 1930-1939', *BQ*, Vol.36, pp.241-51.

school attendance took place in the 1930s, but in fact Sunday schools were not as effective as some thought in drawing children from non-church families into church membership. F.C. Spurr reported in 1931 on an investigation he had made into the beliefs of 100 young adults who had been in Baptist Sunday schools. Only three of them had been brought up in a home in which the father attended church. At the time of Spurr's investigation none had any connection with a church.[147] Much was made of how decline in church attendance had produced 'empty churches': A.C. Underwood described chapels in the North that were once packed and were now sparsely attended, and spoke of ambitious mothers who decided a 'dissenting Bethel' would not help their children's social progress.[148] Yet the *Baptist Handbook* showed that Baptist membership in England in 1930, at 253,614, and even in 1939, at 241,915, was higher than in 1900.[149] Membership may have exceeded attendance, since roll revision was not always undertaken regularly. To focus only on signs of decay, however, was to miss the full picture.

Were there, then, definite signs of renewal? The work carried out during the period of the Discipleship Campaign can be seen as one such sign. Middlebrook said of the Campaign: 'Behind all this flurry of effort was a deep spiritual hunger, a deep longing, dedication of a high order but not enough strategy and "intelligence" in the Army sense.' He indicated that greater use could have been made of P.T. Thomson, the Union's Commissioner for Education (and Union President in 1939-40), in order to engage in a more thorough examination of the changing thought patterns of the 1930s.[150] Aubrey, who had experience in Cambridge of communicating to questioning people, acknowledged in 1933 the pressing need to address 'modern thought'. He urged ministers to preach in such a way as to draw back younger people who had drifted from the churches. However, preaching was not enough. 'The supreme

---

147  *BT*, 12 March 1931, p.84.
148  *BT*, 15 July 1937, p.541.
149  Cited in R. Currie, A. Gilbert and L. Horsley, *Churches and Churchgoers: Patterns of Church Growth in the British Isles since 1700* (Oxford: Clarendon Press, 1977), pp.149-50.
150  Personal Memoir by J.B. Middlebrook.

argument for Christianity', said Aubrey, 'still remains the life of the true Christian, the surrendered disciple.'[151] A year later Henry Townsend also stressed the need for spiritual passion: 'With all our scholarship and exact thinking (and I would not forfeit any hard-won knowledge, Biblical or otherwise) we need to repent and afflict our souls over our failures, and the lack of conviction in our preaching.' He urged young preachers to learn from C.H. Spurgeon and to foster a 'burden of responsibility for the salvation of souls'.[152]

If evangelistic vision was a sign of renewal, another was the desire for a deeper inner life. Concern about this was voiced by H.H. Rowley, who had been a BMS missionary in China. In 1930 Rowley, an outstanding Old Testament scholar, became assistant lecturer in Semitic Languages at University College, Cardiff, and in 1935 Professor of Semitic Languages in the University College of North Wales, Bangor. In 1933 Rowley wrote about the regular (usually monthly) church members' meetings or 'business meetings' held in Baptist churches: 'One of the pressing needs in many of our churches is for a transformation of the Church meeting. It is commonly disgracefully attended, and is a meeting without inspiration. Few members feel any obligation to attend...Its dead formality is only varied when there is trouble in the church, or when the pastorate is under discussion.' Rowley argued that the meeting should be for worship, that financial and other business should occupy as little time as possible, and that there should be the celebration of the Lord's Supper. There could also be time for prayer, for setting apart those taking leadership in the church, and for receiving new members.[153] In similar vein, a Discipleship Group meeting in 1935 stressed prayer retreats. J.W. Ewing, Henry Cook, Middlebrook and Aubrey were asked to pursue this further. It was recognized that many deacons were 'shy of giving spiritual leadership in a church'.[154] There was a widespread desire for renewal

---

151  *BT*, 23 February 1933, p.123.

152  *BT*, 11 January 1934, p.24.

153  *BT*, 24 August 1933, p.576; for Rowley see R.E. Clements, 'The Biblical Theology of H.H. Rowley, 1890-1969', *Baptist History and Heritage*, Vol.38 (Winter 2003), pp.36-63.

154  Minutes of Baptist Union Discipleship Committee, 12 Sept 1935.

among conservative evangelicals across the denominations, which led to the formation of Revival Fellowships. In 1938 the Baptist Revival Fellowship (BRF) was formed.[155]

A further sign of renewal was the way in which young people were contributing to church life. William Taylor Bowie, who became pastor at Church Road, Acton, in 1926, was active together with Ernest Payne in the Baptist Union's Young People's Committee.[156] The Discipleship Campaign in Kent and Sussex was mainly directed to young people, who were encouraged to study the meaning of discipleship. Many made decisions to follow Christ.[157] Charles Brown spoke in 1930 about the significance for church life and evangelism of the responsiveness of young people. Brown had recently baptized his own grandchildren, aged eleven and thirteen.[158] He also noted, however, that by no means all those baptized in Baptist churches remained Baptists, and commented: 'For good or ill, denominational ties are growing slacker all the time.'[159] Mention was made in the *Baptist Times* in 1934 of one congregation where all the children of the church leaders had become either Presbyterians or Anglicans.[160] One young Baptist, Connie Wood, who drove her father, Henry Wood, JP, round the country during his presidential year in 1936-37 – covering 25,000 miles in her sports car – commented: 'Father often talks about the conservatism of Baptists. He is certainly right there. I do not know much about other denominations, but I am sure they could not beat Baptists for refusing to budge.'[161] This conservatism drove some younger people away from Baptist life, but others rose to the challenge to achieve change.

---

155  *The Baptist Revival Fellowship: Constitution and Rules* (London: BRF, n.d.): Spurgeon's College, London, BRF Archive, file TMB; cf. Bebbington, *Evangelicalism in Modern Britain*, pp.231, 251.
156  See E.A. Payne, *William Taylor Bowie, 1902-1952* (London: p.p., 1952).
157  Buffard, *Kent and Sussex Baptist Associations*, p.132.
158  *CW*, 9 October 1930, p.7.
159  *BT*, 23 January 1930, p.61.
160  *BT*, 1 November 1934, p.780.
161  *BT*, 9 July 1936, p.539.

The increasing ministry of women can also be viewed as a sign of progress. J.C. Carlile commented in 1933 on the high profile ministry of Robert and Hettie Rowntree Clifford at West Ham Central Mission. He suggested that there was nothing like their joint ministry to be found elsewhere in the Baptist denomination or indeed in the modern church as a whole. Carlile hoped that there would be a woman President of the Union, although this hope was not to be fulfilled until much later. Hettie had been nominated for the presidency but had not allowed her name to go forward. Instead Robert became President. His presidential message in 1933 touched on themes that both he and his wife felt were important. 'The need of the hour', he stated, 'is a dual ministry.' In this context a woman would have her place 'on an equality with a man'.[162] Rowntree Clifford, acknowledging that many Baptist churches were conservative in their thinking, spoke about the need for change. 'Who ordained our recognised order of service', he asked, 'so that a Church may be split over the singing of an Amen?', perhaps a reference to the revised *Baptist Church Hymnal*. Rather than spending time on such sterile debates, Rowntree Clifford wanted to give priority to encouraging the ministry of women, ministry which in West Ham had helped, he affirmed, to build up 'what is said to be one of the greatest evangelistic and humanitarian centres in the country'. Growth had been experienced at a time when, he estimated, three-quarters of people never entered a church.[163]

The revised *Hymnal* of 1933 was itself another evidence of fresh vitality within Baptist churches. The committee which worked on this was chaired by Carey Bonner, who was Union President in 1931, and the committee included in its membership Wheeler Robinson, F.C. Spurr, W.T. Whitley and Herbert Chown, organist of Brondesbury Chapel, London. They wished to add to the older hymns, which were 'dear to Baptists', some new hymns belonging to the twentieth century. Changes were also made in some tunes, after enquiries among organists, choir-masters, members of choirs and other musical church members had made it clear that many tunes in the existing book were never used. Fresh tunes,

162  *BT*, 4 May 1933, p.297.
163  *BT*, 4 May 1933, p.307.

both ancient and modern, were introduced.[164] Those ministers who were looking for a variety of liturgical approaches could and did use Tait Patterson's *Call to Worship*, with its worship material drawn from different traditions, and F.C. Spurr's *Come, Let Us Worship*.[165] At Highams Park, in East London, under the innovative ministry of Stephen Winward from 1935, Holy Communion became an integral part of the service, not an addendum. This pattern was to have considerable impact after the Second World War, when liturgical revival across all the churches renewed interest in the way Holy Communion was celebrated.[166]

Ecumenical endeavour was arguably a sign of renewal. Although there were serious doubts among Baptists about organic Anglican-Free Church unity, some Baptists committed themselves to seeking more co-operation. Aubrey worked with William Temple, the future Archbishop of Canterbury, in preparations for the Faith and Order Conference in 1937 in Edinburgh. J.H. Rushbrooke, Gilbert Laws, Hugh Martin and C.T. Le Quesne were participants, and Aubrey chaired a group which, crucially, recommended the formation of the World Council of Churches (WCC).[167] But Law was not optimistic about unity. Commenting in 1938 about the Edinburgh Conference, he declared: 'It is a very painful thing to have to say to those who set store by infant baptism that we regard it as a perversion of an ordinance of Christ…Yet nothing less than this is the true Baptist position, and as one who holds it I see no way, except at the cost of truth, of organic union with other Churches.'[168] In the same year, however, Aubrey, as a result of his friendship with Temple and his moderatorship of the Federal Council of the Free Churches, became the

164  Preface, *The Baptist Church Hymnal: Revised Edition, 1933* (London: Psalms and Hymns Trust, 1933), pp.iii-iv.
165  N. Wallwork, 'Developments in Liturgy and Worship in Twentieth-Century Protestant Nonconformity', in Sell and Cross, eds., *Protestant Nonconformity* (2003), pp.118-20.
166  M. Walker, 'Baptist Worship in the Twentieth Century', in Clements, ed., *Baptists in the Twentieth Century*, pp.23-4.
167  W.M.S. West, 'The Reverend Secretary Aubrey: Part III', *BQ*, Vol.34, No.7 (1992), p.331.
168  G. Laws, 'The Edinburgh Conference: What was the Good of it?', *BQ*, Vol.9, No.1 (1938), p.29.

first Free Church person to address the Anglican Convocation of York, and in a fine address he spoke of being 'pledged to ecumenicity'.[169] In line with this thinking, at the Council in March 1939 it was proposed that the Union become a founding member of the WCC. Surprisingly, given his subsequent involvement in the work of the WCC, Payne suggested that so innovative a proposal required an investigative committee, but the original proposal was passed with only five dissenting.[170] The Assembly concurred.

The final example of a sign of renewal was the planting of new churches. In 1930 Charles Brown, arguing for more money for 'church extension', observed: 'There is plenty of money in the Baptist denomination. Motor-cars, amusements, tobacco, wills of deceased Baptists testify to that.'[171] Arthur Dakin echoed the plea for investment in church planting, and by 1934 the Council was encouraging strategic thinking about where churches were and should be located.[172] Wilson Black provided money for the appointment of J.N. Britton in 1935 as Baptist Union Evangelist. At Avenue Baptist Church, Milton Road, Westcliff-on-Sea, Britton had seen church membership almost double in a decade to nearly 800 members. A denominational 'Call to Advance' was announced in 1936 and this became the 'Forward Movement' - a fresh effort at significant church extension. It had a goal of raising £1 million by 1941 for new Baptist churches. Nearly half a million had been raised from 1931 to 1936 and a meeting was held at the Royal Albert Hall in 1936, with Ernest Brown as a speaker, to celebrate the achievements to that date.[173] The stronger economic situation in the South, coupled with the growth in population, meant that in the discussions about new churches the South attracted most attention. In the mid-1930s seven new church sites for Baptist churches were acquired in London.[174] Also, the Free Church Council encouraged the planting of one Free Church in any

---

169   West, 'The Reverend Secretary Aubrey: Part III', pp.331-2.
170   Minutes of the Baptist Union Council, 14 and 15 March 1939.
171   *BT*, 23 January 1930, p.61.
172   *BT*, 26 April 1934, p.303.
173   *BT*, 19 March 1936, pp.209-11; 9 April 1936, p.271; 30 April 1936, p.327.
174   Johnson, *Encounter in London*, p.70.

new housing area. This gave impetus to the trend towards open-membership Baptist churches and so was another factor contributing to ecumenical progress.[175]

CONCLUSION

It was a vision for evangelism that motivated M.E. Aubrey to launch the Discipleship Campaign in 1931. This campaign created its own problems, the most notable being the debate about T.R. Glover's *Fundamentals*. However, the Union was able to make clear its commitment to the evangelical faith. The Council discussed the Declaration of Principle in the mid-1930s to see if any changes needed to be made, and in 1938 the phrase 'our Lord and Saviour Jesus Christ, God manifest in the flesh' was added, together with the statement that the liberty of each church was 'under the guidance of the Holy Spirit'.[176] How did God guide? This issue was crucial for the popular Oxford Group, a contemporary expression of spirituality in this decade. This was also a decade in which Aubrey tried to steer the denomination away from Shakespeare's goal of organic church union. Concern for effective ministry and for renewal was often expressed. In March 1935 the Council had special prayer for 'an outpouring of the blessing of God' and affirmed 'the deepening of spiritual life'.[177] Baptist socio-political activity was less marked, although Aubrey took part in affairs of state, an example being his presentation of a Loyal Address in 1936 to the new King, George VI (following the abdication crisis).[178] In May 1937 Aubrey received high state recognition by being made a Companion of Honour. To what extent, however, did Baptist life affect the wider community? J.C. Carlile, writing in 1939, was convinced that 'something is radically wrong', and he suggested closing some churches, while opening new ones.[179] Reaching a changing

175  Cross, *Baptism and the Baptists*, pp.91-6.
176  Minutes of the Council, 10 and 11 March 1936; Payne, *Baptist Union*, p.212.
177  Minutes of the Baptist Union Council, 5 and 6 March 1935.
178  This was on behalf of the General Body of Protestant Dissenting Ministers of the Three Denominations – Congregational, Baptist and Presbyterian.
179  *BT*, 16 January 1930, pp.33-4.

population was a challenge which Baptists would seek to meet in the coming decades.

*The Baptist Union Council Chamber*
*converted from the gallery of Kingsgate Chapel in 1938-9*

# Chapter 6
# 'EVANGELICAL THROUGH AND THROUGH' (1940-49)

The leading article in the *Baptist Times* for 6 May 1943 said that addresses at the 1943 Assembly by Sydney G. Morris, Union President, and by M.E. Aubrey, showed that 'the denomination is evangelical through and through – but without the dogmatic intolerance which has sometimes marked evangelical emphasis'. F. Townley Lord, the author of the article and by then editor of the *Baptist Times*, commented approvingly on the 'depth and range of Baptist evangelicalism'.[1] Yet David Bebbington suggests that wider British evangelicalism reached its nadir around 1940.[2] Despite this wider decline, among Baptist leaders there was a sense of purpose. Morris' speech included a call for Baptists 'to teach the things that we hold dear, and to teach them clearly, and positively'.[3] Morris had been pastor for thirty years of the vigorous Upper Holloway Baptist Church, and after three years as Southern Area Superintendent he succeeded J.W. Ewing as Metropolitan Superintendent. Morris encouraged many younger ministers, and gave enthusiastic leadership to the Baptist Ministers' Fellowship, a body which from 1939 united the Ministers' Fraternal Union and the Pastoral Session for ministers held at Assemblies. The Union presidents who preceded Morris were all committed to mission: Percy Evans, Principal of Spurgeon's College, R. Wilson Black, the leading promoter of the Forward Movement, and B. Grey Griffith, who had been Home Secretary of the BMS. There were profound Baptist

---

1    *BT*, 6 May 1943, p.1.
2    Bebbington, *Evangelicalism in Modern Britain,* p.252.
3    *BT*, 6 May 1943, p.9.

concerns in this period about a range of issues, but there was also commitment to forward movement in the denomination.

## THE GOSPEL AND THE WAR

The Second World War had many devastating effects. As an example of the impact on London churches, within weeks of the war starting, the Bloomsbury Central Baptist Church congregations - 500 on Sunday mornings and 800 in the evenings - largely scattered. Young men were called up, students dispersed, and Sunday school children were evacuated. In 1941 the London County Council (LCC) requisitioned the Bloomsbury basement as an emergency dormitory and put 250 bunks in it. The LCC also took over one floor of the building as rest rooms and offices for their staff. The church lounge became a dining hall where 150-300 children were fed daily. Townley Lord, Bloomsbury's minister, was concerned to communicate the gospel as widely as possible in this time of upheaval. He had been on the radio since 1936 and had advised the

*Townley Lord*

BBC on religious broadcasts. In 1940 he gave talks on the Forces Programme on radio on 'A man's religion'.[4] At New Road Baptist Church, Oxford, under the leadership of Walter Bottoms (later editor of the *Baptist Times*), a 'Communal Feeding Centre' opened in 1941 which fed as many as 500 people per day.[5] In Cambridge, at Zion Baptist Church, the minister, Vellam Pitts, ensured that the Sunday school buildings were opened for soldiers. Pitts described how 'night after night we dispensed soup, tea, sandwiches, cigarettes and chocolates'.[6] Churches adjusted their work in the light of the dislocation caused by the war.

---

4    Bowers, *A Bold Experiment*, pp.328-33; 362-7.

5    I.M. Randall, ' "Great National Crisis": New Road and the World Wars', in R. Chadwick, ed., *A Protestant Catholic Church of Christ* (Oxford: New Road Baptist Church, 2003), p.276.

6    W.V. Pitts, *Never Old Parchment* (Windsor: Direct Design, 1976), p.103.

Large numbers of Baptist ministers wished to be involved in meeting the needs of men and women in the Forces and many volunteered to be chaplains.[7] By 1942 there were 150 commissioned (full-time) Congregational and Baptist chaplains, about half of whom were Baptists. At that point in the war two had been killed and six were prisoners of war.[8] When ministers became full-time chaplains this affected their churches, which were often left without regular ministry. In addition to the full-time chaplains, there were about 500 officiating (part-time) Baptist chaplains. Aubrey was keen that the pastoral work of chaplains should be encouraged. W. Thorrington Cork, minister of London Road, Lowestoft, and a chaplain from 1942, spoke about the spread of venereal disease among the troops and of the need for pastoral guidance.[9] In 1941 the *Baptist Times* featured contrasting stories from those contacting men and women in the Forces. One Baptist chaplain found little interest in the gospel, whereas another spoke about great evangelistic opportunities. There were also reports from Baptists on active service. A Baptist in the Air Force wrote to say he was feeling isolated.[10] Local Baptist churches sought to help in such cases. A soldier from Yorkshire, Thomas Binns, stationed in Oxfordshire, went to the nearby Baptist church, Little Tew and Cleveley, where Edith Gates was pastor, and found fellowship which helped him to cope with his experiences.[11] In 1943 a Baptist chaplain reported that he had met many 'seekers' unused to formal religion.[12] After the war, Baptists and others would seek to reach these seekers through new evangelistic approaches.

There were some Baptists who were convinced that their beliefs did not allow them to enter the Forces. A few churches were well known for their pacifist witness. Queen's Road, Coventry, was a notable example, with Ingli James reminding the congregation in 1942 that brutality (which was being associated in British minds with the German nation)

---

7    *BT*, 8 February 1940, p.83.
8    *BT*, 30 April 1942, p.211.
9    *BT*, 4 July 1940, p.427. Harrison, *It All Began Here*, pp.136-7.
10   *BT*, 12 June 1941, p.291; 26 June 1941, p.311.
11   *BT*, 5 March 1942, p.112.
12   *BT*, 9 September 1943, p.6.

was 'not peculiar to any one nation'. James made a highly controversial comparison with episodes in Irish history, when 'acts of murder, arson, rape and torture were committed in the name of the British Crown'.[13] A number of pacifists, however, such as the Anglican supporter of the Peace Pledge Union, Maude Royden, and also the highly popular Methodist preacher, Leslie Weatherhead, abandoned their pacifist stance.[14] As Martin Ceadel puts it, 'a pacifist had to believe it was a greater wrong to resist Hitler than to submit to him'.[15] Nonetheless, there were 59,000 British Conscientious Objectors during the Second War, compared with 16,500 during the First. The South-West Tribunal in 1942 reported on 4,056 cases, 662 being Methodists, 531 Anglicans, 439 Brethren (Open and Exclusive), 302 Quakers, 187 Baptists, 170 Christadelphians, 155 Jehovah's Witnesses and 143 Congregationalists. Treatment of COs was more lenient than in the First War, although many faced the possibility of abuse or imprisonment.[16] In June 1940 Aubrey, not himself a pacifist, encouraged churches to protest about discrimination against COs.[17] Later, Aubrey reported that he had been at a tribunal at which he had been expecting to defend a CO, but the hearing was fair and he did not need to speak.[18] Support was given by Percy Evans, Principal of Spurgeon's College, to Bernard Green, a CO who entered Bristol College after the war to train for Baptist ministry. Green was one of the 'Bevin boys' (named after the Minister of Labour, Ernest Bevin), allocated to work down the mines as an alternative to military service.[19]

13   Binfield, *Pastors and People*, p.256.
14   Ceadel, *Pacifism in Britain,* p.294.
15   M. Ceadel, 'Christian Pacifism in the Era of two World Wars', in W. J. Sheils, ed., *The Church and War* (Oxford: Basil Blackwell, 1983), p.403.
16   Dekar in 'Twentieth-Century British Baptist Conscientious Objectors' gives examples.
17   *BT*, 20 June 1940, p.391.
18   *BT*, 21 November 1940, p.663.
19   Conversation with Bernard Green (who became General Secretary of the Baptist Union), 17 July 2002.

An important war-time focus of attention for many Baptists was on prayer. Aubrey applauded King George VI's call to prayer in 1940.[20] The subsequent National Day of Prayer was deemed a success.[21] J.W. Ewing, as Metropolitan Superintendent for almost twenty years, knew London churches well, and he was heavily involved in monthly prayer meetings organized in the capital by the Evangelical Alliance. Other Baptists took part, including Ernest Brown, MP. Anglicans such as William Temple, the Archbishop of York, and Methodists such as W.E. Sangster of Westminster Central Hall, were also speakers.[22] Given the emphasis on prayer, one well-known deaconess, Sister Margaret Evans from Dagenham, found it

*A war-time church - Preston, Paignton, opened in May 1940*

heart-breaking that in some Baptist churches mid-week prayer meetings had ceased. In Dagenham, prayer groups were meeting in homes due to the black-out.[23] Commenting in 1940 on the content of the prayers being made about the war, Aubrey cautioned people from praying as if 'we are right and the Germans are wrong'.[24] A call for special prayer for the Jews was issued in 1944, signed, among others, by J.H. Rushbrooke, President of the BWA; Theo Bamber of Rye Lane Chapel, Peckham; Fred Mitchell, later chairman of the Keswick Convention; Martyn Lloyd-Jones, minister of Westminster Chapel; Colin Kerr, Vicar of St Paul's,

20   *BT*, 30 May 1940, p.343.
21   J. Wolffe, *God and Greater Britain* (London: Routledge, 1994), p.251.
22   *BT*, 20 June 1940, p.404.
23   *BT*, 27 June 1940, p.408.
24   *BT*, 1 August 1940, p.470.

Portman Square, London; and E.J. Poole-Connor, founder of the Fellowship of Independent Evangelical Churches (FIEC). A Day of Prayer was held in Ecclestone Hall, London.[25]

Local Baptist churches sought to respond appropriately to the needs that became evident as the devastation caused by aerial bombardment increased. In London, churches such as the West Ham Mission and Bloomsbury Central Baptist Church, had long experience of large-scale social ministry.[26] At Bloomsbury, four student deaconesses were active in visiting distressed people.[27] Outside London, too, the war affected church life in various ways. Some Baptist congregations were coping with an influx of evacuated children. In 1942 Ruth Henderson Smith, a deaconess who had been a student Sister at Bloomsbury, reported from Clarendon Park, Leicester, that the young minister, A.C. Hardy, was helping evacuees to find accommodation and the church had opened a home for the elderly among the evacuees.[28] Restrictions on travel and the limitations caused by the blackouts during air raids markedly affected the churches. Congregations were depleted by the call-up of members, and shift-work at factories often meant that church members were working in the evenings and at weekends.[29] On the other hand, Ruth Smith, involved in ministry to young people in Leicester, reported that she was glad to be 'young and strong in these momentous days'.[30]

For others, however, the predominant feelings were of confusion, loss and upheaval. Many Baptists, like other Christians, were confused by the common cause that Britain made with Russia, which had been known as a 'godless' Communist state. There was a recurring litany of grief at deaths from bombing and deaths in the Forces. Oldfield Park,

---

25    *BT*, 29 June 1944, p.8.
26    Johnson, *Encounter in London*, p.73.
27    Bowers, *A Bold Experiment*, pp.362-7.
28    *BT*, 12 June 1941, p.291; 29 January 1942, p.55.
29    I am indebted to Douglas Sparkes for several comments from him that I have used in this section. See also articles in *The Layman*, 1941 to 1943, describing the situation in churches across the country.
30    *BT*, 12 June 1941, p.291; 29 January 1942, p.55.

Bath, suffered the loss of forty members in one air raid.[31] Loss of buildings through bombing also caused great war-weariness. The general upheaval affected the Baptist denomination. The BMS moved to High Wycombe, Buckinghamshire, for safety, then returned to Furnival Street, but bomb damage meant a further move, to Kettering. The Baptist Union

*After the blitz: Chatsworth Way,*
*West Norwood*

remained in Church House, but there was considerable disruption, with the top floor being destroyed.[32] In 1940 Henry Cook reported on some of the damage that Baptists had suffered in London: 122 London Baptist churches had suffered damage and thirty-five church premises had been rendered unusable. Some of London's best-known Baptist churches – the Metropolitan Tabernacle, Devonshire Square, the East London Tabernacle, Westbourne Park and West Norwood – had lost their buildings. Outside London, the famous St Mary's Baptist Church, Norwich, renovated in 1940, was destroyed in 1942. Aubrey calculated the damage inflicted on Baptist churches at £6 million. The government pledged itself to provide in due course 'plain substitute buildings'. There was some freedom to move the money received in respect of one site to another, so that suburban churches were helped.[33]

31    Obituary of the minister, C.H. Higgs, *Baptist Handbook* (1969), p.365.
32    Payne, *The Baptist Union,* pp.214-15.
33    M.E. Aubrey, *Our Bombed Churches* (London: Baptist Union, n.d.).

However, churches had to wait for war-damage money until factories and homes were rebuilt.

For some, the result of the war was that their faith was expressed in new ways, although questioning could also lead to a loss of faith. A number of ministerial innovations took place. In Bristol, for instance, the war years saw a group of local ministers – Anglican, Methodist, Baptist, Congregational – build up an adventurous local ecumenical community and shared ministry.[34] In many cases Baptist church members not only drew closer to those in other denominations but also to those outside the churches through the experience of shared suffering. This did not necessarily mean that more people attended the churches during the war, but after the war a new impetus in evangelism was evident. It is significant that interdenominational evangelism attracted a great deal of support from Baptists in the mid-1940s. Perhaps this reflected a degree of impatience with what some church members saw, especially in the light of the war, as petty denominational disputes. The psychological relief experienced at the end of the war also helped to boost evangelistic efforts. After the war many ex-servicemen applied for ministerial training, in part seeking to fulfil a sense of calling to make the world a better place. Ministerial opportunities were considerable, with the Lancashire and Cheshire Association, for example, reporting in 1943 that 94 of the 210 churches

*A war-time wedding, 1944.*
*Monica Lord, daughter of Townley Lord, marries*
*Roy George at Bloomsbury Central Baptist Church*

---

34    Hastings, *A History of English Christianity*, p.392.

in the Association were without ministers.[35] A new generation of Baptists sought to rise to the challenges of post-war society.

## 'AN EXALTED CONCEPTION OF THE CHRISTIAN MINISTER'

The subject of ministry was addressed during as well as after the war, with two significant books about Baptist views of ministry appearing in 1944. They took up the issue of whether Baptist ministry was to be understood simply in terms of the local church, or whether an ordained person was a minister of the whole Church. Arthur Dakin of Bristol College, in *The Baptist View of the Church and Ministry* expounded the former position. His book arose from a conference of Baptist College Principals. At the request of the other College Principals, Dakin prepared an outline and, after discussing it, the Principals suggested it would be better for Dakin to express 'a definite point of view'. Aubrey's introduction to the book made it clear that it went out with the commendation of the Principals as a whole, 'though not necessarily with their concurrence at all points'. Dakin was well aware of the importance of belief in the Church universal, but most of his book dealt with the local congregation. For him it was fundamental that 'converted people are the units which make up the community'.[36] To Baptists this was not controversial. Ernest Payne, who opposed Dakin's view of the ministry, had also stated in 1939 at the BWA Congress that the church was 'a spiritual fellowship made up of converted men and women'.[37]

It was in Dakin's view of ministry that this localism became somewhat controversial. Dakin stated that:

> ...a Baptist minister is one who is actually doing to the full the work of the minister in a Baptist church ... Baptists have no 'order' of ministry in the sense that there is in the church a class of men made distinctive by some special endowment of divine grace regarded as

---

35    Sellers, *Our Heritage*, p.104.
36    A. Dakin, *The Baptist View of the Church & Ministry* (London: Carey Kingsgate Press, 1944), p.26.
37    West, *To be a Pilgrim*, p.54; West, *Baptists Together,* pp.67-8.

being confirmed by an ordination ceremony, or the laying on of hands, or in any other way. In actual practice the minister is given a standing different from that of ordinary members of the church, but this is ... not in any sense [due] to some special grace or 'holiness' not available to others.[38]

For Dakin, if a Baptist minister was not presiding over a congregation (but was, for example, a Baptist Union or BMS officer, or college tutor), 'he would for the time being cease to be a Baptist minister, just as a deacon ceases to be a Baptist deacon when he gives up the office.' Among Baptists, declared Dakin, 'ministry is defined primarily in terms of the local community, and not in terms of a central authority or of an ideal whole. To give up this principle would be to alter profoundly the whole Baptist view both of church and ministry.'[39]

A.C. Underwood, in his *History of the English Baptists*, considered that Dakin had set out the position commonly held among Baptists. Yet Underwood also believed that Baptists were not isolationists, concerned only with the local Baptist community.[40] Dakin readily acknowledged this, but claimed that the minister 'is not first a minister of the Church of God in some general way...Rather the situation is exactly the reverse, first a minister of the local church and then by reason of that a minister of the Church of God.'[41] Payne, from 1940 Senior Tutor at Regent's Park College, and a fine historian, strongly disagreed with Dakin's view. Before Dakin's book was published, Payne saw a manuscript copy and read it with increasing dismay. He responded by drafting a criticism of Dakin's approach, arguing that Baptist tradition was more complex than Dakin allowed. Wheeler Robinson, to whom Payne showed his own draft manuscript, favoured its publication. Payne's friend and life-long confidant, J.O. Barrett, minister of Fuller Chapel, Kettering, said of Payne's draft: 'You rather give me the impression of taking him [Dakin]

38    Dakin, *The Baptist View of the Church & Ministry*, p.42.
39    Ibid., pp.44-5.
40    Underwood, *A History of the English Baptists*, p. 267. For responses at the time, see *The Fraternal*, September 1944.
41    Dakin, *The Baptist View of the Church & Ministry*, pp.47-8.

across your knee!'[42] Payne's work could not be published as an explicit critique of a book that had the support of college Principals and was by the respected Dakin, who was nominated in 1944 as Union Vice-President. But Kingsgate Press was willing to publish a study by Payne: the title *The Fellowship of Believers: Baptist Thought and Practice Yesterday and Today* was suggested by Percy Evans.[43]

In *The Fellowship of Believers* Payne looked at church, ministry and sacraments in Baptist thought and practice over the previous three centuries. Eight years later he would publish an enlarged second edition, with chapters on worship and discipline. Payne acknowledged the encouragement of Wheeler Robinson, who wrote a foreword in which he suggested that although local church independence was a valuable safeguard of Christian liberty, it could 'become a form of selfishness alien to the Spirit of the Body of Christ, and far from the teaching and example of the New Testament'.[44] A.C. Underwood, reviewing the books by Dakin and Payne for the *Baptist Times*, noted a fissure in Baptist thinking. Dakin's trenchant defence of congregationalist views was popular among Baptists, but Payne had shown that much Baptist churchmanship in the seventeenth and eighteenth centuries was higher than in the 1940s. Underwood commended Payne's study, which he hoped would be considered by ministers, deacons and lay preachers.[45] Payne's thinking was influential. In 1946 R.C. Walton, who had trained at Bristol College and who in 1943 was appointed General Secretary for SCM in schools, wrote *The Gathered Community*. In this he maintained, following Payne rather than Dakin, that 'a Baptist church is a local

---

42    J.O. Barrett to E.A. Payne, 8 April 1944: Regent's Park College Oxford, Angus Library, Payne papers. See E.A. Payne, *A 20ᵗʰ Century Minister: John Oliver Barrett, 1901-78* (London: p.p., 1978).

43    West, *To be a Pilgrim*, pp.60-1; E.A. Payne, *The Fellowship of Believers: Baptist Thought and Practice Yesterday and Today* (London: The Kingsgate Press, 1944). For Payne's account of Free Church tradition, see E.A.Payne, *The Free Church Tradition in the Life of England* (London: SCM, 1944).

44    Payne, *Fellowship of Believers*, 2nd edn., 1952, pp.3, 6.

45    *BT*, 24 May 1945, p.7.

manifestation of the universal Church, and, therefore, Baptist ministers are ministers of Christ's Church'.[46]

*Ministry in a small church: a deaconess welcomes babies at a dedication service*

Walton's book was the product of discussions among thirteen people (mainly ministers) who met as a study group from 1941 onwards. Walton had read Payne's manuscript and, when his own work was nearing completion, Walton asked Payne and Hugh Martin of SCM to read his manuscript.[47] Links between a number of the group members who worked with Walton on *The Gathered Community* had been made at Bristol Baptist College, where most of the ministers had trained, and also

---

46    R.C. Walton, *The Gathered Community* (London: Carey Kingsgate Press, 1946), p.147.

47    Ibid., pp.8-10.

through the SCM and the BMS. Group members included Gwenyth Hubble, Assistant General Secretary of SCM and then Principal of Carey Hall, Birmingham; Marjorie Reeves, who was to become a distinguished Oxford historian and Vice-Principal of St Anne's College, Oxford; Norman Moon, later a tutor at Bristol College; Walter Bottoms, minister of New Road, Oxford, who had worked for the Young People's Department of the BMS; Alex Wilson, Director of Visual Aids at the BMS; Emlyn Davies, Welsh National Secretary of SCM, and Stephen Winward of Higham's Park, Walthamstow. The theologically diverse SCM still had wide support, although the conservative evangelical Inter-Varsity Fellowship (IVF) was a growing force in universities and colleges.[48] SCM continued to be influential in Baptist circles, not least through its publishing work, and helped to promote broader views of the church.

Broader thinking about ecclesiology was embodied in an important document approved by the Baptist Union Council in 1948, *The Baptist Doctrine of the Church*. The acceptance of this statement represented a substantial victory for the thinking of Payne and of Walton's group. The document stressed the place of Baptists within the 'one holy Catholic Church', set out a high view of the sacraments, in which 'Christ is really and truly present', and said that Baptists had from the beginning held 'an exalted conception of the Christian minister'. The minister's authority, the statement said, comes from the call of God in personal experience and, after the testing of the call and training, the minister is invited 'to exercise his gift in a particular sphere. The minister's authority therefore, is from Christ through the believing community'. The document explicitly repudiated Dakin's position, stating: 'Many among us hold that since the ministry is the gift of God to the Church, and the call to exercise the function of a minister comes from Him, a man who is called is not only a minister of a local Baptist church but also a minister of the whole Church of Jesus Christ.'[49] This document was produced in the same year in which the World Council of Churches (WCC) was formed

---

48    Bebbington, *Evangelicalism in Modern Britain*, pp.252-3.
49    'The Baptist Doctrine of the Church', in R. Hayden, ed., *Baptist Union Documents, 1948-1977* (London: Baptist Historical Society, 1980), pp.4-11.

in Amsterdam. Payne was one of the four Union representatives at Amsterdam, an indication of his influential position. Although some of the ideas in *The Baptist Doctrine of the Church* were never really understood in local churches, they were of key importance for Baptists involved in ecumenical conversations.[50]

There could be something of a gulf between this exalted conception of ministry and the realities of Baptist life. A new, well-planned Home Work Fund was established in 1943 to deal with ministerial stipends and other issues, but later in the decade a Council member alleged that Baptists had 'the worst-paid ministry of any of the leading denominations in this country'.[51] There was discussion in 1945 about the large number of short pastorates, which prevented churches getting to know their ministers. First pastorates were seen by some ministers as stepping stones.[52] On the question of settlements, one person commented in 1946 that, when a church became vacant, a list of possible preachers to 'fill the pulpit' for a Sunday was compiled. Within this list was an array of potentially suitable pastors. Church members, however, often divided into competing camps, with people in each camp wanting the person of their choice.[53] F.J. Humphrey, however, as chairman of the Superintendents' Board, believed that the Board's success in the work of settlement was, on the whole, remarkable. There were difficulties, and the number of ministers seeking changes was high, but Humphrey did not consider that condemnation of the whole system was justified.[54] In reply to claims that chaplains coming home from the war were finding it difficult to settle, one church secretary said that his church had decided only to look at chaplains for the pastorate. The church approached three, in turn, but each said 'no', two because they did not want to move north

---

50   West, *To be a Pilgrim*, p.70. For a record of ecumenical discussions from a participant see W.M. S. West, 'Baptists in Faith and Order – a Study in Baptismal Convergence', in Clements, ed., *Baptists in the Twentieth Century*, pp.55-75.

51   Sparkes, *The Home Mission Story*, pp.107-16, 119, citing *Report of the Council for 1949*.

52   *BT* 13 December 1945, p.8 (Leslie Chown).

53   *BT*, 24 January 1946, p.8 ('Hopeful').

54   *BT*, 7 February 1946, p.6.

and one because the stipend offered was too low, despite being above the minimum.[55] Problems were not always due to inadequate procedures.

Most Baptist churches were looking for male ministers. Gwenyth Hubble, who transferred from the list of probationers in 1943, was the only new woman minister to be accredited in the 1940s. Hubble, who had a BA and BD, was praised by H. Pilcher of the Essex Lay Preachers' Association, who reported in May 1943 that he had recently heard two women preach, one of them Hubble, and he was sure that God was speaking through them. Indeed he had never attended services more effectively conducted. Pilcher said that in some congregations there was no opportunity to listen to women preaching and wondered if any Baptist pulpits were closed to women.[56] Pulpits may or may not have been officially closed, but it was not obvious that female ministers were welcomed. It was noted in 1943 that the rules for ministerial recognition referred only to 'he', but this was understood, the Union's Ministerial Recognition

*Gwenyth Hubble*

Committee explained, 'to cover the other sex'.[57] In 1946 Sister Helen Britton, a deaconess at the West Ham Central Mission, who had a Diploma in Theology, expressed a desire to enter Baptist ministry. A group was appointed by the Ministerial Recognition Committee to examine the question.[58] Britton was turned down. The committee viewed 'with grave apprehension any tendency there might be for deaconesses to apply for ministerial recognition', suggesting that such applications might be seen as implying that deaconesses were inferior to ministers.[59]

---

55   *BT*, 14 February 1946, p.10.

56   *BT*, 27 May 1943, p.4.

57   Minutes of the Baptist Union Ministerial Recognition Committee, 10 February 1943, bound with BU Council minutes, Angus Library.

58   Ibid., 26 and 27 June 1946.

59   Ibid., 9 and 10 October 1946.

## TRAINING FOR EFFECTIVE MINISTRY

The concern for a fuller understanding of Baptist ministry was accompanied by a continuing concern for high standards of ministerial training. What was happening in the colleges? The foundation stone of the new Regent's Park College had been laid in Oxford in 1938 and a year later the College Council decided to go ahead with the erection of sixteen study bedrooms. Thus the College was fully established in Oxford before the war began and all new building work was halted. In 1942, R.L. Child, who had succeeded Aubrey at St Andrew's Street, Cambridge, became the Regent's Park Principal in succession to Wheeler Robinson.[60] The other colleges continued throughout most of the decade under the same Principals – Arthur Dakin at Bristol, Henry Townsend at Manchester, A.C. Underwood at Rawdon and Percy Evans at Spurgeon's. In 1938 Evans had persuaded the Spurgeon's College Council that the college should affiliate to the Baptist Union. He noted that most former Spurgeon's students served in the Union or the BMS; that eleven members of the College Council were on the Union Council, and that of the twenty-nine ministers who were president of the Union from 1897 to 1933, ten were from Spurgeon's.[61] Evans was instinctively opposed to isolationist ideas and was a significant bridge between the Spurgeonic constituency and the Union as a whole.

On the wider denominational front, a Baptist Polity Sub-Committee was looking at a number of issues, including ministerial training. At a meeting in September 1941, Henry Bonser, the North Eastern Superintendent, submitted a confidential report to the group. The other members present were P.T. Thomson, the Union's Commissioner for Education, J.O. Barrett of Fuller Chapel, Kettering, Wilson Black, Percy Evans, A.S. Langley, the historian, Gordon Fairbairn, the Union's legal adviser, and Arnold Clark, Union treasurer. Bonser reported that 1,578 churches in the Baptist Union had pastoral oversight and 448 had none. The churches with pastoral oversight had 1,141 accredited ministers and

---

60    Cooper, *From Stepney to St Giles'*, pp.89-90, 96-9.
61    Minutes of the Spurgeon's College Council, 15 December 1938: Spurgeon's College, London.

321 who were unaccredited. Evidence suggested, according to Bonser, that there would be a shortage of accredited ministers after the war. There would probably also be financial stringency and therefore stipendiary problems. Serious consideration, he suggested, should be given to the fact that there were increasing numbers of unaccredited ministers, and he proposed that a decrease in the number of such ministers, apart from those who were lay pastors, was desirable. Bonser's conclusion, which indicated that he had doubts about the quality of at least some unaccredited ministers, was: 'It is essential that recruits for the Ministerial lists are men of adequate personality, evangelistic zeal and training.'[62]

Although Bonser did not analyse the age profile of Baptist ministers, this profile was part of the problem. In 1931, no less than sixty per cent of serving Baptist ministers were over fifty, and only fourteen per cent were under forty.[63] This profile, however, was to change in the post-war period: Aubrey said in 1943 that he had received from chaplains the names of about 100 men in the Forces who wanted to become ministers.[64] Four months later, in the light of the Polity Sub-Committee findings and information from Aubrey, college representatives recommended that as many 'suitable men' as possible be trained. As had happened before, it was proposed that the entry of untrained ministers into positions of full ministerial responsibility should be discouraged. A third proposal was that the Council should be asked to consider recognizing a new order of ministry which would combine ministerial service with secular work.[65] The issue of untrained ministers was to be an on-going feature of discussions about ministry in the denomination, and the idea of bi-vocational ministry was not pursued formally until much later. The point about increasing numbers in training, however, was to prove significant: all the colleges were filled after the war. Percy Evans spoke enthusiastically in 1946 about those 'arriving from the Forces, from bomb disposal units, and from coal mining' with 'an

---

62    Minutes of Baptist Union Baptist Polity Sub-Committee, 15 September 1941.
63    Brown, *A Social History of the Nonconformist Ministry*, p.230.
64    *BT*, 6 May 1943, p.7.
65    Minutes of the United Collegiate Board, 17 September 1943.

experience of God and of men'.[66] The numbers involved were very high. The colleges processed nearly 500 applications from servicemen for ministerial training and about one-third were accepted.[67]

One new factor in this period was the establishment of the interdenominational London Bible College (LBC).[68] The central figures in the beginnings of LBC in 1943 were A.J. Vereker, the secretary of the Crusaders' Union, and Douglas Johnson, General Secretary of the IVF. It had been hoped that Martyn Lloyd-Jones, minister of Westminster Chapel, would become LBC's Principal, but he declined. Graham Scroggie, minister at the Metropolitan Tabernacle, who had his own Bible correspondence course, took the post, but served for only a few months. In 1943 Lloyd-Jones proposed that Ernest Kevan, minister of Upper Tooting Baptist Church, whose background was in Strict Baptist ministry but who became an accredited Baptist Union minister, should join the LBC staff, and in due course Kevan became LBC's Principal.[69] Other Baptist ministers such as J.W. Ewing, former Metropolitan Superintendent, George Beasley-Murray, then at Ashurst Drive, Ilford, Stephen Winward, at Higham's Park, and Frank Fitzsimmonds, at New Malden, taught at LBC on a part-time basis. There was some consternation, however, in 1944-5, when LBC appeared to be offering training for Baptist ministry. With so many ex-servicemen seeking training, Kevan considered that LBC could make courses available for one or two years to prepare people to enter denominational colleges. Given the misunderstandings, Kevan agreed that LBC should state that it did not prepare for denominational ministry but that it helped towards that end.[70]

---

66   Percy Evans, 'Rain after Drought', *Spurgeon's College Magazine*, Spring 1946, p.18.
67   *BT*, 9 January 1947, p.7.
68   See I.M. Randall, *Educating Evangelicalism: The Origins, Development and Impact of London Bible College* (Carlisle: Paternoster Press, 2000), chapters 1-3.
69   I.H. Murray, *David Martyn Lloyd-Jones Vol.2: The Fight of Faith, 1939-1981* (Edinburgh: Banner of Truth Trust, 1990), p.93.
70   Minutes of LBC Faculty Meetings, 19 December 1944, 13 February 1945; 16 May 1945: LBC, London.

Although increased numbers of students entered Baptist colleges in the aftermath of the Second World War, the exigencies of the war also increased the number of non-collegiate ministers – those not trained in Baptist colleges. Partly this was because of temporary pastoral appointments in churches whose ministers had taken up posts as chaplains. Also, some churches that became vacant just before or during the war were ready to appoint non-collegiate ministers. For example Alan Redpath, who became minister of Duke Street, Richmond, in 1940, was an accountant who had been an evangelist with the interdenominational National Young Life Campaign.[71] Under Redpath's innovative ministry in the 1940s, the membership at Duke Street increased from 180 to over 400. Redpath was followed at Duke Street by Stephen Olford, who had been an evangelist in the Open Brethren.[72] Seymour Price, General Manager of the Baptist Insurance Company, who was President of the Union in 1944-45, affirmed the variety of ways in which ministerial formation could take place, and Price had discussions with Ernest Kevan at LBC. Price's father had been brought up among the Strict Baptists. In his presidential address in 1944, Price argued for equal honour to be given to everyone - collegiate and non-collegiate alike – entering ministry. At the same time, he called for all those beginning Baptist ministry to be accredited, whether by going to a Baptist college or by taking the Baptist Union examination.[73]

The question of training through colleges that were not Baptist continued to be discussed in the later 1940s. Applications to enter accredited Baptist ministry through taking the Union examination came from students of various colleges, for example the Bible Training Institute, Glasgow, and All Nations, in London, which was primarily a missionary college. In 1947 the Ministerial Recognition Committee discussed a request from Signalman W.G. Guttridge, from Stoke Newington, who had not secured a place at Spurgeon's College and had

---

71    *Christian*, 24 April 1947, p.1.
72    For the Brethren in this period see R.N. Shuff, *Searching for the True Church: Brethren and Evangelicals in mid-Twentieth-Century England*, Carlisle: Paternoster Press, forthcoming.
73    *BT*, 4 May 1944, p.8.

asked about study at LBC. Aubrey said that no adverse reflection was intended on LBC, but it was impossible to recognize a college from outside the denomination as offering full Baptist ministerial training.[74] The Ministerial Recognition Committee, in looking at unaffiliated colleges, consulted with Methodists, Congregationalists and Presbyterians. These denominations utilized only their own colleges for ministerial training. Percy Evans stated that the Baptist college principals were against recognizing LBC for this purpose. He pointed out that the next LBC Principal, after Kevan, might not be a Baptist. Also, Baptist colleges considered they could train as many Baptist ministers as were needed.[75] Earlier in the century Shakespeare had sought to raise the standard of training and ministry; the 1940s threw up new issues about the relationship of Baptist ministry to broader evangelical life.

BAPTIST REVIVAL

It was Theo Bamber, who had trained at Spurgeon's and been the minister of the large Rye Lane Chapel in Peckham since 1926, who emerged in the 1940s as a significant figure calling for evangelical renewal in the denomination. Bamber, a commanding leader, was deeply dissatisfied with much denominational life in England, Baptist life included. In March 1939 Bamber addressed a London audience of 2,000 people, most of them younger people, on personal revival. Those supporting the meeting included Martyn Lloyd-Jones, Westminster Chapel's minister, and Anglican, Independent and Brethren leaders.[76] A year later, Bamber arranged what he termed a service of repentance.[77] This idea was promoted in the *Christian Herald*, edited by T. Wilkinson Riddle, who had been minister of George Street Baptist Church, Plymouth. A few months after this, A. Eric Wood, pastor of Wood Grange, Forest Gate, who had been helped by the Christian Endeavour

74   Minutes of the Baptist Union Ministerial Recognition Committee, 29 January 1947.
75   Minutes of the Baptist Union Ministerial Recognition Committee Sub-Committee re Unaffiliated Colleges, 13 June 1949.
76   *Christian*, 2 March 1939, p.7.
77   *BT*, 29 February 1940, p.132.

movement, arranged a further meeting with the theme of repentance, and several ministers attended.[78] An interdenominational network of evangelical ministers was developing in London. Central to this group was Colin Kerr, Vicar of St Paul's Church, Portman Square. Calls to pray for revival were made at a meeting in 1942 at Kingsway Hall, London, at which Kerr, Bamber and the Methodist, Joe Brice, who was associated with Cliff College, Derbyshire, were the speakers. Kingsway Hall was used by many Christian organizations, but this event was seen as particularly 'enthusiastic'.[79]

Theo Bamber had considerable interest in pan-denominational evangelicalism, but he was also a committed Baptist. At the 1942

*Theo Bamber*

Assembly, he moved a motion as a rider to the regular report from the Council. Bamber suggested – in what would become a recurring theme - that 'the basic weakness of our churches is a defective relationship to the living Lord', and he proposed that the Council should take steps which would bring the churches to the experience of revival. Reporting for the *Baptist Times,* William Taylor Bowie, minister at Church Road, Acton, explained that the Assembly had real sympathy with this sentiment but many felt that the Council report itself stressed such matters and in the light of this Bamber's

motion was rejected. It is not clear that the Council had in fact covered Bamber's concerns, but Aubrey demonstrated at the Assembly that he was not complacent about the spiritual state of the church or the nation. He condemned, for example, members of the Cabinet who were making speeches on Sundays. For Aubrey, however, revival would come not only through a renewed relationship with Christ but also through a renewal of the church's understanding of its place in God's purposes.

---

78    *Christian Herald*, 13 June 1940, p.402.
79    *Christian Herald*, 13 August 1942, p.108.

Aubrey's main contribution to the 1942 Assembly was to stress that Baptists were 'impenitent High Churchmen'. He said that outsiders often failed to understand that Baptists had a high doctrine of the church and exacting standards of church membership.[80]

Meetings between some London ministers concerned about 'the low level of spiritual life in the churches' led to Theo Bamber, Geoffrey King, minister of the East London Tabernacle, Angus McMillan, minister of Lewin Road Baptist Church, Streatham, and others, forming the Baptist Revival Fellowship (BRF) in 1938.[81] In the early 1940s this organization began to make its presence felt. Although the BRF commenced in a small way, it could not be ignored, and was destined to have increasing impact among conservative evangelicals. Rye Lane Chapel had over 1,000 members and was the largest church in the Metropolitan Area. Most London churches which forty years earlier had attracted over 1,000 people were now much smaller. In the North East, one of the largest churches was Wellington Street, Stockton-on-Tees, where another BRF member, Leslie Larwood, was pastor. Melbourne Hall, Leicester, where Leslie Land was minister from 1947, had the biggest membership of any Union church. The largest group of Baptist churches in 1946, however, had under fifty members,[82] and the BRF, with its concern for revival within local churches, sought to reach out to these congregations. Bamber, who was at Rye Lane until his retirement in 1961, had a gift for motivating others, and under his ministry about forty younger people went into full-time Christian service.[83]

The first major public meeting of the BRF was held in Bloomsbury Central Baptist Church in April 1942. Fred Cawley, a tutor at Spurgeon's College, described how a 'youthful "Spurgeonic" platform drew a

80   *BT*, 30 April 1942, pp.210, 212.
81   *The Baptist Revival Fellowship: Constitution and Rules* (London: BRF, n.d.): Spurgeon's College, BRF Archive, file TMB; *Fundamentalist*, February 1939, p.47.
82   *BT*, 21 February 1946, p.8.
83   I am indebted to Ron Luland, who came from Rye Lane Chapel, studied at Spurgeon's College, and in 1950 became minister of St George's Street, Macclesfield, for his reminiscences.

congregation that packed the building'. The opening devotions were led by Ronald Park, of Griffin Road, East Plumstead, and later of Muswell Hill, and the speakers were John Pritchard of the 700-member West Croydon Tabernacle, Geoffrey King, and Theo Bamber, 'who, characteristically', said Cawley, 'stressed the power of the Holy Spirit'.[84] But not all were impressed by this new movement. A 'London Baptist Minister's Wife' objected in 1943 to the announcements and the pamphlets emanating from the BRF. This was a reference to the 'Clarion Call' to Baptist ministers issued by the BRF in that year. She said that her husband worked hard and supported the Union, the BMS, the LBA, and the Ministers' Fraternal. Many ministers like him, she insisted, did not want something else to be organized. She saw the BRF as superfluous, since what it emphasized was basic to Baptist belief.[85] Although the theme that the Baptist denomination was already a revival fellowship was taken up by others, this view had little influence on BRF members. Leslie Long, then BRF Secretary, wrote to the *Baptist Times* to thank all who had written expressing approval or disapproval of the new body and to say that he would present the views expressed to Aubrey.[86] There is no evidence of Aubrey's response.

Baptists who hoped for imminent revival were in many cases also looking for the imminent, premillennial return of Christ. Interest in the prophetic elements in Scripture was certainly not limited to BRF members. In 1940 Ernest Brown, MP, was reported as having created a sensation among the 1,500 people at the Baptist Union Assembly (numbers were lower in war time) by declaring that the book of Daniel foretold the rise of Hitler when it said – Brown used the Moffat translation – that a 'despicable creature' would arise.[87] It was within BRF circles, however, that such views were most commonly discussed. Booklets written by Bamber included *His Glorious Appearing*. Meetings to emphasise these themes were held in 1943, and speakers were largely those who appeared on BRF platforms. Ronald Park wrote in that year

---

84   *The Christian*, 30 April 1942, p.3.
85   *BT*, 14 October 1943, p.4.
86   *BT*, 11 November 1943, p.6.
87   *Christian Herald*, 16 May 1940, p.338.

in the *Advent Witness*, the magazine of the premillennial Advent Testimony and Preparation Movement, that 1943 might be the year in which Christ would return. There was speculation that the rise of Mussolini in Italy could signal a revived Roman Empire, which some biblical interpreters saw prophesied in Scripture, although some writers in the *Advent Witness*, such as E.G. Rudman, minister of Mitcham Lane, Streatham (and from 1947 at Holland Road, Hove), abjured dogmatic views.[88] Dogmatism was certainly rife. In 1943 Stanley Baker, one of the Essex Five, discussing the BRF, warned about 'heresy-hunting', picturing this in ominous terms as 'sectarian goose-stepping'. Baker's call was for united evangelism.[89] It is significant that such an evangelistically-minded pastor was critical of aspects of the BRF's approach.

Undaunted by criticism, the BRF published in 1949 a call to share in the 'Opening of the Door to Mid-Century Revival'. The leaflet publicizing this call listed the BRF's regional correspondents. Of the thirty people who apparently had some responsibility within the BRF, fifteen had been trained at Spurgeon's and three at other Baptist colleges. Eight were non-accredited ministers, three were accredited non-collegiate ministers, and there was one lay person. The Spurgeonic connection was clearly strong. By now the BRF was more explicitly drawing the kind of doctrinal boundaries which had worried Stanley Baker. Scripture, said the leaflet, was 'a unified revelation of the mind of God through men, inerrant and infallible'. Trenchant points were made about Baptist life. Baptist ministry was better educated but less effective; churches were on average seventy-five per cent empty; membership revision, if undertaken, would reveal a loss of twenty-five per cent of the membership; there were few missionary candidates; young people did not know the power of the Holy Spirit; many new members had no 'saving faith'; very little teaching on the Holy Spirit or the Second Advent was taking place; and modernist teaching was

---

88    *Advent Witness*, January-February 1943, p.225; March-April 1943, pp.233-4.
89    *BT*, 18 November 1943, p.4.

robbing the pulpit of authority.[90] This unremittingly gloomy analysis was intended to convince Baptists of the need for revival.

## MAKING CONVERSION THE GOAL

Of more interest to many Baptists in the 1940s than talk of imminent revival or the return of Christ was how to be more effective in day-to-day evangelism. Arthur Dakin, as Union President, said in 1945: 'We need to bring the idea of conversion back into the forefront of our church life, making it the goal of our teaching and the aim of our prayer.' In the light of much that was happening among British evangelicals he stated that he wanted to commend evangelicalism but not emotionalism.[91] Throughout and after the war the Union's Forward Movement continued, and congregations received help with new initiatives. The congregation at Welwyn Garden City, for example, which had begun in 1928, with twenty people, had ninety members in 1940, and with the help of the Forward Movement a new building was completed. Pollard's Hill, Mitcham, was established by the South West Group of the LBA to serve the 16,000 people who were living on a new housing area in Mitcham that had no Free Church. Meetings began in 1938 in a school. The church building, erected later, was in a modern style, with chairs rather than pews. Sister Bertha Beal, a deaconess, undertook pioneer work at Pollard's Hill and the local Lay Preachers' Federation provided preachers.[92] At Chingford, Essex, in the same period, another deaconess, Sister Winifred Willmott, led a team under the auspices of the Forward Movement. In eight months twenty-one new members joined and in 1940 five were awaiting baptism. Previously the church had made contact with only a few children, but now a large Sunday school had developed.[93]

The Forward Movement was not the only stimulus to evangelism. Ministers took local initiatives. At Winton, Bournemouth, Arthur Coffey,

---

90   *Opening of the Door to Mid-Century Revival* (London: BRF, n.d.): Spurgeon's College, BRF Archive, file TMB.
91   *BT*, 3 May 1945, p.8.
92   *BT*, 25 January 1940, p.54; 1 February 1940, p.70.
93   *BT*, 20 June 1940, p.390.

the minister, utilized special speakers whose visits were advertised widely. Ernest Brown, MP, Townley Lord, W.D. Jackson, Southern Area Superintendent, and William G. Channon, who moved from Elim Pentecostal to Baptist ministry and became minister of the Metropolitan Tabernacle in 1944, were among the speakers used – as Coffey put it - to 'stir people in the town'. At these meetings extra chairs had to be placed down the aisle.[94] Wilson Black, commenting on the progress of evangelism nation-wide, noted that ministers in the South seemed to have more conversions than those in the North, and Henry Townsend pointed to 'a sort of [Northern] hard-headedness and independence'.[95] In 1946 Townley Lord said a friend of his had been preaching in a Northern chapel to a congregation of eight. The friend asked whether this was usual and was told that several members were on holiday. The previous Sunday there had been a normal congregation: seventeen people, in a building accommodating 900![96] Nonetheless, Black's observation about Baptists in the North was a generalization. Stanley Voke, at Bethesda Free Church, Sunderland, had Sunday evening congregations of 700. At a baptismal service in 1946, early in Voke's ministry there, twenty-seven were baptized and twenty more young people came forward to confess Christ.[97]

The war may have contributed to more awareness of spiritual issues. At the Shoreditch Tabernacle, where Ernest Clifford was minister, four men and three women were baptized in June 1942. At the end of the service an appeal was made in which others who wished to be baptized were invited to give their names to a deaconess of the church, and during the singing of the final hymn six people came down the aisle. They were not known to the Tabernacle - they included, it later transpired, a doctor, a Rugby International and Cambridge Blue, and a soldier – but all were baptized immediately.[98] This sparked off a debate about the relationship between conversion, baptism and church membership. Normal Baptist

---

94    *BT*, 14 February 1946, p.14.
95    Townsend, *Robert Wilson Black*, p.66.
96    *BT*, 17 January 1946, p.1.
97    *BT*, 5 December 1946, p.19.
98    *BT*, 11 June 1942, p.293.

practice in the 1940s was that a number of baptismal classes – perhaps six – preceded baptism. In *Concerning Believer's Baptism* (1943), F.C. Bryan, then minister of Tyndale Baptist Church, Bristol, who strongly advocated such classes for applicants for baptism and membership, set out what could be covered in them and described the appointment of visitors from among the church members who would interview candidates.[99] George Beasley-Murray, by contrast, believed that baptism was the climax of conversion, with appropriate teaching following baptism.[100]

*A women's meeting led by a deaconess*

Whatever the views about this issue, baptismal services were commonly evangelistic, and in most Baptist churches in this period they took place on Sunday evenings, when larger congregations could be attracted.[101]

Initiatives in evangelism were celebrated, but difficulties confronted evangelistic endeavour. House-to-house surveys found that in some new housing areas only one home in ten had a Bible. Younger members of the Baptist Women's League were holding house or 'cottage' meetings in such areas.[102] Aubrey remained deeply concerned about falling Baptist membership, which, he said in 1942, reflected 'the serious decline in

99   F.C. Bryan, 'Preparation, Administration and Visitation', in F.C. Bryan, ed., *Concerning Believer's Baptism* (London: The Kingsgate Press, 1943), pp.66-72; 76-8.
100  G.R. Beasley-Murray, 'The Sacraments', *The Fraternal*, October 1948, pp.3-7; Cross, *Baptism and the Baptists*, pp.387-95.
101  Bryan, 'Preparation, Administration and Visitation', pp.72-6.
102  *BT*, 25 June 1942, p.318.

religious interest and firmly held Christian faith which has been going on for many years'. He advocated methods relevant to a society in which there was less respect for the spoken word and in which meetings of all kinds were less well attended. From time to time, Aubrey raised contentious issues. He was pleased that a rigid Calvinism which hindered mission had gone, but he saw belief in an imminent second coming of Christ as a 'dangerous doctrine', cutting the nerve of mission. When he added (with doubtful historical warrant) that some who discouraged William Carey had held these views, it was certain that he would be challenged.[103] The challenge came from Geoffrey King, who found Aubrey's article invigorating but described the reference to the Second Advent as 'unfortunate and misleading'. King contended that the 'Second Advent preacher is usually the most ardent missionary enthusiast and to the fore in home evangelism'. Many critics, he believed, were entirely misinformed about this teaching.[104]

It seemed that in some rural areas difficulties were particularly acute. Cyril Petch, from Isleham, an active lay preacher, knew the situation of small churches in rural areas and suggested that many had no real leadership and were living on the past. The age group 14-18, he maintained, had largely disappeared from rural churches.[105] After the war, however, teams of young people gave specific assistance to village chapels in the Midlands.[106] In 1949 the Union analysed data about 755 village Baptist churches in nine areas of the country. About 400 had ministerial oversight, 200 of these being served by full-time ministers, 134 by part-time ministers, and 85 by lay pastors. But 220 were without ministerial oversight and were unable to provide a manse or qualify for Union help. Information was incomplete, but it is probable that thirty

---

103  *BT*, 11 June 1942, p.294.

104  *BT*, 9 July 1942, p.343.

105  *BT*, 2 September 1943, p.6. Petch was to become a central figure in the Baptist Men's Movement.

106  F.M.W. Harrison, *It All Began Here: The Story of the East Midland Baptist Association* (London: East Midland Baptist Association, 1986), p.140; conversation with Bernard Green, former General Secretary of the Union, 17 July 2002.

churches which might have afforded a minister were unable to attract one. Churches without oversight were growing weaker, numerically and spiritually, and making little impact. Several ideas about leadership – most in fact already being tried - were offered: the use of teams of younger lay people; partnership between churches; encouragement to probationers to settle in rural areas; and greater use of able lay people who had retired. 'The ideal', said the report, 'is a cultured, gifted, consecrated preacher in every village pulpit'. Chapels were also encouraged to modernize their premises and to try to obtain a manse where they did not have one.[107]

Baptists were not alone in struggling to modernize. The Church of England's significant report, *Towards the Conversion of England*, produced in 1945, received considerable acclaim, but Adrian Hastings suggests that the Church of England was tied by its venerable customs and pastoral amateurishness.[108] Methodists had some success with their evangelistic 'Commando Campaigns', in which many Baptists participated.[109] A young British evangelist, Tom Rees, who had worked for the Children's Special Service Mission (CSSM), initiated large-scale interdenominational meetings, particularly for young people, in the Westminster Central Hall and then in the Royal Albert Hall. Early speakers included C.S. Lewis, Martyn Lloyd-Jones, and W.E. Sangster. Rees purchased Hildenborough Hall, a large country house in Kent, and turned it into a popular Christian conference centre. His 'Faith for the Times' campaigns in London, with evangelistic speakers such as Theo Bamber, Alan Redpath, Colin Kerr and A. Lindsay Glegg (a businessman and pastor of Down Lodge Hall, Wandsworth), drew many Baptists. Townley Lord, reporting on an Albert Hall meeting, observed that those present were predominantly 'enthusiastic church-going types'. Some of Bamber's views, Townley Lord commented, were not shared by all, but

---

107  Minutes of Baptist Union Council 15 and 16 November 1949.
108  Hastings, *History of English Christianity*, p.437.
109  C.A. Roberts, ed., *These Christian Commando Campaigns* (London: Epworth Press, 1945).

Lord 'felt the power of his direct and at times passionate evangelical appeal'.[110]

Further initiatives came from North America. In the spring of 1946 a twenty-seven-year-old American evangelist, Billy Graham, a Southern Baptist, was part of a small Youth for Christ (YFC) team that came to Britain. Tom Rees gathered about sixty people to meet the Americans at the Bonnington Hotel in London. Evangelistic events across Britain began to be advertised as 'on the American Youth for Christ pattern'.[111] The reception given to the highly contemporary approach being used was mixed. Stanley Baker, then minister of Bordesley Green Baptist Church in Birmingham, who was arguing in March 1946 for an Order of evangelists and community chaplains, was dubious about young Americans seeking to convert Birmingham. He said that 'some of us, trying to serve church, community and county, yet seeking to remain conscientious pastors and youth leaders, face physical breakdown and spiritual despair', and he was looking for experienced people as pastors and evangelists. He was deeply sceptical about a 'hand-counting huckster whose perorations drip with emotion'.[112] Billy Graham persuaded him otherwise, and Baker then telephoned his acquaintances urging support for Graham's Birmingham youth meetings. Numbers attending these meetings rose to 2,500.[113] The initial YFC British tour was followed by six months of mission which Graham conducted throughout Britain from October 1946, and by further transatlantic trips in the next two years.[114] Evangelism, not least among Baptists, was to be profoundly affected by Graham's methods.

110   BT, 13 April 1944, p.6; J. Rees, Stranger than Fiction (Frinton-on-Sea: p.p., 1957), pp.24-5.
111   BT, 21 March 1946, p.13.
112   BT, 7 March 1946, p.8.
113   Report by Billy Graham: Wheaton College, USA, Billy Graham Archives, CN 318, Box 54, Folder 13.
114   Christian, 8 April 1948, p.9.

## THE STATE OF THE CHURCHES

In 1944 the Council 'anxiously debated', as Payne put it, the 'State of the Churches'. A group was convened by Henry Cook, Metropolitan Superintendent, to look at 'spiritual welfare' in Baptist churches.[115] Although the group did not embrace the pessimism of the BRF about the denomination, it did take the situation seriously. Among those who worked with Cook on the group's report were Arthur Dakin, Ingli James (previously of Queen's Road, Coventry, and now East Midland Superintendent), R. Rowntree Clifford from West Ham, Grey Griffith of the BMS, Theo Bamber, Geoffrey King, J.C. Rendall (East Midland Superintendent from 1947), H.L. Watson of Richmond, Liverpool (later North Western Superintendent), and Aubrey. When meetings were held at Regent's Park College, Oxford, Payne was also present. In 1946 the group produced a report entitled, 'Speak - that they go Forward'. This was published as a book under the same title, and 25,000 copies were produced. The book emphasized revival but rejected any simple formula, and stressed the importance of the message of the gospel, the ministry (seen as 'the key to most of our problems'), and, naturally, evangelism. It was recommended that every Association should have an Evangelistic or Spiritual Advance Committee.[116] Cook followed *Speak – that they go Forward* with *What Baptists Stand For* (1947), and also gave the Louisa Curtis Lectures at Spurgeon's in 1949 on the subject of evangelism.[117]

There was further discussion of spiritual welfare in 1947 in the context of national austerity and hopes for post-war reconstruction. Henry Cook produced a form of covenant for churches, reminiscent of some older Baptist church covenants, to guide Baptist members in renewing their commitment to Christ and each other.[118] 50,000 copies of

---

115  Payne, *Baptist Union*, p.227.
116  H. Cook, *Speak - that they go Forward: A Report on the Spiritual Welfare in the Churches of the Baptist Denomination* (London: Baptist Union, 1946).
117  These were published: H. Cook, *The Theology of Evangelism* (London: Carey Kingsgate Press, 1951).
118  Minutes of the Council, 12 and 13 March 1946.

the covenant were issued in response to requests.[119] At the March 1947 Council, Cook pressed home his conviction that 'only through a re-vitalised and re-spiritualised Church could the people be converted'. There were reports at the Council of open-air meetings taking place across the country, some using motor cars and loud speakers.[120] Bamber, however, was not satisfied. At the November 1947 Council he called for the Assembly, the Associations, and all churches in membership with the Union, to encourage the re-emphasis of the 'great evangelical principles' of 'our beloved denomination'.[121] Churches, Bamber argued, should be evangelizing forces, not social fellowships, and he stressed the importance of spiritual qualities produced by 'the teaching of the Word of God rather than by the theories of man'. He attributed decline in Baptist membership to various factors: Baptists moving to other churches because they were failing to find spiritual help in Baptist churches; Baptists lapsing from their faith; and lack of new converts.[122]

There was a feeling that *Speak - that they go Forward*, while offering a very good diagnosis, was short on practical suggestions. In his follow-up book, *What Baptists Stand For*, Cook encouraged Baptists to advocate their particular historic doctrine of the church, based on the teaching of the New Testament.[123] Bamber's suggestion was that principals and tutors in Baptist colleges should be encouraged to 'emphasise to their students the authority and sufficiency of the Bible and the need for clear conviction, challenging preaching and holiness of life'. Geoffrey King and Bamber commended the idea of Union and Association Spiritual Welfare Commissioners. After discussion, the Council agreed the formation of an 'Evangelisation and Spiritual Welfare Committee'.[124] All sections of the Council were committed to these priorities. Indeed what King and Bamber envisaged did not seem to others to be very different from Aubrey's Discipleship Campaign

---

119  *BT*, 20 March 1947, p.8.
120  Minutes of the Baptist Union Council, 11 and 12 March 1947.
121  Minutes of the Baptist Union Council, 18 and 19 November 1947.
122  Ibid.
123  H. Cook, *What Baptists Stand For* (London: Carey Kingsgate Press, 1947).
124  Minutes of the Baptist Union Council, 18 and 19 November 1947.

Messengers. It is possible that Bamber would only be fully satisfied when ideas that he put forward were implemented. The March 1948 Council again emphasized the need for the preaching of the gospel, biblical exposition in the churches, prayer, holiness of living and personal witness.[125]

*Sister Elsie leading a young people's fellowship*

In many of these discussions about the state of the churches there was a lack of input from lay people in Baptist congregations. However, many lay women and men were active in denominational life through the Baptist Women's League and the Baptist Laymen's Missionary Movement respectively. In 1944 the Laymen's Missionary Movement, founded in 1917, which had supported the BMS, changed its name to the Baptist Men's Movement (BMM), and from then on related both to the BMS and to the Union. The principal aims of the movement were to mobilize laymen in the churches to 'give united and effective witness in

---

125  Minutes of the Baptist Union Council, 9 and 10 March 1948.

every department of life', to 'win men outside the churches for the service of Christ and His Kingdom', and to 'support Baptist endeavours'. G.W. Harte, of Elm Road, Beckenham, who in 1953 became the first minister to serve as BMM President, introduced the idea of men's Contact Clubs, and by the end of the war these had been formed in seventy-two Baptist churches.[126] Many who were members of the BMM, and who attended its annual conference at Swanwick, were deacons or in other leadership positions in Baptist churches.

An obvious resource for future Baptist renewal was younger lay people. Arnold Clark, Union Treasurer, praised the Boys' Brigade for its Bible teaching and its spiritual priorities.[127] Christian Endeavour Societies were also important. It was reported in January 1941 that 2,000 CE societies were meeting in Baptist churches.[128] Given their strong commitment to developing young people as effective Christians, this represented huge potential for Baptists. In 1948 Stanley Turl, Organising Secretary of the Baptist Lay Preachers' Federation, contacted the national CE secretary, Andrew Wright, a Baptist minister, about recruitment of lay preachers from CE societies, and a leaflet was produced.[129] There was considerable discussion in 1944 about whether local churches were welcoming young people. Brenda Holloway from Moseley, Birmingham, who had worked in youth clubs for several years, said in the *Baptist Times* that one younger person in her church had objected to notions of young people as the 'church of the future'. They wanted to be the church of today. Young people were seen as blasé and independent, but Holloway argued that they needed love and understanding. Also, they had energy to offer.[130] In universities and colleges, Baptist students might be involved in the SCM or the IVF. In 1947 the Baptist Students' Federation (BSF), which would shape many

---

126  K.W. Bennett, *God at Work with Men* (1997), pp.20, 23-4; cf. *World Outlook*, No. 159 (1945), p.1.
127  *BT*, 18 April 1940, p.244.
128  *BT*, 16 January 1941, p.28.
129  Minutes of the Baptist Union Lay Preachers' Federation Committee, 6 October 1948; bound with BU Council papers, Angus Library.
130  *BT*, 14 December 1944, p.8.

Baptist leaders, was formed.[131] The BSF annual conference was an important meeting-point, and the BSF organized evangelistic campaigns in churches.[132]

There were, however, noticeable inter-generational tensions in some Baptists churches. In the 1940s the wearing of hats by women during church services was still quite widespread, and one Baptist member, 'A.G.R.', protested about a young woman who had not followed this custom at a communion service. The pastor of the church suggested that 'only hard-boiled Church of England parsons took notice of that these days', but 'A.G.R.', who had been a Baptist for thirty years, had never before seen hatless women at communion.[133] The *Baptist Times* commented on the number and the vigour of the letters that followed. One respondent asked tersely whether A.G.R. had nothing better to do at communion than observe hats. A.G.R.'s attitude was condemned by one correspondent as 'pettiness and spiritual immaturity', another enquired whether at A.G.R.'s church the female baptismal candidates wore hats, and still others reported on changes in the custom of hat-wearing. One Baptist church apparently had 'numberless young women with uncovered heads', and this was welcomed since they were 'under the sound of the gospel message'. No-one offered a whole-hearted defence of obligatory hat-wearing. Vellam Pitts, however, at Zion Baptist Church, Cambridge, had one intriguing story: in an Anglican church in Cambridge a young woman 'had such striking hair and arranged it with such effect that it became a distraction to the worshippers'. Although the church did not insist on hats, she was asked to wear one.[134]

Other aspects of the life of the churches provoked debate and disagreement. There were several letters in the *Baptist Times* in 1944 on the subject of clerical attire. J. Clement Connell, pastor at Herne Hill, London, and later a tutor at London Bible College, was sympathetic to

131   The Robert Hall Society and the John Bunyan Society for Baptist students had existed in Cambridge and Oxford respectively since early in the century.
132   Payne, *Baptist Union*, pp.227-8. A few years later the older Baptist Theological Students' Union, dating from the 1920s, was amalgamated with the BSF.
133   *BT*, 10 September 1942, p.453.
134   *BT*, 24 September 1942, p.475.

the practice of many ministers, including younger ones, who wore a clerical collar and also a gown. Others opposed such practices.[135] Much debate also took place about hymns and church music, with numerous complaints being aired about the state of Baptist worship. Organs were uniformly used in Baptist churches; when church music was criticized no other instrument was mentioned. The merits of new and old hymns were compared. The Keswick Convention had produced a new hymnbook and it was noted that many hymns of a highly subjective nature or with ecstatic language, which had been in the previous Keswick hymnbook, had been eliminated.[136] Many Baptist congregations used Keswick hymns and Sankey's *Sacred Songs and Solos*, as well as the Baptist hymnal. But in the midst of one debate, a despairing G.P.L. Pickering wrote that 'it is well-nigh heart-breaking to read in 1944 a plea for even a partial return to *Sankey's*'.[137] One correspondent said despairingly that a recent service had started with the hymn, 'Come on, my partners in distress'. There was a call for ministers to give more thought to hymns and for colleges to provide more training on this matter.[138]

Finally, attention was given to new possibilities in the conduct of services of communion and baptism. T. Ernest Wilmshurst from Redhill wrote in 1942 in the *Baptist Times* that the laying on of hands at believers' baptism was neglected in Baptist practice, 'with the consequent lack, so often deplored by our leaders, of the evidences of the Holy Spirit's presence and power among us, which in apostolic days was normally the experience of the baptised believer'.[139] W. Powell from Worthing said that he had witnessed 'definite blessing' by the laying on of hands at baptism. A.D. Robertson from Brighton quoted the popular devotional author and Baptist minister, F.W. Boreham, who had been deeply impressed by a laying on of hands he had witnessed at a service in Stockwell, London.[140] Stephen Winward, who saw his small church in

---

135  *BT*, 31 August 1944, p.3.
136  *Life of Faith*, 3 August 1938, p.838.
137  *BT*, 30 November 1944, p.6.
138  *BT*, 22 June 1944, p.4.
139  *BT*, 1 January 1942, p.4.
140  *BT*, 22 January 1942, p.40; 19 February 1942, p.88.

Walthamstow grow to over 300 members, together with Stanley Voke, then minister at Woodside, South Norwood, shared a concern to have more hymns with a rich devotional and theological content for use at the Lord's Supper. They produced a book, *Hymns of Worship and Communion*, with about 180 hymns 'collected from all the communions and hymnals of the Church Universal'. It was advertised in 1946 as obtainable for one shilling.[141] Emphasis was being placed on all the parts of public worship, not just on the sermon, as means of encounter with God.

## THE STATE OF THE UNION

At the same time as changes such as these were taking place among the churches, the Union was examining the need for modifications to its organization. Stanley Baker said in 1942 that during the time he had been representing the Essex Association on the Union Council there had been scarcely ever more than half a dozen ministers present under the age of forty-five. He said that younger ministers found ready acceptance in interdenominational fellowships and he was concerned that the situation he was describing would weaken the denomination in the post-war era. Leslie Chown, another member of the Council, agreed, but said that as long as the older ministers who were well known as the fathers of the denomination allowed themselves to be nominated to the Council they would be elected.[142] Another allegation, that the West Country was under-represented on the Council, led to more general discussion. The Council of the Lancashire and Cheshire Association maintained that there was inadequate representation from the provinces generally. At one stage, of the seventy elected and co-opted members of the Union Council, thirty-five were from London. Also, it was suggested there were always more people present at the Council from the South because of the relative ease with which they could travel to London. Elections by postal

---

141 S.J. Voke and S.F. Winward, *Hymns of Worship and Communion* (London: Henry E. Walter, 1946); *BT*, 10 October 1946, p.8.
142 *BT*, 11 June 1942, p.291; 25 June 1942, p.319.

ballot were implemented in 1949 as a way to address one aspect of the problem.[143]

Another change was the increasing role of the Women's Department of the Union. The BWL prided itself on being open to new thinking, and in 1943 it organized a meeting for young businesswomen which about seventy attended. Violet Hedger chaired, and the topic was 'How to attract young women into our churches'. The six young women who spoke were in favour of Baptist churches being more progressive, friendly and attractively presented. They wanted churches to stress both spiritual and social ministry.[144] Three years later, Lois Chapple, a missionary in China who had been appointed to work with Doris Rose at the BWL, spoke about women's attitudes after the war and suggested that there was more response to religion from young men than young women.[145] Within the churches, many women's groups that were not in the BWL - sometimes Young Wives' Clubs - linked up to the Union's Women's Department. Some younger ministers' wives, however, baulked at the expectation that they would lead women's groups, sing in the choir and - as one twenty-five-year-old minister's wife put it - do '101 other things' happily done by wives who 'love to fuss around'. She was adamant that she was not a speaker or leader. 'I cannot sing', she continued, 'and certainly have not the patience to smooth out petty squabbles between "half-baked" Christians.' Her gift, she felt, was her sense of humour.[146] Women offered the churches new perspectives in the post-war period.

*Lois Chapple as a young deaconess*

Ministry to young people was given fresh attention by the Union. Popular youth rallies and very well attended summer schools were run by the Young People's Departments of the Union and the BMS.

---

143  Minutes of the Baptist Union General Purposes Committee, 1 July 1942.

144  *BT*, 18 November 1943, p.3.

145  *BT*, 17 January 1946, p.7.

146  *BT*, 19 February 1948, p.6 (Letter from 'P.E.C.').

However, at a Youth Rally at Bloomsbury in 1946, Jean Sansom, one of the young women present, said that as she looked down from the balcony she was surprised to see 'many grey and hairless heads'.[147] Some who responded to Sansom said they were young at heart, or suggested that grey hairs might not mean great age.[148] But for many young people in this period entertainment such as the cinema was more attractive than a youth meeting. A survey in 1942 of a hundred girls in the 14-18 age group, living in the North West, showed that most went at least twice a week to the cinema. Sunday school attendance had been widespread in this group up to age fourteen, when they left secondary school, but had then dropped rapidly.[149] These statistics prompted calls for the name 'Sunday School' to be dropped. The Council's response was to encourage churches to prepare material relevant to young people, such as guidance on 'the purpose of God for sex'.[150] Post-war features of youth work included special courses on sex education for youth leaders and the creation of a Fellowship of Baptist Clubs. In 1945 the number of such clubs was increasing rapidly.[151]

Baptist social enterprises, too, were being reviewed. The social involvement of deaconesses was in a process of change: there were over fifty deaconesses working in the churches in the 1940s, but there was uncertainty about their role. Sister Gertrude Kendall was succeeded by Miss E. Samuel Webb as Principal of the Training College. When Webb resigned, the leadership passed, for the first time, out of female hands, with H.H. Sutton, former Southern Area Superintendent, becoming Principal. In

*Sister Margaret Wilmshurst and Sister Florence Hill in 1940*

---

147   *BT*, 16 May 1946, p.10.
148   *BT*, 23 May 1946, p.6.
149   *BT*, 17 September 1942, p.461.
150   Minutes of the Baptist Union Council, 14 and 15 March 1944.
151   *BT*, 3 May 1945, p.9.

1945 Wilson Black provided money for the purchase of 'Struan', a property in Wimbledon Park, for deaconess training, but in 1948 there were only five deaconesses being trained. During the war the far-reaching call-up of women affected intake.[152]

In 1949 discussion took place about new uniforms for deaconesses. This led to changes: for new deaconesses, a navy blue dress and hat, and black or navy shoes, with shade of stockings optional, became the norm.[153] Attitudes to traditional Baptist concerns such as temperance were also changing. The Union committee looking after temperance took the view in 1942 that applicants for ministerial training should be asked if they were abstainers. If they were not, this would not necessarily preclude ministry, but would be noted. This approach was carried,

*Sister Jenny Clark wears the new deaconess uniform*

but almost half the Council had reservations about the proposal.[154] The debate indicated varied approaches to matters traditionally regarded as fixed..

Social changes were partially responsible for fresh thinking about the pastoral support and development of those in ministry within the Union. The *Report of the Committee on Baptist Polity* was presented to the Council on 17 November 1942.[155] The Committee had been working on this report for six years. The problems of churches without pastoral oversight were well known, but even where there was ministerial oversight there were difficulties. In an echo of what had been said in the *Report on Ministerial Efficiency* a decade before, a proposal was passed

---

152   Townsend, *Robert Wilson Black*, pp.114-19; Payne, *Baptist Union*, pp.228-9; D.M. Rose, *Baptist Deaconesses*, pp.20-2.

153   Minutes of the Baptist Union Deaconess Sub-Committee Re Uniform, 4 November 1949; bound with BU Council papers, Angus Library.

154   Minutes of the Baptist Union Temperance Committee, 30 June 1942; Minutes of the Council, 17 and 18 November 1942; bound with BU Council papers.

155   *Report of the Committee on Baptist Polity*, presented to the Baptist Union Council on 17 November 1942: Minutes of the Baptist Union Council, 17 November 1942.

on to the United Collegiate Board that in college training there was a need to give more attention to pastoral aspects. The minimum stipend was judged to be much too low, which was another recurring theme in Baptist reports.[156] What was new in this report was the emphasis on superintendents providing spiritual leadership. It stated:

> The General Superintendents have now been at work among our churches for twenty-seven years, and we have no hesitation in saying that they have abundantly justified the institution of their office...The original conception of their office was primarily one of spiritual leadership...We believe the time has come to take more seriously this view of the office, and to give our General Superintendents larger opportunities of exercising such a ministry.[157]

Henry Bonser, commenting on this aspect, said that superintendents did not wish to be regarded as 'a bench of bishops or a spiritual cabinet', but rather as general practitioners, who have 'unique opportunities to feel the spiritual pulse of the denomination, to diagnose its ailments and prescribe remedies'.[158] Shakespeare's episcopal notions seemed very distant in the 1940s.

However, some younger leaders were not satisfied with the current Union leadership. A group of younger ministers which took the name 'Focus' had begun to meet in the late 1930s and this group became more prominent in the 1940s. The early ministerial members included J.O. Barrett from Kettering, William Taylor Bowie from Acton, Frank Bryan from Bristol, Frank Buffard from Yeovil, R.L. Child from Bristol, H. Ingli James from Coventry, J.B. Middlebrook from Huddersfield, Guy Ramsay from Ferme Park, J.C. Rendall from Harrow-on-the-Hill, and Ernest Payne. They served some of the most strategically placed churches in the Union, and from their ranks came a College Principal,

156  *Report of the Committee on Baptist Polity* (London: Baptist Union, 1942), pp.7-8, 10-11, 13; bound with BU Council Minutes, Angus Library.
157  *Report of the Committee on Baptist Polity*, p.17.
158  H Bonser, 'Recollections of a General Superintendent', *BQ*, Vol.XIII (1949-50), pp.173-4.

four superintendents, and General Secretaries for both the Baptist Union and the BMS. Two lay members of 'Focus', Ronald Bell and Charles Jewson, occupied important public and business positions. The group met regularly on the evening before the Union Council – at first using the name 'Supper Club' - and, in addition, met once a year in Oxford, when there was greater leisure and freedom to consider denominational matters. In 1943 Middlebrook, by then Home Secretary of the BMS, expressed unhappiness about the way Focus members sat 'in a bunch' at Council meetings.[159] Certainly the group acted in concert, although Payne, looking back, wondered if members might have achieved more if they had done this 'more often and more vigorously'.[160] To Aubrey, the Focus group was an irritant without clear alternative policies, rather than a creative force for meeting the challenges of the time.[161]

It was generally acknowledged that the Union's new Home Work Scheme proved to be a successful replacement for the Sustentation Fund. A great deal of work was done by Gordon Fairbairn, together with Clark and Aubrey, to produce the revised Scheme. It set a new minimum ministerial stipend of £250 per annum, pledged the resources of the Union to maintaining minimum stipends, and also included provision for special financial support for 'initial pastorates'. A Settlement Covenant replaced the time limits which had been a feature of the original Ministerial Settlement and Sustentation Scheme, and this arrangement soon found favour with churches and ministers.[162] A post-war Victory Thanksgiving Fund of £150,000 was raised in 1945-6: £100,000 for new buildings and £50,000 for developing European Baptist work. European advance was expressed in 1949-50 in the formation of the European Baptist Federation (EBF).[163] In 1948, O.D. Wiles, a former army

---

159  J.O. Barrett to E A Payne, 18 May 1943: Regent's Park College Oxford, Angus Library, Payne papers.
160  Ernest Payne Diaries, Vol. V, pp.255-6: Regent's Park College Oxford, Angus Library, Payne papers.
161  West, *Baptists Together*, p.58.
162  Sparkes, *The Home Mission Story*, chapter 8; Bonser, 'Recollections of a General Superintendent', pp.177-8.
163  See Green, *Crossing the Boundaries*, pp.8-14..

chaplain who had received the DSO and MC, was appointed Union Deputy General Secretary.[164] A year later Aubrey launched a 'Baptist Advance', which called for renewed Baptist dedication. To some extent these various new initiatives mirrored the hopes for a better society after the war. Politically, the Labour Government held out this promise. Perhaps the election as Union President for 1948-9 of Ernest Brown, whose trade union contacts had contributed considerably to good labour relationships during the war, reflected hopes for a new era.[165]

UNITY AND DISUNITY

As part of this new era, there was a renewed commitment to the search for Christian unity. If the nation could come together, could not the churches do the same? Already the Baptist Union had identified about sixty-five 'union churches'; these were Free churches that practised both the baptism of infants and believers.[166] In this respect a significant Free Church event, in September 1940, was a meeting in Baptist Church House which created the Free Church Federal Council (FCFC), bringing together the older National Free Church Council and the Federal Council of Evangelical Free Churches, dating from Shakespeare's era. Wilson Black was committed to this project and he, together with S.W. Hughes (Free Church Council Secretary), Henry Townsend, Percy Evans and Aubrey, were the Baptists who were mainly involved in the efforts to achieve union.[167] The new organization adopted the Declaratory Statement of the Federal Council, and (through a scheme prepared and financed by Wilson Black) had its headquarters in Tavistock Square, London, at what had been the offices of the Free Church Council. S.W. Hughes (Baptist Union President in 1949) was the FCFC Secretary. Morris West suggested that the formation of the new body was driven by desires for a united Free Church voice in speaking to the government and the country, and for more integrated Free Church activity, a coherent Free

164   Payne, *Baptist Union*, pp.224-34.
165   Bebbington, 'Baptist Members of Parliament in the Twentieth Century', p.260.
166   Cross, *Baptism and the Baptists*, pp.91-6.
167   Jordan, *Free Church Unity*, pp.227-9; Townsend, *Robert Wilson Black*, pp.122-9.

Church emphasis, and advance towards Free Church Union.[168] Much of this vision would prove unrealizable.

A more far-reaching achievement, which would have thrilled Shakespeare, took place in September 1942, when the British Council of Churches (BCC), representing most of the main Protestant bodies in Britain that 'confess the Lord Jesus as God and Saviour', was inaugurated. Again the setting was Baptist Church House. T.G. Dunning from the Union offices, Grey Griffith of the BMS, Hugh Martin, J.H. Rushbrooke and Aubrey were the Baptist representatives on the BCC.[169] A service of inauguration took place in St Paul's Cathedral, and in his speech on that occasion William Temple, Archbishop of Canterbury and the first President of the BCC, looked forward, at least implicitly, to the coming together of Roman Catholics and Protestants.[170] The BCC was to be the central British ecumenical body for the next half-century, drawing together official representatives of all the main non-Roman Churches of England, Scotland, Wales and Northern Ireland. Although relationships between Anglicans and the Free Churches had improved markedly since the early part of the century, there were still tensions. There was concern in the 1940s about a small number of Baptist ministers leaving the denomination to join the Church of England and the Baptist Union noted that for some younger ministers Anglican liturgy was attractive.[171]

In 1945, against the background of ecumenical advance, the new Archbishop of Canterbury, Geoffrey Fisher, drew together forty-four Anglican and Free Church leaders for theological discussions. Free Church theologians explored the subject of Protestant Catholicity. The Baptist representatives in these talks were R.L. Child and Percy Evans, both college Principals, Ingli James, a superintendent, and Ernest Payne,

---

168   *BT*, 27 September 1990, p.13.
169   For Baptist service to the ecumenical movement, see A.R. Cross, 'Service to the Ecumenical Movement: The Contribution of British Baptists', *BQ*, Vol.38, No.3 (1999), pp.107-22.
170   F.A. Iremonger, *William Temple: Archbishop of Canterbury* (London: Oxford University Press, 1948), pp.413-14.
171   Minutes of the Baptist Union Ministerial Recognition Committee, 10 February 1942, bound with BU Council papers, Angus Library.

a college tutor. Two books resulted from the discussions among the Anglicans, and the Free Church group produced a report and a book, *The Catholicity of Protestantism*.[172] In November 1946 Fisher preached a sermon at Cambridge University in which he invited the Free Churches to 'take episcopacy into their systems'. He mooted the idea of a measure of inter-communion, something long called for by the Free Churches.[173] In the following year, R.L. Child took up the subject of continued Baptist suspicions about unity. He was well aware of Baptist fears about loss of liberty and sacrifice of principle, as well as the lack of conviction that organic unity was Christ's purpose. Child hoped that Baptists would continue to be involved in ecumenical conversations. His challenge was blunt and prophetic: 'Finally', he pleaded, 'let us recognise that the real hindrance to Christian unity today lies, as always, not in the presence or absence

*R.L. Child*

of any outward organisation nor in the possession or otherwise of various types of ministry or sacraments. It lies in the absence of any genuine desire among the followers of Jesus to draw closer to one another in mutual commitment and service.'[174]

The problems that attempts at church union encountered were illustrated in the case of the discussions in the 1940s between the Baptist Union and the Churches of Christ, a denomination which at the end of the decade had 140 churches in membership.[175] In 1942, as Baptist Union President, Wilson Black, a former member of the Churches of Christ, proposed that a group of five representatives of the Churches of Christ should meet with a similar group from the Baptist Union to discuss

172  R.N. Flew and R.E. Davies, eds., *The Catholicity of Protestantism* (London: Lutterworth, 1950).
173  Payne, *Baptist Union*, pp.219-20.
174  R.L. Child, *Baptists and Christian Unity* (London: Carey Kingsgate Press, 1948), pp.3-8, 14.
175  D.M. Thompson, *Let Sects and Parties Fall* (Birmingham: Berean Press, 1980), p.204.

possibilities for closer co-operation. These discussions took place, with Black, Percy Evans, Gilbert Laws, C.T. Le Quesne and Wheeler Robinson representing the Baptists, but problems soon arose over the practice of open membership by some churches in the Baptist Union, a practice which was unacceptable to the Churches of Christ. Although this difference in approach to the question of membership was a barrier to union, nonetheless, proposals for closer co-operation were produced in 1948 and were approved by the Baptist Union Council and subsequently by the Churches of Christ Central Council. A useful pamphlet, *Infant Baptism Today* (1948) was published, which drew attention to some disquiet about infant baptism that was then evident in Reformed and Anglican Churches. In the event, despite the hopes that were generated by these discussions, little was achieved, and they came to an end in 1952.[176]

The final major ecumenical landmark of the decade, which was truly ecumenical in the sense of being world-wide, was the formation in Amsterdam in 1948 of the World Council of Churches. Some Baptists had reservations about membership of the WCC, and the Southern Baptist Convention, the largest Baptist body in the world, did not join. However, Henry Cook, addressing the BWA Congress in Copenhagen in 1947, encouraged Baptist participation. It was against this background, and the backdrop of renewed Anglican-Free Church conversations, that the report *The Baptist Doctrine of the Church* was published in 1948. This report, as well as painting a theological picture, sought to commit Baptists in England to involvement with the whole Church.[177] The Union delegates appointed to Amsterdam were C.T. Le Quesne, who was Union President in 1946-7, Percy Evans, Payne, and Aubrey, with Ernest Brown, T. G. Dunning and Hugh Martin as alternates. Ernest Brown and Aubrey were later appointed members of the WCC Central Committee. The WCC drew in representatives from forty countries and 147 churches or denominations. J.H. Rushbrooke, as President of the BWA, played an important role in world developments, and until his death in 1947

176  Thompson, *Let Sects and Parties Fall*, pp.184-5; Payne, *Baptist Union*, p.221.
177  Cross, *Baptism and the Baptists*, pp.155-7.

Rushbrooke brought European affairs to the attention of British Baptists.[178]

Other developments in the 1940s showed both the practical contribution and the limitations of ecumenism. One area of practical action was education. An ecumenical delegation in 1941 led by the then Archbishop of Canterbury, Cosmo Lang, and which included from the Free Church side the veteran Methodist, J. Scott Lidgett, as well as Wilson Black and Henry Townsend, met with the Secretary of State for Education, R.A. Butler, and agreed principles about religious education in schools. It was agreed that there should be religious education in all schools and a daily act of worship. The principles outlined were acceptable to all the denominations; although state grants to church schools continued, the education controversies that had divided the Anglicans and the Free Churches no longer generated the same feelings. Discussions about education were now taking place in a very different religious climate from that of forty years before: one in which the Free Churches were no longer confident of their strength. Before and after the meeting with Butler, the issues were discussed at the Education Committee of the Baptist Union. Baptist Union representatives supported a completely national system of education, but that hope was not achieved. The new provisions for religion in schools were embodied in the 1944 Education Act.[179]

An unexpected war-time ecumenical enterprise was 'The Sword of the Spirit', launched in 1940 with the Roman Catholic Archbishop of Westminster, Cardinal Hinsley, as President.[180] Meetings organized in London 1941 were hugely successful, resulting in a remarkable demonstration of unity by leaders of the Catholic, Anglican and Free Churches. Later the ecumenical aspect disappeared and the Sword of the Spirit became a purely Roman Catholic body. Hinsley was keen to have

178  Green, *Tomorrow's Man,* p.132.
179  Lockhart, *Gordon Cosmo Lang,* pp.368-9; Iremonger, *William Temple,* pp.569-78; Bebbington, 'Baptists and Politics since 1914', in Clements, ed., *Baptists in the Twentieth Century,* p.89.
180  S. Mews, 'The Sword of the Spirit', in W.J. Sheils, ed., *The Church and War* (Oxford: Basil Blackwell, 1983), pp.420-1.

shared prayer as well as action between Catholics and Protestants but the idea was somewhat ahead of its time.[181] Those who were suspicious of any co-operation with Catholics were quick to protest. Theo Bamber was a speaker at a Protestant Truth Society Rally opposing the Sword of the Spirit, held in the Caxton Hall in October 1941.[182] In some Baptist Union meetings a more open attitude prevailed. The growth of the Sword of the Spirit was described by Dunning at the Union's Moral and Social Questions Committee early in 1942. At that point some unofficial meetings were being planned between Catholic leaders and a few Protestant representatives. Dunning was involved in these discussions and his report was received with much interest.[183] When this matter came to the whole Council, however, there were reservations. Percy Evans and Wilson Black put a motion expressing concern about the religious liberty of Protestants. Although they withdrew the motion, there were deep-seated worries about co-operating with Catholics, since in parts of Europe where Catholics were dominant Protestant life was often restricted.[184]

It was not only those standing on what was seen as the conservative wing of the denomination who had concerns over ecumenical developments. In 1941 Wilson Black had contact with a group of Baptist ministers in Liverpool who were anxious that moves towards union with other denominations could weaken or betray Baptist principles. Black himself was not opposed to all expressions of unity. He gave considerable support to the Free Church Federal Council in its work. In the case of the Liverpool ministers, however, he encouraged them to make their hesitations known. The group included K.C. Dykes of Wavertree, who became Principal of Manchester College in 1949, W.E. Moore of Page Moss Lane, who became a tutor at Rawdon in 1956, and H.L. Watson of Richmond, Liverpool, who became North Western Superintendent in 1949. These ministers were by no means ultra-conservatives. They set out a *Declaration* of Baptist principles – including what they called the 'truly

181  Hastings, *English Christianity*, p.396.
182  *Christian*, 16 October 1941, p.14.
183  Minutes of the Baptist Union Moral and Social Questions Committee, 11 February 1942, bound with BU Council minutes, Angus Library.
184  Minutes of the Baptist Union Council 10 and 11 March 1942.

High Church doctrines' of believers' baptism and Christ's living presence in the Lord's Supper - and, with Wilson Black's help, this declaration was sent to all Baptist ministers. In all, 342 Baptist ministers, including four college principals, signed the declaration.[185] For Baptists the ecumenical route was never going to be free from tensions of this kind.

CONCLUSION

By 1939 it was reckoned that not more than ten per cent of the population in England attended church regularly. Although this was probably an under-estimate, the perception of being a small minority created, as Ernest Payne put it, a 'spiritual pressure', and to this was added in the next few years the loss of life and the widespread physical destruction caused by the war.[186] Baptists responded in a number of different ways. Townley Lord, who saw the denomination as 'evangelical through and through', was one of many who stressed evangelism. His booklet, *The Great Decision*, was the Union's best-selling publication. But Baptists displayed some uncertainty and were at times divided over issues such as ministry, the nature of spiritual renewal, aspects of worship, and ecumenical involvement. Was there a way by which the denomination's different evangelical streams, which tended to espouse either narrower or broader views, could flow together in the post-war period? Some, such as the conservative evangelical Baptist Revival Fellowship, were to express serious doubts about what they saw as a tendency to play down theological distinctives. Others, too, were concerned about current trends - in society, in the churches and in theological thought. Henry Townsend, of Manchester College, alleged in 1940 that 'theological liberalism has utterly failed ministers and Churches'.[187] The most hopeful place to find significant Baptist unity was undoubtedly in evangelism. What became more prominent from the mid-1940s and especially in the 1950s was

---

185  Townsend, *Robert Wilson Black*, pp. 110-14; Cross, *Baptism and the Baptists*, pp.161-3.
186  E.A. Payne, 'The Protestant World', in S. Neill, ed, *Twentieth Century Christianity* (London: Collins, 1962), pp.182-3.
187  *BT*, 15 February 1940, p.104.

renewed evangelistic endeavour in England, a thrust to a considerable extent associated with younger evangelicals. The tensions over the nature of the evangelicalism espoused in the denomination were not, however, destined to be readily resolved.

*A further reminder of the cost of war: Mare Street, Hackney, was another of the London churches destroyed by bombing*

# Chapter 7
# 'QUICKENED EVANGELISTIC ACTIVITIES' 1950-59

T he *Baptist Handbook* for 1950 showed 208,888 members of Baptist churches in England. This compared with the figure for English Baptist membership at the beginning of the century of 239,114. The annual number of baptisms in the early 1950s, at about 5,000, was running at approximately half the level of twenty years earlier, a massive reduction. The 1956 *Handbook*, however, showed 7,211 baptisms, and this much higher level was repeated for a further year, with 6,791 baptisms being reported.[1] Commenting in 1957 in the *Baptist Times*, Ernest Payne, the Union General Secretary, said that the 'heartening figures are the fruit of the quickened evangelistic activities of our churches and the church extension which is taking place in many parts of the country'.[2] For the remainder of the decade, however, baptisms reverted to previous levels and at the end of the 1950s the number of members shown in the *Handbook* was 200,100.[3] This suggests the 'evangelistic activities' were limited in their long-term impact. But Payne was right when he wrote in 1958 that there had been 'a renewed spiritual interest and wistfulness in many different quarters' and that 'Christians

---

1    'Summary of Statistics for the British Isles', in the *Baptist Handbook* (1950), p.237.
2    *BT*, 31 January 1957, p.3.
3    The Congregationalists were declining more rapidly, and in 1955, for the first time, the number of members of Baptist churches in England exceeded the number of Congregationalists: R. Currie, A. Gilbert and L. Horsley, *Churches and Churchgoers: Patterns of Church Growth in the British Isles since 1700* (Oxford: Clarendon Press, 1977), p.151.

were no longer on the defensive, as they had been for at least thirty years.'[4] Callum Brown, in *The Death of Christian Britain*, highlights 1955-59 as a period of religious revivalism mirroring a general emphasis in Britain on family, home and piety.[5] Baptist activity reflected to some extent this wider picture.

## THE UNION AND ITS LEADERSHIP

In 1950 M.E. Aubrey had been General Secretary of the Union for a quarter of a century. In anticipation of his retirement he was nominated and then elected to serve as Union President in 1950-51, during his last year as Secretary. A nomination committee to seek his successor was set up under the chairmanship of Percy Evans, who was then completing twenty-five years as Principal of Spurgeon's College. After meeting five times, the committee approached Ernest A. Payne and in January 1950 Payne was interviewed by Evans, Hugh Martin of the SCM Press, as a member of the Union Council, and Arnold Clark, Union treasurer. Payne was surprised by the approach. Together with others in the Focus group he had often been critical of directions taken by the Union. In addition he had not had much contact with the Spurgeonic tradition. Finally, he was deeply involved in ecumenical affairs.[6] Payne doubted if he had the gifts for the job – for example, he was not at his best speaking to large audiences – and he did not want to leave his post as tutor at Regent's Park College. Others, however, were convinced that he was the right person to follow Aubrey, and he allowed the interviewing committee's recommendation to go to the Council. Payne was duly commended by the Council to the 1950 Assembly and the recommendation was unanimously accepted.[7] He served as General Secretary for three consecutive terms, until 1967.

---

4    Payne, *The Baptist Union,* p.238.
5    C.G. Brown, *The Death of Christian Britain* (London: Routledge, 2001), pp.172-3.
6    West, *To be a Pilgrim*, pp.74-5.
7    Minutes of the Baptist Union Council, 14 and 15 March 1950; West, *Baptists Together*, p.72.

Ernest Payne was born in 1902. His family was involved in the Downs Baptist Church, Clapton, where he was baptized in 1917; and in 1922, after obtaining a degree in Philosophy from King's College London, he entered Regent's Park College to train for missionary service with the Baptist Missionary Society. Family circumstances meant that he was not

able to fulfil this vision. However, in 1928, after further studies in Oxford and in Germany, he began home ministry at Bugbrooke Baptist Church, Northamptonshire. From 1932 to 1940 he worked for the BMS as Young People's Secretary and then Editor. Payne became a noted writer, especially in the historical field. When his *Free Church Tradition in the Life of England* was published in 1944 it was the best brief history of Dissent available.[8] Payne also became involved in the Baptist World Alliance. In 1940, at the age of thirty-eight, he was appointed to the staff at Regent's Park College, where he was able

*E.A. Payne*

to develop his considerable teaching as well as writing gifts. He was also increasingly relied upon by the Union in ecumenical dialogue. In such conversations, Percy Evans sometimes referred to Payne as his 'armour bearer'. From the 1920s onwards, Payne's links beyond Baptist life were with the SCM and the developing ecumenical movement. While at university he had attended meetings of the London Inter-Collegiate Christian Union, which formed part of the Inter-Varsity Fellowship, but he did not feel fully at ease with the theological approach of the Christian Union and 'the kind of conversion' that characterized the more conservative stream of evangelical life.[9]

8    E.A. Payne, *The Free Church Tradition in the Life of England* (London: SCM, 1944); cf. D. Cornick, 'Twentieth-Century Historians of English Protestant Nonconformity', in A.P.F. Sell and A.R. Cross, eds., *Protestant Nonconformity in the Twentieth Century* (Carlisle: Paternoster Press, 2003), pp.66-71.
9    West, *To be a Pilgrim,* chapters 1-3; p.17.

Yet Payne was not restricted in his sympathies. He wished to have greater contact with the Spurgeonic element in the denomination and Percy Evans had promised to help him. In March 1951, however, a month before Payne took office, Evans died suddenly. For Payne the loss was devastating. In his acceptance speech as General Secretary, Payne said that 'the fact that Dr Evans and the tradition he represented had supported his nomination ... had been one of the decisive factors influencing his decision to accept the nomination'.[10] He was to write years later of the sky darkening on the day of Evans' death.[11] An essentially shy person, Payne spoke in early May 1951 of how he had been tempted since his

*B. Grey Griffith*

appointment to run away from the task, especially when he heard of the loss of Percy Evans, but he had been encouraged by the kindness of those around him.[12] In particular, Payne looked to Grey Griffith, who, having retired from the BMS, was the Union's 'elder statesman par excellence'.[13] Others with whom Payne worked closely were Seymour Price, chairman of the Ministerial Recognition Committee, Arnold Clark, Gordon Fairbairn, and O.D. Wiles, Deputy General Secretary. But without Evans the task of holding different elements in the denomination together was – as Payne anticipated - to prove much more difficult.[14]

Despite the difficulties, Payne's early years as General Secretary were marked by advances. The Superannuation Fund reached £300,000 and was still growing, while continued appeals for the Baptist Forward Movement, which dated from the 1930s, had brought in £1 million. The new Home Work Scheme proved successful, with the Fund rising from

10    *BT*, 11 May 1950, p.2.
11    Article by E.A. Payne on P.W. Evans, April 1974, cited by West, *To be a Pilgrim*, p.76.
12    *BT*, 3 May 1951, pp.7-8.
13    Thomson, 'A Round Unvarnish'd Tale' (unpublished manuscript, 1979), p.26.
14    E.A. Payne Diary, Vol. VII, p.358: Regent's Park College Oxford, Angus Library, Payne papers.

£32,620 in 1951 to £47,064 a year later. This was an enormous boost.[15] In his first year in office Payne visited fifty churches and addressed twenty-four other meetings across the country. He was appreciated for the efficient way he conducted Union business and he created a feeling of shared loyalty and a sense of purpose among those who worked with him.[16] The Women's Department of the Union added new responsibilities such as the Baptist Women's League, the Hospitality and Younger Women's Committees, and the Baptist Union Adoption Society.[17] The work of the superintendents also developed under Payne's leadership. J.O. Barrett took the view, as he put it to Payne, that the superintendents should form 'a cabinet having regular discussions on evangelism, the deployment of denominational resources, etc.', and should not confine themselves to administrative matters connected with ministerial settlement and grants to churches. This was the strategy Payne adopted, and he made it his policy to attend the monthly superintendents' meeting.[18]

On the international front, one of Payne's first tasks was to be involved with the Golden Jubilee Congress of the Baptist World Alliance. The 1950 BWA Congress, held in Cleveland, Ohio, USA, brought together 20,000 registered delegates and saw 40,000 gathering for special open meetings. Although only forty-six British Baptists travelled to Cleveland, the place of British Baptists within the development of the Alliance was recognized. As an indication of this recognition, Payne was approached before the 1950 Congress to ask if he would consider the post of Associate General Secretary of the BWA and it was indicated to him by Theodore Adams, an influential American, that acceptance of the post would lead to his subsequent appointment as BWA General Secretary. Payne was firm in his refusal.[19] English Baptist involvement in the

---

15    Payne, *Baptist Union*, p.241.
16    *BT*, 8 May 1952, p.3; West, *Baptists Together*, p.73.
17    Payne, *Baptist Union*, p.229.
18    E.A. Payne, *A 20ᵗʰ Century Minister: John Oliver Barrett, 1901-78* (London: p.p., 1978), p.15.
19    West, *To be a Pilgrim*, pp.70-72. For the Cleveland Congress see A.T. Ohrn, ed., *Eighth Baptist World Congress, Cleveland, Ohio, 1950* (London: BWA, 1950).

leadership of the BWA was, however, guaranteed by the election of Townley Lord as President of the Alliance. British Baptists worked hard to ensure as many participants as possible attended the 1955 Congress in London. About 8,000 delegates from forty countries registered, half from the USA and about 1,700 from Britain. The Royal Albert Hall and Arsenal Football Club's Highbury Stadium, which accommodated 65,000 people, were venues used. Geoffrey Fisher, Archbishop of Canterbury, was among those who gave addresses at the beginning of the Congress.[20]

Baptist Union leaders were also active in Europe. Nine Baptists came to the 1955 Congress from the Soviet Union. There had been no Russians at BWA Congresses since 1928 but in 1954 Ernest Payne and Townley Lord had made a personal visit to the All-Union Council of Evangelical Christians-Baptists in the Soviet Union. In the year following the Congress, Payne and Lord were able to make contact with Hungarian and Czechoslovak Baptists during visits to Budapest, Bratislava and Prague. Townley Lord travelled extensively as BWA President, and both he and Payne contributed to stronger Baptist links across Europe. Henry Cook, another English Baptist active among European Baptists, was European Baptist Federation President, 1952-4, and Acting Secretary, 1956-9. In between, Cook was Baptist Union President. European Baptists gathered for Congresses in Copenhagen in 1952, and West Berlin in 1958, with English Baptists playing a full part.[21] Mrs Ruth Pepper, who had been a deaconess at West Ham, and Mrs Ernest [Eva] Brown, both Presidents of the BWL in the 1940s, contributed to drawing together Baptist women in Europe. An International Baptist Seminary was established in Rüschlikon, near Zurich, Switzerland, in 1949, and this became a centre for European

*Eva Brown*

---

20    *BT*, 28 April 1955, p.9; see A.T. Ohrn, ed., *Baptist World Alliance Golden Jubilee Congress, London, 1955* (London: Carey Kingsgate Press, 1955), pp.19-21, for Fisher's address.

21    Green, *Crossing the Boundaries*, pp.21-3, 36-42.

Baptist life.[22] In 1952 the first post-war BWA student conference was held at Rüschlikon, with students participating from countries in Europe that had been at war with one another. Among the group from Britain, attending under the auspices of the Baptist Student Federation, were John Nicholson and Basil Amey, both of whom would become prominent in ecumenical affairs.[23]

During the 1950s, Baptist Union Presidents took up a variety of themes relating to the life of the denomination. Aubrey's concern, as it had been during his secretaryship, was for evangelistic progress, under the title 'Baptist Advance'. Arnold Clark, President in 1952-3, gave a fine presidential address on worship, and in particular the Lord's Supper. He argued that the Lord's Supper lost its meaning if it was seen only as a Memorial Service. It was certainly a remembrance, but Clark wished to stress that the 'Risen Saviour is with us waiting to be received by us.' For Clark the Lord's Supper was a Sacrament. With reference to baptism he made a plea for the description 'Holy Baptism'.[24] R.L. Child, as President in 1954, was similarly passionate about worship, particularly preaching: 'We urgently need today', he urged, 'a revival of the kind of preaching which grips and searches the heart and conscience, and confronts men inescapably with the claims of Christ. There has been a remarkable and welcome return in recent years to Biblical theology...Yet it is equally important that, as congregations, we should approach the ministry of the Word with more spiritual passion and eagerness.'[25] Sir Herbert Janes, President in 1956-7, was a successful builder and civic leader, becoming Mayor of Luton. He gave prominence to the theme of the gospel and society. Janes was active as a lay preacher and led the Baptist cause at Stopsley, a branch of Park Street Baptist Church, Luton.[26]

---

22    Payne, *Baptist Union*, p.249; Green, *Crossing the Boundaries*, pp.94-5.
23    I am indebted to Basil Amey, later BMS Assistant Home Secretary and Editor, and Assistant General Secretary, British Council of Churches, for his recollection of the 1952 conference.
24    *BT*, 1 May 1952, pp.1-3.
25    *BT*, 6 May 1954, p.2.
26    West, *To be a Pilgrim*, pp.80, 105.

Although the mid-1950s saw some advances in Union life, these were combined with set-backs. 'The year 1957', Douglas Sparkes comments, 'was not an encouraging one for the denomination'. Decline in church membership continued, the BMS had a large deficit, and giving to the Home Work Fund was £4,000 less than the target figure.[27] It was evident at this point that Ernest Payne was physically tired. His schedule was hectic. In March 1958 he became Moderator of the Free Church Council, which involved a number of ecumenical responsibilities, while Baptist commitments and also meetings with others in the wider church took him to different parts of Europe in the summer. In mid-September he collapsed completely and a heart specialist diagnosed a coronary thrombosis. During his recovery period, Payne, who was then fifty-six, wondered whether he should resign from the post of General Secretary. He decided that he should continue, however, and by the time of the 1959 Assembly he was active again. His scheme for a celebration of the Baptist Union's Ter-Jubilee over a period of four years, from 1959 to 1963, was launched in 1959, and was advocated by the Union President, J.B. Middlebrook, BMS Home Secretary. Payne's hope had been for a joint appeal with the BMS, but that was not agreed. The appeal had three main emphases: commemoration and education; evangelism; and finance, with the aim of raising £300,000. Payne's vision was that the four years of celebration would change the mood of the denomination.[28]

EVANGELISM – THE TURNING OF THE TIDE?

The denominational mood at the beginning of the decade was influenced by some heartening statistics. With an increase in baptisms in 1949 of nearly ten per cent over the previous year, Aubrey claimed – as others had before - that there was definite evidence in support of 'our contention that the tide has at last begun to turn'.[29] Individual examples were adduced of

27    Sparkes, *The Home Mission Story*, p.121.
28    West, *To be a Pilgrim*, pp.110-14.
29    *BT*, 12 January 1950, p.8.

effective evangelism. At the Stockton-on-Tees Baptist Tabernacle equipment had been installed to relay services outside the church. A programme of hymns and sacred music was played before evening services, and twelve young people – called 'Fishers' – invited people into the church. A report in 1950 said that three young men had recently professed conversion.[30] The Baptist Revival Fellowship noted in 1950 how many young people were present for what had become an annual BRF meeting, held in Bloomsbury Central Baptist Church.[31] Nor was it only young people who were responding. Major interdenominational evangelistic meetings were held in 1951, to coincide with the Festival of Britain, in the Methodist Westminster Central Hall, Westminster Chapel, and the Royal Albert Hall. Speaking in 1951 about Baptist Advance, Aubrey reported that from his talks with ministers and deacons he believed 'the fire has begun to burn in many places'; he highlighted particularly the number of middle-aged and older people responding to his messages. Some were making 'a surrender' for the first time and others were anxious to 'get back'.[32]

The Union Council was keen to hear about and encourage such developments. After the Council meeting in March 1951, Townley Lord reported that the perception was that 'the spiritual vitality of our church life is on the increase'. Evangelism was being stressed. A pamphlet that had been produced for use in house-to-house visiting had proved to be very popular, with about 350,000 copies having been requested by the churches.[33] The same emphasis was to be found in the Associations. The Kent and Sussex Association had a Mid-Century Crusade in 1949-51, and baptisms in the Association in 1950 reached their highest level since 1911, while at the Northern Association annual Assembly in 1953 there was a feeling that revival might not be far away.[34] In the same year Hubert

---

30   *BT*, 2 February 1950, p.7.
31   *BT*, 25 May 1950, p.9.
32   *BT*, 8 February 1951, p.9.
33   *BT*, 22 March 1951, p.8.
34   F. Buffard, *Kent and Sussex Baptist Associations* (Faversham: Kent and Sussex Baptist Associations, 1963), pp.136-7; *BT*, 28 May 1953, p.7. R.D. Brown wrote

Watson, North Western Superintendent, called for a reappraisal of Baptist priorities. He was troubled by announcements often heard in church services about pantomimes, reviews, cabarets and dances.[35] The Baptist Revival Fellowship was in sympathy with such sentiments. In January 1954 the BRF *Bulletin* spoke about 'a stupor reflected in the absence of prayer meetings' in many Baptist churches and also 'indifference to personal evangelism'. But the BRF also discerned a new spiritual impetus and this was expressed in a BRF Ministers' Retreat in February 1954, which attracted forty-six ministers to Barnes Close, near Birmingham.[36]

It is important to note this stress on revival in the early 1950s, since it is sometimes thought that heightened spiritual awareness in this period was associated largely with Billy Graham, the American evangelist. The scale of the three-month Graham campaign in 1954 - March to May - at the Harringay Arena (normally used for boxing and skating events), was certainly unprecedented. There was an aggregate attendance of over two million at all associated meetings, including 120,000 at Wembley Stadium on the closing day. It was the nearest that Graham came to reaching his dream, expressed in 1946, of saving Britain out of 'the abyss'.[37] Even before Graham arrived, Townley Lord was enthusiastic. He had received a letter from Graham saying millions of Americans would be praying for awakening in London. Lord's response was: 'May the awakening come! May 1954 see spiritual revival not at Harringay only but in all our churches throughout the land.'[38] The campaign was sponsored by the Evangelical Alliance. Townley Lord, as the respected editor of the *Baptist Times* (which almost doubled its readership under his editorship), was

---

the hymn 'Thou, Lord, hast given Thyself for our healing', for the Mid-Century Crusade.

35  Sellers, ed., *Our Heritage*, pp.115-16. Watson was Union President in 1963.

36  *Baptist Revival Fellowship Bulletin*, No.41, January 1954, pp.1, 3. Spurgeon's College, BRF Archive, *Bulletin* file.

37  Report by Wes Hartzell: Wheaton College, USA, Billy Graham Archive, Collection 224, Box 1, Folder 17. Also W. Martin, *The Billy Graham Story: A Prophet with Honour* (London: Hutchinson, 1991), pp.94-5, 106.

38  *BT*, 7 January 1954, p.3.

*A remote rural church could muster plenty of support for the reopening after*
*refurbishment, Newton St Petrock, Devon, 1955*

able to promote his perspective on the meetings. He spoke of Graham's biblical preaching, of the absence of excessive emotionalism, and of how people responded to the appeal at the end of meetings and went forward in a dignified way. He insisted that what some had disparagingly called 'Americanism' was not a feature of the Crusade.[39]

Nonetheless, there were critics. Martyn Lloyd-Jones, the minister of Westminster Chapel, declined to take part in ministers' meetings held in conjunction with the Harringay meetings. He included in his public prayers at Westminster Chapel on 1 March 1954 the 'brethren' who were 'ministering in another part of the city', but a week later, in a letter to Elizabeth and Fred Catherwood (his daughter and son-in-law), he spoke of reports from the campaign as 'most confusing'.[40] One *Baptist Times* correspondent, a few days after this, while confirming that the meetings

---

39    *BT*, 4 March 1954, p.5.
40    I.H. Murray, *David Martyn Lloyd-Jones. Vol.2: The Fight of Faith, 1939-1981* (Edinburgh: Banner of Truth Trust, 1990), p.338.

were not charged with emotion, thought that some who came forward to the front had no idea why they did so.[41] In the North of England, as elsewhere, there were very conservative Baptists who considered that Graham, with his ecumenical contacts and revivalist techniques, seemed to be compromising the gospel.[42] Criticisms were also to emerge from other quarters. In February 1956 Michael Ramsey, then Bishop of Durham and soon to become Archbishop of York, made vague charges in the Durham diocesan magazine, *The Bishoprick*, about Billy Graham having taught unacceptable doctrines at a mission in Cambridge.[43] The common assertion was that Graham was teaching narrow Fundamentalism. Lloyd Harding, however, minister of the Baptist Church in Aston, Birmingham, claimed that during the Cambridge mission Graham won over nearly all his critics.[44]

Among those won over, according to Townley Lord, were journalists. He said that the daily newspapers had given the Crusade unprecedented coverage and that journalists who had attended scornfully had come away thoughtfully.[45] Some Baptist ministers who had reservations changed their opinions. The Rawdon-trained minister of Park Road Baptist Church, Rushden, A. Stuart Arnold, said that if he had been asked two years previously about Graham he would have replied that he was 'another American hot-gospeller'. Now Arnold saw him as someone given 'an exceptional gift by God'. At Harringay, Arnold argued, Graham's preaching had been scriptural, and there had been no emotion in the meetings. He believed that as a result of Harringay, the churches had gained new confidence.[46] Others confirmed this verdict. Godfrey Robinson, minister of Main Road Baptist Church, Romford, who had been Young People's Secretary of the BMS, wrote about lessons learned

41   *BT*, 11 March 1954, p.8.
42   Sellers, ed., *Our Heritage: The Baptists of Yorkshire, Lancashire and Cheshire*, p.127.
43   O. Chadwick, *Michael Ramsey: A Life* (Oxford: Clarendon, 1990), pp.24–5, 92.
44   *BT*, 29 December 1955, p.2.
45   *BT*, 18 March 1954, pp.1, 7.
46   *BT*, 25 March 1954, p.1.

from Harringay regarding prayer, the place of the Bible, and the utilization of people's gifts.[47] Robinson's thinking was partly influenced by his conversion among the lay-led Open Brethren. Many Brethren members were involved in Harringay and a number of Brethren were to find their way into Baptist life. In 1955 Ernest Payne, although dissimilar to Graham in several respects, believed the campaign had shown 'that the spiritual mood of our land is one of readiness for decision'.[48] In similar vein, Townley Lord spoke of a changed spiritual attitude, 'from prevailing coldness and indifference to increasing warmth and growth'.[49]

Billy Graham was concerned to try to ensure that the results of Harringay were conserved. At the end of April 1954 he spoke at Bloomsbury to Baptist ministers and emphasized the responsibility of the churches for evangelism and nurture. The campaign, he stressed, would be a failure unless the churches moved forward. Graham spoke of 'God's golden hour'.[50] Baptist Union leaders, including Payne and R.L. Child, had smaller meetings with Graham, and Cyril (from 1959 Sir Cyril) Black, MP, the son of Wilson Black, was a strong Graham backer.[51]

Although London ministers had been particularly involved in the campaign, the effects were felt nationally, not least through land-line relays. At Hay Hill Baptist Church, Bath, for example, people queued to enter a relay meeting.[52] In early May 1954 Graham met with 2,400 ministers and clergy in Westminster Central Hall, London, to reflect on the events of the previous three months. It was reckoned that most Baptist churches in London had received information about people who had responded at Harringay and who required follow-up. Two Baptist

---

47  *BT*, 27 May 1954, p.9.
48  West, *To be a Pilgrim*, p.92.
49  J.C. Pollock, *Billy Graham* (London: Hodder & Stoughton, 1966), p.201.
50  *BT*, 29 April 1954, p.8.
51  Minutes of the Baptist Union General Purposes and Finance Executive, 12 January 1954; Minutes of the Baptist Union Council, 9 and 10 March 1954; 28 April 1955; H. Kingsley, *Crusader: The Life and Times of Sir Cyril Black* (Old Woking: p.p., 1996), p.71.
52  *BT*, 6 May 1954, p.3.

churches reported forty conversions each, and one church was arranging a baptismal service for thirteen people.[53] In 1955 Graham preached at the final gathering of the Baptist World Congress held in the Arsenal football stadium. In the years following Harringay numerous ministers in the Baptist Union, as well as other denominations, attributed their conversion to the Harringay meetings.[54]

Evangelism in England had been stimulated in a number of ways. Youth for Christ (YFC), with which Graham was closely associated in the 1940s and 1950s, became the channel for significant evangelistic enterprise.[55] Some British evangelists, such as Eric Hutchings, modelled themselves on Graham. A gathering called in 1958 by another British evangelist, Tom Rees, who spearheaded large rallies in London which many Baptist young people attended, revealed that evangelists who had previously felt discouraged were heartened.[56] New initiatives were evident. In 1958 a team from Spurgeon's College formed a 'South Coast Venture Team' for a mission in Brighton. A music group led by Bryan Gilbert, a student at Spurgeon's, was part of the team.[57] A year later Gilbert and his associates were involved in evangelism in coffee bars in Liverpool.[58] In the same period the Union Council was discussing the vital need to evangelize. Cyril Black wanted a Secretary for Evangelism, the role that Douglas Brown had fulfilled in the 1920s, and offered to contribute to the costs, but no decision was made. Lewis Misselbrook, minister of Leavesdon Road, Watford, produced evangelistic literature for Baptist churches. His books, *Winning the People for Christ* and *Training in Visitation*, were widely used.[59] Hubert Janisch, chairman of the Union's

53  *BT*, 27 May 1954, p.8.
54  I.M. Randall, 'Conservative Constructionist: The Early Influence of Billy Graham in Britain', *The Evangelical Quarterly*, Vol.67, No.4 (1995), pp.330-1.
55  For insights see D.J. Jeremy, 'Businessmen in Interdenominational Activity: Birmingham Youth for Christ, 1940s-1950s', *BQ*, Vol.33, No.7 (1990), pp.336-43.
56  J. Rees, *Stranger than Fiction* (Frinton-on-Sea: p.p., 1957), p.88.
57  *BT*, 14 August 1958, p.12.
58  *BT*, 28 May 1959, p.4.
59  L. Misselbrook, *Winning the People for Christ* (London: Carey Kingsgate Press, 1956); L. Misselbrook, *Training in Visitation* (London: Carey Kingsgate Press,

Evangelism Committee, reported to the Council in 1959 that London Baptists had been engaged in an 'Alive to God Campaign' and that Ter-Jubilee celebrations included a strong stress on evangelism.[60] The denomination was united in its evangelistic commitment.

## CHURCH PLANTING AND CHURCH RENEWAL

What effect did the widespread stress on evangelism have at local church level? There were existing Baptist churches that were growing. Discussion took place in the *Baptist Times* concerning factors which helped or hindered church growth. Mrs D.A. Taylor, from Bromley, said in September 1950 that during the previous twenty years she had experienced a number of Baptist churches in the different towns where she had lived. She had received 'warm welcomes' in some churches and 'freezing stares' in others, and her view was that 'warm' churches flourished while 'cold' ones were moribund.[61] Morgan Derham, minister at Theydon Bois, Essex, probably reflected the views of many ministers when he observed a few months later that the key to advance lay 'not in stunts and spasmodic spurts, but in solid, patient pastoral work'.[62] Sudbury, Middlesex, was an example of growth. Under the ministry of Edmund Heddle, who had studied at London Bible College, the church doubled in three years from about fifty to over a hundred members.[63] Derham and others viewed the role of the minister and other leaders as crucial to growth. The role of deaconesses in this period was also highlighted. Twenty deaconesses were leading Baptist work on expanding housing estates.[64]

---

1957).

60  *BT*, 14 January 1960, p.1.

61  *BT*, 7 September 1950, p.6.

62  *BT*, 14 December 1950, p.8.

63  Minutes of the Baptist Union Ministerial Recognition Sub-Committee, 3 December 1952. Edmund Heddle later became a member of the Baptist Union Council and chairman of the Ministry Main Committee.

64  *BT*, 28 April 1955, p.7.

New churches were being started. A survey in 1954 reported that forty-two new Baptist causes had been established since 1946 and said that Associations had plans for another thirty.[65] Larger churches planted outreach causes and Associations also took strategic initiatives. The Home Work provisions for initial pastorates meant that a minister could begin work in a new area before a church had been formally constituted, although often new congregations were brought into being under lay leadership. In 1957 the Area Superintendents painted a detailed picture in the *Baptist Times* of church extension across the country. The reports offer an insight into the outreach being undertaken by Baptists in different regions. In the North East, J.O. Barrett, an influential Union figure, who was

*People arriving for the opening of Dalton Baptist Church, Huddersfield, April 1955 - an 'estate' church led by Sister Christine Perrett, with a Home Work Fund initial pastorate grant*

appointed Area Superintendent in 1949, was concerned to encourage imaginative thinking about the task of contemporary mission. He described Baptist causes started on a number of new estates in the North East: the Dalton estate in Huddersfield; Moortown in Leeds; Priory Road in Hull; Berwick Hills in Middlesborough; Brecken Bank in Keighley; Simonside in Jarrow; and West View and Owton Manor in Hartlepool. Relatively few of these congregations were led in the first place by ordained ministers: the common pattern was for the initial leader to be a deaconess or a layman.[66] Most of these 'estate' churches were meeting in

65   *BT*, 18 March 1954, p.8.
66   *BT*, 16 May 1957, p.9.

rented buildings, mainly schools. In one case the venue was a cricket pavilion. A number of new buildings were erected, although the style of some of them was later described as 'somewhere between a local authority clinic and a Scout hut'.[67]

The situation in the North West, as Hubert Watson explained, was different in certain respects from elsewhere in the country. A number of Baptist churches were suffering badly as a result of the declining populations in their surrounding communities. The majority of Baptist church buildings that had been erected 80-100 years before were now too large for the congregations and were often a liability. The emphasis, Watson commented, was commonly on existing churches 'holding on' rather than expanding. There was some new extension in the North West, however, for example in Liverpool, at Speke, Maghull and Kirkby; in Manchester, on the large Wythenshaw estate; and in Carlisle, on the Belah estate. Often primary or secondary schools were used for Sunday services, and the common format was to have a Sunday school in the morning and an adult service in the evening.[68] Local Baptist committees also launched campaigns in which they sought to raise funds for the erection of new church buildings. In a number of instances local authorities issued strict guidelines about building work, which often increased the costs. Despite the great efforts made by people from other Baptist churches around, a number of the new council estate churches of the 1950s, such as that planted at Belah, Carlisle, ultimately failed to survive.[69]

There was evidence of advance in the Midlands. Within the East Midland Area, W.J. Grant reported, sixteen new ventures had been launched in the 1950s. At Scunthorpe a Baptist witness had been resuscitated; in Leicester new Baptist work had begun at Braunstone and

---

67    Sellers, ed., *Our Heritage: The Baptists of Yorkshire, Lancashire and Cheshire*, p.114.
68    *BT*, 30 May 1957, p.9.
69    Sellers, ed., *Our Heritage: The Baptists of Yorkshire, Lancashire and Cheshire*, p.115.

at Stocking Farm, where Alex Wright, a Spurgeon's student, was leading a new cause; and at Bilborough, in Nottingham, Richard Hamper, who had been minister at Botley and Eynsham, Oxford, had started working with young people on a new housing estate in 1956 and a church was formed in April 1957 with forty-three members.[70] The West Midland Area had seen considerable outreach activity, as reported by A. J. Klaiber, who was an observant commentator on Baptist affairs from the superintendents' perspective. In Birmingham seven new Baptist causes had been established and were now provided with buildings in which to meet. Coventry had three new Baptist congregations, and in addition Overslade (in Rugby), Stafford, Walsall, Wolverhampton and Dudley all had new ventures. Gloucestershire had two new causes, at Lower Tuffley and Matson. A number of these extension congregations had ministers supported by the initial pastorate scheme.[71]

*Overslade Baptist Church, Rugby*

Reporting on the Metropolitan Area, the Superintendent, W.D. Jackson, paid tribute to the visionary work that had been done by Henry Cook, his predecessor, and by Charles Johnson, the Secretary of the LBA. The first initial pastorate in the LBA was at New Addington, Croydon, in 1948. Pioneer causes followed at Bonneville in Balham; Temple Hill in Dartford, Kent; Northolt Park in Harrow, Middlesex; Monks Gate in Ilford, Essex; Morden Park, Surrey; and Enfield, Middlesex. Two of these new congregations were led by deaconesses. Jackson emphasized the strategic use of the War Damage funds available from the government, which were being used in this period not only to rebuild churches that had been damaged by bombing but also to construct new church buildings on

---

70   *BT*, 1 August 1957, p.6.
71   *BT*, 5 September 1957, p.9.

different sites.[72] This was especially crucial given the shifts in London's population. There was concern in this period, however, that the considerable number of Baptist church members who had moved out of London, often to live in commuter areas around the city or in new towns, were losing contact with Baptist churches. A reunion in one London Baptist church revealed that many who had once been active members did not regularly attend a place of worship after moving.[73]

*Stone-laying at Ramridge, Luton, 12 July 1956*

The Central and Eastern Areas were affected in a different way by the movement taking place of large numbers of people out of London. Douglas Hicks, Central Area Superintendent, reported that in Stevenage, Hertfordshire, where 70,000 Londoners were to be re-housed, a new site

---

72    *BT*, 15 August 1957, p.7.
73    *BT*, 24 August 1950, p.8.

had been purchased for a church and Baptists were meeting in a community centre. There were twelve initial pastorates in the Area. Hicks highlighted Cotton Mill, St Albans, and Ramridge, Luton, where Peter Tongeman, a Spurgeon's student, was leading the work. At Kidlington, Oxfordshire, six students from Regent's Park College had taken responsibility. Different models of church planting were in evidence from the Midlands to the outskirts of London.[74] In the Eastern Area, F.C. Bryan highlighted the huge challenge of starting Baptist churches in rapidly-growing London 'overspill' towns like Harlow and Basildon, each with a population of 60-80,000 people. He reported that the Soham church had bought a site on a new housing area. Other extension work was taking place in Barnwell in Cambridge; on the Heartsease estate to the north-east of Norwich; on the Gunton estate in Lowestoft; in the Holly Lodge Mission in Ipswich; at Harold Hill, Essex; and in the Grays, Upminster and Halstead areas.[75]

In his report on the Southern Area, H.V. Larcombe highlighted the work of deaconesses. Sister Margaret Smith was leading a new endeavour in Parkstone, Dorset; Sister Muriel Scott was pioneering an outreach from Holland Road Baptist Church, Hove, at Hangleton Valley; and Sister Ruth Phillips was the leader of a work on a new estate in the Redhill, Surrey, area. In the

*Crawley Baptist Church, 1954*
*This replaced a bombed building*

Southampton area there was an extension congregation at Thornhill, and there was growth in various parts of Sussex – in Crawley, in Chichester and in Moulescoomb, an estate in Brighton. At Moulescoomb, R.E. East, who had previously been pastor at Whetstone, Leicestershire, had recently

74    *BT*, 19 September 1957, p.9.
75    *BT*, 4 July 1957, p.6.

baptized eighteen people, all of whom who had become part of this pioneering venture, thereby doubling the membership of the new church in the first nine months of East's ministry. East was receiving initial pastorate funding, and in this report emphasis was again placed on the vital support being given to such initial pastorates by the Home Work scheme. As was the case elsewhere in the country, several of the new congregations were meeting in schools.[76]

H.H. Pewtress reported on the Western Area. Here, as in some other parts of England, the provision of ministry for small Baptist churches in rural areas presented a huge challenge. Across England as a whole, two-thirds of Baptist churches were reckoned to be country churches. Of the 320 Baptist churches in the West

*A caravan solves the problem - a bachelor minister living on site on a new estate, 1956*

Country, 140 had memberships of under twenty people. Financial support of a minister was virtually impossible in such situations, unless chapels were grouped together in some way. There was, however, some urban growth taking place in the West of England. Bristol, known traditionally for the strength of its Baptist witness, had four large housing estates and Baptist work was starting on two of these. There was new impetus at Lawrence Weston and Little Stoke, with the help of the Bristol Association. Halcon, Taunton, was received into the Western Association as an independent church, as a result of extension ministry by two other churches into a new housing estate. In Plymouth, 17,000 new houses were being built and new Baptist churches had been established on three estates.[77] The impression given by these reports was of considerable

---

76    *BT*, 20 June 1957, p. 8.
77    *BT*, 31 October 1957, p.8.

investment of time, energy and financial resources by Baptists in church extension.

Yet while some churches were growing, others were in decline. In some cases people were leaving Baptist churches and were joining other denominations. In 1950 a *Baptist Times* correspondent, Desmond Hall, said: 'I could name five local churches run and staffed by renegade Baptists.'[78] Whether this was typical or not, it seemed from an analysis done in Kent and Sussex at the end of the 1950s that there was a degree of dissatisfaction in Baptist congregations. This study looked at 316 removals from rolls – 214 women and 102 men. Of these, 76 were removed for non-attendance, 69 because they had moved, and 51 because they had joined another denomination. Some had been removed from membership through a process of church discipline - over issues like marriage to a non-Christian (11) and 'unworthy conduct' (9). The evidence suggests that church discipline, a procedure that expressed the Baptist desire for high standards of membership, was still practised. However, it was probably often the case that those at odds with their church simply resigned. Of those in the survey who had resigned, most did not state what precipitated their resignation, but some referred to quarrels in the church (17) or home influences (14). At a time of great emphasis on younger people, a worrying aspect of this survey was that many of those being lost to Baptist churches were under thirty.[79]

Retention of members was a particularly acute issue for city centre churches, as more Baptists in the 1950s moved to the suburbs. The famous Union Chapel in Oxford Road, Manchester, was demolished in 1950. Attention was given to models for renewing congregations. Cemetery Road, Sheffield, under the leadership of S.F. Clark, was attracting 250 people on Sunday mornings and 300 on Sunday evenings. As car ownership increased, members who owned cars brought others to church. A cup of tea was available in the church lounge after the evening service. During the week, the church lounge was used as a meeting place.

---

78    *BT*, 7 September 1950, p.6.
79    *BT*, 12 March 1959, p.1.

At Broadmead Baptist Church, Bristol, there was a similar pattern of people travelling in from the suburbs. It was reckoned that one in four of the Broadmead members had a car. At King's Road, Reading, the morning services were described as 'semi-liturgical', whereas a 'People's Service' took place on Sunday evenings. London Road, Portsmouth, a church of 450 members, had 250 attending in the morning and 400-500 in the evening. The emphasis was on preaching.[80] There was also concern to reach people living in the inner cities. At Bloomsbury Central Baptist Church, twenty-five young adults organized Visitation Campaigns in 1955 and 1957, visiting 2,000 local residents to invite them to worship and offer practical help. Townley Lord applauded this 'first class piece of evangelism'.[81]

Questions were also being asked about how to foster the inner dimensions of church life. At Bloomsbury, the Thursday evening Prayer and Bible Study meeting was revived in 1955; it took place at 6.30 p.m., with light refreshments beforehand to assist people coming direct from work.[82] There was denominational discussion about the renewal of worship. In 1950 correspondents in the *Baptist Times* discussed having music during the distribution of the bread and wine at communion. This practice, which was increasing, seemed to some to suggest that Baptists were afraid of silence. W.J. Vincent, the organist at Brown Street, Salisbury, argued, however, that the Chorale Preludes of Bach (for example) were helpful in a 'spiritual approach to the Sacrament'.[83] A.J. Tugwell, from London Road, Portsmouth, was thankful that in his experience 'a good deal of the cacophony today published under the pseudonym of music is excluded'.[84] In the early 1950s Alec Gilmore, minister at Kingsthorpe, Northampton, contributed to discussions on 'Baptists and Worship', setting out the place of invocation, confession, and silence, and arguing that the sacraments helped believers offer their

---

80   *BT,* 19 February 1959, pp.8-9.
81   Bowers, *A Bold Experiment,* p.369.
82   Ibid., p.376.
83   *BT,* 6 July 1950, p.9; 3 August 1950, p.3.
84   *BT,* 17 April 1958, p.9.

lives to God.[85] There was evidence of a rising sacramentalism in Baptist worship. Ernest Payne, who was always keen to stimulate the thinking of younger ministers, encouraged Gilmore, who was in his first pastorate, to explore the issue of baptism more fully.[86] A range of possibilities for renewal was emerging.

ECCLESIOLOGICAL ISSUES

The call by Geoffrey Fisher, Archbishop of Canterbury, for Free Churches to take episcopacy into their system eventually resulted in a formal document, *Church Relations in England* (1951). A Baptist committee set up in 1951, chaired by Arthur Dakin, made clear its opposition to making inter-communion dependent on some kind of acceptance of episcopacy. Nonetheless, Baptist ecumenical activity continued. The Baptist Union document, *The Doctrine of the Church* (1948), was part of a volume produced for the WCC's Faith and Order Conference in Lund (1952) which discussed 'The Nature of the Church' and 'Inter-Communion'.[87] At the Baptist Assembly in 1951, when the Union President was H.R. Williamson, Foreign Secretary of the BMS, Geoffrey Fisher was a speaker. It was a historic moment: the first time that the Archbishop of Canterbury had been at the Assembly.[88] Fisher, who was greeted with prolonged applause, expressed appreciation of M.E. Aubrey, who was retiring. Fisher explained that Aubrey's address to the Convocation of York in the 1930s had led him to commit himself to the ecumenical movement. Fisher spoke of Aubrey's integrity and courage within the British and World Councils of Churches. In response, Williamson suggested Fisher's request to adopt episcopacy was asking a great deal, since Free Churches had 'expurgated it 400 years ago'. But

---

85   *BT*, 5 June 1952, p.9; 2 July 1953, p.2.
86   I am indebted to Keith Jones, Rector of the International Baptist Theological Seminary, Prague, for this recollection from Alec Gilmore.
87   Cross, *Baptism and the Baptists*, p.156; West, *Baptists Together*, p.106.
88   When Cosmo Lang addressed the Assembly he was Archbishop of York.

*Interior of Mare Street Baptist Church, Hackney, a new building after bombs destroyed the old chapel. Behind the communion table is an open baptistry, so the pulpit is no longer the dominant central feature.*

Williamson believed that Fisher had brought Anglicans and Baptists nearer to Christ and one another.[89]

Few Baptist leaders were sympathetic to submitting to episcopacy. Payne insisted in 1952 that Baptists were fully part of the One, Holy, Catholic and Apostolic Church and that 'in their fellowship and service, and in their sacramental worship, they have known the presence of their Lord and the power of the Holy Spirit'.[90] Baptists saw nothing inferior in their ecclesiology. A year later Hugh Martin, preaching at St Paul's Cathedral as Moderator of the Free Church Federal Council, suggested that many Free Church people could see that episcopacy had value, but could not agree that it was essential.[91] Henry Townsend, who had retired from the principalship at Manchester in 1949, objected to parts of Martin's address and insisted on Baptist distinctives.[92] In response,

---

89    *BT*, 3 May 1951, p.2.
90    E.A. Payne, *The Free Churches and Episcopacy* (London: Carey Kingsgate Press, 1952), pp.12-13.
91    *BT*, 14 May 1953, p.5.
92    *BT*, 21 May 1953, p.7.

Martin said he was not prepared to let differences over baptism obscure more important matters on which Baptists agreed with other Christians.[93] A few months later, in November 1953, the Union published a response to the Lund conference report. This response welcomed the description of the Church as 'a company of the sanctified – forgiven, justified and born anew in Christ', but said that the report's views on the eucharist and baptism needed explanation and further study, and claimed that practices such as the worship of Mary had no scriptural warrant.[94]

This raised the specific question of whether there could be any unity with the Roman Catholic Church. Fear of Rome was still a notable feature among evangelicals. Anti-ecumenical convictions found institutional expression in the establishment in 1952 of the British Evangelical Council (BEC). Among the founders was E.J. Poole-Connor, National Commissioner of the Fellowship of Independent Evangelical Churches (FIEC). The American International Council of Christian Churches (ICCC) - a fiercely anti-ecumenical organization – envisaged a British ICCC branch, but the BEC did not wish to be an appendage of the American body, aspects of whose stance it did not find acceptable.[95] George Beasley-Murray, who joined the staff at Spurgeon's College in 1950, wrote an article in 1955, 'Is the World Council of Churches Antichrist?' In much Protestant tradition the Pope had been seen as Anti-Christ and the WCC was now being given that label in some quarters. Beasley-Murray saw this as a misinterpretation of Revelation and a misunderstanding of the WCC. Indeed he commended one WCC paper -

---

93    *BT*, 28 May 1953, p.7.
94    'The Response of the Baptist Union of Great Britain and Ireland to the Report of the Third World Conference on Faith and Order', Baptist Church House, November 1953; Minutes of the Baptist Union Council, 17 and 18 November 1953.
95    For background, see H. Jones, 'The Doctor and the British Evangelical Council', in H.R. Jones, ed., *D. Martyn Lloyd-Jones: Unity in Truth* (Darlington: Evangelical Press, 1991), pp.7-19; D.G. Fountain, *E.J. Poole-Connor, 1872-1962* (Worthing: Henry E. Walter, 1966), chapters 7 and 8. E.A. Payne wrote a defence of the WCC against the background of ICCC criticisms: E.A.Payne, 'Some Illusions and Errors', *Ecumenical Review*, Vol.10, No.3 (1958), pp.294-319.

*Christ the Hope of the World* – as one of the finest declarations on eschatology he had read. He concluded robustly: 'I should be grateful to God if the general theology of the World Council of Churches, and the deep spirituality manifested therein, characterized our own Denomination. In fact, we fall far short of it.'[96]

Beasley-Murray's perception was that it was important for Baptists to engage in ecclesiological and inter-church debates, and he involved himself in ecumenical activity. Contention about such issues was to become fierce. Older ecclesiological tensions, such as between open and closed membership or open and closed communion churches, were now less evident. By the mid-1950s a very large number of Baptist churches allowed into membership those who had not been baptized as believers.[97] A major new feature was the emergence of strident voices questioning Baptist involvement in the ecumenical movement and urging withdrawal from the BCC and WCC. When the Metropolitan Tabernacle re-joined the Union in 1955, after sixty-eight years outside, three Baptists from America commented to Beasley-Murray that a fire that had damaged the Tabernacle was a judgment on the church being in the Union. 'No wonder', they said, 'God burned it down.'[98] At the BRF conference at the end of 1957, Theo Bamber asserted that it was time the BRF spoke about ecumenism. He argued that Anglicans had conceded nothing in ecumenical discussions. 'Rome is adamant', he stated sombrely, 'Canterbury is dominant and Baptists are quiescent, if not subservient.' He foresaw a 'new Nonconformity' standing outside any 'artificial scheme for unity',[99] an idea that a number of Baptists were to espouse.

---

96  *BT*, 29 December 1955, p.6.
97  Minutes of the Baptist Union Council, 12 and 13 Nov 1956. Ruth Trevithick from Yorkshire moved to Ealing in 1957 and was unable to find a Baptist Union church with a closed membership: *BT*, 18 July 1957, p.6.
98  Minutes of the Baptist Union Council 15 and 16 November 1955; *BT*, 12 January 1956, p.7.
99  T.M. Bamber 'Christian Unity', paper given to the BRF Conference at High Leigh 26 November 1957.

Shifts were taking place in Baptist identity. The historic ecclesiological identity of Baptists had been shaped by the Dissenting/Nonconformist tradition, but with the formation of the BCC and WCC some Baptists were finding a wider ecumenical identity, while others opposed that vigorously. Free Church work continued, however, and Ernest Payne served as Moderator of the Free Church Federal Council in this period. For much of the 1950s, Payne was heavily involved in the work of the Central Committee of the WCC, and from the 1954 WCC Assembly, at Evanston, USA, he had the distinction of being the Central Committee vice-chairman. In delicate discussions, Payne had the ability to draft resolutions which satisfied different parties.[100] For those Baptists wary of such wider co-operation, fellowship was to be found in evangelical organizations such as the Keswick Convention. In 1951 two Baptists, Francis Dixon and Geoffrey King, were among the Keswick speakers, and it was suggested that thousands of Baptists were

*Queues at West Croydon Tabernacle for the induction of Geoffrey King as minister, 4 September 1954*

---

100   Thomson, 'A Round Unvarnish'd Tale', p.35.

among the over 8,000 people at the Convention.[101] A new thrust in the 1950s was represented by the Puritan and Reformed Studies Conference, which began in 1950 and to which Martyn Lloyd-Jones gave support. Volumes of Puritan theology were re-published by a new publishing house, the Banner of Truth. This Puritan revival would colour post-war conservative evangelicalism. The Westminster Fellowship, a monthly meeting for ministers chaired by Martyn Lloyd-Jones, attracted several Baptist ministers.[102]

The nature of the church members' meeting in Baptist churches was also changing. Writing in 1952, Ernest Payne identified two tendencies observable after the Second World War. Some churches had returned to an earlier practice of transacting business relating to the pastorate and to admission and transfer of church members on Sundays, usually after the evening service. Other churches had tried to revive the mid-week church members' meeting by introducing themes such as Christian witness for discussion. There was wide recognition, said Payne, that the sense of responsibility that had in an earlier period been a mark of church membership had been dangerously weakened. Church discipline as part of Baptist church life had not disappeared, but was far less prominent. In earlier centuries, Baptist church meetings had often dealt with instances of individual members whose conduct was thought to have fallen short: issues frequently addressed had included excessive drinking, sexual impropriety, or involvement in doubtful entertainment. Payne believed that there was a need to articulate a more definite code of conduct adapted to the twentieth century. He also raised the possibility of a renewal of the life of the church meeting, which had became a 'business meeting', but believed it was too early to say that this was taking place.[103]

Another issue was the nature of baptism and the Lord's Supper. In 1951 the Baptist college principals produced *The Lord's Supper: A Baptist Statement*, edited by R.L Child, which stressed that the Lord's

---

101   *BT*, 9 August 1951, p.2.
102   Bebbington, *Evangelicalism in Modern Britain*, pp.261-2.
103   E.A. Payne, *The Fellowship of Believers* (London: Carey Kingsgate Press, 1952), pp.101-6.

Supper was 'not only commemorative but also communicative', that Jesus Christ was 'truly present'.[104] Much more attention, however, was given

*George Beasley-Murray*

to baptism. When Neville Clark wrote in 1956 that 'the New Testament view of baptism is of a rite that is effective rather than merely symbolic', he was accused of following Catholic writers, but J.R.C. Perkin, at Altrincham Baptist Church, Cheshire, drawing from his own research on baptism, contended that Clark had gone back to the New Testament.[105] Concern to be true to the New Testament also characterized the writings of George Beasley-Murray, whose massive contribution to the baptismal debate made him 'the foremost Baptist sacramentalist' in this area.[106] Beasley-Murray was one of the Baptist ministers who co-operated in the production of a book in 1959, *Christian Baptism*, which was a landmark in Baptist

thinking about baptism.[107] Like Alec Gilmore (the editor of the volume), Neville Clark, and other contributors, Beasley-Murray, by then Principal of Spurgeon's, argued that baptism was 'an effective sign: in it Christ and faith come together in the meeting of conversion'.[108] When the

104   R.L. Child, *The Lord's Supper: A Baptist Statement* (London; Carey Kingsgate Press, 1951), pp.19-20.

105   *BT*, 5 July 1956, p.6; cf. Cross, *Baptism and the Baptists*, pp.225-7. Perkin had received an Oxford DPhil for his work on baptism.

106   Cross, *Baptism and the Baptists*, pp.225-7.

107   Editorial, *The Fraternal*, July 1959, p.4.

108   G.R. Beasley-Murray, 'Baptism in the Epistles of Paul', in A. Gilmore, ed., *Christian Baptism: A Fresh Attempt to Understand the Rite in terms of Scripture, History and Theology* (London: Lutterworth, 1959), p.148. The other contributors included A.W. Argyle and W.M.S. West, both tutors at Regent's Park College, R.E.O. White, then at Birkenhead, and Stephen Winward.

sacramentalism found in *Christian Baptism* was strongly criticized by some *Baptist Times* correspondents, Beasley-Murray replied that Scripture militated against the 'reduced baptism' that was being widely championed.[109]

An analysis of fault lines in evangelical life was offered in 1957 by W.E. Sangster, the Methodist Home Mission Secretary, speaking at the Baptist Assembly. He argued that in all denominations the gap between conservative and liberal evangelicals was a hindrance to evangelism. The *Baptist Times* report spoke of the 'left and right wings' of the Baptist denomination: those on the right wing were referred to as conservative evangelicals or fundamentalists.[110] One correspondent, Roy Williams from Coseley, said that he had been reared in the liberal tradition and he believed that Baptist Assemblies were biased in favour of that position. He suggested 'it is time we heard more voices from the more conservative groups'. Walter Bottoms, who had taken over from Townley Lord as *Baptist Times* editor, asserted that Assembly speakers were 'chosen without bias by a Programme Committee, all members of which are Evangelicals, and who include representatives of both sides of theological outlook'.[111] It was too simple to speak of two 'sides' in the denomination. For example, Beasley-Murray, who identified with the Inter-Varsity Fellowship rather than with SCM, was happy to work within the WCC. What was evident in the 1950s was that some Baptist leaders had a more 'catholic' vision of the Church, while others were suspicious of this trend.

MINISTRY – QUANTITY AND QUALITY

Questions about the church inevitably raised questions about ministry. The role of the minister was changing, as J.O Barrett, the North Eastern Superintendent, pointed out in 1952: 'The old idea of the minister as called to spend his time in conducting Sunday services and a weeknight

---

109  *BT*, 10 December 1959, p.8.
110  *BT*, 9 May 1957, pp.1, 2.
111  *BT*, 30 May 1957, p.7. Walter Bottoms moved to the *Baptist Times* from the post of Central Area Superintendent.

devotional service…and in pastoral visitation of his congregation, is outmoded in the actual situation which many of our churches face, with a small congregation surrounded by a population only a minute fraction of which has any church connection.'[112] Later in the same year, R.L. Child, the Regent's Park College Principal, commented on the interest in the theology of ordination, an interest which partly sprang from theological dialogue with the Church of England. Against the background of queries among Baptists regarding the role of the minister, Child argued that ordination was an act of God in which a person already gifted by God was set apart to 'ministerial functions'. The chief purpose of the ordination service, said Child, was 'to recognize that fact, and to claim for the ordinand the gift of the Holy Spirit, and the guidance and blessing of God'.[113] In Child's view, the authority of the ordained person lay in the Spirit's power and ordination to ministry was intended to be permanent.[114]

*Many mid-century ministers, like G.W. Sterry of Heath Street, Hampstead, normally wore clerical dress*

Such a high view of ministry was bound to generate debate, and in May 1954 the General Purposes and Finance Executive of the Union asked a group of eight people to prepare a statement on ordination. The group was chaired by David S. Russell, recently appointed as Principal of Rawdon College, with J.O. Barrett as secretary. Three of the members were lay people. The report, *The Meaning and Practice of Ordination among Baptists*, was completed in 1957 after nine residential group meetings. It defined ordination as 'the act, wherein the Church, under the guidance of the Holy Spirit, publicly recognises and confirms that a Christian believer has been gifted, called and set apart by God for the work of the ministry

---

112   *BT*, 11 September 1952, p.7.
113   *BT*, 30 October 1952, p.9.
114   *BT*, 13 November 1952, p.9.

and in the name of Christ commissions him for his work'.[115] The work of ministry was seen in traditional terms as 'the ministry of the Word and Sacraments', to be exercised normally, but not exclusively, in a local congregation. If any ministry involved 'leadership of the Church's worship, the administration of the ordinances of Baptism and the Lord's Supper, the proclamation of the Gospel and the teaching of the faith, the work of pastoral care and Christian service', then ordination was seen as appropriate.[116] There was a growing practice in this period for ordinations to take place in the new minister's home church rather than in the new sphere of ministry.[117] The 1957 report followed the thinking of Payne about ministry, rather than the views expressed in the 1940s by Arthur Dakin.

Although the Ordination report was the result of considerable theological work, some Council members encouraged further study, since they thought that the report did not go far enough in setting out a theology of ministry.[118] Other concerns about ministry were raised by a Union Commission on the Ministry which reported in 1958. This produced some disturbing statistics about trends in ministry. Before 1910 there had been worries about the position of about 400 unaccredited ministers, but most of them were accredited under the new arrangements. In 1910 there had been 1,012 accredited and only 96 unaccredited ministers serving Union churches in England. By 1957, however, there were 883 accredited ministers and 403 unaccredited ministers in local church ministries, with 81 ministers in other spheres.[119] The unaccredited figure had increased significantly. In addition, about a quarter of churches had no pastoral oversight. The report by the Commission on Ministry also looked at current problems being experienced by all ministers, whether accredited or not. It identified a number of causes for a loss of confidence in

---

115  *The Meaning and Practice of Ordination among Baptists* (London: Baptist Union, 1957), p.22.
116  Ibid., pp.23-4.
117  *BT*, 2 December 1954, p.7.
118  *BT*, 21 March 1957, p.1.
119  Minutes of a Baptist Union Commission on the Ministry, 23 January 1958.

ministry, leading to an overall decline in ministerial numbers: low stipends, frustration about the role - churches wanted a 'general Factotum' rather than a pastor and teacher - and ease of transfer to other occupations, particularly teaching and social work.[120]

At the start of the decade, with the denomination benefiting from the post-war bulge in ministerial recruits, there had been no particular worries about ministerial supply.[121] By 1953, however, there was talk of making better use of lay pastors because recruitment to ordained ministry was insufficient.[122] In 1957 Ernest Payne and Henry Bonser (former North Eastern Superintendent and Union President in 1953) analysed the decrease in the number of ministers in pastoral service. It was noted that because of the number of ministers approaching retirement, the shortage would become greater.[123] A year later, as the situation regarding ministerial supply continued to deteriorate – the shortfall in recruitment was about ten per year - the Commission on Ministry made the stark prediction that 'if the present trends continue unchecked, the spiritual health of the churches will continue to decline and grave harm may result to our denominational witness'. The recommendations made by the Commission were that greater efforts should be made to increase the minimum stipend, to provide motor cars for ministers, to utilize retired ministers, to present the claims of ministry to a younger generation, and to develop ministerial teams.[124]

The issue of stipends was a pressing one. In 1951 John Giles of Littleover, Derby, called the standard (minimum) stipend 'ludicrous', although his comparison of the stipend of £295 per annum with the commencing salary of a newly qualified day school teacher, which was £300, led some to suggest that he was overstating his case. After considerable correspondence in the *Baptist Times*, J.O. Barrett made what

---

120   Minutes of the Baptist Union Council, 11 and 12 March 1958; cf. Sparkes, *An Accredited Ministry*, pp.45-6.

121   Minutes of a Baptist Union Committee *re* the Ministry, 26 July 1951.

122   Minutes of a Baptist Union Committee *re* the Ministry, 28 January 1953.

123   *BT*, 21 March 1957, p.8.

124   Minutes of the Baptist Union Council, 11 and 12 March 1958.

was widely viewed as an authoritative statement when he concluded that the 'plain and painful truth' was that a married minister with children, who was in an aided (i.e. aided by the Home Work Fund) church, could not make ends meet.[125] S.G. Morris, who chaired the superintendents' monthly board meetings, noted in 1955 that the average working wage in Britain was reckoned to be over £600 per annum, while the aim of the Baptist Union was to achieve a ministerial stipend of £400 plus manse. The 1955 figure was £355. By the later 1950s, many British workers were earning

*J.O. Barrett*

three times as much as before the Second World War, and it was very difficult to see how the Union could match such increases. The committee considering these issues recommended, among other things, that ministers in aided churches should be permitted to undertake approved paid employment in addition to pastoral duties.[126]

Yet there were many positive aspects to ministry in the 1950s. In 1954 there was comment on the inspiring Baptist Assembly services each year at which young ministers and deaconesses were transferred to the Union's accredited list. In that year there were sixty-two new ministers and one new deaconess.[127] Considerable time and energy were also devoted to facilitating ministerial settlements within the Union and J.O. Barrett spoke about 'the deeply religious spirit' of the meetings of the superintendents at which discussions on settlements took place. When meeting with the deacons and members of local churches, superintendents emphasized that seeking a minister was 'a profoundly spiritual task', and they encouraged the churches to spend time in prayer.[128] Many ministers

---

125 *BT*, 18 January 1951, p.7; 11 September 1952, p.7; Sparkes, *The Home Mission Story*, pp.119-20.

126 *BT*, 1 September 1955, p.6; Sparkes, *The Home Mission Story*, pp.120-3.

127 *BT*, 13 May 1954, p.6.

128 *BT*, 18 September 1952, p.2.

who settled in churches found their work fulfilling. When Arthur Dakin retired from Bristol College, Payne spoke of ministers trained under him as having 'steadiness of character, realism, and a deepened sense of vocation'.[129] Demand for the ministry of deaconesses was increasing, and H.M. Angus and his wife oversaw the training of deaconesses at 'Struan' in the early 1950s. Angus had worked for the BMS in India and at home. One trainee deaconess in this period, Joy Baines, said that she came to know Christ in reality as Master and Lord at the Baptist Assembly Youth Rally and then offered herself for deaconess work.[130]

*Struan, 1951 - Left to right: Revd H.M. Angus, Mrs Barbara Angus, Sisters Christine Perrett, Joan Allen, Jenny Clark, Joy Baines, Elizabeth Goodwin, Daphne Pearce (below), Monica McFale (above), Muriel Roskiley and Margaret Smith*

New emphases were also to be found in ministry. In 1952 Leslie Jenkins, minister at Long Crendon, near Aylesbury, who had trained at Spurgeon's, wrote to the *Baptist Times* suggesting that the ministry of

---

129   *BT*, 15 October 1953, p.8.
130   *BT*, 7 May 1953, p.4. Joy Baines later married a minister, Leslie Gregory.

healing was relevant to Baptist life. He referred to healing in the New Testament and to examples of seventeenth-century Baptists who believed in anointing with oil and prayer for the sick. Two leading seventeenth-century Baptists, William Kiffin and Hanserd Knollys, were described by Jenkins as having been 'instrumental in the healing of extreme cases of illness'. Although anointing with oil for healing had been rare in recent Baptist life, interest was growing. Jenkins noted that some Baptists had been joining Pentecostal churches, where prayer for healing was common. He concluded: 'I am sure that a consideration of the subject of Divine Healing would lead to a deepening of the spiritual life of Christian people through a more practical faith in the power of prayer.'[131] By 1959 Donald Nield, minister at Cippenham, Slough, who had trained at Manchester College, said that healing groups were now part of the ministry of churches of several denominations.[132] One Baptist participant in regular healing services, Helen Wylie, spoke about many people receiving mental, spiritual and physical help.[133] Fresh thinking about ministry was evident.

## MINISTERIAL AND LAY EDUCATION

Thinking about ministry raised issues of training. In reporting the findings of the Union Commission in 1958, the headline in the *Baptist Times* was 'Grave decline in quality and numbers entering ministry'. There was no doubting the reduction in numbers seeking training. K.C. Dykes, Principal of Manchester College, noted that, whereas there used to be three applicants for every college place, applications had now halved.[134] But what about quality? L.G. Champion, Arthur Dakin's successor as Principal at Bristol, who had degrees from Bristol, London and Heidelberg, was disturbed by the remarks about quality having declined. Champion had been a member of the commission that produced the 1958 report on ministry and he was impressed with the sense of vocation and

---

131  *BT*, 6 March 1952, p.7.
132  *BT*, 1 October 1959, p.6.
133  *BT*, 23 August 1962, p.7.
134  *BT*, 20 March 1958, p.8.

*L.G. Champion*

readiness to learn that characterized those preparing for ministerial work. The problems, he argued, were largely in the churches, and he urged that ministers should have the opportunity to give imaginative leadership. The *Baptist Times*' editor, Walter Bottoms, defended the comments about quality, pointing out that the rising number of unaccredited ministers meant there had been 'a great – not to say alarming – increase in the proportion of churches served by those who have not had the benefit of a full, ministerial training course'.[135]

The fact that someone in ministry had not been to a Baptist college did not, of course, mean that they had received an inadequate education, but it did seem that some wishing to enter Baptist ministry in this period had relatively little awareness of Baptist life. In 1952 Brash Bonsall, who had trained at All Nations Bible College, applied for Union ministerial recognition. He was a member of Lion Walk Congregational Church, Colchester, and had been baptized as a believer. Bonsall, later the founder and Principal of Birmingham Bible Institute, had been rejected for Congregational ministry and had been advised to apply to the Baptist Union. The Ministerial Recognition Committee could not support his application.[136] Another applicant who had studied at All Nations was Noel Stanton. In presenting his case to the Ministerial Recognition Committee, Stanton referred to 'the blessing which has already attended my ministry in various Churches throughout the country'. It was agreed that Stanton could take oversight of a church, and in 1957 he became lay pastor at

---

135  R. Hayden, 'The Stillness and the Dancing', in R. Hayden and B. Haymes, eds., *Bible, History and Ministry: Essays for L G Champion on his Ninetieth Birthday* (Bristol: Bristol Baptist College, 1997), p.6; *BT*, 10 April 1958, pp.5-6.

136  Minutes of the Baptist Union Ministerial Recognition Sub-Committee, 10 September 1952.

Bugbrooke, where Payne had been minister.[137] Several applicants for accreditation had studied at LBC.[138] Ernest Kevan, LBC's Principal, was keen to ensure that LBC students seeking to enter Baptist ministry were loyal to the denomination.[139]

Training for women was a continuing issue. Few women applied for ministerial training in the 1950s. Violet Hedger, who had become an accredited minister in 1926, led worship at the Baptist Assembly in 1952. After much discussion about deaconess training it was decided that 'Struan' should close, and from 1955 deaconesses were trained at Carey Hall, Birmingham. When the Baptist deaconesses were transferred there they constituted only eight of the forty-eight students. Carey Hall was mainly engaged in training women for service with the Baptist, Presbyterian and Congregational Missionary societies. Gwenyth Hubble, who was Principal, went on to work for the World Council of Churches.[140] Fred Cawley, Principal of Spurgeon's from 1950 to 1955, argued in 1951 that the status of deaconesses should be equal to that of ministers.[141] The Union Council noted in 1953 that thirty of the fifty-five deaconesses in active ministry were serving as if they were ministers. The Council members took the view, however, that there was little demand for women ministers by Baptist churches, although they accepted that in the future this might alter.[142] If thirty churches were happy with women who were

---

137  Minutes of the Baptist Union Ministerial Recognition Sub-Committee, 20 and 21 June 1956.
138  Minutes of the Baptist Union Ministerial Recognition Sub-Committee, 17 April 1956.
139  Randall, *Educating Evangelicalism*, p.104.
140  Minutes of the Baptist Union Council, 16 and 17 November 1954; Payne, *Baptist Union*, pp.243-4; H. Martin, *Fifty Years of Carey Hall, 1912-1962* (Birmingham: The Council of Carey Hall, 1962), p.8. The BRF lodged a strong protest in 1958-9 about the theological position of Carey Hall – *Baptist Revival Fellowship Bulletin*, Nos.59 and 60 (October/December 1958 and January/March 1959). Gwenyth Hubble moved from Carey Hall in 1960, to work for the World Council of Churches, first in New York and then in Canada.
141  Minutes of the Women's Training College Curriculum Sub-Committee, 4 January 1951.
142  Minutes of the Baptist Union Council, 17 and 18 November 1953.

effectively their ministers, the conclusion that there was little demand for women ministers seems strange.

Within the Baptist colleges, fresh challenges were evident. Eric Worstead, Vice-Principal of Spurgeon's, described in 1954 the rising costs that colleges were experiencing. Income from investments was declining and some Local Education Authorities gave nothing to 'sectarian training'. Many larger churches in the Union contributed little money to the colleges. Smaller churches gave proportionately more support, but three-quarters of churches gave nothing.[143] No doubt some did not feel confidence in the colleges, and this could make College Councils cautious. In 1957 Worstead, by then Spurgeon's Principal, wrote in the *Baptist Times* about how he had been spiritually affected by a conference of the Oxford Group (or MRA - Moral Re-Armament), a movement that had helped a number of Baptists in the 1930s.[144] Geoffrey King, minister of West Croydon Tabernacle, raised this matter at the College Council in June 1957. Over the course of five meetings, the identification of the Principal with a movement that was very broad in its religious sympathies was discussed. The Council then concluded that it was 'contrary to the well-being of the College that its Principal should be associated with M.R.A.', and Worstead resigned.[145] Worstead's personal assessment of his spiritual journey was that he had been given a closer attachment to the Bible and the Church's wider witness.[146]

---

143   *BT*, 14 January 1954, p.8.
144   See Chapter 5 above.
145   Minutes of the Spurgeon's College Executive Committee held on 1 July, 2, 10 and 30 September 1957; Minutes of the Spurgeon's College Council held on 18 June, 12 July, 4 and 13 September 1957. See P. Beasley-Murray, *Fearless for Truth: A Personal Portrait of the Life of George Beasley-Murray* (Carlisle: Paternoster Press, 2002), p.89.
146   Eric Worstead to the author, 10 June 1995.

The colleges were able to make progress in certain areas. In 1956, the centenary of the founding of Spurgeon's College, a new college chapel was opened. Ernest Payne laid the first stone and recalled the eleven 'Spurgeon's men' who had been presidents of the Union. Of the fifteen leaving students in 1956, ten were going into home ministry and five overseas.[147] Four students from Russia came to study in England in 1956, and Michael Zhidkov and Matthew Melnik, who went to Spurgeon's and Bristol respectively, would become significant Baptist leaders.[148] At Rawdon, David Russell developed lay as well as ministerial training, while at Manchester K.C. Dykes placed emphasis on worship, the spiritual development of ministers and world issues.[149] L.G. Champion, at Bristol, appointed Norman Moon and Harry Mowvley as tutors, and created a fine chapel for worship.[150] In 1957, through the work of R.L. Child, Regent's Park College obtained permission to take students for non-ministerial courses, although preference was to be given to those training for Baptist ministry. Child retired in 1958, to be followed by G.

*Regent's Park College, Oxford*

Henton Davies. After distinguishing himself in academic studies at Cardiff, Oxford, Marburg, and London, Henton Davies went into pastoral ministry and was then on the staff of Bristol College. From 1951 to 1958 he was Professor of Old Testament Studies, University of Durham.[151]

Old Testament scholarship continued to be a field in which Baptists made a substantial contribution. H.H. Rowley, who from 1945 was

147   *BT*, 12 July 1956, p.9.
148   Green, *Crossing the Boundaries*, pp.26-31; Payne, *Baptist Union*, p.248; West, *To be a Pilgrim*, p.106.
149   Sellers, ed., *Our Heritage: The Baptists of Yorkshire, Lancashire and Cheshire*, pp.107, 118.
150   Hayden, 'The Stillness and the Dancing', pp.6-7.
151   Cooper, *From Stepney to St Giles'*, pp.101-7.

Professor of Semitic Languages and Literature, University of Manchester, and the author of over thirty books, was a leading representative of the Biblical Theology movement, as evidenced by such books as *The Unity of the Bible* (1953). Rowley's work on apocalyptic themes, on archeology and the history of ancient Israel, and on theology and mission, established him as a major international scholar, who as R.E. Clements put it, made Old Testament research widely known and popularly accessible.[152] The area of mission, which was of particular interest to Rowley as a former missionary, was considered in a number of his books, such as *The Biblical Doctrine of Election* (1950). For Rowley, biblical criticism helped rather than hindered biblical theology and he had outstanding ability to deal clearly with complex issues in Old Testament scholarship. Rowley saw his work as being in continuity with that of his mentor, Wheeler Robinson, and in turn Rowley's endeavours were a source of inspiration for younger scholars.[153] R.E. Clements, following pastoral ministry in the 1950s, lectured from 1960 in the Department of Hebrew and Semitic Languages, University of Edinburgh, moving in 1967 to the University of Cambridge. Clements had a special interest in the Nonconformist contribution to nineteenth-century biblical scholarship.[154]

New initiatives were evident in lay education. There were about eighty Union-affiliated associations of Baptist lay preachers and about fifty lay preachers came together each year at a preachers' conference. The flow of new people into lay preaching was steady. A Baptist Union Diploma in Religious Knowledge for lay leaders was introduced and in 1954 this was awarded to twenty-one candidates, of whom ten were women. Although the scheme was popular, there was some dissatisfaction

---

152  R.E. Clements, 'The Biblical Theology of H.H. Rowley, 1890-1969', *BQ*, Vol.38, No.2 (1999), pp.70-82.

153  J.T. Williams, 'The Contribution of Protestant Nonconformists to Biblical Scholarship in the Twentieth Century', in A.P.F. Sell and A.R. Cross, eds., *Protestant Nonconformity in the Twentieth Century* (Carlisle: Paternoster Press, 2003), pp.11-12.

154  In 1985 R.E. Clements became Professor of Old Testament Studies, King's College London.

with the way preaching was tested by older lay preachers. It seemed that a few experienced lay preachers were not sufficiently appreciative of promising young candidates.[155] In 1955 fifteen lay pastors and thirty lay preachers qualified for Union recognition.[156] There were also local initiatives in training. In the North East, for example, courses began in 1951 to train younger people for leadership, stimulated by an evangelistic campaign in Cleveland in which 100 people professed conversion.[157] The BWL, with branches in three-quarters of the churches in the Union, placed emphasis on training. The BWL President in 1957, Mrs G.C. Batten, had been a lecturer at Stockport College of Further Education.[158] Baptist educators worked both within and outside the churches.

## INITIATIVES WITH CHILDREN AND YOUTH

An ongoing concern for Baptists was integrating children into church life. George Beasley-Murray addressed the 'Church and the Child' from a theological standpoint.[159] It was calculated that only ten per cent of those in Baptist Sunday schools stayed involved in church life beyond the age of fourteen, and the decline accelerated throughout the 1950s. In 1959 a loss of 21,000 children in the previous year was reported.[160] Society was changing, with car ownership making it easier for families to go out on Sundays and TV offering recreation at home. But other issues within Sunday schools were apparent. Jean Green, the Union's Sunday School adviser, compiled a forthright report in 1956 after visiting seventy Baptist churches. She wrote: 'With the exception of a few outstandingly good

---

155 Minutes of the Diploma Management Committee, 7 October 1954.
156 *BT*, 5 May 1955, p.6.
157 *BT*, 22 November 1951, p.9.
158 *BT*, 2 May 1957, p.9.
159 G.R. Beasley-Murray, 'The Church and the Child', *The Fraternal*, April 1943, pp.9-13. For background see W.M.S. West, 'The Child and the Church: A Baptist Perspective', in W.H. Brackney, P.S. Fiddes and J.H.Y. Briggs, *Pilgrim Pathways: Essays in Honour of B.R. White* (Macon, Ga.: Mercer University Press, 1999), pp.88-92.
160 *BT*, 23 April 1959, p.8.

Beginners and Primary departments, the work among the younger children can generally only be described as dull.' Most teachers had no training and the children inevitably compared the 'low standard of teaching, poor equipment and general unsatisfactory environment' with their day schools. Green continued: 'We can no longer expect children and young people to spend an hour a week sitting in dreary surroundings listening to badly presented lessons which have little meaning in their own experience.' It was a devastating critique. Green called for imaginative leadership in churches and asked whether these issues were discussed at church members' meetings.[161]

As in other denominations in this period, work among 'teens and twenties' seemed to be more effective. About 2,000 young Baptists filled Westminster Chapel at the end of the Assembly each year for an evening Youth Rally. At the 1951 rally the Baptist Youth Movement was launched. The rally's organizers were W.T. Cowlan, Director of the Union's Young People's Department, and Godfrey Robinson, Young People's Secretary, BMS, who co-authored, with Stephen Winward, the best-selling book for new Christians, *The Way*. They emphasized four themes - conversion, church involvement, evangelism and citizenship.[162] Interest grew rapidly, and seven thousand Baptist young people packed the Royal Albert Hall in 1952. The chairman on that occasion, Godfrey Robinson, said that it was easier to get a ticket for Saturday's cup final than for the rally. Youth choirs took part and testimonies to personal faith were given, with speakers including J. Godfray (later Sir Godfray) Le Quesne, a barrister; Cynthia Allegro, a former ballet dancer then training as a deaconess; Charlton Athletic's famous and popular Bert Johnson, 'who leads young fellows to Christ in his two Bible classes'; W.M. Knight, a Jamaican Baptist who was studying at Regent's Park College; and Marianne Freye, who had travelled 10,000 miles in India on a motor bike in the course of her work as a BMS missionary. The rally's aims were to bring Christian challenge and to broaden horizons. David Russell,

161  *BT*, 3 April 1952, p.8.
162  *BT*, 3 May 1951, p.8.

chairman of the Young People's Committee, was the main speaker and urged young people to witness to their contemporaries.[163]

Another aspect of Baptist engagement with young people was ministry in universities and colleges. The Baptist Students' Federation was intended to foster evangelism and fellowship, and by 1960 the BSF had grown to nineteen societies, with a total membership of over 600. The annual BSF conference attracted about 130 students.[164] One important aim was that members should be equipped to have an impact in society. R.L. Child, Union President in 1954, encouraged young people to consider teaching as a profession.[165] Grey Griffith wanted to see BSF members thinking seriously about the call to ministry, and he insisted in 1957 that the lack of passion in the churches about trained ministry must be addressed.[166] In the same year, H.H. Rowley, as Union President, made

*Students from Aberystwyth, Bristol and London on a BSF Mission at Earls Hall Baptist Church, Southend, Essex, September 1959*

---

163  *BT,* 8 May 1952, p.9.
164  *BT,* 15 September 1960, p.11.
165  *BT,* 6 May 1954, p.2.
166  Minutes of a Baptist Union Commission re the Ministry 28 November 1957.

a similar point. Rowley was in close touch with students in Manchester University, and he wanted to encourage younger people to engage in study of their faith. Addressing Baptists who were suspicious of degrees, he stated: 'A trained minister is none the worse for having a university degree, though many of the best ministers I have known have had none.' He commended the kind of person who could take the gospel in an effective way outside the church.[167]

Alongside the denominational societies in universities were the inter-denominational student groups to which Baptists belonged. In 1952 Hugh Martin noted that the Student Christian Movement had branches in 242 British universities and colleges and that seventy-seven theological colleges were associated with SCM. There were about 10,000 student members. The Baptist Union gave a grant towards the support of a Baptist on the SCM staff, and there were many links between SCM and the Union leadership.[168] But student support for SCM was falling. SCM was also losing its earlier evangelistic thrust. The Christian Unions (CUs) associated with the Inter-Varsity Fellowship, by contrast, were conducting large-scale university missions in the 1950s, with evangelicals such as John Stott, Rector of All Souls' Church, Langham Place, London, delivering thoughtful evangelistic messages. The emphasis of the SCM was on meetings to which speakers of various theological viewpoints were invited.[169] During the 1950s the *Baptist Times* included information from both SCM and IVF leaders. In 1956, for example, Oliver Barclay, IVF General Secretary, stressed that in some colleges CUs were the only organized form of Christian witness. Philip Lee-Woolf, for SCM, claimed that many students had 'first heard the gospel through the agency of the S.C.M.'.[170]

Within the local Associations and through the Young People's Department of the Union many different types of outreach to young people

---

167  *BT*, 2 May 1957, pp.2, 3.

168  *BT*, 7 February 1952, p.8.

169  Bebbington, *Evangelicalism in Modern Britain*, pp.253, 259-61; O. Barclay, *Evangelicalism in Britain, 1935-1995* (Leicester: IVP, 1997), p.66.

170  *BT*, 6 September 1956, p.7.

took place. The Yorkshire Association organized an effective annual Campaign Camp which encouraged young people in areas of discipleship.[171] The Union's Young People's National Council, chaired by Paul Rowntree Clifford, organized Summer and Easter events and Fellowship Tours, and was active in forming links with local church Youth Fellowships. W.T. Cowlan, who had come to the Baptist Union in 1949 from the Free Church Federal Council, moved to pastoral ministry in Taunton in 1955, and W. David Jackson, of Histon Baptist Church, joined the Union's Young People's Department. Conferences arranged for young people explored issues connected with Baptist life. J.N. Schofield, a lecturer in Old Testament at Cambridge, reported from one conference of under twenty-fives in 1953: these young Baptists, he said, were committed to youth activities but many were not regular at public worship or church members' meetings and they felt that their ideas were often turned down by the churches. Schofield concluded that this situation was contributing to the decline in Baptist membership.[172]

Although attitudes to worship and church meetings among younger Baptists caused concern, young people were, nonetheless, seeking to reach out to others in their age group. This was being done in new ways. Open Youth Clubs – 'open' in the sense of not placing conditions on attendance – were increasingly to be found in churches of most denominations.[173] Some older youth movements were now in decline, such as the National Young Life Campaign and Christian Endeavour, although there were still about 1,000 CE Societies in Baptist churches in the 1950s. Newer movements, such as Youth for Christ (YFC), were growing. George Cumming, the minister of Victoria Drive, Eastbourne, described in 1956 YFC-initiated evangelism in which a café, called The Rendezvous, was taken over to reach 'teddy boys and teddy girls' in the town. A band played and there was a five-minute talk. Although the young people often

171 Sellers, ed., *Our Heritage: The Baptists of Yorkshire, Lancashire and Cheshire*, p.118.
172 *BT*, 1 October 1953, p.2.
173 P. Ward, *Growing up Evangelical: Youthwork and the Making of a Subculture* (London: SPCK, 1996), pp.63-4.

interrupted the speaker, conversations always followed.[174] The use of new styles of music was to become increasingly important. The programme at the Baptist youth meeting at the Assembly in 1955, in Westminster Chapel, included a song from Bryan Gilbert, 'who brought novelty to the programme by accompanying himself on the guitar'.[175] New forms of communication were being encouraged.

## ENGAGEMENT WITH SOCIETY

Outreach was taking place within a changing society. In 1954 a *Baptist Times* article reported on racial tension in places like Brixton and Birmingham. It was estimated that up to 20,000 people from the Caribbean had come to Britain in one year. There was no shortage of work: the Midland Region of the Ministry of Labour alone reported 45,000 vacancies. The article continued: 'We must integrate our new neighbours into the full life of the community. Here the churches have a big part to play.'[176] To help with housing shortages, the Birmingham Friendship Housing Association and the Baptist Union purchased two houses in Aston.[177] Baptist ministers in Southampton and Plymouth were involved in seeking to meet new arrivals.[178] In Wednesbury, in the Midlands, local factories were employing West Indians, and after Wednesbury Baptist Church invited some West Indians to the services large numbers began to attend. Donald Hepburn, pastor of East Street Baptist Church, Kingston, Jamaica, conducted Jamaican-style services at Wednesbury, with a Caribbean choir singing spirituals in what one report called an 'uninhibited manner'. The church emphasized that it was 'not in favour of any Colour Bar that may exist in the town and the surrounding

174  *BT*, 2 February 1956, p.5.
175  *BT*, 5 May 1955, p.8.
176  *BT*, 18 November 1954, p.2.
177  Minutes of the Baptist Union General Purposes and Finance Executive, 10 April 1956.
178  Minutes of the Baptist Union Moral and Social Questions Committee, 21 June 1955; 4 October 1955.

area'.[179] When race riots took place in Notting Hill, London, in 1958, David Shewan and Robert Cooper, ministers at Westbourne Grove and Westbourne Park Baptist churches respectively, spoke of their determination to work for reconciliation.[180]

*A Sunday evening service at Wednesbury led by Pastor Donald Hepburn from Kingston, Jamaica, assisted by Caribbeans from the local congregation*

Churches, organizations and individuals were active in many forms of social activity, as they had been throughout the century. The Baptist Women's League, for example, continued to be responsible for the hostel in London, Newington Court, which usually accommodated between forty and fifty girls from Baptist churches who were working in the capital, often as secretaries. The Baptist Men's Movement was keen to be involved in missionary and social enterprises, and became interested in the agricultural work of the BMS. In the 1950s David Stockley, a BMS

179  *BT*, 13 October 1955, p.2; 28 June 1956, p.9.
180  *BT*, 11 September 1958, p.9.

missionary in Pakistan, trained students who became pioneers in agricultural innovation, and the BMS set up Operation Agri to support his work. Operation Agri developed as a wider scheme for the provision of tools, seed and livestock for people with whom BMS missionaries were working, and was recommended to the BMM and accepted at its 1961 Annual Meeting at Swanwick. Many Baptist churches took up the project with enthusiasm. Cyril Petch, the dynamic Secretary and Chief Commissioner of the BMM from 1959, as a farmer, magistrate and County councillor, gave significant leadership to this enterprise.[181] Other initiatives took place locally. In Yorkshire, the Association had set up a Commission of Christian Witness in 1949, which engaged with issues such as evangelism, education, and Christian ethics, and which helped to nurture future Baptist leaders who saw the need for the gospel to relate to pressing needs within society.[182]

Ernest Payne, writing in 1951, addressed particular social issues that were of concern at the time: 'The whole country', he stated, 'is acutely troubled by the problem of juvenile delinquency.' Often problems were associated with family breakdown. Initiatives were being taken in this area. The Carnegie United Kingdom Trust gave a grant of £15,000 to enable the building of a Boys' Home in connection with the West Ham Central Mission. In the early 1950s many churches were looking at ways to engage constructively with disaffected young people, especially because the public had been shocked by instances of violent crime involving young people.[183] In the same period Vernon Baptist Church was working among prostitutes in the King's Cross area of London where the church was situated. Arnold Clark, the Union treasurer, encouraged the Union in its social care work. This included a home for unmarried mothers, 'The Haven', in Yateley, Surrey, and also the Baptist Union Adoption Society, both operating under the auspices of the Union's Women's Department.

---

181  K.W. Bennett, *God at Work with Men* (Pontesford, Shrewsbury: BMM, 1997), pp.34-6; *World Outlook*, No.249 (1967), p.5.
182  Sellers, ed., *Our Heritage: The Baptists of Yorkshire, Lancashire and Cheshire*, p.109.
183  *BT*, 19 July 1951, p.7.

In the 1950s adoption was much more common than was later the case, and over fifty babies born each year to mothers in the Haven were adopted by Christian families. Arnold Clark took a particular interest in this aspect of Baptist work. Baptist churches were also seeking to help alcoholics in Britain - estimated at nearly half a million.[184]

Historic Baptist concerns also remained evident, as illustrated again by Arnold Clark, who advocated temperance and Sunday observance, and opposed gambling, including raffles.[185] T.G. Dunning, the Union's Director of Education, Temperance and Social Service, became secretary of the Churches' Temperance Council. He was Union President in 1958. Clifford Cleal, formerly on the BCC staff, led a new Union Citizenship department, assisted by John Hough, Jean Green and then Dorothy Taylor. During the 1950s issues featuring prominently were temperance, gambling and holding professional sports on Sundays. Clifford Cleal and his colleagues did outstanding work, broadening the agenda in significant ways. Industrial Mission, for example, was included.[186] Some Baptist concerns arose because of likely Parliamentary legislation. Responding to the Royal Commission on marriage and divorce, Baptists opposed devaluation of marriage, but noted that Baptist ministers could conduct re-marriages of divorcees in church.[187] There was Baptist opposition in 1957 to Premium Bonds, which were equated with gambling.[188] In other cases new legislation was welcomed. Baptist MPs were aware that many Baptists supported suspension of the death penalty.[189] New issues emerged, such as artificial insemination and the growing threat of nuclear weapons. The problem of smoking was increasingly raised in relation to

184 *BT*, 1 May 1952, pp.1-3, 8; Payne, *Baptist Union*, p.229.
185 *BT*, 1 May 1952, pp.1-3.
186 Bernard Green, retired General Secretary of the Union, to the author, 16 February 2004.
187 *BT*, 10 October 1957, p.5.
188 Bebbington, 'Baptists and Politics since 1914', in Clements, ed., *Baptists in the Twentieth Century*, p.87.
189 Minutes of the Baptist Union Moral and Social Questions Committee, 19 June 1956. At that point there were ten Baptist MPs, mainly representing constituencies in Wales.

addiction and lung cancer. Ronald Thorns from West Worthing said in 1957 that there were Baptists who 'shout from the rooftops that they are total abstainers; yet very often they are slaves to the nicotine addiction'.[190]

*Baptist Union Council in session, 1955*
*Henry Cook presides, with E.A. Payne on his right*

Wider political involvement by Baptists, both nationally and internationally, was on a much reduced scale in the post-war period. Of the three Baptist MPs representing constituencies in England in 1959, Stanley Awbery (Bristol, Central) and Clifford Kenyon (Chorley, Lancashire), were Labour, and Cyril Black (Wimbledon) was Conservative. Under Townley Lord's editorship the *Baptist Times* generally avoided politics, although after Bottoms became editor in 1956 politicians from the main parties were invited to contribute.[191] It was impossible to avoid moral questions raised by political action. At the Union Council in November 1956, Godfray Le Quesne introduced a

---

190  *BT*, 30 May 1957, p.7.
191  Bebbington, 'Baptists and Politics since 1914', pp.78-9. During most of the 1950s a Conservative government was in power.

resolution deploring 'the action of Great Britain and France in invading Egypt without the authority of the United Nations'. The invasion had taken place because Egypt's President Nasser had nationalized the Suez canal. Sir Herbert Janes, Union President, was among those who supported the British action. After sharp disagreement a compromise resolution supporting the UN was agreed.[192] Clifford Kenyon, MP, a lay pastor and a member of the Union Council, lamented the 'cowardly compromise' by Baptists.[193] By contrast, Theo Bamber, a premillennialist, saw resolutions as of 'negligible' value: the world was heading towards 'a baptism of blood without parallel in the history of the human race, to be brought to a climax by the appearing of our Blessed Lord'.[194]

Baptists were still, however, active in such areas as academic life, business and the media. Among the academics were A.O. Rankin, Professor of Physics in the Imperial College of Science and Technology, and a Fellow of the Royal Society. Baptists working in industry arranged conferences to discuss questions of mutual concern. Among the conference contributors in 1957 were J.W. Johnson, managing director of several companies in the Rossendale Valley; C.F. Allister of Ealing, assistant production manager of McVitie & Price; Harry Crowe, a foreman in the Ipswich Gas Company; and L.W. Jordan, accountant at Eastern Electricity Board.[195] The media was also an area of Baptist interest. In 1949 R.C. Walton and E.H. Robertson, both Baptist ministers, were appointed to the BBC's School Education and Religious Broadcasting Departments respectively. Robertson was succeeded in 1955 by another Baptist, Douglas Stewart. In 1952 Robertson stressed at the Baptist Assembly the important place of religious broadcasting.[196] There was much discussion of the influence of television, and Norman B. Jones

---

192  Minutes of the Baptist Union Council, 12 and 13 November 1956; *BT*, 22 November 1956, p.8. Herbert Janes said he would resign the presidency if Godfray Le Quesne's motion was passed. Godfray was the son of C.T. Le Quesne.

193  *BT*, 29 November 1956, p.7.

194  *BT*, 13 December 1956, p.7.

195  *BT*, 3 October 1957, p.8.

196  *BT*, 8 May 1952, p.7.

from Waterbarn, Lancashire, produced imaginative epilogues for Granada Television. Despite hesitations, a baptismal service from Richmond, Liverpool, was televised, with the Union Council supporting such opportunities for public witness.[197]

## CONCLUSION

The 1950s saw Ernest Payne placing his stamp firmly on the life of the Union. He was not a naturally dominant type of personality, but the Council and the committees of the Union were contexts in which he was able to put his gifts to good use. However, the activities of the Council were seen by some in the churches as rather remote. With his high view of the universal Church, Ernest Payne gave considerable attention to ecumenical affairs, and Adrian Hastings sees him as the leading ecumenical figure in England from the 1950s onwards. Like Shakespeare, Payne found it difficult to secure affirmation from some Baptists. Hastings comments that Payne's ecumenical commitments 'caused some disquiet on the part of his Baptist constituency – perhaps more at home than abroad'.[198] Unease at home was to grow and cause tensions in the 1960s. Those churches in the 1950s which saw local evangelism as a priority were likely to have been more impressed by the evangelistic vision conveyed by Billy Graham than by an ecumenical agenda. Yet the Union leadership was also deeply concerned about reaching post-war society. An important part of the Union's Ter-Jubilee emphasis was on evangelism and social action. But high levels of evangelistic activity did not guarantee sustained church growth. At the end of the decade there were over 8,000 fewer Baptist members than at the beginning. In the 1950s, however, Payne's hope of Baptists responding to 'a renewed spiritual interest' was widely shared, and many Baptists were pleased to be part of a Union which was – to use a term employed during the Ter-Jubilee – 'Alive to the Gospel'.

---

197  Minutes of the Baptist Union Council, 18 and 19 November 1952.
198  Hastings, *A History of English Christianity*, p.470.

# Chapter 8
# 'A SPECTRUM OF THEOLOGICAL VIEWS' 1960-69

The 1960s, according to Callum Brown, saw the Christian-centred culture which had conferred identity on the people of Britain, rejected.[1] The decade was a turning point in a number of ways. The post-war austerity of the 1950s gave way to greater affluence. The religious world was rocked by Bishop John Robinson's provocative book, *Honest to God*, published in 1963, which called for a new understanding of God. 350,000 copies were in print within a year.[2] In the same year Beatlemania was reaching its height. There were Baptists who were seeking to respond to the changing culture, and new experiments in outreach were to be found. A desire for authentic spiritual experience was also evident. In addition, Baptists were concerned to understand their own identity. The celebrations of 150 years of the Baptist Union, promoted by Ernest Payne over four years up to 1963, produced a growing self-awareness among Baptists, resulting in fruitful discussions about the nature of the church, its ministry, ordination, baptism and the place of children in the churches. An appeal was launched for £300,000 which, although not fully achieved, contributed significantly to mission at home. But this was also a period of tension and of theological polarization. An editorial in the *Baptist Times* in 1968 suggested: 'Baptists probably cover as wide a spectrum of theological views as other denominations'.[3] Although this was rather an over-statement, the spectrum of views that did exist made the 1960s a difficult decade.

1    C.G. Brown, *The Death of Christian Britain* (London: Routledge, 2001), p.193.
2    J.A.T. Robinson, *Honest to God* (London: SCM, 1963); J.A.T. Robinson and D.L. Edwards, *The Honest to God Debate* (London: SCM, 1964).
3    *BT*, 1 February 1968, p.5.

REACHING OUT

The decade began with expressions of concern about Baptist decline in England. There were some hopeful signs: the number of churches was increasing, there was talk of 'Missionary Congregations',[4] and since 1949 seventy-five schemes for initial pastorates had been aided from the Home Work (renamed Home Mission in 1970) Fund. But each Baptist congregation was, on average, becoming smaller. Fewer new members were being attracted and churches were not particularly successful in holding young people. The number of baptisms declined.[5] The average loss of members overall was about 3,000 per year. However, such total figures did not highlight regional variations. An analysis of decline from 1911 to 1961, published in the *Baptist Times* in 1962, suggested that over that fifty-year period the loss of members from Baptist churches in the North of

*A new church opens at Thetford, Norfolk, 1964*

England was approaching half the membership. In the South the figure was about one-sixth. Church membership in Lancashire and Cheshire, which in 1960 was 19,574, fell to 13,164 a decade later. Norman B. Jones, who moved from Waterbarn, Bacup, Lancashire, to become Superintendent for the North West in 1961, and David S. Russell, Principal of Rawdon College, near Leeds, tried to provoke churches in the North to look realistically at their difficulties.[6]

As a response to the changing cultural patterns and the challenges of the 1960s, some Baptists explored new methods of reaching out. Walter Fancutt, then working for the Mission to Lepers, wrote in 1962

4     *BT*, 6 April 1967, p.5.
5     *BT*, 4 May 1961, p.7.
6     *BT*, 19 July 1962, pp. 8-10; Sellers, *Our Heritage*, pp.123-4, 130.

about new opportunities for churches to grasp.[7] One person who attempted this was Bryan Gilbert, with his music group, the Venturers, later led by another Spurgeon's student, Michael Wood. The Spurgeon's College faculty discussed the group and expressed 'its strong distaste for this kind of music with Gospel songs'; although George Beasley-Murray, the Principal, himself a fine musician, was personally supportive.[8] Café

*The Venturers, 1964*

evangelism was tried at Leominster in 1963 under the leadership of the minister, Eric Hayden. Young people came into a café taken over by the church, sat round tables, and talked and listened to taped or live music provided by groups like the Venturers.[9] A similar coffee bar was in operation in Dagenham. In autumn 1963, a mission to Dagenham was led by the Principal, tutors and students from Spurgeon's College. The influence of new approaches was evident, with 1,000 young people attending a Saturday cinema club during the mission.[10] Four years later, Alister Mogford, an eighteen-year-old engineering apprentice involved in Baptist life in Stevenage, spoke of the needs of teenagers on drugs, and said: 'If we are to convert teenagers, the Church must reform, or the Church will die.'[11]

While newer schemes were generally well received, there was also considerable allegiance among Baptists to the style promoted by Billy Graham in the 1950s and again in 1966, when Graham returned to Britain. One British evangelist who saw himself as playing a Graham-like role was Eric Hutchings. In 1960, after an Eric Hutchings' crusade

---

7   *BT*, 25 October 1962, p.6.
8   P. Beasley-Murray, *Fearless for Truth: A Personal Portrait of the Life of George Beasley-Murray* (Carlisle: Paternoster Press, 2002), pp.102-3.
9   *BT*, 14 February 1963, p.1.
10  *BT*, 17 October 1963, p.2.
11  *BT*, 21 December 1967, p.4.

in the Bingley Hall, Birmingham, Trevor Stout, minister of Bearwood Baptist Church, said that fourteen people associated with his church had 'been brought to the point of personal decision for Christ'. He believed this experience was typical. D.H. Sleigh, from Smethwick, agreed and said that the *Sunday Mercury* had been impressed by the absence of 'emotional histrionics' at the crusade. By contrast a *Baptist Times* reporter, Brian Cooper, of St Anthony's College, Oxford, considered Hutchings was 'inclined to be too emotional, too fond of threatening hell'. There was, therefore, sharp disagreement.[12] The *Baptist Times* editor, Walter Bottoms, received many letters testifying to the value of the crusade, criticizing Cooper's negative comments, and indicating the large number of Baptist lay people and ministers who were supportive of Hutchings. It was claimed that 3,500 people had responded to the evangelistic appeals made at the crusade.[13] Cooper was unrepentant, arguing that the leading clergy in Birmingham had opposed the crusade.[14] Nonetheless, the high degree of Baptist support for this exercise in traditional evangelism was significant.

In areas such as Birmingham, the West Indian segment of the population was growing in the 1960s. Asians were also coming to Britain, settling in areas such as Southall, Middlesex. It soon became apparent that Baptist churches had to take steps to meet the challenges of a changing society. At the Union's Citizenship Committee in January 1960 some ministers shared their experiences of West Indians attending their churches.[15] It was evident that advice and help was needed, and a month later the Union's General Purposes and Finance Committee recommended that the BMS and the Union should share the cost of bringing a Jamaican Baptist minister over to give advice about integrating West Indians into Baptist churches and to help with communication in both directions.[16] At the May meeting of the

---

12    *BT*, 21 July 1960, p.7.
13    *BT*, 28 July 1960, p.7.
14    *BT*, 11 August 1960, p.4. He did not name the clergy.
15    Minutes of the Baptist Union Christian Citizenship Committee, 11 January 1960.
16    Minutes of the Baptist Union General Purposes and Finance Executive, 16 February 1960.

Committee it was reported that M.E.W. Sawyers, a respected Jamaican Baptist – minister of Georgetown Baptist Church and former President of the Jamaican Baptist Union – was willing to come to Britain for six months. The Union and the BMS would cover the costs. When Sawyers arrived, in April 1961, he was sponsored by the Union, the BMS and Baptist churches in North London.[17]

The visit by Sawyers was one initiative. Other initiatives were being taken by several Baptist churches, especially in London, Birmingham and Manchester. Charles Karunaratna, after ministry in Ceylon, became associate minister at the West Ham Central Mission in 1963. At Ferme Park, Hornsey, a special event for West Indians in 1960 was attended by the local MP, the Mayor of Hornsey, and Mr de Sousa, Secretary of the West Indian Commission. One of the newly-elected Ferme Park deacons, Roy Lewis, was a West Indian. There were suggestions in the *Baptist Times* that Lewis had special responsibility for West Indians, but the Ferme Park minister, Geoffrey Haden, replied that he would have the same responsibilities as other deacons, although Haden emphasized that Lewis' outstanding work at Ferme Park had attracted West Indians.[18] When Sawyers arrived in Britain in 1961 he made Ferme Park his base. During his six months he spoke to many West Indians and when he returned to Jamaica in October 1961 he reflected: 'Over and over again, they have told me that they were made to feel they were not wanted by the churches.' In addition, their church-going was ridiculed at work. Sawyers wondered whether British reserve was misinterpreted as unfriendliness and argued that Baptist churches needed to do more to involve West Indians. He praised Ferme Park, under Geoffrey Haden, and Small Heath, Birmingham, firstly under Norman Moon and subsequently under Bernard Mason.[19]

---

17    Minutes of the Baptist Union General Purposes and Finance Executive, 31 May 1960.
18    *BT*, 23 June 1960, p.16; 11 August 1960, p.7.
19    *BT*, 26 October 1961, p.1.

Further encouragement was given to British Baptists seeking to reach out to West Indians three years later when G.H.L. Gayle from St Ann's Bay, Jamaica, came to Britain for twelve months.[20] On his arrival in 1964, Gayle was welcomed officially at a meeting in Small Heath, which the Deputy Mayor of Birmingham attended. There were reports of progress in integrating West Indians in Baptist churches. Dennis Horwood, minister at Woodgrange, Forest Gate, appointed a twenty-eight year old West Indian, Heckford Sharpe, as his lay assistant. Sharpe, a sorter in the Post Office, had previously been in a Caribbean Baptist group meeting in a Moravian Church. In Nottingham, Mansfield Road Baptist Church, under Bernard Green's leadership, attracted many West Indians.[21] At Rosemary Street Baptist Church, Mansfield, a Jamaican, Samuel Case, was elected a deacon. Arthur Neave, the minister, said this was the 'crowning joy' of his ministry.[22] In 1964 it was reported that Willesden Green, London, had appointed two West Indian deacons. The Union Council was being urged by Norman Jones to oppose all racial discrimination.[23] Gayle, analysing his year in Britain, said in March 1965 that Baptists might welcome Jamaicans but they were reluctant to adapt church structures.[24] In the meantime, black-majority Pentecostal churches

*G.H.L. Gayle*

such as the New Testament Church of God were growing.[25] Former Baptists were joining these churches. Of 40,000 West Indians in Birmingham, only 101 were members of Baptist churches. Many more would have been Baptists when they lived in the Caribbean.[26]

---

20   See Minutes of the Baptist Union Council of 7 May 1963 for discussion.
21   Conversation with Bernard Green, retired General Secretary of the Baptist Union, 17 July 2002.
22   *BT*, 1 March 1962, p.1.
23   *BT*, 19 November 1964, p.1.
24   *BT*, 11 March 1965, p.1.
25   W.J. Hollenweger, *The Pentecostals* (Peabody, Mass.: Hendrickson, 1988), p.188; Hastings, *A History of English Christianity*, pp.558-60.
26   *BT*, 11 March 1965, p.2.

*London Baptist Association rally in Trafalgar Square, 1962*

The denominational leadership was committed to reaching out to all sectors of society, but this was not always happening effectively. A perceptive report, edited by Roger Hayden, of Waterbarn, was produced in 1966 on Baptist churches in North East Lancashire. It seemed that in many churches in the cotton towns there was a lack of commitment to mission, Sunday schools were divorced from church life, and meetings for prayer and Bible study were not flourishing.[27] At the same time, 1966 saw a major Billy Graham Crusade in Britain, and London Baptists gathered in large numbers in Trafalgar Square for open-air witness. These contradictory signals provoked considerable debate at the Union Council in November 1966. Lewis Misselbrook, chairman of the Evangelism Committee and minister at Park Road, Rushden, feared complacency. He favoured a motion urging the Union to give more priority to evangelism, but it seemed unlikely to gain support.[28] L.G. Champion, Principal of Bristol College, later commented that the two-hour debate had exposed rather than illuminated problems.[29] In February 1967 the Baptist Union set up a working group on evangelism.[30] This reflected wider evangelical concerns. The Evangelical Alliance, which had a significant role under its General Secretary, Gilbert Kirby, and which in this period opened its membership to organizations as well as individuals, produced a report suggesting alternatives to 'crusade' evangelism.[31]

NEW SPIRITUAL EXPERIENCES

Worries about the inner life of the churches paralleled concerns about their outward witness. The 1960s was a period in which attention was given to renewal of worship. Liturgical thinking found expression in

27  BT, 10 February 1966, p.9; Sellers, Our Heritage, pp.124-5.
28  Minutes of the Baptist Union Council, 15 and 16 November 1966.
29  BT, 24 November 1966, p.1.
30  Minutes of the Baptist Union General Purposes and Finance Executive, 21 February 1967.
31  I.M. Randall and D. Hilborn, One Body in Christ: The History and Significance of the Evangelical Alliance (Carlisle: Paternoster Press, 2001), pp.270-4.

*Orders and Prayers for Church Worship* (1960), compiled by Ernest Payne and Stephen Winward. The introduction set out a powerful case for freedom and liturgy: 'We must avoid on the one hand the dangers taught us by history of an inflexible and fixed liturgy which leaves no room for the freedom of the Holy Spirit. On the other hand, we must avoid that "squalid sluttery" and uninspired disorder which comes from disregarding the traditional pattern and forms of Christian worship.'[32] Winward, under whose ministry from 1938 to 1966 Higham's Park, Walthamstow, grew from a small congregation to a church of over 300 members, emphasized the Reformation pattern of Word and Sacrament. He established weekly communion as integral to worship, and encouraged the congregation to use set responses following Scripture reading and prayers. In 1964 Winward set out in *The Reformation of our Worship* what he called 'the fruit of past experience and continuing experiment'.[33] This was a follow-up to his *Responsive Prayers and Praises for Minister and Congregation*. He also expressed indebtedness to Neville Clark's *Call to Worship*.[34] Winward and Clark were Baptist members of an ecumenical Joint Liturgical Group formed in 1963.[35]

Stephen Winward's vision had a profound influence on many younger ministers. At a Baptist ministers' conference on worship held in 1962, one of the participants, John Freshwater, minister of Norbury Baptist Church, London, reported that of the eighty present most were in their first ten years of ministry. Payne gave a paper on 'Our Free Church Tradition and Worship', Neville Clark, then minister of Amersham-on-the-Hill Free Church, spoke on the Liturgical Movement, and Stephen Winward gave an address on baptism and the Lord's Supper. For one

---

32  *Orders and Prayers for Church Worship* (1960), compiled by E.A. Payne and S.F. Winward (London: The Baptist Union, 1960), pp.xiv-xv.

33  S.F. Winward, *The Reformation of our Worship* (London: Carey Kingsgate Press, 1964), Preface. Winward wrote a number of books and co-authored several others with Godfrey Robinson.

34  Winward, *Reformation of our Worship*, p.7; N. Clark, *Call to Worship* (London: SCM, 1960).

35  See R.C.D. Jasper, ed., *The Renewal of Worship: Essays by Members of the Joint Liturgical Group* (London: Oxford University Press, 1965).

participant this was the most exciting conference he had attended.[36] Michael Walker, who in 1967 followed Winward at Higham's Park, later wrote: 'Nonconformists found the catholic that lurked in their souls and catholics explored the freedom of extemporaneous prayer. Transcendence and immediacy were introduced to each other after a long period of illegal separation.'[37] By 1967, Ithel Jones, Principal of the South Wales Baptist College, could speak as President of the Union about a renewal of worship through the liturgical movement. He claimed that Baptists were feeling that their worship was 'drab, unexciting, almost completely lacking in what one might call the vertical dimension'. But liturgical developments had taken place. Some Baptist churches had made the communion table central. Jones was not, however, complacent. Many local congregations were growing weaker, he argued, and renewal was urgent.[38]

Congregation at worship, Bloomsbury 1961

---

36    *BT*, 22 November 1962, p.10; M.F. Williams, 'Swanwick Conference on Worship', *The Fraternal*, No.128 (April 1963), pp.20-3. Clark was later Principal of the South Wales Baptist College.

37    M. Walker, 'Baptist Worship in the Twentieth Century', in Clements, *Baptists in the Twentieth Century*, p.24.

38    *BT*, 27 April 1967, pp.1, 9.

One group which sought to further renewal in worship and theology was the 'Cassock Club'. It was created by a group of ministers who had trained at Regent's Park College in the 1950s. At the end of the 1954 Probationer Ministers' Conference, J.O. Barrett, who was leading communion, concluded the service with the words 'please pass the communion cups to the end of the row before leaving'. The Regent's Park group consequently decided there was a task to do in the area of liturgical renewal, and resolved to meet to discuss liturgy, systematic theology, and the practical issues of their ministry. In the 1960s the group members were all in local church ministry: Don Black, Ferme Park, Hornsey; Neville Clark, Amersham-on-the-Hill; John Freshwater, Norbury; Viv Lewis, Union, Loughton, Essex; H. Alan Smith, Westgate, Bradford; Geoffrey Taylor, Dewsbury; Maurice Williams, South Street, Exeter; and Jamie Wallace, Westbourne Park, Paddington. Some were to move into wider ministry. Their wider influence was felt in the writings of Neville Clark and of Jamie Wallace, in the preaching of Maurice Williams at Assemblies, and within the Union Council. The cassock was something that most chose to wear, indicating their liturgical commitment. The Cassock Club met each summer term in Oxford, for four days, and the programme included study of Karl Barth's *Christian Dogmatics* or some other theological work, papers from group members, periods of silence, and corporate worship.[39]

The work which went into the publication of the new *Baptist Hymn Book* (*BHB*) in 1962 was another example of the interest in Baptist worship in this period. Hugh Martin, manager of SCM Press, was appointed chair of the editorial committee by the Psalms and Hymns trustees, Eric Sharpe, minister of New Road, Oxford, who was the leading Baptist hymnologist, was chairman of the music committee, and Stephen Winward was also involved. R.W. Thomson, the Union's Assistant General Secretary from 1960, was secretary of the Psalms and Hymns Trust. In this period few Baptist churches used any instruments in worship apart from organ and piano. In most services four or five

---

39   I am indebted to Don Black and Roger Hayden for this information. See Don Black, 'The Cassock Club', *BQ* 40, July 2004, pp.436-9.

traditional hymns were sung. The new book was designed to widen the range of music used and also to encourage structured acts of worship.[40] It was a great success. Soon over 100,000 copies had been sold and Thomson estimated later that it was being used in ninety-nine per cent of Baptist churches.[41] This was a sign of the degree of liturgical uniformity in the denomination in the early 1960s. There were some complaints about Geoffrey Beaumont's new tunes being included in the new *BHB*, but one fifteen-year-old, Barbara Rogers, wrote to the *Baptist Times* to say that she had learned the new tunes at her youth club and they were very popular.[42] In the next few years, books of contemporary songs and choruses were introduced into Baptist services alongside the *BHB*.

It is sometimes thought that liturgical renewal was at odds with the charismatic or neo-Pentecostal movement that emerged in the 1960s. The movements had their own distinctives, but also shared concerns. In 1960 Dennis Bennett, an Episcopalian clergyman, announced to his parish in Van Nuys, California, that he had received 'the fullness of the Spirit' (often to be termed the baptism of the Spirit) and had spoken in tongues.[43] Payne and Winward's *Orders and Prayers*, published in the same year, under the heading 'Pentecostal Worship', spoke about the Spirit endowing believers with 'gifts' to enable them to 'participate in the worship of the assembly'.[44] Like many ministers within charismatic renewal, Winward introduced small groups into church life. These groups, eventually numbering seventeen, formed the backbone of the church.[45] Kenneth Bird, minister at Hay Hill, Bath, took up discussions initiated by Winward, emphasizing 'the Charismatic Ministry and freedom of expression in worship' in the early church.[46] Two years later

---

40    M. Ball, 'Baptist Praise and Worship', *BQ*, Vol.40, No.4 (2003), pp.197-8.
41    *BT*, 15 March 1962, p.10; R.W. Thomson, 'A Round Unvarnish'd Tale' (unpublished manuscript, 1979), p.8.
42    *BT*, 29 March 1962, p.6.
43    P. Hocken, *Streams of Renewal: The Origins and Early Development of the Charismatic Movement in Britain* (Carlisle: Paternoster Press, 1997), p.108.
44    *Orders and Prayers*, p.xii.
45    *Baptist Union Directory, 1986-87* (London: Baptist Union, 1987), pp.304-5 (S.F. Winward's obituary).
46    *BT*, 25 February 1960, p.10.

Philip Hughes, an Anglican scholar, visited California and wrote about 'indications of a new movement of the Holy Spirit'.[47] New spiritual power appeared to be evident, often involving a post-conversion experience of the Spirit. One of those who read Hughes' report was Douglas McBain, then minister of Wishaw Baptist Church in Scotland. In 1963 McBain began to speak in tongues and he became central to charismatic renewal in Baptist circles.[48] Soon after, Gordon Hunt, minister of Chapel Park Road Baptist Church, St Leonard's, and David Jones, assistant minister at Beulah, Bexhill, had experiences of charismatic renewal.[49]

These fresh spiritual experiences were to find early acceptance among some within the Baptist Revival Fellowship. For some, this was the answer to longings for revival. At the BRF's annual conference in 1960, Martyn Lloyd-Jones, minister of Westminster Chapel, gave two addresses, at a time when major attention was being given to the theme of revival. Ernest Payne, unusually, attended the conference and, as one participant, Hugh Wrigley from Ryde, put it, Payne 'strove in his remarks to establish a link between himself and the conference through an emphasis on prayer'.[50] Lloyd-Jones, whose leadership would influence a number of Baptists, suggested in 1963 that interest in Pentecostal spirituality showed a 'longing for something deeper'.[51] In March 1964 Malcolm Piper, minister of New Addington Baptist Church, Croydon, wrote to Alec Steen, Secretary of the BRF and minister at Queensberry Street, Old Basford, Nottingham, to suggest inviting a speaker to the BRF conference who had 'personally experienced the baptism of the Holy Spirit recently'. Piper knew of renewal in St Paul's Church, Beckenham, and Piper's Baptist fraternal had recently heard the

47    'Editorial', *The Churchman*, September 1962, p.131.
48    D. McBain, *Fire over the Waters: Renewal among Baptists and others from the 1960s to the 1990s* (London: DLT, 1997), pp.37-8.
49    Hocken, *Streams of Renewal*, pp.261-2, n.27.
50    *Baptist Revival Fellowship Bulletin,* No. 66, October/December 1960, pp.1-3: Spurgeon's College, BRF Archive, *Bulletin* file.
51    I.H. Murray, *David Martyn Lloyd-Jones. Vol.2: The Fight of Faith, 1939-1981* (Edinburgh: Banner of Truth Trust, 1990), pp.480-2.

vicar, George Forrester.[52] Piper's hope was realized. At the 1964 BRF conference David Pawson, minister of Gold Hill Baptist Church, Buckinghamshire, spoke to the 250 people present on the baptism of the Spirit. Several ministers, including BRF committee members such as Harold Owen from Carey, Reading, and Henry Tyler, soon to move to Buckhurst Hill, Essex, testified that they received this experience during the conference.[53]

The Union was to feel the tensions caused by the new spiritual emphases. This was a period of growth in numbers for the BRF, which in 1966 had 1,200 members, of whom 440 were ministers.[54] The 1967 BRF Conference, held at 'The Hayes', Swanwick, had as its subject 'Revival and Reformation', with speakers addressing ecumenical affairs as well as spiritual renewal. Leslie Larwood, minister at the large West Croydon church, noted a growing concern among many BRF members that it was no longer a 'Revival' Fellowship. Many items other than revival were dealt with, he maintained, in the BRF Committee, whereas the main purpose of the Fellowship was never mentioned.[55] Amid growing questions about renewal within Baptist structures, several Baptists left Union life to set up new churches which emphasized baptism in the Spirit and spiritual gifts such as speaking in tongues, prophecy and healing. One person who exemplified this trend was Terry Virgo, a young member of Holland Road Baptist Church, Hove, a 500-member church, who entered into the experience of the baptism of the Spirit in 1962. The Holland Road minister, E.G. Rudman, who was active in the BRF, encouraged Virgo to speak about his experience. After studying at LBC, Virgo became pastor of an independent church and later launched a new network of churches (later entitled New Frontiers)

---

52    M.W.B. Piper to T.A. Steen, 9 April 1964: Spurgeon's College, BRF Archive, file 1964/65; cf. Hocken, *Streams of Renewal*, pp.63-5.
53    Hocken, *Streams of Renewal*, pp.133-5. The next two BRF conferences continued this emphasis.
54    *BT*, 1 December 1966, p.2.
55    *Baptist Revival Fellowship Bulletin*, No.91, April/June 1967, p.1: Spurgeon's College, Spurgeon's College, BRF Archive, *Bulletin* file.

committed to seeking to restore what he saw as New Testament church life.[56]

Whereas some Baptists were leaving the denomination to set up new groups, others remained committed Baptists while involving themselves heavily in interdenominational activities. A significant number of younger Baptists seemed to be more attracted to interdenominational evangelical activity, such as that expressed in outreach events organized by British Youth for Christ, than to similar events that were distinctively Baptist. This did not necessarily mean that there was a loss of interest in being Baptist, since for some it was clear that wider co-operation brought positive benefits. Others were doubtful about certain expressions of pan-denominational spirituality. In 1962 a *Baptist Times* columnist, 'Kairos', attacked the interdenominational Keswick movement, dismissing it as a 'coterie'. He was not impressed by leaders drawn, he claimed, mainly from the 'low' Church of England and the Brethren. Theo Bamber (who had retired from Rye Lane in the previous year and was Pastor Emeritus) was outraged, arguing that Keswick enabled Anglicans, Baptists, Brethren and others to experience united fellowship. He accused denominations of not wanting biblical unity.[57] Debates about transdenominational and ecumenical co-operation continued. L.G. Champion argued in 1968 that it was wrong to make 'evangelical' and 'ecumenical' mutually exclusive terms.[58]

The signs were that the future for many Baptists was going to be less denominationally bound than the past. Ernest Payne contributed to this process with his wide vision of spiritual experience. In 1966 he commended Pope John XXIII's *Journal of a Soul*. It was, he said, 'a remarkable book, which may well come to be regarded as the generation's devotional classic'. Payne, who was at its British launch, believed it had much to say to Protestant readers about the Christian life. The Delegate from the Pope who was at the launch told Payne that for

---

56    T. Virgo, *No Well-Worn Paths* (Eastbourne: Kingsway Publications, 2001).
57    *BT*, 16 August 1962, p.3; *Baptist Revival Fellowship Bulletin*, No.73, September/October 1962, pp.3-4.
58    *BT*, 25 January 1968, p.4.

daily meditation he was reading Billy Graham's *Peace with God*.[59] A year later the Fountain Trust, formed in 1964 as an agency for pan-denominational charismatic renewal, held a conference at High Leigh conference centre, Hertfordshire, which drew Anglicans (both evangelical and Anglo-Catholic), Baptists, Brethren, Presbyterians, Pentecostals and members of the Salvation Army. Most ministerial participants were in the early years of their ministry. The Trust was led by an evangelical Anglican clergyman, Michael Harper, who for a time in 1965 was assisted by Frank Wilson, minister of Willesborough Baptist Church, Ashford, Kent.[60] The theme at High Leigh was 'The Holy Spirit and the Church'. David Pawson gave addresses and A. Morgan Derham, recently appointed General Secretary of the EA in succession to Kirby, was one of the Baptist ministers present.[61] Spiritual experience, which at times seemed to promote division, was also drawing Baptists into new expressions of unity.

## RENEWED BAPTIST IDENTITY

Did this mean that Baptist identity was being eroded? To address the issue of identity an important denominational conference was held at 'The Hayes', Swanwick, from 23 to 26 May 1961. It was Ernest Payne's idea.[62] A statement was produced setting out a number of the issues discussed by the 271 representatives present. There was a call for Baptist local church independency to be balanced by inter-dependency, a position that Payne supported. The place of Associations was stressed, and a Commission was later set up to address issues of associating. A report produced in 1964, at which point a second denominational conference was held, commended giving greater power to Associations, and it was agreed later that Associations should nominate and elect fifty

---

59    E.A. Payne, General Secretary, letter to ministers, October 1966, No.10: Regent's Park College Oxford, Angus Library, Payne papers.

60    Hocken, *Streams of Renewal*, pp.115-22, 258, n.34.

61    McBain, *Fire over the Waters*, pp.46-7. McBain gives the names of other Baptists present.

62    West, *To be a Pilgrim*, p.122.

of the Council members. This was a significant move towards seeing the Union as 'an association of Associations'.[63] The abolition of a rule preventing people aged over forty from beginning training to be full-time accredited ministers was an important change made as a result of the 1961 conference deliberations. There was also a widely-held conviction that discussions should be set in the ecumenical context.[64] The 1961 conference had an effect: over the next decade many of the issues raised were addressed. Neville Clark described the conference report as 'like an advance agenda for the actual Union business of the sixties'.[65]

*1964 Baptist Union Assembly at Westminster Chapel,*
*the regular mid-century venue*

---

63   For the vote, see *Baptist Handbook* (London: Baptist Union, 1970), p.99.
64   Statement approved by the Denominational Conference. See also *The Report of the Commission on Associations* (London: Baptist Union, 1964); *BT*, 28 May 1964, pp.1,2.
65   N. Clark, 'Servant of the Union', in J.H.Y. Briggs, ed., *Faith, Heritage and Witness* (London: Baptist Historical Society, 1987), p.14. These were essays in honour of Morris West.

At the same time, it was evident that there were theological strains within the denomination. A rousing address at the 1960 Assembly by Howard Williams, minister at Bloomsbury and Union President in 1965, prompted six months of correspondence in the *Baptist Times*. One correspondent, P.W. Howe, from London, said that Williams' address had played down judgment and sin, but R.H. Wheatcroft, minister at Charnwood Road, Shepshed, considered it was like 'a gust of fresh air'.[66] In July 1960 Irwin Barnes, minister of Beechen Grove, Watford, suggested the correspondence showed that the denomination contained two schools of theological thought – presumably more liberal and more conservative – and was 'dissipating its energies in a fratricidal shooting-match between them'. Barnes called for humility and asked that 'our Fundamentalist friends' admit that their emphases did not exhaust 'the unsearchable riches of Christ'.[67] Both 'schools of thought' found it difficult to hear this message. Raymond Brown, minister of Upton Vale, Torquay (later Principal of Spurgeon's), subsequently commented that for evangelicals at the time Williams was 'a rather threatening figure',[68] while for his part Williams was hurt by conservative criticisms. Williams was especially upset when the LBA withdrew support for a series of lectures organized at Bloomsbury with William Barclay from the University of Glasgow, Rex Mason from Spurgeon's College, and Michael Walker from Higham's Park as speakers. Williams later complained of 'those LBA evangelical rotweilers appointed to guard the property of the faith'.[69]

Another area of strain was organizational. Considerable energy was invested in seeking a united Baptist headquarters to house the Union and the BMS and thus encourage closer co-operation. This hope had been dashed before, much to Ernest Payne's disappointment, but it was agreed by the Assembly in 1961 that it should be denominational policy.[70] The

---

66    *BT*, 9 June 1960, p.6; F. Bowers, 'H. Howard Williams: Preacher, Pastor – Prophet without honour?', *BQ*, Vol.37, No.7 (1998), pp.316-35.
67    *BT*, 21 July 1960, p.7.
68    Bowers, *A Bold Experiment*, pp.392-7.
69    Ibid.
70    *BT*, 11 May 1961, p.1.

wider background was the celebration of 150 years of Baptist Union life and the desire for closer integration of the two organizational centres of Baptist activity. Leslie Larwood of West Croydon and Geoffrey Haden of Ferme Park were asked to prepare a leaflet about integration for the benefit of the churches.[71] A number of sites in London for a united headquarters were investigated. There was then discussion about relocation out of London. A move to Watford looked possible at one stage. In 1965 the Beechen Grove church in Watford was open to pursuing discussions about the potential use of its site. However, none of the ideas materialized.[72] Some of the protracted discussions between officers of the Union and the BMS were described by R.W. Thomson as 'very bitter'.[73] In 1967, after further schemes had come to nothing, Roger Hayden asked: 'How long, may we ask, can the majority of the denomination be in general agreement about this matter of closer relations between the union and the society, and the officers and elected representatives at them continue to drag their feet?'[74]

Crucial to Baptist identity was the doctrine of the church. Here divergent views were evident. A significant theological contribution was made with the publication in 1963 of *The Pattern of the Church*. The authors were Neville Clark, Alec Gilmore, minister at West Worthing, Morris West, who had been a tutor at Regent's Park College and was then minister of Dagnall Street, St Albans, and Stephen Winward. Two of these, Clark and West, would later become College Principals.[75] This book stood firmly in the tradition of higher views of church, ministry and sacraments. Thus Neville Clark claimed that proper 'catholic Order' needed 'structural embodiment in association synod and national assembly, where deliberative decisions under the word of God and the

---

71  Minutes of the Baptist Union General Purposes and Finance Executive, 9 January 1962.

72  Minutes of the Baptist Union General Purposes and Finance Executive, 5 January 1965.

73  Thomson, 'A Round Unvarnish'd Tale', p.47.

74  *BT*, 16 March 1967, p.3. For the efforts that were made, see D.C. Sparkes, *The Offices of the Baptist Union of Great Britain* (Didcot: Baptist Historical Society, 1996), chapters 4 and 5.

75  A. Gilmore, ed., *The Pattern of the Church* (London: Lutterworth Press, 1963).

guidance of the Spirit have authority appropriate to sphere and function'.[76] This had resonance with the thinking of the Commission on Associations about interdependency. By contrast with this approach, in 1964 the BRF produced an important booklet, *Liberty in the Lord*, signed by sixteen Baptist ministers, which criticized – as many Baptists had done before – what it saw as centralizing tendencies in the Union. It was suggested in *Liberty in the Lord* that inter-church authority over local churches would break with the New Testament pattern and 'would radically alter the nature of our Union as Baptists'.[77] Walter Bottoms, however, editor of the *Baptist Times*, reviewing *Liberty in the Lord*, considered that the authors had 'weakened their own case by faulty exegesis and church history, and confused thinking'.[78]

A.D. Gilbert, in *The Making of Post-Christian Britain* (1980), has argued that *Liberty in the Lord* was an important publication because it recognized, from a denominational perspective, that denominational patterns were being eroded by secularization, and also because it was articulating the views of many conservative evangelicals.[79] This highlights something of the tension in *Liberty in the Lord*. Although its first two chapters argued, from the New Testament and from Baptist history, for the autonomy of the local church, overseen by local elders, it was sympathetic to movements that were 'seeking closer outward and visible fellowship with those of like doctrinal convictions', and highlighted fellowship of this kind emerging 'across denominational frontiers'.[80] The stress on Baptist distinctives was somewhat undermined

---

76   N. Clark, 'The Fullness of the Church of God', in Gilmore, ed., *The Pattern of the Church*, p.107.
77   *Liberty in the Lord* (London: Baptist Revival Fellowship, 1964), pp.9-11, 15-16, 41, 48. Of the sixteen, those who were members of the study group or wrote papers were A. Morgan Derham (editoral secretary of Scripture Union), David Kingdon (Principal, Irish Baptist College), Ronald Luland (Wootton), Samuel Nash (Leigh-on-Sea), I.J.W. Oakley (who moved from Aylesbury to be a tutor at the Irish Baptist College in 1964) and Herbert Ward (Kingston-upon-Thames).
78   *BT*, 7 May 1964, p.10; 21 May 1964, p.4.
79   A.D. Gilbert, *The Making of Post-Christian Britain* (London: Longman, 1980), p.150.
80   *Liberty in the Lord*, pp.33-4.

by the citing of Martyn Lloyd-Jones' Westminster Fellowship, which was not a Baptist group, as a prototypical example of evangelical trends. It seemed that the BRF was open to a less Baptist type of future. Yet the authors of *Liberty in the Lord* were also adamant that those Baptists who were sympathetic to the ecumenical movement, to the liturgical movement, or to a higher view of ministry, were abandoning traditional Baptist convictions.[81] Baptists holding differing views of the church, emphasizing either the local church or the church catholic, found it difficult to appreciate each other's positions.

In part the articulation of Baptist positions was the responsibility of the General Secretary, and Ernest Payne had shouldered that task. In 1965 Payne made it clear that he intended to retire at the age of sixty-five, in 1967. He suffered a further heart attack in March 1966, but after recovering he was able to stay on until August 1967. In the farewell to Payne at the 1967 Assembly, L.G. Champion spoke and presented Payne with a *Festschrift*. It was entitled *Outlook for Christianity* and it was, fittingly, a compilation by distinguished authors.[82] Payne highlighted four things which had given him special satisfaction: his attempts to improve provisions for ministers and deaconesses; the links he had made with eastern Europe; the contribution he had been able to make to the denomination's worship; and his ecumenical ministry. He also had regrets. Commenting on the failure to bring together the Union and the BMS he said: 'I thought the iron was hot enough, but cold water was poured on it, so we must go on striking until it is hot enough to fuse one organisation'. Finally he appealed for unity, using a familiar argument regarding Baptist identity: there was a line of Baptist history through John Bunyan, C.H. Spurgeon, F.B. Meyer and Billy Graham, and another through John Clifford, H.E. Fosdick and Martin Luther King. Payne believed that both traditions were necessary for a full expression of worship, witness and service.[83]

It was David S. Russell, Payne's successor as General Secretary, who had to pick up this challenge to forge a shared Baptist identity.

---

81   Ibid., pp.34-45.
82   L.G. Champion, ed., *Outlook for Christianity* (London: Lutterworth, 1967).
83   West, *To be a Pilgrim*, pp.152-4.

Russell's name was proposed during discussions at the General Purposes and Finance Committee in April 1966 and it was agreed that he be recommended to the Council to be nominated at the 1967 Assembly.[84] At the April Council a note was read from Payne expressing pleasure at Russell's nomination. Supportive speeches were given by J.B. Middlebrook of the BMS, Cyril Petch of the Baptist Men's Movement,

*David S. Russell*

Professor H.H. Rowley, and Geoffrey Rusling, Vice-Principal at Spurgeon's.[85] The Assembly endorsed the appointment. Russell was aware, however, that there was a perception that the Council was resistant to the views of conservative evangelicals. From the beginning of his secretaryship, therefore, he sought to embrace as many as possible.[86] David Russell's background had given him insights into the varied hues of Baptist life. Born in 1916 in Whitburn, he was educated at Rutherglen Academy and Glasgow University, gaining an MA in 1938 and a BD in 1941. His theological studies, at the Scottish Baptist College and Trinity College, Glasgow, were followed by a degree in Hebrew and Aramaic, and subsequently a research degree at Regent's Park College. Alongside these studies he undertook ministry at Castlegate Baptist Church, Berwick-on-Tweed, and at Woodstock Road, Oxford. In 1945 he moved to London, to Church Road, Acton, exercising an effective ministry there until becoming Principal at Rawdon in 1953.[87]

By the time Russell became General Secretary he had considerable experience of local church ministry and wider leadership. He was also a fine biblical scholar. His research thesis was 'The Method and Message

---

84   Minutes of the Baptist Union General Purposes and Finance Executive, 5 April 1966.

85   Minutes of the Baptist Union Council, 15 April 1966.

86   Interview with David Russell, 8 October 2002.

87   G.W. Rusling, 'David Syme Russell: A Life of Service', in J.H.Y. Briggs, ed., *Bible, Church and World* (London: Baptist Historical Society, 1989), pp.4-8.

of Jewish Apocalyptic', for which he was awarded a DLitt. During the 1960s and 1970s he published important works in the field of apocalyptic studies. Above all, Russell was a preacher, pastor and evangelist, and as he took up office the needs of mission were at the forefront of his thoughts. He was quickly made aware, however, that as well as external challenges there was internal unrest among ministers and this led, in September 1967, to the convening of a 'Committee on Causes of Dissension within the Denomination'.[88] This group included conservative evangelicals such as Hugh Butt, West Midland Area Superintendent. There was pressure for evangelicals who were not ecumenically inclined to be represented on the Union's Advisory Committee for Church Relations (ACCR), set up in 1963 and chaired by George Beasley-Murray, Spurgeon's Principal.[89] Russell was actively involved in seeking to address these tensions, but of three conservative evangelicals on the Council who were nominated to the Church Relations committee two would not stand. Two other Council members who represented the BRF constituency, Stanley Voke, from Walton-on-Thames, and Leslie Larwood, spoke appreciatively of Russell's handling of these situations.[90]

During 1968 and 1969 Russell continued to give attention to issues concerned with Baptist identity. His ebullient approach meant that he was happy to engage in discussions with groups and he asked to visit churches that expressed concerns about the evangelical stance of the Union. In January 1968 he emphasized that membership in a Baptist church was based on conscious acceptance of Christ as Saviour and

---

88    D.S. Russell, 'Reflections on the General Secretaryship of the BU, 1967-1982' (unpublished paper), Regent's Park College Oxford, Angus Library, D/RSL/A1, pp.1-3.
89    The members of the Committee were L.G. Champion, Principal of Bristol College; W. Davies and W. J. Grant, Area Superintendents from South Wales and East Midlands respectively; R.L. Child, retired in Oxford; Alberic Clement, BMS Home Secretary; W.M.S. West of St Albans; and four lay people, H.F. Gale of Bedford, E.E. Iremonger of Oxford, J.G. Le Quesne, QC, and Miss M. Russell of Hitchin. See Cross, *Baptism and the Baptists,* p.246.
90    Minutes of the Baptist Union General Purposes and Finance Executive, 12 December 1967; Minutes of the Baptist Union Council, 12 and 13 March 1968. See comments by A. Morgan Derham, *Christian,* 12 January 1968, p.16.

Lord.[91] There was a perception at this point that some BRF members were on a path to secession from the Union: the Union was seen by them as pro-ecumenical, the Declaration of Principle was viewed as inadequate, and the Union was believed to be seeking to undermine local church independence.[92] Efforts were nonetheless made to stress common ground, although this was not helped by a controversy which erupted in February 1968 over a paper by David Kingdon, Principal of the Irish Baptist College, given at the 1967 BRF Conference. The published booklet, *Baptists at the Crossroads* (1968), suggested that if evangelicals took no action they would lose what was distinctively evangelical in the 'coming great Church'. Kingdon suggested that the options were reforming or separating from the Union.[93] Some BRF members insisted that secession was not their policy. Stanley Voke, worried about feelings running high, warned that the Union could experience 'another Downgrade, leaving us with a weakened witness and a divided denomination'.[94] Haddon Willmer, from Leeds University, urged controversialists to take each other seriously and sympathetically, which was not happening.[95]

At the 1968 Assembly George Beasley-Murray became Union President, and, in keeping with his well-known commitment to evangelism, took as his theme 'Renewed for Mission'. Beasley-Murray also worked with Russell to address the theological tensions in the Union and to encourage the work of the Committee looking at the causes of dissension. In December 1968 dissension became more evident with the formation of the Baptist Renewal Group, drawing together those who wanted a broader and more ecumenical theological agenda. Paul Rowntree Clifford, President of the Selly Oak Colleges, Birmingham,

---

91    Russell, 'Reflections on the General Secretaryship', p.3.
92    *BT*, 11 January 1968, p.4.
93    D.P. Kingdon, *Baptists at the Crossroads: Past and Present* (Baptist Revival Fellowship, 1968), p.11.
94    *BT*, 21 March 1968, p.4.
95    *BT*, 28 March 1968, p.4.

was chairman of this Group and Alec Gilmore publicized its vision.[96] Others flatly opposed such a vision. In May 1969 it was reported that some BRF leaders were contemplating forming an evangelical Baptist fellowship outside the Union, and it was arranged that Russell and Beasley-Murray would meet the BRF committee.[97] Russell reported to the Union officers in September 1969 that the meeting had been an unhappy event.[98] A month later Russell, desperate to avoid fragmentation, wrote to all Union ministers to allay fears about a drive towards centralization and to stress the liberty of each Baptist church under the guidance of the Holy Spirit.[99] The many replies Russell received were generally affirming. One retired minister, T. Wilkinson Riddle, then aged eighty-five, recalled how he had tried to support J.H. Shakespeare in his difficult times. 'Nothing is more pernicious', said Riddle with reference to those opposing the Union's stance, 'than ignorance wedded to enthusiasm.'[100]

## UNITY AND SEPARATION

The ecumenical issue was one significant legacy of Shakespeare's leadership that caused continued controversy in this period. Although there had always been Baptists who were wary of church union, when the Baptist Union joined the World Council of Churches at its inauguration, few queries had been raised. In the 1960s this changed dramatically. At the 1960 BRF Conference, Payne was questioned about

---

96  *BT*, 5 December 1968, p.16; 26 December 1968, pp.1,2; Baptist Renewal Group, unpublished paper, June 1969. The Baptist Renewal Group papers are in the possession of Roger Nunn and I am grateful to him for his help. In 1968 Nunn moved from Walsgrave and Shilton to work for the British Council of Churches as Assistant Youth Secretary and then Youth Secretary.
97  Minutes of the Baptist Union Advisory Committee on Church Relations, 11 July 1969.
98  Minutes of a Meeting of Officers, 8 September 1969.
99  A special letter from D.S. Russell, General Secretary, to all ministers, October 1969, Spurgeon's College, BRF Archive, General Papers.
100 T. Wilkinson Riddle to D.S. Russell, 4 October 1969: Regent's Park College Oxford, Angus Library, D/RSL, 5/3.

ecumenism and he assured BRF members that there were no negotiations in progress for Church union under the auspices of the BCC or the WCC.[101] From 1962 to 1971 Payne chaired the BCC's executive committee. Theo Bamber, from an anti-ecumenical standpoint, stated in 1962 that 'all Baptists who count' – a sarcastic reference to the Union leadership - would be part of the sheep-fold of the World Church, which, he predicted, would be 'more of a lion's den' than a sheep-fold. Bamber anticipated that a President of the Baptist Union would soon visit the Pope, and noted how Anglicans, the Orthodox Church and Roman Catholics were coming together.[102] Michael Ramsey, the Archbishop of Canterbury, held Anglo-Catholic convictions, but it was evangelicals who were to emerge as the growing section of the Church of England, and, significantly, at the historic National Evangelical Anglican Congress at Keele University in 1967 they stated: 'We desire to enter this ecumenical dialogue fully.'[103] By contrast, Bamber believed that 'the general view of our [BRF] members is unsympathetic and many would declare to be hostile'.[104]

Why did a stronger anti-ecumenical rhetoric emerge in this period? One reason was that a more open stance towards Roman Catholics on the part of some Protestants produced an opposite reaction by others. G.E. Wyatt from Woking argued in January 1962 that ecumenically-inclined Baptist leaders were out of touch with ordinary Baptists in their tendency to 'flirt with Rome'.[105] Angus McMillan, at Lewin Road, Streatham, giving a lecture a month later on Protestantism, stated categorically: 'The teaching of Rome is utterly divorced from Scripture and Apostolic teaching therein.'[106] W.D. Jackson, Metropolitan Superintendent, as Union President in 1962, said that while Baptists cherished individual

---

101  *Baptist Revival Fellowship Bulletin*, No. 66, October/December 1960, pp.1-3: Spurgeon's College, BRF Archive, *Bulletin* file.
102  *Baptist Revival Fellowship Bulletin*, No.71, January/March 1962, pp.1-2: BRF Archive, *Bulletin* file.
103  *Keele '67, The National Evangelical Anglican Congress Statement* (London: National Evangelical Anglican Congress, 1967), p.37.
104  *Baptist Revival Fellowship Bulletin*, No.80, July/September 1964, pp.1-3.
105  *BT*, 11 January 1962, p.6.
106  *BT*, 15 February 1962, p.6.

Catholics as friends they regarded the Roman Church as the enemy of the truth. One rather untheological criticism he made of Catholic parish life was that funds were raised by football pools.[107] For George Beasley-Murray, writing in the *Baptist Times* in June 1962, the Roman Church was 'an unreformed Church with many abuses', and talk of union seemed to him irresponsible. Yet he spoke of many biblical scholars who were Catholics and he commended dialogue. G. Henton Davies, Principal of Regent's Park College, expressed substantial agreement with this stance.[108] This was at a time when Payne was commenting positively on the Second Vatican Council. The BWA did not send observers to Vatican II, which disappointed Payne. An attempt at the Baptist Union Council in 1964 to reverse that decision did not succeed.[109] Long-standing anti-Catholicism fostered an anti-ecumenical spirit.

Schemes for church union in Britain also caused some Baptists anxiety. An ecumenical Faith and Order Conference was held at Nottingham in 1964 and the 550 delegates from fifteen denominations who were present passed a resolution inviting BCC member churches to work for unity by 1980.[110] Evangelicals were represented in some strength at this conference.[111] Theo Bamber's perspective, however, was that there would have to be a choice between withdrawal from the ecumenical movement or 'acceptance of this all embracing, world-church objective'.[112] His language was similar to that used by Martyn Lloyd-Jones. Evangelicals saw little to encourage them in Congregational-Presbyterian discussions about unity, and fear of domination by liberal theology led to strong statements being made by Lloyd-Jones at the Evangelical Alliance's 1966 National Assembly. He spoke of denominations being 'prepared to put everything into the melting pot in

---

107  *BT*, 3 May 1962, p.8.
108  *BT* 21 June 1962, p. 9. Beasley-Murray returned to this theme in a booklet, *Reflections on the Ecumenical Movement* (London: Baptist Union, 1965), p.11. This booklet was one in a series entitled 'Living Issues', published by the Baptist Union.
109  Minutes of the Baptist Union Council, 10 and 11 March 1964.
110  *BT*, 24 September 1964, p.1.
111  *Christian*, 25 September 1964, p.1.
112  *Baptist Revival Fellowship Bulletin*, No.81, October/December 1964, p.4.

order that a new world Church might come out of it'.[113] Although a report by an EA commission – which included Baptist ministers Godfrey Robinson and John Caiger - saw no widespread desire for a 'united evangelical church', this was precisely the hope of some Baptists. Ronald Luland from Bedford, a BRF member, believed the EA report failed to represent the views of Baptists contemplating secession from the Union. Leslie Larwood, however, insisted that the Union upheld basic Christian doctrine.[114]

Other factors contributed to tensions. There was a conservative evangelical perception that the Union leadership, although evangelical in a wider sense, wanted to marginalize conservatives. For their part, conservatives considered that they were true to traditional Baptist commitments, for example, in their view of the authority of scripture.[115]

For some the sense of alienation from the Union increased when Walter Bottoms castigated *Liberty in the Lord* for what he termed its confusion, misunderstanding, failure to do justice to the views it opposed, and its 'suggestion that the Church's one foundation of unity is identity of theological views, instead of her Lord'. Paul Tucker, of the East London Tabernacle, like others who felt that conservatives had been misjudged, demanded that the allegations be substantiated.[116] Also, at local Baptist level there was often little understanding of the wider ecumenical world. Some did move from local pastorates into ecumenical activity, for instance Glenn Garfield Williams, of Dagnall Street, St Albans, who was appointed to the significant ecumenical post

*Glenn Garfield Williams*

113 Evangelical Alliance, *Unity in Diversity: The Papers Given at the National Assembly of Evangelicals at Westminster, London, in October 1966* (London: Evangelical Alliance, 1967), p.9. In fact the Anglican-Methodist union scheme failed in 1969.
114 *BT*, 27 October 1966, pp.1, 2, 12.
115 *Liberty in the Lord*, pp.32-5.
116 *BT*, 7 May 1964, p.10; 21 May 1964, p.4.

of General Secretary of the Conference of European Churches (CEC).[117] But in a letter to ministers in 1963, reporting on his experiences in the USA and at the Faith and Order Conference in Montreal, Canada, Payne acknowledged: 'You may feel that they are all rather remote from the life and witness of most Baptist congregations in Britain.'[118]

The Union leadership, for its part, felt that its ecumenical stance reflected the views of most churches in the Union. In response to the Nottingham Conference of 1964, the Union's Advisory Committee on Church Relations produced a major report entitled *Baptists and Unity*. This acknowledged that there was probably 'no other major denomination in which there is such widespread doubt concerning the present desire and movement to recover the unity of the Church'. The report rejected the idea of church unity by 1980, saying that this would endanger Baptist unity, but advocated continued Union membership of the BCC and WCC. It was presented to the Council by George Beasley-Murray, chairman of the ACCR, and adopted in March 1967 - to mixed reaction.[119] Those in the BRF and elsewhere who wanted to see the Union disengaging from all ecumenical involvement were unimpressed by the ACCR report.[120] Earlier in the year Beasley-Murray himself had been condemned by the Protestant Truth Society for sharing a platform with a Roman Catholic priest on the staff of the BBC, Agnellus Andrew.[121] On the other hand, Baptists who wanted to see progress in

117  R. Gurney, ed., *CEC at 40* (Geneva: CEC, 1999), chapters 1-3. Glenn Garfield Williams served CEC from 1961 to 1986.
118  E.A. Payne, General Secretary, to ministers, Letter No.1, September 1963.
119  See G.R. Beasley-Murray, *et. al.*, *Baptists and Unity* (London: Baptist Union, 1967).
120  *Baptist Revival Fellowship Bulletin*, No.91, April/June 1967, pp.5-6. The Baptist Union of Ireland published an anti-ecumenical contribution: *Thy Word is Truth* (Belfast: Baptist Union of Ireland, 1971). For further responses to *Baptists and Unity* see Cross, *Baptism and the Baptists*, pp.248-52.
121  For this see Beasley-Murray, *Fearless for Truth*, pp.135-9. Beasley-Murray asked Father Agnellus three questions about his personal faith, and on receiving affirmative answers said: 'Then I humbly own you as a brother in Christ'. Beasley-Murray defended his action in *The Christian and Christianity Today*, 10 February 1967, p.12.

terms of ecumenical involvement were disappointed because they considered the *Baptists and Unity* report to be 'rather fence-sitting and cautious'.[122]

In March 1968 a pro-ecumenical statement, *Baptists for Unity*, was prepared. This booklet was the result of discussions by a group of ministers in the Midlands: Robert Brown of Hearsall, Coventry; Peter Coleman of Coseley; Roger Nunn of Walsgrave and Shilton; Donald Smith of the Church of the Redeemer, Birmingham; and Michael Taylor, of Hall Green. The foreword was by Paul Rowntree Clifford. Michael Taylor, who prepared the final draft of the booklet, argued that mission and unity belonged together. *Baptists for Unity* suggested that although Baptists of a more radical outlook and those of more conservative outlook might differ in their ideas of unity, they were at one in believing that 'mission is the most urgent task of the Church' and that there should be a united missionary effort.[123] The agenda for ecumenically-inclined Baptists that was set out in *Baptists for Unity* created such interest that a wider group of ministers came together to plan a conference, which was held at Hothorpe Hall, Market Harborough. It was this which in turn led to the formation of the Baptist Renewal Group.[124] All Baptist churches were asked to comment on the *Baptists and Unity* report so that it could be revised. Only 635 replied, and it was evident from these replies that there were fears about a loss of Baptist freedoms. 1,500 did not reply and were assumed to be content with the report.[125] At the 1969 Assembly, Beasley-Murray presented *Baptists and Unity Reviewed*. His speech was acclaimed by prolonged applause. Raymond Brown was among those who urged acceptance of the report. The voting was 1,125 for the report and 356 against.[126] The growing Baptist Renewal Group,

122  Roger Nunn to the author, 28 April 2004.
123  M. Taylor, ed., *Baptists for Unity* (Coventry: Reynolds Press, 1968), pp.8-9; *BT*, 11 April 1968, p.7.
124  Minutes of the Baptist Renewal for Mission Conference Committee, held at Selly Oak, 5 September 1968; Cross, *Baptism and the Baptists*, p.252.
125  Minutes of the Baptist Union Advisory Committee on Church Relations, 26 September 1968.
126  *BT*, 1 May 1969, pp.1, 16.

which by that time had 135 members, considered that the vote revealed 'a more open-minded and forward-looking attitude to ecumenism in the denomination at large than had hitherto been shown'.[127]

In thinking about ecumenical documents such as *Baptists and Unity*, Baptists did not operate from the top down, but were guided by the views of local churches, which Roger Hayden argued was advantageous.[128] Local flexibility was possible. Thus 'The People Next Door', an ecumenical programme of mission, was readily embraced by many Baptist congregations.[129] Other local churches, however, were intent on leaving the Union, since they feared, as David Russell reported, a 'total eclipse of evangelical truth in the Baptist ministry'.[130] In the midst of these pressures, Russell continued to act in an eirenic way. In March 1969 the Council received a request from George Stirrup of Manor Park, London, that details of local churches withdrawing from the Union should be published. Russell responded that names *were* published, but not private correspondence.[131] Amongst churches that left the Union from the mid-1960s were West Street, Dunstable; Trinity, Gloucester; Melbourne Hall, Leicester; Vicarage Road, Leyton; Thomas Cooper, Lincoln; and the People's Church, Everton, Liverpool, which withdrew against the wishes of its minister.[132] At Hester's Way, Cheltenham, the minister, Basil Howlett, hoped the church would withdraw, but there were disputes about the Trust deeds and Hester's Way became something

---

127  Baptist Renewal Group, unpublished paper, June 1969. At this stage the joint secretaries of the Group were Peter Coleman and Roger Nunn.
128  *BT*, 20 April 1967, p.4; Harrison, *It All Began Here,* p.157.
129  This emerged from discussions within the Executive Committee of the Home Council of the Conference of British Missionary Societies. Basil Amey was the BMS member of the Executive.
130  Minutes of the Baptist Union Council, 29 March 1968.
131  Minutes of the Baptist Union Council, 11 and 12 March 1969; *Baptist Revival Fellowship Bulletin*, No.98, Jan./March 1969, pp.1-5.
132  See Minutes of the Baptist Union Council, 16 and 17 November 1965; Minutes of Meeting of Officers, 2 June 1967; Minutes of the Baptist Union Council, 12 and 13 March 1968.

of a test case for Trust matters. The congregation resigned from the Union in 1967, but re-joined later.[133]

Robert Horn, minister of Horley Baptist Church, noted in the July-September *BRF Bulletin* that after fair debates the 1969 Assembly had voted by seventy-five per cent to affirm Union membership of the BCC and WCC. Churches, he considered, could not sever this link except by withdrawing from the Union. Horn reported that following the Assembly a letter had gone to all BRF ministerial members raising the possibility of an evangelical fellowship of Baptist churches.[134] The BRF was, however, deeply divided over this issue. Geoffrey King, the LBA's Commissioner for Evangelism and a BRF leader since the 1940s, and Stanley Voke, who had warned against separation, both resigned from the BRF Committee in protest at the direction being taken. Voke's experiences of those who withdrew to form new movements had not convinced him 'that any better situation is gained by such division'.[135] Leslie Larwood, Hugh Butt and E.G. Rudman had previously resigned from the BRF committee.[136] Thus at the end of 1969 Bamber was the only figure in the BRF leadership who was well known in the denomination. Bamber continued to shoulder his responsibilities, but he was gloomy about the future. Writing to David Russell on 19 July 1969 to express pleasure at Russell's wish to meet BRF representatives, he made his own views about the Union clear. 'We do not think', Bamber

---

133    Minutes of the Baptist Union General Purposes and Finance Committee, 11 July 1967; *BT*, 1 January 1970, p.3; 26 March 1970, p.7; 7 May 1970, p.1. Basil Howlett, who had trained at Manchester College, became an FIEC minister.

134    *Baptist Revival Fellowship Bulletin*, No.100, July/September 1969, pp.4-6. The Evangelical Fellowship of Congregational Churches was formed by evangelicals who did not want to be part of the United Reformed Church, formed in 1972.

135    S. Voke to T. Bamber, 27 November 1969: Spurgeon's College, BRF Archive, file TMB; Minutes of BRF Committee Meeting, 17 November 1969: BRF Archive, file BRF Minutes, 1968-75.

136    Minutes of BRF Committee Meetings, 25 April 1967; 26 June 1967: BRF Archive, file BRF Minutes, 1966-68.

stated, 'the Denomination is really troubled about the possible withdrawal of evangelicals'.[137]

## MINISTERS AND THE CHALLENGES OF MINISTRY

The tensions within the Union were felt by many ministers. Whereas some left the Union on theological grounds, others were unhappy for different reasons. There was talk in the early 1960s of an exodus from the ministry of dissatisfied ministers. Several factors may be identified. George Beasley-Murray, speaking in 1960 at the annual rally of the Baptist Men's Movement, urged wider sharing of pastoral work in churches and suggested that ministers were leaving because they lacked active congregational support.[138] An article in the *Baptist Times* a year later raised other issues. The chief reason for wastage was said by many to be low stipends. Other ministers believed they could make 'a better contribution towards the saving of the souls of needy men and women and boys and girls when they are freed from the restrictions imposed upon them by an earnest, but narrow-minded, set of deacons'. A number of ministers became school teachers or social workers. One young minister, it was alleged, had left the ministry after attracting a number of teenagers with no previous church connection who came to the church's youth club and Bible class and on Sunday evenings filled five rows in church. Older members criticized their dress and showed no enthusiasm when about twenty of the teenagers applied for baptism and church membership. The minister resigned.[139] Arthur Dakin, from his experience as a Principal, could not believe that this was anything other than an isolated example, but others disagreed.[140]

In 1961 an influential study of the ministry entitled *The Doctrine of the Ministry* was produced by L.G. Champion, J.O. Barrett (who retired in 1963 as North Eastern Superintendent), and Morris West. The Union

---

137  T.M. Bamber to D.S. Russell, 19 July 1969: Spurgeon's College, BRF Archive, file TMB.
138  *BT*, 14 April 1960, p.16.
139  *BT* 19 January 1961, p.9.
140  *BT*, 26 January 1961, p.6; 2 February 1961, p.6. The minister was not named.

Council suggested it should be carefully considered by churches and ministers. The study began with the 'teaching of the New Testament about Christian ministry' and then turned to the 'theological basis of the ministry'. It chose three phrases to summarize New Testament teaching: 'the people of God', 'the body of Christ', and 'the community of the Spirit', and it argued that 'the nature and functions of Christian ministry are determined by the ministry of the whole Church'. Some among Christ's disciples were 'authorised to exercise special functions of leadership'.[141] Baptist thinking was traced through history, with reference to various historic confessions of faith. The study then turned to practical implications for contemporary ministry. Here there was an emphasis on 'the whole community' of churches in the Union working together, a perspective which queried extreme independency. Local churches should accept the spiritual leadership provided by the Union and find ministers from among those duly accredited. At a time when ministers were questioning their role, this study wanted to encourage a clearer appreciation of 'the nature of the ministers' status and authority'.[142]

There was a widespread stress in this period on churches identifying those with appropriate gifts for ministry, an issue that was more pressing because of the shortage of ministers. The functions appropriate to ministry were defined by Champion, Barrett and West as: preaching and teaching the Gospel, leading worship, administering baptism and the Lord's Supper, and caring for people. These were not seen as exclusively the minister's tasks, but normally the church would appoint a minister to fulfil these functions. All members of the church were, nonetheless, viewed as being responsible for the total ministry of the church. It is significant that mission as a responsibility of ministers was not mentioned.[143] In the light of ministerial shortage, an analysis of ministerial recruitment and wastage patterns within the Union was undertaken by R.E.O. White, minister of Boreham Wood Free Church (later Principal of the Scottish Baptist College), and was published in

141  L.G. Champion, *et. al.*, *The Doctrine of the Ministry* (London: The Baptist Union, 1961), p.12.
142  Ibid., pp.37, 41.
143  Ibid., p.44. I am indebted to Roger Hayden for this observation.

1963. He showed that there was no difficulty in recruiting ministers, but retaining them was problematic. A significant number left the ministry for other work – mainly school teaching - within ten years of their ordination. Over ten years, White estimated, there had been a loss of 305 ministers, although he did not note that some had gone abroad. White wanted pastors who would be effective in applying scripture to people's lives. He asked about the age at which people entered ministry. Some began Baptist college training after 'A' levels and the average age of those entering Baptist colleges was twenty-two. Young ministers were dealing with complex personal and marital problems.[144]

The early 1960s also saw debates about women in ministry, with a Union committee considering 'women in the service of the denomination'. A *Baptist Times* editorial in 1962 noted that Congregationalists had fifty-four women ministers, while Baptists had two, neither now in pastoral charge. One was Margaret Jarman, a former deaconess, who had trained at Spurgeon's and was working for the Union.[145] Some Baptists believed that Paul's statement, 'I permit no woman to teach', was timeless.[146] Cynthia Allegro, a deaconess, pointed, however, to the example in John's Gospel of the woman at the well, who told a whole city, including men, about Jesus.[147] Henton Davies argued that the thrust of scripture showed the equality of men and women before the fall and in salvation.[148] Constance Nash, another deaconess, could not believe she had acted against God's will in responding to the Superintendent's suggestion and taking pastoral charge of a small church in Donnington Wood, Wellington, which had not had a minister for fifty years. The church had since had conversions and baptisms.[149] Despite these discussions, Ruth Matthews, who began ministry in 1964 in Salisbury and later had a joint ministry in Swindon with her husband, John, spoke of the limited awareness in the churches that women could

---

144  *BT*, 7 February 1963, p.9; 14 February 1963, p.8; 21 February 1963, p.8..
145  *BT*, 8 March 1962, p.5.
146  *BT*, 3 May 1962, p.6.
147  *BT*, 17 May 1962, p.6.
148  *BT*, 31 May 1962, p.10.
149  *BT*, 7 June 1962, p.10.

be ministers.[150] During the 1960s, Allegro and three other deaconesses sought recognition from the Ministerial Recognition Committee, chaired by W.G. Channon, minister of Purley Baptist Church. Allegro's congregation, Wolston, near Coventry, where she was Deaconess, paid for her college training at Rawdon (she was the first female student at Rawdon) and in 1965 she became minister at Wolston.[151] By the end of the decade there were ten women on the accredited list.

Growth in awareness of the West Indian contribution to Baptist life led to Samuel Reid, a West Indian who had graduated with distinction from Regent's Park College, taking up a pastorate at Moss Side, Manchester, early in 1962.[152] There were 10,000 West Indians in the Moss Side area. The Moss Side church had a 1,200-seater building but only a small and dispirited congregation, wondering how to reach an area that had become known for crime. Norman Jones, the Area Superintendent, was asked to help, and the churches at Fallowfield and Chorlton – led by John Nicholson and J.H. Swanson – gave financial and other assistance. The church's schoolroom was carpeted and transformed into an attractive sanctuary.[153] It was sometimes stated that Reid was the first West Indian Baptist to hold a pastorate in Britain, but George Cousens had become pastor of Four Ways Baptist Church, Cradley Heath, Staffs, in 1837.[154] What was new at Moss Side in the 1960s was that Reid had the freedom to introduce forms of worship with which West Indians were familiar. A Caribbean choir was also formed and a 'Rally of the Apostles' was held 'Jamaican style' in November 1962.[155] In London, Gordon Fitch, as LBA assistant secretary and then Secretary, promoted new initiatives: Hubert Myrie, who had trained at Manchester

---

150   Minutes of the Baptist Union General Purposes and Finance Executive, 11 January 1966; *BT*, 22 December 1966, p.4.
151   N. Morris, *Sisters of the People: The Order of Baptist Deaconesses, 1890-1975, CCSRG Research Paper 2* (Bristol: University of Bristol, 2002), p.25. Allegro's brother was John Allegro, a Methodist scholar.
152   Minutes of Meeting of Officers, 5 January 1962.
153   *BT*, 15 March 1962, p.15.
154   *BT*, 26 April 1962, p.8. For background see D. Killingray, 'Black Baptists in Britain, 1640-1950', *BQ*, Vol.40, No.2 (April 2003), pp.69-89.
155   *BT*, 29 November 1962, pp.1, 2, 9.

College, was appointed by the LBA to work among fellow West Indians.[156]

At the end of the decade a report was produced by a small group chaired by Norman Jones, entitled *Ministry Tomorrow* (1969). Commissioned by the Council, it looked at future ministerial recruitment, selection, accreditation, ordination and settlement. There was a perception that ministry among Baptists was marked by rigidity rather than flexibility. 'To foster a relevant and contemporary ministry', said the report, 'is to assist materially in the growth of a relevant and contemporary Church'.[157] A significant problem was perceived to be that congregational patterns were ill equipped to face the fast changing world. The Baptist denomination had many small churches, often struggling to maintain paraphernalia appropriate to larger communities. The report envisaged a much-reduced number of full-time ministers in the future. It considered that small churches created frustration, with ministers 'denied the diverse kind of community that would stretch them'. They would not give their best 'where they are expected to be ecclesiastical mechanics with the expertise to maintain the machinery and produce bigger churches and rising budgets'.[158] The report is popularly remembered for the fact that it foresaw the Union reaching a point at which churches would be able to support only 400 full-time paid ministers, a reduction of about two-thirds.[159] This forecast was dropped, but many of the recommendations of *Ministry Tomorrow*, for example those regarding the spiritual care of ministers, were accepted and made a significant contribution to Baptist thinking about ministry.

Some Baptist ministers and churches in the 1960s were trying to work more closely together in order to be more effective. Five churches in the Huddersfield District began to hold united deacons' meetings and

---

156  *BT*, 11 March 1965, p.9.
157  *Ministry Tomorrow: The Report of the Commission on the Ministry* (London: Baptist Union, 1969), p.6.
158  Ibid., p.7.
159  D.C. Sparkes, *An Accredited Ministry* (Didcot: Baptist Historical Society, 1996), p.46. For the forecast of 400 ministers see *Ministry Tomorrow*, p.26.

mid-week meetings.[160] J.J. Brown moved to Dagenham, Essex, in 1962 to give ministerial leadership to a group of four congregations.[161] In the North West, four churches in Rochdale agreed to work as a team in 1962, the North Cheshire Fellowship was formed from six churches, and a Fellowship was established in St Helens, mid-Cheshire. The role of lay leaders in this process was crucial. James Beardwood, Eric Hitchon and Ted Marston were among lay leaders of high calibre who were utilized in the North West.[162] Superintendents often encouraged teams and groupings of churches. Three superintendents, F.C. Bryan, H.L. Watson and W.J. Grant, became Union Presidents in the 1960s and brought their perspectives on local church and team ministry to the attention of the denomination. The Swanwick Conference deliberations and *Ministry Tomorrow* also proposed the recognition of 'Supplementary' ministers, who were to be fully trained theologically but employed by churches on a non-stipendiary basis, earning their living through secular work. The numbers in this form of ministry were never high, but it represented creative thinking about team work.

There was also continued creative thinking about the sacraments. R.E.O. White wrote *The Biblical Doctrine of Initiation* (1960), on baptism, and a number of articles on this subject appeared in the same year in the *Fraternal*. There was talk of a 'domestic debate' about baptism. In February 1960 R.L. Child, former Principal of Regent's Park College, argued in the *Baptist Times* that baptism was an efficacious sign.[163] George Beasley-Murray wrote a week later on the subject of baptism and the sacramental view. He defined a sacrament as 'the Word of God in action', contrasting this with preaching as the Word of God in free speech. He argued that in Acts and in the letters of Paul 'baptism is viewed as the entrance into the Christian life' and saw no difficulty in reconciling this with justification by faith. In the New Testament, he

---

160  *BT*, 12 October 1961, p.9.
161  *BT*, 19 October 1961, p.15.
162  Sellers, ed., *Our Heritage: The Baptists of Yorkshire, Lancashire and Cheshire*, pp.121, 125; Sister Muriel Westcott, Norman Jones and J.J. Brown, 'Team Ministry', *The Fraternal*, No.152 (April 1969), pp.19-30.
163  *BT*, 4 February 1960, p.8.

argued, baptism was inseparable from turning to God in faith, on the basis of which God justifies, gives the Spirit and unites a person to Christ.[164] Many Baptists viewed baptism as purely a symbol, or perhaps, as W.G. Channon had argued in *Much Water and Believers Only* (1950), as a means of blessing. The minister of Totterdown, Bristol, L.J. Stones, was so upset by the 'higher' views of baptism being advocated, and in particular the advocacy of prayers for the gift of the Spirit on those being baptized, that he said in 1959 he might have to renounce his baptism to show that he was justified by faith alone.[165]

Debate continued throughout the 1960s. Beasley-Murray's comprehensive study, *Baptism in the New Testament*, appeared in 1962. In the same year L.G. Champion published a book, *Baptists and Unity,*

Baptism in the open air
at Old Southwick, Wiltshire, 1965

which argued that among Baptists there had always been those willing to reach out to fellow Christians. Champion believed that Baptists must consider the place of infant baptism and of children in the church. At the same time he welcomed Beasley-Murray's scholarly exposition of New Testament practice and theology' as a 'call to all sections of the Church to consider afresh the meaning of baptism'.[166] In 1966 Beasley-Murray produced *Baptism Today and Tomorrow* and Alec Gilmore produced *Baptism and Christian Unity*. The effect of these scholarly writings, especially those of Beasley-Murray, who in 1966 used the phrase 'faith-

164   *BT*, 11 February 1960, pp.9-10.
165   *BT*, 4 June 1959, p.1; 10 September 1959, p.6; W.G. Channon, *Much Water and Believers Only* (London: Victory Press, 1950), pp.32-3.
166   L.G. Champion, *Baptists and Unity* (London: Mowbrays, 1962), pp.52-3.

baptism', promoted a higher and more sacramental view of baptism.[167] In parallel with this development was the more central position being given to the Lord's Supper, especially in the thinking of Stephen Winward and Neville Clark. In 1972 Clark edited, with the Anglican, R.C.D. Jasper, the book *Initiation and Eucharist: Essays on their Structure by the Joint Liturgical Group*. But the attention given by Baptists to the meaning of the Lord's Supper was far less than that given to baptism and to the ministry.[168]

## EDUCATION AND TRAINING

As an indication of the crucial role of the Baptist colleges in relation to ministry, three college Principals, Champion, Beasley-Murray and Ithel Jones, were Union Presidents in the 1960s. But questions were raised about training: those dropping out of ministry often did so within five years of leaving college.[169] There were debates in the colleges about the theology of John Robinson, Bishop of Woolwich. Keith Robbins, a member at Victoria Park, Bristol, suggested that lack of engagement with *Honest to God* was alienating young graduates like himself from the denomination.[170] Beasley-Murray, who encouraged students at Spurgeon's to obtain theological degrees and engage with current issues, described *Honest to God* as a calamity and opposed Robinson point by point. Neville Clark queried what he called the 'diatribe' by Beasley-Murray, suggesting *Honest to God* might be a catalyst.[171] Union tensions over London Bible College subsided under the principalship of Gilbert Kirby and the vice-principalship of H.D. McDonald, an accredited Union

---

167 Cross, *Baptism and the Baptists*, chapters 6 and 7, esp. pp.235-43.

168 N. Clark and R.C.D. Jasper, eds., *Initiation and Eucharist: Essays on their Structure by the Joint Liturgical Group* (London: JLG, 1972). See M. Walker, *Baptists at the Table* (Didcot: Baptist Historical Society, 1992), p.201.

169 Minutes of the Baptist Union Ministerial Recognition Committee, 5 and 6 Oct 1960.

170 Keith Robbins was to have a distinguished academic career, holding chairs of history at the Universities of Bangor and Glasgow and serving as Principal of St David's College, Lampeter, and Vice Chancellor of the University of Wales.

171 *BT*, 18 April 1963, p.6; 23 May 1963, p.7; 30 May 1963, p.6.

minister. The Union agreed that those securing a BD at LBC could become probationers after two years in ministry.[172] One highly significant change in college life was the merger in 1964 – after several failed attempts - of the Rawdon and Manchester Colleges. Rawdon was rather isolated, not having a university nearby that offered the kind of theological teaching David Russell and the tutors felt was needed, and it was in financial difficulties. David Russell initiated and played a major part in the merger discussions. He and K.C. Dykes, Manchester's Principal, became joint Principals of the new Northern Baptist College in Manchester.[173]

Ernest Payne was keen to raise the profile of education in several areas. The valuable work of the Particular Baptist Fund, which gave book grants to ministers, was highlighted by Payne and by Theo Valentine of Teddington, the Fund's Secretary.[174] As part of the Union's Ter-Jubilee celebrations a range of booklets was published. Payne spoke about materials to teach a new generation Baptist history and principles.[175] Hubert Janisch, chairman of the Union's Evangelism Committee (and known in the wider Free Church world as Moderator of the Free Church Federal Council), reported that the booklets were selling very well. In the event an amazing one million copies were circulated. Payne wrote a number of these booklets, including *The Prayer Call Resounded*, which recalled the impact of the eighteenth-century revival on Baptist life.[176] Morris West, who as editor of the *Baptist Quarterly* in the

---

172 Minutes of the Baptist Union Ministerial Recognition Committee, 5 and 6 October 1960. From 1968 applicants for accredited Baptist ministry who had not been trained at a Baptist college in Union membership were required to attend the Union's Residential Selection Conference (RSC).

173 P. Shepherd, *The making of a northern Baptist college* (Manchester: Northern Baptist College, 2004), pp.207-17.

174 In 1967 the Fund was 250 years old. Thomas Powell, Fund Secretary from 1935 to 1962, started a history of the PBF. This work was completed by Theo Valentine: T. Valentine, *Concern for the Ministry* (Teddington: Particular Baptist Fund, 1967), pp.v, vi, 41.

175 W.M.S. West, *To be a Pilgrim*, p.132.

176 *BT*, 14 January 1960, p.1; E.A. Payne, *The Prayer call Re-Sounded* (London: Baptist Union, 1959).

1950s established it as a crucial contributor to discussions about Baptist identity, wrote a best-selling booklet, *Baptist Principles*. Payne had aimed to raise £300,000 during the four years 1959-63, and although this was not quite achieved, substantial sums were made available for theological education. £20,000 was given to the new Northern College, £15,000 to Regent's Park College for a lecturer in Reformation, Free Church and Baptist history, and £20,000 for bursaries was allocated between the five other colleges.[177]

There were other aspects of the interest in education. The Union's traditional concern for those in the educational sector was seen, for example, in conferences for Baptists teaching in primary and secondary schools. Within higher education, Ernest Payne strongly encouraged the work of the Baptist Students' Federation and the chaplains who served them, seeing the BSF as one of the growing points of the denomination. Against the rapid growth in the number of students in colleges and universities in Britain, the BSF groups were enormously significant, especially in the 1950s and 60s, in encouraging and training future leaders within the denomination. These future leaders included John Nicholson, Peter Saunders, Gwynne Edwards and Roger Hayden, all of whom became superintendents; David Staple, who became General Secretary of the Free Church Federal Council; Basil Amey, who was BMS Assistant Home Director and Editor, and later Assistant General Secretary of the British Council of Churches; B.R. White, who was tutor and then Principal, Regent's Park College; Paul Ballard, who became Professor, Religious and Theological Studies, at Cardiff University; and lay people such as Faith Bowers, John Biggs and John Briggs, who served on many Union committees.[178]

The field of training and education for adults was one in which there were areas of progress. Building on the advances made during Cyril Petch's period of leadership, the Baptist Men's Movement began, in 1969, a programme of Christian education. Rex Mason from Spurgeon's

---

177  Minutes of the Baptist Union General Purposes and Finance Executive, 20 February 1962; 5 June 1962.

178  West, *To be a Pilgrim*, p.89. For more on Faith Bowers, John Biggs and John Briggs, see Chapter 10.

College was BMM President that year and he launched the programme with the theme 'Men Made Ready For Mission'.[179] The Union stressed 'stewardship' and discipleship training. Lay Preachers' Federation Conferences in this period, held in Oxford, attracted about sixty people. There were also local and regional initiatives. The East Midland Association placed emphasis on the training of lay preachers through correspondence courses and a fair number took the Baptist Union Diploma in Religious Knowledge. So many people were interested in training that extra conferences had to be arranged. The Leicestershire deacons met in conference in 1964, with 170 deacons from twenty-six churches participating.[180] The BWL was also active in seeking to equip women. A Women's Forum was arranged at Baptist Church House in 1960 to consider the needs of overseas students. One of the speakers, Mary Trevelyan, adviser to overseas students in the University of London, spoke about what could be done for overseas students arriving in Britain.[181]

The education of children was a further issue. J.O. Barrett and Morris West wrote on the 'Child and the Church', emphasizing the responsibilities of parents and the church for children, at the time of the dedication of infants and as children grew up.[182] Afternoon Sunday Schools were largely abandoned as leisure activities increased, and the concept of 'Family Church' was introduced. Children were present for about twenty minutes of worship with the whole congregation on Sunday mornings before going to their classes. Evening services, which had traditionally been the best-attended services, saw numbers decline as the focus shifted to the morning.[183] Family Church was publicized in 1963 by H.A. Hamilton's book, *The Family Church in Principle and Practice*. It was taken up by Alec Gilmore at Kingsthorpe, Northampton, and

---

179  Bennett, *God at Work with Men*, p.43.
180  Harrison, *It All Began Here: The Story of the East Midland Baptist Association*, p.153.
181  *BT*, 7 April 1960, p.8.
182  J.O. Barrett, *Your Child and the Church* (London: Baptist Union, 1960); W.M.S. West, 'The Child and the Church', *The Fraternal*, January 1961, pp.15-19.
183  *BT*, 13 March 1969, p.5.

Bruce Keeble at Shirley Baptist Church, in the Birmingham area. Keeble reported in 1964 on his experiences. Children, in his view, were to be regarded as part of the catechumenate, together with adults linked to the

church but not members. Keeble explained that after twenty-five minutes of worship together on a Sunday morning, groups engaged in study. In practice, although children had small groups, adults stayed in one large group and were addressed by the minister.[184] This became the normal Baptist Sunday morning pattern by the end of the 1960s. The material often used in Baptist Sunday

*Children leaving Sunday School at the new church in Basildon, Essex, 1964*

Schools had been from the National Sunday School Union (later the National Christian Education Council), but Scripture Union material became increasingly popular.[185]

In view of discussions about the place of children, Bernard Green prepared a paper in the early 1960s which was discussed at the Union Council. At the suggestion of the Young People's Committee of the Union the Council appointed a small study group in 1963 to produce a statement on the Baptist view of the child and the church. The chairman of the group was Geoffrey Rusling, and the secretary was Harry Mowvley, who had considerable experience of Family Church at Cotham Grove, Bristol. The report, *The Child and the Church*, was presented to

---

184  L.B. Keeble and W.H. Campbell, 'Family Church: An Appreciation and Assessment', *The Fraternal*, No.134, October 1964, pp.18-22.
185  Sellers, ed., *Our Heritage: The Baptists of Yorkshire, Lancashire and Cheshire*, pp.122-3.

the Council in March 1966. In the same period the *Baptist Quarterly* published articles on the subject by Beasley-Murray, Michael Walker and R.E. Clements, who became a lecturer in Old Testament at Cambridge in 1967.[186] *The Child and the Church* report dealt with theological issues, ecumenical questions relating to infant baptism, the catechumenate, and care of children. The debate at the Council centred on the idea of the catechumenate, which some Council members vehemently criticized. In his brief introduction to the printed report Payne drew attention to the fact that the report questioned whether the church was to be defined simply as a fellowship of believers. It suggested that children were 'in the church' in the sense that they were in fellowship with believers. The report stated: 'The conversion theology which dominates Baptist doctrines of baptism and the Church is, in itself, silent about the infant.' The report called for on-going theological work.[187] In the event little action was taken.

Various initiatives were taken for young people in their teens and twenties. For teenagers, the Union's Young People's Department began a magazine entitled *B.Y.*, designed to appeal especially to those not yet committed. Green Hills, Worthing, a new conference and training centre for Baptist youth, was opened in 1962 with accommodation for sixty young people.[188] In this period BMS summer schools were attracting over 3,000 young people.[189] A 'Time for God' scheme was launched to give young people leaving school opportunities for mission. But many local churches were struggling to retain young people, especially those who felt Baptist thinking was narrow. Marion Parsons, a seventeen-year-old, working in (as she put it) a very non-Christian office, was appalled at Baptist attitudes to the Roman Catholic Church. She had a non-

---

186  See articles in the *Baptist Quarterly*, Vol.21, Nos.5 and 6.
187  Minutes of the Baptist Union Young People's Department Committee, 7-8 June 1963; *The Child and the Church: A Baptist Discussion* (London: Baptist Union, 1966), pp.4, 9, 11; West, *Baptists Together*, pp.113-18. Ministers in the Radlett Fellowship, from four Baptist churches in north-west London and Middlesex, produced a critical response, *The Gospel, the Child and the Church*.
188  *BT*, 26 April 1962, p.2.
189  *BT*, 3 August 1961, p.1.

Christian friend who had gone to a Catholic service and had come away thinking there was something in the Christian faith. If anti-Catholicism was the Baptist position, Marion Parsons said, then 'I'm out'.[190] Christian Endeavour was still active, but was declining. One Baptist youth group in Sydenham left the Christian Endeavour and Miss W. Henfrey-Smith, aged twenty, suggested in the *Baptist Times* that CE seemed to be for the 'in-set'.[191] This verdict was challenged: Wallingford Baptist Church reported that in 1958 the church had only four young people but since a CE had started twenty-nine young people from non-Christian backgrounds had been baptized.[192] Despite overall church decline, there were examples of effective work with young people.

*'Plenty of life now at Walkley'*
*A church in 'a working-class district' of Sheffield, 1964*

---

190  *BT*, 17 May 1962, p.6.
191  *BT*, 15 June 1967, p.4.
192  *BT*, 31 August 1967, p.8.

## CHURCH IN A CHANGING SOCIETY

Many of the problems in society at large were addressed at Association meetings or national assemblies. At the 1960 Assembly J.G. Diefenbaker, the Canadian Prime Minister, who was a Baptist, expressed his commitment to ending racial discrimination and also stressed his opposition to nuclear weapons.[193] A year later South Africa, with its apartheid regime, withdrew from the Commonwealth, and the Assembly passed a resolution expressing abhorrence of the doctrine of apartheid. Some Baptists were involved in the Campaign for Nuclear Disarmament. Baptists were, however, divided on the legitimacy of nuclear weapons as a deterrent. The Union Council rejected a document proposed by the Yorkshire Association criticizing the mounting arms race. There was little evidence at this stage of the pacifist element that had been an earlier feature of Baptist life. By now Baptists were clearly split three ways in their political affiliation. Walter Bottoms kept a close eye on the political arena and before the 1964 General Election there were articles in the *Baptist Times* from advocates of each of the three main political parties. The Union's Christian Citizenship Department, under the direction of Clifford Cleal, put out a pamphlet before the election entitled *Public Issues*.[194]

One issue which united Baptists and others was injustice, particularly where governments acted brutally towards people. There was considerable Baptist involvement, led by Ernest Payne and David Russell, in protests about the treatment of Baptists in communist countries. Payne was one of the founders of Amnesty International in 1961. In the same year Baptists were stirred up by the treatment of Angolans by the Portuguese regime of Dr Salazar. Rebellion against the regime broke out in that year and in response to a massacre of Portuguese settlers there were terrible reprisals by the authorities. At the 1961 Assembly, Clifford Parsons, the BMS Africa Secretary, gave a moving speech which led to a resolution being passed that registered

---

193   *BT*, 5 May 1960, p.1.
194   *BT*, 10 September 1964, p.5; D.W. Bebbington, 'Baptist Members of Parliament in the Twentieth Century', *BQ*, Vol.31, No.6 (1986), pp.78-9.

'grave disquiet at the reports of large-scale terrorism by the armed European community' and appealed to the Portuguese authorities for restraint.[195] Three Southend Baptist ministers, Len Addicott, Eric Blakebrough and George Thompson Brake, formed an 'Angola Action Group' to raise awareness of the atrocities being committed by the Portuguese. Ernest Payne and others went to see Lord Home, Foreign Secretary, and London Baptist ministers met MPs and Government Under-Secretaries. Baptists formed area groups, most notably in Manchester, to bring pressure on the British government to urge the Portuguese to exercise restraint.[196] The Methodist, George Thomas, MP, later Speaker of the House, presented a petition to the Commons and on the same day it was announced that Britain would no longer send arms to Portuguese territories overseas.[197]

Many other more domestic moral issues attracted the attention of Baptists in this period. Compared to the previous decade, the 1960s brought a range of new challenges. There were worries about standards on TV and about X-rated films. Mary Whitehouse was an active campaigner for moral responsibility in broadcasting. It was acknowledged that there was growing promiscuity among young people – the 'new morality' as it was called. During a debate in Parliament in 1964 Sir Cyril Black, MP, expressed the hope that there might be a clear statement made against sex before marriage. There was also considerable discussion in the Union's Christian Citizenship Committee about abortion and changes to the divorce laws. In debates taking place in 1966 in relation to changes in the law on homosexual practice, Sir Cyril Black said that homosexuals were 'a body of wrongdoers performing an unnatural act'. In response, Dr A.K. Thomas, from Pinner, wrote to the *Baptist Times* to say that he completely opposed Black's position over legislative changes. Thomas, who saw homosexual practice as an aberration but not a vice, argued against the existing restrictive

---

195  B. Stanley, *The History of the Baptist Missionary Society, 1792-1992* (Edinburgh: T & T Clark, 1992), p.454.

196  *BT*, 15 June 1961, p.1; 29 June 1961, p.1; 13 July 1961, p.3; 20 July 1961, p.4; 2 November 1961, p.1.

197  L. Addicott, *Cry Angola!* (London: SCM, 1962), p.104.

legislation.[198] Parliament would later liberalize the position regarding homosexual acts, abortion, and divorce.

More attention was being paid by some Baptists in this period to engagement with working life. Eric Blakeborough and then Thornton Elwyn worked for the South London Industrial Mission. Howard Williams spoke at the 1960 Assembly and in a powerful address called for churches to engage seriously with working people.[199] A BWL survey of women in Baptist churches noted that 63 of every 100 Baptist church members were women and found that about half of the BWL groups meeting on weekdays during the day-time were experiencing losses from women going to work. Almost half the women attending the BWL groups were not church members.[200] The Union was keen to highlight the role that Baptists played through their work and also through their charitable giving. Eric Grief, Union President in 1961, was a life deacon of Long Sutton Baptist Church, Lincolnshire, a businessman and a magistrate. A former high court judge, Sir Donald Finnemore, became Union President and used media opportunities to talk about his faith.[201] Sir Herbert Janes was reckoned to have given away half a million pounds to Baptist causes. Edward Vinson, a fruit farmer in Faversham, was the country's largest strawberry producer and a Baptist benefactor. Sir Edmund Davies (later Lord Edmund-Davies, a Lord of Appeal), a member at Haven Green, Ealing, and later of the Welsh Baptist Church in Eastcastle Street, London, was the British judge who presided over the longest trial of modern times.[202]

Baptists were also maintaining some of their traditional areas of concern, although priorities and policies were changing. In the past much socio-political action had taken place through Free Church co-operation, but the distinctive Free Church alliance was slowly breaking down. Leslie Cooke, a Congregational minister who worked for the WCC in Geneva, thought closer Free Church-Anglican links through the BCC

---

198   *BT*, 24 February 1966, pp.4, 6.
199   *BT*, 12 May 1960, p.8.
200   *BT*, 3 November 1960, p.9.
201   *BT*, 4 August 1966, p.3.
202   *BT*, 23 April 1964, p.9. This was the 'great train robbery' trial.

were having an effect on the Anglican Church and that 'the prophetic note' was now often heard from that quarter.[203] Many Baptists supported the Inter-Church Aid Department, later Christian Aid, a Division of the BCC. Commitment to temperance was still evident among many Baptists, but zeal for that cause was declining. Another traditional cause was Sunday observance. John Wood, who was on the Christian Citizenship Committee and was Parliamentary Secretary of the Co-operative Union Ltd., considered shops had little desire for Sunday trading.[204] Of more concern was the increasing number of Sunday sports events. In response to the Wolfenden Report on 'Sport and the Community', the Christian Citizenship Committee saw no objection to facilities for recreation on Sunday afternoons and evenings, provided that opportunities for worship were preserved and commercialism avoided, but it opposed professional sport on Sundays.[205] Battles waged against this development would, however, prove unsuccessful.

CONCLUSION

When Ernest Payne retired he spoke about the ecumenical vision which had been so important to him and expressed his delight that he had been able to represent Baptists in the wider church. He was deeply disappointed, however, that revival and renewal had not come to Baptist churches. Nonetheless, he had confidence for the future.[206] Decline in the 1960s had certainly been drastic in some places, although there were many examples of churches reaching out. In the later 1960s, David Russell became deeply involved in the demanding questions facing Baptists in areas such as spirituality, Baptist identity and unity. Writing to Baptist ministers in January 1969, Russell said that he had been reading a recent book, *A Study of the Evangelical Alliance in Great*

---

203  *BT*, 24 March 1960, p.1.
204  The Baptist Union's Christian Citizenship Committee issued occasional bulletins with comment on current developments.
205  Minutes of the Baptist Union Christian Citizenship Committee, 4 October 1960.
206  West, *To be a Pilgrim*, p.153.

*Britain*,[207] and had found it instructive in thinking about the Baptist denomination. Seeking unity was an issue of great concern to Baptists and the issue was causing pain, as at times it had done in the story of the Evangelical Alliance. Russell spoke about the recent Baptist Revival Fellowship conference, 'Renewed for Mission', and also about the Baptist Renewal Group, with its commitment to ecumenical experiment. Some described these bodies as standing for 'extremes' in the denomination, but Russell did not agree. Rather he saw them as representing emphases which could produce much good 'if there is an openness of heart and mind and a readiness to effect changes with a deep concern for the whole flock of God'.[208] Change was certainly coming. For Baptists, as for wider society, the 1960s represented a turning point. Many of the older certainties disappeared and the new order that emerged posed challenges which were met in different ways by those of differing theological hues.

---

207  J.B.A. Kessler, *A Study of the Evangelical Alliance in Great Britain* (Goes, Netherlands: Oosterbaan & Le Cointre, 1968).
208  D.S. Russell, General Secretary, letter to ministers, No.4, January 1969, pp.1-2.

*Baptist Church House, 4 Southampton Row, Holborn, in mid-century*

# Chapter 9
# 'BREACH IN THE FELLOWSHIP' (1970-79)

The theological tensions evident in the Baptist Union in the 1960s intensified in the early 1970s. A further denominational conference was held in 1970 and among other things it provided a forum for discussing theological issues. In the following year, controversy that followed an address on the topic, 'How much of a man was Jesus Christ?', given at the 1971 Assembly by Michael Taylor, the recently-appointed Principal of Northern Baptist College, contributed to withdrawals of ministers and churches from the Union. David Russell involved himself deeply in the ensuing intense debates. Writing to ministers who were considering withdrawing from the Union because of the content of the address, Russell insisted that such a move would 'cause an unnecessary and grievous breach in the fellowship'.[1] Part of Russell's contribution in this difficult period, as Geoffrey Rusling put it, was 'to absorb the indignation, righteous and sometimes less than righteous, which came from different quarters by phone, letter and personal confrontation'.[2] The issue of Christology was not, however, the only question occupying the attention of Baptists. The 1970s saw new ecumenical initiatives and the growth of charismatic influence. Baptists who participated in ecumenical partnerships or charismatic renewal often found in them fresh vision, although others were, for various reasons, doubtful or even opposed to these developments. There was also continued uncertainty about ministry. But at the end of the decade a Union Working Group produced a report on the state of the churches

---

1   D.S. Russell to H.G. Owen, 16 June 1971: BRF Archive, file 1971/72.
2   G.W. Rusling, 'David Syme Russell: A Life of Service', in Briggs, *Bible, Church and World*, p.14.

which was entitled *Signs of Hope*.[3] Although there had been breaches of fellowship among Baptists, hopeful indicators appeared to be present.

## CHRISTOLOGY IN FOCUS

In discussion about the programme for the 1971 Assembly, the in-coming President, G. Henton Davies, suggested the themes of the centrality of God, Christ, the Holy Spirit and the Cross. He insisted that he wanted to bring some theocentric thought into the Assembly as he felt that addresses given in the 1960s had emphasized the human element in the situation faced by Christians.[4] In the event, invitations were sent to John Huxtable, General Secretary of the Congregational Church, to speak on 'How dead is God?', to B.R. White, soon to be Davies' successor at Regent's Park College, to address the topic 'Is the Holy Spirit a Ghost?', and to Michael Taylor to tackle the subject 'How much of a man was Jesus Christ?'. It was Taylor's contribution which aroused

*Michael Taylor*

controversy. At the outset of his address, delivered on the Tuesday evening, Taylor said that he had no wish to disown the Nicene Creed, with its affirmation that Jesus Christ was 'true God of true God', but later in the address he explained that he thought he must stop short of saying categorically 'Jesus is God', and he understood that the New Testament probably stopped short of it as well. For Taylor, God was present in Christ 'as God is in all men', but in Jesus God 'acted in a unique and decisive way for our salvation'. That, said

---

3    *Signs of Hope: Report of the Denominational Enquiry Group* (London: Baptist Union, 1979). The Group members were J.H.Y. Briggs, Peter Clark (Solicitor), Don Cranefield (minister of Bromley Baptist Church), F.A. Goodwin (Director of Evangelism, LBA), W.C.R. Hancock (Superintendent, South Eastern Area), Clarice Morgan (involved in the women's network in the Union), D.F.G. Pusey (Lecturer), John Tucker (minister of Thomas Helwys, Nottingham), W.V. Thompson (minister at Melksham and later Western Baptist Association Secretary), and Muriel Warwick (who represented the Bristol Association on the Council). The group met eleven times: *BT*, 29 March 1979, pp.1, 10.

4    Minutes of Assembly Programme meeting, 25 June 1970.

Taylor, was the conclusion that he had reached at this stage in his intellectual pilgrimage, but he stressed that he did not say that he was right and those who disagreed were wrong. He asked that others should share their opinions with him.[5]

Opinions about the address differed sharply. Henton Davies stated when Taylor had finished that he did not agree with all that had been said.[6] When David Russell moved the customary thanks to the Assembly speakers, John Nainby, minister at Buckhurst Hill, Essex, who had trained at Regent's Park College, protested against Michael Taylor being included. Ernest Payne, by contrast, privately considered Taylor's address 'one of the most impressive and moving given from the Baptist Union platform for many years'.[7] On the Thursday afternoon of Assembly week, at a Baptist Union Council meeting, Stanley Voke raised the issue – as the minutes record it - of 'the theology of one address during the Assembly'. George Beasley-Murray, as chairman of the Council, suggested that a notice be put in the *Baptist Times* giving an assurance that the views of speakers at the Assembly were not necessarily representative of the Council's position. There was lengthy discussion, in which it was pointed out that Michael Taylor had not been informed that the matter was to be raised. Payne successfully moved that the debate be adjourned.[8] Voke wrote to Taylor on 30 April to reiterate his concerns, and in his reply Taylor expressed his thanks 'for what I have been told was the helpful way in which you did what you felt you

---

5    M.H. Taylor, 'The Incarnate Presence: how much of a man was Jesus Christ?', unpublished manuscript, in M.H. Taylor's personal papers, and BRF Archive, file 1971/72; *BT*, 6 May 1971, p.7.

6    G. Henton Davies confirmed and expanded on his position in a written statement in December 1971, which he gave to the officers of the Baptist Union: G. Henton Davies to M.H. Taylor, 18 January 1972, in Taylor's personal papers.

7    Ernest Payne Diary, Vol.XII, pp.721-2: Regent's Park College Oxford, Angus Library, Payne papers. At the same time, Payne told Lois Chapple that the Assembly programme was 'a very unwise one': E.A. Payne to L. Chapple, 3 August 1971: Regent's Park College Oxford, Angus Library, Payne papers, A/3.

8    Minutes of the Council, 29 April 1971; P. Beasley-Murray, *Fearless for Truth: A Personal Portrait of the Life of George Beasley-Murray* (Carlisle: Paternoster, 2002), p.146.

had to do at the Council'.[9] At a meeting of Union Officers on 7 May 1971, Russell reported that letters about Taylor's address were fewer than he had expected, that the general tone was kind but critical, and that some were favourable.[10] The debate seemed restrained.

Two weeks later the situation had changed markedly. At the Advisory Committee for Church Relations on 20 May, Russell said he had been appalled by the tone of some letters he had now received, though others were fair. He was replying to each one.[11] The most significant sign that a crisis loomed for the Union was when Russell received a letter (dated 25 May 1971) from members of the Baptist Revival Fellowship Committee saying that they could not remain in constitutional association with those who would not affirm categorically that Jesus was God. The BRF members were the BRF Chairman, H.G. Owen, who had moved from Reading to Percy Street, Woking; C.P. Collinson, Priory Street, Dudley; R.M. Horn, Horley; E.M. Kirk, Malden Road, Cheam; R.S. Luland, Russell Park, Bedford; Percy Nuttall, Stuart Road, Liverpool; John Pretlove, Walkley, Sheffield; George Stirrup, Day's Lane, Sidcup; H.C. Tyler, Ilford; A.J. Waterman, High Barnet; and James Wood, West Street, Crewe. They wanted a clear statement on the deity of Christ from the Council and from Taylor. If Taylor could not do that, they considered he should not remain at Northern College or as an accredited Baptist minister. Russell replied immediately to say that he would take the BRF letter to the Union's General Purposes and Finance Committee. In response, Harold Owen stated that for the BRF mere re-affirmation of the Union's Declaration of Principle, with its statement that Christ was 'God manifest in the flesh', would not suffice.[12]

---

9    S.J. Voke to M.H. Taylor, 30 April 1971; M.H. Taylor to S.J. Voke, 5 May 1971: in Taylor's personal papers. David Russell had written to Taylor about Voke's desire to be as helpful as possible: D.S. Russell to M.H. Taylor, 30 April 1971, in Taylor's personal papers.

10   Minutes of a Meeting of Baptist Union Officers, 7 May 1971.

11   Minutes of the Baptist Union Advisory Committee on Church Relations, 20 May 1971.

12   BRF committee members to D.S. Russell, 26 May 1971; D.S. Russell to H.G. Owen, 26 May 1971; H.G. Owen to D.S. Russell, 10 June 1971: BRF Archive, file 1971/72.

In the meantime, the *Baptist Times* was featuring letters for and against Taylor's address and Taylor himself was receiving many letters. T. Henry Lovegrove, minister at Mill Road, Wellingborough, said on 13 May 1971 that he was in serious disagreement with what had been said but it was clear to him that Christ had a very real and personal significance for Taylor.[13] There were further responses in similar vein. Stanley Sharpe, minister of Willesden Green, London, expressed disagreement with Taylor but welcomed the stimulus offered. Others were deeply concerned. Norman Moss, minister of Queen's Road, Wimbledon, said that Taylor was in 'a state of paralysed uncertainty about the person of Jesus Christ'. 'If Jesus is not God', Moss stated trenchantly, 'then the worship offered to Him in our Baptist churches is idolatry.'[14] A further perspective was offered by C.T. Cook from Bromley, who as editor of *The Christian* had often analysed evangelical life. He admired Taylor's humility, frankness and seriousness. However, Cook's opinion was that the paradox of the Incarnation raised questions requiring the kind of discussion that could not take place at an Assembly.[15] Some correspondents commended Taylor's intellectual honesty, although Donald Bridge, minister of Enon, Sunderland, insisted that Taylor's critics, too, were thoughtful. 'When we reject a theology, we do so not because we have stopped thinking years ago, nor because we are frightened of new ideas', said Bridge, 'but because we have an ultimate authority'... 'the Christ clearly and consistently revealed in the New Testament'.[16]

Churches also began to make their views known. Critical comment was offered by Bromham Baptist Church, Bedfordshire, and by South Lee, London. Stanley Costin, the South Lee church secretary, wrote to say that the pastor and deacons of the church wished to protest against the address. Taylor's position, he continued, 'appears to us to be quite heretical in that he denies the essential deity of our Lord and Saviour

---

13    *BT*, 13 May 1971, p.3.
14    *BT*, 20 May 1971, p.3.
15    *BT*, 27 May 1971, p.3.
16    *BT*, 24 June 1971, p.3.

Jesus Christ'.[17] A number of churches that had been contemplating withdrawing from the Union now took steps to put that into effect. In May 1971 the Metropolitan Tabernacle, London, ended its Union membership. Russell met with Peter Masters, the minister, and with the deacons, but Russell reported in July 1971 that it had been clear at this meeting that they were adamant about withdrawing.[18] On the other hand, there were churches that expressed support for what they saw as Taylor's way of approaching theology. Writing on behalf of the church in Stoneygate, London Road, Leicester, the ministers, Jim Findlay and Bernard Monk, together with the church secretary, R.O.A. Dixon, affirmed the need for just such honest and open exploration of the meaning of the gospel.[19] Bernard Monk, who was one of many correspondents who wrote to Taylor to express personal support, considered that Taylor's address was 'one of the best I have ever heard at a BU Assembly'.[20]

David Russell, characteristically, sought to answer in detail the letters he was receiving. Writing to Harold Owen on 16 June 1971, he said that he had gone back to earlier debates about the Declaration of Principle. He explained that although the Union had not attempted to define the Declaration's statement about Jesus Christ as 'God manifest in the flesh', at the time when that wording was adopted the Council had spoken of Christ 'as of one nature with God, the unique manifestation, the incarnation of deity and verily and in effect one in the quality of His being with the eternal God'. Russell said that it was not for him to defend Taylor's words and that he would have worded things differently, but Russell strongly defended Taylor's right to express himself as he did on the basis of his acceptance of the Declaration of Principle. Russell also noted that Taylor stated he did not disown the Nicene Creed.[21] Meetings of Council members and Union officers were held, and on 25 June

---

17    J.H. Burrell, secretary, Bromham Baptist Church, to M.H. Taylor, 8 May 1971, in Taylor's personal papers; *BT*, 10 June 1971, p.3.

18    Minutes of the Baptist Union General Purposes and Finance Committee, 6 July 1971.

19    *BT*, 3 June 1971, p.3.

20    B.J. Monk to M.H. Taylor, 23 May 1971: in Taylor's personal papers.

21    D.S. Russell to H.G. Owen, 16 June 1971: BRF Archive, file 1971/72.

Russell spoke about the spate of letters he was receiving. David Pawson, who had moved from Gold Hill to Commercial Road, Guildford, had asked for a special Union commission on the matter to be appointed,[22] and at a well-attended public meeting at Bloomsbury, Pawson gave an address, 'How much of a God is Jesus?', which was later printed. Derek Moon, minister of Littlehampton Baptist Church, arranged for the booklet by Pawson to be sent to all ministers.[23] The degree of bad feeling in the Union was indicated by the fact that Walter Bottoms, in the *Baptist Times*, alleged that Pawson had laid himself open to the accusation of teaching the heresy that Christ was not fully man.[24]

There was little enthusiasm among Union leaders for the kind of commission suggested by David Pawson. Ernest Payne's reaction was probably typical of them when he recorded in his diary his hope that 'the storm would blow itself out'.[25] Michael Taylor himself had been willing to write on Christology for the *Baptist Times*, which published a series of articles on the subject, but Taylor came to the opinion that there was little wisdom in pursuing the debate in public. He considered that the reaction in some quarters seemed to overrate the importance of his address and he also asked whether there was freedom to make this kind of theological exploration in the denomination.[26] But the pressure on the Union leadership continued. An LBA Council meeting in September 1971, with sixty-nine members present, passed by forty-three votes to fifteen a resolution by Sir Cyril Black, President of the Union in 1970-71, which spoke for those who believed that Taylor's address appeared

---

22 Minutes of a Meeting of Baptist Union Officers, 25 June 1971.

23 J.D. Pawson, *How much of a God is Jesus?* (Littlehampton, p.p., 1971); D.J. Moon to ministers, 27 October 1971.

24 *BT*, 11 November 1971, p.3. Pawson defended himself: *BT*, 18 Nov 1971, p.4. He was also defended by Douglas McBain, Andrew McKie and Norman Moss, the three ministers who had organized the Bloomsbury meeting: *BT*, 25 November 1971, p.3.

25 Ernest Payne Diary, Vol.XIII, p.723.

26 *BT*, 15 July 1971, p.2. In a private letter to Walter Bottoms, Michael Taylor also expressed concern that the debate could be centred on him personally, rather than on the theological issues: M.H. Taylor to Walter Bottoms, 22 May 1971, in Taylor's personal papers.

'to throw doubt upon the Authority, Deity and Sinlessness of Jesus Christ'. An amendment by Godfray Le Quesne and Gordon Hastings, minister of the 600-member Sutton Baptist Church, declaring that while some saw Taylor's address as inconsistent with the Declaration of Principle others were 'thankful for an attempt to restate traditional doctrine in contemporary terms', was defeated by forty-three votes to twenty. The motion that was passed asked the Council to seek to repair the harm done to the denomination.[27] A number of London ministers, such as C.W. Beckett, of College Lane, Harrow, and Gwynne Edwards, of Fillebrook Baptist Church, Leytonstone, wrote to Michael Taylor to assure him that they did not support the motion that had been passed.[28]

*Sir Cyril Black*

By this stage Michael Taylor had received a large number of letters, some critical, some commendatory, and some which did not necessarily agree with what he had said but voiced concern for him personally in the light of the controversy that had ensued. As an instance of this kind of concern, the deacons of Perry Rise, Forest Hill, London, wrote to Taylor on 26 September to say that, although direct discussions might show that 'our understanding of the truth as it is in Jesus differs from yours', nonetheless they wished to affirm Taylor's honesty and integrity and to express sorrow for the way in which Taylor had been 'vilified'. Douglas Sparkes, the Perry Rise minister, who in 1976 became Metropolitan Area Superintendent, added a note to Taylor to say that his own feelings were those articulated in the letter, but that discussion in the deacons' meeting had come from the deacons themselves and the letter was an expression of their heartfelt concern. For Sparkes the spirit exhibited by the deacons was an encouraging sign.[29] The Northamptonshire Baptist Ministers'

27  *BT*, 30 September 1971, p.12. Gordon Hastings wrote to Payne to say that the voting was a fair reflection of the thinking of London Baptists: G. Hastings to E.A. Payne, 6 October 1971: Payne papers, A/3.
28  C.W. Becket to M.H. Taylor, 30 September 1971; R.G. Edwards to M.H. Taylor, 11 October 1971: in Taylor's personal papers.
29  A.F. Collins, church secretary, on behalf of the minister and deacons, to M.H. Taylor, 25 September 1971; D.C. Sparkes to M.H. Taylor, 26 September 1971: in

Fraternal spoke of the affectionate consideration felt for Taylor, in his 'present time of trial', by all the Fraternal members. 'With your Northamptonshire connections', said George Green on behalf of the ministers, 'we feel that we have an affinity with you and that you belong to us.'[30]

Northern College was also receiving letters. In response to a letter from the members of Bognor Regis Baptist Church, which regretted that someone training ministers had apparently questioned the belief that Christ was 'God manifest in the flesh', J.R. Hulme, JP, chairman of the Northern College governors, replied that personally he had been impressed by the vision shown in Taylor's Assembly address and that corporately the governors fully supported Taylor's principalship.[31] Hulme answered other letters in the same vein. Responding to Wakefield Baptist Church, Hulme emphasized that Taylor subscribed to the Union's Declaration of Principle, and that there did not, therefore, seem to be grounds to refer, as the Wakefield church meeting had done, to an 'apparent denial of the deity of Christ'.[32] The support for Taylor expressed by Hulme was formally recorded by the governors as a whole at a governors' meeting on 6 October, at which they resolved: 'From our knowledge of Principal Taylor, from the evidence of his work in the College and from the evidence of his devotion and dedication to Jesus Christ as Lord, we affirm our confidence in him as Principal of the College and give him our full support. We further believe it to be essential to a College that freedom of speech be assured to the College Principal and that his academic integrity be respected.' There was one abstention and no dissenters.[33]

It was, therefore, against a background of sharply conflicting opinions within the Union that the General Purposes and Finance

---

Taylor's personal papers.

30   G.S. Green to M.H. Taylor, 17 November 1971, in Taylor's personal papers.

31   D.T. Morris, secretary, Bognor Regis Baptist Church, to J.R. Hulme, 20 July 1971; J.R. Hulme to D.T. Morris, 23 July 1971: in Taylor's personal papers.

32   H.F. Rudd, church secretary, Wakefield Baptist Church, 19 January 1972; J.R. Hulme to H.F. Rudd, 26 January 1972; in Taylor's personal papers.

33   Governors' Meeting, 6 October 1971, cited by Shepherd, *The making of a northern Baptist college*, pp.233-4.

(GP&F) Committee met on 5 October 1971 and discussed how to proceed. George Beasley-Murray wanted a resolution that 'this Council records its belief that the address by the Rev. Michael Taylor does not apparently do justice to the teaching of the New Testament concerning our Lord Jesus Christ', but this proposal was defeated by fourteen votes to six. The GP&F resolution which was agreed, with one voting against, recognized the concern felt by some who judged that Taylor's address failed to do justice to the teaching of the New Testament about the deity of Christ; affirmed the task of theological restatement; and described the Assembly address as an individual attempt made, with integrity, by a member of the Baptist community expressing faith in the living Christ as a contribution to debate. The Council was invited by the GP&F Committee to reaffirm the Declaration of Principle, specifically Christ as 'Lord and Saviour' and 'God manifest in the flesh', and to state that it was 'unequivocal in its profession of the deity of Christ as also of His humanity'. Beasley-Murray suggested he should not preside in the forthcoming Council when the matter was discussed, but the Committee thought he could express his views on the proposed resolution without leaving the chair.[34]

The Council, held on 9 and 10 November 1971, was a tense affair. Stanley Voke moved the first of five amendments to the GP&F resolution. Voke's view was that Taylor's address had failed to do justice to New Testament teaching about the deity of Christ. Beasley-Murray was given leave to speak from the chair in favour of Voke's amendment. It was, however, lost by a large majority. Other amendments which sought to re-emphasize the Declaration of Principle were also defeated, as was an amendment by E.A. Payne which stressed the Baptist heritage of liberty. Although Payne's amendment was not carried, it was agreed to include it as an addendum to the resolution. The addendum noted that 'the Union has always contained within its fellowship those of different theological opinions and emphases, believing that its claim for toleration involved tolerance and respect within its own ranks'. Sir Cyril Black wanted to add 'consistent with acceptance of, and loyalty to, the

---

34    Minutes of the Baptist Union General Purposes and Finance Committee, 5 October 1971.

doctrinal clauses of the constitution', but his proposal was defeated.[35] A slightly revised version of the GP&F resolution was passed (with the Payne addendum), with 180 in favour and four abstaining. It might have seemed that peace could prevail. However, Beasley-Murray was unable to associate with this position and resigned as Council chairman.[36] Cyril Black was amazed that his own amendment had been rejected, since it seemed that there was now no limit to the views acceptable in the Union. Black suggested, with justification as it turned out, that this might prove to be the issue on which the 'parting of the ways' would be reached.[37]

A 'PARTING OF THE WAYS'

Five days after the Council, the BRF held its annual conference at Swanwick. At the conference, BRF members agreed a statement that Michael Taylor's address 'was a denial of the essential Biblical truth concerning the Deity of our Lord Jesus Christ'. The BRF statement continued: 'We believe the B.U. Council's Resolution of November 10th, 1971 failed to discern and declare all this.' In the view of BRF members, the Council had affirmed the Declaration of Principle concerning the deity of Christ and yet allowed a view that denied it. Then came the signal of the parting of the ways: 'We cannot in conscience', said the statement, 'remain associated with the life of a Union which has decided to tolerate the denial of the Deity of our Lord Jesus Christ amongst its accredited ministers.' Some ministers, it was indicated, were going to resign from the accredited list in the immediate future and others would do so later. These ministers believed efforts over years to influence the Union to a more biblical position had been largely in vain. This

---

35 Minutes of the Baptist Union Council, 9 and 10 November 1971.
36 Beasley-Murray, *Fearless for Truth*, p.148-50. Beasley-Murray later said his experience at the Council meeting was the most embarrassing he had ever undergone. There was clearly resentment at Council about the way he spoke: G.R. Beasley-Murray to D.S. Russell, 17 November 1971. A copy of this letter is in the Payne papers, A/3.
37 *BT*, 2 December 1971, p.3.

statement was passed with 155 in favour, 14 against and 24 abstentions.[38] Others were at the conference but were not eligible to vote. A meeting chaired by Henton Davies, which drew together five BRF representatives and four Union representatives, including Russell and Beasley-Murray, was held on 25 November 1971, and at that meeting Henton Davies emphasized that he disagreed with what Taylor had said, but supported his right to say it.[39]

The BRF Conference statement was sent out by the BRF, together with a letter dated 1 December 1971, to all ministers and churches of the Union. The letter was signed by Harold Owen as chairman of the BRF, Alec Steen as secretary, and John Waterman as treasurer, plus six other committee members. The BRF leaders explained that the Union's Declaration of Principle had hitherto been understood to state clearly and unequivocally the full eternal deity of Christ and to limit membership in the Union to those who held this truth unreservedly. The BRF letter then referred specifically to the addendum to the November Council resolution, which was being interpreted exactly as Black had foreseen. Those signing the BRF letter indicated that since the issue was in their view a matter of the heart and basis of the Christian faith, they were resigning from the Union's accredited ministerial list. They made it clear that they believed there was no reasonable hope of the 1972 Assembly reversing the decision of the Council.[40] This letter of 1 December was followed up by one of 10 December 1971 announcing that the BRF committee was convening a meeting to pray and confer about the formation of an Association of Evangelical Baptist Churches (AEBC).[41] This was not a new idea. It had been mooted two years before, an indication that the events of 1971 only confirmed for some a direction that they had already taken.

38  BRF Statement, agreed at the BRF Conference at Swanwick, 15-18 November 1971: BRF Archive, file 1971/72.
39  Notes of a Meeting of Representatives of Baptist Union and Baptist Revival Fellowship, 25 November 1971: BRF Archive, file 1971/72.
40  BRF Letter to all Ministers, Deacons and Churches of the Baptist Union, 1 December 1971: BRF Archive, file 1971/72.
41  R.S. Luland, on behalf of the BRF Committee, 10 December 1971: BRF Archive, file 1971/72.

A very different view of the November 1971 Council was set out in a letter from David Russell to all Union ministers. Russell reported on what he called the 'most important single item on the Council's agenda', the debate relating to Michael Taylor's address. He said that many hours of hard thinking and earnest praying had gone into the important matters involved, but not everyone would be satisfied with the Council statement. There were those who were deeply troubled about the truth of the gospel being undermined while there were also those (often the same people) who were appalled at the prospect of a heresy-hunt. The Council, said Russell, affirmed the deity of Christ and the Declaration of Principle, and asked for tolerance and mutual trust. He was aware that there were those contemplating leaving the Union and he emphasized that he believed the denomination was made up of 'humble, devout and earnest Christian men and women and churches which stand securely in the evangelical tradition'. Finally he asked for ministers and churches to think long and hard before endangering the fellowship and weakening the witness, and he hoped for 'a new dedication to our Lord, a new reliance on the Holy Spirit, a new commitment to one another and a new resolve to make known his saving Gospel to our generation'.[42]

Ministers receiving letters both from the Union's General Secretary and from the BRF were faced with choices. For some, resignation from the Union was inevitable, given their long-term dissatisfaction. In early December Russell reported on eighteen resignations from the accredited list.[43] But many letters to the BRF deplored the BRF leadership's actions. Adrian Thatcher at Abingdon, for example, wrote that 'the Church at Abingdon is far too busy proclaiming the gospel of Christ to consider your divisive partisan statement'.[44] Lewis Misselbrook, at Chelmsley Wood, Birmingham, begged BRF leaders to recall that it was 'possible to be quite right in doctrine and quite wrong in spirit'.[45] In

42   General Secretary's letter to ministers, November 1971: Payne papers, A/3.
43   Minutes of a Meeting of Baptist Union Officers, 3 December 1971; Minutes of the Baptist Union General Purpose and Finance Committee, 7 December 1971.
44   A. Thatcher to T.A. Steen, 4 January 1972: BRF Archive, 1971/72 file. Adrian Thatcher later became an Anglican. He wrote extensively in the fields of spirituality and ethics.
45   L.R. Misselbrook to T.A. Steen, 13 January 1972: BRF Archive, file 1971/72.

some cases, positions became firmer after the November 1971 Council. On 4 December eleven ministers from Merseyside wrote a letter to Russell, which they hoped was free of 'theological vindictiveness', stating that, although Taylor had said much that was 'salutary and necessary about orthodox formulations of belief', they believed his Christology was 'seriously at variance with that of the New Testament'. They appealed to him to step down as Principal of Northern 'and give place to another who would receive wider confidence among the churches'.[46] The LBA's December council unanimously welcomed the Union Council's affirmation of the Declaration of Principle but regretted that the Council 'feels unable to make clear that any statement which fails to do justice to the deity of our Lord Jesus Christ ... goes beyond the bounds of liberty of opinion and theological restatement'. The Council was asked by the LBA to re-consider what had become the rather notorious 'addendum'.[47]

Considerable energy now began to be applied to the question by Sir Cyril Black. On 20 December 1971 he wrote to Payne to say that it was clear to him from many interviews and much correspondence that the addendum had created the bad impression he foresaw, despite Russell's explanations about it. 'If matters are left as they are', Black continued, 'there is no doubt that there will be massive withdrawals of Ministers and Churches from the Baptist Union.'[48] Payne's view, which he expressed to Cyril Black in January 1972, was that it was better to leave things as they were.[49] But by that stage it was difficult to see the advantages of inaction. A number of churches as well as ministers were leaving the

---

46    Letter from B.F. Harrison, J.A. Pollard, J. Fisher, F.E. Finch, W.J. Pemberton, S.T. Lewis, K. Barker, R. Cave, T.F. Hughes, P. Nuttall and E. Hammond to D.S. Russell, 4 December 1971. Bryan F. Harrison, of Page Moss Lane, Liverpool, was the principal drafter, and wrote to Taylor to say that he hoped what was said was 'free of rancour': B.F. Harrison to M.H. Taylor, 4 December 1971, in Taylor's personal papers.
47    Letter to all churches in the LBA and members of the LBA Council, December 1971, referring to the LBA Council of 9 December 1971, at which 73 members were present: Payne papers, A/3.
48    Sir Cyril Black to E.A. Payne, 20 December 1971, Payne papers, A/3.
49    E.A. Payne to Cyril Black, 8 January 1972, Payne papers, A/3.

Union, including some larger churches of 200-300 members such as Carey, Reading, and Percy Street, Woking. The new Baptist group, the AEBC, was formed in 1972; a year later fifty-six ministers belonged to its Ministers' Fellowship.[50] At the Union GP&F Committee on 11 January 1972 an attempt was made to deal with the problems caused by the 'addendum', by stating in respect of the deity and humanity of Christ that the Council 'cannot identify itself with any position which would deny this fundamental tenet of our faith'. It was agreed that a letter from Russell to this effect would go to ministers and churches.[51]

Sir Cyril Black, however, was now convinced about his course of action. In a letter to the *Baptist Times*, on 30 December 1971, he stated: 'There is still the final court of appeal. It is to the assembly that we must look.'[52] With this in mind, a small group worked together to construct an Assembly resolution. Those involved were Black himself, Beasley-Murray, Norman Moss from Wimbledon, Andrew McKie of Chatsworth Way, West Norwood, and Douglas McBain of Lewin Road, Streatham. Beasley-Murray produced an article which he hoped to publish in the *Baptist Times*, but when Walter Bottoms told him that the correspondence about the Christological issue was closed he produced a booklet, *The Christological Controversy in the Baptist Union*. At the March 1972 Council, Russell reported that he had received 625 letters, many supporting the Council and many others extremely critical of the 'addendum'. Beasley-Murray proposed and it was accepted that a resolution to the 1972 Assembly should say that the addendum in no way sought to weaken the Declaration of Principle.[53] On 20 March 1972, Beasley-Murray sent his booklet to all ministers. It was being maintained, Beasley-Murray said, that the Union's troubles were due to division between 'an outmoded right wing theology and a progressive

50 *Evangelical Times*, February 1972, p.1. The AEBC Constitution had a 'self-execution' clause by which it would be terminated after ten years. On 3 October 1981 a decision was made at the annual AEBC Assembly to close the AEBC. I am indebted to Graham Harrison for this information.
51 Minutes of the Baptist Union General Purposes and Finance Committee, 11 January 1972.
52 *BT*, 30 December 1971, p.3.
53 Minutes of the Baptist Union Council, 14 and 15 March 1972.

theology which takes account of the realities of our time'; the difference, he suggested, could be more objectively described as between a small group of theologians maintaining a theological novelty and the consensus of theologians past and present.[54] Beasley-Murray believed that if the denomination did not declare its position it would call in question its existence.[55]

The communication from Beasley-Murray elicited a strong response from Payne, who wrote on 6 April 1972 that Beasley-Murray had 'pushed the denomination nearer disaster at a moment when your friends hoped you were going to exercise the kind of restraining influence which we surely have the right to expect from you'.[56] Walter Bottoms, writing in the *Baptist Times* on 13 April, described Beasley-Murray's claim about the precarious position of the denomination as false.[57] Payne, in a further letter to Beasley-Murray, dated 18 April, said: 'You have been stirring up trouble instead of calming it, and have contributed thereby, more than perhaps any other single individual, to the very difficult and dangerous situation we now face'.[58] In reply, Beasley-Murray emphasized that he had wanted a Council statement that the Union was not responsible for or implicated in what Assembly speakers said. In his view Payne was 'above all responsible for the Council declining that advice'.[59] By now the resolution to be put to the Assembly by Sir Cyril Black was known, as was an amendment to be moved by L.G. Champion, seconded by Bernard Green. Payne wrote to Black on 14 April saying he believed the Champion amendment would be very widely supported. In Yorkshire, Lancashire and the Midlands, according to Payne, there was a feeling that Beasley-Murray's action was ill-timed and his language intemperate. Black replied that he did not anticipate

54    G.R. Beasley-Murray, covering letter, 20 March 1972: Payne papers, A/3.
55    G.R. Beasley-Murray, *The Christological Controversy in the Baptist Union* (Rushden: Stanley L Hunt, n.d. [1972]), pp.1, 5.
56    E.A. Payne to G.R. Beasley-Murray, 6 April 1972: Payne papers, A/3.
57    *BT*, 13 April 1972, p.2.
58    E.A. Payne to G.R. Beasley-Murray, 18 April 1972: Payne papers, A/3.
59    G.R. Beasley-Murray to E.A. Payne, 20 April 1972: Payne papers, A/3.

Champion's amendment being carried.[60] The stage was set for the Assembly debate on 25 April 1972.

At the Assembly, Cyril Black, seconded by Beasley-Murray, put his motion. Two paragraphs were singled out by Black as of particular importance:

> We firmly and unhesitatingly place on record our conviction that the Declaration of Principle represents the basic requirements for fellowship in the Baptist denomination and that we attach high importance to the loyal and wholehearted acceptance of it. In particular we assert the unacceptability of any interpretation of the person and work of Jesus Christ our Lord which would obscure or deny the fundamental tenet of the Christian faith that Jesus Christ is Lord and Saviour, truly God and truly Man.

> We recall that the rule of Ministerial recognition stipulates that 'all persons who become or remain Ministers or Probationers accredited by the Union are required to accept the Declaration of Principle as contained in the constitution of the Union'.

Two amendments from conservatives who wanted a stronger statement, and one amendment that was at odds with the whole resolution, were decisively defeated. Champion and Green then put their amendment, calling for the removal of the two paragraphs emphasized by Cyril Black. Their concern was that the paragraphs might encourage heresy hunts in the future. This final amendment was lost by a large majority. The original resolution was then carried overwhelmingly, with 1,800 delegates voting in favour, 46 against and 72 abstentions.[61] After the debate Russell wrote to Payne saying he was sorry Champion's amendment had not received greater support, but that Cyril Black's statement had produced a measure of unity. Russell hoped that the discussions of the previous months would be seen as 'a non-event in the

---

60    E.A. Payne to Cyril Black, 14 April 1972; Cyril Black to E.A. Payne, 17 April 1972: Payne papers, A/3.

61    *BT*, 27 April 1972, p.7.

life of our Union'.[62]  Black's perspective was different. Writing to Russell on 25 April 1972, he said: 'Most of our Ministers and lay people are much more conservative than are what might be described, not unkindly, as the "professional" Committee men who tend to dominate the Finance and General Purposes Committee and the Council of the Union. The strength of this conservative element in the denomination cannot any longer be ignored.'[63]

## ECUMENICAL ISSUES

The fear among some Union leaders was that the 1972 vote signalled the beginning of a heresy hunt by conservatives. Speaking to a late-night gathering of the Baptist Renewal Group during the 1972 Assembly, Payne raised the issue of whether 'men and women of liberal outlook' would remain in a Baptist Union 'which had taken a lurch to the right'.[64] On ecumenical questions, however, the denomination continued to exhibit the same mixture of caution and openness that had been characteristic of its approach. The only new development was that some ministers who had been militantly anti-ecumenical left the Union. Membership of the BCC and WCC had been an issue of conscience for them in the 1960s, before the Christological debates began. In January 1970, Theo Bamber, who died later that year, spoke about the need to safeguard the interests of those who were disturbed by the commitment of the Union to the WCC.[65] But Sir Cyril Black, as Union President in 1970-71, said that he saw no conflict between being both ecumenical and evangelical.[66] Later he appealed, 'as a conservative evangelical', for an acceptance of the fact that the majority of Baptists favoured membership of the BCC.[67] At the same time, Black made it clear in 1973 that he

---

62   D.S. Russell to E.A. Payne 27 April 1972: Payne papers, A/3.
63   Cyril Black to D.S. Russell, 25 April 1972, quoted by Beasley-Murray, *Fearless for Truth*, pp.159-60.
64   Ernest Payne diary, Vol.XIII, p.746.
65   *BT*, 15 January 1970, p.3.
66   *BT*, 23 April 1970, p.6.
67   *BT*, 30 April 1970, p.6.

opposed any compromise of Baptist principles regarding the baptism of believers.[68]

It seemed to Gordon Hastings of Sutton Baptist Church, writing in 1971, that the ecumenical picture was fairly mixed. Despite set-backs over Anglican-Methodist union, talks were continuing. Official inter-communion between Anglican and Free Church members, a long-held Free Church aspiration, had been achieved. Baptists were active at local level in ecumenical ventures, and although many evangelicals were upset that the BCC and the WCC appeared to be reluctant to talk about evangelism and mission, Baptists were finding many areas of shared belief and concern with other traditions.[69] Increased contacts with Roman Catholics in the early 1970s represented

*The principle of the baptism of believers - baptism during a televised service, Altrincham, May 1976*

a new development for Baptists. In January 1970 it was reported that the Baptist Renewal Group was in dialogue with the Catholic Renewal Movement.[70] A few months later a group called 'One for Christian Renewal' was formed. It declared denominations to be 'not only meaningless but a hindrance'. Adrian Hastings, in his survey of the twentieth century, viewed this new group as 'almost wholly insignificant',[71] but its initial conference, which drew 300 people from twelve denominations at Swanwick, suggests that this expression of grass-roots ecumenism cannot be so easily dismissed.[72] During 1971 there was further progress, with Baptist Renewal Group and Catholic Renewal Movement members gathering for a weekend conference.[73]

---

68   *BT*, 11 January 1973, p.8.
69   *BT*, 15 April 1971, p.6.
70   *BT*, 21 January 1970, p.2. In the mid-1980s the Baptist Renewal Group became the Broad Alliance of Radical Baptists.
71   Hastings, *A History of English Christianity*, p.549.
72   *BT*, 4 June 1970, p.12.
73   *BT*, 21 January 1971, p.2.

Some of the actions of the WCC appeared to be less constructive. Questions raised in 1970 about the WCC's Programme to Combat Racism, which was apparently giving money to South African guerrilla groups. Payne, who was better placed than any other Baptist to understand the WCC, explained that the money went to welfare programmes.[74]  Many Baptists, however, were puzzled. Alfred Grimwade from Beckenham, writing to the *Baptist Times* in 1970, expressed a view that was typical of much lay opinion. Everyone, he believed, wanted the end of apartheid, but giving money to guerrillas was appalling.[75]  It was clear that Baptists and other denominations were divided over whether violent social change could be justified.[76]  In December 1970 Suffolk Baptists, by a majority of ninety per cent, deplored both apartheid and grants to freedom fighters.[77] David Russell, who was a delegate to the Central Committee of the WCC and was deeply involved in struggles for human rights and religious freedom, was involved in the debate.[78] Russell, together with John Huxtable, Secretary of the Congregational Church, who was also a WCC Central Committee delegate, tried unsuccessfully to modify the way funds were used. Although a supporter and advocate of the Special Fund to Combat Racism, with its humanitarian objective, Russell thought it unwise that money for this purpose had apparently been transferred from the WCC's central funds, to which all member churches contributed whether or not they were supportive of the Special Fund. Lighthouse Road Baptist Church, Bow, saw the support given by the WCC to guerrilla groups as a reason for the Union to leave the WCC.[79]

The early 1970s saw one major victory for institutional ecumenism – the coming together of the Congregational Church of England and Wales and the Presbyterian Church of England to form the United

---

74    *BT*, September 1970, p.1; cf. West, *To be a Pilgrim,* pp.177-9.
75    *BT*, 17 September 1970, p.3; 8 October 1970, p.3.
76    Minutes of the Baptist Union Council, 10 and 11 November 1970; E.A. Payne, *Thirty Years of the British Council of Churches, 1942-1972* (London: BCC, 1972), pp.27-8.
77    *BT*, 3 December 1970, p.3.
78    *BT*, 1 October 1970, pp.1, 12; 4 February 1971, p.1.
79    I am grateful to David Russell for these observations.

Reformed Church (URC) in 1972.[80] There was also one significant failure. For the second time the Church of England failed to achieve the necessary majority in favour of unity with the Methodist Church, despite Methodist enthusiasm.[81] More informal ecumenical discussions continued. In May 1973 the URC issued an invitation to Roman Catholics, Anglicans, Methodists and Baptists to attend talks. Beasley-Murray, supported by Morris West, urged Baptist involvement from the outset.[82] David Russell was present at a two-day conference at Mansfield College, Oxford, in December 1973. There were eight representatives from the Baptist Union, eight from the URC, eight Roman Catholics, and smaller numbers from the Church of England, the Methodist Church, the Churches of Christ, the Free Church Federal Council, the Lutheran Council of Great Britain, and the Greek Orthodox Church. Considerable discussion took place of a scheme for local ecumenical progress put forward by Donald English, then a Methodist theological tutor.[83] The Churches' Unity Commission was set up and in 1974 the Baptist Union Council decided to join it.[84] Later, Donald English would become chairman of the ecumenical Nationwide Initiative in Evangelism, which had support from the Archbishop of Canterbury, Donald Coggan, as well as from David Russell and other leaders.[85]

Donald English was right to highlight the fruitfulness of local ecumenism – what became known as Local Ecumenical Projects (LEPs)

---

80    Although this was a success, a significant number of churches stayed outside the URC. Within Congregationalism two new groups emerged: the Congregational Federation (about 300 churches) and the Evangelical Fellowship of Congregational Churches (about 130 churches).

81    Hastings, *A History of English Christianity*, pp.623-6.

82    Cross, *Baptism and the Baptists*, pp.255-6.

83    Notes of a meeting, 'Talks about Talks', 10-11 December 1973, held at Mansfield College, Oxford. The notes are in Donald English's personal papers, at Westminster College, Oxford.

84    Cross, *Baptism and the Baptists: Theology and Practice in Twentieth-Century Britain*, pp.253-6.

85    *BT*, 23 November 1978, p.1. See R. Whitehead and A. Sneddon, *An Unwanted Child? The Story of the NIE* (London: BCC/CCBI, 1990), and B. Hoare and I. Randall, *More than a Methodist: The Life and Ministry of Donald English* (Carlisle: Paternoster Press, 2003), pp.145-55.

– particularly against the background of the Sharing of Buildings Act and the scarcity of land for new church buildings. In Skelmersdale New Town, Lancashire, where Norman Giller settled as Baptist minister in 1969, an Ecumenical Centre took shape with members of the Anglican, Baptist, Methodist and United Reformed Churches sharing a team ministry.[86] Another example was in Sheffield. St Thomas's Anglican Church and Mulehouse Road Baptist Church in Crookes began joint worship in 1977 when the Anglican building was undergoing extensive refurbishment. An LEP was inaugurated in 1982.[87] South West Manchester saw the emergence of an Ecumenical Group of Baptist and URC causes. In new towns like Warrington, Runcorn and Mosborough, ecumenical life was seen as normal by Baptists.[88] Milton Keynes was also noted for ecumenical experiment. Whaddon Way in North Bletchley became an Anglican/Baptist experiment in 1973 and later an LEP.[89] Developments in Swindon in the 1970s led to the formation of Swindon Central Church (Methodist, Baptist and URC).[90] In these contexts, fresh thinking about issues of infant and believer's baptism had to take place. At LEPs like Blackbird Leys, Oxford, which was Anglican, Baptist, Methodist and URC, parents of new-born children were offered infant dedication or baptism, with most opting for baptism.[91]

Many Baptists found this kind of local co-operation much more amenable than national ecumenical schemes involving attempts to unite denominational bodies. The national discussions which did take place in

---

86    I. Sellers, ed., *Our Heritage: The Baptists of Yorkshire, Lancashire and Cheshire, 1647-1987* (Leeds: Yorkshire Baptist Association and Lancashire & Cheshire Baptist Association, 1987), p.135. Skelmersdale was accepted into Baptist Union membership in 1973: Minutes of the Council, 13 and 14 November 1973.

87    R. Warren, *In the Crucible: The Testing and Growth of a Local Church* (Crowborough: Highland Books, 1989), chapters 8 and 9.

88    Sellers, ed., *Our Heritage: The Baptists of Yorkshire, Lancashire and Cheshire*, p.145.

89    R. Simpson, *How We Grew a Local Ecumenical Project* (Bramcote: Grove Pastoral Series, No.17, 1984).

90    H. Dunscombe, *Footprints of Faith: A History of Central Church, Swindon* (Swindon: p.p., 2nd edn., 1990).

91    M.J. Quicke, 'Baptists and the Current Debate on Baptism', *BQ*, Vol.29, No.4 (1981), pp.153-68.

the 1970s were about churches covenanting together rather than about institutional unity. In January 1976 the Churches' Unity Commission set out *The Ten Propositions* for discussion, and Baptists agreed to consider what 'covenanting together' with other denominations (excluding Roman Catholics) might mean. Morris West presented the *Propositions* document to the Council in 1976, and it was agreed that it be sent to the churches for their response. The proposals included acceptance of different forms of baptism. Proposition Five spoke of 'mutually acceptable rites': the Union's notes said that this did not mean a uniform common rite of baptism and did not preclude so-called re-baptism.[92] The Council debated the responses in November 1977. About seventy per cent of the Union membership responded, with many churches reporting that they were co-operating ecumenically at local level but were wary of national schemes. The Union felt unable to recommend the *Propositions* as a way forward for Baptists.[93] The Baptist reply, *Visible Unity in Life and Mission,* concluded: 'It is our clear judgment that at present no unqualified recommendation to accept the Ten Propositions can be made.' There was considerable concern about a covenant that barred administering believer's baptism to those baptized as infants.[94]

Although rejection of *The Ten Propositions* probably reflected the views of most Baptists, some wanted deeper ecumenical involvement. Paul Rowntree Clifford, President of Selly Oak Colleges, Birmingham, was a convenor in January 1978 of a conference of forty Baptists, including Hugh Cross of Grove Hill and Highfield, Hemel Hempstead, who was Ecumenical Officer for England for the BCC from 1979, David Tennant, General Secretary of the Birmingham Council of Christian Education, Michael Taylor and Michael Ball of Pontypridd. A statement, 'We Want to Covenant', was signed.[95] At a meeting at the 1978

---

92   *A Statement to the Churches in membership of the Baptist Union of Great Britain and Ireland* (London: Baptist Union, 1976), pp.2-3.
93   Cross, *Baptism and the Baptists*, pp.256-9.
94   *Visible Unity in Life and Mission: Reply by the Council of the Baptist Union of Great Britain and Ireland to the Ten Propositions of the Churches' Unity Commission* (London: Baptist Union, 1977), p.3.
95   *BT*, 26 January 1978, p.5. For Clifford's ecumenical vision, see P.R. Clifford, *An Ecumenical Pilgrimage* (London: West Ham Central Mission, 1994), chapter 11.

Assembly, David Savage, Merseyside Ecumenical Officer, said Baptists in LEPs were disappointed by the Union response to the Propositions. Other speakers at the meeting included John Nicholson, then BCC Ecumenical Officer for England, David Wilcox of Abingdon, and David Russell. A pro-ecumenical '1980 Group' was set up, convened by Roger Nunn of Manvers Street, Bath, who had been central to the formation of the Baptist Renewal Group.[96] At WCC level, English Baptists were involved in discussions in the 1970s about baptism, eucharist and ministry. Morris West, who became Principal of Bristol Baptist College in 1972, was a central figure. In 1979 an important Consultation on Baptism was held at Southern Baptist Seminary, Louisville, USA, with Beasley-Murray, Morris West and John Nicholson taking part. Equal numbers of believer-baptist and paedobaptist scholars met to discuss baptism.[97] Despite the setbacks, Baptist ecumenical involvement continued.

MINISTRY TOMORROW

The subject of ministry remained important, with new topics being raised. A sabbatical leave scheme for ministers was introduced. There was fierce debate about *Ministry Tomorrow*, especially over its suggestion that in the future the denomination would have only 400 full-time ministers. Beasley-Murray argued in January 1970 that the report's suggestion of one Baptist minister per 300 church members meant that Manchester would have only three ministers. He saw this as a policy of retrenchment.[98] By contrast, John Nicholson, then with the North Cheshire Fellowship of Baptist Churches, considered the figures to be

---

96   Cross, *Baptism and the Baptists*, pp.262-3.
97   W.M.S. West, 'Towards a Consensus on Baptism? Louisville 1979', *BQ*, Vol.28, No.5 (1980), pp.225-32; W.M.S. West, 'Baptism: Report of the Faith and Order Consultation, Louisville 1979', *BQ*, Vol.28, No.5 (1980), pp.232-9; W.M.S. West, 'Baptists in Faith and Order – A Study in Baptismal Convergence', in K.W. Clements, ed., *Baptists in the Twentieth Century* (London: Baptist Historical Society, 1982), pp.70-3.
98   *BT*, 22 January 1970, p.4.

realistic and argued for team ministry as the strategy for the future.[99] It was announced in early 1971 that, in order to do justice to *Ministry Tomorrow,* the Council would meet for three instead of two days. David Russell sought to ward off some of the criticisms being made, explaining before the Council that the report did not *recommend* 400 ministers but saw this as the number the denomination would require and be able to sustain.[100] The report was considered by the Council in March 1971. Special attention was given to the idea of supplementary ministers, with Bernard Green emphasizing that this scheme was not intended to enable churches to have cheap part-time ministry. The introduction of supplementary ministers was affirmed. The Council was not, however, inclined to accept the report in full: Norman Jones, who had chaired the Commission that produced the report, spoke about a 'failure of nerve'.[101]

One important proposal in *Ministry Tomorrow* was the transfer of all deaconesses to the Ministerial list. This idea was put to the deaconesses in 1970, when a majority opposed the idea. The matter was then discussed by a Ministry Working Group set up in 1972. The Group reported that there were thirty-five deaconesses in active service and suggested that, as the Union now had sixteen women ministers, and all the deaconesses were doing ministerial work, it was sensible to make them all ministers.[102] In September 1974 the deaconesses voted on whether they supported this move. Although only four definitely wanted to seek ministerial recognition, with others unsure or opposed, they accepted at a meeting in January 1975 that their function had become ministerial.[103] Tributes were paid to the fine work of the existing deaconesses, such as Brenda Partridge, who was undertaking full social and pastoral ministry in Bristol, Elsie Drewett and Winifred Waller at New Addington, Barbara Stanford at Bloomsbury, and Daphne Pearce

---

99   *BT,* 12 February 1970, p.4.
100  *BT,* 25 February 1971, p.6.
101  Minutes of the Baptist Union Council, 15-17 March 1971; *BT,* 25 March 1971, pp.1, 6.
102  N. Morris, *Sisters of the People: The Order of Baptist Deaconesses, 1890-1975, CCSRG Research Paper 2* (Bristol: University of Bristol, 2002), p.32.
103  Deaconess Committee Minutes, 17 September 1974; 23 January 1975; Minutes of the Baptist Union Council, 11 and 12 March 1975.

and Sylvia Owen at West Ham.[104] In June 1975 all serving deaconesses

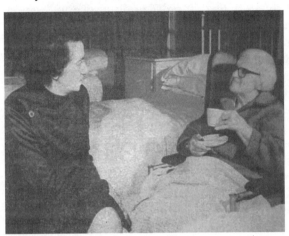

*Barbara Stanford - for over 40 years a pastor in Bloomsbury as deaconess, minister, and hospital chaplain*

were transferred to the accredited list of m i n i s t e r s . Addressing an audience before the Assembly in 1977, as he was about to become Union President, Ernest Payne saw it as significant that 'at last the Christian church is ready to give a much more adequate recognition to women'.[105]

The idea in *Ministry Tomorrow* of groupings of churches was taken up in 1971 by David Russell, who sought to show that this was not a way of reducing ministerial oversight, nor a procedure which would weaken the position of the local church. Rather, he argued, what was being encouraged was associating together. Above all, Russell wanted to counter the sense of gloom about the future and to see churches as effective 'converting agencies'.[106] Some responded that if the denomination was serious about such a vision it should be aiming for an increase rather than a reduction in ministers. The report continued to be discussed, with 55,000 copies sold. It included a graph that attracted attention, since this appeared to show the virtual demise of the Baptist

---

104  *BT*, 15 May 1975, pp.6-7.
105  Cited by Morris, *Sisters of the People*, p.33. Ironically, there were some churches that had been happy to have a deaconess in pastoral charge who would not accept a woman as their ordained minister. I am indebted to Douglas Sparkes for this comment: D.C. Sparkes to the author, 28 February 2004.
106  *BT*, 29 April 1971, p.7.

*Reaching out: some of the congregation at a parade service,
Brickhill Baptist Church, Bedford, 1979*

denomination by the early twenty-first century.[107] Douglas McBain felt
that it 'promoted little more than the idea of a seemly denominational
funeral'.[108] Geoffrey Haden, the Metropolitan Superintendent, who was
critical of the report from the beginning and made this clear to London
ministers, claimed in 1973 that the figure of 400 ministers had
discouraged young people from offering themselves for ministry. By that
time a new examination of the evidence, which Haden welcomed,
suggested that much higher ministerial numbers would be required.[109]

107  *Ministry Tomorrow: The Report of the Commission on the Ministry* (London:
     Baptist Union, 1969), p.6.
108  D. McBain, *Fire over the Waters:Renewal among Baptists and others from the
     1960s to the 1990s* (London: DLT, 1997), p.50.
109  Minutes of the Baptist Union Council, 13 and 14 November 1973; *BT*, 22
     November 1973, p.1.

There were other problems for those contemplating ministry which were quite unrelated to *Ministry Tomorrow*. Considerable disquiet was evident in 1970 about the problems of students in Baptist colleges finding churches. Anthony Giller, house president at Bristol, wrote a letter to the *Baptist Times* in February 1970 entitled 'Give students a chance'. He said he was speaking on behalf of thirty other Bristol students and reported that at that stage in the academic year only two of the students who were seeking settlement were anywhere near achieving it. Some were looking at non-ministerial work. The divine call, said Giller, seemed to be in jeopardy.[110] Giller himself did not enter Baptist ministry at the end of his training. Norman Jones, as Secretary of the Superintendents' Board, replied that for some years there had been a 'cult of youth' but that churches were now asking for pastoral experience. He also explained that there was a total of 120 students and ministers on the 'list', either seeking settlement for the first time or looking to change pastorates. There were 130 churches seeking ministers. Jones accepted that there might be problems in individual cases, for example if students were not able or willing to move to certain areas, or if there was not a match of theological views. However, he sought to reassure the students that in the previous year all the students completing their training in Baptist colleges had settled.[111]

It was one thing to settle in ministry; it was another thing to be satisfied and to stay in ministry. One reason given for feeling unsettled and in some cases leaving the ministry was financial. Kenneth Smith of Bromley, who had taken over from Arnold Clark as Union treasurer, had to deal with the problem for the Union of government control of rises in wages. It proved impossible to persuade the government that ministerial stipends should be exempt from controls because they were already depressed in comparison with other incomes.[112] Correspondence in the *Baptist Times* in the 1970s showed that in many cases the wives of

110  *BT*, 26 February 1970, p.3.
111  *BT*, 5 March 1970, p.6.
112  D.C. Sparkes, *The Home Mission Story* (Didcot: Baptist Historical Society, 1995), p.125.

ministers were in paid employment to make up the needed family income. This had implications for the way in which ministerial families were seen by the churches. Where wives of ministers were in paid employment they could no longer take on the role of 'archetypical mother figure', as one minister's wife put it.[113] Another minister's wife, however, wrote that she could not work outside the home because she had two small children. The family, she explained, was on family income supplement and other benefits. They could not afford a car whereas in the congregation many families had not one but two cars.[114]

A low level of income was by no means the only problem faced by ministers. Barrie Petterson, who had studied at Rawdon College and had begun ministry at Urmston, Manchester, in 1964, spoke in 1971 about his own frustrations in ministry. He said that he had found churches dominated by people who did not have vision, had found it hard to survive financially, and had felt he had no freedom to work outside the church. He had left ministry at that point and, like a number of other Baptist ministers in this period, had begun to work in social care.[115] The article by Petterson provoked differing reactions. Kenneth Witting, who had trained at Spurgeon's and had been in ministry since the 1940s, wrote to say that he did not recognize the descriptions given by Petterson.[116] Gwynne Edwards, by contrast, from Fillebrook, Leytonstone, who was soon to move to Brown Street, Salisbury, spoke of frequent anguish of soul and identified with Petterson's feelings. He knew the frustrations of 'hymn sandwiches' at 11.00 a.m. and 6.30 p.m. and of some visiting which operated at a superficial level, and he also referred to the 'seven-year itch' which resulted in a proportion of ministers leaving pastoral ministry. Despite all this, his sense of calling remained.[117]

There was no doubt that expectations regarding ministry – by ministers and congregations - were changing, and this often created

---

113  *BT*, 31 May 1973, p.6.
114  *BT*, 15 August 1974, p.5.
115  *BT*, 28 January 1971, pp.6-7.
116  *BT*, 11 February 1971, p.9.
117  *BT*, 18 February 1971, p.4.

tensions. Alec Gilmore spoke in 1971 about some of the deeper issues involved in what he called a crisis in ministry. In the wider society, social services seemed to a large extent to have taken over the traditional role of the minister. There was also considerable questioning of belief. Yet Gilmore was not gloomy. He believed that the crisis could be addressed, but doing so required ministers to be more relevant and imaginative in their preaching, and congregations to reappraise church life, including the use of buildings.[118] Some Baptists found it difficult to adjust to the more informal style of church life that was spreading. By 1973 there was talk of ministerial 'dog collars' being 'out of fashion'. Joan Booth, from Eynesford, Kent, was disappointed at this development,[119] but Kenneth Jarvis, minister at Rayner's Lane, Harrow, presumed she had never worn a dog collar or she would know it was not an enjoyable experience. More seriously, he argued that the media portrayed those in dog collars as 'amiable buffoons'.[120]

In an article in 1971 on the theology of ministry, Neville Clark argued for a view of ministry as 'in the world and for the world'; ministry which 'lives on the boundaries' of Church and world.[121] Some who left pastoral ministry for 'secular' employment still saw themselves as ministers. T. Ashworth Taylor, who had been in pastoral ministry during the 1950s and 60s, conducted a survey in 1973, contacting 400 Baptist ministers who had left the ministry. Of the 188 who replied, over one hundred were in education, mostly teaching religious education, and over fifty were in social services. Many made the point that they saw their ministry carrying on.[122] In 1976 John Nicholson noted that some ordained ministers had asked to remain on the accredited list because in certain professions, such as religious education, they were serving as

---

118  *BT*, 22 April 1971, pp.4, 7.
119  *BT*, 5 July 1973, p.4. For the informal style at baptisms, see Cross, *Baptism and the Baptists*, pp.399-400.
120  *BT*, 26 July 1973, p.5.
121  N. Clark, 'The Ministry: A Review and Assessment', *BQ*, Vol.24, No.4 (1971), p.153.
122  *BT*, 8 November 1973, pp.6-7.

ministers.[123] Other ministers became chaplains. Paul Cattermole, who became an army chaplain in 1977, was awarded an MBE for service in Northern Ireland. A few became industrial chaplains, and Thornton Elwyn, who had moved from local church ministry into chaplaincy in 1967, called in 1975 for more discussion in churches about the daily life of people in the congregations.[124] In some cases the link between the church and the world was made because churches were led by lay pastors who had other employment. David Pringle, a college lecturer, led Poynton Baptist Church in the 1970s and church membership grew dramatically from twenty-one to 210 during the decade.[125]

What about ministerial training? The Union's Commission on the Colleges looked at the period 1968-73. Over these years Bristol had an average of 32.3 students, Northern 20, Regent's Park 16.5 and Spurgeon's 53.6. The suggestion was made that the number of colleges be reduced to three, since it was thought 30-35 students were necessary to provide 'academic stimulus and a live Christian fellowship'.[126] It was significant that the Union took the initiative in looking at training, but no action was taken over reducing to three colleges. The most notable innovations in training took place at Northern College, where the Alternative Pattern of Training was pioneered. Michael Taylor had in mind 'not a quasi-academic community but one that is actively engaged in mission in an actual situation'.[127] After the Christological controversy student numbers at Northern briefly fell to single figures. However, the new pattern of training, in which students worked in churches three days a week, proved enormously popular and Northern's numbers reached a record of over forty in the mid-1980s. David Goodbourn, John Nicholson, and Brian Haymes, minister of Mansfield Road, Nottingham,

---

123   J.F.V. Nicholson, *The Ministry: A Baptist View* (London: Baptist Publications, 1976), p.23.

124   *BT*, 13 February 1975, p.6.

125   Sellers, ed., *Our Heritage: The Baptists of Yorkshire, Lancashire and Cheshire*, pp.131, 152. See D. Pringle, 'The Church that Grew', *The Fraternal*, No.173 (May 1975), pp.7-11.

126   *BT*, 16 January 1975, p.1.

127   M.H. Taylor, 'Ministerial Training and Theological Education', *The Fraternal*, No. 164 (May 1972), pp.18-26.

joined the team at Northern.[128] Goodbourn, aged twenty-five, had been responsible for student work at the Baptist Union for two years and had then undertaken educational work as director of the Baptist World Poverty Education Programme. He developed lay training at Northern, working with Methodists and the URC.[129] Church-based training models spread. Increasingly, especially after the removal of the 'age 40' limit, those entering college tended to be people with considerable work experience. This was in tune with the desire on the part of the churches for more experienced people as pastors. Training evolved to meet new situations.

## A 'NEW THING'

The charismatic movement, which grew considerably in 1970s, was marked by speaking in tongues, informal worship, an emphasis on prayer for healing, and a stress on community.[130] In 1973 Douglas McBain reported in the *Baptist Times* on the world-wide growth of the movement, noting that there had been no evaluation of how it had affected Baptist life and urging greater interest in it. He suggested that Baptists needed to share in this 'new thing'.[131] In fact there was discussion in Union committees. David Russell, at the Advisory Committee on Church Relations in September 1971, reported on problems in some churches due to charismatic groups.[132] In that summer, however, a major international charismatic conference, organized by the Fountain Trust, took place in Guildford, and the participation of over thirty Roman Catholics showed that renewal could be inclusive. It clearly reached beyond conservative evangelicals. Indeed, because a Roman Catholic, Kevin Ranaghan, was a speaker at Guildford, Harold Owen of the BRF was wary.[133] Baptists who were involved included McBain, who

128  Shepherd, *The making of a northern Baptist college*, pp.228-53.
129  *BT*, 17 May 1973, p.1.
130  Bebbington, *Evangelicalism in Modern Britain,*, pp.229-48.
131  *BT*, 18 October 1973, p.7.
132  Minutes of the Baptist Union Advisory Committee on Church Relations, 24 September 1971.
133  McBain, *Fire over the Waters*, p.53.

*David Pawson, an early leader in the charismatic worship, conducts an Easter sunrise service on a hill outside Guildford*

became the first Baptist on the Advisory Council of the Fountain Trust, David Pawson of Guildford, and Alan Braybrooks from Bognor Regis. At the Advisory Committee on Church Relations in February 1972, Morris West presented a BCC report suggesting a new approach, as indicated in the minutes: 'It was clear that blanket condemnation of the [charismatic] movement was no longer possible following the Guildford Conference. It would be important to consider how best to keep in touch with those participating in the movement.'[134]

The *Baptist Times* carried a considerable number of letters on the subject. Eileen Parkman from Cippenham, Slough, who became a supplementary minister, said the experience of baptism in the Holy Spirit had revolutionized her life. The secretary of the Buckinghamshire Association, J.C. Webster, noted how renewal was spreading. Lois Chapple, of the BWL, spoke of her 'deeper experience' of the Holy Spirit's infilling, accompanied (without her seeking) by the gift of

---

134 Minutes of the Baptist Union Advisory Committee on Church Relations, 4 February 1972.

tongues.[135] Articles followed by McBain, W.H.T. Richards, a Pentecostal pastor in Slough, and two scholars sympathetic to Pentecostal spirituality, Walter Hollenweger, from Birmingham University, and James Dunn, Nottingham University. One enthusiast, David Gardner from Hastings, claimed many Baptists were discovering the power of the Spirit, and he commended Richards' 500-member congregation.[136] By this time some Baptist congregations were emerging as models of renewal. Jim Graham, who succeeded Pawson as minister of Gold Hill, was seeing growth. Gold Hill was featured in the *Baptist Times* in 1974. Graham reported on congregations of 500 in the morning and 300-400 in the evening. Church membership was just over 300. He described the evening services: 'We have a lot more spontaneity in praise and freedom in worship. It would not be unfamiliar for hands to be uplifted, or to have clapping within the congregation. There would be an opportunity for the Gifts of the Spirit to be used. The main Gift used in the evening services so far has been prophecy…Perhaps the most significant evening service is our evening communion service which would now probably run for two hours with much freedom.'[137]

With no evaluation of renewal among Baptists available, there were requests that the Baptist ministers' journal, The *Fraternal*, might carry an article on the subject. This did not happen, although Stephen Winward, now at the Selly Oak Colleges, Birmingham, and also minister of Victoria Road, Sutton Coldfield, wrote on developments in worship. He spoke of some Baptist churches as 'stimulated, modified and in some cases transformed' by charismatic influence and noted the tendency to have 'open' periods in worship when people were encouraged to contribute praise, prayer, testimony or ministry. For Winward the liturgical and charismatic movements were both seeking the same end, 'the full and active participation of all the people of God in worship'.[138] In 1975 the superintendents commented on 'the growing influence' of

---

135   *BT*, 3 February 1972, p.3; 25 May 1972, p.3.

136   *BT*, 7 December 1972, p.3.

137   *BT*, 5 September 1974, p.7.

138   S.F. Winward, 'Recent Trends and Developments in the Liturgical Movement', *The Fraternal*, No.165 (September 1972), p.11.

the charismatic movement in the denomination. An informal group, serviced by Don Black, the Union's Director of Social Responsibility (later Secretary for Mission), was asked to pursue investigations further.[139] It was intended to seek comment, for instance from someone whose work had been disrupted by charismatic renewal and from a Roman Catholic in touch with the movement. In the event the working group interviewed some Baptist ministers, a House Church leader, and Tom Smail, Secretary of the Fountain Trust. Work continued until 1978, when a report on 'Charismatic Renewal' was received by the Council.[140]

By this time it was clear that there were two distinct streams emerging within charismatic renewal. The report noted a tendency in some charismatic churches 'away from fellowship with other Baptists'. There were acute divisions in some Baptist churches affected by this outlook. The opposite tendency was that those involved in renewal reached out both ecumenically and 'towards their fellow Baptists'.[141] Andrew Walker, in *Restoring the Kingdom* (1985), charted the divisions within the first stream - the House Church movement or Restorationism (expressing the belief that a New Testament model of the church could be restored).[142] *Restoration* magazine began in 1975, edited by Bryn Jones, in Bradford, and Arthur Wallis, who in 1974 wrote: 'I see no future for denominations, but a glorious future for the body of Christ.'[143] In 1976 Jones launched the Dales Bible Week, Harrogate, which was soon attracting 9,000 people. New fellowships began, as people left Baptist and other churches. Saltersgill, a church in the YBA, welcomed

---

139  Minutes of the Baptist Union Advisory Committee on Church Relations, 8 September 1975.
140  Minutes of the Baptist Union Advisory Committee on Church Relations, 27 January 1976; 13 February 1976. Report dated 13 February 1978.
141  'Report to the Council on Charismatic Renewal', 17 and 18 March 1978, in P.S. Fiddes, *Charismatic Renewal: A Baptist View* (London: Baptist Publications, 1980), p.7. The members of the Working Group were Donald McKenzie, Edmund Heddle and Geoffrey Rusling, all representing the Ministry Department, John Briggs and Don Black from the Mission Department, Hugh Logan representing the superintendents, and David Russell. Paul Fiddes joined the Group for the preparation of a commentary, for which he was primarily responsible.
142  A Walker, *Restoring the Kingdom* (London: Hodder & Stoughton, 1985).
143  *Renewal*, No.52 (1974), p.16.

a house church group, and David Tomlinson gave leadership. Later the church left the Association.[144] Tomlinson subsequently became an Anglican clergyman. Terry Virgo's network proved attractive to some BRF leaders. Another example of movement into Restorationism was Basingstoke Baptist Church, led first by Michael Pusey, a BRF member, and then Barney Coombs, who had Brethren and Pentecostal influences and had been a deacon at East Acton Baptist Church.[145] Restorationists tended to reject congregational church government in favour of the authority of apostles and elders. Michael Walker, minister at Elm Road, Beckenham, in the 1970s, spoke of 'a new breed of authoritarians'.[146]

On the other hand, there were many examples of Baptist ministers and members affected by charismatic renewal who were committed to the Baptist denomination. The features within the charismatic movement identified by the 1978 Charismatic Renewal report – for example, committed fellowship, use of spiritual gifts, participatory worship, and responsible giving – all had commonalities with Baptist tradition. The charismatic movement also offered informal expressions of spirituality that mirrored cultural changes. For Baptists as well as others, 'renewal created a Christian version of the counter-culture'.[147] In the 1970s, David Pawson, Douglas McBain, Jim Graham, and the pastor of Beulah, Bexhill-on-Sea, Edmund Heddle (Chairman of the Ministry Main Committee and a member of the Group that produced the Charismatic Renewal report), were prominent Baptist exponents of charismatic renewal. They did not espouse the narrower outlook of Restorationism. The ecumenical stance of the Fountain Trust, of which McBain and Graham became trustees, was important in the 1970s (it closed in 1980). Baptists who attended Trust meetings appreciated the leadership of Tom

144  Sellers, ed., *Our Heritage: The Baptists of Yorkshire, Lancashire and Cheshire*, p.138.
145  P. Hocken, *Streams of Renewal: The Origins and Early Development of the Charismatic Movement in Britain* (Carlisle: Paternoster Press, 1997), p.135; *Renewal*, No.60 (1975-76), p.18.
146  M. Walker, 'Baptist Worship in the Twentieth Century', in K.W. Clements, *Baptists in the Twentieth Century* (London: Baptist Historical Society, 1983), pp.27-9.
147  Bebbington, *Evangelicalism in Modern Britain*, p.233.

Smail, the Trust's Director from 1975. Those who compiled the Charismatic Renewal report met with Smail and welcomed the way he included charismatic experience 'in the one event of Christian initiation' and also the way he gave the experience 'a Christological content'.[148]

It was this view of charismatic experience that Douglas McBain expounded. In a crucial series of articles in the *Baptist Times* in June/July 1975 he spoke of baptism in the Spirit in terms of Christian initiation, with the Holy Spirit and gifts for ministry being received upon initiation into Christ. He also associated this process with its 'sacramental expression' in water baptism.[149] McBain argued against Restorationist thinking and urged positive attitudes within the denomination to renewal.[150] By the end of the decade this message was becoming widely accepted, although the Union would continue to lose members to Restorationism. Charismatic leaders in the mainline denominations

*Douglas McBain*

tried to distance themselves from the unattractive elements within some new fellowships – spiritual superiority, intolerance of women holding office in churches, and heavy-handed leadership. Thus Bob Gordon, the most prominent exponent of charismatic renewal within the URC, speaking to Baptists in 1979 at an Oxfordshire and East Gloucestershire Association conference, claimed that renewal was rarely divisive if wise pastoral guidance was applied. He accepted, however, that some charismatics had 'rather too much brashness for their own good'.[151] In the same year David Russell referred to some charismatically-influenced churches that had broken with the Union and to others which opposed the charismatic movement, but he also pointed to churches where charismatic spirituality had brought new life.[152]

---

148   Fiddes, *Charismatic Renewal: A Baptist View*, p.6.
149   *BT*, 19 June 1975, p.2; 26 June 1975, p.2.
150   McBain, *Fire over the Waters*, p.207.
151   *BT*, 26 April 1979, p.16.
152   *BT*, 26 April 1979, p.8.

## THE TIDE A LONG WAY OUT

There were clear signs of new life and growth in the 1970s and in certain cases this was directly linked with charismatic renewal. In the South East, Gold Hill and Guildford, which with new premises became known as the Millmead Centre, were the primary examples. Gold Hill more than doubled its membership to over 400 from the mid-1960s to 1980. At the beginning of the 1970s there were 350 members at Guildford; by the end there were 600, making it the largest Baptist church in England. The North of England, which had seen considerable decline in many Baptist churches, now began to experience new growth. At Altrincham, Paul Beasley-Murray was seeking to apply

*The new Millmead Centre, Guildford*

some of the Church Growth thinking that had been developed at Fuller Theological Seminary in the USA and which was supported in Britain by the Bible Society. Membership at Altrincham grew from 93 in 1971 to over 200 by 1980. Other Baptist churches in the North which saw growth in this period included Ansdell, Lytham St Anne's, which went from 62 to 198 members under the leadership of Nigel Wright, and Moortown, Leeds, with Ralph Drake as minister, which increased from 223 to 327 members. [153]There was also advance in the South West. A report from Teignmouth, where Ian Burley was minister, spoke of conversions and growth. The church was hiring a local theatre for morning services because the 200-seater building could not accommodate the congregations.[154]

---

153  Sellers, ed., *Our Heritage: The Baptists of Yorkshire, Lancashire and Cheshire*, p.152.
154  *BT*, 26 July 1979, p.12.

*During Richard Hamper's ministry in the 1960s and 1970s Queen's Road, Coventry, became the Christian youth centre for the city.*

In other places, however, churches were struggling. Colin Marchant, an associate minister of the West Ham Central Mission and chairman of the Newham Churches Docklands Group, said that in Docklands 'the church's tide is still a long way out'. Almost all the existing churches had closed and New Beckton Baptist Church was the only church building in nearly six square miles of dereliction.[155] Social problems were increasing, with local authorities worried about young people of thirteen and fourteen drinking alcohol at discos and coming to school with hangovers. Churches became involved - at High Road, Ilford, for example, there was outreach to those who were members of 'skinhead' gangs and to other teenagers, and Queen's Road, Coventry, opened a successful youth centre. Enid Bichard, the Union's former Adoption

---

155   *BT*, 17 August 1978, p.3.

Officer, was appointed as a Christian social worker in the South West Durham Group of Baptist churches.[156] A ground-breaking example of community action was at Bunyan, Kingston-upon-Thames, where the church launched the Kaleidoscope Youth and Community Project under the leadership of Eric Blakebrough. The youth club, advice centre, hostel, and other ministries were featured in two television documentaries, and Blakebrough wrote about his experiences of mission to the drug scene in London.[157] The struggles of the churches to address community problems were producing creative initiatives.

Particular attention was being paid to ministry in multi-ethnic areas. Many Baptists were opposed to the Immigration Act of 1971, which they saw as harsh. It meant that illegal immigrants could be deported without trial.[158] Racial tensions were illustrated in 1973 when a Baptist church in Essex housed in its manse an Asian refugee family referred to them by the Ugandan Resettlement Board when Idi Amin evicted Asians from Uganda. Local residents complained about the Asian family, and the church realized the gulf between its thinking and that of the wider community. Dialogue helped to resolve the problem.[159] There were continued heart-searchings about the extent to which people from various ethnic backgrounds were being integrated into churches. Arthur Dobson, secretary of Braemar Avenue, Wood Green, said in 1973 that he knew of four churches, including his own, that had made great efforts to integrate West Indians, but generally West Indians preferred their own services.[160] Three articles in *The Fraternal* in 1974 offered different perspectives. Donald Hudson, from the West Bradford Fellowship, spoke out of two decades of experience in India with the BMS about sensitivity to other cultures. Donald Monkcom in South Norwood, who had served with the BMS in the West Indies, believed in multi-racial churches but acknowledged that most Black church-goers in Britain were attending Black churches. Donald Cranefield, in Southall, which became home to

---

156   *BT*, 2 April 1970, p.12; 8 March 1973, p.6.
157   E. Blakebrough, *No Quick Fix* (Basingstoke: Marshall Pickering, 1986).
158   *BT*, 28 June 1973, p.2.
159   *BT*, 4 January 1973, p.1.
160   *BT*, 12 July 1973, p.5.

many Asians, encouraged different congregations, including an Asian Christian Fellowship.[161] In 1979 Edwin Robertson, at Westbourne Park, rightly discerned a new Islamic revival and called for greater understanding of Islam.[162]

Within the Union there were initiatives which involved evangelism and social action, especially at local level. It was a compelling conviction of David Russell's that these two things should be seen as indissolubly wedded, and he argued his case in influential articles in 1974 entitled 'The Wholeness of the Gospel'.

David Russell's thinking about the gospel – 'the whole gospel for the whole man in the whole world' – brought a comprehensive theological and practical dimension to the Union's work. His insights were taken up by Associations and in Union developments. Norman Jones was appointed as Head of the new Mission Department and Lewis Misselbrook, who had been engaged in innovative outreach at Chelmsley Wood, Birmingham,

*The Boys' Brigade band from Southall Baptist Church leads a 'Southall Aflame' march in the early 1970s*

was appointed to the Department to encourage evangelism in the churches. He launched through the Department his programme 'Discovering Your Gifts'.[163] Many Baptist churches also had 'One Step Forward' events, during which Bryan Gilbert and others challenged people to take a step in their spiritual journey.[164] Each year the Baptist Youth Movement's 'Time for God' scheme attracted dozens of young people who gave several weeks or months to Christian service. There was redevelopment of church property for sheltered housing, for example through the Baptist Men's Movement's Housing Association. Spurgeon's

---

161  *The Fraternal*, No.169 (February 1974), pp.5-22.
162  *BT*, 20 December 1979, p.4.
163  I am indebted to Bernard Green for material in this section.
164  *BT*, 2 September 1976, p.3.

Homes, which stemmed from C.H. Spurgeon's orphanages, moved their work into smaller units.[165] A physically handicapped-able bodied (PHAB) summer school was run by Geoff Evans, who had been the Yorkshire Association's Youth Officer and was appointed Baptist Youth Officer in Lancashire, with his salary paid by the county authority.[166]

The student population doubled in the 1960s to over half a million and more Baptist ministers became involved in student chaplaincies.[167] Michael Quicke, the Baptist Students' Federation Secretary from 1967, encouraged the BSF groups, but several were losing impetus and it was decided in 1977 to wind up the Federation. Its demise was deeply regretted by Ernest Payne, who had argued for its strategic role.[168] Other changes were taking place in Baptist involvement in higher education. The Union's General Purposes and Finance Committee expressed unhappiness over trends in the Student Christian Movement.[169] After SCM produced a book, *Towards a Theology of Gay Liberation* (1977), Philip Gathercole, minister at Milton, Weston-Super-Mare, interviewed Viv Broughton, an SCM staff member, who in his remarks accused the church of homophobia.[170] Most Baptists in tertiary education were now typically involved in the Christian Unions affiliated to the Universities and Colleges Christian Fellowship (UCCF, formerly IVF). But Payne had been right to stress the BSF's role in nurturing Baptist leadership. In 1979, when Douglas Johnson, IVF General Secretary for forty years, listed well-known 'student' churches, no Baptist churches featured in the list.[171] A number of younger Baptists were tending to drift away from Baptist life.

---

165  *World Outlook*, July 1979, p.25. This became Spurgeon's Child Care.
166  Sellers, ed., *Our Heritage: The Baptists of Yorkshire, Lancashire and Cheshire*, p.139.
167  *BT*, 14 May 1970, p.5.
168  West, *To be a Pilgrim*, p.89.
169  Minutes of the Baptist Union General Purposes and Finance Committee, 6 April 1971.
170  *BT*, 31 March 1977, p.7; M. Macourt, ed., *Towards a Theology of Gay Liberation* (London: SCM, 1977).
171  D. Johnson, *Contending for the Faith* (Leicester: IVP, 1979), p.245. The IVF became the UCCF in 1975.

The wider trend in Britain and elsewhere was towards united action by evangelicals, rather than denominational action. The International Congress on World Evangelization, held in 1974 at Lausanne, Switzerland, had great influence on evangelical thinking about evangelism and social responsibility.[172] Many Baptists supported the Nationwide Festival of Light in the early 1970s, with its attempt to counter 'moral pollution'. Robert (Bob) Archer, minister of St George's Place Baptist Church, Canterbury, believed the campaign had the unanimous support of the local Council of Churches.[173] At a Festival gathering in Trafalgar Square in 1976, 42% of the attenders were Anglican, 22% Baptist and (next largest) 9% Pentecostal or charismatic. Baptist involvement was significant.[174] Not all Baptists, however, enthused about pan-evangelical thinking. Michael Taylor, commenting on Evangelical Alliance discussions about a decade of evangelism, argued that the priority should be responsible participation 'in the ordering and re-ordering of our life together in God's world'.[175] R.V. Moore from Leeds, who had moved south, complained in 1975 that at its spring assembly the Essex Association had featured TEAR Fund, the evangelical relief agency, but ignored the BU/BMS World Poverty Education Programme.[176] Ralph Stephens, for the Association, replied that at the spring assembly Don Black from the Union had been the speaker.[177] Much pan-evangelical consciousness would find its focus in organizations like TEAR Fund and the Evangelical Alliance.

Michael Taylor's concept of participation was being worked out in various ways. On behalf of the Union, Don Black wrote extensively on issues such as world poverty, unemployment, religious education in schools, apartheid in South Africa, and the EEC. Black was able to meet

---

172 This created the Lausanne Movement: see John Stott, ed., *Making Christ Known: Historic Mission Documents from the Lausanne Movement, 1974-1989* (Carlisle: Paternoster Press, 1996).
173 *BT*, 7 October 1971, p.3
174 D.W. Bebbington, 'Baptists and Politics since 1914', in KW Clements, ed., *Baptists in the Twentieth Century* (London: Baptist Historical Society, 1982), p.87.
175 *BT*, 8 February 1979, p.5.
176 *BT*, 30 October 1975, p.5.
177 *BT*, 13 November 1975, p.5.

many political figures, including MPs at the House of Commons and overseas visitors such as Desmond Tutu from South Africa. Ron Goulding, General Secretary of the European Baptist Federation, prepared a booklet, *Baptists in Europe*, to encourage greater European participation.[178] Ronald Allison, a member of Duke Street, Richmond, was appointed Press Secretary to the Queen. For Christians in the arts, the inter-denominational Arts Centre Group was important. The pop singer, Cliff Richard, a member of the Millmead Centre, was involved. Roy Castle, the TV and stage entertainer, attended Gold Hill.[179] Many Baptist Christians who never made headlines saw themselves as called

to live as Christians in the world. S.F. Dean from Romford, a local trade union secretary for the guards at Liverpool Street station, reported that two out of four local union representatives were Baptists. Dean commented that he had often found more understanding at union meetings than at church business meetings.[180] The temperance movement now attracted less commitment among Baptists, but Glenis Mills, a member of Bromley Baptist Church, who was training to be a teacher, was secretary of the

*European friendships: Nell Alexander receives a samovar from Russian Baptists led by Alexei Bichkov*

Beckenham Youth Temperance Council and drew attention to problems related to alcohol.[181] Baptists were operating in varied spheres of society, but fewer were as prominent as had been the case earlier in the century.

---

178  For Ron Goulding, see B. Green, *Crossing the Boundaries: A History of the European Baptist Federation* (Didcot: Baptist Historical Society, 1999), pp.58-67.

179  Developments in the Arts were covered in the magazine *Third Way*, launched in 1977 and edited by a Baptist, John Capon.

180  *BT*, 1 February 1973, p.5.

181  *BT*, 5 June 1975, p.7.

## THE UNION AND THE CHURCHES

David Russell was active at home and overseas in connection with the WCC, the Conference of European Churches, the BWA, and the EBF. He was delighted by the successful 1979 EBF Congress in Brighton. Russell and Alec Gilmore, General Secretary of the United Society for Christian Literature (and chair of the Union's Ministerial Recognition Committee), founded Eurolit, facilitating supplies of books to Baptists in eastern Europe.[182] Under Russell's leadership Union life was re-organized. It was agreed following a report in 1969 that there would be three Main Committees: Mission, Ministry and Administration. Later, in 1970-1, a number of changes of personnel took place. R.W. Thomson, Assistant General Secretary, retired, and Ernest F. Clipsham moved to the pastorate at Cottingham Road, Hull. Norman Jones, appointed in 1971 as Head of Mission, had to retire through ill-health after three years, to be replaced by Don Black. Geoffrey Rusling, Vice-Principal of Spurgeon's College, became Head of Ministry in 1971. J.B. Morris, Head of Administration, died in 1977. Russell's own health was a cause for concern and in 1977 he suffered a heart attack. On the retirement of Gordon Fairbairn, Union legal adviser for over three decades, Richard Fairbairn, his son, became honorary solicitor. It was Richard Fairbairn's vision and persistence that brought the Retired Baptist Ministers' Housing Society into being in 1974, which greatly improved housing provisions for retired ministers.[183] Union activity was evident.

The increasing influence of ecumenical and post-denominational perspectives had implications for the life of the Union and for Baptist identity. Stanley Turl of the West Ham Mission argued that Free Church roots were still important and that Baptists should not pour all their energies into wider ecumenical co-operation.[184] George Mann, a Baptist

---

182  Rusling, 'David Syme Russell: A Life of Service', pp.12-19. In contrast to organizations that used the policy of Bible smuggling, they developed legally negotiated programmes and exports. From 1984 Gilmore was also Director of Feed the Minds.

183  D.C. Sparkes, *Autumn Gold: The Story of the Retired Baptist Ministers' Housing Society* (Didcot: Retired Baptist Ministers Housing Society, 1999).

184  *BT*, 11 January 1979, p.1.

minister, was the Secretary of the Free Church Federal Council from 1970 (having been the Assistant Secretary) and he was followed in 1979 by another Baptist, Richard Hamper, minister of Queen's Road, Coventry. In 1979 the Baptist Union Council discussed what was a common statement by that time, 'I am a Christian first and a Baptist second', and Morris West, President of the Union 1979-80, argued, as had David Russell, for the concept of 'Baptist Christians'.[185] Consumer choice was increasingly governing attitudes to churches. The question being asked by those moving to a new area and visiting churches was often – is this a live church? A sense of Baptist identity was particularly weak among young people and there was discussion in 1973 of a perceived trend towards people being baptized in Baptist churches but not becoming church members.[186]

Baptist identity was also traditionally linked to the church members' meeting. In his booklet, *Baptist Principles*, the third edition of which was published in 1975, Morris West addressed the problem of poor attendance at the church meeting. This was an issue that had been raised throughout the century. West referred to the common practice for members who attended the church meetings to arrive after the opening hymn, prayer and Bible reading, 'in time for the business'. The worship setting, West argued, was essential: the meeting was not one in which a group gathered to do 'the business of the church' (he objected to the widely-used term 'business meeting'), but one in which believers gathered to seek to know and do the will of Christ. Discussion should cover pastoral care, evangelism, the work of the organizations in the church, and societal concerns. The decline of the church meeting was seen by West as one of the reasons for the lack of advance of Baptists. For him, a Baptist church without a regular, well-attended church meeting was something other than a Baptist church.[187] Some Baptist churches, such as Bugbrooke, Northamptonshire, were dropping the name 'Baptist'. An ITV documentary about Bugbrooke in 1974 reported that the chapel had purchased a local manor house for community-based

---

185   *BT*, 22 November 1979, pp.6-7.
186   *BT*, 24 May 1973, p.12.
187   W.M.S. West, *Baptist Principles* (London: Baptist Union, 3$^{rd}$ ed., 1975), pp.14-16.

living.[188] Later, Bugbrooke was to cause the Union particular anxiety, but it was not unusual in moving away from its Baptist roots.

Other churches wished to remain explicitly Baptist, but were experimenting with new forms of congregational life. In 1970 Baptist congregations in Shirley and district, Southampton, came together to form a group with a membership of almost 500, a joint diaconate and a team ministry.[189] E.H. Robertson, at Westbourne Park, London, addressed the problem of small Sunday evening services. He began to link up with a Black church that did not have its own premises. The presence of the members of Mount Zion Spiritual Baptist Church swelled the evening congregations to the extent that Westbourne Park was almost filled.[190] Arthur Liston, North Eastern Superintendent from 1975, who had been minister of Horfield, Bristol (then the largest church in the Union), believed that radical action was needed among the churches. In the early 1970s the Bradford District discussed a team ministry strategy and this led to two new Fellowships with Team Ministries being set up in Bradford in 1975. One of these represented a pioneering effort in inner-city ministry. David Milner, Donald Hudson (a supplementary minister), and two newly-settled ministers from Northern College, John Shaw and Ernest Whalley, formed a team with five churches. Another Bradford group, the South West Fellowship, had four churches and two ministers, but this group ended in the 1980s. Liston was known for his forward thinking, and hoped to encourage more groups, but he died in 1976.[191]

There was a concern by some that genuinely representative team ministry should include women as well as men. Although at Union and local level Baptist leadership was still overwhelmingly male, this situation was questioned. At a conference at Bristol Baptist College in

---

188  *BT*, 4 July 1974, p.2.
189  *BT*, 29 October 1970, p.2.
190  E.H. Robertson, 'That Sunday Evening Service', *The Fraternal*, No.177, October 1977, pp.29-34.
191  Sellers, ed., *Our Heritage: The Baptists of Yorkshire, Lancashire and Cheshire*, p.141-2. A consultation on team ministry was convened at Northampton by the Department of Ministry in 1976 and a report was published: *Team Ministry among Baptists* (London: Baptist Union, 1976).

1977, on 'Men and Women', it was stated that local churches had twice as many women in membership as men, but twice as many male as female deacons. It was also noted that there had never been a woman president of Union.[192] A year later this was rectified. Nell Alexander, a member of Zion Baptist Church, Cambridge, served in 1978-79. She was known for her active involvement in national Baptist life, for example as chairperson of the Union's General Purposes and Finance Committee, and also for her work in the field of drama. At that stage she was one of only twenty women on the Union Council. Many women as well as men were studying through the Union's new Christian Training Programme (CTP) and in 1979 it was announced that over 2,000 students had enrolled in CTP since it began in 1974.[193] A new generation of women was questioning the role of the BWL, and a revised 'Baptist Women's Work' was launched in 1979. The

*Nell Alexander*

number of women in Baptist ministry was increasing, but the *Baptist Times* noted in 1977 that it was 'no secret' that women ministers found it hard to get a call to a first pastorate and equally hard later to move to another.[194] Change in this area was still slow.

One marked change during the 1970s was in styles of worship. Ralph Martin, a lecturer at London Bible College, Manchester University, and then Fuller Seminary, was a leading Baptist scholar writing on worship.[195] Attention was being given to renewing worship through drama, dance and music. The Baptist Music Society, formed in the 1960s, contributed to connecting theory and practice. Graham Kendrick, the son of Maurice Kendrick, the Putney Baptist minister, was

---

192   *BT*, 7 April 1977, p.1.
193   *BT*, 1 March 1979, p.9.
194   *BT*, 28 April 1977, p.1.
195   Cross, *Baptism and the Baptists*, pp.444-6.

to be influential in this field.[196] Kendrick, who later joined the Ichthus Fellowship in London, became the leading writer of new songs. A new Baptist hymnbook supplement appeared, entitled *Praise for Today*, with 100 modern hymns, and many churches began to use *Youth Praise* and *Sound of Living Waters*. Michael Taylor wrote *Guidelines: Variations on a Theme* to cultivate new thinking about the use of different media in worship and the place of gifts such as speaking in tongues.[197] Overhead projectors were introduced in worship. Candles at Advent and Easter began to appear in some Baptist churches. Traditional Baptist mid-week meetings – for prayer and Bible study - were replaced in many churches by home groups. The YBA's Commission of Christian Witness produced widely-used material reviewing issues in worship and fellowship. New forms of musical expression affected thinking about Baptist Assemblies. In 1973 Harry Weatherley, minister at Barrow-in-Furness, urged that Assemblies utilize the musical talents of young people.[198]

Union leaders worked hard throughout the later 1970s and beyond to address the 'them and us' that had been a feature of denominational life. Residential assemblies in Liverpool and then Nottingham were enthusiastically received. Compared to earlier decades, more serving local church pastors were Union presidents in the 1970s, which encouraged the sense of connection between the churches and the Union. Godfrey Robinson, who had built up Main Road, Romford, to over 500 members and then moved to the similarly-sized Bromley Baptist Church, was to have been President in 1972-3, but to the shock of the denomination he died of a heart attack at the age of fifty-seven.[199] His place as President was taken by J.J. Brown, senior minister of the Dagenham Baptist Group. Other presidents were D.H. Hicks, who had

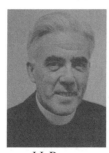

J.J. Brown

---

196  *BT*, 20 April 1972, p.7; cf. G. Kendrick, *Worship* (Eastbourne: Kingsway, 1984).
197  M. Taylor, *Guidelines: Variations on a Theme* (London: Stainer and Bell Ltd., 1973), pp.83-93.
198  *BT*, 24 May 1973, p.8.
199  *BT*, 29 April 1971, p.1.

been the Central Area Superintendent; George Cumming, minister of Victoria, Eldon Road, Eastbourne; Stanley Turl from the West Ham Central Mission; and F.A. Goodwin, minister at Hinckley in the East Midlands. It was always a presidential aim to foster good relationships between the Union leadership and the churches.

A test of Union responsiveness came at the 1977 Assembly when, after the annual report, Douglas McBain asked from the floor that the Union examine 'the reasons for our numerical and spiritual decline'. McBain's intervention took the platform by surprise. Although Ernest Payne was resistant to the motion, after Paul Beasley-Murray questioned the way McBain's point was handled there were hurried consultations and a resolution was passed (with some dissent) that an enquiry group should look at issues of decline.[200] Weatherley, in June 1977, saw 'signs of hope', and this expression was taken up.[201] John H.Y. Briggs, of the History Department at Keele University, chaired the group, and its report, *Signs of Hope,* produced in 1979, represented an important analysis of Baptist life. Decline from 1952 to 1977 was delineated. In 1952 there were 205,013 members enumerated in the *Handbook,* whereas in 1977 there were 147,200. This overstated the decline, since from 1972 churches not in the Union were no longer included. But from 1952 to1977 decline was twenty-two per cent. Some losses were readily explained: the controversies of the early 1970s resulted in fifty-two churches, with 6,210 members, leaving the Union. The commission was concerned about churches that were 'closed in outlook', but concluded that 'there does seem to be ... an unwillingness to be bound by precedent, a new concern to proclaim the eternal gospel in terms relevant to the contemporary scene, and a greater willingness to serve the needs of the community in the name of Christ'.[202]

A few months after *Signs of Hope* was published, a new movement emerged within the Union. Following the 1977 Assembly there were

200  *BT*, 28 April 1977, p.3; 12 May 1977, p.5; P. Beasley-Murray, 'The Assembly: A deliberative body?', *The Fraternal*, No.180 (July 1977), p.19. West, *To be a Pilgrim*, p.191. The group that was set up was the Denominational Enquiry Group.
201  *BT*, 30 June 1977, p.5.
202  *Signs of Hope,* 1979, pp.8, 9, 25, 44.

informal discussions which led to a meeting in February 1978 between Raymond Brown, Principal of Spurgeon's College from 1973 (when George Beasley-Murray moved to the USA), Douglas McBain and Paul Beasley-Murray. A further meeting, with an enlarged group, took place at the 1978 Assembly, and at subsequent discussions in Gorsley, near Ross-on-Wye, the details of the launch of the new movement, with the title 'Mainstream', were agreed. The sub-heading was 'Baptists for Life and Growth', and the first newsletter affirmed wholehearted commitment to the Gospel 'as expressed in the Union's Declaration of Principle' and to the denomination's life and work.[203] The evangelicals who came together in Mainstream wished to avoid separatism and also non-charismatic/charismatic divides. The early Mainstream leadership included Raymond Brown, president, Patrick Goodland from Gorsley, chairman, David Coffey, secretary, Peter Grange of Kirby Muxloe, treasurer, and Jack Ramsbottom of Kidlington, Oxfordshire, secretary of the annual conference. Mainstream was publicly launched at a late-night extra at the 1979 Assembly which attracted 700 people. David Coffey interviewed ministers about experiences of church growth and Paul Beasley-Murray spoke on the same topic. Precious Stones, the dance and drama group from Lewin Road, Streatham, took part. Peter Wortley, Secretary of the LBA, wrote in the *Baptist Times* about the joyful spirit that was evident.[204] Mainstream was a new element contributing to a vision for renewal.

CONCLUSION

The early 1970s was a period of considerable anxiety for the Union. The rate at which ministers and churches were leaving the Union was unprecedented. Not all of this was due to the Christological controversy, although that became a focus. Pressure had been building up within conservative ranks to leave the Union and form a separate Baptist fellowship. In fact those who left tended to go in divergent directions and no enduring anti-Union Baptist denomination was created. By the later

---

203  *Mainstream Newsletter*, No.1 (March 1979), p.1.
204  *BT*, 5 May 1979, p.4.

1970s, the Union had regained a sense of hope. In May 1977 Douglas McBain applauded the crucial role played by David Russell in achieving much greater unity, and he encouraged 'the large hearted toleration, and clear-minded evangelicalism of which we are capable'.[205] Michael Taylor continued to call for a new articulation of Christology in *The Plain Man's Guide to the Incarnation* (1977),[206] but by now the interest of ministers in the Union was in issues of 'life and growth'. The Christological orthodoxy of the Union was widely regarded as settled. Ecumenical debates continued. In 1979 Lighthouse Road Baptist Church, Bow, proposed that the Union leave the WCC. The vote was 2-1 against leaving and an amendment endorsing David Russell's approach was carried 4-1. This, nonetheless, left a dissatisfied minority, and by the end of 1979 nine churches had left the Union, including the 500-member Lansdowne Baptist Church, Bournemouth.[207] There was realism within the Union about the challenges it faced, and the authors of *Signs of Hope* struck a prophetic note with their belief that as new life came to Baptist churches 'the ongoing work of the Spirit may well demand new institutions and structures'.[208] The next two decades were to see this being worked out.

205  *BT*, 19 May 1977, p.2.
206  Michael Taylor, *The Plain Man's Guide to the Incarnation* (Loughborough: ONE Publication, 1977). For the wider Christological debates of the later 1970s see Clements, *Lovers of Discord*, chapter 8.
207  *BT*, 26 April 1979, p.7; Minutes of the Baptist Union Council, 13 and 14 November 1979.
208  *Signs of Hope*, p.36.

# Chapter 10
# 'THE BAPTIST WAY OF BEING THE CHURCH'
# 1980-89

In the 1980s English Baptists witnessed, on the whole, a measure of progress. Growth in membership of churches in the Union in 1984 was the largest for sixty years. Baptisms in that year were 1,900 more than the 1983 figure, with a total of 8,159 people baptized. Mission England, which took place in 1984 with Billy Graham as its leading figure, played an important part in this growth.[1] There was also considerable interest among English Baptists in church growth theories.[2] A further increase in Baptist membership was reported in 1987, against a background of general decline in the mainline denominations.[3] The charismatic movement was an ingredient contributing to growth, although it also brought division. Douglas McBain spoke in 1986 about charismatic renewal's commitment to mission, ecumenical harmony and spiritual growth, but also its authoritarianism, exclusivism and unrealistic expectations.[4] Bernard Green, who became Union General Secretary in 1982, worked with others on crucial issues relating to renewal, inter-church relationships, ministry, mission and Baptist identity. During his time as General Secretary he wrote a monthly 'Yours Personally' letter in the *Baptist Times* as well as regular letters to ministers, theological students, and church and Association secretaries. Introducing a Union

1  *BT*, 6 February 1986, p.1.
2  Church growth thinking was dealt with in *Signs of Hope: Report of the Denominational Enquiry Group* (London: Baptist Union, 1979). See chapter 9 above.
3  *BT*, 31 December 1987, p.7.
4  McBain, *Fire over the Waters,* p.122. The address in which McBain set this out was on the state of renewal.

report on small churches entitled *Half the Denomination* (1983), Green said that his prayer was that it would be used 'to awaken new hope and expectancy' in place of 'frustration and even despondency'.[5] In various ways this change of mood became evident.

## THE SOCIO-POLITICAL CONTEXT

In April 1979, on the eve of the General Election, the *Baptist Times* carried articles by James Callaghan, David Steel and Margaret Thatcher, pressing their respective cases for the Labour, Liberal and Conservative parties.[6] The Conservatives, under Margaret Thatcher, were elected, taking over from Labour, and the 1980s saw the dominance of 'Thatcherism'. With the move of the Conservative Party to the right and the Labour Party to the left, some Baptists took an interest in other political possibilities, especially of the centre. Geoffrey Locks, who had taken over the editorship of the *Baptist Times*, followed the tradition of Walter Bottoms in reporting political developments, and in 1981, with reference to politicians who had left Labour and formed what became the Social Democratic Party (SDP), asked: 'Will the New Labour win Free Church Votes.'[7] 'New Labour' was to become a common term. There was also debate about Christian political parties, an idea supported by W.C.R. (Bill) Hancock, South Eastern Area Superintendent, who undertook considerable research in the political area. At the 1983 election, Ian Twinn, a senior lecturer in Planning and a member of St Andrew's Street, Cambridge, was elected as Conservative MP for Edmonton. He was the only Baptist representing an English constituency.[8] Five other Baptists stood unsuccessfully, four on the Liberal/SDP Alliance ticket. A poll of clergy in 1985 showed that of 115 Baptist ministers who took part, two-thirds supported the Liberal/SDP

---

5    B. Green, introduction, *Half the Denomination* (London: Department of Ministry, 1983), p.i.
6    *BT*, 19 April 1979, pp.4-5.
7    *BT*, 29 January 1981, p.2.
8    D.W. Bebbington, 'Baptist Members of Parliament in the Twentieth Century', *BQ*, Vol.31, No.6 (1986), p.273. Sir (Herbert) Raymond Gower represented a Welsh constituency.

Alliance.[9] Two years later a survey of the Union's Council members found strong support for the Alliance.[10]

*Assembly 1983*

Many Baptists expressed their views on particular issues. In the mid-1980s government proposals to deregulate Sunday shop-opening hours roused strong feelings. A remarkable 50,000 letters of protest were written, many reckoned to be from Christians. A revolt of backbench MPs meant that the government's bill was defeated.[11] Responses to social questions were often articulated by Don Black, who had contributed an enormous amount to Union work since 1970, as Director of Social Responsibility, Head of the Department of Mission, and Secretary for Social Affairs from 1985. Black's view was that when responsibility for social affairs was separated from responsibility for mission, there was a greater opportunity to bring social issues to the attention of the Baptist

9    *BT*, 23 May 1985, p.1.
10   *BT*, 19 March 1987, p.13.
11   *The Times*, 16 April 1986, p.1.

constituency.[12] Especially through articles that he wrote, and also in personal conversations, Black expressed in eloquent terms his concerns about issues such as the deep division in Britain between wealthy 'yuppies' and those struggling with poverty, the world's nuclear weapons, and the government's Nationality Bill of 1981, with its additional limits on immigration to Britain. In 1984, 800 Assembly delegates voted overwhelmingly for a resolution, proposed by Bernard Green, General Secretary, which stated that the existence of nuclear weapons was contrary to the purpose of God. A proposal for an immediate nuclear freeze also gained overwhelming support.[13]

Although Baptists were willing to lobby central government, most Baptist socio-political action was at local level. Baptists who stood in local government elections had greater chance of success than if they attempted to gain a seat at Westminster. In 1985 Rob Wheway, for example, a member of Hearsall Baptist Church, Coventry, became the first Liberal to be elected to the city council for sixty years.[14] Those Baptists who were socially and politically involved were often those most acutely aware of the degree of social fracture in Britain. Riots in the 1980s, in Brixton, Tottenham, Toxteth, Bristol and Birmingham, showed the tension that existed in parts of inner-city Britain. Stuart Cook, at Kenyon, Brixton, and Stanley Woods, JP, in Handsworth, Birmingham were among Baptist ministers reaching out to ravaged communities. In Rochdale, Graham and Kate Routley developed community work among the large Asian population.[15] Some problems were seen as linked with unemployment: in certain areas ninety-five per cent of Black school leavers failed to find jobs. Several Baptist churches assisted in the

---

12    Conversation between Don Black and Roger Hayden, 19 January 2003.
13    *BT*, 7 May 1981, p.2; 10 May 1984, p.7; *Baptist Union Directory, 1984-85* (London: Baptist Union, 1985), pp.37-8. D.D. Black, 'Nuclear Issues – Where are we in the Baptist Denomination?', *The Fraternal*, Vol.207 (April 1984), pp.15-19. The vote for a nuclear freeze was 731 in favour, 16 against and 2 undecided. Unilateral nuclear disarmament by the UK was also supported, but not so decisively: 456 in favour, 227 against and 64 undecided.
14    *BT*, 12 December 1985, p.3.
15    A Report by Graham and Kate Routley, 1 January 1980, Baptist Union Council papers; Sellers, ed., *Our Heritage,* p.149.

organization of work experience. Spurgeon's Child Care, formerly Spurgeon's Homes, opened foster homes and day centres in the 1980s, forging partnerships with Local Authorities and churches. Concern about deprivation led the Yorkshire Baptist Association, through its Secretary, Keith Jones, to arrange consultations on poverty. A Baptist mill-owner from Huddersfield proposed a scheme in 1986 to train unemployed young people as dry stone wallers.[16] There was concern among Baptists to empower the disadvantaged.

But questions were being raised as to what role Christians could play in a society where traditional Christian values were of less and less consequence. Marriage was one illustration of the changes taking place. Before the Second World War there had been roughly one divorce for every hundred marriages annually, whereas during the 1980s the number of divorces per year was nearly half the number of marriages. In 1988, twenty-five per cent of all births took place outside marriage.[17] Other topics generating debate and highlighting dilemmas included the ethical implications of using surrogate motherhood to help childless couples. Homosexual relationships constituted another issue receiving increasing attention. In response to the London Borough of Haringey's policy of encouraging positive images of homosexuality, a London Baptist minister, David Rushworth Smith, at Westbury Avenue, went on a 59-day fast in 1987. Haringey received a mass petition (with 30,000 signatures) from local people asking that its pro-gay policies be re-considered.[18] Within the Church of England there were divisions about policies regarding homosexual relationships, and although Baptists generally supported traditional teaching, there were exceptions.[19]

Several Baptists received honours for their contribution to society. A knighthood was awarded to Godfray Le Quesne, who had distinguished himself in the legal profession, ending his full-time career as Chairman of the Monopolies Commission. As well as being prominent in wider Union affairs, he was the secretary of Heath Street Baptist

---

16   *BT*, 6 March 1986, p.9.
17   P. Clarke, *Hope and Glory: Britain 1900-1990* (London: Allen Lane, 1996), p.366.
18   *BT*, 5 March 1987, p.1, 7.
19   *BT*, 29 January 1987, p. 15.

Church, Hampstead, and was a long-term chairman of the Council of Regent's Park College. In 1980 Tom Fleming, the son of a Baptist minister, received an OBE. Fleming, who spoke at the Union Assembly in 1985, had an illustrious career as an actor and commentator, becoming especially well known for his coverage of royal events. As an actor he was the first person to play the part of Jesus in front of television cameras. Professor Graham Ashworth of Salford University, who was associate minister of Carey Baptist Church, Preston, received a CBE for his services to the Civic Trust of the North-West.[20] Mary M. Towy-Evans, secretary of the Blackheath and Charlton Baptist Church, who served as Moderator of the BCC's Division of Community Affairs Board, was honoured for her contribution as a senior civil servant. At a time when Bryan George, Education Adviser for the Union, was in touch with many Baptist school-teachers who were finding their jobs difficult,[21] Margaret Evans, a member of Ashurst Drive Baptist Church, Ilford, received an OBE for her achievements as head of Seven Kings High School, a 1,200-student multi-cultural comprehensive.[22]

THE UNION AND ITS LEADERSHIP

David Russell, Union General Secretary until his retirement in 1982, was awarded a CBE, primarily for his advocacy of human rights and religious freedom in Central and Eastern Europe. At home, Russell worked hard, as had Payne, to bring the Union and the BMS together in one building, but he did not achieve this during his period as Secretary. However, there was a range of achievements. Russell was able to launch a Strategy Building Scheme in 1980, following the example of Baptists in

---

20   *BT*, 3 January 1980, p.1. Graham Ashworth was Union President in 2000-1.
21   *BT*, 31 October 1985, p.15.
22   *BT*, 16 January 1986, p.13.

Scotland.[23] The purpose was to release finance for capital building schemes by churches and to assist projects of strategic importance. In its first year it raised £75,000.[24] As Joint Chairman of the United Navy, Army and Air Force Board, Russell brought Baptist chaplains more fully into denominational life.[25] Finally, Russell produced *A Call to Commitment*, which built both on his own work, particularly the 'Wholeness of the Gospel', and also on *Signs of Hope*, presenting a challenge and offering proposals for action – in worship and prayer, evangelism, learning, caring, serving and leadership.[26] When David Russell concluded his secretaryship, the *Baptist Times* judged that he had given constructive leadership through his reorganization of the Union and his *Call to Commitment* and had made a notable contribution to Baptist and ecumenical arenas. One critical observer valued his role within the Union in 'restoring the balance of the evangelical view'.[27]

David Russell's successor, Bernard Green, was born in 1925 into a Baptist family near Kettering, went to public school in Wellingborough, and, after working down the mines as a pacifist alternative to military service, studied at Bristol and Regent's Park Colleges. He had highly valued pastoral ministries at Yardley in Birmingham, Mansfield Road in Nottingham, and Horfield in Bristol. While in Nottingham he was a chaplain to students and in Nottingham and Bristol he was involved in local radio broadcasting. In addition, he served on several

*Bernard Green*

23    D.S. Russell, 'Reflections on the General Secretaryship of the BU, 1967-1982' (unpublished), Regent's Park College Oxford, Angus Library, D/RSL/A1, p.14.
24    G.W. Rusling, 'David Syme Russell: A Life of Service', in J.H.Y. Briggs, *Bible, Church and World* (London: Baptist Historical Society, 1989), p.13.
25    Ibid, p.14.
26    Russell, 'Reflections on the General Secretaryship of the BU', p.14; *A Call to Commitment – Baptist Christians through the 1980s* (London: Baptist Union, 1980).
27    *BT,* 22 April 1982, p.2.

Union committees and was a member of commissions looking at 'The Child and the Church' and the future of the Baptist colleges. In April 1980 he wrote, by request, an article in the *Fraternal* on 'What Baptists Ought to be Thinking about in the Next Ten Years'. Green urged, among other things, exploration of the role of Associations in education and training, inspiration, fellowship, evangelism, social responsibility and

*Douglas Sparkes*

prayer; greater co-operation between the Union and the BMS; a critical examination of the life of local churches; and creative involvement in 'the struggles of humanity'.[28] His outline of hopes and aims was well received. In the following year, the Council agreed unanimously that Green be proposed to the 1982 Assembly as the next General Secretary.[29] Bernard Green was elected by the Assembly. Douglas Sparkes, Metropolitan Area Superintendent, was elected Deputy General Secretary, a post which now carried authority to represent the Union as required.

Bernard Green came to his new role committed to the ideal of denominational variety and also personally committed to being in close pastoral contact with the denomination, not operating from a distant head office. Speaking to the 400 people at the Mainstream Conference at Swanwick in January 1982, and probably with an eye to his forthcoming position, he argued that 'the concept that we must gather like to like and all be the same theologically' was stultifying. He affirmed those people lifting their hands joyfully in worship and also those sitting quietly yet rejoicing just as deeply. The Holy Spirit's work could, he suggested, be seen in different ways.[30] In June 1982 he wrote in the *Fraternal* about 'The Way Forward', stressing freedom in fellowship and warning against frustrations over matters such as church members' meetings that were 'leading in some places to authoritarian structures which may produce conformity but threaten true *koinonia*'. Green called for the

---

28    B. Green, 'What Baptists Ought to be Thinking about in the Next Ten Years', *The Fraternal*, No.191 (April 1980), pp.3-6.

29    *BT*, 12 March 1981, p.1.

30    *BT*, 28 January 1982, p.6.

transformation of what had become 'dull routine'.[31] In September 1982 Green reported that he had been engaged in 'talk-back' sessions with ministers and lay people across the country.[32] At the Council meeting in November 1982, Green offered 'signposts', building on the programme set out by David Russell. Green's wider-ranging address encouraged Baptists to direct energy to helping young people; asked for development of special ministries for city and rural situations; expressed hope for a revitalized 'nonconformist conscience' in public affairs; and called for further ecumenical development and renewal of churches and Associations.[33]

The expectation of those examining the life of the Union in the 1980s was that inspirational leadership would help churches to move forward.[34] This was expressed forcibly in 1981 by Douglas McBain in a Mainstream publication, *No Gentle Breeze*, in which he argued that when 'vigorous life in the churches is not reflected in the support they give to their centralised institutions it is essential that the establishment abandons a policy of maintaining the status quo and undertakes one of vigorous self-reform'. It was vital, in his view, that the Council and its committees should become catalysts for change.[35] A leaflet produced by Green in 1985 showed that change was in his mind. Recalling the signposts he had set out in 1982, he gave examples of advance: the appointment of Association missioners; inner city and ecumenical projects; day centres operating in churches; and new-style Association assemblies and family days.[36] Green and Sparkes were assisted by a relatively new team: Bill Hancock as Secretary for Ministry; Paul Mortimore, from Crofton, Orpington, as Secretary for Lay Ministries and

---

31    B. Green, 'The Way Forward', *The Fraternal*, No.200 (June 1982), p.5.
32    B. Green, General Secretary, to ministers and theological students, September 1982. Regent's Park College: Angus Library, Bernard Green papers.
33    'Signposts for Strategy', with Minutes of the Baptist Union Council, 9 and 10 November 1982.
34    Report in November 1980 from the Committee on the General Secretaryship, with Minutes of the Baptist Union Council.
35    D. McBain, *No Gentle Breeze: Baptist churchmanship and the winds of change* (Mainstream, 1981), pp.6, 17.
36    *On the Move* (London: Baptist Union, 1982).

the Christian Training Programme; Tom Rogers, previously at Gillingham, Kent, as Secretary for Evangelism; Don Black as Secretary for Social Affairs; Rita Milne as Secretary for Women's Work; Paul Montacute as National Youth Officer; Bryan George, who had held senior posts in education, as Education Adviser; and Barry Walton, previously at Clarence Road, Southend, as Home Mission Secretary.[37] It was a team with considerable and varied experience.

The vision for a united headquarters for the Union and the BMS, which had been discussed for fifty years, became a reality at the end of the 1980s. This followed protracted discussions about the possibility of redeveloping Church House.[38] Reg Harvey, minister of Regent Place, Rugby, became Secretary of the BMS at the same time as Bernard Green became Union Secretary. The two leaders were long-standing personal friends: both had been in pastoral ministry in the Midlands in the 1950s and 1960s. Both were committed to the 'Wholeness of the Gospel' (David Russell's theme), and to one mission, at home and overseas. In 1984 they issued a joint 'Prayer Call'.[39] They also further developed joint Assemblies for the Union and the BMS. The trend was towards residential Assemblies and Bernard Green spoke in the 1980s of the 'joyous worship', the 'warmth of fellowship', and the increasing numbers of young people at these events. The renewed impetus for a shared head office came against this background.[40]

*Residential Assemblies tried different locations like the Spa Royal Hall at Bridlington*

37    *Baptist Union Directory, 1985-86* (London: Baptist Union, 1986), pp.3-7.
38    For details, see D.C. Sparkes, *The Offices of the Baptist Union of Great Britain* (Didcot: Baptist Historical Society, 1996), pp.45-7.
39    B. Green, General Secretary, to ministers and theological students, May 1984.
40    B. Green, General Secretary, to ministers and theological students, April 1985; May 1988.

*Baptist House, Didcot*

From 1986, the Union's Working Group on Baptist Church House, and a parallel BMS Working Group, met frequently. In 1987 the Union Council agreed that in the light of the expressed wish of both the Union and the BMS to have joint head offices, steps should be taken to dispose of Baptist Church House, which had all the problems of an ageing listed building, and to seek alternative premises which would house a joint BU/BMS headquarters.[41]

Douglas Sparkes undertook on-site searches for suitable premises in London and other places. Then the Union's treasurer, David Nixon, from Wokingham, identified a modern office building in Didcot, Oxfordshire. Didcot, a town of 16,000 people, was not widely known around the country, but was to become a major development area in the South Oxfordshire Structure Plan. After the Didcot offices were recommended by the BU/BMS Joint Working Group (ten in favour, two against and no

---

41    Sparkes, *The Offices of the Baptist Union*, pp.47-8.

abstentions), a historic joint meeting of the Union Council and the General Committee of the BMS was held at Bloomsbury on 18 October 1988. David Staple, General Secretary of the Free Church Federal Council and a member of the Union Council and the Society's General Committee, ably chaired the proceedings. Votes were taken in the two bodies. The Union majority in favour of the move to Didcot was 91% (117 in favour and 11 against), and the BMS majority was 89% (116 in favour and 15 against).[42] When the sale of Baptist Church House and the purchase and equipping of the Didcot offices (called Baptist House) had to be implemented, Bernard Green was ill with a heart attack and Douglas Sparkes acted in his place. Baptist Church House was sold to London Regional Transport and the official opening at Didcot was on 23 September 1989. The move gave the Union, the BMS, and the *Baptist Times* modern offices, with new IT provision, and excellent conference facilities. Money was also released for Home Mission, the Union Bursary Fund and scholarships, the Ministers' Pension Fund, and Baptist Loan Fund facilities to provide help with local church building projects.[43]

Engagement with local churches was emphasized by the Union Presidents. Of the Presidents in the 1980s, six were local church ministers: Fred Wilson, minister of Carey, Preston; Frank Cooke of Purley; Norman Wright of Main Road, Romford; David Coffey from Upton Vale, Torquay, who was the youngest President of the Union to that point; Margaret Jarman of the West Coventry Fellowship; and Colin Marchant of the West Ham Central Mission. There was a move away from the older concept of the presidency as an honour bestowed at the end of a person's career, although this could still be appropriate, as when

*Margaret Jarman, the first woman minister to be BU President*

---

42    *BT*, 27 October 1988, p.7; Minutes of the Council, 8 and 9 November 1988; Sparkes, *The Offices of the Baptist Union*, pp.50-2.

43    Sparkes, *The Offices of the Baptist Union*, pp.52-4; B. Green to the author, 16 February 2004.

David Russell served in 1983-84. There were three lay Presidents in the 1980s: Stanley Browne and David Charley, who had both distinguished themselves in the field of medicine, and John Biggs, a lecturer in chemistry at Hull University. Charley encouraged the trend towards greater social involvement by evangelicals.[44] Margaret Jarman, the first woman minister to be President, contributed to what would be an increasing interest among Baptists in contemplative spirituality. She led prayer retreats and was the first person to chair the Baptist Union Retreat Group, formed in 1988.[45] David Coffey pressed home the theme of 'Bridge-building', calling for dialogue with the Black churches, independent evangelical leaders, and the house church movement. He was concerned that the ecumenical map in England was too small.[46]

While these were constructive developments, there were other sides to Union life. By 1980, Bugbrooke Baptist Church, Northamptonshire, had grown to over 500 people, and although Lewis Misselbrook spoke warmly of its exploration of community, there were complaints that it was splitting up families.[47] Noel Stanton, Bugbrooke's pastor, replying to criticisms by a former member, Mrs L. Mackinney from Margate, asked forgiveness for past imperfections.[48] But allegations of excessive control over members continued. Also, Bugbrooke's relationship with wider Baptist life was virtually non-existent. It was starting new communities close to other Baptist churches without consultation. After protracted correspondence, Bernard Green, Roy Freestone (the Area Superintendent), and Peter Clark (Area Pastoral Committee chairman) met with Stanton and other Bugbrooke leaders in February 1986.[49] In the same period the Evangelical Alliance asked Bugbrooke to resign its

---

44    *BT*, 29 April 1982, p.11.
45    *BT*, 12 November 1987, p.2.
46    *BT*, 1 May 1986, p.1; cf. D. Coffey, *Build that Bridge* (Eastbourne: Kingsway, 1986). Internationally, Coffey co-led, with the Archbishop of York, a British Churches' delegation in May 1986 to the then Soviet Union.
47    *BT*, 10 April 1980, p.1; 24 April 1980, p.4.
48    *Renewal*, No.102, December 1982/January 1983, p.7; No.103, February/March 1983, p.7.
49    Bernard Green, 'Report to the Baptist Union Council', October 1986.

membership.[50] The Union Council in November decided that it was no longer possible to see Bugbrooke as a Baptist church 'in the way in which Baptists have always biblically and theologically regarded it'. It was emphasized that the decision was not made for anti-charismatic reasons.[51] In response to Green's letter conveying this decision, Stanton said it would be seen as the Union preferring 'Baptist tradition rather than living radical life in the power of the Spirit'. Bernard Green stressed that there were 'many churches in full membership of the Union which are experiencing new life in the power of the Holy Spirit and we rejoice in this'.[52]

## THE CHURCH GROWTH MOVEMENT

Paul Beasley-Murray, writing in 1992, identified the same 'new life'. His view was that 'in the 1980s a new spirit of optimism and commitment to church growth and church planting emerged.' One reason for this, according to Beasley-Murray, was Baptist involvement in the church growth movement.[53] In 1978 Derek Tidball, who had been minister of Northchurch Baptist Church, Berkhamsted, and was then a tutor at London Bible College, was involved in organizing the first British Church Growth Consultation, sponsored by the Evangelical Alliance and LBC. The main speaker was Peter Wagner from the School of World Mission, Fuller Seminary, USA.[54] A year later Lewis Misselbrook said that in the mid-1970s it would have been difficult to find a dozen English Baptist churches that were growing steadily, whereas now there were

---

50   See S. Cooper and M. Farrant, *Fire in our Hearts: The Story of the Jesus Fellowship* (Eastbourne: Kingsway, 1991), pp.227-30.
51   Minutes of the Baptist Union Council, 11 and 12 November 1986. At this point Bugbrooke called itself the Jesus Fellowship Church (Baptist).
52   B. Green to N. Stanton, 13 November 1986; statement by Noel Stanton (undated) and comment by Bernard Green, 18 November 1986: papers at Baptist Church House, Didcot.
53   P. Beasley-Murray, *Radical Believers: The Baptist way of being the church* (Didcot: Baptist Union, 1992), p.118.
54   I.M. Randall, *Educating Evangelicalism: The Origins, Development and Impact of London Bible College* (Carlisle: Paternoster, 2000), p.177.

about 200.[55] The inaugural meeting of the British Church Growth Association was at Baptist Church House in 1981, when the speakers included Tidball and an Anglican, Eddie Gibbs.[56] Roy Pointer, a Baptist minister who trained at LBC and did research at Fuller Seminary, was also involved. In 1984, Pointer, then Church Growth Consultant with the Bible Society, wrote *How Do Churches Grow?*, urging churches to deploy leadership, utilize small groups, define evangelistic tasks, and identify members' ministries.[57] Bible Society courses were attended by considerable numbers of Baptists.

An examination of 330 Baptist churches with over fifty members was undertaken by Paul Beasley-Murray, then senior minister at Altrincham Baptist Church, and Alan Wilkinson, Senior Fellow (Administration) in the Manchester Business School. The results were published in 1981 in *Turning the Tide*. This survey found that six out of every ten of the churches in the sample were growing, but that 'in the so-called growing churches, on average, no more than 16 people were being won for Christ in a five-year period'. But the study was intended to go beyond description. It analysed growth against 'seven vital signs' proposed by Peter Wagner: the key role of the pastor as leader, mobilization of the laity, churches of adequate size, homogeneous churches, the use of celebrations, congregations and cells, the use of proven evangelistic methods, and seeing outreach as primary. The study suggested that growing British Baptist churches exhibited most of these signs, although growth was not dependent on size or homogeneity. Beasley-Murray and Wilkinson developed a model of growth that was praised by Wagner for its thoroughness and for the way it integrated 'internal growth with expansion growth; quality with quantity'. These principles were ones that had been developed in the light of experience at Altrincham.[58]

---

55   L.R. Misselbrook, 'Perspective on Growth', *Mainstream Newsletter*, No.1 (March 1979), p.2.
56   *Renewal*, No.95, October/November 1981, p.4.
57   R. Pointer, *How Do Churches Grow?* (Basingstoke: Marshall, Morgan & Scott, 1984), pp.7, 115-41.
58   P. Beasley-Murray and A. Wilkinson, *Turning the Tide* (London: The Bible Society, 1981).

There were, however, queries about the church growth approach. Michael Walker, tutor at the South Wales Baptist College, argued that the temptation was that congregations wanting to escape the depressive atmosphere of decline would shape worship to meet consumer needs. This, he suggested, tended to foster services that cultivated the sense of well-being that the secular world claimed almost as a basic human right. He wrote: 'Using the insights of sociology and market research, it [church growth theory] plots the course of action that will lead to expansion. Goals are set and success is looked for.' As some saw it, the movement did not affirm the traditional Baptist commitment to biblical preaching. Walker quoted the example of a speaker he had heard who had advised ministers to pay less attention to preaching and more to congregational management, on the basis that 'anyone can get up and spout'.[59] Such a statement, however, was not typical of church growth advocates. Others pointed out that the recent growth to be found among Baptists was from a low starting level. Donald Cranefield, LBA President in 1976, observed that churches with 300-600 members half a century earlier now had 30-80 members. 'The graph line', he remarked, 'falls as relentlessly as the tide'.[60]

This raised questions about the place of small churches. The report, *Half the Denomination*, highlighted the fact that half the congregations within the Union had fewer than fifty members and a majority of those had no full-time ministerial oversight. In many rural areas, said the report, church life presented 'a scene of desolation'. Methodists had engaged in wholesale closure of village chapels, while many Baptist causes were composed only of older people. But small churches were to be found in inner-city communities as well as in villages. A considerable section of *Half the Denomination* was devoted to questions about leadership, since many small churches cited 'lack of leadership' as the biggest obstacle to their progress. As with similar Union studies previously, it suggested better use of lay preachers and lay pastors, and

59    M. Walker, 'Baptist Worship in the Twentieth Century', in Clements, ed., *Baptists in the Twentieth Century,* pp.29-30. Michael Walker moved to the college from Elm Road Beckenham in 1981.

60    D. Cranefield, *Survival* (London: p.p., 1976), p.1.

it also called for a move away from the concept of a small church as a scaled-down version of a large one. Bernard Green hoped the report would be used in forward-looking mission, enabling churches to 'abandon false independence or resistance to change so that this important half of the denomination can become a true missionary spearhead'.[61] In the Bristol Association the report led to the appointment of Tom Elsby as a 'consultant' to smaller churches, but in general little action was taken.

There were examples of small and large churches that were growing. Some were newly planted, such as a church in Sussex which started meeting in the home of two medical doctors, David and Helen Skipp, in 1977, and by 1980 had outgrown a youth centre in Haywards Heath with seating for 150 people. Other examples of growth in the South included Locks Heath, Hampshire. The principles of the initial pastorate scheme continued to operate, with a number of new causes receiving financial support from Home Mission to enable them to call a minister.[62] In 1982 the Union launched a church planting initiative.[63] Often individual churches began extension work, in much the same way as in the 1950s. In the Midlands, West Bridgford, Nottingham, under the leadership of Peter Nodding, engaged in starting new congregations.[64] An example of growth in the West Country was Zion, Creech St Michael, which grew from thirty-five members in the early 1980s to 175 by 1986. David Goodyear, the minister, was joined by two others to form a leadership team.[65] In the Northern Association, where there were 224 baptisms in 1985 (more than in any year since 1923), the Association Secretary, David Neil, considered that the Association's churches generally accepted the principles of church growth and renewal.[66]

A different contribution to thinking about growth came in the 1980s from John Wimber, the leader of the Vineyard Christian Fellowship in

61  B. Green, introduction, *Half the Denomination*, p.i.
62  *BT*, 28 January 1980, pp.8-9.
63  *BT*, 17 November 1982, pp.1, 7.
64  Peter Nodding later wrote *Local Church Planting* (London: Marshall Pickering, 1994).
65  *BT*, 11 April 1985, p.7; 6 March 1986, p.7.
66  *BT*, 1 May 1986, p.21.

Los Angeles. Wimber's approach had been influenced by Church Growth, but he came to believe that an essential element of authentic evangelism was 'signs and wonders', as seen in the ministry of Jesus and in the Acts of the Apostles. This came to be known as 'power evangelism' and in 1985 Wimber published a book with that title. The best-known leader within the Anglican charismatic movement, David Watson, of St Michael-le-Belfry in York, gave his backing to Wimber in 1981.[67] Later that year, Roy Pointer contacted Douglas McBain, then director of the newly-formed Manna Ministries Trust, and suggested that Wimber might be invited to visit some Baptist and other churches to talk about ministry in the power of the Holy Spirit. McBain responded, and a series of meetings in Britain took place in 1982. This was followed by an international conference in 1984 in London with the title 'Third Wave', a term used by Peter Wagner to describe a new movement following on historically from Pentecostalism and the charismatic movement.[68]

## 'THE PRESENT MOVE OF THE HOLY SPIRIT'

For many Baptists, what Wimber brought was an intensified form of charismatic renewal. In Lytham St Anne's, Ansdell Baptist Church hosted Wimber and his team for a weekend. When an associate of Wimber's, Lonnie Frisbee, climbed into the pulpit and said 'Come, Holy Spirit', the results were remarkable. Nigel Wright, the minister, later recalled: 'Within seconds the Spirit of God had fallen upon a large proportion of the congregation'. Many of those present began to tremble, speak in tongues and prophesy.[69] Inevitably, Wimber's approach produced widely differing reactions. As Peter Wortley, the LBA Secretary, noted in 1984, some feared that searching for the miraculous

---

67    For David Watson see T. Saunders and H. Sansom, *David Watson* (London: Hodder & Stoughton, 1992).

68    McBain, *Fire over the Waters*, pp.89-96.

69    N. Wright, 'A Pilgrimage in Renewal', in T. Smail, A. Walker and N. Wright, *Charismatic Renewal: The Search for a Theology* (London: SPCK, 1993), p.27. See also, N. Wright, 'A Baptist Evaluation', in D Pytches, ed., *John Wimber: His Influence and Legacy* (Guildford: Eagle, 1998), pp.244-56.

would be a diversion from 'the proper aim of the church to lead people, the healthy as well as the sick, to God and his salvation'.[70] But Wimber had supporters. Brian Butcher, pastor at Banbury, reported that after the 1984 Wimber Conference he and his wife had shared their experiences with the Banbury church and had seen 'God move across the congregation'.[71] Wimber returned to Britain in 1985, attracting 7,500 people to seminars in Brighton, London and Sheffield.[72] Debates about Wimber continued. Max Turner, who was a supplementary Baptist minister at North Bushey, an LBC staff member, and a fine New Testament scholar, argued that documented healings were taking place.[73]

Significant numbers of Baptist churches in England were involved in charismatic renewal by the early 1980s. A consultation took place at Ansdell Baptist Church in July 1981 which drew together fifty Baptist ministers who had an interest in discussing some of the implications of renewal. The small group of ministers in the North West who initiated this consultation described how they had spent time developing a covenant relationship in order to pastor one another. The purpose of the meeting at Ansdell was to 'discuss, pray and explore together concerning the ways in which ministers involved in the present move of the Holy Spirit in renewal can grow together, work together, and discover new depths of commitment to one another'. Jim Graham and Douglas McBain were invited to explore the possibility of their exercising ministries of encouragement and guidance.[74] By 1983 the initial group in the North West had expanded to eight ministers and for a time Douglas McBain gave what Michael Beaumont, the pastor in Sale, called

---

70  *BT*, 15 November 1984, p.2.
71  B. Butcher, 'Wimber at Westminster', *Mainstream Newsletter*, No.19 (April 1985), pp.6-7.
72  *BT*, 14 November 1985, p.6.
73  M. Turner, 'Spiritual Gifts Then and Now', *Vox Evangelica*, Vol.XV (1985), pp.7-64. Turner's most substantial books on pneumatology were *The Holy Spirit and Spiritual Gifts – Then and Now* and *Power from on High* (both 1996).
74  *Renewal*, No.96, December 1981/January 1982, pp.13-14; N. Wright, 'Gleanings from the North West', *Mainstream Newsletter*, No.9 (January 1982), pp.4-6.

'apostolic input into our lives'.[75] Monthly celebrations at Heywood and Sale provided a focus for expressions of charismatic renewal among Baptists in the area.

One influence on thinking about 'apostolic' issues was the Dales Bible Week, where speakers advocated submission to the leadership of apostles and elders. Although some Baptists became interested in 'apostolic input', most did not accept the model of what was then often called 'shepherding'. Haddon Willmer of Leeds University characterized the 'enthusiasm for authoritative Eldership' as a religious form of the 'conservative security-seeking' evident in society.[76] Restorationists, however, viewed their role differently. Bryn Jones and Arthur Wallis, who were major speakers at the Dales, saw the traditional churches as seriously deficient. In 1981 Clifford Fryer, who had been at Lewin Road, Streatham, reviewed Wallis' recently-published *The Radical Christian*, which argued for abandoning inherited ecclesiastical structures. Fryer suggested that established denominations could not afford to ignore the alarm sounded by Wallis.[77] The idea of a 'denominational ceiling', beyond which further development was impossible in historic denominations, was a favourite Restorationist concept.[78] Numerous Baptist churches lost members to Restoration groups. Nonetheless, Trevor Hubbard, Superintendent for the North West, said at the 1982 Assembly that there was evidence of winds of change blowing through the denomination, and that this was in part due to charismatic renewal.[79]

Some of the problems as well as the benefits of charismatic renewal were highlighted by Bernard Green, who was dealing with a number of churches experiencing division. It was reported in March 1982 that charismatic leaders in Witney, Oxfordshire, had closed the Baptist chapel and three associated village causes.[80] In another Baptist church people

75    M. Beaumont, 'Growing together in committed covenant relationships', *Mainstream Newsletter*, No.13 (April 1983), p.3.
76    *Mainstream Newsletter*, No.12 (January 1983), p.7.
77    Clifford Fryer, 'What does God want for his Church', *Renewal*, August/September 1981, No.94, pp.10-11.
78    *Crusade*, January 1981, p.22.
79    *BT*, 29 April 1982, p.5.
80    *BT*, 11 March 1982, p.3.

were told they could only be members if they signed a written covenant promising 'total obedience to the leaders of the church'.[81] A polemical Restorationist book, *Built to Last*, by Ron Trudinger, saw changes at Basingstoke Baptist Church as a move from more traditional structures to biblical patterns.[82] Roger Hayden wrote a thoughtful critique of Trudinger's thinking.[83] Bernard Green spoke in July 1982 about churches that were replacing church meetings with the rule of elders and he argued for the practice of the church meeting from the New Testament.[84] There were numerous discussions about 'When is a Baptist Church a Baptist Church?', and in some cases steps had to be taken where churches developed constitutions that were in breach of the original Trusts. At the 1983 LBA assembly, which attracted 300 people, Green spoke of unhealthy attempts to have instant blessing, prophecies which in some cases claimed to be above scripture, and authoritarian elderships.[85] Green welcomed a wider understanding of ministry that was emerging in the 1980s, but he stressed the importance of commitment to the primary ministry of Word and Sacraments.[86]

Disputes took place among those committed to charismatic ministries. By the 1980s there were at least ten distinct Restorationist networks, including a group of churches which developed out of Basingstoke Baptist Church; Harvestime churches under Bryn Jones; Coastlands, later New Frontiers, led by Terry Virgo; Pioneer, with Gerald Coates as leader; and Roger Foster's Ichthus Fellowship in London.[87] All these groups, each with their own emphases, attracted

81  A. Walker, *Restoring the Kingdom: The Radical Christianity of the House Church Movement* (Guildford: Eagle, 1998), pp.274-5.
82  R. Trudinger, *Built to Last: Biblical Principles for Church Restoration* (Eastbourne: Kingsway Publications, 1982), p.14.
83  R. Hayden, 'Baptists, Covenants and Confessions', in *Bound to Love: The Covenant Basis of Baptist Life and Mission* (London: Baptist Union, 1985), pp.24-36.
84  *BT*, 8 July 1982, p.7.
85  *BT*, 19 May 1983, p.7.
86  B. Green, General Secretary, to ministers and theological students, April 1987.
87  N. Wright, 'The Nature and Variety of Restorationism and the "House Church" Movement', in S. Hunt, M. Hamilton and T. Walter, *Charismatic Christianity: Sociological Perspectives* (Basingstoke: Macmillan Press, 1997), pp.60-76.

people previously within mainline denominations. There were also divisions within local charismatic congregations. In 1981 about 200 people left the Millmead Centre in Guildford, although two years later there was a considerable influx of new members, a new ministerial team and the introduction of two morning services.[88] In Baptist life overall, although the growth in Union membership in 1984 was the biggest for sixty years, total membership in Union churches was still below the 1980 figure, partly because of Baptist losses to the 'apostolic' networks.[89] But some Baptists who went to events like the Dales Bible Week were not convinced by all the claims made there. Alan Pain, minister at Sutton Coldfield, commented in 1983 that he found some of the preaching at the Dales unsatisfactory, but he was glad that about 100 out of his 380 members attended and he hoped for dialogue with Restorationists.[90]

In the early 1980s a number of Baptist churches interested in Restorationism linked themselves with Terry Virgo, prominent examples being Bracknell Baptist Church and Queen's Road, Wimbledon. Others who worked closely with Virgo had previously been Baptists, such as John Hosier, who taught at Moorlands Bible College. When Ben Davies went to Bracknell as minister in 1964 the church was a small village congregation. Sustained growth led to the building of a 1,000-seater building.[91] The tendency was for Baptist churches submitting to 'apostles', such as Virgo, to lessen their involvement in Association life. In 1986 a *Baptist Times* editorial suggested that 'sections of the restoration movement are causing unnecessary spiritual havoc in many of our churches', and considered that in this difficult period Baptists who understood charismatic renewal had an important role to play.[92] Nigel Wright, who from 1987 was tutor in Christian Doctrine at Spurgeon's College, in a key book, *The Radical Kingdom*, probed Restorationist thinking. Wright emerged as the foremost Baptist theological thinker

---

88   *Renewal*, No.105 June/July 1983, p.10.
89   *BT*, 6 February 1986, p.1.
90   A. Pain, 'The Dales Bible Week, Friend or Foe?', *Mainstream Newsletter*, No.13 (April 1983), pp.4-8.
91   *BT*, 2 February 1989, p.7.
92   *BT*, 16 January 1986, p.2.

dealing with ecclesiology and spirituality in relation to renewal. He was critical of the 'rigid and slavish attempt' by some Restorationists 'to decode the New Testament and to bring life into a sterile conformity with it', and he argued for a view of renewal that embraced the whole church.[93] It was such inclusive renewal that most Baptists welcomed.

EVANGELICAL RENEWAL

Charismatic renewal in the 1980s was linked, at least in part, to wider currents of evangelical renewal. There was a growing evangelical identity among Baptists, as Paul Beasley-Murray has argued, which meant that they benefited from 'the general evangelical renaissance in England'.[94] This renaissance, evident since the 1950s, was given fresh energy in the 1980s by the appointment of the Director of Youth for Christ, Clive Calver, aged thirty-four, as General Secretary of the Evangelical Alliance. Under his leadership, from 1983 to 1997, the Alliance grew rapidly. In the early 1980s the number of individual EA members was 900-1,000, and by the mid-1990s individual membership reached 50,000. The number of churches in membership grew from under 1,000 to almost 3,000.[95] Calver was keen to unite the evangelical community and the historic evangelical identity of Baptists meant they responded to this enterprise. In 1984 Bernard Green, as part of his concern that the Union should accept those with differing doctrinal positions and different approaches to ecumenism, met with the new EA leadership.[96] Other pan-evangelical organizations, such as Tearfund, also attracted the support of many Baptist congregations and individual members. Doug Balfour, General Director of Tearfund from 1995, was a member of a Baptist church. John Briggs, Head of the History Department at Keele University, whose own background included

---

93    N. Wright, *The Radical Kingdom* (Eastbourne: Kingsway, 1986), pp.19, 140. For aspects of spiritual experience, see N. Wright, *The Fair Face of Evil* (London: Marshall Pickering, 1989).
94    Beasley-Murray, *Radical Believers*, p.118.
95    Membership Statistics for the Evangelical Alliance, produced in 2000: held in the EA offices. About a quarter of the churches in membership of the EA are Baptist.
96    B. Green to the author, 16 February 2004.

involvement in evangelical bodies such as Crusaders, the Inter-Schools Christian Fellowship, and the Cambridge Inter-Collegiate Christian Union, considered that in many respects Baptists provided a bridge between ecumenical and evangelical movements.[97]

Even before Calver's appointment, several Baptist leaders were involved in the EA and were among those seeking to draw evangelicals together.[98] In September 1981 fifty-two evangelical leaders, drawn from most of the major denominations and evangelical groupings in England, met to discuss the Evangelical Alliance and future evangelical co-operation. A further conference was held in September 1982. One Baptist who presented a paper in September 1981, A. Morgan Derham, recalled that in the late 1960s, when he was EA General Secretary, he had not believed bridges could be made between separatist and broader evangelicals. This, however, was now happening. Another Baptist who contributed to the consultation process was Raymond Brown, Principal of Spurgeon's College. At the 1982 conference, David Watson spoke about his evangelistic missions and festivals, seeking to show that he upheld biblical ecumenism. Two of the speakers at these conferences who represented the independent evangelical position, Peter Lewis from Nottingham, and Robert Horn, had both been Baptist Union ministers but had left the Union in the 1970s. Whereas the 1960s and 1970s had seen separatist thinking exercising considerable influence, a new mood of co-operation was emerging.[99] It was this new spirit which Calver would foster and which many Baptists welcomed.

In parallel with and drawing from the fresh initiatives within broader evangelicalism, Mainstream was seeking to give a higher profile to 'life and growth' in the Union. Membership of Mainstream was through subscription to the *Newsletter*, initially edited by Paul Beasley-Murray.

---

97     J.H.Y. Briggs, ed., *Faith, Heritage and Witness* (London: Baptist Historical Society, 1987), p.63-4; F. Bowers, 'John H.Y. Briggs MA, FSA, FRHistS: An Appreciation', in A.R. Cross, ed., *Ecumenism and History: Studies in Honour of John H.Y. Briggs* (Carlisle: Paternoster Press, 2002), pp.1-20.

98     Randall and Hilborn, *One Body in Christ*, p.280.

99     Notes of Evangelical Leaders' Conferences, 9-11 September 1981; 22-24 September 1982, held in the EA Offices, 186 Kennington Park Road, London SE11 4BT; cf. Randall and Hilborn, *One Body in Christ*, pp.280-1.

At a meeting of the Mainstream executive in March 1982, David Coffey, Mainstream secretary, who became the Union's Secretary for Evangelism in 1988, outlined the positive contribution Mainstream had made to the denomination. He considered that evangelicals were being taken more seriously, were better informed, and had a stronger representation on the Union Council. The Mainstream executive judged that there was a need to be clearer about Mainstream's aims, such as 'seeking to express the breadth and variety of evangelical life within the Denomination'.[100] At one stage in the early 1980s, all the members of the Mainstream executive were members of the Union Council.[101] Mainstream's leadership was well aware that theirs was not a homogeneous movement. The majority of participants, Douglas McBain suggests, belonged to the traditional evangelical section represented by Raymond Brown, president of Mainstream. A second group was charismatic, with McBain himself a leading figure. Thirdly, there were those such as Paul Beasley-Murray who were seeking to forge a progressive (though not necessarily charismatic) evangelicalism.[102] Beasley-Murray argued for the place of charismatics within Baptist life, noting that at Mainstream there were 'more hands raised than ever seen at all Baptist Assemblies put together'.[103]

The boundaries between these groups within Mainstream were not fixed. B.R. White, Principal of Regent's Park College, who spoke at the first Mainstream Swanwick Conference in January 1980 and joined the Mainstream executive, did not fit neatly into one of the three categories. White gave a profoundly challenging address at Swanwick, later published as *Opening Our Doors To God*, in which he argued for an appreciation of the activity of the Holy Spirit in the liturgical and charismatic movements, urged that the Lord's Supper should be central to spirituality, and made a powerful appeal: 'Can you not hear him summoning us to give ourselves to that worship which feeds the hunger

---

100   Minutes of the Executive Committee of Mainstream, 22 and 23 March 1982: Mainstream archive, held by Adrian Argile.
101   D. Coffey, 'Mainstream', *Mainstream*, No.63 (September 1998), p.5.
102   McBain, *Fire over the Waters*, pp.108-9.
103   *Mainstream Newsletter*, No.7 (April 1981), p.1.

---

of God's people for him, not only a hunger for programmes, not a hunger for theology only (though I believe theology is vitally important)...but a hunger for him.'[104] Similarly probing themes were taken up at the 1981 Swanwick conference by the Union President, Stanley Browne. Other participants at the 1981 conference included David Russell, George Beasley-Murray, Jim Graham, John Briggs, Graham Ashworth, and Myra Blyth, who was soon to become BCC Youth Secretary. Lewis Misselbrook noted the testimonies from Neville Atkinson of Stockton-on-Tees, Michael Flowers (consultant at the Leeds Royal Infirmary), Anne Wilkinson of Altrincham (Youth Secretary for Christian Aid), John Freer (a solicitor and lay preacher), Mali Browne (a recent President of the BWL, and the wife of Stanley Browne), and Tom Rogers of Gillingham.[105]

Some wanted more. McBain suggested in 1981 that it was largely from churches affected by charismatic spirituality that candidates for ministry in many denominations, including the Baptist Union, were coming, and he argued that the charismatic movement had the potential to renew Baptist life. McBain wrote: 'It is all too easy for the negative forces of ecclesiastical inertia to kill off enthusiasm among the people of God. I understand why it is that some Christians despair of the very institutions in which they were nurtured...I do not share their pessimism...What I am advocating is not a contracting out of our present responsibilities but the most determined contracting into them.'[106] Mainstream continued to embrace both charismatics and those cautious about the movement. At the 1982 conference, speakers included Bernard Green, Fred Wilson, Bill Hancock, Douglas McBain and Michael Eastman, leader of the Frontier Youth Trust and a member of Main Road, Romford.[107] Following this conference, the Mainstream executive discussed tensions that had been evident, due partly to different perspectives on how to stimulate change. Raymond Brown circulated an article by Tom Smail which suggested that the charismatic movement had

---

104  B.R. White, *Opening our Doors to God* (Ilkestone: Mainstream, 1980), p.16.
105  *BT*, 29 January 1981, p.6.
106  McBain, *No Gentle Breeze*, pp.14, 32
107  *BT*, 28 January 1982, p.7; McBain, *Fire over the Waters*, pp.108-9.

to die,[108] but this view did not gain much support, and the *Mainstream Newsletter* affirmed: 'Some of us in Mainstream are enthusiastic towards the charismatic movement, others much less so, but we are committed to accepting one another in one fellowship for life and growth.'[109]

These sentiments were in tune with those of wider evangelicalism and it was not surprising that some Baptists became deeply involved in pan-evangelical enterprises. Ian Coffey, the brother of David, who had been at Earl's Hall, Southend, and then with Saltmine Trust, became the EA field director in 1988 and spoke of the need for a 'theology of diversity' within evangelicalism.[110] The same approach was evident at Spring Harvest, started in 1979 as a modern version of Keswick by Clive Calver and Peter Meadows, whose field was communications. Five years later Spring Harvest was Britain's largest Christian Convention. By 1988 about 50,000 people were participating, with meetings being held over three weeks in the Easter period on sites at Minehead and Skegness. Speakers were drawn from charismatic and non-charismatic camps, from historic denominations and from new churches. Several Baptists were speakers in the 1980s: Alan Redpath, Jim Graham, David Coffey, Paul Beasley-Murray, Ian Coffey, Steve Chalke of Oasis Trust, and Stephen Gaukroger of Stopsley, Luton. One-third of those attending Spring Harvest were Anglicans, one-third were Baptists and one third were from other denominations.[111] Many Baptists were finding their identity in pan-evangelicalism.

---

108 Minutes of the Executive Committee of Mainstream, 22 and 23 March 1982: Mainstream archive; cf. *Grassroots*, Vol.8, No.1 (1982); McBain, *Fire over the Waters*, pp.113-14.

109 'Statement by the Mainstream Executive', *Mainstream Newsletter*, No.10 (April 1982), p.1. During the 1980s about 2,000 copies of the *Mainstream Newsletter* were produced.

110 J. Edwards, 'The Evangelical Alliance: A National Phenomenon', in S. Brady and H. Rowdon, eds., *For Such a Time as This* (London: Scripture Union, 1996), p.53.

111 *BT*, 22 April 1982, p.1; 10 May 1984, p.15; 27 March 1986, pp.1, 2; P. Beasley-Murray, 'Renewal in Baptist churches', *Renewal*, No.130 (March 1987), pp.27-8; McBain, *Fire over the Waters*, p.135.

ECUMENICAL PILGRIMAGE

Others hoped that a new ecumenical identity might be forged. The ecumenical '1980 Group' published a pack in 1981, 'Baptists and the Covenant', and over 500 were sold.[112] The Fellowship of Baptist Churches for Covenanting (FBCC) was formed at a meeting in October 1981 which represented fifty-four churches. The FBCC, whose first moderator was Chris Ellis, Swindon Central Church, stressed that its members were loyal to the Baptist Union while seeking to take steps towards covenanting with other denominations.[113] In 1982 the national covenant scheme was accepted by the URC and the Methodist Church, but narrowly rejected by the Church of England, and discussions about covenanting ended.[114] The ecumenical impetus, however, continued. British Council of Churches' leaders, among whom were Baptists such as Basil Amey, the BCC Assistant General Secretary, engaged in re-thinking, and the BCC's 1984 spring Assembly resolved to consult member churches about 'a process of prayer, reflection and debate together centred on the nature and purpose of the church in the light of its calling in and for the world'. This 'Inter-Church Process' (ICP) was launched in May 1985.[115] It offered hope of a broader expression of unity, including not only Roman Catholics but also Black-led churches.[116] Bernard Green was in favour. From 31 August to 4 September an ICP conference was held at Swanwick, with fifteen Baptist Union representatives participating. This conference marked a shift from co-operation to commitment, articulated in the Swanwick Declaration, *Not Strangers but Pilgrims*.[117]

---

112 R. Nunn, chairman of the '1980 Group', circular letter of 14 October 1981.

113 *BT*, 5 November 1981, p.1; Cross, *Baptism and the Baptists,* p.263.

114 *BT*, 27 May 1982, pp.1 and 6; 8 July 1982, p.1; 15 July 1982, pp.8-9. The FBCC came to an end as from 1 October 1982: C.J. Ellis to FBCC member churches, personal members and friends, August 1982: in papers held by Roger Nunn.

115 *BT*, 23 May 1985, p.3.

116 C.J. Ellis, *Together on the Way: A Theology of Ecumenism* (London: British Council of Churches, 1990), pp.4-5.

117 *Not Strangers but Pilgrims: Report of the Swanwick Conference, 31 August to 4 September 1987* (London: ICP, c.1987).

Baptists were engaged in exploring the ICP over the next two years, in parallel with discussions going on in other denominations. In December 1987 Green wrote to all Union churches to invite full discussion of a proposal that the Union join the ICP. He also corresponded with superintendents, colleges, individual churches and ministers. Churches were asked to respond with a view to a full discussion at the Council in November 1988, with the March Council preparing proposals for a major debate at the 1989 Assembly.[118] During 1988, study, discussion and prayer about the Process took place in Associations. In September 1988 a document about the thinking thus far was sent to the churches, followed by a further document in which Bernard Green answered ten major questions that had been asked. The

*The March 1989 Council considers proposals for the 1989 Assembly. This was the last Council meeting at Southampton Row.*

---

118   B. Green to churches in the Union, December 1987, cited by Cross, *Baptism and the Baptists*, pp.278-9.

Advisory Committee on Church Relations produced a commentary.[119]
Baptists were also involved in consultations about the ICP through the
EA. At a meeting of the EA's executive in June 1988 two Baptists,
Robert Amess, minister of Duke Street, Richmond (and later EA
chairman), and Ian Coffey, reported that the BCC had requested the EA's
involvement in providing written comments and criticisms in connection
with the ICP proposals. It was agreed that Amess, Coffey and Kenneth
Prior, an Anglican, would take this forward.[120]

Baptist worries about the proposed new ecumenical bodies, Churches
Together in England (CTE) and the Council of Churches for Britain and
Ireland (CCBI), had to do especially with Roman Catholic involvement.
The *Baptist Times* of 16 February 1989 contained letters from some who
were unhappy – Michael McGill at Green Street Green, Kent; Peter Clark
at Leamington Spa; and Colin Frampton at Springfield Gardens,
Upminster, Essex. On the other hand, Douglas Sparkes, Deputy General
Secretary, spoke about how much Baptists could gain.[121] Derek Tidball,
Senior Pastor at Mutley, Plymouth, reported that the issue had been
discussed at the Mutley church meeting. The majority had been in favour
of participation but others had been unsure and some were opposed.[122]
The contrasting attitudes of evangelical ministers were highlighted by
articles in March 1989 in which Michael McGill said 'No' and Michael
Bochenski from Blackburn said 'Yes' to participation in the ICP.[123] At
the Council later in the month, the vote indicated very strong backing for
participation; it was decided that a two-thirds majority was necessary at
the Assembly to carry the proposal.[124] Bochenski then set out more fully
his reasons for a 'yes' vote: the basis and aims of ICP, the success of

119 'Churches Together in Pilgrimage: A Commentary by the Baptist Union Advisory
    Committee on Church Relations on the revised proposals of the Inter-Church
    Process' (January 1989). See Minutes of the Advisory Committee on Church
    Relations, 15 March and 23 September 1988.
120 Minutes of the Executive Committee of the Evangelical Alliance, 22 June 1988.
121 *BT*, 16 February 1989, p.15.
122 *BT*, 23 Feb 1989, p.5.
123 *BT*, 9 March 1989, pp.10-11; 16 March 1989, pp.8-9.
124 Minutes of the Baptist Union Council, 14 and 15 March 1989; *BT*, 23 March 1989,
    pp.1 and 13.

local ecumenism, and evident common ground with Catholics.[125] Morris West, an experienced ecumenical figure, stated that a 'yes' vote would not commit any local Baptist church to ecumenical involvement; conversely a 'no' vote would not inhibit local commitment.[126]

About 1,400 delegates were present at the 1989 Assembly, which was held in Leicester. The vote took place on 19 April, with John Briggs of Keele University, as chairman of the Advisory Committee on Church Relations, presenting the resolution and urging that delegates vote in favour of membership of the new ecumenical bodies. Briggs stressed that the basis of belief of the new bodies was faithful to the New Testament and he argued that the recovery of evangelical confidence within

*BU President, John Biggs, introduces the ICP debate at Assembly. John Briggs, ready to propose the resolution, is on the extreme left.*

ecumenical circles in the past thirty years meant that this was not the time to retreat into a Baptist ghetto. Douglas McBain, now Metropolitan Area Superintendent, seconded the resolution. An amendment by Anthony Jones of Millom, Cumbria, proposed that Baptists should opt for associate membership in the new bodies. This position was opposed by Hugh Cross, Ecumenical Officer for England for the BCC, who described it as 'Laodicean' – neither hot nor cold. The amendment failed. Sixteen delegates spoke in favour of the resolution, including former Union Presidents such as Fred Wilson of Preston who commended the ICP because its emphasis on the local church marked a 'return to Baptist principles'. Eleven speakers opposed the resolution, including Daniel

---

125  M. Bochenski, 'Churches Together in Pilgrimage', *Mainstream Newsletter*, No.32 (April 1989), pp.2-4.
126  *BT*, 23 March 1989, p.5. For the wider context, including the publication of *The Next Steps for Churches Together in Pilgrimage*, see D. Palmer, *Strangers no Longer* (London: Hodder & Stoughton, 1990), pp.69-80.

Connoll of Burnley, a former Roman Catholic. The voting was seventy-four per cent in favour, 1,035 voting for the resolution and 364 against.[127]

*The ICP debate: Fred Wilson at the 'Yes' microphone,*
*with a queue of delegates waiting behind him*

The vote caused considerable heart-searching among those who opposed participation in CTE and CCBI. Writing in the *Baptist Times* in May 1989, Michael McGill pointed out that those who dissented represented twenty-five per cent of the Union and stated that he was considering his own position.[128] By November 1989 thirteen churches had left the Union, and more followed later. Some of the churches leaving had in any case little meaningful relationship with the Union. In November 1989, the *Baptist Times* listed the names of sixty-five churches which had asked the Union to note that they dissociated themselves from the decision that the Union should be in full membership of the new bodies. At the Union Council meeting that month, George Beasley-Murray remarked that as someone who had been involved in much ecumenical work he was in the ironic position of being a deacon of a church that had dissented from the Union's decision, and he observed that Roman Catholic involvement was a key issue for many Baptists. Ruth

127   *BT*, 27 April 1989, pp.1, 8-9.
128   *BT*, 18 May 1989, p.11.

Matthews, who had long ecumenical experience – she and her husband, John, had led the Tabernacle Baptist Church, Swindon, into becoming an ecumenical congregation in the 1970s - drew attention to the important role which Black-led churches would play in future inter-church developments.[129] This aspect attracted much less attention, but was of great significance.

The 1980s also saw ecumenical progress at WCC level. In 1974 the Faith and Order Commission of the WCC, meeting in Accra, Ghana, produced a document, *One Baptism, One Eucharist and a Mutually Recognized Ministry* (1974). There were further discussions, for example at the Fifth WCC Assembly, in 1975 in Nairobi. A crucial stage in the discussions about baptism came in 1979 in Louisville.[130] Morris West played a critical role on the Faith and Order Standing Commission and his arguments helped to shape the final version of *Baptism, Eucharist and Ministry* (*BEM*), which was produced at Lima in 1982. It was agreed at Lima that the text should be sent to the churches of the WCC for their responses. *BEM* was published in more than thirty languages and sold nearly a million copies worldwide, becoming the most widely-discussed ecumenical document of the twentieth century.[131] The Baptist Union response was based on comments from Associations, ministers' fraternals, superintendents, churches, colleges and individuals.[132] Baptists welcomed the *BEM* statement that 'baptism upon personal profession of faith is the most clearly attested pattern in the New Testament documents', but the Union's response objected to *BEM*'s affirmation that any practice that might be interpreted as 're-baptism' must be avoided. This was 'wholly unacceptable in its present form', since it prevented an

---

129  *BT*, 23 November 1989, p.13.
130  W.M.S. West, 'Towards a Consensus on Baptism? Louisville 1979', *BQ*, Vol.28 (1980), pp.232-9.
131  K. Clements, 'The Larger Context: Morris West, Servant of World Ecumenism', pp.19-29, in West, *Baptists Together*.
132  Minutes of the Baptist Union Advisory Committee on Church Relations, 19 October 1982; Minutes of the Council, 10 and 11 November 1982. For responses see Cross, *Baptism and the Baptists*, pp.274-5.

individual coming to the conviction that Christian obedience required believer's baptism.[133]

Issues of baptismal policy were often discussed locally. Baptists such as Gethin Abraham-Williams, Ecumenical Officer/Executive Secretary to the Milton Keynes Christian Council, were giving leadership in local ecumenism. In 1983 Keith Jones, Secretary of the Yorkshire Association, produced an important document, *Baptismal Policy in LEPs*, arguing for LEP guidelines on baptismal policy that recognized the churchmanship of those in partnership.[134] Some LEPs, such as Southgate Church, Bury St Edmunds, where Jonathan Edwards was minister, operated baptismal policies which were not constitutionalized.[135] However, any new LEP with Baptist participation had to submit its proposed constitution to the Union's Advisory Committee on Church Relations to ensure that principles such as the church meeting were safeguarded. Jones' work was utilized by the Union's Working Group on LEPs, WORGLEP, an ACCR sub-group. The ACCR, then chaired by Neville Clark of South Wales Baptist College, did not wish to expose Baptist divisions over ecumenism. In 1984 WORGLEP produced a report, *With Charity and With Conviction*, compiled by Douglas Sparkes, which encouraged Baptist participation in LEPs, provided Baptists were able to teach believer's baptism.[136] In an ecumenical setting there would be infant baptisms, but Baptist ministers had no obligation to conduct these. A WORGLEP enquiry about baptism, sent in 1987 to seventy-one LEPs, produced forty-one responses. These indicated the ways in which Baptists

---

133  *Baptism, Eucharist and Ministry*, Faith and Order Paper No.111 (Geneva: WCC, 1982), p.4; 'Baptist Union of Great Britain and Ireland', in M. Thurian, ed., *Churches respond to BEM: Official responses to the "Baptism, Eucharist and Ministry" text*, Vol.1, Faith and Order Paper 129 (Geneva: WCC, 1986), pp.70-1; Cross, *Baptism and the Baptists*, pp.275-8. Some of the matters that worried Baptists were not in the text but in the official 'commentary'.

134  K.G. Jones, *Baptismal Policy in LEPs: A Discussion Document* (Leeds: YBA, 1983, revised 1989).

135  Cross, *Baptism and the Baptists*, p.303. Southgate Church was Baptist, URC and Anglican. Jonathan Edwards went in 1991 to Station Road, Orpington. In 1998 he became South Western Area Superintendent.

136  D.C. Sparkes, ed., *With Charity and With Conviction* (Didcot: Baptist Union, 1984), pp.12, 14.

were dealing with issues – particularly the question of baptism – raised by the ecumenical pilgrimage.[137] There were other matters to be resolved, but freedom to practise believer's baptism was often central.

## MINISTRY AND LEADERSHIP

In parallel with the growth of ecumenical ministries there was progress in Baptist ministry. Numbers coming out of training were increasing in the early 1980s. Estimates were that fifty-one people would enter ministry from the Baptist colleges in 1980, fifty-seven in 1981 and sixty-four in 1982. There was an annual loss of about fifty-five, about half through retirement and death in service. The number of churches seeking ministers was increasing. Support for initial pastorates created new ministerial opportunities, with eighteen initial pastorates being supported in 1982. About forty churches now had an assistant minister or were looking for one, which represented a considerable increase in the number of team ministries.[138] The ability of churches to support more ministers was partly due to the underlying growth in prosperity in this period.[139] Discussions about ministerial supply and demand continued throughout the 1980s. The prediction in the later 1980s was that the buoyant state of applications to Baptist colleges, the increasing numbers of ministers of other denominations wanting to enter Baptist ministry, and ministers returning from overseas, might mean that newly trained ministers would find it harder to settle. Thought was given to abolishing the supplementary ministry.[140] Perspectives on ministerial openings were in marked contrast to the thinking in *Ministry Tomorrow* (1969).

Thinking about training also changed, especially as more mature students entered colleges. In 1989 the average age of students entering Spurgeon's was 32.4 years and three-quarters had already served as

---

137  D.C. Sparkes, 'The "Rebaptism" Issue', unpublished paper (January, 1988).
138  See Donald Black, 'Ministerial Supply and Demand', for Baptist Union Council, 26 September 1980; *BT*, 4 June 1981, p.2.
139  For figures see A.H. Halsey and J. Webb, eds., *Twentieth-Century British Social Trends* (Basingstoke: Macmillan, 2000), p.328.
140  *BT*, 28 April 1988, p.17.

assistant ministers, elders or deacons. About a quarter were from Baptist backgrounds and eighty per cent saw themselves as charismatic.[141] Paul Beasley-Murray, Principal at Spurgeon's from 1986, developed the Spurgeon's Adaptable Leadership Training Programme (SALT). The Spurgeon's staff in the 1980s included Frank Fitzsimmonds, vice-principal, succeeded by Michael Nicholls, with Peter Manson directing pastoral studies. At Northern, Michael Taylor became Director of Christian Aid in 1985, and was succeeded by Brian Haymes. Ernest Whalley further developed Northern's congregational-based mode of training. Research flourished at Regent's Park under the principalship of B.R. White, who was the denomination's foremost scholar in the field of Baptist history. Rex Mason, an outstanding communicator and a fine Old Testament scholar, who had previously taught at Spurgeon's, was senior tutor at Regent's Park,[142] and Malcolm Goodspeed, minister at Woolwich, was appointed tutor in mission and lay training, partly in response to the *Half the Denomination* report.[143] At Bristol, Morris West, a leading ecumenical statesman, was Principal, and from 1977 Keith Clements, of Downend, Bristol, was tutor in theology.[144] LBC had several Baptists on the staff, including Donald Guthrie (whose *New Testament Theology* was published in 1981), Mary Evans, Peter Hicks, Jack Ramsbottom, Derek Tidball, and Peter Cotterell, Principal from 1990.[145]

Debates continued about women in ministry and some within the Union leadership feared that the issue might cause a split in the Union.[146] Shirley Dex, lecturer in economics at Keele University and a member at Newcastle-under-Lyme, stated in 1987 that women leaders, including

---

141  *BT*, 21 December 1989, p.10.
142  Rex Mason published several books in the 1990s. He brought together preaching and Old Testament study in *Preaching the tradition: Homily and hermeneutics after the exile* (Cambridge: CUP, 1990).
143  *BT*, 3 July 1980, p.7; 21 Feb 1985, p.1.
144  N.S. Moon, *Education for Ministry: Bristol Baptist College, 1679-1979* (Bristol: Bristol Baptist College, 1979), pp.96-7.
145  Randall, *Educating Evangelicalism*, chapter 9.
146  Douglas Sparkes to the author, 28 February 2004.

women ministers, were often made to feel invisible.[147] Of the 225 members of the Union Council in 1985-6, only twenty-seven were women.[148] In 1988 David Pawson addressed the subject of women in leadership in an interview at the Mainstream conference, pronouncing that 'leadership is male' and that there was a need 'to break the effeminate image of the Church of God in this country'.[149] Anne Mansfield from West Bridgford responded in the *Baptist Times* that it was not the ministry of women that would deter people from joining churches but the lack of love and sensitivity characterizing remarks such as Pawson's.[150] Paul Beasley-Murray and B.R. White, as Mainstream leaders and Principals of colleges training women and men for ministry, stressed Baptist affirmation of women as pastors, and spoke of women who had been 'martyrs, heroines and saints'.[151] David Butler, of Devonshire Avenue, Southsea, by contrast, argued that it was churches led by men that were growing.[152] John Nicholson, North Eastern Superintendent, replied that there were also growing churches led by women and noted that Baptists believing in biblical principles reached differing conclusions on this topic.[153] Jane Hassell, minister at Victoria Park, Bow, commented that a predominantly male leadership had not brought 'revival growth' in the past hundred years.[154]

Attention was also given to ministry beyond the local church. There was a concern to enable Area Superintendents to give effective leadership

---

147  *BT*, 22 October 1987, p.6. See also S. Dex, 'The Church's Response to Feminism', *BQ*, Vol.31, No.7 (1986), pp.320-5. The whole of this issue of the *Baptist Quarterly* was devoted to issues connected with women in ministry. The contributors were Edward Lehman, Shirley Dex, Margaret Jarman, Ruth Matthews, Carol McCarthy, and John Briggs.
148  For further details see A.R. Barker, 'Women's Roles in the Baptist Churches', Westminster College, Oxford, MTh thesis (1996), pp.24-6.
149  *BT*, 28 January 1988, p.10. See his later book: D. Pawson, *Leadership is male* (Guildford: Eagle, 1997).
150  *BT*, 18 February 1988, p.13.
151  *BT*, 3 March 1988, p.11.
152  *BT*, 11 August 1988, p.11.
153  *BT*, 18 August 1988, p.15.
154  *BT*, 28 September 1988, p.15. See also J. Hassell, 'My Best Men are Women', *Mainstream Newsletter*, No.24 (January 1987), pp.7-9.

in mission. Area reorganization created a Western and a South Western Area. During the 1980s new appointments were made in each of the Areas. In the North, Keith Hobbs (North West), who followed Trevor Hubbard, and John Nicholson (North East), were both deeply involved in ecumenical affairs. Gwynne Edwards (South West), Roger Hayden (Western), and Peter Tongeman (South East), who became superintendents in 1986, came from Geoffrey Reynolds' Area (Southern) and were influenced by the ideas he formulated about the leadership role of superintendents. Roy Freestone (Central) was a powerful ecumenical influence on the Superintendents' Board. The West Midland Area was served by Neil Hall, whose wife, Rosalie, was also a minister. Eddie Pilling, in the East Midland Area, David Harper in the Eastern Area, and Arthur Thompson, in London, concentrated their attention on local ministerial and congregational issues. A major emphasis was on pastoral help for ministers and Bernard Green said in 1987 that the superintendents were dealing with a range of problems, including higher levels of ministerial marriage breakdown.[155]

Several Associations appointed Association Ministers in the 1980s and other new ministries emerged. In some cases these new developments were due to the recognition that the tasks expected of superintendents were too great. David Harper and Roger Hayden, before they were superintendents, raised issues in the Council which led, in 1978, to the first review of the superintendency. A number of changes took place, including the replacement of Area Committees by Area Pastoral Committees. Greater emphasis was placed on pastoral care for ministers, through superintendents and the Area team.[156] In parallel with (or in some cases anticipating) wider Union re-thinking, local initiatives were taken and teams were developed. The Northern Association was served by Edgar Wright in the 1970s. Association appointments in the 1980s included Gordon Thomas in Berkshire; David Keenan in Devon and Cornwall; Graham Wise in Hertfordshire; Michael Ridgeon in Kent;

---

155  *BT*, 9 April 1987, p.17. There was earlier discussion about marital problems among ministers at the Ministry Main Committee, 5 February 1981.
156  'Report of the Working Group on the General Superintendency to the Baptist Union Council', November 1978; D. Harper to the author, 2 February 2004.

Patricia Hinchsliff in Lancashire and Cheshire; Peter Wortley in London; David Neil in Northern; and Keith Jones in Yorkshire. The YBA was the first Association to appoint a missioner: Harry Weatherley moved in 1983 from South Parade, Leeds, to take up this post.[157] Other initiatives included Steve Flashman being seconded by the Union for music ministry, and Steve Chalke establishing Oasis Trust, with help from Home Mission. Initially Oasis Trust provided accommodation for homeless young people, but other social work developed. In 1988 (after three years of operation) the Trust had thirty-two people working full time.[158]

Variety was also evident in lay ministry. Declining involvement in the Baptist Women's League led to its closure, the replacement being a National Council of Baptist Women, with Yona Pusey as a leading figure in national and European women's work.[159] The *Baptist Times* had several women writers, notably Brenda Forward and Gwenda Bond. There was a stress on the creative arts, with Greenbelt, a trans-denominational Christian arts festival, attracting 28,000 people each August Bank Holiday.[160] The medium of dance was used by the Tyndale Dancers, from Tyndale Baptist Church, Bristol. David Goodbourn argued that Family Church needed re-shaping, and advocated dramatic all-age worship.[161] To emphasize broadening thinking about ministry, the Lay Preachers' Federation became the Federation of Lay Ministries.[162] The high quality Christian Training Programme courses were popular, with most new students being aged 25-40. Lay pastors, preachers and deacons all benefited. Frank Cooke, of Purley Baptist Church, set up a trust to help with lay training.[163] Increasing numbers of lay people became involved in Christian counselling and prayer for healing. A Union Health

---

157   *BT*, 4 October 1984, p.17; Sellers, ed., *Our Heritage: The Baptists of Yorkshire, Lancashire and Cheshire*, pp.154-5.
158   *BT*, 18 February 1988, p.4.
159   For Europe, see Y. Pusey, *European Baptist Women's Union: Our Story, 1948-1998* (Oakham: EBWU, 1998).
160   *BT*, 21 August 1980, p.6; 18 September 1980, p.4.
161   *BT*, 16 January 1986, p.12.
162   *Baptist Union Directory, 1985-86* (London: Baptist Union, 1986), p.13.
163   *BT*, 31 January 1980, p.11.

and Healing Advisory Group, chaired first by Dr Stanley Thomas, a missionary with the BMS for thirty-one years, and then by Sheila Smith, a professional counsellor, produced publications in the 1980s and held national and regional conferences. In 1982 the Group's *Bulletin* welcomed the interest in the ministry of healing.[164]

Discussion in the 1980s about how worship could be more inclusive highlighted the needs of members of Baptist congregations with learning and physical disabilities. In 1981, the International Year of Disabled People, some of the worship at the Union Assembly was led by two people in wheelchairs, Sandra and Richard Creed.[165] The Union's Physically Handicapped Able Bodied Residential Course had a long

*Enthusiastic worshippers at a BUild conference*

waiting list.[166] Camberley Baptist Church reported in 1982 on ministry which it offered for disabled people. A number of those worshipping at Camberley were in wheelchairs and four had recently been welcomed into membership after baptism.[167] At Chipping Norton, Gerald Force was involved in ministry to adults and children with learning difficulties. He described teaching groups in his church that might include some children who were unable to speak or hold a

---

164  Roy Freestone, former Central Area Superintendent, to the author, 27 February 2004; *Baptist Health and Healing Bulletin*, No.11 (1982), p.1.

165  *BT* 30 April 1981, p.5.

166  *BT*, 13 August 1981, p.6

167  *BT*, 4 March 1982, p.3.

pencil.[168] Faith Bowers, convenor of the Union's Working Group on Mental Handicap and the Church, reported in 1985 on an ecumenical conference that had taken place, partly at the Group's initiative, to share experiences from different denominations. This event, held at the headquarters of the charity, Mencap, identified major concerns: the need to communicate properly with those who had learning disabilities and the need for an adequate theology in this area.[169] The Union's Working Group led to the formation of BUild, the Baptist Union initiative with people with learning disabilities.[170]

## INITIATIVES IN MISSION

The increasing diversity of British society in the 1980s presented its own set of challenges. The multi-faith, multi-ethnic background was illustrated when Jim Chauhan was appointed by the West Midland Association to work in mission in the region. He was born in Kenya, was a Hindu by family background, and was a member of a West Midlands Baptist church. Some Baptist churches were now Black-majority churches, one example being Small Heath, Birmingham. The Small Heath minister, W.A. (Bill) Dixon, was white, but the number of Black ministers gradually increased. Desmond Gordon, for example, who trained at Bristol, served with the BMS in Trinidad from 1974-9 and then became minister at Church End, Finchley, London. Another Black minister, Glenford Gordon, from Birmingham, who also trained at Bristol, became pastor at Acock's Green, Birmingham, in 1988. The growth of Black-majority churches of various denominations led to the founding in March 1985 of the West Indian Evangelical Alliance (WIEA), later the African and Caribbean Evangelical Alliance (ACEA), with Philip Mohibir as chairman. A congregation of 450 people attended its launch, at Rye Lane

---

168   *Mainstream Newsletter*, No.7 (April 1981), pp.11-12.
169   *BT*, 17 October 1985, p.4.
170   F. Bowers, 'The Story of BUild', *The Fraternal*, Vol.242 (April 1993), pp.7-9. See also F. Bowers, ed., *Let Love be Genuine: Mental Handicap and the Church* (London: Baptist Union, 1985; A. Cross, *Baptism and the Baptists*, pp.450-3.

Chapel, Peckham. A report in the EA's *Idea* in 1985 noted that the WIEA was seeking to represent about 1,500 local churches.[171]

In 1988 Philip Mohobir was succeeded at the WIEA by Joel Edwards, a pastor in the New Testament Church of God, who had studied at LBC.[172] Edwards spoke of 2,000 Black-led churches that had little contact with white churches.[173] Although most of the growth that had brought about this situation was among those whose roots were in the Caribbean or Africa, significant ministry was also taking place through and among people whose background was elsewhere. After training at Spurgeon's, V. Fred George, from Sri Lanka, settled at East Barnet in 1969. Delvin Knower, also from Sri Lanka, came to Spurgeon's after study in America, and then served in three pastorates. Home Mission funded workers in Birmingham, Bradford, and Forest Gate and Clapham in London. In Birmingham, Small Heath opened an Advice Centre for Asians. Many Baptists co-operated with other Christians in inner-city initiatives. Two Baptists, Colin Marchant from the West Ham Central Mission and Michael Eastman from the Frontier Youth Trust, were among the speakers at an event in 1981 when five urban mission agencies launched the Evangelical Coalition for Urban Mission (ECUM), with Eastman as Secretary.[174] Marchant observed that ECUM drew younger evangelicals, especially those concerned about radical discipleship. He noted the role of American writers like Ronald Sider and John Howard Yoder.[175] ECUM was launched on the day riots erupted in Brixton and Toxteth, and concern about these riots led to the establishment of the Archbishops' Commission on Urban Priority Areas.[176]

Writing in the mid-1980s, Colin Marchant found hopeful signs in the city. He described the emergence in inner-city areas of London of hundreds of new churches, many Black, some Asian and others multi-

---

171  *Idea*, Summer 1985, p.3.
172  J. Edwards, *Lord, Make us One – but not all the same!* (London: Hodder & Stoughton, 1999), chapter 3.
173  *Idea*, Summer 1988, p.7.
174  *BT*, 30 April 1981, p.3.
175  C. Marchant, *Signs in the City* (London: Hodder & Stoughton, 1986), pp.93, 107, 124.
176  T. Chester, *Awakening to a World of Need* (Leicester: IVP, 1993), p.162.

racial. Baptists were active, with Stephen Peake in Leyton one example of a Baptist minister re-opening a closed church, and in February 1984 the LBA called a consultation on church planting.[177] In Merseyside, the Merseyside and Region Churches Ecumenical Assembly (MARCEA), in which Keith Hobbs (North Western Superintendent from 1989) was deeply involved, had encouraged the growth of relationships and trust across traditions, and this enabled the churches to respond to the Toxteth riots.[178] Marchant noted that many emerging inner-city churches were 'baptistic', stressing conversion, community, freedom in worship, and the authority of scripture.[179] Anglicans were also involved. John Stott, the foremost Anglican evangelical leader, saw ECUM as probably the most important evangelical initiative of recent years.[180] Michael Eastman had an influence on the major Anglican report, *Faith in the City*, produced in 1985. Indeed Robert Runcie, Archbishop of Canterbury, remarked at the National Evangelical Anglican Congress in 1988 that momentum for *Faith in the City* had come from evangelicals linking theology with worship, witness and social action.[181]

By 1988, when Colin Marchant was Union President, he was able to speak to the Assembly about having lived through a revolution in East London. In order to introduce Assembly members to aspects of the inner city, he organized walking tours, for example to Kenyon Baptist Church, Brixton. Kenyon had experienced decline, but in the early 1980s Christians from the Caribbean brought new life. Jamaican-born Gladstone Davidson, the church secretary, spoke of the Kenyon church as his home. Other Assembly visits were to Docklands (West Ham Central Mission), Kingston, Southall and King's Cross.[182] In his Assembly address, Marchant recalled that when he went to West Ham in 1965 he found decline and depression. Much had changed: there were now more

---

177  Marchant, *Signs in the City*, pp.88-9.
178  I am grateful to Keith Hobbs for this observation. For more see D. Sheppard and D. Worlock, *Better Together* (London: Hodder & Stoughton, 1988).
179  *BT*, 4 October 1984, p.12.
180  *Third Way*, February 1982, p.9.
181  R. Steer, *Church on Fire: The Story of Anglican Evangelicals* (London: Hodder & Stoughton, 1998), p.330.
182  *BT*, 28 April 1988, pp.1, 2, 3.

Muslims than Methodists, and Baptists were outnumbered by Hindus and Sikhs. Mission had to recognize this new situation. Emphasizing that inner-city mission also involved issues of justice, Marchant stated: 'In a black church you can't just sing hymns and forget that some of your congregation got roughed up last night and your kids are unemployed.'[183] Marchant related how Plaistow Baptist Church, in Lawrence Hall, had seen six new churches planted, while in Newham nearly sixty new churches had started in the previous fifteen years.[184] Although many of these new churches were not Baptist, Bernard Green noted that the 1988 Assembly had a large percentage of first-time delegates, quite a number from new churches that had recently joined the Union.[185]

*Assembly Choir, 1988*

Although the inner city was attracting considerable attention, other initiatives were taking place. Baptists were heavily involved in Billy

183  *BT*, 28 April 1988, pp.10, 14-15.
184  Ibid.
185  B. Green, General Secretary, to ministers and theological students, May 1988.

Graham's Missions, nationally in 1984 and in Sheffield in 1989. The total attendance at the 1984 stadium meetings across the country was over one million people, and approaching 100,000 responded to Graham's appeal.[186] These events gave significant impetus to local evangelism. A song book, *Mission Praise* (1983), was produced, which came to be used in many Baptist churches. Baptists were also active in the Nationwide Initiative for Evangelism (NIE), which Donald English, President of the Methodist Conference in 1978-9, chaired until 1983, when some of the work of NIE was passed to the BCC Standing Committee on Evangelism. NIE came into being partly as a result of an initiative by the BCC. At the Dedication Service for NIE, in January 1979, 120 Christian leaders, including Baptists, gathered for a service in Lambeth Palace Chapel. Donald English believed that 'the leaders of most of the Christians in England took a decisive step towards reconciliation and stronger trust within the body of Christ'.[187] The NIE event that had the highest profile was a National Assembly in September 1980 in Nottingham.[188] The Baptist Union Mission Department was represented by Don Black and Lewis Misselbrook. Black found the Assembly remarkable, and hoped it would be an incentive to deeper mission.[189]

Throughout the 1980s Baptists engaged in varied expressions of local mission, especially involving younger people. Bernard Green, like David Russell, was convinced that the front line of mission was the local church; the task of the Unions and Associations was to undergird, encourage, and provide resources for the churches.[190] As one example of significant local advance, under the fine preaching and pastoral ministry of Michael Quicke, from 1980, the congregation at St Andrew's Street Baptist Church, Cambridge, more than quadrupled, a centre was opened

---

186   G. Reid, *To Reach a Nation* (London: Hodder & Stoughton, 1987), pp.56, 61.
187   An Address given at the Dedication Service of the NIE by Donald English, NIE Papers. See R. Whitehead and A. Sneddon, *An Unwanted Child?: The story of NIE* (London: BCC/CCBI, 1990).
188   51% were Anglicans, 12% were Methodists, 11% were Baptists, 10% were URC, 4% were Catholics and 12% were 'others' – including Brethren, Pentecostals, Independents and Black-majority churches.
189   Report on NIE, Minutes of Mission Main Committee, 29 September 1980.
190   B. Green to the author, 16 February 2004.

which served 4,000 people each week, including those who were homeless and jobless, and the full-time church staff team grew to fourteen.[191] In 1982 John Perry, minister at Cippenham, Slough, became the Co-ordinator of Partnership Missions, which facilitated teams of people, of all ages, taking part in mission exchanges between Britain and North America. Other forms of ministry were undertaken by Task Force teams of young people. Terry Dunnell, the Union's Youth Officer, was one of those active in making connections with Baptist young people's fellowships.[192] The Task Force teams were available to help Home Mission churches and in 1986 twenty-five churches had 150 young people working with them. A year later Bernard Green noted a growth within Baptist churches in the number of young people turning to Christian faith.[193]

The Yorkshire Baptist Association, with Keith Jones as Secretary, initiated audits of local neighbourhoods around churches as part of the YBA's Advance '87 Programme. The Church of England was also utilizing parish audits. Using these ideas, the Union developed Action in Mission, known as AIM, which offered resources for churches seeking to engage in mission. It was launched at the 1988 Assembly.[194] Tom Rogers, Union Secretary for Evangelism, and Don Black, Secretary for Social Affairs, jointly promoted AIM, stressing that it involved both evangelism and social action, areas that had sometimes been divided from one another. Indeed churches were urged to concentrate on the aspect in which they had been weak, whether this was evangelistic or societal. In this way AIM was an agent of change in Baptist life, cutting across previous prejudices about priorities in mission. Part of the scheme was that a small team from outside the church that was using AIM came to assist in assessing mission possibilities. As Bernard Green noted in February 1988, AIM owed much to the vision of Tom Rogers; his untimely death meant that he was not able to develop it in the Union as he had hoped. Nonetheless, by 1989 about 600 Baptist churches were

---

191  M.J. Quicke, *360-Degree Preaching* (Carlisle: Paternoster Press, 2003), p.13.
192  The Alliance of Baptist Youth (ABY) replaced the Baptist Youth Movement.
193  B. Green, General Secretary, to ministers and theological students, February 1987.
194  *Action in Mission Evaluation* (Didcot: Baptist Union, 1990).

sharing in AIM, and baptisms and church growth was to result. David Wilcox, of Abingdon, was one minister who spoke of AIM as a catalyst for advance in Christian service.[195]

## BAPTIST IDENTITY

Issues of Baptist identity, which were both national and international, did not arise in the context of overall Baptist decline. Although some churches left the Union over ecumenical issues, more churches were joining than were leaving. Booklets published by the Union on 'Baptist basics', on 'Baptist heritage', and on 'Evangelism', sold in large quantities.[196] In 1982 giving to Home Mission reached record levels. A year later Rex Mason, chairman of the Home Mission Fund working group, did raise concerns about the financial situation of the Fund,[197] but when John Biggs took over from Mason he discerned 'signs of hope'.[198]

*Baptism at Gretton, Northamptonshire, 1988*

Alongside Union initiatives there was international advance. At the fourteenth Baptist World Congress, held in Toronto, Canada, in July 1980, over 20,000 people from ninety-three countries were registered.[199] There was considerable BWA concern to support witness in Eastern Europe, and David Russell was very active in this area. By the end of the decade, with communist governments collapsing in many countries,

---

195 *BT*, 28 April 1988, p.9; B. Green, General Secretary, to ministers and theological students, February 1988; F. Bowers to the author, 4 March 2004.
196 B. Green. General Secretary, to ministers and theological students, May 1983.
197 *BT*, 19 March 1981, p.2.
198 Sellers, ed., *Our Heritage: The Baptists of Yorkshire, Lancashire and Cheshire*, p.158.
199 *Baptist World*, July-August 1980, p.5. This represented a peak of congress attendance. The 1985 Congress, in Los Angeles, attracted about 8,000 people. Many Southern Baptists attended their own Convention instead of the BWA Congress.

European Baptists faced new opportunities. Following the death in 1988 of Gerhard Claas from Germany, who was General Secretary of the BWA from 1980, Denton Lotz, an American who had spent fifteen years in Europe, became General Secretary. Under Claas and then Lotz the BWA became more truly international, with Baptists from the non-Western world increasingly taking leadership.[200] The BWA Youth Congress in Glasgow in 1988 attracted more than 7,000 young people, with the British Baptist Youth Officer, Paul Montacute (President of the BWA Youth Department), central in planning this event.[201]

But challenges continued. L.G. Champion, former Principal of Bristol College, gave a lecture at the annual meeting of the Baptist Historical Society in 1979 in which he argued that new structures of church life were needed 'as an effective means of communicating the

gospel and sustaining both faith and fellowship amid the radical changes occurring in contemporary society'. He called for 'a clearer, more coherent and more widely accepted theology than prevails among us at present'.[202] A group of five Baptist ministers responded to this challenge. They were Keith Clements, tutor at Bristol College, Richard Kidd of Botley, Oxford, Paul Fiddes, tutor at Regent's Park College, Roger Hayden of Haven Green, Ealing, and Brian Haymes of Mansfield Road, Nottingham. The

*Paul Fiddes*

work of this group resulted in *A Call to Mind* (1981), which looked at the issues of secularism, Christian ministry, hope, the Christian faith within the context of other faith communities, and the Church. In his essay, 'On Being the Church', Brian Haymes commented: 'Theological reflection is ... not a luxury for the few but a necessity for all. It may be difficult, even uncongenial and disturbing at times, but it is essential for the life of

200  I.M. Randall, 'Pro-existence: The BWA in the 1980s', in BWA volume (forthcoming).

201  Minutes of the BWA Executive Committee, 7-9 March 1989: Falls Church, Virginia, USA, BWA offices, BWA Archives.

202  L.G. Champion, 'Evangelical Calvinism and the Structures of Baptist Church Life', BQ, Vol.28 (1980), p.206.

the Church'.[203] From the end of the 1980s, Paul Fiddes, the Union's leading writer in the field of contemporary theological thought, demonstrated what it means to 'take the risk of talking about God' in three important books, *The Creative Suffering of God* (1988), *The Promised End* (2000), and *Participating in God* (2000), and these informed his considerable participation in the important Union committees on which he served.[204]

The group that produced *Call to Mind* continued its work and became convinced that a crucial issue for Baptist identity was authority. The background was the stress on heavy authority by leaders in Restorationist churches. In 1983 Paul Fiddes produced *A Leading Question*, which offered a theological discussion of the issues of ordained ministry, local leadership, wider oversight and authority in the church.[205] As the group considered authority in Baptist life the members concluded that if authority was a problem it was in large measure because of the loss of the concept of 'covenant'. This led to a second book, *Bound to Love* (1985), which looked at a covenantal basis for Baptist life and mission. The chapters examined historical, theological, communal and mission dimensions of covenant, with the authors seeking to recover an image which 'used to play such a luminous part within the Baptist tradition', but which had by the later twentieth century been lost or was at best 'barely appreciated in its richness and depth'.[206] Three of the members of the group that produced *Bound to Love*, Paul Fiddes, Richard Kidd and Brian Haymes, were to be appointed as college principals. The work of this group on the theme of covenant was to prove significant.[207]

---

203 B. Haymes, 'On Being the Church', in K.W. Clements, *et al*, *A Call to Mind: Baptist Essays Towards a Theology of Commitment* (London: Baptist Union, 1981), p.35.

204 Paul Fiddes, *The Creative Suffering of God* (Oxford: Oxford University Press, 1988); *The Promised End* (Oxford: Blackwell, 2000); and *Participating in God* (London: DLT, 2000). See also P. Fiddes, *Past Event and Present Salvation: The Christian Idea of Atonement* (London: DLT/ Westminster Press 1989).

205 P.S. Fiddes, *A Leading Question* (London: Baptist Publications, 1983).

206 Fiddes, *et. al*., *Bound to Love*, pp.4-5 (Introduction).

207 For a full account of this group, see P.S. Fiddes, *Doing Theology in a Baptist Way* (Whitley Publications, Oxford, 2000).

A year after the production of *Bound to Love*, Brian Haymes, by then Principal of Northern College, delivered some lectures to the Yorkshire Baptist Ministers' Fellowship Annual Retreat and Conference, and these were published as *A Question of Baptist Identity* (1986). This proved to be a 'tract for the times', initiating wide-ranging discussion. Haymes suggested that there were important features of Christian identity to which Baptists had witnessed 'as a way of being Christ's Church'. He argued that these were worth developing and guarding, but that they were in danger of being lost.[208] Haymes was disturbed by three trends in particular. First, there was the 'polarity experienced in all the British churches around such matters as theological perceptions, the liturgical movement, the theology of mission and Charismatic renewal'. Second, there was the rise in the last fifteen years of what he called 'non-rational conservatism', a view that was impatient with 'demanding questions of belief and practice'. The third issue was the rise of 'personality cults within the church'.[209] In his subsequent chapters, Haymes examined the nature of the 'true' Church, the question of authority, the tradition of Dissent, and the necessity of right belief. He concluded with a call to undertake the task of 'articulating and discovering the faith by which we live'.[210]

The call from Haymes found an echo within Mainstream. In the January 1986 issue of the *Mainstream Newsletter*, a number of aims of Mainstream were set out, including study conferences 'tackling contemporary theological, pastoral and social issues'.[211] Accordingly, in 1987 Mainstream convened a consultation to consider Haymes's important reflections, and a booklet, *A Perspective on Baptist Identity*, was produced, edited by David Slater, minister at Kingsbridge, Devon, and secretary of Mainstream.[212] The first contribution was by Derek Tidball, who expressed appreciation for what Haymes had said, while

---

208  B. Haymes, *A Question of Identity* (Leeds: Yorkshire Baptist Association, 1986), p.1.
209  Ibid., p.4.
210  Ibid., p.29.
211  *Mainstream Newsletter*, No.21 (January 1986), p.2.
212  D. Slater, ed., *A Perspective on Baptist Identity* (Mainstream, 1987).

also raising some serious queries. He felt that conservative evangelicalism remained a vital force and that this factor had not been properly recognized by Haymes. He also suggested that it was a serious omission for a book dealing with Baptist identity to lack any real mention of mission. Finally, Tidball questioned if it was adequate to talk about the Bible as a 'basic resource' or 'major resource' and suggested that this language offered a weak view of biblical authority. Tidball's conclusion was that deeper analysis was required. 'Our tradition', he said, 'has not always been successful at meeting the needs of the people in the context of their times. There have been times when it has done so gloriously – but not today. The challenge is to mould our tradition and to do it again.'[213]

Other contributors to this volume dealt with the themes of association, ministry, worship and confession. Some related matters like church meetings had already been examined within the Mainstream newsletter.[214] B.R. White, addressing the issue of Baptist associating, argued for wider 'fellowship' as the lifestyle of the gospel. *Inter*dependence, he concluded, was the mark of the converted – the search for independence was Adam's sin.[215] Alastair Campbell, minister at Broadmead, Northampton, and then Research Fellow at Spurgeon's, also probed Association life. Nigel Wright, tutor in Christian Doctrine at Spurgeon's, examined 'The Baptist way of being the Church'. Wright had earlier argued for the church being seen as 'a charismatic-organic community'.[216] Here he urged a reassessment of Baptist heritage to take seriously the ecclesial life of the sixteenth-century Anabaptists and also the Reformation centralities: scripture, faith and grace. 'Baptists', Wright claimed, 'are by definition evangelical. A departure from evangelical theology entails a fatal loss of Baptist identity.'[217] Mike Nicholls of Spurgeon's surveyed differing approaches to ministry, and Stephen Ibbotson, of Harris Street, Peterborough, saw worshipping communities

---

213  Ibid., pp.7-16.
214  For example, *Mainstream Newsletter*, No.16 (April 1984), pp.2-10; *Mainstream Newsletter*, No.20 (September 1985).
215  Slater, ed., *A Perspective on Baptist Identity*, p.29.
216  *Mainstream Newsletter*, No.20 (September 1985), p.5.
217  Slater, ed., *A Perspective on Baptist Identity*, pp.41-4.

as evangelical, catholic and charismatic.[218] The final chapter by George Beasley-Murray, who had returned to England from the Southern Baptist Seminary, Louisville, Kentucky, supported Haymes' plea for a contemporary expression of Baptist faith. Beasley-Murray believed, like Haymes, that 'visionary theological thinking' was essential to enable the gospel to be more effectively communicated.[219] This was a call for a mission vision of Baptist identity.

CONCLUSION

The 1980s saw changes in the leadership of the Baptist Union, as David Russell, who had led the Union through a difficult period, handed over to Bernard Green. Like Payne and Russell, Green gave himself to the task with utter dedication and the decade saw the vision of Green for an inclusive Baptist community being increasingly fulfilled. A number of Baptists, such as those involved in Mainstream, drew from the thinking and experience of those outside the English Baptist scene in such areas as church growth, social action and spiritual renewal, and sought to adapt these for Baptist life. Early Mainstream conference speakers included the Methodist leader, Donald English, and the American Baptist, Tony Campolo, an outspoken social commentator. At the Mainstream conference in 1986 the speakers included Richard Foster, an American Quaker; Sister Margaret Magdalen, an Anglican nun who as Margaret Evening had been a Baptist missionary in Congo; and Wilfred Fahrer, a Mennonite pastor.[220] Baptists gained from both the growth in evangelicalism and openness to the ecumenical movement. There were tensions in the churches over styles of ministry, but the number of people entering ordained ministry was increasing and the greater confidence about witness in the inner cities was also significant. In the April 1989 *Mainstream Newsletter*, the editor, Terry Griffith, involved in inner-city ministry in Hackney, said that the Mainstream leadership had been discussing possible aims, such as the deepening of evangelical faith and

218  Ibid., pp.66-73.
219  Ibid., pp.75-85.
220  *BT*, 23 January 1986, pp.1, 10.

life among Baptists, the rediscovery of distinctive Baptist identity and the encouragement of mission-minded leadership.[221] These were themes that would help to shape the Baptist way of being the church in the last decade of the century.

---

221  T. Griffith, 'Mainstream in the Future', *Mainstream Newsletter*, No.32 April 1989, p.1.

# Chapter 11
# 'IMAGINATIVE AND EFFECTIVE STRATEGIES' 1990-1999

The last decade of the twentieth century saw significant developments taking place within the life of the Union. Nigel Wright wrote in the *Mainstream Newsletter* in January 1990 that the 1990s could be an opportunity 'for Baptists to turn a corner in their experience of denominational life' and look at 'extensive change in the largely Edwardian structures of the Union'.[1] This was to prove to be the case. In the light of the retirement of Bernard Green in 1991 and of Douglas Sparkes in the following year, the Council initiated a process of consultation about their successors. In March 1990 the Council nominated forty-eight-year old David Coffey and thirty-nine year old Keith G. Jones as Secretary and Deputy Secretary.[2] Coffey had been Union Secretary for Evangelism since 1988. As Union President in 1986-7 he had demonstrated his desire to be inclusive with his theme 'Build that Bridge', in which he pressed for bridges of acceptance within local churches, of understanding in the denomination, of tolerance between Baptists and other Christians, and of compassion into the world.[3] Jones, who had ten years of experience of wider Baptist life as the Yorkshire Baptist Association Secretary, was deeply committed to a radical evangelical stance. He combined appreciation of discipleship, liturgy, and sacraments, with a strong awareness of issues of peace and justice.[4] The two had been friends for several years. The 1990 Assembly gave

---

1    *Mainstream Newsletter*, No.35 (January 1990), pp.2-4.
2    *BT*, 15 March 1990, p.1.
3    D. Coffey, *Build that Bridge* (London: Baptist Union, 1986).
4    *BT*, 19 September 1991, p.9. Some of his thinking was later embodied in K.G. Jones, *A Believing Church* (Didcot: Baptist Union, 1998).

enthusiastic backing to the joint nomination. In 1991 warm tributes were paid to the work of Bernard Green and Douglas Sparkes (who became the Union's Historical Research Scholar), and Coffey and Jones were inducted to their new posts, with Donald English, President of the Methodist Conference, preaching the induction sermon.[5]

## LISTENING AND LEADING

David Coffey, the son of a Baptist minister, was working for the Social Services Department of Surrey County Council when he experienced a call to ministry at a Keswick Convention meeting. His home church was Union Street, Kingston upon Thames. David Coffey's initial application

*David Coffey*

to train for Baptist ministry was turned down by the London Baptist Association and he spent a period as a student pastor at Chessington Evangelical Free Church. His second application to the LBA was accepted and he trained at Spurgeon's College under George Beasley-Murray. From 1967 to 1988 he had three pastoral ministries, at Whetstone, Leicester, at North Cheam, Surrey, and Upton Vale, Torquay. His presidency and then his appointment as Secretary for Evangelism, following the death of Tom Rogers, brought him to the centre of denominational life.[6] Coffey, who had been influenced by the thinking of evangelicals such as John Stott, had a broad vision of mission. In 1991 he stated: 'I understand Mission to mean church planting and evangelism, social action and prophetic protest, a world mission commitment and a Kingdom of God awareness of international affairs and environmental concerns.'[7] Keith Jones, who

---

5     *BT*, 18 April 1991, p.1. Keith Jones was taught mission studies by Donald English during Jones' training in Manchester.

6     *BT*, 9 May 1991, p.7.

7     *BT*, 25 March 1991, p.8; conversation with David Coffey, 17 July 2002.

was from Bradford, sensed God saying: 'Follow me into the ministry' at a Campaign Camp in 1967 run by the YBA. After working for Bradford City Council in transport management, Jones trained for ministry at Northern College under Michael Taylor. Professor F.F. Bruce at Manchester University was his personal tutor. Following pastoral ministry in Barnoldswick, Jones became YBA Secretary in 1980. Within the Union, he chaired the General Purposes and Finance Executive and then the Council. His appointment as Union Deputy Secretary included responsibility for ecumenical issues and for the forty Union staff at Didcot.[8]

Coffey and Jones wanted to take seriously the Baptist understanding of discerning the mind of Christ for the Union by gathering Baptists together in the setting of worship to listen and debate. During 1991 they set up and attended twelve 'Listening Days' across the country. These covered the Union's Areas and involved meeting with 3,000 people. There were, as Coffey saw it, key issues to discuss: the identifying marks of Baptists, the purpose of Associations, training for mission-minded ministry, and the best way to organize financial resources. Coffey argued for ways of being the church 'which will overcome the considerable cultural barriers facing those beyond the church'.[9] The process of 'listening to the family', as Jones called it, began with a meeting at which LBA representatives talked to Coffey, Jones and David Nixon, the Union treasurer. LBA speakers - Adele Blakebrough-Fairbairn of Kingston upon Thames, Fred George of East Barnet, Bob Almond of Welling, and John Colwell of Catford - discussed sexism, racism, ministerial support and Baptist diversity.[10] Superintendents such as David Harper, Eastern Area, assisted at Listening Days, and Coffey used the superintendents as a sounding board. Listening Day findings from across the country were disseminated through two new publications, *Baptist Leader* and *SecCheck*, and a draft document was produced in

---

8    *BT*, 19 September 1991, p.9. Keith Jones was the youngest chair of the Baptist Union General Purposes and Finance Executive and the Council.
9    *BT*, 25 March 1991, p.8.
10   *BT*, 11 April 1991, p.11.

*The Superintendents Board, 1992*
*Left to right, front row: General Secretary David Coffey, Eddie Pilling, Board*
*Chairman Morris West, Secretary for Ministry Malcolm Goodspeed, Douglas*
*McBain; middle: David Harper, Geoffrey Reynolds, Neil Hall, Roger Hayden; back:*
*Peter Tongeman, Eric Watson, Roy Freestone, Peter Manson, Gwynne Edwards,*
*John Nicholson, Keith Hobbs*

1992 entitled 'Towards 2000'. Coffey and Jones later spoke of the vibrant Listening Day meetings as 'an adventure in spirituality'.[11]

'Towards 2000' was a ten-year plan, designed to take Baptists forward with a common mission strategy. The plan was received by the residential Council meeting at Kinmel Hall, North Wales, and a statement of intent was agreed:

> Seeking God's guidance through the Holy Spirit, under the Lordship of Christ, and in response to the concerns of the Churches, we, the Baptist Union Council, commit ourselves: to encourage, support and initiate imaginative and effective strategies in evangelism and other aspects of God's mission, to develop our distinctive Baptist identity, to strengthen our associating by mutual commitment at every level, to promote the greater sharing of people, money and other resources.[12]

---

11   *SecCheck*, Issue No.9, Summer 1994.
12   *Baptist Leader*, Issue No.3 Summer 1992.

The published document, *A Ten Year Plan Towards 2000: Incorporating the National Mission Strategy* (1993) was taken to the Assembly.[13] The themes outlined were to be worked out over the remainder of the decade. The Listening Day process also produced *A 'Green Paper' on Council Restructuring* with various points for debate.[14] In 1994 the Council approved a proposal that this Green Paper, which suggested major changes to the Council, be referred to Associations, colleges and interested committees, with a view to establishing a Task Group on Council Restructuring. There was a desire to see more women, people from minority ethnic groups, lay people, and under-thirties on the Council.[15]

As thinking about change continued, there were those who urged the Union leadership to move faster and show more imagination. In 1994 the Mainstream executive endorsed the 'Towards 2000' proposals, but wanted to see the process of change accelerated. In particular there was a call for more effective personal support for ministers.[16] A second series of Listening Days was held in 1995. The *Baptist Leader* of autumn 1995 set out several issues emerging in the Listening Days. One crucial question was consistently raised: what kind of Baptist Union was required for the twenty-first century? Another frequently-mentioned issue was the need to give priority to prayer in the decision-making process of the Union. Churches and ministers were also seeking reforms to strengthen associating. David Coffey's own commitment was indicated by the question: do we share the common vision that every local church should have a trained leadership enabling it to be a missionary congregation?[17] It was clear in 1995 that there was much still to be done, and the November 1995 Council unanimously agreed to

---

13  *A Ten Year Plan Towards 2000: Incorporating the National Mission Strategy* (Didcot: Baptist Union, 1993).
14  *A 'Green Paper' on Council Restructuring* (Didcot: Baptist Union, 1994) For the debate already going on, see *BT*, 22 October 1992, p. 6.
15  *BT*, 31 March 1994, p.2.
16  *Mainstream*, No.50 (June 1994), p.11; *BT*, 27 January 1994, p.3.
17  *Baptist Leader*, Issue No.12, Autumn 1995, pp.1-2. David Coffey wrote an edited version of what was in *Baptist Leader* for the *Baptist Times*, 18 January 1996, pp.7, 13.

recommend to the Assembly the re-appointment of Coffey and Jones, who were given a lengthy standing ovation.[18] From 1996 discussion of 'Towards 2000' merged with new strands of thinking in the Union.

Others shared in denominational leadership. A number of changes of Union personnel took place in the early 1990s. In 1991 Derek Tidball, like Coffey already a past-president of the Union, became Secretary for Mission and Evangelism. Tidball had a particular interest in relating mission to a changing societal context. Bill Hancock, Secretary for Ministry (and a former Area Superintendent), retired in 1991, to be replaced by Malcolm Goodspeed, tutor at Regent's Park College. After twenty-one years of influential work for the Union, Don Black also retired in 1991, and Anne Wilkinson-Hayes, aged thirty-three, became Executive for social affairs. Hilary Saunders, aged thirty, became Administration Officer at Didcot. Members of the new, younger Union team were welcomed at the Council in November 1991.[19] Experienced staff such as David Lovegrove, Finance Officer, continued to serve the Union. Some painful decisions had to be taken following a Home Mission deficit, and it was decided, very reluctantly, that it was necessary to shed ten jobs at Didcot, which included seven redundancies and the decision to end the Christian Training Programme. By the time David Nixon stood down as Union treasurer in 1996, the financial situation had improved. Many tributes were paid to Nixon's work during his ten years as treasurer.[20] There were also hopes for a stronger partnership between the Union and the BMS in the light of the move to Didcot.[21] In 1996 Alistair Brown, minister of Gerrard Street Baptist Church, Aberdeen, became BMS General Director, and Coffey and Brown became a familiar duo at Baptist Assemblies.

Leadership was also evident in the contribution of Union Presidents. Derek Tidball, President in 1990-91, and at age forty-two the youngest president to date, gave a frank analysis of decline in Union membership. His call was for ministers to preach the Word, challenge the cultural

18   *BT*, 16 November 1995, p.2.
19   Minutes of the Council, 12 and 13 November 1991.
20   *BT*, 28 March 1996, p.2.
21   *Baptist Leader*, Issue No.3, Summer 1992.

*status quo*, and be willing to suffer.[22] Roy Jenkins, who founded 'Christians against Torture', took as his presidential theme, 'Cry Freedom'. Jenkins had moved from the pastorate of Ararat, Cardiff, to become Senior Producer, Religious Programmes, BBC Wales.[23] Eric Westwood, President in 1992-3, had served for two decades with the BMS in Brazil, before becoming Northern Baptist Association Missioner. Three Presidents in the 1990s, Tidball, Westwood and Douglas McBain, had trained at LBC; this recognition of LBC-trained ministers was in marked contrast to the situation earlier in the century.[24] Brian Haymes, who became President in 1993, and in the following year moved from Northern Baptist College to become Principal at Bristol, reiterated his deeply-felt concerns about the need to value Baptist tradition and identity.[25] Steve Gaukroger, from Stopsley, Luton, who moved to Gold Hill in 1996, travelled about 900 miles per week during his presidency in 1994-5. He found that Association meetings were usually poorly attended and elderly, but some Associations were developing in imaginative ways.[26]

The Presidents in the second half of the decade represented different aspects of Union life, although there were no women elected to the presidency in the 1990s. Peter Tongeman and Douglas McBain were both Area Superintendents. Tongeman had been Secretary of the Young People's Department of the Union. John James, from Penarth Tabernacle, South Glamorgan, and Michael Bochenski, from Dagnall Street, St Albans, were local church pastors. Bochenski, who was involved in Mainstream and in the Baptist Ministers' Fellowship, stimulated discussion in 1993 by arguing for reform of the superintendency to achieve broader representation, including women; a more effective settlement process; better pastoral care of ministers; and

---

22   *BT*, 3 May 1990, pp.1, 2, 6.
23   *BT*, 18 April 1991, p.1.
24   Randall, *Educating Evangelicalism,* pp.279-80. Malcolm Goodspeed had also trained at LBC.
25   *BT*, 22 April 1993, p.7. In 2000 Brian Haymes became minister of Bloomsbury Central Baptist Church.
26   *BT*, 16 March 1995, p.2.

Area strategies for mission.[27] V. Frederick George, minister from 1969 at East Barnet, President in 1997-8, was the first person from an Asian background to hold the presidency. In January 1996 George wrote on 'Race and Racism', urging recognition of the contribution of Black and Asian spirituality and scholarship to theological exploration, worship and mission. He called for an environment in local churches in which it was the norm to consider the gifts of Black members when looking for leaders, and a commitment among wider church bodies to ensuring that Black and Asian members were represented.[28]

The call by Fred George and others to ensure that the leadership of the Union was more representative of the Union's growing diversity was taken up by the Council. In March 1996 the Council adopted a resolution

in which there was encouragement and affirmation of the contribution of different races and cultures, recognition that racism was sinful and a denial of God's view of humanity, acknowledgement that racism within individuals and churches had to be challenged, and support for the ongoing work of the Union's Racial Justice Task Group. Fred George proposed the motion, and several speakers from London and Birmingham spoke movingly of their experiences of racism both outside and inside the churches.[29] A year later, when Fred George was

*Fred George*    Union President, he promoted Racial Justice Sunday. Together with Pat White, deputy moderator of the Churches' Commission for Racial Justice and convenor of the Union's Racial Justice Task Group, Fred George encouraged local initiatives. Nottingham and Derby had a Black Baptist Support Group, with learning being facilitated by leaders from the New Testament Church of God. London had 'Reach In, Reach Out', and Birmingham also had a group, 'Progress Within'.[30]

---

27    *BT*, 16 September 1993, p.6.
28    *Mainstream*, No.55 (January 1996), p.9.
29    *BT*, 28 March 1996, p.3.
30    *BT*, 4 September 1997, pp.8-9.

Progress in the area of women in ministry continued to be slow.[31] Pam Neville gave up-to-date statistics in 1990. There were ninety-four women on the accredited list, sixty-nine in pastorates or other Christian work. Twenty women were in colleges, training for ministry and seven were looking for a church.[32] Ten years later there were 155 women on the accredited list. Although this represented advance, after having had women in ministry for eighty years fewer than seven per cent of accredited Baptist ministers were women.[33] Several women Baptist ministers did, however, exert influence in the affairs of the Union in the 1990s. Ruth Matthews and Ruth Bottoms served with distinction as moderators of crucial Union committees. Vivienne Lassetter became the Union's Ministries Adviser. Creative work on mission issues was undertaken by Anne Wilkinson-Hayes, who challenged Baptists to move on from 'sticking plaster ministry' to tackling the real reasons why people were marginalized.[34] Keith Jones, who moved to Prague in 1998, on his appointment as Rector of the International Baptist Theological Seminary, argued that Baptists had been impoverished by not having the insights of gifted women in senior leadership.[35] By the end of the decade, Myra Blyth, who had been an executive director with the WCC in

*Patricia Took*

Geneva, had replaced Keith Jones as Deputy General Secretary, and Patricia Took, minister of Cann Hall and Harrow Green Baptist Church,

---

31  See articles by Edward Lehman, Shirley Dex, Margaret Jarman, Ruth Matthews, Carol McCarthy and John Briggs in *BQ*, Vol.31, No.7 (1986).
32  *BT*, 25 January 1990, p.4. Dianne Tidball, 'Walking a Tightrope: Women training for Baptist ministry', *BQ*, Vol.33, No.8 (1990), pp.388-95. For the Church of England, see S. Gill, *Women and the Church of England* (London: SPCK, 1994).
33  I am indebted to Douglas Sparkes for the statistics.
34  *Mainstream*, No.51 (November 1994), p.4.
35  *BT*, 4 July 1996, p.12.

Leytonstone, had been appointed Area Superintendent for London, the first woman superintendent in the Union.[36]

## FORMS OF MINISTRY

In November 1994 the Council received a major paper from the Faith and Unity Executive, chaired by John Briggs: *Forms of Ministry Among Baptists: Towards an Understanding of Spiritual Leadership.* This was the product of work done by the influential Doctrine and Worship Committee, chaired by Paul Fiddes. From 1992 the Advisory Committee on Church Relations had been replaced by the Faith and Unity Executive with its feeder committees: Church Relations, Local Ecumenical, International, and Doctrine and Worship. *Forms of Ministry*, presented by Paul Fiddes, referred to work done in the 1950s and 1960s on ordination and ministry.[37] It was hoped that this further study would assist consideration of Baptist identity and practice.[38] It aimed to 'reflect theologically upon the needs for ministry', especially in the light of recommendations for the recognition of youth specialists and more thorough processes of training and recognition for lay pastors and preachers.[39] It had been suggested that 'lay' be dropped from these titles.[40] Drawing from Fiddes' own theological work, *Forms of Ministry* argued for the distinction between 'pastoral oversight' (*episkope*) and 'pastoral service' (*diakonia*). Pastoral oversight was seen as the activity of the 'minister', who was called to a 'way of being'; the minister also had a responsibility to act as the 'representative of the Universal

---

36    *BT*, 20 November 1997, p.2. Pat Took was appointed in 1998 and Myra Blyth in 1999.

37    *The Meaning and Practice of Ordination among Baptists* (1957); *The Doctrine of the Ministry* (1961); *Ministry Tomorrow* (1969).

38    Faith and Unity Executive, Doctrine and Worship Committee, *Forms of Ministry Among Baptists: Towards an Understanding of Spiritual Leadership* (Didcot: Baptist Union, 1994), p.53.

39    Ibid., pp.14-15.

40    Papers had been produced entitled *Called to be a Pastor* and *Called to be a Preacher*.

Church'.[41] Paul Fiddes' presentation of this material to the Council was, according to the *Baptist Times*, 'received with something approaching awe'.[42]

Part of the process of consideration of Baptist identity, and one mentioned in *Forms of Ministry*, was work being done on superintendency. A Task Group on this subject was set up in March 1994, with Brian Haymes as moderator and Douglas Sparkes as facilitator.[43] The group had twenty meetings and engaged in consultations within and beyond the denomination. Geoffrey Reynolds, Southern Area Superintendent, was a consultant representing the superintendents. Haymes presented the report, entitled *Transforming Superintendency*, to the November 1996 Council. The major question addressed was what form of superintendency was needed.[44] The group made a large number of recommendations. These included the recommendations that the pastoral care of ministers should become the primary task of superintendents; that Associations should develop a mission and pastoral policy; that greater responsibility for the life of the churches should lie with the Associations; that new guidelines for the settlement process should be drawn up; and that each superintendent should be called to exercise a ministry with some national dimensions, with central funding of the stipends of superintendents being preserved.[45]

The Task Group had clearly raised issues that required discussion, not only about superintendency but also about Associations. Although the review had highlighted considerable concern among ministers about the settlement process, the report was positive. Chris Norrish, chairman

41  *Forms of Ministry Among Baptists*, pp.23, 30-1.
42  *BT*, 17 November 1994, p.2.
43  *BT*, 31 March 1994, p.3. The group was Michael Bochenski, Ruth Gouldbourne (Bedford), Andrew Rollinson (Newcastle), Hazel Sherman (Bristol Baptist College), John Weaver (Regent's Park College), Arthur Jennings (Hemel Hempstead), Stan Jones (Church Secretary, Cheltenham) and Catherine Joughin (Secretary, Essex Baptist Association).
44  *Transforming Superintendency: The Report of the General Superintendency Review Group* (Didcot: Baptist Union, 1996), p.3.
45  *Transforming Superintendency*, pp.24-45; cf. *BT*, 21 November 1996, pp.1, 3 and 5.

of the Superintendents' Board, expressed the gratitude of the superintendents for the way the review was undertaken.[46] David Harper, Eastern Area Superintendent, chaired the Superintendents' Board through the final stages of the review. The Task Group members had no doubt from their investigations that churches and ministers saw pastoral care of ministers as the top priority for superintendents. This might mean their being released from other tasks.[47] Brian Haymes, in an address to the Council in March 1997, argued that care for ministers was to be seen in the context of the mission of God and that for superintendents to have pastoral care as a primary focus did not rule out other tasks. Haymes wanted superintendents who were 'pastoral theologians'. He also argued that it was not possible to separate ministers from churches, and so there must be care for churches. However, in this area there should be more thorough partnerships with Associations.[48] There was considerable debate at the Council over questions such as the size of Areas and the number of superintendents. The Council received the report and passed it on for further work.[49]

In the meantime, discussions were going on about other forms of ministry. It was agreed at the Council in March 1990 that no further appointments would be made to the accredited list under the 'Supplementary Minister' category. Part of the thinking behind supplementary ministry had been the anticipated problems in supporting full-time ministers, but during the 1980s the situation had changed.[50] In 1993 a scheme was proposed for Union recognition of youth specialists. Iain Hoskins was now National Youth Officer, Paul Montacute having moved to the BWA. The ideas about recognition caused lively debate at the Council meetings, with the November 1994 Council agreeing that youth specialists could be eligible to receive denominational recognition.[51] Preliminary consideration was also given to the

---

46   *BT*, 23 November 1995, p.2.
47   *BT*, 21 November 1996, pp.1, 3 and 5.
48   *BT*, 20 March 1997, pp.1 and 10.
49   *BT*, 27 March 1997, p.2.
50   Minutes of the Baptist Union Council, 13 and 14 March 1990.
51   *BT*, 17 November 1994, pp.2, 4.

recognition of evangelists, and in 1995 this proposal was agreed. The Council also wished to affirm the ministry of 'lay' pastors, while recognizing some of the difficulties of terminology that were involved.[52] In 1996 John Nicholson recalled that ten years previously, just before he became North Eastern Superintendent, the YBA had embraced a strategy aimed at finding some form of ministerial leadership for every YBA church. With the exception of some small churches that did not want such leadership, that had been achieved.[53]

It was pointed out in 1991 that there were high numbers of people in training for ministry, and it was anticipated that they would be able to find positions because of the increase in team ministries and other new opportunities.[54] Statistics from the Ministry Department suggested that about twenty additional full-time pastoral positions were being created each year.[55] But over-supply of ministers soon became a concern. In 1993 a proposal was brought to the Council that colleges be asked to restrict student intake. One issue was that older ministers were finding it difficult to move since churches preferred younger ministers. After a passionate debate, the proposal was passed by eighty-five votes to fifty-five. Those who opposed it thought the denomination would be left unprepared for growth, while others argued that the numbers entering ministry were considerably in excess of the number of retirements, resignations, transfers and deaths.[56] Paul Jackson, from Westbourne Park, said the Council seemed to have a split personality: it was endorsing a Mission Strategy which included planting new congregations, while reducing numbers for ministry.[57] Nigel Wright regretted the 'air of uncourageous retrenchment communicated by the Council's decision' and reminded *Baptist Times* readers of *Ministry Tomorrow* (1969), which

---

52   *BT*, 17 November 1994, p.4.
53   *BT*, 22 February 1996, p.11.
54   *BT*, 12 September 1991, p.3.
55   Minutes of the Baptist Union Council, 12 and 13 November 1991.
56   Minutes of the Baptist Union Council, 9 and 10 March 1993; *BT*, 18 March 1993, p.2.
57   *BT*, 1 April 1993, p.12.

had envisaged only 400 ministers being supported. Instead of a reduction, the tide has been in the opposite direction.[58]

Later in 1993, however, there were letters in the *Baptist Times* from those who were finding it difficult to move to another church, or who were suffering from ill health but were not ill enough for medical retirement.[59] Letters of sympathy concerning these situations appeared from Philip Cooke, chairman of the Baptist Ministers' Pension Fund Committee, from Ruth Matthews, chair of the Ministry Executive Committee, and from Chris Norrish.[60] A year later more questions were asked about ministerial targets. The targets discussed (fifty-five students coming into ministry from colleges and five from the Residential Selection Conference), represented a considerable cut-back from the ninety-one ministerial students who had started in the colleges in 1990. In 1994, Michael Quicke - Principal of Spurgeon's from 1992, after Paul Beasley-Murray moved to pastoral ministry at Victoria Road South, Chelmsford - gave an update, reporting that the number of Baptist ministerial students was down in all colleges. Although Spurgeon's had 100 new students in total, most were on part-time courses, were starting an MTh in Applied Theology (in-service training for ministers), were Eastern European students, or were from non-Baptist churches, particularly London African congregations. Quicke emphasized that the core activity at Spurgeon's remained Baptist ministerial formation, but in that area decline was evident: only eighteen new students were Baptist Union ministerial.[61]

Nonetheless, there were constructive developments in ministry. A number of Baptists wrote on preaching and pastoral work. Neville Clark contributed two fine books.[62] Mark Greene, Vice-Principal at LBC, challenged preachers to address work-place issues.[63] In 1998 Paul

---

58    *BT*, 22 April 1993, p.6.
59    *BT*, 1 July 1993, p.11.
60    *BT*, 15 July 1993, p.11.
61    *BT*, 10 November 1994, p.6.
62    N. Clark, *Preaching in Context* (Bury St Edmunds: Kevin Mayhew, 1991); N. Clark, *Pastoral Care in Context* (Bury St Edmunds: Kevin Mayhew, 1992).
63    M. Greene, *Thank God it's Monday* (London: Scripture Union, 1994); M. Greene, *The Three-eared Preacher* (Northwood: London Bible College, 1998).

Goodliff, who the following year became Central Area Superintendent, wrote *Care in a Confused Climate*.[64] There was considerable interest among Baptist ministers in chaplaincy work in hospitals, higher education and the armed forces. In 1990 Caroline Pullman, a twenty-eight-year-old Baptist minister trained at Bristol, became the first woman chaplain to the Royal Navy. Stephen Heap, minister at Blackbird Leys, Oxford, was appointed full-time Baptist chaplain to higher education in London in 1992.[65] John Boyer pioneered sports ministry, initially through his work as chaplain to Manchester United. Other Baptist ministers served in ecumenical teams in hospitals, prisons and industry, while David Holmwood was a chaplain at Heathrow Airport.

Chaplaincy, together with accreditation of youth specialists and evangelists, indicated the increasing diversity in Baptist ministry, and the Council returned in 1996 to the report, *Forms of Ministry*. Douglas McBain argued for superintendents as mission enablers; John Maile, of West Wickham and Shirley, Kent, was concerned about misleading ideas of the minister as omni-competent; Roger Martin, of Leigh Road, Leigh-on-Sea, affirmed a range of ministries; and Paul Fiddes, noting that the phrase about ministers 'called to a way of being' had caused misunderstanding, argued that there were different 'ways of being' for all Christians.[66]

RETHINKING THE UNION

Re-thinking of the Union was taking place. Writing in 1990, Nigel Wright hoped to see the Union cultivating a new spirit of warmth and personal affirmation, reforming its structures and engaging in sustained decentralization, and acting as a resource agency. He suggested a plan to be implemented by the year 2000.[67] Wright elaborated on these ideas in

---

64    P. Goodliff, *Care in a Confused Climate: Pastoral care and postmodern culture* (London: Darton, Longman and Todd, 1998).

65    There was tripartite support for Stephen Heap from the Union, the LBA and Bloomsbury Central Baptist Church: Bowers, *A Bold Experiment,* p.438.

66    *BT*, 4 April 1996, p.4.

67    *Mainstream Newsletter*, No.35 (January 1990), pp.2-4.

*Challenge to Change* (1991), in which he suggested ways to renew church meetings – for example by less use of voting procedures and more reliance on consensus – Associations and the Union.[68] David Coffey strongly encouraged local churches and groupings of churches to use the book to inform the debate on identity.[69] Wright made a formative contribution to this debate. In 1993 Coffey predicted a shaking of some denominational structures, including superintendency, Association life, home mission, and the Union's central services.[70] New thinking was embodied in a paper presented to the Council by the Faith and Unity Executive in March 1994, *The Nature of the Assembly and the Council of the Baptist Union of Great Britain*. Like *Forms of Ministry*, this was prepared by the Doctrine and Worship Committee, chaired by Paul Fiddes. The paper drew from ideas in *Call to Mind* and *Bound to Love*, and stated that concepts such as '*covenant, fellowship (koinonia)* and *body*' could be used 'to understand the theological basis of union between Christian churches in general, and Baptist churches in particular'.[71]

The implications of God's covenant with humankind through Jesus Christ and the commitment of church members to each other were explored in terms of local church life, Associations, the Council, and the Assembly. *The Nature of the Assembly* argued that wider assemblies were ecclesial, having as their aim discerning the mind of Christ.[72] The relationship between Council and Assembly was seen as a balance of mutual trust, with the Assembly giving weight to the decisions of Council without being bound by them. Several proposals for reforming the Council and Assembly were offered for consultation.[73] During the process of consultation, McBain encouraged reform and also 'the

---

68   N. Wright, *Challenge to Change: A Radical Agenda for Baptists* (Eastbourne: Kingsway Publications, 1991).
69   Ibid., p.9.
70   *BT*, 23 September 1993, p.2.
71   *The Nature of the Assembly and the Council of the Baptist Union of Great Britain* (Didcot: Baptist Union, 1994), p.4. Faith Bowers, sub-editor of the *Baptist Quarterly*, was secretary of the committee.
72   Ibid., pp.10-12.
73   Ibid., p.25.

investment of time, energy and spirituality within the existing structures'. Restorationists, who continued to cause tensions, did not value such an investment, but McBain considered that they had 'lost their novelty appeal'.[74] *The Nature of the Assembly* was accepted in November 1995,[75] and the Council made some adjustments to its composition and practices. The Council hoped for more women, young people and ethnic minorities through co-option, although Ruth Bottoms noted in 1996 that the number of women was down from forty-five to thirty-six.[76]

Those involved in Mainstream were also discussing restructuring. A paper entitled 'Mainstream – a Word and Spirit Network' was presented to the annual Mainstream Conference in January 1994 as an agenda document and a summary of changes that were underway. The paper considered that existing denominational structures were appropriate to a previous time. 'However', it continued, 'new wine is being poured into our Union. Structures must serve this new life: new wine skins are needed.' Michael Bochenski, commenting later in 1994, hoped that those who might be critical of Mainstream's initiatives would note the situation as it actually existed in Associations. In some there was new life, with events being arranged which included imaginative worship, workshops and activities for the family. But overall, Bochenski argued, Associations were failing to connect with ninety-five per cent of Baptists, except in indirect ways, and were failing to relate to a large number of churches.[77] In a Mainstream editorial in June 1994 about a proposed new 'Word and Spirit' network, with regional Mainstream groups, Bochenski welcomed such possibilities as supplementing Association life.[78] Within two years these were in operation.

In the light of comments about more radical changes, David Coffey brought to the November 1995 Council, held in Reading, a proposal for a Denominational Consultation. In presenting this, Coffey suggested that there was a need to identify the unifying factor in the changes within the

---

74    *Mainstream*, No.52 (January 1995), pp.4, 6.
75    *BT*, 23 November 1995, p.3.
76    *BT*, 28 March 1996, p.2.
77    *BT*, 17 March 1994, p.12.
78    *Mainstream*, No.50 (June 1994), p.7.

Union. For him, this crucial factor was the missionary vision. Frances Godden, Joint Secretary of the East Midland Association, and Michael Quicke, stirred the Council to enthusiasm for a consultation. Some members had reservations, fearing that past tensions could be aroused, but as Quicke gave a passionate endorsement of Coffey's proposal and declared 'we are with you', there was applause.[79] Commenting a few weeks later, Coffey talked about 'a day to remember'. The Denominational Consultation, Coffey believed, was going to highlight frustrations: some ministers and churches were frustrated with Association life, others considered the Union too remote, and some felt marginalized because their radical agenda was not being addressed. Colleges could think their vision was not

*Coffee break at the Consultation*

shared by the wider Baptist community and staff at Baptist House could feel their work was unappreciated. Within all this ferment, Coffey hoped that mission would be the prism through which discussions at the consultation were viewed.[80] It was hoped that the vibrancy which Coffey, Jones and others had found as people had come together for the Listening Days would be conveyed to the Council through the consultation.[81]

In January 1996, as Coffey looked forward to the consultation - to be held at Swanwick in September of that year – he described at the Mainstream Conference the circumstances in which he had proposed that it be held. At the Reading Council meeting there had been what Coffey perceived as 'a particular sense of God speaking not only through words, but through the climate of the meeting'. The Council members as a whole, Coffey believed, had experienced a deep awareness that the church was facing, with varying degrees of helplessness, the stark needs of a morally and spiritually sick society. Coffey connected this experience with other events which he considered significant, such as a

---

79    Minutes of the Council, 7 and 8 November 1995; also *BT*, 16 November 1995, p.2.

80    D.Coffey 'The Denominational Consultation', *Baptist Leader*, Issue No.3, Winter 1995, pp.1-2.

81    K.G. Jones to the author, 24 March 2004.

prophecy given at Mainstream in the 1980s and a Dawn 2000 prayer retreat in the autumn of 1995 when a number of leaders met to pray for the nation.[82] The preparatory material for the consultation included a book of Bible Studies, *Beginning with God*, prepared by the Doctrine and Worship committee. This was also used by those praying for the gathering. In July 1996, as the consultation was imminent, Keith Jones called for a wide sharing of spiritual insights – insights from women, from diverse communities and from ecumenical and evangelical networks.[83] Invitations to attend the consultation had gone to members of Council and to others who, it was hoped, would help to ensure that the voices of younger people, women and minority ethnic groups were heard.

The main work of the consultation took place in thirty-eight small groups of seven or eight people. Two facilitators had been invited, the

senior facilitator being Hilary Ineson, from the Church of England's Board of Education, and they played a major role. The only input at plenary level was from Brian Haymes, who spoke on the Baptist view of the church, and from Tom Houston, of the continuing Lausanne Committee on World Evangelization, who analysed the social context for contemporary mission. Ellie Kreider, a Mennonite who with her husband Alan was based at Regent's Park College, led worship. The groups looked at issues like associating, justice, leadership, ministry and mission, and finance (in the light of falling Home Mission contributions), and views were fed back by the facilitators. The need for new ways of associating emerged as a priority issue. Among the many who offered comments about their

*Voting at the Denominational Consultation 1996*

---

82   *BT*, 25 January 1996, p.5.
83   *BT*, 4 July 1996, p.12.

experience of the consultation were Pat White, who said that she was glad to offer Black Baptist perspectives, and Carolyn Talkes, chair of the East Midland Alliance of Baptist Youth, who spoke of a sense of excitement about what God was going to do and say.[84] In evaluating the consultation, Coffey stressed that the reformation of a historic denomination was about generational change, and that there would a need for patient perseverance. At the same time, Coffey and Jones reported that the vast majority of participants in the consultation had agreed – much to their surprise own in some cases – that it was a great success.[85]

At the November 1996 meeting of the Council, in Bristol, Michael Quicke again caught the Council's mood when he said that in his thirty years of experience of Council meetings he had never known a greater sense of anticipation that God was doing something new in the Union. He was convinced that the process in which the denomination was engaged was of the Holy Spirit. Council members showed, by acclamation, that they agreed.[86] It was decided to form a six-person reference group to work on the implications of the consultation, especially in relation to mission and associating. At the consultation there had been a clear desire to implement new ways of associating 'for both effective local co-operative mission and quality pastoral care'. There had also been a hope that mission could be a higher priority for superintendents, and Geoffrey Reynolds expressed agreement with this view. Of the areas of ministry undertaken by superintendents, the emphasis tended to be on pastoral care of ministers, oversight of churches, and facilitating ministerial settlement, and the priority of care for ministers had been affirmed in *Transforming Superintendency*.[87] In the light of other issues, discussion about *Transforming Superintendency* was put on hold, but its focus on translocal ministry would prove decisive.

---

84    *BT*, 3 October 1996, pp. 1 and 2 and supplement.
85    *Baptist Leader* and *SecCheck*, Issue No.15, Winter 1996, p.1.
86    Minutes of the Council, 14 and 15 November 1996.
87    *Baptist Leader* and *SecCheck*, Issue No.15, Winter 1996, p.1.

## THE INTER-CHURCH PROCESS

Another decisive issue for Baptists in the early 1990s was their relationship with the Inter-Church Process. Many evangelicals welcomed the opportunities opened up by Churches Together in England (CTE). George Carey, the new Archbishop of Canterbury, was both evangelical and ecumenical. Donald English, the leading evangelical in Methodism, hoped that Baptists and Methodists would together promote evangelism.[88] A number of Baptist ministers were very active ecumenically. Keith Clements moved from Bristol Baptist College in 1990 to become Co-ordinating Secretary for International Affairs for the Council of Churches for Britain and Ireland (CCBI), and in 1997 became General Secretary, Conference of European Churches (CEC). Roger Nunn, of Manvers Street, Bath, became Field Officer (South) for CTE in 1990. Hugh Cross was Ecumenical Moderator of the Milton Keynes Christian Council from 1991 until he retired in 1995, when he received an MBE. Simon Oxley became Ecumenical Officer, Greater Manchester Ecumenical Council, in 1992, and then Executive Secretary for Education, WCC, in 1996. After ecumenical ministry in Milton Keynes, Gethin Abraham-Williams became General Secretary of the Covenanted Churches in Wales in 1990 and later of Churches Together in Wales. In 1999 David Goodbourn, who had earlier been a tutor at Northern Baptist College, became the first lay person to be General Secretary of Churches Together in Britain and Ireland (CTBI, formerly CCBI). In the latter part of the century Baptists filled several offices in the ecumenical movement.[89]

Other Baptists, however, opposed all such ecumenical participation. Following the pro-ecumenical vote at the 1989 Assembly, a new Baptist group, FAB, came into being, linking those who were unhappy about 'Churches Together'. David Rushworth Smith, of Crich, Derbyshire, was editor of *FAB* newsletters. The name FAB was short for fabulous. A young pastor had said that what was being done to oppose involvement

---

88    *BT*, 26 July 1990, p.11.
89    A.R. Cross, 'Service to the Ecumenical Movement: The Contribution of British Baptists', *BQ*, Vol.38, No.3 (1999).

in 'Churches Together' was 'fab'. The name stuck.[90] In the first *FAB* newsletter, in November 1990, Rushworth Smith explained that he had written to every church in the *Baptist Handbook*[91] to ask for their opinion about Churches Together. Approximately half of those who had responded were in favour of the Inter-Church Process, as they understood it, while the rest were against or were making up their minds. The *FAB* newsletter queried the way the vote had been counted at the 1989 Assembly, arguing that if abstentions had been counted the vote in favour of ICP participation would have been just below the two-thirds majority required. Among the 500 people on the FAB mailing list were those urging links with the Evangelical Alliance, the (anti-ecumenical) British Evangelical Council, the Fellowship for Revival (formerly the Baptist Revival Fellowship) and the Reformed Baptist Carey Conference.[92]

Given the apparent division in the denomination, it was agreed at the March 1991 Council that David Coffey should communicate with churches about ecumenical issues and in particular the Union's membership of 'Churches Together'.[93] At the time of the 1991 Assembly in Bournemouth, more than eighty churches had written to the Union to say they wished to dissociate from 'Churches Together', and at least twenty-five had resigned from the Union.[94] At the Assembly, FAB convened a fringe meeting which attracted about 170 supporters.[95] David Coffey arranged a consultation at Fairmile Court, Cobham, Surrey, in December 1991, when six ministers who dissented from the 1989 vote met with six people who supported the decision taken. A book, *Evangelicals and Ecumenism*, was subsequently produced. Those writing in favour of CTE membership were Michael Bochenski, Faith Bowers, Douglas McBain and David Coffey. Those against were Robert Amess of Duke Street, Richmond, John Balchin of Purley, and Andrew Rigden

---

90    *FAB*, No.7 [Autumn 1992], p.12. FAB was also taken to stand for the Fellowship of Anxious Baptists.
91    Properly the *Baptist Directory* at this date.
92    *FAB*, No. 1 (November 1990), pp.1-8. Rushworth Smith's letter to the churches is dated August 1990.
93    Minutes of the Baptist Union Council, 12 and 13 March 1991.
94    *FAB*, No.7 [Autumn 1992], pp.2, 10.
95    *FAB*, No. 4 [1991], p.3.

Green of Upton Vale, Torquay.[96] In the following year Coffey answered in detail questions put to him by FAB and argued that his commitment to Christ led necessarily to commitment to 'Churches Together'.[97]

In 1992-3 the Union's Faith and Unity Executive asked for the views of ministers and churches about the way CTE was working. A CTE Review Group was set up in September 1993 and in June 1994 it completed its report. This review became part of the wider 'Called to be One' process, established among the twenty-two member churches of CTE, which asked for comments about understandings of the 'visible unity of the church'. The Baptist Union's Review Group encouraged continuation in ICP, a stance later confirmed by the Council. A provisional Baptist response to the issue of visible unity was drawn up by the Faith and Unity Executive and sent in October 1994 by Keith Jones to the CTE's General Secretary, Martin Reardon, convenor of the CTE Working Party. The Baptist response offered different models of unity affirmed by Baptists, from full mutual recognition of other denominations to a loose 'Evangelical Alliance' unity based on certain core beliefs.[98] The CTE Working Party, which included two Baptists, Roger Nunn and Hazel Sherman (previously at Bristol Baptist College), produced the book *Called to be One* (1996).[99] Although *Called to be One* opposed 're-baptism', Baptists continued to press for the rights of conscience of each person wanting to be baptized, even those already baptized as infants and subsequently confirmed.[100]

Of more immediate concern to the Union leadership was the decision due to be taken at the 1995 Assembly at Plymouth. In the run-up to the Assembly, David Coffey and Keith Jones wrote in *Baptist Leader*, the *Baptist Times* and *SecCheck* about the issues. Keith Jones explained that within ecumenical circles Baptists were arguing for a Baptist

96  M.I. Bochenski, ed., *Evangelicals and Ecumenism: When Baptists Disagree* (Didcot: Baptist Union, 1993).
97  *FAB*, No.4 [Autumn 1992], pp.1-9.
98  *Churches Together in England: The 'Called to be One' Process: Provisional Answers to the Seven Questions* (October, 1994).
99  Cross, *Baptism and the Baptists,* p.284.
100 *Called to be One* (London: CTE, 1996), on 'Christian Initiation and Church Membership'.

understanding of mission, baptism, ecclesiology and ministry, and also for a strong Trinitarian statement of belief.[101] Coffey recognized the unease felt by some about Roman Catholic membership of Churches Together and referred to a recent declaration, *Evangelicals and Catholics Together*, produced by seven Roman Catholic and eight evangelical Protestant leaders in North America.[102] He spoke about misunderstandings and disagreements between evangelicals and Catholics and said he was grateful to FAB for making Baptists face contentious issues. There were those who felt that since ecumenism included those with whom they disagreed, they had to register dissent or leave the Union. Others affirmed ecumenism on the basis of a Trinitarian confession of faith. Coffey noted that Baptists had opposed Unitarians joining CCBI, and this position had been established. Coffey's argument was that it was possible to dissent from *within* the ecumenical movement and that it was important to cross bridges to reach those with different views.[103]

A number of correspondents in the *Baptist Times* disagreed with Coffey. There was reference to ecumenical involvement by Baptists being 'a bridge too far'.[104] By this stage the FAB network was suggesting that all churches should be able to register their desire to opt into CTE, rather than the Union having a register only of those who opposed CTE membership. This possibility was reiterated in the *Baptist Times* by Ian Burley, who had been Consultant in Evangelism, Baptist Union of Wales, and had moved in 1991 to Oakes and Milnsbridge, Huddersfield. Burley saw the idea that all churches could register their views, for or against CTE, as constructive.[105] A good deal of the focus of anxiety had been about Roman Catholic involvement in Churches Together, but Mike Smith from Golcar, Huddersfield, who had originally trained for and

---

101  K.G. Jones, 'Committed, but critical', *SecCheck*, Issue No 11, Spring 1995, pp.1-2.
102  D. Coffey, 'Misunderstandings and Disagreements', *Baptist Leader*, Issue No.11 (Spring 1995), p.1; for the full text of the Declaration see *First Things*, Vol.43 (May 1994), pp.15-22.
103  Coffey, 'Misunderstandings and Disagreements', pp.1-2; *BT*, 30 March 1995, pp.7 and 11.
104  *BT*, 20 April 1995, p.15.
105  *It's FAB*, No.13 (December 1994), p.1; *BT*, 23 February 1995, p.11.

entered Anglican ministry before becoming a Baptist minister, declared in a letter in April 1995 to the *Baptist Times* that his biggest problem was not co-operation with Roman Catholics but with liberal Protestants. In the same issue Paul Sheppey, minister at Barnoldswick, maintained that he knew many fine Christians living out their faith in the Roman Catholic communion.[106]

At the Plymouth Assembly in the following month, the motions to continue membership of CTE and CCBI were put by Peter Wortley, LBA Secretary, and Steve Gaukroger. An amendment from Ian Burley, proposing that churches should be able to register whether or not they wished to be associated with continuing membership, was defeated. The votes in favour of Baptist involvement were higher than had been the case in 1989: 90.21% for CTE and 81.2% for CCBI. David Coffey, who hoped no group of Baptists would be marginalized, stated: 'We have had good relationships with those Baptists who have not wished to become involved with the ecumenical instruments and we hope that these will continue.'[107] Writing in June 1995 about the Assembly decision, Alec Gilmore, a veteran in the ecumenical arena, perceptively suggested that Baptists were no longer so worried about ecumenism since it had in fact become inter-church co-operation.[108] It did seem that the churches of the Baptist Union had, as a whole, decided that Roman Catholics were fellow-pilgrims. In 1998, at the invitation of Douglas McBain, then President of the Union, Basil Hume, Cardinal Archbishop of Westminster, addressed the Baptist Assembly. He received a prolonged ovation. David Coffey emphasized Baptist appreciation of Hume's deep spirituality and his courageous stand on issues such as abortion, euthanasia and the protection of the family.[109]

---

106  *BT*, 20 April 1995, p.15.
107  *BT*, 18 May 1995, p.3. During the 1990s over twenty former Baptist Union churches joined the Fellowship of Independent Evangelical Churches (FIEC). I am indebted to Rod Badams of the FIEC for this information.
108  *BT*, 1 June 1995, pp.5 and 13. For Alec Gilmore and ecumenism see J.A. Newton, 'Protestant Nonconformists and Ecumenism', in Sell and Cross, eds., *Protestant Nonconformity in the Twentieth Century*, pp.372-3.
109  *BT*, 14 May 1998, p.2.

Locally, many Baptists now had considerable ecumenical experience. Increasingly, there were more formalized arrangements for local partnerships. In 1990 the Consultative Committee for Local Ecumenical Projects in England (CCLEPE) published *Constitutional Guidelines for a Local Ecumenical Project.*[110] The Baptist Working Group, WORGLEP, and the Methodist Church published a *Baptist/Methodist Agreement on Baptismal Policy* for LEPs a year later. This said that if Methodists in an LEP were re-baptized they had to transfer to the Baptist membership roll.[111] A CTE consultation took place in 1994 on the future of LEPs and at this meeting LEPs were re-designated Local Ecumenical Partnerships. This consultation recommended the establishment of a group to explore theological issues. Baptist participants in the group, which met during 1995-96, were Chris Ellis of Cemetery Road, Sheffield, Paul Fiddes, Roger Hayden, Western Area Superintendent, Keith Jones, and Morris West as a consultant.[112] A 1996 LEP document, *Baptist/United Reformed Church Agreed Guidelines on Baptismal Policy*, followed the Baptist/Methodist agreement, but added recourse to outside help over disagreements about baptismal policy.[113] The same year saw the publication of *Called to be One.* Tony Peck, Secretary of the YBA, was encouraged that this set unity in the context of mission, but considered that a clear vision for ecumenism in the next century was lacking.[114]

## BAPTIST IDENTITY – CORE VALUES

Another area in which there was a lack of clear vision, according to David Coffey, was contemporary Baptist thinking about the church. Writing in 1994, he spoke of his gratitude for his evangelical roots and

---

110 Minutes of the Baptist Union Council, 13 and 14 November 1990.
111 See E. Welch and F. Winfield, *Travelling Together: A Handbook on Local Ecumenical Partnerships*, (London: CTE, 1995), pp.107-9. Cross, *Baptism and the Baptists*, p. 299.
112 *Pilgrim Post*, Vol.21, pp.15-18; Cross, *Baptism and the Baptists*, p.301.
113 Baptist Union of Great Britain and United Reformed Church, *Agreed Guidelines for Baptismal Policy in Local Ecumenical Partnerships* (Didcot: Baptist Union, 1996).
114 *SecCheck*, Issue No.14, Summer 1996, p.2.

his continuing debt to that stream of Christian tradition. Coffey was a member of the Evangelical Alliance Council, and the Union's Mission Department became an EA member. But Coffey noted that it was widely accepted that evangelicals had not been strong in their ecclesiology. He asked whether Baptists had been influenced by evangelical thinking which lacked 'a rich understanding of a distinctive Baptist doctrine of the Church'. He also argued for the central place of mission in Baptist identity.[115] It did seem that younger Baptists felt less sense of commitment to Baptist values and one response by the Union to the issue of younger leadership was the setting up of a Young Leaders' Forum. Philip Clements-Jewery, a part-time chaplain at Liverpool University, commented that Baptist students who came to Liverpool for higher education often went to 'magnet congregations' - largely Anglican or independent evangelical. A consultation for Baptist chaplains in higher education, of whom there were over sixty, showed that this was a widespread trend.[116]

Others, however, wanted to highlight positive features in some of the newer developments. In 1991 it was noted that a recent census had shown that eighty-four per cent of Baptists identified themselves as evangelical. The census also showed that although from 1979 to 1985 there had been a three per cent decline in Baptist attendance, there had been growth of two per cent from 1985 to 1989, which contrasted with decline in other mainstream denominations.[117] The strength of Baptist evangelicalism was not surprising: in 1943 F. Townley Lord of Bloomsbury had referred to the denomination as 'evangelical through and through'.[118] Certainly there was a range of evangelical thinking within Baptist life, but Rob Warner argued in the *Mainstream Newsletter* that the census refuted any claim

---

115 *BT*, 28 April 1994, p.7.
116 *BT*, 20 October 1994, p.8; cf. paper by David Hart, 19 December 1991, 'Baptist Union – Student Ministry Policy'. These chaplains were almost all ministers in Baptist churches who undertook chaplaincy duties. Many Baptist students joined the Christian Unions linked to the Universities and Colleges Christian Fellowship (UCCF).
117 *BT*, 26 April 1991, p.6.
118 *BT*, 6 May 1943, p.1.

that what characterized Baptists was 'unusual theological diversity'.[119] Nigel Wright advocated the values of the sixteenth-century Anabaptists as potentially helpful in finding a more radical Baptist identity. He spoke warmly in 1992 about the formation of an Anabaptist Network and a new journal *Anabaptism Today*.[120] In thinking about identity, the Evangelical Alliance was an important point of reference for many Baptists. Steve Chalke, as closing speaker at the 1996 EA Assembly, declared that many people in the television world – in which he was heavily involved - perceived evangelicals as 'bigoted and uninformed'. Chalke applauded the Assembly's outward-looking evangelicalism.[121]

The four English Baptist College Principals, Paul Fiddes, Brian Haymes, Richard Kidd and Michael Quicke, made a significant contribution to thinking about Baptist identity in 1996 with a joint publication, *Something to Declare*, which explored the Union's Declaration of Principle. Their study argued that the Declaration was designed to hold together in

*Baptism in a swimming pool, Kingsteignton Baptist Church, Devon, 1994*

covenant a wide Baptist family and that it was an important affirmation that Baptist theology had one clear centre, Jesus Christ.[122] The authors believed that in debates about baptism, Baptists needed a Declaration that provided them with strength of principle and genuine openness to others.[123] Ted Hale, of the Abbey Centre, Northampton, and Nigel

---

119  *Mainstream Newsletter*, No.41 (July 1991), p.2. The figure of 84% was to rise to 87% in a later survey.
120  *BT*, 24 September 1992, p.10. Nigel Wright pursued some of these themes in *Disavowing Constantine* (Carlisle: Paternoster Press, 2000).
121  *Idea*, January-March 1997, p.9.
122  P. Fiddes, *et al.*, *Something to Declare* (Oxford: Whitley Publications, 1996), p.25.
123  Ibid., p.38.

Wright, from 1995 senior minister at Altrincham, offered responses to the Principals' book. Hale found no basis in the New Testament for the idea of covenant being proposed.[124] Wright welcomed the Principals' approach, in particular their suggestion that the Declaration struck the same Christological note as the Barmen Declaration of 1934 (drafted by Karl Barth). But Wright queried some of the Principals' statements. For example, they described the Declaration as holding together Baptists with 'widely differing theological understandings'. Wright argued that 'diversity', if true to the Declaration, had to be within the boundaries of commitment to the deity of Christ, the Trinity, the absolute authority of Christ, scriptural authority, the doctrine of baptism, and conversion.[125]

*Something to Declare* referred to a Union discussion document, *Believing and Being Baptized: Baptism, so-called Re-baptism, and Children in the Church*, published in 1996. This represented the work of the nine members of the Doctrine and Worship Committee meeting over three years under the chairmanship of Paul Fiddes. The Council unanimously accepted the document in November 1995. The majority of the group members refused to regard infant baptism as baptism 'in the proper theological meaning of the word'. A minority saw it as potentially a significant staging point in a process of initiation. If followed by a declaration of faith, it could, for them, have baptismal significance.[126] Although *Believing and Being Baptized* was not widely read in the churches, it was nonetheless highly significant. It spoke about salvation as a spiritual journey in which baptism was normally near the beginning of Christian discipleship. For those coming to faith from outside the Christian community, baptism would be located relatively close to conversion, whereas for those nurtured within the community baptism

---

124   *BT*, 29 August 1996, p.6.
125   *BT*, 29 August 1996, p. 6.Nigel Wright expanded on aspects of his thinking in *The Radical Evangelical* (London: SPCK, 1996).
126   *BT*, 23 November 1995, p.2. The committee that produced *Believing and Being Baptized: Baptism, so-called Re-baptism, and Children in the Church* (Didcot: Baptist Union, 1996) was Paul Fiddes, Faith Bowers, G. Abraham-Williams (General Secretary of the Covenanted Churches in Wales), David Coffey (ex-officio), Chris Ellis, Brian Haymes, Peter Hicks (Director of Ministry at LBC), Keith Jones, Douglas McBain, and Nigel Wright.

marked the point when they professed faith and when God bestowed his Spirit in a new way. The document envisaged those baptized as infants and nurtured in other Christian traditions being received into Baptist membership without being baptized as believers, but with baptism being administered where a request was made out of an informed conscience.[127]

*Churches still sometimes baptize in the sea or river - here at Iseleham, formerly the scene of C.H. Spurgeon's baptism*

A number of other books in this period contributed to ongoing debates about baptism.[128] The most creative of these was *Reflections on the Water: Understanding God and the World through the Baptism of Believers.* This was edited by Paul Fiddes and there were chapters by Roger Hayden, Chris Ellis, Fiddes himself, Brian Haymes, Richard Kidd, and Hazel Sherman, now minister of Kensington Baptist Church, Brecon. There was also a response from an Anglican theologian, Christopher Rowland.[129] This book represented an important theological contribution by significant Baptist thinkers.[130] Ellis proposed that to use the term sacrament 'suggests the power of symbols to link us with the depths of reality, and points us to the use by God of material means to mediate His saving action'. He also considered that baptism was not an isolated event,

---

127  *Believing and Being Baptized*, pp.10-12, 24-29.

128  For example, D. Pawson, *Fourth Wave: Charismatics and Evangelicals* (London: Hodder & Stoughton, 1993), which built upon D. Pawson, *The Normal Christian Birth* (London: Hodder & Stoughton, 1989); D. Bridge and D. Phypers, *The Water that Divides: A Survey of the Doctrine of Baptism* (Fearn, Ross-shire: Christian Focus, 2ⁿᵈ ed., 1998).

129  P.S. Fiddes, ed., *Reflections on the Water: Understanding God and the World through the Baptism of Believers* (Oxford: Regent's Park College, 1996). This was part of a series of Regent's Study Guides.

130  For commentary see Cross, *Baptism and the Baptists*, pp.345-8, 381-4.

'but a focus of what is continually taking place' in the process of salvation.[131] Paul Fiddes took the view that Baptists should be quite willing to recognize that there were elements of faith and divine grace in infant baptism, but he also argued that in the baptism of infants the scope of grace and faith was narrower than in the baptism of believers.[132]

Aspects of this discussion were related to the issue of children in Baptist life. A Union consultation had been held in Scarborough in 1985 about children and Holy Communion. David Tennant, Head of the Church Education Department, Westhill College, from 1980 to 1997, was deeply involved in discussions about the theology of childhood.[133] He addressed the Council in 1994, introducing a resolution from the Union's Children's Working Group which urged churches 'to identify the needs of the children in their locality, and explore a strategy of working with them'. The resolution asked for an investigation of the resourcing of children's advocacy, which involved questions about representing and protecting children. It was agreed that the Group should carry on working in this area.[134] In 1995 Anne Dunkley, who was chairing the Children's Working Group, reported to the Council on their new 'Safe to Grow' guidelines, based on the government's principles in 'Safe from Harm'. Children's advocates were to be appointed in churches. There was a need to protect children and also leaders. With some amendments, the Council accepted the guidelines.[135] Anne Dunkley was among those who undertook further work on child development in Baptist communities. She gave the Whitley Lecture in 1999-2000, on children and Baptist tradition.[136]

---

131  C. Ellis, 'Baptism and the Sacramental Freedom of God', in Fiddes, ed., *Reflections on the Water*, p.36.

132  P.S. Fiddes, 'Baptism and Creation', in Fiddes, ed., *Reflections on the Water*, p.60.

133  See D. Tennant, 'Anabaptist Theologies of Childhood and Education', *BQ*, in five parts: 1982-1985.

134  *BT*, 17 November 1994, p.2.

135  *BT*, 16 March 1995, p.2; 23 November 1995, p.2. Some other denominations adapted 'Safe to Grow'.

136  Anne Dunkley, *Seen and Heard: Reflections on Children and Baptist Tradition* (Oxford: Whitley, 1999); cf. P. Martin and D. Tennant, 'Believers' Baptism, the Fellowship of Believers and Faith Development' *BQ*, Vol.39, Nos.2 and 3 (2001),

The later 1990s saw debate about the idea of the whole denomination covenanting together around core values, following the thinking of the Principals in *Something to Declare* and in their follow-up booklet, *On the Way of Trust*. At the November 1995 Council, Roger Hayden proposed a covenant to mark the millennium, and in what the *Baptist Times* described as 'a moment of pure theatre', Hayden gave a cheque for £100 to the Head of Finance and Administration, Philip Putman, to start a Millennium fund.[137] Although the idea of a new fund was not pursued,[138] a 'core values' Task Group was set up.[139] Five core values 'for a gospel people' were suggested by the Group. Churches should be prophetic, inclusive, sacrificial, missionary-minded and worshipping communities.[140] Many Baptist churches used an attractive booklet produced by the Union, *Five Core Values*, for study purposes. 'Focus Days' were held around the country to discuss ways forward, and on 12 September 1998 the Council held a special meeting to report on the Focus Days. Following this, David Coffey commended (in *Baptist Leader*) six themes: listening to God through prayer and meditation on scripture, meaningful belonging and open relationships, exploration of partnership in mission, quality care of ministers and families, generous sharing and efficient use of resources, and developing welcoming (Open Door) churches.[141] Core values for renewal were central.

## PRAYER AND PRAISE

The first item in the list in *Baptist Leader* was spirituality. Perhaps the most dramatic event of the 1990s in the area of spiritual experience was 'the Toronto Blessing', which originated at a Vineyard Christian

---

pp.96-104, 121-31.
137  *BT*, 16 November 1995, p.2.
138  *BT*, 28 March 1996, p.3.
139  The members were Bernard Green, Anne Wilkinson-Hayes, Andy Bruce (Mansfield Road, Nottingham), Stephen Greasley (Pear Tree Road, Derby), Chris Andre-Watson (Kenyon, Brixton), John Claydon (Durham City) and Hilary Willmer (Leeds).
140  *BT*, 1 October 1998, p.1.
141  *Baptist Leader*, Issue No.20, Autumn 1998.

Fellowship in Toronto, Canada, and arrived in Britain, at the Anglican Holy Trinity Church, Brompton (HTB), in May 1994. People began to 'laugh in the Spirit', exhibit physical contortions, and even make animal noises. *The Times* journalist, Ruth Gledhill, reported on 18 June 1994 that 'Toronto Blessing' was becoming popular as a nickname for 'mass fainting'.[142] A number of Baptist churches were soon affected, notably Queen's Road, Wimbledon, Lewin Road, Streatham, Herne Hill, and Bookham, Surrey.[143] The Evangelical Alliance's ACUTE group convened a meeting to discuss the phenomenon at the Ibis Hotel, London, 19-20 December 1994. Clive Calver and Joel Edwards (who was to be Calver's successor), drew together twenty-three leaders with differing views. Among the Baptists present, Robert Amess of Duke Street, Richmond, was cautious about the phenomenon, while Rob Warner was favourable. Derek Tidball, Principal of LBC, gave a paper on tensions caused by revivals. Six months later the EA convened a further consultation with about sixty present. Speakers included David Coffey, who argued for deeper examination of the theological issues at stake in the 'Blessing', and urged stronger commitment to evangelical unity.[144]

Because the Toronto Blessing was causing much debate in both charismatic and non-charismatic churches, not least in Baptist churches, several Baptist leaders addressed the issue. David Coffey wrote an article, 'When the Spirit Comes', in *Baptist Leader*, which generated considerable correspondence. Coffey acknowledged that in some churches there had been spiritual refreshing, while in others there had been tension and division. He suggested that it was important for Christians to avoid judging others without searching their own hearts. There was, he argued, a need to be aware of 'the danger of claiming that there is something ultimate and complete about our current religious experience or discovery'. There was 'fresh light and truth to break forth

---

142  R. Gledhill, 'Spread of Hysteria Fad Worries Church', *The Times*, 18 June 1994, p.12.
143  *BT*, 30 June 1994, p.2.
144  ACUTE is the Alliance Commission for Unity and Truth among Evangelicals. A third ACUTE consultation was held in December 1995, but by this time the impact of the movement was waning. See Randall and Hilborn, *One Body in Christ*, pp.316-29.

from God's word'. Coffey called for biblical, historical and theological reflection, and recommended writers who were analysing contemporary experience from different perspectives. Above all, Coffey looked for spiritual renewal that led to full-orbed mission: 'We know from the past', he wrote, 'that Renewal which goes deep into the life of the church possesses a reforming zeal which is personal, ecclesiastical and social in its dimension.'[145] In the January 1995 issue of *Mainstream*, Chris Ellis described his experience of personal renewal, and Michael Bochenski, the editor, discussed 'renewing renewal'. The emphasis was on a broad vision of renewal in the churches.[146]

Debates about music in worship continued. In the late 1980s Bernard Green welcomed the 'vitality and warmth' experienced in Baptist Assembly worship and fellowship.[147] Assembly music in the early 1990s was described by some as 'happy clappy', but Ken Davies, from Horsham, who had committed his life to God fifty years before through Arthur Coffey (David Coffey's father), welcomed the fresh life evidenced in the 1992 Assembly. Pauline Stutton of Gillingham commented that she was not 'happy clappy' but she had experienced new joy in her Christian life.[148] This period also saw the production by the Psalms and Hymns Trust of a new Baptist hymnbook, *Baptist Praise and Worship* (1991), the result of the work of three groups - an editorial committee (chairman, Alec Gilmore), music advisory committee (chairman, Michael Ball) and worship advisory committee (chairman, Michael Walker). The book contained a fine mixture of older and contemporary hymns, and also liturgical responses.[149] In 1999 the comprehensive survey of Baptist worship, *Baptist Worship To-day,* produced by Chris Ellis (who in 2000 became Principal of Bristol Baptist College), showed that most churches were using several hymnbooks and also overhead projectors to display the words of hymns. Most also used blocks of sung material as well as

---

145  D. Coffey, 'When the Spirit Comes', *Baptist Leader*, Issue No.10, Winter 1994/95, pp.1-2. David Coffey also wrote on the Toronto Blessing in *BT*, 5 January 1995, p.5.
146  *Mainstream*, No. 52 (January 1995).
147  B. Green. General Secretary, to ministers and theological students, May 1988.
148  *BT*, 28 May 1992, p.11.
149  *BT*, 31 October 1991, p.13.

hymns interspersed through the service. Changing patterns of worship meant that *Baptist Praise and Worship* did not achieve the acceptance that earlier Baptist hymnbooks had done.[150] More use was made, however, of the liturgies in the new *Patterns and Prayers for Christian Worship*.[151]

Initiatives were taken in order to help people leading worship. The Baptist Music Society became the Baptist Music Network in 1991, publicizing resources through its magazine, *Baptist Music*. Paul Lavender, later minister of Tanterton, Preston, became Training Officer for the Network.[152] Also in 1991, a guide for contemporary worship leaders, *Faith and Festivity*, by Paul Beasley-Murray, was published.[153] In 1992 *Worship File* was launched, edited by Stuart Jenkins, who moved from Higham's Park to Cheadle Hulme in that year. *Worship File* contained responsive readings, new hymns, material for preachers, and items for special occasions, especially for the Christian Year. An issue in 1995, for example, concentrated on Communion liturgies for Lent, Passiontide and Easter.[154] Keith Jones gave considerable attention to the place of the Lord's Supper in Baptist worship, and in 1999 his Whitley Lecture on this topic, *A Shared Meal and a Common Table*, was published.[155] Ian Millgate, in the Union's Ministry Department, became *Worship File* editor in 1996. New influences became evident, for example

---

150  C.J. Ellis, *Baptist Worship To-day* (Didcot: Baptist Union, 1999), pp.14, 17; cf. M. Ball, 'Baptist Praise and Worship', *BQ*, Vol.40, No.4 (2003), pp.196-214. Michael Ball, a former minister of Sutton Baptist Church, refers to the *Baptist Church Hymnal* (1900), the revised *Baptist Church Hymnal* (1933) and the *Baptist Hymn Book* (1962), before analysing in detail the production of *Baptist Praise and Worship*.

151  *Patterns and Prayers for Christian Worship* (Oxford: OUP, 1991). See R. Gouldbourne, 'Praise and Prayer', and also N. Clark, 'Baptist Praise and Worship', *BQ*, Vol.35, No.2 (1993), pp.90-4, 95-100.

152  For the new name and new thinking, see *Baptist Music*, Vol.5, No.3 (1991).

153  P. Beasley-Murray, *Faith and Festivity* (Eastbourne: MARC, 1991); cf. N. Wallwork, 'Developments in Liturgy and Worship in Twentieth-Century Protestant Nonconformity', in Sell and Cross, eds., *Protestant Nonconformity,* pp.122-4.

154  *Worship File*, Winter 1995, pp.S65-S82

155  K.G. Jones, *A Shared Meal and a Common Table: Some reflections on the Lord's Supper and Baptists* (Oxford: Whitley, 1999).

material from Celtic sources or from the Taizé community.[156] The most famous centre of Celtic tradition was Iona, off the west coast of Scotland, and in 1995 John Bell from the Iona Community introduced the community's music to the Baptist Assembly at Plymouth. Roy Searle moved from the pastorate of Enon, Sunderland, in 1992 to become Director of the Northumbria Community, which gave attention to Celtic tradition. As a member of the Mainstream executive, Searle was well placed to introduce this stream of spirituality to that constituency.[157]

Further developments in the area of spirituality came through the work of the Baptist Retreat Group, formed in 1988. In 1990 Pam Neville surveyed the ministry of the Group. Five retreats were being organized in that year. Neville explained that it was at St Mary's Anglican Convent, Wantage, that Margaret Jarman had come to the conviction that a Baptist Retreat Group should be formed. In the 1980s Springfield St Mary, Oxford, a branch house of St Mary's Convent, was becoming increasingly used by Baptist ministers for retreats. Most Baptists, however, Pam Neville noted, had been ignorant until recently of the value of contemplative spirituality.[158] By the early 1990s, many Baptists were discovering the writings of Henri Nouwen and Gerard Hughes. At the 1991 Assembly, Gerard Hughes, a Jesuit, spoke on 'The Spirituality of Freedom', and won rapt attention and warm applause.[159] Evangelical writers such as Joyce Huggett and Richard Foster were influential in this period, with Foster introducing many evangelicals to classic writers from the Catholic and Orthodox traditions. The Retreat Group began to produce a range of publications. In 1995 Bernard Green, Margaret Jarman, who from 1997 was at the Community of the Prince of Peace, Alfreton, Barry Vendy, of John Street, Stroud, and John Rackley, of Manvers Street, Bath, brought together accounts of personal spiritual journeys in *Travellers' Tales*.[160]

---

156  See *Baptist Music Magazine*, Vol.8, No.3 (1995).
157  *BT*, 27 January 1994, p.2
158  *BT*, 8 March 1990, p.7.
159  *BT*, 18 April 1991, p.1.
160  *Travellers Tales* (n.p.; Bernard Green, *et. al.*, 1995). John Rackley became Union President in 2003-4. There was a foreword to *Travellers Tales* by Malcolm Goodspeed, Head of the Ministry Department.

Although the 1990s brought new thinking and moved some Baptists in fresh directions, many Baptists continued to find the kind of spirituality experienced at events such as the Keswick Convention and Spring Harvest satisfying. David Coffey was a Keswick speaker and Council member. In the 1990s both Keswick and Spring Harvest

*A March for Jesus*

emphasized Bible teaching, inspirational preaching that called for a response, seminars, and corporate worship shaped by the influence of contemporary song-writers. In 1990 there were 75,000 people at Spring Harvest, about one-third of them Baptists. Ian Coffey and Steve Gaukroger were leading Spring Harvest figures.[161] From 1996, Baptists had their own holiday Bible week, entitled 'Leading Edge'. Baptists also joined with others in large praise walks with the title 'March for Jesus'.[162]

*Doug Hollidge leads worship at Leading Edge*

A further link between Baptists and wider expressions of evangelical spirituality was that David Peacock, who had been full-time director of music at Upton Vale, Torquay, and then became head of a new music department at LBC, co-ordinated the music at a number of Baptist Assemblies.[163] Many Baptists were drawn to inclusive expressions of evangelical

---

161   *BT*, 19 April 1990, pp.1, 12.
162   G. Kendrick, *March for Jesus* (Eastbourne: Kingsway, 1992); I. Cotton, *The Hallelujah Revolution* (London: Warner Books, 1996), chapter 1.
163   Randall, *Educating Evangelicalism*, p.260.

spirituality which they saw as embracing the breadth of evangelicalism to be found in denominational life in England.

## MISSION AND SOCIETY

One of the pan-denominational emphases of the 1990s was church planting. At a two-day Union conference in 1990 on this issue, which attracted forty specialists, Geoffrey Reynolds, Southern Area Superintendent, stressed the importance of Associations having a church planting strategy. This was based on his own experience in the 1980s. Movement of industrial and office development out of London had resulted in very substantial residential growth in the Thames Valley, and later around Swindon, and many Baptist churches established new congregations in these areas. Similar developments then took place in Hampshire. Not all the Southern Area's church planting ventures succeeded, but many new churches had become established. The Southern Area Ministry Team attended conferences on church growth. Association conferences were also held. Considerable sums of money were raised for new church premises and Home Mission initial pastorate grants made a major contribution towards the support of ministry. Stuart Christine, Oasis director for church planting and tutor at Spurgeon's College, was another speaker at the 1990 conference. Different models of church planting were offered, such as local churches planting other churches, as had happened in Peterborough under the leadership of Stephen Ibbotson.[164]

The most spectacular examples of church planting and growth were among Black-majority Baptist congregations. Kingsley Appiagyei, in West Norwood, reported that when he came from Ghana to study at Spurgeon's in the late 1980s a group of eight people began to meet in his flat. By 1991 the group had become a Ghanaian Baptist Fellowship of 180, in West Norwood, London. A year later, when this congregation was applying to join the Union, there were 350 worshippers, ninety-five per

---

164  *BT*, 19 July 1990, p.5. I am grateful to Geoffrey Reynolds for his comments.

cent Ghanaian.[165] Another predominantly Ghanaian congregation, Calvary Charismatic Baptist Church, which began in 1994 with Francis Sarpong as minister, had almost 400 members two years later. Loans from the London Baptist Property Board and the Union Corporation helped this church to acquire a former car showroom for worship.[166] A number of ethnically diverse congregations were growing. Willesden Green, London, with Philip Robinson as

*Many older churches were adapted for contemporary worship, with pews removed and screens installed. This example is the church at Bovey Tracey in Devon.*

minister, more than doubled in size during the 1990s, to over 600 members. Growth was also seen in Birmingham. Clifford Fryer reported in 1992 on Cannon Street Memorial, Handsworth, a 280-member church that was eighty per cent Black and was part of the Birmingham Baptist Inner City Project. The Project missioner, Christine Parkinson, ran 'create and celebrate' days for Black and Asian leaders, mostly aged under thirty-five. Another church, Small Heath, was converting a derelict property into shops and accommodation for single women and their children.[167] In 1994, a group of African Caribbean churches in London and the Midlands, the Progressive Baptist Convention of Europe, joined the Union.[168] Not surprisingly, when there was reference at the Union

165  *BT*, 11 March 1991, p.11. K. Appiagyei, 'Reaching Africans in London: An Ethnic Ministry', *The Baptist Ministers' Journal*, Vol.238 (April 1992), pp. 6-10.

166  *BT*, 20 June 1996, p.1.

167  *BT*, 16 July 1992, p.6.

168  *BT*, 17 November 1994, p.3. The parent body in the USA is African American and was the Convention to which Martin Luther King belonged.

Council to promoting church planting among ethnic communities the response was that ethnic minority churches were already leading the way.[169]

A thoughtful debate took place at the Council in November 1995 about the role of the Union's Mission Department in developing strategies for church planting. A survey of the thinking of Association representatives about church plants had shown that 8% were enthusiastic, 20% were negative and 72% were non-committal. The Mission Department was asked to develop training to facilitate appropriate church planting. David Ronco, at Port Hill, Hertford, queried the very high figures for projected new churches that had been talked about in 1992 at the church planting Dawn 2000 Congress.[170] In 1992 it had been calculated that in the period since 1980 Baptists had been involved in the planting of 183 new churches, with the Southern Area leading the field (37 new churches), followed by the North West (22), then the North East and London (19 each), the South East (17) and the Eastern Area (16). The other Areas averaged a dozen new churches each.[171] In the mid-1990s there were doubts about whether this rate of church planting could be significantly increased. There were also tensions over denominational church planting. Baptists like Hugh Cross argued that all new churches should be ecumenical, but others in the denomination, such as David Spriggs, Evangelism Secretary at the EA, and Stuart Murray, who succeeded Stuart Christine at Spurgeon's, did not share this view.[172]

In many areas of witness Baptists were certainly thinking pan-denominationally. The Union Council encouraged local Baptist churches to co-operate with others in the Decade of Evangelism, which was launched in January 1991.[173] 'On Fire', an ecumenical celebration of Pentecost in 1994, which developed out of an idea of Steve Chalke's, was well supported, but on the whole the Decade did not produce much in the way of initiatives. Baptists showed much more interest in Alpha courses,

---

169  *BT*, 3 April 1997, p.2.
170  *BT*, 16 Nov 1995, p.3.
171  *BT*, 2 April 1992, pp.8-9.
172  *BT*, 22 July 1993, p.9.
173  Minutes of the Baptist Union Council, 13 and 14 November 1990.

*Roy Castle with children at Great Ormond Street.*
*A popular entertainer and a Baptist, he and his*
*wife Fiona witnessed strongly to their faith when*
*he developed lung cancer.*

which provided a non-threatening setting within which people were introduced to the Christian faith. Alpha was a product of Holy Trinity Church, Brompton. In 1997 approaching 5,000 Alpha courses were being run all over the world, including 350 in Baptist churches in Britain. A year later the Baptist figure had risen to 500.[174] Another approach to evangelism which aroused interest was 'seeker sensitive' services for unchurched people, developed especially by Willow Creek Community Church in the USA. Bill Hybels, the Willow Creek senior pastor, spoke at the Baptist Assembly in 1994 and groups of Baptist ministers visited Willow Creek. At the Mainstream Conference in 1994, Roger Sutton, from Altrincham, showed how the Altrincham church's monthly 'seeker service' operated.[175]

Those within the Union thinking about mission faced both difficulties and opportunities. The giving to Home Mission faltered in the early 1990s. In 1994, however, there was a recovery, and David Nixon was able to announce that the Home Mission target of £2.5 million had almost been reached.[176] In the same year a new Baptist Women's Mission Network was launched. The intention was 'to encourage, equip and enable women within Baptist churches, and beyond, in the ecumenical sphere, to become fully integrated at all levels in the Church's life and mission so that their gifts might be used to the full'. The administrator of

174   D. Hilborn, *Picking up the Pieces*, (London: Hodder & Stoughton, 1997), pp.210–14; S. Hunt, *Anyone for Alpha?: Evangelism in a post-Christian society* (London: Darton, Longman and Todd, 2001).
175   *BT*, 27 January 1994, p.2.
176   *BT*, 16 March 1995, p.3.

the network was Shirley Lane, who had chaired the executive of the National Council of Baptist Women.[177] Further changes took place in 1997 when the Christian Training Programme finally ceased and when approval was given to replacing the Union's Mission Department with a Department for Training and Research in Mission. It had proved difficult to fill the post of Secretary for Mission and Evangelism after Derek Tidball moved to LBC as Principal, and it was out of the Denominational Consultation that the idea had come of a Department for Research and Training in Mission. The Council also committed itself to a 'Policy for Growth and Church Planting'.[178] In 1998 Derek Allan, minister in Redcar, became Head of the Union's Mission Department. There were three Mission advisers: Iain Hoskins, Darrell Jackson and Graham Sparkes.[179]

Baptist mission in the 1990s was marked by social action as well as evangelism. In 1990 Eric Blakebrough received an MBE for his work among drug addicts.[180] Oasis Trust, directed by Steve Chalke, took several initiatives. The Trust became responsible for Haddon Hall, a church near London Bridge that was near to closure. In 1990 it also opened a new hostel for the homeless in south London.[181] Another initiative by Chalke, Christmas Cracker restaurants, raised about £1 million in 1990 for social projects in Africa and India. Christmas Cracker had 420 outlets over the Christmas period, with thousands of young people involved. The seed-bed of the idea was a restaurant that Chalke set up during his ministry at Tonbridge Baptist Church. He also launched Radio Christmas in Tonbridge, and this led in 1991 to Christmas Cracker radio stations. The BBC produced a documentary about what was done.[182] Later Oasis Trust began training youth specialists for work in church and

---

177  *BT*, 21 April 1994, p.10.
178  *BT*, 3 April 1997, p.2.
179  Iain Hoskins had been National Youth Officer, Darrell Jackson had been Devon and Cornwall Association Youth Representative, and Graham Sparkes had been minister of Christ Church, Kings Langley.
180  E. Blakebrough, *No Quick Fix* (Basingstoke: Marshall Pickering, 1986).
181  *BT*, 8 March 1990, p.3.
182  *BT*, 21 March 1991, pp.1, 9; 19 Dec 1991, pp.11-12.

*Steve Chalke launches Christmas Cracker*

community settings. The emphasis on both social action and evangelism was encouraged by the Union. Help for mission initiatives was available through Home Mission 'Green Shoots' grants. The 1994 Assembly saw a presentation by Andy Bruce, chair of the Union's Social Action Committee, and Anne Wilkinson-Hayes, of 'Against the Stream', a scheme to help fund projects in needy areas. The first 'Against the Stream' grants were made to churches in Toxteth and Dagenham.[183]

Political interest was also evident. John Biggs spoke to MPs in 1990 about environmental issues.[184] In 1996 the *Baptist Times* noted an article written by Tony Blair, leader of the Labour Party (and soon to be Prime Minister), with the title 'Why I am a Christian'.[185] At that point John Major was Prime Minister, and Lord McColl, a member of Herne Hill Baptist Church and Professor of Surgery at Guy's and St Thomas's hospitals, was his Parliamentary Private Secretary.[186] Seminar papers were offered by Baptists prior to the 1997 General Election.[187] Graham

---

183  *BT*, 5 May 1994, p.3; 28 July 1994, p.3.

184  *BT*, 31 May 1990, p.1.

185  *BT*, 18 April 1996, p.5.

186  *BT*, 1 August 1996, p.11.

187  Keith Jones, Faith Bowers and Michael Bochenski offered perspectives in a series of seminars at the Bloomsbury church and in the *Baptist Times*: *BT*, 20 March 1997, p.5. These were published as *Baptist Perspectives: Seminar papers given January-March 1997 prior to the General Election* (London: Bloomsbury Central Baptist Church, 1997).

Dale, who studied at LBC and then worked for the EA, became director of the Christian Socialist Movement.[188] Baptists were also among those addressing employment problems. A hard-hitting report, *Unemployment and the Future of Work* (1997), was produced by an ecumenical group, chaired by David Sheppard, Bishop of Liverpool, with Bill Allen, tutor at Spurgeon's, as a member. Simon Jones, convenor of the Baptist Union's 'Future of Work' Study Group, who was also involved, noted the almost deafening silence about unemployment from political parties.[189] World debt was another major concern. In the mid-1990s a campaign began, and in 1997 Ann Pettifor, director of Jubilee 2000 (as the campaign was called), met with thirty Baptist representatives at Didcot. Wilkinson-Hayes was delighted with the discussions.[190] Leading

*Another march of witness for Christ's Kingdom: churches supported demonstrations focusing on debt relief and fair trade*

---

188   See G. Dale, *God's Politicians: The Christian Contribution to 100 years of Labour* (London: HarperCollins, 2000).

189   *BT*, 10 April 1997, p.1.

190   *BT*, 17 April 1997, p.3.

Christian aid agencies as well as denominations ranged behind the campaign. In May 1998, 70,000 people, many from churches, formed a human chain in Birmingham to highlight the issue to world leaders at an economic summit. Following this, the British government called for a review of debt relief.[191]

Other societal developments raised issues of justice which Baptists sought to address. There was concern about the treatment of minorities. In 1991 Jim Chauhan, who was director of the Asian Ministry Partnership in the West Midlands and was supported by Home Mission, argued that the Gulf War was alienating many British Asians and that many white Christians had only a superficial understanding of the issues.[192] As well as increasing ethnic diversity there was also the question of religious diversity. Inter-faith dialogue was on the agenda. The Joppa Group, a group of Baptists seeking to wrestle with questions posed by a multi-faith society, produced a booklet in 1992 on the issue, and Paul Weller, a member of the Joppa Group and Head of the Religious Resource and Research Centre at Derbyshire College of Higher Education, contributed articles for the *Baptist Quarterly*.[193] Questions were also being increasingly raised - and answered in different ways - within the denominations about appropriate responses to issues concerning homosexuality.[194] The Union issued guidelines to the ministerial recognition rules, stating that homosexual orientation was not a reason for exclusion from Baptist ministry but that homosexual genital practice was regarded as unacceptable in the pastoral office and that ministers were expected not to advocate homosexual or lesbian genital relationships as acceptable alternatives to male/female marriage partnership.[195]

---

191   *BT*, 12 March 1998, p.1, 21 May 1998, p.1.

192   *BT*, 14 February 1991, p.1.

193   Clinton Bennett, *et. al.*, *A Baptist Perspective on Interfaith Dialogue* (Alcester: Joppa Publications, 1992); P. Weller, 'Freedom and Witness in a Multi-Religious Society: A Baptist Perspective', *BQ*, Vol.33, Nos.6 and 7 (1990), pp.252-64 and 302-15.

194   See *Faith, Hope and Homosexuality: A report by the Evangelical Alliance's Commission on Unity and Truth among Evangelicals* (London: ACUTE, 1998).

195   The Ministry Main Committee formally accepted these guidelines in February 1988. They were later made available to the Baptist Union Council; *BT*, 13 August

Despite the stress on involvement in society, the picture of Baptist advance in England during the 1990s was mixed. David Staple, General Secretary of the Free Church Federal Council, applauded the Council's vision for mission, but noted that Home Mission giving was inadequate.[196] In 1995 the annual figure for baptisms fell below 4,000 for the first time. David Coffey and Darrell Jackson, the Union's evangelism co-ordinator, asked questions. Were people being challenged about baptism? Was youth work effective?[197] Iain Hoskins reported in 1995 that 300 young people were leaving Baptist churches every week and that eighty-five per cent of teenagers had no church connection. He expressed sympathy with the idea of youth churches.[198] Derek Tidball argued in 1996 that postmodern culture's challenge to comprehensive interpretations of reality, such as the Christian story, had to be faced.[199] Despite the worries that Baptist churches were not communicating effectively in a postmodern context, baptisms were up by fifteen per cent in 1997 compared to the year before.[200] Writing in 1998, Darrell Jackson noted that in the previous two years Baptist membership had continued to decline, although baptisms had increased. There were indications of more people attending Baptist churches, but many were not becoming members. Jackson noted that since *Turning the Tide* had been published in 1981, Baptist membership had fallen by 6,900.[201] A year later Jackson's analysis of the changing relationship between attendance and membership was confirmed. Research showed that against a background of a fourteen per cent decline in churchgoing in the 1990s, attendance at Baptist churches had grown by thirteen per cent.[202]

1992, p.8. I am indebted to Malcolm Goodspeed for his help.
196  *BT*, 19 December 1991 p.12.
197  *BT*, 31 October 1996, pp.1 and 5.
198  *BT*, 8 June 1995, p.10.
199  D.J. Tidball, 'Postmodernity', *Mainstream* (January 1996), pp.11–18.
200  *BT*, 1 January 1998, p.1
201  *BT*, 19 November 1998, p.5.
202  *BT*, 2 December 1999, p.1; cf. G. Davie, *Religion in Britain since 1945: Believing without Belonging* (Oxford, Blackwell, 1994).

RELATING AND RESOURCING

After the Denominational Consultation in September 1996 the major question was: 'What kind of Baptist Union is required to respond to God's call to mission as we enter a new millennium?' David Coffey and Peter Wortley, moderator of the Council, indicated that the full agenda set out by the consultation would occupy the denomination's thinking for a long time to come.[203] The Denominational Conference Reference Group that was set up had Tony Peck, Secretary of the YBA, as convenor; in November 1997 Peck reported to the Council, meeting in Tonbridge, that the denomination appeared to be reaching a crucial stage in implementing the new vision. He spoke about an interim statement reaffirming the Baptist way of being the church, a covenant based on trust, commitment to justice, agreed models of translocal leadership, including superintendency, commitment to close partnership with the BMS, and commitment to working ecumenically wherever possible. The future would involve a greater emphasis on a relational approach to association life and on holistic mission. He said that many felt the future direction of superintendency was unclear. A one-day Council meeting was arranged for September 1998 to discuss issues of associating, leadership and superintendency. Also a Baptist Leaders' Conference was planned for 1999 at Wembley. Associations were in the meantime to come up with action plans.[204]

A Task Group was set up to pursue the over-riding theme of reform of the Associations that had come out of the Consultation. This group was chaired by Nigel Wright. Within the terms of reference set out for this Group by the Council, the first aim given to it was to further the concerns of the denominational consultation and the Council for 'a radical revision of our Associating'.[205] Comment on the future of associating was invited

---

203  *BT*, 3 October 1996, p.iv. Peter Wortley was Union President, 2001-2.
204  *BT*, 27 November 1997, p.4.
205  *Relating and Resourcing* (Didcot: Baptist Union, 1998), Appendix 1. Members of the Task Group were Peter Grange, East Midland superintendent; Carolyn Green, YBA; Chris Haig, North Western Association; David Hall, Sussex Association; Keith Jones; Jacqui Keenan, Devon and Cornwall Association; John Newman, Union treasurer; and Rob Warner, Queen's Road, Wimbledon. The committee was

and received from various quarters. Mainstream noted in January 1998 that some welcomed what they saw as radical ideas emerging from the consultation, but others observed unnecessary caution. Tony Peck, described by Michael Bochenski as the Union's busiest man, spoke from his experience in Yorkshire about regional teams as the best way forward in the leadership, encouragement and resourcing of associating.[206] For some, Mainstream had been important as a way of developing relationships within the Union, a point made by John Weaver, tutor at Regent's Park College, as he looked back in 1998 on twenty years of Mainstream. Peter Grange, however, Area Superintendent of the East Midlands, who had also been fully involved in Mainstream, considered that much of its original vision remained unfulfilled. Although there had been pioneering work, generally the hoped for life and growth in Baptist churches had not happened.[207]

The articulation of this kind of critique was a clear challenge to the Task Group on Associating. Its report, *Relating and Resourcing*, called for a rediscovery of 'the reality of associating'. There should, it considered, be mutually supportive 'relationships, clusters and networks'. But it also affirmed regional and national structures. A crucial recommendation of *Relating and Resourcing* was for the merging of the existing twenty-nine Associations and the Areas in order to create approximately sixteen new regional associations. Each of these would be served by a regional team comprising a variety of ministries including visionary, pastoral, evangelistic and others. There would be at least two regional ministers in each Association. Together with the General Secretaries and the heads of department at Didcot, these would form a national leadership team. Another radical recommendation was that regional ministers would be employed and paid locally. Home Mission funds would be reallocated for this purpose.[208] These were far-reaching proposals, and the Council gave itself three days in April 1998 so that *Relating and Resourcing* could be thoroughly discussed.

---

serviced by Philip Putman, Head of Finance and Administration.
206  *Mainstream*, No.61 (January 1998), p.13.
207  *Mainstream*, No. 63 (September 1998), p.20.
208  *Relating and Resourcing*, pp.10-15; *BT*, 26 March 1998, pp.1 and 8.

Nigel Wright, as the Task Group convenor, presented the report. The Council agreed that the reality of associating had largely been lost and that this should be recovered through the building of networks. The keynote was flexibility. The proposal to replace the existing Associations prompted vigorous discussion. A straw poll indicated ninety-one in favour, twenty-one against and twenty-eight abstaining. There were also reservations about the proposal that regional teams be responsible for the tasks of leading Associations in mission, oversight of the churches, inter-church associating and the pastoral care of ministers. The liveliest debate was over the idea that regional ministers should be called, employed and paid locally by the Associations. On a straw poll about this recommendation, seventy-one were in favour, fifty-two were against, and thirty abstained. This move, which was ultimately to be accepted, had not been envisaged in *Transforming Superintendency*. The idea in *Relating and Resourcing* of a national leadership team was agreed. At the end of the debate three substantive resolutions were passed. These recognized *Transforming Superintendency* as foundational; welcomed *Relating and Resourcing*, commending it for wide discussion; and invited the Denominational Consultation Reference Group to set up task groups to develop a Millennium Covenant and to oversee implementation of Council recommendations.[209]

The 1998 Assembly saw a spirited debate on restructuring.[210] Further steps included widespread consultation and the special Council meeting in September 1998. The thinking in *Relating and Resourcing* proved to be pivotal. In March 1999 the Council agreed a new framework for Associations. The plan was for twelve in England and one in Wales, with 1 January 2002 as the starting date. Associations would facilitate clustering. Regional team leaders would be appointed and regional teams would have responsibility for mission and pastoral care. A National Strategy Team would deal with mission strategy and a National Settlement Team would take the settlement aspects of the work of

---

209   *BT*, 2 April 1998, p.1; 16 April 1998, pp.4, 5.
210   *BT*, 14 May 1998, p.1.

*Baptist Leaders' Day at Wembley 1999*

superintendents.[211] As part of the process of engaging the churches, the Baptist Leaders' Day, held at Wembley Conference Centre in March 1999, which attracted 2,600 people, was a boost to confidence. Douglas McBain outlined the challenge of church decline and four speakers addressed areas of renewal: Tony Peck on the renewal of the local church; Nigel Wright on renewing relationships; Brian Haymes on the renewal of ministry; and Lynn Green, minister of Wokingham Baptist Church, on renewing mission. David Coffey, the *Baptist Times* editorial commented, demonstrated his credentials as a leader. He gave a keynote address on Isaiah chapter 35 in which he emphasized that the focus was not 'narrow denominational interests'. Indeed he saw 'documents, reports, dreams and personal ambitions' being relinquished, and he urged those present to say together: 'For the King and his Kingdom'. Coffey was questioned by Harvey Thomas, former Conservative Party conference organiser and a member of a London Baptist church.[212] At the end of 1999, Coffey affirmed his belief that 'God is leading us on this journey of reform for his missionary purposes'.[213]

---

211   *BT*, 1 April 1999, p.7.
212   *BT*, 18 March 1999, pp.1, 2, 5, 7, 10.
213   *BT*, 23 September 1999, p.11.

CONCLUSION

At the beginning of the 1990s Bernard Green had spoken of signs of hope. New churches were being planted, AIM was being used in 600 churches, a flexible Home Mission scheme was in operation, leadership training was taking place, the move to Didcot had been achieved, and there were hopes for a new era in BU-BMS partnership. The challenges which he saw ahead included the decade of evangelism, international issues, and ecumenical developments.[214] In a number of areas Bernard Green's optimism proved well-founded. For example, nearly 200 Baptist churches were planted during the decade.[215] Progress was also seen in the ecumenical field. The Union Council statement in 1992, which encouraged imaginative and effective strategies in evangelism and other aspects of God's mission, reflected the priorities espoused by David Coffey and Keith Jones. At the end of the decade the English Church Census showed that there had been areas of growth. In Yorkshire, for example, Baptist congregations had grown by nineteen per cent during the 1990s after a fall of six per cent in the 1980s. Attendance at Baptist worship (in Union and non-Union churches) had risen from 270,900 people in 1989 to 277,600 in 1998. In that year 209,000 people were Baptist church members.[216] As well as mission, the commitment of the Council 'to develop our distinctive Baptist identity, to strengthen our associating by mutual commitment at every level', proved to be a strategic focus in the 1990s. Far-reaching changes were agreed. It was the hope of the Union leadership that these changes would mean that the Union was better equipped to face the new challenges of the twenty-first century.

214  *BT*, 4 January 1990, p.6.
215  *BT*, 2 December 1999, p.1
216  *BT*, 16/23 December 1999, p.5.

# Chapter 12
# CONCLUSION
# 'REJUVENATING CHANGE'

The Baptist denomination in England, like other historic denominations, has seen massive changes through the course of the twentieth century. At the beginning of the century the Free Churches displayed enormous optimism. Seeing themselves as part of a cohesive movement, with shared beliefs that resonated with some of the aspirations of the wider society, they felt that the future belonged to them. In 1900 to be connected with a church was respectable, and the Free Churches had themselves gained respectability. J.H. Shakespeare, the Baptist Union General Secretary, was the embodiment of this positive outlook. Under Shakespeare's leadership, in the first two decades of the twentieth century, the structures of the Baptist Union which were to exist for most of the century were put in place. The denomination had a sense of confidence. By the end of the century, the religious outlook was quite different. The church attender, of whatever denomination, had, as Adrian Hastings put it, 'become, just slightly, an oddity' in a predominantly secular society.[1] It was in this period, especially under David Coffey as General Secretary, that the Baptist Union's structures, and more fundamentally the thinking that lay behind them, began to be questioned publicly by significant numbers of Baptists. This re-evaluation led to the articulation of a new vision of what it meant to be a Baptist community.

Questions about the ministry have been at the forefront of many discussions in the Union. Shakespeare, wishing to ensure that Baptist ministers were effective as preachers and pastors and were well supported, promoted accreditation procedures, central funding and the superintendency. He believed that he was dealing with considerable dissatisfaction among ministers and churches, and although there were

---

1    Hastings, *A History of English Christianity,* pp.xv-xvi.

different opinions about the degree of frustration that existed, it seemed clear that action was needed.[2] The machinery that was put in place to ensure proper ministerial accreditation and standards addressed pressing problems, but many challenges remained. A Union report, *Matters Affecting the Efficiency of the Ministry* (1930), articulated these challenges. The absence of a widely-accepted theology of ministry led to a further report, in 1957, on *The Meaning and Practice of Ordination among Baptists*. In the 1960s, when significant numbers of ministers were leaving pastoral ministry, the reports on *The Doctrine of the Ministry* (1961) and *Ministry Tomorrow* (1969) were produced. *Ministry Tomorrow* was wide of the mark in estimating greatly reduced numbers of full-time ministers. Later the fresh buoyancy in Baptist life led to the very different concern that too many people were training for ministry. Principles were agreed in the 1990s for accrediting evangelists and youth specialists. The report, *Forms of Ministry among Baptists* (1994), led to an acceptance of diversity while maintaining the uniqueness of ordained pastoral ministry.

As well as diversity in forms of ministry, there was also much greater diversity by the end of the century in those entering ministry. One of the outcomes of the Denominational Conference in 1961 was the abolition of a rule preventing people aged over forty from beginning training to be full-time accredited ministers, and this altered the age profile of those entering ministry. Prior to the 1960s virtually all those entering training were in their early twenties, whereas by the end of the century the average age was early thirties.[3] This had the effect of reducing the years that people spent in ministry. At the same time, more churches were appointing paid youth leaders and children's workers, partly as a response to the increasing demands of such work. Diversity was also seen in the increasing numbers of women in ministry. Although progress in this area was painfully slow, there were important landmarks. These included the ordination of the first women Baptist ministers in the 1920s, the transfer of serving deaconesses to the accredited ministerial list in 1975, and in 1997 the appointment to the superintendency of Patricia Took, whom David Coffey described as bringing 'a unique

2    Sparkes, *The Home Mission Story,* p.29.
3    *BT,* 21 December 1989, p.10.

combination of spirituality, gifting and personality to the ministry of superintendent'.[4] Ethnic diversity was also increasingly evident. At the end of the century Black ministers were leading congregations in London that were the fastest-growing in the Union: Trinity, West Norwood, and Calvary Charismatic, Stratford, both with over 800 members in 1999, were the largest shown in the Union's 1999-2000 *Directory*.[5]

Ministers were involved in shaping the spirituality of the churches. Daily prayer and Bible reading were regarded as basic to Baptist spirituality.[6] At various times, however, there were calls for Baptists to seek a deeper spiritual experience. In the inter-war period these invitations were issued at the Keswick Convention and at the Keswick-style revival meetings held by Douglas Brown, as well as emanating from the Oxford Group.[7] Amongst a section of the Baptist community, represented partly by the Baptist Revival Fellowship, there was a stress in the 1940s and 1950s on personal and corporate revival. Although M.E. Aubrey, as Union General Secretary until 1951, was sympathetic to this theme, it seemed that those who expressed most forcibly their concern about the spiritual state of the churches, such as Theo Bamber of Rye Lane Chapel, Peckham, felt that they did not influence Union life. There was, however, a movement of spiritual renewal which gradually achieved a more central place within Baptist churches: the charismatic movement. Although all the major denominations were affected from the 1960s onwards by this new impetus, among Free Churches the most potent effect was on Baptist congregations. Some grew substantially, although there were also splits.[8]

Expressions of spirituality, whether personal or corporate, had links with the changing social context. From the 1960s, with an increasingly informal culture in Britain, the trend in worship was towards more

---

4    *BT*, 20 November 1997, p.2.
5    *The Baptist Union Directory: 1999-2000* (Didcot: Baptist Union, 2001).
6    S.F. Winward, 'Baptist Spirituality', in G.S. Wakefield, ed., *A Dictionary of Christian Spirituality* (London: SCM, 1983), pp.36-8.
7    For the wider picture in the 1920s and 1930s see I.M. Randall, *Evangelical Experiences: A study of the Spirituality of English Evangelicalism, 1918-1939* (Carlisle: Paternoster Press, 1999).
8    D.W. Bebbington, 'Evangelism and Spirituality in Twentieth-Century Protestant Nonconformity', in Sell and Cross, eds., *Protestant Nonconformity*, p.212.

participation and spontaneity. Change was evident, for example, in the practice of baptism. Whereas up to the 1960s ministers dressed formally for baptisms, ordinary dress became fairly common.[9] There was also a tendency to disengage from socio-political affairs. From the 1930s internal Baptist Union issues began to take on greater significance than political and social issues.[10] By the 1950s there was what Bebbington terms 'a psychology of withdrawal', due to a feeling that before dealing with the nation there was a need for Baptist life itself to be put in order.[11] In 1906 there were seventeen Baptist MPs, fifteen Liberal and two Labour, in the House of Commons. In 2001, by contrast, Andrew Selous, a member of Hockliffe Street, Leighton Buzzard, Conservative MP for South West Bedfordshire and Parliamentary Chairman of the Conservative Christian Fellowship, was the only Baptist MP at Westminster.[12] The number of Baptists taking an active part in the 'public square' declined. By the 1990s only a few Baptist figures impinged on the public consciousness. These included Steve Chalke, who appeared regularly on TV programmes; Sir John Houghton, Director of the Meteorological Office and a major spokesman on ecological concerns; Eric Ives, Pro-Vice Chancellor of Birmingham University and Professor of History; David Cook, Fellow of Green College, Oxford, and a panel member of the BBC radio programme, the 'Moral Maze'; Michael Taylor, Director of Christian Aid until 1997 and later Professor of Social Theology, Birmingham University;[13] and Justin Phillips, a member of Haven Green and Deputy Editor of Radio 4's 'The World Tonight'.[14]

Nonetheless, the Baptist Union sought to have a voice in national affairs. During his General Secretaryship, E.A. Payne attempted to give attention to both ecclesiastical and socio-political affairs, and David S.

9    Cross, *Baptism and the Baptists,* pp.199-200.
10   M. Goodman, 'A Faded Heritage: English Baptist political thinking in the 1930s', *BQ,* Vol.37, No.2 (1997), p.61.
11   D.W. Bebbington, 'Baptists and Politics since 1914', in Clements, ed., *Baptists in the Twentieth Century,* p.81.
12   *BT,* 15 January 2004, p.1.
13   *BT,* 26 April 1991, p.6. See M.H. Taylor, *Not Angels but Agencies: The ecumenical response to poverty* (London: SCM, 1996).
14   *BT,* 14 April 1994, p.7.

Russell, who followed him, was honoured for his tireless work on behalf of human rights. By the time Bernard Green became General Secretary, in the 1980s, it was becoming common for Baptist leaders to make their voice heard through ecumenical channels and also through the agency of the rapidly-growing Evangelical Alliance, led by Clive Calver. This trend continued in the 1990s, when Joel Edwards, of the Black-majority New Testament Church of God, succeeded Calver as EA's Director. Adrian Hastings described Edwards as 'perhaps, all in all, the most significant ecclesiastical figure of the 1990s'.[15] Whereas at the beginning of the twentieth century Baptists had co-operated closely with other Free Churches in pursuing their wider socio-political agenda, at the end of the century most Baptists saw themselves operating as part of both wider ecumenical bodies and pan-evangelical communities and organizations.[16] By the end of the 1990s, the political campaigns early in the twentieth century on behalf of the Free Churches, led by nationally-known Baptist ministers like John Clifford and F.B. Meyer, were hard to imagine.

The changing configuration of inter-church relationships created enormous tensions for Baptists, as it did for all denominations, and at times ecumenical questions consumed a great deal of the energy of the Union's leadership. J.H. Shakespeare's vision, articulated in his book *The Churches at the Cross-Roads* (1918), for a united Church in England, meant that he was seen by Hastings as 'the most deeply and consistently ecumenical of all the Church leaders of the time'.[17] Yet any moves towards structural church unity raised profound questions about Baptist ecclesiology. Despite Shakespeare's standing, his thinking in this area failed to gain much Baptist support. Shakespeare's approach, however, was taken up and developed by Ernest Payne, who became a leading statesman within the World Council of Churches. Payne's high view of Church and ministry was also embodied in *The Baptist Doctrine of the Church* (1948), and in other publications by Payne himself and by the Union. Other Baptists, however, considered that such thinking, with its associated hopes for moves towards wider unity, threatened Baptist distinctives such as believer's baptism, evangelical faith, and the

---

15    Hastings, *A History of English Christianity*, p.xlvi.
16    Randall and Hilborn, *One Body in Christ*, chapter 12.
17    Hastings, *A History of English Christianity*, p.98.

ecclesiological integrity of the local church. Anti-ecumenical feeling in the 1960s and 1970s, combined with other theological tensions, led to a number of churches and ministers, in some cases associated with the Baptist Revival Fellowship, leaving the Union. Others, by contrast, especially through the Baptist Renewal Group, encouraged ecumenical commitment.

It appeared from the votes taken at the Assemblies in 1989 and 1995 that, like many other evangelicals, most Baptists were increasingly committed to pursuing and deepening inter-church co-operation.[18] Although some who left the Union saw it as shackled by unbiblical traditions, within ecumenical circles the Union was seen as progressive in such areas as the use of technology in the service of mission.[19] Baptist

involvement in both ecumenism and evangelicalism is well illustrated by the commitments of John Briggs, who became Principal of Westhill College, Birmingham, in 1997 and also Pro-Vice-Chancellor of Birmingham University. Professor Briggs was deeply involved in a number of significant evangelical projects, such as the *Lion Handbook of Christianity*. He served the Union in a wide variety of ways, for example as the first chair of the Faith and Unity Executive. Within the Baptist World Alliance he served in several capacities. Ecumenically, Briggs

*John Briggs*        was a member of the executive committee of the WCC from 1991 to 1998 and was part of a committee exploring issues raised by the Orthodox Church. On 7 March 2001, Briggs preached at a service in Bloomsbury Baptist Church to mark the end of the Free Church Council, which became the Free Churches Group in association with Churches Together in England. Briggs also became convenor of the Group.[20] As one of the most influential lay

---

18    I.M. Randall, 'Unity in the Gospel: Catholic-Evangelical Relationships', *One in Christ*, Vol.38, No.1 (2003), pp.16-30.

19    I am indebted to John Briggs for this observation.

20    F. Bowers, 'John H.Y. Briggs MA, FSA, FRHistS: An Appreciation', in A.R. Cross, ed., *Ecumenism and History: Studies in Honour of John H.Y. Briggs*

people in the Baptist denomination, Briggs both exemplified and shaped trends in Baptist life.

New thinking about ecumenism formed part of a wider debate about Baptist identity. Shakespeare did much to enhance a sense of Baptist identity, while also creating the potential for future fissures. Historically, the centre-piece of Baptist identity has been the doctrine of the church. Payne's creative thinking, which was expressed in a number of ways (for example in the Focus Group and through his historical writings) portrayed a broader vision of ecclesial life while still affirming congregationalism.[21] Although Payne's conception of the 'Church catholic' had limited impact on grass-roots Baptists life, it did provoke further questions about Baptist identity. These were taken up in the later 1970s and 1980s by Brian Haymes and others, who formed a group that wrote several significant booklets, and by a new Baptist movement, Mainstream, dedicated to life and growth among Baptists. Like the Focus Group, Mainstream became a seed-bed for fresh ideas. Some of the new perspectives, especially about the renewal of local churches and about translocal relationships, were fed into discussions in the 1990s through those active in wider renewal, such as Douglas McBain and Nigel Wright. The creation of the Faith and Unity Executive Committee and the Doctrine and Worship Committee in this period was a sign of theological confidence in the Union, with issues of doctrine and ecumenical relationships being more thoroughly analysed by participants such as Paul Fiddes, the Union's leading theologian involved in ecumenical dialogue.[22] In 2002 Fiddes was appointed Professor of Systematic Theology in the University of Oxford.

---

(Carlisle: Paternoster Press, 2002), pp.1-20. I am also indebted to Basil Amey. Briggs took over as convenor from Rosalind Goodfellow, of the URC.

21    For Payne as a Free Church historian, see D. Cornick, 'Twentieth-Century Historians of English Protestant Nonconformity', in Sell and Cross, eds., *Protestant Nonconformity in the Twentieth Century*, pp.66-72.

22    I am grateful to Keith Jones, former Deputy General Secretary of the Union, for some of these observations. For an example of Paul Fiddes' work in the field of ecumenical theology, see P.S. Fiddes, 'The Church and Salvation: A Comparison of Orthodox and Baptist Thinking', in A.R. Cross, ed., *Ecumenism and History: Studies in Honour of John H.Y. Briggs* (Carlisle: Paternoster Press, 2002), pp.120-48.

The twentieth century saw Baptists establishing a world-wide and a European-wide identity through the BWA and the European Baptist Federation. In the 1990s David Coffey played an important international role, as President of the EBF at a time when post-communist Europe was experiencing massive change, and as Vice-President of the BWA when non-Western Baptist life was becoming increasingly significant. David Coffey was elected to the BWA Presidency from 2005.[23] In his leadership, Coffey committed himself to the broader Baptist community, to other evangelicals, and to ecumenism. Within the Baptist Union, David Coffey, Keith Jones and others were concerned to strengthen associating and thus Baptist identity. However, by the beginning of the twenty-first century, as Nigel Wright, by then Principal of Spurgeon's College, observed, it was difficult, in the great majority of Baptist churches in Britain, to find more than a few people who would describe themselves as 'cradle' or 'pedigree' Baptists. This created an opportunity for a new agenda for Baptists. In terms of crossing over traditional denominational boundaries, there was a new freedom, but this also, Wright noted, involved an indifference to denominational values. It was against this pervasive post-denomination background that Baptist churches in Britain had to forge a fresh identity.[24] The attempt being made by some within the Baptist denomination to create a stronger sense of both a national and transnational Baptist community, and to build stronger relationships, was a particularly challenging one, since it was taking place within the wider context of a general breakdown in denominational loyalty.[25]

Relationships within the broader Baptist community raised the question of the nature of the relationship between the Baptist Union and

23  For Europe, see B. Green, *Crossing the Boundaries: A History of the European Baptist Federation* (Didcot: Baptist Historical Society, 1999), chapter 7. As evidence of the changes in the BWA, the 1990 Congress was in Seoul, South Korea, and the 1995 Congress was in Buenos Aires, Argentina. Also, in 1995 Nilson Do Amaral Fanini, President of the Brazilian Baptist Convention, became BWA President, followed in 2000 by Billy Kim from South Korea.
24  N.G. Wright, *New Baptists, New Agenda* (Carlisle: Paternoster Press, 2002), chapter 4. Wright was President of the Union, 2002-3, and produced this book to launch his presidency.
25  I am indebted to my colleague at Spurgeon's, John Colwell, for highlighting this tension.

the BMS. By the end of the century they were in the same building at Didcot, but beyond that had relationships changed? To a large extent the two bodies continued to operate separately. There were hopes that wider Baptist fellowship would be fostered through the Fellowship of British Baptists, a body which in the 1990s brought together Baptist churches in Great Britain in membership with the Baptist Unions of Scotland, Wales and Great Britain, and also the BMS, with its relationship to all three of these Unions.[26] At the end of the century, however, there was little tangible progress in this area. Within the BMS itself, Alistair Brown's appointment as General Director in 1996 led to new directions. The 1999 BMS *Annual Review* spoke of a review that had taken place of the Society's corporate identity. The BMS was to become known as BMS World Mission, describing itself as 'a leading Christian mission organisation' aiming to share life in all its fullness with the world's people by 'enabling them to know Christ', 'alleviating suffering and injustice', and 'improving the quality of life'. BMS World Mission also opened the BMS International Mission Centre, taking ownership of what had been Carey Hall and then St Andrew's Hall, Selly Oak. Alan Pain, of Sutton Coldfield, became the Centre Director. The later 1990s saw rapid growth in the number of BMS volunteers and short-term workers, as well as a steady flow of long-term missionary candidates.[27] Under its new leadership, BMS was growing and developing in fresh ways.

Baptist leaders were also looking at how well equipped churches were to undertake contemporary mission in a postmodern context in Britain. Issues such as this were addressed at the Denominational Consultation at Swanwick in 1996, only the third such consultation held since the Second World War. It was David Coffey's hope that mission would be the focus of discussions. He was also well aware of the fact that, as at the beginning of the century, there was a great deal of frustration with the functioning of the Union.[28] By now there was a

---

26   This body replaced meetings of officers of the three Unions and the BMS.
27   *Annual Review*, BMS World Mission, 1999, p.1. I am grateful to Jo Sutherland and John Howes of BMS World Mission for their help. Constitutionally, the name Baptist Missionary Society was retained.
28   D. Coffey 'The Denominational Consultation', *Baptist Leader*, Issue No 13, Winter 1995, pp.1-2.

widespread concern about how to be relevant to a new cultural climate. At the 1996 Consultation the importance of re-imagining the Union for a new century was emphasized, as was the need to create a new structural framework for associating within the Union. The results of these discussions and of the production of two key reports, *Transforming Superintendency* and *Relating and Resourcing*, were some radical decisions. The most far-reaching was the decision to do away with the structure of Areas and Associations, replacing them with thirteen Regional Associations (twelve in England and one in Wales).[29] Local churches were also encouraged to form local 'clusters', which need not be exclusively Baptist. In addition, Area Superintendents were to be replaced by teams of regional ministers, employed by the Associations rather than the Union. The implementation of these changes, which reflected the thinking in *Relating and Resourcing*, meant that crucial parts of the Union's structure that had been put in place by Shakespeare early in the twentieth century were dismantled.

To what extent, however, were these changes within the Union in the 1990s producing, as David Coffey and Keith Jones hoped, a new thrust in mission? The English Church Attendance Survey of 1998 offered some encouragement. Over the period 1989 to 1998 the churches in the Baptist Union had an increased Sunday attendance of two per cent, from 226,700 to 232,200, although the Old Baptist Union, a group with just over 1,000 members which joined the Baptist Union in this period, was in decline. Grace Baptists and Gospel Standard Strict Baptists also declined. Independent Baptist attendance, however, increased by twenty-seven per cent to 24,400.[30] Darrell Jackson, who was engaged in research into mission, deduced from the census that the typical Baptist was a forty-one year old female living in the suburbs and belonging to a congregation of 160 people. Mrs Average Baptist was five years younger than the average worshipper in the Church of England, but in African Caribbean congregations the average age was twenty-seven. One worrying trend was that the twenties and thirties age group was under-represented in Baptist

---

29  One of the proposed regions, in the South East, became the South East Partnership, linking the North Downs, Kent and Sussex Associations. In addition there was the Old Baptist Union Association, a non-geographical association.
30  Brierley, *The Tide is Running Out,* p.39.

congregations. However, increasing numbers of people were coming to faith in their fifties.[31] It seemed that at the end of the 1990s Baptists were sensing that the future held out new hope. The Assembly at Blackpool in 1998, held over a weekend for the first time to allow more people to attend, was applauded for its professionalism and vitality.[32]

It is easy to look back on the twentieth century and focus on dismal features in Baptist life. Attendance has not kept up with population growth and many chapels now have small congregations. The huge Sunday schools of the first half of the century have disappeared. But the picture is not all bleak. There has been evangelistic success, for example through the Billy Graham campaigns and Alpha courses. Individual churches are reaching out to their local communities and beyond. One Baptist church, Frinton Free Church, with 550 members, was chosen by ITV for two hour-long broadcasts to mark the new millennium. David Beer, the minister, drew in Cliff Richard and the London Community Gospel Choir to take part. Churches have rediscovered a long tradition of social action by evangelicals and have developed significant social projects. Spiritual renewal and growth has taken place: as well as Black-majority congregations, churches with large congregations at the end of the century included Gold Hill, Chalfont St Peter, where Steve Gaukroger was senior minister, Trinity Hill, Sutton Coldfield, which had grown under the ministry of Alan Pain, and Tonbridge, Kent, with Derek Hills as senior minister. Each of these was attracting over 700 people to Sunday worship at the turn of the century.[33] David Bebbington argues that up to the 1960s many chapels were retreating before secularizing forces and that the charismatic movement brought 'rejuvenating change' and new confidence.[34] Several factors contributed to the more hopeful indicators in Baptist life towards the end of the century, but underlying all the advances was an openness to rejuvenating change.

---

31  *BT*, 16/23 December 1999, p.5.
32  *BT*, 14 May 1998, p.1.
33  *BT*, 18/25 December 2003, p.1. The attendance at Gold Hill was 1,200.
34  Bebbington, 'Evangelism and Spirituality in Twentieth-Century Protestant Nonconformity', p.215.

# APPENDIX
## SUPERINTENDENTS 1914-2000

**Central**

| | |
|---|---|
| C.T. Byford | 1915-1920 |
| F.J. Walkey | 1920-1942 |
| W.R. Miller | 1942-1955 |
| W.W. Bottoms | 1955-1956 |
| Douglas H. Hick | 1956-1973 |
| Hugh D. Logan | 1974-1982 |
| Roy A. Freestone | 1982-1999 |

**East Midland**

| | |
|---|---|
| C.G. Croome | 1915-1923 |
| Gummer Butt | 1924-1929 |
| J.T. Dawson | 1929-1932 |
| C.H. Weaver | 1932-1943 |
| H. Ingli James | 1943-1946 |
| J.C. Rendall | 1947-1956 |
| W.J. Grant | 1957-1968 |
| Arthur H. Bonser | 1969-1983 |
| Edmund Pilling | 1984-1994 |
| Peter Grange | 1994-2001 |

**Eastern**

| | |
|---|---|
| N.H. Patrick | 1915-1924 |
| R.C. Griffin | 1925-1934 |
| W.H. Tebbit | 1934-1950 |
| Frank C. Bryan | 1950-1958 |
| J.H.G. Adam | 1958-1973 |
| Edward T. Smalley | 1973-1982 |
| David Harper | 1982-1998 |

**Metropolitan**

| | |
|---|---|
| J.W. Ewing | 1915-1934 |
| Sydney G. Morris | 1934-1939 |
| Henry Cook | 1939-1954 |
| W.D. Jackson | 1954-1961 |
| G.W. Haden | 1961-1976 |
| Douglas C. Sparkes | 1977-1982 |
| Arthur Thompson | 1982-1989 |
| Douglas McBain | 1989-1997 |
| Patricia M. Took | 1997-2000 |

**North-Eastern**

| | |
|---|---|
| J. Gyles Williams | 1915-1922 |
| Henry Bonser | 1923-1949 |
| John O. Barrett | 1949-1963 |
| Sydney F. Clark | 1964-1975 |
| Arthur Liston | 1975-1976 |
| Tasker R. Lewis | 1976-1985 |
| J.F.V. Nicholson | 1986-1994 |
| D. Iain Collins | 1995-1997 |
| W. Ernest Whalley | 1998-2001 |

**North-Western**

| | |
|---|---|
| Hector V. Thomas | 1915-1924 |
| J.M.D. Robertson | 1924-1933 |
| Herbert Motley | 1934-1949 |
| Hubert L. Watson | 1949-1960 |
| Norman B. Jones | 1960-1971 |
| A. Trevor Hubbard | 1972-1989 |
| Keith D. Hobbs | 1989-2001 |

**South Eastern**

| | |
|---|---|
| W.C.R. Hancock | 1981-1985 |
| P.H.K. Tongeman | 1986-1994 |
| David Taylor | 1995-2000 |

**South Wales**

| | |
|---|---|
| J. Meredith Jones | 1915-1934 |
| Griffith H. Harris | 1934-1946 |
| H. Ingli James | 1947-1956 |
| William Davies | 1956-1970 |
| George Evans | 1971-1981 |
| Peter G. Saunders | 1981-1991 |
| Peter D. Manson | 1992-2000 |

**South Western**

| | |
|---|---|
| R. Gwynne Edwards | 1986-1998 |
| J. Page Edwards | 1998-2000 |

**Southern**

| | |
|---|---|
| Thomas Woodhouse | 1915-1930 |
| Sydney G. Morris | 1931-1934 |
| H.H. Sutton | 1934-1945 |
| W.D. Jackson | 1946-1954 |
| H.V. Larcombe | 1954-1961 |
| Vivian C. Lewis | 1961-1977 |
| W.C.R. Hancock | 1977-1981 |
| G.G. Reynolds | 1981-1999 |

**West Midland**

| | |
|---|---|
| R.M. Julian | 1915-1924 |
| J. Ivory Cripps | 1925-1945 |
| A.J. Klaiber | 1945-1957 |
| Charles Hardiman | 1957-1965 |
| B. Hugh Butt | 1966-1970 |
| E. Ellis Mold | 1971-1979 |
| Neil B. Hall | 1980-1995 |
| Brian Nicholls | 1995-2001 |

**Western**

| | |
|---|---|
| Frank Durbin | 1915-1928 |
| Gummer Butt | 1929-1937 |
| A.J. Nixon | 1938-1951 |
| H.H. Pewtress | 1951-1965 |
| Ralph Darvill | 1966-1974 |
| Ronald A. Cowley | 1974-1986 |
| Roger Hayden | 1986-2000 |

# BIBLIOGRAPHY

Many of the primary source references are to the minutes of the Baptist Union Council and associated committees. These are bound together into a series of volumes which are held as part of the main English Baptist archive at Regent's Park College Oxford, Angus Library.

Amey, B., 'The Free Church Federal Council', *The Journal of the United Reformed Church History Society*, Vol.7. No.3 (2003)

Aubrey, M.E., *Baptist Deaconesses: their training and work* (London: Baptist Union, n.d.)

Aubrey, M.E., *Our Bombed Churches* (London: Baptist Union, n.d.)

Aubrey, M.E., 'The Future of our Ministry', *BQ*, Vol.1 (1922-1923)

Avery, W.J., 'The Late Midland College', *BQ*, Vol.1 (1922-3)

Bacon, F., *Church Administration* (Bristol: Bristol and District Association of Baptist Churches, 1981 [with subsequent reprintings and revision])

*Baptist Handbook* (London: Baptist Union) - published annually

*Baptist Church Hymnal: Revised Edition, 1933* (London: Psalms and Hymns Trust, 1933)

Bassett, T.M., *The Baptists of Wales and the Baptist Missionary Society* (Swansea: Ilston Press, 1991)

Beasley-Murray, G.R., *Baptism in the New Testament* (London: Macmillan, 1962)

Beasley-Murray, G.R., 'The Sacraments', *The Fraternal*, October 1948

Beasley-Murray, P, *Fearless for Truth: A personal portrait of the life of George Raymond Beasley-Murray* (Carlisle: Paternoster Press, 2002)

Bebbington, D.W., 'Baptists and Fundamentalism in Inter-War Britain', in K. Robbins, ed., *Protestant Evangelicalism: Britain, Ireland, Germany and America, c1750-c1950* (Oxford: Blackwell, 1990)

Bebbington, D.W., 'Baptists and Politics since 1914', in K.W. Clements, ed., *Baptists in the Twentieth Century* (1982)

Bebbington, D.W., 'Baptist MPs in the Nineteenth Century', *BQ*, Vol.29, No.1 (1981)

Bebbington, D.W., 'Baptist Members of Parliament in the Twentieth Century', *BQ*, Vol.31, No.6 (1986)

Bebbington, D.W., *Evangelicalism in Modern Britain: A History from the 1730s to the 1980s* (London: Routledge, 1995)

Bebbington, D.W., 'Nonconformity and Electoral Sociology, 1867-1918', *Historical Journal*, Vol.27, No.3 (1984).

Bebbington, D.W., ed., *The Baptists in Scotland: A History* (Glasgow: The

538THE ENGLISH BAPTISTS OF THE 20TH CENTURY

Baptist Union of Scotland, 1988)

Bebbington, D.W., ed., *The Gospel in the World* (Carlisle: Paternoster Press, 2002)

Bebbington, D.W., *The Nonconformist Conscience: Chapel and Politics, 1870-1914* (London: George Allen and Unwin, 1982)

Bebbington, D.W., 'The Oxford Group Movement between the Wars', in W.J. Sheils and D. Wood, eds., *Voluntary Religion* (Oxford: Blackwell, 1986)

Bebbington, D.W., & Larsen, T., eds., *Modern Christianity and Cultural Aspirations* (Sheffield Academic Press, 2003)

Belden, K.D., *Reflections on Moral Re-armament* (London: Grosvenor Books, 1983)

Bell, G.K.A., *Documents on Christian Unity, 1920-4* (London: Oxford University Press, 1924)

Bell, G.K.A., *Randall Davidson: Archbishop of Canterbury* (London: Oxford University Press, 1952)

Bendor-Samuel, T.H., *Keeping the Faith* (Croydon: FIEC, 1992)

Bennett, K.W., *God at Work with Men* (Pontesford, Shrewsbury: BMM, 1997)

Binfield, J.C.G., *Pastors and People: The Biography of a Baptist Church, Queen's Road, Coventry* (Coventry: Queen's Road Baptist Church, 1984)

Binfield, J.C.G., *So Down to Prayers: Studies in English Nonconformity, 1780-1920* (London: J.M. Dent & Sons, 1977)

Binfield, J.C.G., 'Strangers and Dissenters: The Architectural Legacy of Twentieth-Century English Nonconformity – Context, Case Study and Connexion', in Sell and Cross, eds., *Protestant Nonconformity in the Twentieth Century*.

Blomfield, W.E., 'A Few Reflections on my Presidential Experiences', *BQ*, Vol.2 (1924-1925)

Bonser, H., 'Recollections of a General Superintendent', *BQ*, Vol.XIII (1949-50)

Bowers, Faith, *A Bold Experiment: The Story of Bloomsbury Chapel and Bloomsbury Central Baptist Church, 1848-1999* (London: Bloomsbury Baptist Church, 1999)

Brackney, W.H., Fiddes, P.S., and Briggs, J.H.Y., eds., *Pilgrim Pathways: Essays in Honour of B.R. White* (Macon, Ga.: Mercer University Press, 1999)

Brierley, P., *Religious Trends: 2000/2001, No.2* (London: Christian Research Association, 1999)

Brierley, P., *The Tide is Running Out* (London: Christian Research Association, 2000)

Briggs, J.H.Y., *The English Baptists of the Nineteenth Century* (Didcot: Baptist Historical Society, 1994)

*Bristol Baptist College: 250 years, 1679-1929* (Bristol: The Baptist College, 1929)

Brown, C.G., *The Death of Christian Britain: Understanding Secularisation, 1800-2000* (London: Routledge, 2001)

Brown, R., *The English Baptists of the Eighteenth Century* (London: Baptist Historical Society, 1986)

Brown, K.D., *A Social History of the Nonconformist Ministry in England and Wales, 1800-1930* (Oxford: Clarendon Press, 1988)

Bryan, F.C., 'Preparation, Administration and Visitation', in F.C. Bryan, ed., *Concerning Believer's Baptism* (London: The Kingsgate Press, 1943)

Buffard, Frank, *Kent and Sussex Baptist Associations* (Faversham: Kent and Sussex Baptist Associations, 1963)

Campbell, R.J., *The New Theology* (London: Chapman & Hall, 1907)

Carlile, J.C., *My Life's Little Day* (London: Blackie, 1935)

Ceadel, M., 'Christian Pacifism in the Era of two World Wars', in W. J. Sheils, ed., *The Church and War* (Oxford: Basil Blackwell, 1983)

Ceadel, M., *Pacifism in Britain, 1914-1945: The Defining of a Faith* (Oxford: Clarendon Press, 1980)

Chadwick, R., ed., *A Protestant Catholic Church of Christ* (Oxford: New Road Baptist Church, 2003)

Champion, L.G., *Bristol and District Association of Baptist Churches, 1823-1973* (Bristol: p.p., 1973)

Child, R.L., *Baptists and Christian Unity* (London: Carey Kingsgate Press, 1948)

Child, R.L., '"The Ministry and the Sacraments": A Free Church Point of View', *BQ*, Vol.9, No.3 (1938)

Childs, Sir Wyndham, *Episodes and Reflections* (London: Cassell & Co., 1930)

Clements, K.W., 'Baptists and the Outbreak of the First World War', *BQ*, Vol.26, No.2 (1975)

Clements, K.W., ed., *Baptists in the Twentieth Century* (London: Baptist Historical Society, 1982)

Clements, K.W., *Lovers of Discord: Twentieth Century Theological Controversies in England* (London: SPCK, 1988)

Clements, R.E., 'The Biblical Theology of H.H. Rowley, 1890-1969', *Baptist History and Heritage*, Vol.38 (Winter 2003)

Clifford, Paul Rowntree, *Venture in Faith: The Story of the West Ham Central Mission* (London: Carey Kingsgate Press, 1950)

Cockett, F.H., *Partnership in Service: A Brief History of the Western Baptist Association, 1823-1973* (Bridport, n.p., [n.d. but 1973])

Cook, H., *Charles Brown* (London: The Kingsgate Press, 1939)

Cook, H., *Speak - that they go Forward: A Report on the Spiritual Welfare in the Churches of the Baptist Denomination* (London: Baptist Union, 1946)

Cook, H., *The Theology of Evangelism* (London: Carey Kingsgate Press, 1951)

Cook, H., *What Baptists Stand For* (London: Carey Kingsgate Press, 1947)

Cooper, R.E., *From Stepney to St Giles': The Story of Regent's Park College, 1810-1960* (London: Carey Kingsgate Press, 1960)

Cox, J., *The English Churches in a Secular Society: Lambeth, 1870-1930* (Oxford: Oxford University Press, 1982)

Cross, A.R., *Baptism and the Baptists: Theology and Practice in Twentieth-Century Britain* (Carlisle, Paternoster Press, 2000)

Cross, A.R., 'Dr Hugh Martin: Publisher and Writer, Part 1', *BQ*, Vol.37, No.1 (1997).

Cross, A.R., 'Revd Dr Hugh Martin: Ecumenist, Part 2', *BQ*, Vol.37, No.2 (1997).

Cross, A.R., 'The Holy Spirit: Key to the Baptismal Sacramentalism of H. Wheeler Robinson', *Baptist History and Heritage*, Vol.36, Nos.1&2 (2001)

Cross, A.R., 'Service to the Ecumenical Movement: The Contribution of British Baptists', *BQ*, Vol.38, No.3 (1999)

Currie, R., Gilbert, A. , and Horsley, L., *Churches and Churchgoers: Patterns of Church Growth in the British Isles since 1700* (Oxford: Clarendon Press, 1977)

Dakin, A., *The Baptist View of the Church & Ministry* (London: Carey Kingsgate Press, 1944)

Dekar, P.R., 'Twentieth-Century British Baptist Conscientious Objectors', *BQ*, Vol.35, No.1 (1993)

Dix, K., *Strict and Particular: English Strict and Particular Baptists in the Nineteenth Century* (Didcot: Baptist Historical Society, 2001)

Doyle, B.M., ' "Through the Windows of a Baptist Meeting House": Religion, Politics and the Nonconformist Conscience in the Life of Sir George White MP', *BQ*, Vol.36, No.6 (1996)

Dunkerley, R., ed., *The Ministry and the Sacraments* (London: SCM Press, 1937)

Edmonds, G., *The Free Church Fellowship, 1911-1965: An Ecumenical Pioneer* (Gerrards Cross: Free Church Council, 1965)

Ellis, C.J., *Baptist Worship To-day* (Didcot: Baptist Union, 1999)

Ellis, C.J., *Gathering* (Canterbury Press, 2004)

Elwyn, T.S.H., *The Northamptonshire Baptist Association* (London: Carey Kingsgate Press, 1964)

Evans, Percy, 'Rain after Drought', *Spurgeon's College Magazine*, Spring 1946

Flew, R.N., and Davies, R.E., *The Catholicity of Protestantism* (London: Lutterworth, 1950)

Fountain, D.G., *E.J. Poole-Connor, 1872-1962: Contender for the Faith* (Worthing: Henry E. Walter, 1966)

Fullerton, W.Y., *F.B. Meyer: A Biography* (London: Marshall, Morgan & Scott [1929])

Fullerton, W.Y., 'The Stockholm Congress and Exhibition', *BQ*, Vol.1 (1923)

Gilbert, A.D., *The Making of Post-Christian Britain: A history of the secularization of modern society* (London: Longman, 1980)

Gill, R., *The 'Empty' Church Revisited* (Aldershot: Ashgate, 2003)

Gilmore, A., ed., *Christian Baptism* (London: Lutterworth, 1959)

Gilmore, A., ed., *The Pattern of the Church: A Baptist view* (London: Lutterworth, 1963)

Gouldbourne, R.M.B., *Reinventing the Wheel: Women and Ministry in English Baptist Life* (Oxford: Whitley Publications, 1997)

Glover, T.R., *Fundamentals* (London: Baptist Union, 1931)

Glover, T.R., *The Free Churches and Re-Union* (Cambridge: W Heffer & Sons, 1921)

Goodman, M., 'A Faded Heritage: English Baptist political thinking in the 1930s', *BQ*, Vol.37, No.2 (1997)

Goodman, M., 'Numerical Decline amongst English Baptists, 1930-1939', *BQ*, Vol.36, No.5 (1996)

Grant, J.W., *Free Churchmanship in England, 1870-1940* (London: Independent Press [n.d. but 1940])

Grass, T., 'Strict Baptists and Reformed Baptists in England, 1955-76', in *Baptist Myths* (forthcoming, Paternoster, 2005)

Green, Bernard, *Crossing the Boundaries: A History of the European Baptist Federation* (Didcot: Baptist Historical Society, 1999)

Green, Bernard, *Tomorrow's Man: A Biography of James Henry Rushbrooke* (Didcot: Baptist Historical Society, 1997)

Griffin, S.C., *Forgotten Revival* (Bromley: Day One Publications, 1992)

Hamer, D.A., *Liberal Politics in the Age of Gladstone and Rosebery* (Oxford: Clarendon Press, 1972

Harrison, F.M.W., *It All Began Here: The Story of the East Midland Baptist Association* (London: East Midland Baptist Association, 1986)

Hastings, A., *A History of English Christianity, 1920-2000* (London: SCM, 4th ed., 2001)

R. Hayden, 'The Stillness and the Dancing', in R. Hayden and B. Haymes, eds., *Bible, History and Ministry: Essays for L G Champion on his Ninetieth Birthday* (Bristol: Bristol Baptist College, 1997)

Hayden, R., 'Still at the Crossroads?: Revd J.H. Shakespeare and Ecumenism', in K.W. Clements, ed., *Baptists in the Twentieth Century* (1982)

Hayden, R., ed., *Baptist Union Documents, 1948-1977* (London: Baptist Historical Society, 1980)

Hayden, R., *English Baptist History and Heritage*, 2nd edition, (Didcot: BUGB 2005).

Hogg, W.R., *Ecumenical Foundations*, (New York: Harper & Brothers, 1952)

Iremonger, F.A., *William Temple: Archbishop of Canterbury* (London: Oxford University Press, 1948)

Jaeger, C., *Never to Lose my Vision: The Story of Bill Jaeger* (London: Grosvenor Books, 1995)

Jarlert, A., *The Oxford Group, Group Revivalism and the Churches in Northern Europe, 1930-1945* (Lund, Sweden: Lund University Press, 1995)

Jewson, C.B., *The Baptists in Norfolk* (London: Carey Kingsgate Press, 1957)

Johnson, W.C., *Encounter in London: The Story of the London Baptist Association, 1865-1965* (London: Carey Kingsgate Press, 1965)

Jones, B.P., *The King's Champions* (Cwmbran, Gwent: Christian Literature Press, 1986)

Jordan, E.K.H., *Free Church Unity: History of the Free Church Council Movement, 1896-1941* (London: Lutterworth Press, 1956)

Kendall, E.E., *Doing and Daring* (Rushden: Stanley L. Hunt, 1955)

Kidd, R.L., ed., *Something to Declare: A Study of the Declaration of Principle* (Oxford: Whitley Publications, 1996)

Klaiber, A.J., *et al.*, *The Baptist Union General Superintendents* (London: Baptist Union, 1949)

Koss, S., *Nonconformity in Modern British Politics* (London: B.T. Batsford, 1975)

Langley, A.S., *Birmingham Baptists: Past and Present* (London: The Kingsgate Press, 1939)

Laws, G., 'The Edinburgh Conference: What was the Good of it?', *BQ*, Vol.9, No.1 (1938)

Lee, G., 'Women in Baptist Ministry in the 20th Century' (unpublished paper, 2001)

Lenwood, F., *Jesus - Lord or Leader?* (London: Constable & Co., 1930)

Lockhart, J.G., *Cosmo Gordon Lang* (London: Hodder and Stoughton, 1949)

Lord, F.T., *Baptist World Fellowship* (London: Carey Kingsgate Press, 1955)

Machin, G.I.T., *Churches and Social Issues in Twentieth-Century Britain* (Oxford: Oxford University Press, 1998)

Machin, G.I.T., *Politics and the Churches in Great Britain, 1869 to 1921* (Oxford: Clarendon Press, 1987)

Machin, I., 'Reservation under Pressure: Ritual in the Prayer Book Crisis, 1927-1928', in R.N. Swanson, ed., *Continuity and Change in Christian Worship* (Woodbridge, Suffolk: Boydell Press, 1999)

Manley, K., ' "The right man in the right place": W.T. Whitley in Australia (1891-1901)', *BQ*, Vol.37, No.4 (1997)

Martin, Hugh, ed., *Towards Reunion: What the Churches Stand For* (London: SCM Press, 1934)

Marty, M., *Modern American Religion: The Noise of Conflict, 1919-1941* (Chicago: University of Chicago, 1991)

Mason, R., 'H. Wheeler Robinson Revisited', *BQ*, Vol.37, No.5 (1998)

Matheney, M.P., Jnr, 'Teaching Prophet: The Life and Continuing Influence of Theodore Henry Robinson', *BQ*, Vol.29, No.5 (1981)

McBain, Douglas, *Fire over the Waters: Renewal among Baptists and others from the 1960s to the 1990s* (London: Darton, Longman & Todd, 1997)

McCaig, A., 'The Pastors' College Jubilee', *The Sword and the Trowel*, June 1906

McLeod, H., *Class and Religion in the Late Victorian City* (London: Croom Helm, 1974)

McLeod, H., '"Thews and Sinews": Nonconformity and Sport', in D.W. Bebbington and T. Larsen, eds., *Modern Christianity and Cultural Aspirations* (Sheffield Academic Press, 2003)

Mews, S., 'The Sword of the Spirit', in W.J. Sheils, ed., *The Church and War* (Oxford: Basil Blackwell, 1983)

Micklem, N., *The Religion of a Sceptic* (London: Acton Society Trust, 1976)

Moncrieff, H., *Roots of Labour* (Yeovil: Linden Hall, 1990)

Moon, N.S., *Education for Ministry: Bristol Baptist College, 1679-1979* (Bristol: Bristol Baptist College, 1979)

Morgan, D., *Span of the Cross: Christian Religion and Society in Wales 1914-2000* (Cardiff: University of Wales Press, 1999)

Morris, N., *Sisters of the People: The Order of Baptist Deaconesses, 1890-1975, CCSRG Research Paper 2* (Bristol: University of Bristol, 2002)

Mountain, J., *My Baptism and what led to it*, 2<sup>nd</sup> edn. (London: n.p., n.d.).

Mountain, J., *Rev. F.C. Spurr and Keswick* (Tunbridge Wells: n.p., 1921)

Munson, J.E.B., 'The education of Baptist ministers, 1870-1900', *BQ*, Vol.26 (1976)

Munson, J., *The Nonconformists: In search of a lost culture* (London: SPCK, 1991)

Murray, I.H., *David Martyn Lloyd-Jones Vol.2: The Fight of Faith, 1939-1981* (Edinburgh: Banner of Truth Trust, 1990)

Nicholls, M., *Lights to the World: A History of Spurgeon's College, 1856-1992* (Harpenden: Nuprint, 1994)

Nicoll, William Robertson and Butcher, J.W., *The Children for the Church: The Young Worshippers' League* (London: Hodder & Stoughton, 1913).

Payne, E.A., *A 20<sup>th</sup> Century Minister: John Oliver Barrett, 1901-78* (London: p.p., 1978)

Payne, E.A., *Henry Wheeler Robinson* (London: Nisbet & Co, 1946)

Payne, E.A., 'Public Prayer', *BQ*, Vol.2 (1924-1925), pp.128-32.

Payne, E.A., *The Baptist Union: A Short History* (London: Carey Kingsgate Press, 1959)

Payne, E.A., *The Baptists of Berkshire* (London: Carey Kingsgate Press, 1951)

Payne, 'The Development of Nonconformist Theological Education in the Nineteenth Century, with Special Reference to Regent's Park College', in E.A. Payne, ed., *Studies in History and Religion* (London: Lutterworth Press, 1942)

Payne, E.A., *The Fellowship of Believers: Baptist Thought and Practice Yesterday and Today* (London: The Kingsgate Press, 1944). Second edition 1952.

Payne, E.A., *The Free Church Tradition in the Life of England* (London: SCM, 1944).

Payne, E.A., 'The Protestant World', in S. Neill, ed, *Twentieth Century Christianity* (London: Collins, 1962)

Payne, E.A., *William Taylor Bowie, 1902-1952* (London: p.p., 1952)

Peaston, A.E., *The Prayer Book Tradition in the Free Churches* (London: James Clarke & Co., 1964)

Pickering, W.S.F., *Anglo-Catholicism* (London: SPCK, 1989)

Pitts, W.V., *Never Old Parchment* (Windsor: Direct Design, 1976)

Price, Charles, & Randall, I.M., *Transforming Keswick* (Carlisle: Paternoster/OM, 2000)

Price, S.J., 'The Office of Church Secretary', *BQ*, Vol.2 (1924-1925)

Randall, I.M.,'"Arresting People for Christ": Baptists and the Oxford Group in the 1930s', *BQ*, Vol.38, No.1 (1999)

Randall, I.M., 'A Good Bench of Bishops?', in S. Murray Williams, ed., *Translocal Ministry* (Didcot: Baptist Union, 2004)

Randall, I.M., ' "Capturing Keswick": Baptists and the Changing Spirituality of the Keswick Convention in the 1920s', *BQ*, Vol.36, No.7 (1996)

Randall, I.M., *Educating Evangelicalism: The Origins, Development and Impact of London Bible College* (Carlisle: Paternoster Press, 2000)

Randall, I.M., *Evangelical Experiences: A Study of the Spirituality of English Evangelicalism, 1918-1939* (Carlisle: Paternoster Press, 1999)

Randall, I.M., ' "Great National Crisis": New Road and the World Wars', in R. Chadwick, ed., *A Protestant Catholic Church of Christ* (Oxford: New Road Baptist Church, 2003)

Randall, I.M, *Spirituality and Social Change: The Contribution of F.B. Meyer* (Carlisle: Paternoster Press, 2003)

Randall, I.M. & Hilborn, D., *One Body in Christ: The History and Significance of the Evangelical Alliance* (Carlisle: Paternoster Press, 2001)

Rapp, D.R., 'A Baptist Pioneer: The exhibition of film to London's East End working classes, 1900-1919', *BQ*, Vol.40, No.1 (January 2003)

Rees, J., *Stranger than Fiction* (Frinton-on-Sea: p.p., 1957)

REKABAS, *An Adventure for God* (London: Kingsgate Press, 1934)

Reynolds, G.G., *First among Equals* (Didcot: Baptist Union, Southern Area, 1993)

Rignal, C., *Manchester Baptist College, 1866-1916* (Bradford & London: William Byles & Sons Ltd, 1916)

Roberts, C.A. , ed., *These Christian Commando Campaigns* (London: Epworth Press, 1945)

Robbins, K., *The Abolition of War: The 'Peace Movement' in Britain, 1914-1919* (Cardiff: University Wales Press, 1976)

Robbins, K., ed., *Protestant Evangelicalism: Britain, Ireland, Germany and America, c1750-c1950* (Oxford: Blackwell, 1990)

Robbins, K., 'Protestant Nonconformists and the Peace Question', in A.P.F. Sell and A.R. Cross, eds., *Protestant Nonconformity* (2003)

Robinson, H. Wheeler, 'Hebrew Psychology', in A.S. Peake, ed., *The People and the Book: Essays on the Old Testament* (Oxford: Clarendon, 1925)

Robinson, H. Wheeler, *The Christian Experience of the Holy Spirit* (London: Nisbet & Co, 1928)

Robinson, H.Wheeler, 'The Place of Baptism in Baptist Churches To-day',

*BQ*, Volume 1 (1922-1923)

Robinson, T.H., *Prophecy and the Prophets in Ancient Israel* (London: Duckworth, 1923)

Rodd, C.S., in 'Introduction', H.W. Robinson, *Corporate Personality* (Edinburgh: T&T Clark, 1981, 2<sup>nd</sup> edn.)

Rose, D.M., *Baptist Deaconesses* (London: Carey Kingsgate Press, 1954)

Roxburgh, K., 'Eric Roberts and orthodoxy among Scottish Baptists', *BQ*, Vol.34, No.2 (2001)

Rushbrooke, J.H., ed., *Fifth Baptist World Congress, Berlin, 1934* (London: BWA, 1934)

Rushbrooke, J.H., ed., *Sixth Baptist World Congress, 1939* (Atlanta, Georgia: BWA, 1939)

Rushbrooke, J.H., *et al.*, *The Faith of the Baptists* (London: The Kingsgate Press, 1926)

Sell, A.P.F., & Cross, A.R., eds., *Protestant Nonconformity in the Twentieth Century* (Carlisle: Paternoster Press, 2003)

Sellers, Ian, ed., *Our Heritage: The Baptists of Yorkshire, Lancashire and Cheshire, 1647-1987* (Leeds: Yorkshire Baptist Association and Lancashire & Cheshire Baptist Association, 1987)

Sellers, Ian, 'W.T. Whitley: A Commemorative Essay', *BQ*, Vol.37, No.4 (1997)

Shakespeare, Sir Geoffrey, *Let Candles be Brought In* (London: MacDonald, 1949)

Shakespeare, J.H., *The Churches at the Cross-Roads* (London: Williams & Norgate, 1918)

Shakespeare, J.H., *The Story of the Baptist Union Twentieth Century Fund* (London: Baptist Union Publications Department, 1904)

Sheils, W.J., and Wood, D., eds., *Voluntary Religion* (Oxford: Blackwell, 1986)

Shepherd, Peter, *The making of a northern Baptist College* (Manchester: Northern Baptist College, 2004)

Shepherd, Peter, 'Denominational Renewal', *BQ*, Vol.37, No.7 (1998)

Shepherd, Peter, *The Making of a Modern Denomination: John Howard Shakespeare and the English Baptists, 1898-1924* (Carlisle: Paternoster Press, 2001)

Shuff, R.N., *Searching for the True Church: Brethren and Evangelicals in mid-Twentieth-Century England* (Carlisle: Paternoster, forthcoming)

Sparkes, D.C., *An Accredited Ministry* (Didcot: Baptist Historical Society, 1996)

Sparkes, D.C., *The Constitutions of the Baptist Union of Great Britain*

(Didcot: Baptist Historical Society, 1996)

Sparkes, D.C., *Pensions – Provision for Retired and Disabled Ministers* (Didcot: Baptist Historical Society, 1996)

Sparkes, D.C., 'Percy Illingworth and the last Liberal Government', *BQ*, Vol. 34, No 7 (2002)

Sparkes, D.C., *The Home Mission Story* (Didcot: Baptist Historical Society, 1995)

Sparkes, D.C., *The Offices of the Baptist Union of Great Britain* (Didcot: Baptist Historical Society, 1996)

Spoerri, T., *Dynamic out of Silence* (London: Grosvenor Books, 1976)

Spurr, F.C., *Some Chaplains in Khaki: An account of the work of Chaplains of the United Navy and Army Board* (London: H.R. Allinsen, 1916)

Stanley, Brian, 'Manliness and Mission: Frank Lenwood and the London Missionary Society', *The Journal of the United Reformed Church History Society*, Vol.5, No.8 (1996)

Stanley, Brian, *The History of the Baptist Missionary Society, 1792-1992* (Edinburgh: T & T Clark, 1992)

Stanley, Brian, ' "The Old Religion and the New": India and the making of T.R. Glover's *The Jesus of History*', in D.W. Bebbington, ed., *The Gospel in the World* (Carlisle: Paternoster Press, 2002)

Swanson, R.W, ed., *Unity and Diversity in the Church* (Oxford: Blackwell, 1996)

Talbot, B.R., *The Search for a Common Identity: The Origins of the Baptist Union of Scotland 1800-1870* (Carlisle: Paternoster Press, 2003)

Tatlow, T., *The Story of the Student Christian Movement* (London: SCM Press, 1933)

*The Grounds of our Fellowship*, (n.p.: Free Church Council, [n.d. but 1911])

Thompson, D.M., *Let Sects and Parties Fall* (Birmingham: Berean Press, 1980)

Thompson, D.M., 'The Unity of the Church in Twentieth-Century England: Pleasing Dream or Common Calling?', in R.W. Swanson, ed., *Unity and Diversity in the Church* (Oxford: Blackwell, 1996)

Thompson, J., *Century of Grace: The Baptist Union of Ireland: A Short History, 1895-1995* (Belfast: Baptist Union of Ireland, 1996)

Tidball, D.J., 'Evangelical Nonconformist Home Missions, 1796-1901', University of Keele PhD (1981).

Townsend, H., *Robert Wilson Black* (London: Carey Kingsgate Press, 1954)

Underwood, A.C., *A History of the English Baptists* (London: Carey Kingsgate Press, 1947)

Valentine, T., *Concern for the Ministry* (Teddington: Particular Baptist Fund,

1967)
Vellacott, J., *Bertrand Russell and the Pacifists in the First World War* (Brighton: Harvester, 1980)
Voke, S.J., and Winward, S.F., *Hymns of Worship and Communion* (London: Henry E. Walter, 1946)
Walton, R.C., *The Gathered Community* (London: Carey Kingsgate Press, 1946)
Warrington, K., ed., *Pentecostal Perspectives* (Carlisle: Paternoster Press, 1998)
West, W.M.S., 'Baptists in Faith and Order', in K.W. Clements, ed., *Baptists in the Twentieth Century* (1982)
West, W.M.S., *Baptists Together* (Didcot: Baptist Historical Society, 2000)
West, W.M.S., 'The Child and the Church: A Baptist Perspective', in W.H. Brackney, P.S. Fiddes and J.H.Y. Briggs, eds., *Pilgrim Pathways: Essays in Honour of B.R. White* (Macon, Ga.: Mercer University Press, 1999)
West, W.M.S., 'The Reverend Secretary Aubrey: Part I', *BQ*, Vol.34, No.5 (1992)
West, W.M.S., 'The Reverend Secretary Aubrey: Part II', *BQ*, Vol.34, No.6 (1992)
West, W.M.S., 'The Reverend Secretary Aubrey: Part III', *BQ*, Vol.34, No.7 (1992)
West, W.M.S., *To be a Pilgrim: A Memoir of Ernest A Payne* (Guildford: Lutterworth Press, 1983)
Whale, J.S., 'Jesus - Lord or Leader?', *Congregational Quarterly*, Vol.8, No.1 (1930)
White, B.R., *The English Baptists of the Seventeenth Century* (Didcot: Baptist Historical Society, 1996, 2<sup>nd</sup> edn.)
Wilkinson, A., *Dissent or Conform? War, Peace and the English Churches, 1900-1945* (London: SCM, 1986)
Williams, C., *The Principles and Practices of the Baptists* (London: Baptist Tract Society, 1903)
Williams, J.T., 'The Contribution of Protestant Nonconformists to Biblical Scholarship in the Twentieth Century', in A.P.F. Sell and A.R. Cross, eds., *Protestant Nonconformity* (2003)
Williams, S. Murray, ed., *Translocal Ministry* (Didcot: Baptist Union, 2004)
Wittard, Doris, *Bibles in Barrels: A History of Essex Baptists* (Southend-on-Sea: Essex Baptist Association, 1962)
Whitley, W.T., 'Lambeth and Murren', *BQ*, Vol.5 (1930)
Whitley, W.T., 'Our Theological Colleges', *BQ*, Vol.1 (1922-3)

Whitley, W.T., ed., *Third Baptist World Congress* (London: Kingsgate Press, 1923)

Wolffe, J., *God and Greater Britain* (London: Routledge, 1994)

Wood, H.G., *Terrot Reaveley Glover: A Biography* (Cambridge: Cambridge University Press, 1953)

Wright, N.G., *Challenge to Change: A radical agenda for Baptists* (Eastbourne: Kingsway, 1991)

Wright, N.G., *New Baptists, New Agenda,*(Carlisle: Paternoster, 2002)

Wright, N.G., *The Radical Evangelical: Seeking a place to stand* (London: SPCK, 1996)

# INDEX

Note: BC here = Baptist Church
Figures in italics denote illustration

Prestridge, J.N. 49ff
Pretlove, John 368
Price, Seymour J. 175, 227, 262
Prime Ministers 43, 47, 60, 83, 88, 126,
  158, 194f, 359, 513
Pringle, David 395
Prior, Kenneth 446
prisons 84, 212
prisoners of war 86, 211
Pritchard, John 231
probations/probationer ministers 64, 67f,
  71, 123, 140, 142, 169ff, 186, 223,
  237, 323, 353, 381
Prochazka, Dr, Rector of Baptist
  Seminary, Prague 159
Progressive Baptist Convention of Europe
  509
prophecy/prophets/prophetic ministry
  131, 187, 231, 253
Protestant Peace Conference, Constance,
  Germany (1914) 79
Protestant Truth Society 256, 341
Protestants 86, 252, 256, 284, 327, 338,
  494f
Psalms and Hymns Trust 56, 323, 504
Pullman, Caroline 485
pulpits 11, 26, 46, *283*, 434
Puritan and Reformed Studies Conference
  (1950) 287
Puritan/Reformed theology 287
Pusey, David F.G. 366
Pusey, Michael 400
Pusey, Yona 455
Putman, Philip 502, 518n

Quakers 41, 78, 212, 468
Quicke, Michael 406, 461, 484, 488, 490,
  498

race relations &c 306, 318, 359, 404, 478
Racial Justice Sunday 478
Rackley, John 506
radical discipleship 458

Radlett Fellowship 357n
Ramsay, Guy 249
Ramsbottom, Jack 415, 452
Ramsey, Michael, Archbishop of
  York/Canterbury 270, 338
Ramsgate, Kent 151
Ranaghan, Kevin 396
Rankin, A.O. 311
rates (local) 36f, 84
Raven, Thelma 199
Rawdon College, Leeds 15, 69, 92, 97,
  101, 116, 125, 131, 169, 177, 182,
  224, 256, 290, 314, 348, 353, 393
Rayleigh, Essex 167
Reading, Berkshire 487f
- Carey BC 326, 368, 379, 422
- King's Road BC 185, 281
Reardon, Martin 493
Redcar BC, Cleveland 512
Redhill, Surrey 151, 244, 278
Redpath, Alan 227, 237, 443
Redwood, Hugh 166
Rees, Tom 237f, 272
Reeves, Marjorie 221
Reformation, The 287, 321, 354, 467
Reformed Baptists 4
Reformed Baptist Carey Conference 492
Reformed Churches 254
refugees 78, 86, 404
Regent's Park College, London/Oxford
  21, 69ff, *70*, 77, 86, 92, 101, 104,
  109, 121f, 131, 133, 135, 142, 154,
  159, 174n, 182f, 185, 187, 218, 221,
  224, 239, 249, 252f, 260f, 278, 290,
  299, *299*, 302, 323, 331, 334, 339,
  348, 350, 354, 366f, 422f, 441, 464,
  476, 489, 518
Reid, Samuel 348
relief work 137, 159, 407, 515
religious broadcasting 210, 311
religious equality 36, 47, 54
religious liberty/liberty of conscience
  (including freedom of worship) 52ff,

33
Tottlebank Baptist Church, Lake District 175
Townsend, Henry 117, 139, 163, 178f, 198, 202, 224, 234, 251, 255, 257, 283
'Towards 2000' 474ff
Towy-Evans, Mary M. 422
trades unions 36, 251, 408
tradition 11, 30, 48, 55, 82, 95, 100, 111, 133, 135, 148, 151, 170, 172, 177, 179, 205, 218, 248
Trevelyan, Mary 355
Trevithick, Ruth 285n
tribunals 79, 122, 212
Trinidad 457
Trinitarian belief 494
Trudinger, Ron 437
trusts/trustees 63, 323, 343f, 400, 437, 455
Tucker, John 366n
Tucker, Paul 340
Tugwell, A.J. 281
Tunbridge Wells, Kent 44
- St John's Free Church 98, 120
Turl, Stanley 242, 409, 414
Turner, George 39
Turner, Max 435
Tutu, Desmond 408
Twinn, Ian, MP 418
Tyler, H.C. 368
Tyler, Henry 326

Ugandan Resettlement Board 404
Underwood, A.C. 92, 169f, 177f, 187, 201, 218f, 224
unemployed/umemployment 182, 192, 194, 407, 420f, 460, 514
Unitarians 494
united Baptist headquarters *see* joint headquarters
United Collegiate Board 76, 187, 249
United Free Church of England concept 63, 82, 94ff, 115

United Fund (BU/BMS 1920) 137
United Hungarian Church 90
United Kingdom Alliance 192
United Nations 311
United Navy and Army Board/United Navy, Army and Air Force Board 82, 200, 423
United Reformed Church (URC) 1, 344n, 385f, 496
United Society for Christian Literature 409
United States of America (USA) 47, 49, 89, 119, 122, 124, 169, 200, 263f, 286, 341, 388, 402, 415, 430, 509, 511
unity (between churches,denominations, &c) 6,21,47,48,53,62, 94f, 113, 118, 120, 126, 135, 175ff, 181, 205, 251ff, 257, 284f, 327f, 333, 337-43, 351, 362f, 385, 387, 416, 444, 493, 496, 503, 527
Universities and Colleges Christian Fellowship (UCCF) 406, 497n
universities 19,21,24, 64, 69, 221, 242, 261, 303f, 353f
Upminster, Essex 278
- Springfield Gardens BC 446
Uppsala Cathedral, Sweden 130
urban churches 19, 21, 279, 458f

Valentine, Theo 353
Vendy, Barry 506
Venturers, The 315, *315*
Vereker, A.J. 226
Victory Thanksgiving Fund (BU) 250
villages/village churches 66, 95, 193, 432, 436, 438
Vincent, Samuel 23
Vincent, W.J. 281
Vineyard Christian Fellowship 433, 502f
Vinson, Edward 361
Virgo, Terry 326, 400, 437f
visitation/ house-to-house visitation &c

# PUBLISHED WORKS CITED IN THE TEXT
(Including various reports, but not including works cited in footnotes only)

*A Call to Commitment: Baptist Christians through the 1980s* (London: BUGB 1980) 423

*A 'Green Paper' on Council Restructuring* 475

*A study of the Evangelical Alliance in Great Britain* (1968) 362f

*A Ten Year Plan Towards 2000: incorporating the National Mission Strategy* (Didcot 1993) 475

*Advent Witness* 232

*Anabaptism Today* 498

*Appeal to All Christian People* (Lambeth 1920) 114 and *The Reply of the Churches in membership of the Baptist Union to the 'Appeal to all Christian People'* (1926) 118f

Aubrey, M.E., *Ministers' Manual* (1927) 189

Bamber, Theo, *His Glorious Appearing*, 231

*Baptism, Eucharist and Ministry (BEM)*, Faith and Order Paper 111 (Geneva: WCC 1981) 449f

*Baptists and Unity* 342f

*Baptist Argus* 49

*Baptist Church Hymnal* 56, 204

*Baptist Handbook/Baptist Directory* 8, 14, 27, 64, 154, 201, 259, 492

*Baptist Hymn Book* (1962) 323

*Baptist Layman/Layman* 10

*Baptist Leader* 471, 475, 493, 502f

*Baptist/Methodist Agreement on Baptismal Policy* (1991) 496

*Baptist Ministers' Journal* 9

*Baptist Music* 505

*Baptist Praise and Worship* (1991) 504f

*Baptist Quarterly* 2, 9, 132, 139, 353, 357, 453n, 515

Baptist Revival Fellowship, *Liberty in the Lord* (1964) 332f, 340

*Baptist, The* 7f, 19, 25, 28f, 34, 64ff, 68

*Baptist Times* 6ff, 14, 16f, 23, 26, 28, 30f, 53, 57f, 65ff, 72, 75, 83, 93, 101, 104f, 122, 128, 132, 138, 141, 145, 150, 164f, 169f, 176, 179, 182f, 188f, 192, 197f, 203, 209ff, 219, 229, 231, 242ff, 259, 268, 273f, 281, 289, 292, 294ff, 298, 304, 310, 313f, 316f, 324, 330, 332, 339, 345, 350, 358ff, 367, 369, 371, 379f, 384, 392, 396ff, 401, 412, 415, 417f, 423, 428, 446, 448, 453, 455, 481, 484, 493ff, 502, 513, 520

*Baptist/United Reformed Church Agreed Guidelines on Baptismal Policy* (Didcot: BU 1996) 496

Barth, Karl, *Christian Dogmatics*, 323

Beasley-Murray, G., *Baptism in the New Testament* (1962) 351

Beasley-Murray, G., *Baptism Today and Tomorrow* (1966) 351

Beasley-Murray, G., *Baptists and Unity Reviewed* (1969) 342

Beasley-Murray, G., *Christian Baptism* (1959) 288f

Beasley-Murray, G., *The Christological Controversy in the Baptist Union* (1971) 379

Beasley-Murray, P. and Wilkinson, A., *Turning the Tide* (London: Bible Society 1981) 431, 516

Bebbington, David, *Evangelicalism in Modern Britain* (1995) 6

*Beginning with God* (Doctrine & Worship Committee, BUGB 1996) 489

*Believing and Being Baptized* 1996 (Didcot: BUGB 1996) 499

*Bible Call/Bible Call and*